SEVENTH EDITION

Joining Together

Group Theory and Group Skills

David W. Johnson
University of Minnesota

Frank P. Johnson

ALLYN AND BACON
Boston • London • Toronto • Sydney • Tokyo • Singapore

This book is dedicated to our parents,
Roger W. Johnson and Frances E. Johnson,
who created the basic group to
which we first belonged.

SENIOR VICE PRESIDENT and EDITOR-IN-CHIEF, EDUCATION: Paul A. Smith
EDITORIAL ASSISTANT: Shannon Morrow
MARKETING MANAGER: Brad Parkins
COVER ADMINISTRATOR: Linda Knowles
PHOTO RESEARCHER: Susan Duane
COMPOSITION and PREPRESS BUYER: Linda Cox
MANUFACTURING BUYER: Suzanne Lareau
PRODUCTION ADMINISTRATOR: Deborah Brown
EDITORIAL-PRODUCTION SERVICE: P. M. Gordon Associates
ILLUSTRATOR: Drew Dernavich

Copyright © 2000, 1997, 1994, 1991, 1987, 1982, 1975 by Allyn & Bacon
A Pearson Education Company
160 Gould Street
Needham Heights, MA 02494

Internet: www.abacon.com

Photo credits appear on page 643, which constitutes a continuation of the
copyright page.

Library of Congress Cataloging-in-Publication Data

Johnson, David W., 1940–
   Joining together : group theory and group skills / David W.
Johnson, Frank P. Johnson.—7th ed.
      p.   cm.
   Includes bibliographical references and index.
   ISBN 0–205–30859–7
   1. Social groups.   2. Leadership.   3. Group relations training.
I. Johnson, Frank P. (Frank Pierce), 1935–   . II. Title.
HM716.J64 2000
302.3—dc20   99–25920
                                                        CIP

PRINTED IN THE UNITED STATES OF AMERICA
10 9 8 7 6 5 4 3 2   04 03 02 01 00

Contents

5 *Leadership* 177

6 *Using Power* 229

7 *Decision Making* 273

8 *Controversy and Creativity* 329

11 Learning and Discussion Groups 487

12 Leading Growth and Counseling Groups 517

13 Team Development, Team Training 537

List of Exercises

Preface

We, the authors, know a great deal about groups. We grew up in one. There are seven children in our family. Frank is the oldest. David is in the middle. We are five years apart in age. Although Frank was very bossy as a child and refused to ever believe that David was really not supposed to clean up his room, our relationships survived. As part of a group of seven children, we raised each other and learned about group dynamics in the trenches of trying to decide as a group who gets the extra piece of pie, who sits by the windows in the car, who decides which game we are going to play, who sweeps and who mops, and whether we go to sleep with the light on or off.

Families are not the only group setting. Within all organizations and social systems, and throughout all walks of life, groups are the key setting in which things get done. The need for knowledge of group dynamics and skills in being part of small groups is more important than ever. Our original reasons for writing *Joining Together* included introducing readers to both (a) the theory and research findings needed to understand how to make groups effective and (b) the skills required to apply that knowledge in practical situations. Expertise in working in groups is based on an integration of such knowledge and skills. *Joining Together* is more than a book reviewing current knowledge in the area of small groups, and it is more than a book of skill-building exercises. The theory and exercises are integrated into an inquiry or experiential approach to learning about the dynamics of small groups. Just as "the truth will make you free," throughout one's life, choices, opportunities, and successes are created by (a) knowledge of group dynamics and (b) mastery of the skills required to apply that knowledge in practical situations.

What we know about group functioning is dynamic, not static. It is constantly being revised and updated as new insights are translated into revised theoretical explanations for group behavior and new lines of research. Significant advances in the field continue to be achieved. Much has changed since we published the first edition of this book in 1975. Some theories have been disconfirmed in the intervening years. Other theories have been refined or subsumed into new conceptual systems. This book reflects the new developments in theory and research by taking an updated look at what we know about group dynamics. Although the readers of this book are diverse, *Joining Together* remains focused on the characteristic dynamics found in virtually all groups. Examples are used from all walks of life. Furthermore, because this book is intended to serve as an introduction to the dynamics of groups, we have maintained a balanced, integrative stance when presenting theories and research findings.

The authors wish to thank many people for their help in writing this book and in preparing the manuscript. We owe much to the social psychologists who have influenced our theorizing and to the colleagues with whom we have conducted various types of laboratory-training experiences. We have tried to acknowledge sources of the exercises included in this book whenever possible. Some of the exercises presented are so commonly used that the originators are not traceable. If we have inadvertently missed giving recognition to anyone, we apologize.

We wish to thank Margaret Zimmerman, Virginia Wesleyan University; and Muriel Stockberger, Eastern Kentucky University, for their reviews and suggestions.

Special thanks are extended to our wives, Linda Mulholland Johnson and Jane Miley Johnson, who contributed their support to the development and writing of this book.

Joining
Together

1

Group Dynamics

Basic Concepts to Be Covered in This Chapter

In this chapter a number of concepts are defined and discussed. The major ones are listed below. Divide into heterogeneous pairs. Each pair is to (a) define each concept, noting the page on which it is defined and discussed and (b) ensure that both members of the pair understand the meaning of each concept. Then combine into groups of four. Compare the answers of the two pairs. If there is disagreement, look up the concept in the chapter and clarify it until all members agree on and understand the definition.

Concepts

1. Group
2. Group dynamics
3. Group effectiveness
4. Interdependence
5. Role
6. Norm
7. Recurring-phase theory of group development
8. Sequential-stage theory of group development
9. Primary group
10. Reference group
11. Action research
12. Kurt Lewin

Importance of Groups	Nature of Groups	Types of Groups
We are small group beings We live in groups Groups and quality of life	Group orientation Individual orientation	Pseudo Traditional Effective High performance

Group Structure	Stages of Group Development	Basic Elements of Effectiveness
Roles Norms	**Recurring Stages** Task and emotional expressions Depend, pair, fight–flight Affection, inclusion, control **Sequential Stages** Forming Storming Norming Performing Adjourning	Positive interdependence Individual accountability Promotive interaction Social skills Group processing **Field of Group Dynamics** Nature of group dynamics History of group dynamics Kurt Lewin Nature of book

Dynamics of Promotive Interaction

Creating clear, operational, mutual goals members are committed to.
Communicating ideas and feelings accurately and clearly.
Distributed participation and leadership.
Equal access to power based on expertise, access to information.
Decision procedures flexibly matched with situational needs.
Controversy used to promote creative problem solving, critical thinking.
Conflicts are faced, encouraged, and resolved constructively.

Figure 1.1 Nature of group dynamics.

GROUP DYNAMICS AND ME

The purposes of this book are for the reader to:

1. Understand the theory and research on group dynamics.
2. Improve his or her small group skills.

In order to achieve these purposes, you may wish to think carefully about each of the questions given on page 5.

Self-Diagnosis

Each of the following seven statements describes an action related to group effectiveness. For each statement mark:

5 = I always behave that way   **2** = I seldom behave that way
4 = I frequently behave that way   **1** = I never behave that way
3 = I occasionally behave that way

WHEN I AM A MEMBER OF A GROUP:

_____ **1.** I clarify the group's goals and ensure that the goals are formulated so members "sink or swim" together and are committed to achieving them.

_____ **2.** I facilitate communication by modeling good sending and receiving skills and ensuring communication among all group members is distributed and two-way.

_____ **3.** I provide leadership by taking whatever action is needed to help the group achieve its goals and maintain good working relationships among members, and I encourage all other members to do the same.

_____ **4.** I use my expertise and knowledge to influence the other group members to increase their efforts to achieve our mutual goals, and I let myself be influenced by other members who are knowledgeable and have relevant expertise.

_____ **5.** I suggest different ways of making decisions (such as majority vote or consensus) depending on the (a) availability of time and resources, (b) size and seriousness of the decision, and (c) amount of member commitment needed to implement the decision.

_____ **6.** I advocate my views and challenge the views of others in order to create high-quality and creative decisions.

_____ **7.** I face my conflicts with other group members and present the conflicts as problems to be jointly solved. If we are unable to do so, I request the help of other group members to help us resolve the conflicts constructively.

_____ **Total Score**

THE IMPORTANCE OF GROUPS

Although the scientific investigations of group work are but a few years old,
I don't hesitate to predict that group work—that is, the handling of human
beings not as isolated individuals, but in the social setting of groups—will
soon be one of the most important theoretical and practical fields.... There

*is no hope for creating a better world without a deeper scientific insight into
the . . . essentials of group life.*

Kurt Lewin (1943)

Humans Are Small Group Beings

Our origins are somehow linked with the fate of the Neanderthals. We have never been
proud of our extinct predecessors, partly because of their looks. Nevertheless, the Neanderthals represent a high point in the human story. Their lineage goes back to the earliest members of the genus *Homo.* They were the original pioneers. Over thousands of
years Neanderthals moved out of Africa by way of the Near East into India, China,
Malaysia, and southern Europe. In recent times, 150,000 or so years ago, they pioneered
glacial landscapes and became the first humans to cope with climates hospitable only
to woolly mammoths and reindeer.

There is no anatomical evidence that the Neanderthals were cerebrally inferior to
us (the Cro-Magnons). In fact, they had a larger brain than we do. There is no doubt
whatever that they were our physical superiors. Their strongest individuals could probably lift weights of half a ton or so. Physically, we are quite puny in comparison. But we
gradually replaced the Neanderthals during an overlapping period of a few thousand
years. It may have mainly been a matter of attrition and population pressure. As the
glaciers from Scandinavia advanced, northern populations of Neanderthals moved
south while our ancestors were moving north out of Africa. About 40,000 years ago we
met in Europe. We flourished and they vanished about 30,000 years ago.

There are numerous explanations for the disappearance of the Neanderthals. Perhaps they evolved into us. Perhaps we merged through intermarriage. Perhaps there
was an intergroup competition for food, with the Neanderthals unable to meet our
challenge and dying off in marginal areas. Perhaps the Neanderthals were too set in

their ways and were unable to evolve and refine better ways to cooperate whereas we were continually organizing better cooperative efforts to cope with changing climatic conditions. There seems to be little doubt that we were more able to form and maintain cooperative efforts.

During the time we (the Cro-Magnons) overlapped with the Neanderthals, our ancestors developed highly sophisticated cooperative effects characterized by social organization, group-hunting procedures, creative experimentation with a variety of materials, sharing of knowledge, divisions of labor, trade, and transportation systems. We sent out scouts to monitor the movements of herds of animals we preyed on. The Neanderthals probably did not. We cached supplies and first aid materials to aid hunting parties far away from our home bases. The Neanderthals apparently did not. Neanderthals probably engaged their prey chiefly in direct combat. We developed more efficient ways of hunting, such as driving animals over cliffs and thereby fundamentally changed our relationship with the rest of the animal kingdom. Instead of behaving like lions and other carnivores and going after young and old and sick animals to weed out the less fit, large-scale game drives wiped out entire herds and perhaps entire species. We developed more sophisticated tools and weapons to kill from a distance such as the spear-thrower and the bow and arrow. The Neanderthals probably did not. The Neanderthals used local materials to develop tools. We were more selective, often obtaining special fine-grained and colorful flints from quarries as far as 250 miles away. This took a level of intergroup cooperation and social organization that Neanderthals did not seem to develop. We improved the tool-making process through experimentation and sharing knowledge. The Neanderthals did not. The Neanderthals used stone almost exclusively for tools. We used bone and ivory to make needles and other tools. We "tailored" our clothes and made ropes and nets. Our ability to obtain more food than we needed resulted in trading and the formation of far-ranging social networks. Status hierarchies, the accumulation of wealth, artistic efforts, laws, and storytelling to preserve traditions followed, as more complex forms of cooperation were developed. Whether we replaced or evolved from the Neanderthals, our ingenuity was especially evident in organizing cooperative efforts to increase our standard of living and the quality of our lives. We excelled at organizing effective group efforts.

Humans are small group beings. We always have been and we always will be. As John Donne said, "No man is an island, entire of itself." For 200,000 years humans lived in small hunting and gathering groups. For 10,000 years humans lived in small farming communities. It is only recently, the past 100 years or so, that large cities have become the rule rather than the exception.

We Live in Groups

Membership in groups is inevitable and ubiquitous. All day long we interact first in one group and then in another. Our family life, our leisure time, our friendships, and our careers are all filled with groups. In fact, if a person from outer space conducted a study of the people of Earth, group membership would probably be the dominant characteristic noted. We are born into a group called the family, and we would not survive the first few years of our lives, the first few weeks, or even the first few minutes without membership in this group. It is within our family and peer groups that we are socialized into ways of behaving and thinking, educated, and taught to have certain perspectives on ourselves and our world. Our personal identity is derived from the way in which we are perceived and treated by other members of our groups. We learn, work, worship, and plan in groups. As humans we have an inherent social nature: Our life is filled with groups from the moment of our birth to the moment of our death.

Groups and the Quality of Your Life

As the effectiveness of our groups go, so goes the quality of our life. **Understanding group dynamics is central to maintaining a viable family.** For thousands of years, family life has been one of the sustaining values of civilization. Anthropologist Margaret Mead observed that the family is the toughest institution humans have. Yet the structure of the family has been changing. First, there was the demise of the extended family. Second, there was the demise of the nuclear family. One out of four children today is being raised by a single parent. In order to build and maintain a constructive family life within the diverse demands of modern life, individuals have to have a thorough knowledge of group dynamics and the small group skills.

A **knowledge of group dynamics is central to effective businesses and industries.** During the first half of the twentieth century, mass production made the United States the world leader in manufacturing. In the 1980s and 1990s, companies turned to the high productivity generated by small groups. Ford Industries, for example, formed **problem-solving groups** to deal with shop floor problems, **interface groups** to work on problems that cut across work groups, **opportunity teams** to oversee implementation of new technology and facilities improvements, **special project teams** to manage specific events such as auto shows, **linking teams** to deal with issues that require input from several shifts and departments, **launch teams** to coordinate process and design needed to launch a successful new project, **vendor quality teams** to develop ongoing communication with suppliers both inside and outside the company, and **resource committees** to provide consulting and training on request (Banas, 1988). What makes organizations viable today is their ability to create teams dominated by a culture of learning, continuous improvement, and adaptation (see Chapter 13).

Understanding group dynamics is central to education. The paradigm of teaching is changing from lecture and individual work to cooperative learning (Johnson, Johnson, & Holubec, 1998a, 1998b). Instead of listening to lectures and taking notes, students work in small groups to maximize both their own learning and the learning of their classmates. Cooperative learning typically produces higher achievement, more positive relationships, and greater psychological health than does competitive or individualistic learning (Johnson & Johnson, 1989) (see Chapter 11).

A **knowledge of group dynamics is central to the long-term maintenance of psychological health.** We are in an epidemic of depression, anxiety, and mental illness (Seligman, 1988). Two major surveys of mental illness in the United States, for example, showed that, contrary to expectations, younger people were much more likely to have had a depressive episode in their lives than were older people (Robins et al., 1984, reported in Seligman, 1988). The rate of depression over the last two generations has increased roughly tenfold as people are experiencing much more depression now than they did two generations ago, feeling hopeless, giving up, being passive, having low self-esteem, and committing suicide. Being involved in supportive groups prevents the occurrence of psychological problems, and the use of supportive and caring groups are the ideal mode of treatment of psychological problems (see Chapter 12).

Knowing group dynamics theory and having small group skills can change your life. It can make you more employable and lead to greater career success. It can improve your friendships. It can lead to more caring and loving family relationships and greater competence as parents. It can promote greater psychological health and increased ability to cope with stress and adversity. **When it comes to group functioning, knowledge does give power.** But knowledge of group dynamics in and of itself is not sufficient to promote effective functioning—social skills are also required. To promote effective group functioning you must both know what an effective group is and have the necessary social skills.

Because it takes both knowledge and skills to build and maintain effective groups, **this book has two purposes:**

1. To provide you with a systematic analysis of the theory and research on group dynamics.
2. To provide you with experiences needed to develop group skills.

Now that the importance of groups is clear, there is a need to understand what is and is not an effective group.

Exercise 1.1: Your Solitary Activities

1. List everything you do in a typical day from the moment you wake up to the moment you fall asleep.
2. Delete from your list all the activities you perform with groups of people and see what is left.
3. Form a group of three and discuss the results.

Exercise 1.2: Who Am I?

We are all members of groups. If we are asked to describe who we are, most of us include information about the groups to which we belong. "I'm a student at the University of Minnesota," "I'm a member of the hockey team," "I'm a Johnson," "I'm a male," "I'm an American," and so forth. Membership in groups may be formal ("I'm an employee of IBM"), aspiring ("I want to be rich"), marginal ("Sometimes I'm invited to Ralph's parties, sometimes I'm not"), voluntary ("I'm a Baptist"), and nonvoluntary ("I'm a female"). To a large extent, our memberships define who we are as individuals.

1. We can all describe ourselves in many ways. Write ten different answers to the question "Who am I?" on a sheet of paper. Answer in terms of groups you belong to, beliefs you hold, and your roles and responsibilities.
2. Rank your answers from most important to your sense of self to least important to your sense of self.
3. Form a group of three, and share your self-descriptions. Count how many memberships are represented in the triad. Discuss the role of groups in your view of who you are as a person.
4. Count how many group memberships are represented in the class.

Exercise 1.3: Saving the World from Dracula

The purpose of this exercise is to provide an introduction to group dynamics. A problem-solving situation is used.

1. Form heterogeneous groups of four.
2. The group's task is to formulate a plan to save the world by stopping Count Dracula from initiating a new reign of terror by vampires. Your group is to establish:
   a. How vampires may be destroyed.
   b. How to protect yourself from vampires.
   c. A vampire's strengths and weaknesses that must be overcome and exploited.
   d. When (time of day) vampires may be destroyed.
3. Complete the task by creating a plan and then ranking the items from most important to least important. Read the situation sheet. Your *goal* is to rank items from most important (1) to least important (10) and write out a rationale as to why you ranked the items as you did.
   a. Working by yourself, *individualistically,* rank the items from most important (1) to least important (10). Write out a rationale explaining your ranking.
   b. Working *cooperatively* in your group, rank the items again, coming to consensus. Write out a rationale explaining the group's ranking. There should be one ranking and rationale from the group.
4. Score your own and your group's ranking:
   a. Compute the absolute difference (ignore plus and minus signs) between your individual ranking and the experts' ranking.
   b. Compute the absolute difference (ignore plus and minus signs) between your group's ranking and the experts' ranking.
   c. A perfect ranking will have a score of zero. The lower your score, the more accurate your ranking. The criteria for success are:

0–20	Excellent
21–30	Good
31–40	Poor
41+	Terrible

5. When the group has solved the problem, answer the following questions:
   a. What is the group's goal?
   b. What were the patterns of communication among group members?
   c. How did leadership emerge in the group? Who provided what types of leadership in your group?
   d. What determined how influential each member was in the group?
   e. What method of decision making was used and how effective was it?
   f. Why or why not did members challenge each other's conclusions?
   g. What conflicts arose among group members and how were they managed?
   h. How do you simultaneously participate in a group and observe the processes the group uses to complete its tasks?
   i. What actions by group members helped (and hindered?) the team in completing its task?

THE DANGER OF DRACULA

You are a group of scientists who specialize in public health. Your mandate is to prevent epidemics and threats to the general health of the public. Your current concern is the possibility of a proliferation of vampires resulting from the release of Count Dracula from his grave where he has been trapped for over a hundred years.

Voivode Dracula (1431–1476) was Vlad III, Prince of Wallachia (a province of Romania bordered to the north by Transylvania and Moldavia, to the east by the Black Sea, and to the south by Bulgaria). He was known (a) as a brilliant, courageous, cunning, and clever general who defeated the Turkish army; and (b) as Vlad the Impaler for impaling tens of thousands of victims on sharpened stakes. In 1459, on St. Bartholomew's Day, for example, Dracula had thirty thousand of the citizens of the city of Brasov impaled, arranging the stakes in various geometric formations in front of the city. He was also a noted statesman and scholar. His mighty brain, iron resolution, and immense cruelty made him a formidable adversary. Although supposedly killed in battle in 1476 by the Turks, it soon became apparent that he had become a vampire. He adopted the title of Count and terrorized that region of Europe until he was imprisoned in his grave in the late 1800s by a team of English scientists and adventurers. The exact whereabouts of his grave were hidden to prevent any misguided soul from freeing him.

Archeologists excavating an ancient castle in Transylvania have uncovered Count Dracula's crypt and coffin. When they open the casket they will release Count Dracula once more on the world. Not believing in the danger, the archeologists are inviting television crews to film the opening, hoping the publicity will help them raise money. You, however, know the truth. Vampires do exist and once released, Count Dracula will create at least five more vampires a day, each of which will create five more vampires a day. In a very short time, vampires could be terrorizing the whole world. Your group has the responsibility of preventing this world disaster by destroying Count Dracula before he can begin. Your plan must include:

a. The procedures you will use to destroy Dracula.
b. The procedures you will use to protect yourself from Dracula.
c. A description of Dracula's strengths and weaknesses that must be overcome and exploited.
d. When (time of day) Dracula will be destroyed.

Pooling the resources of your group, you have twelve relevant items. **Your task is to rank these items according to their importance for your quest to prevent a reign of terror by Count Dracula,** starting with 1 for the most important item and ending with 12 for the least important one.

How to Destroy Dracula	Protection Procedures	Dracula's Strengths and Weaknesses	When (Time) We Will Destroy Dracula

SAVING THE WORLD FROM DRACULA RANKING SHEET

Rank the following items according to their importance for saving the world from Dracula, starting with 1 for the most important to 10 for the least important.

1	2	3	4	2–4	3–4
Item	Your Ranking	Group Ranking	Experts' Ranking	Individual Difference Scores	Group Difference Scores
1. Oak stake					
2. Diagram/map of Dracula's castle and key to Dracula's crypt					
3. Human ability to cooperate					
4. Table detailing sunrise and sunset in Transylvania					
5. 44-magnum revolver and shells					
6. Branch of wild rose					
7. Sharp ax and several cloves of garlic					
8. Tickets: plane to Budapest, train to Transylvania, car to castle					
9. Collapsible steel cage					
10. Cross, holy water, communion wafers					
Total					

HOW TO CREATE AN EFFECTIVE GROUP

I will pay more for the ability to deal with people than for any other ability under the sun.

John D. Rockefeller

Not all groups are effective. In fact, most groups may be less effective than they should be. To be effective, a group must (a) achieve its goals, (b) maintain good working relationships among members, and (c) adapt to changing conditions in the surrounding organization, society, and world. In order to ensure the groups you belong to are effective,

Table 1.1 **Guidelines for Creating Effective Groups**

1. Establish clear, operational, relevant group goals that create positive interdependence and evoke a high level of commitment from every member.
2. Establish effective two-way communication within which group members communicate their ideas and feelings accurately and clearly.
3. Ensure that leadership and participation are distributed among all group members.
4. Ensure that the use of power is distributed among group members and patterns of influence vary according to the needs of the group as members strive to achieve their mutual goals.
5. Match the method of decision making with the (a) availability of time and resources, (b) size and seriousness of the decision, and (c) amount of member commitment needed to implement the decision. The most effective way of making a decision is usually by consensus.
6. Encourage structured controversies in which members advocate their views, disagree, and challenge each other's conclusions and reasoning in order to create high quality and creative decisions.
7. Ensure members face their conflicts of interests and use integrative negotiations and mediation to resolve them constructively.

you must follow a set of guidelines to ensure that the group's goals are achieved, good relationships among members are maintained, and the group adapts to changing conditions (see Table 1.1). These guidelines provide (a) a direction in building an effective group, (b) a framework for diagnosing how well a group is functioning, and (c) a means for motivating group members to improve (compare actual performance with ideal performance (see Table 1.2).

Guideline 1: Establish clear, operational, relevant group goals that create positive interdependence and evoke a high level of commitment from every member. Groups exist for a reason. People join groups to achieve goals they are unable to achieve by themselves. To be effective, the goals must be clear so that all members understand the nature of the goals, the goals must be operational so that members understand how to achieve the goals, the goals must be relevant to members' needs so that they commit themselves to achieve the goals, and the goals must create positive interdependence among members. Group goals and social interdependence are discussed in Chapter 3.

Guideline 2: Establish effective two-way communication within which group members communicate their ideas and feelings accurately and clearly. Communication is the basis for all human interaction and group functioning. Members must send and receive messages effectively in order to exchange information and transmit meaning. Competition among members must be minimized. Two-way communication is required for effective group work. Communication among group members is discussed in Chapter 4.

Guideline 3: Ensure leadership and participation are distributed among all group members. All members are responsible for providing leadership. The equalization of participation and leadership makes certain that all members are involved in the group's work, committed to implementing the group's decisions, and satisfied with their membership. It also (a) assures that the resources of every member are fully utilized and (b) increases the cohesiveness of the group. Leadership is discussed in Chapter 5.

Table 1.2 **Comparison of Effective and Ineffective Groups**

Effective Groups	Ineffective Groups
Goals are clarified and modified so that the best possible match between individual goals and the group's goals is achieved; goals are structured cooperatively so all members are committed to achieving them.	Members accept imposed goals; goals are competitively structured so that each member strives to outperform the others.
Communication is two-way, and the open and accurate expression of both ideas and feelings is emphasized.	Communication is one-way, and only ideas are expressed; feelings are suppressed or ignored.
Participation and leadership are distributed among all group members; goal accomplishment, internal maintenance, and developmental change are underscored.	Leadership is delegated and based on authority; participation is unequal with high-power members dominating; only goal accomplishment is emphasized.
Ability and information determine influence and power; contracts are built to make sure individuals' goals and needs are fulfilled; power is equalized and shared.	Position determines power; power is concentrated in the authority system; obedience to authority is the rule.
Decision-making procedures are matched with the situation; different methods are used at different times; consensus is sought for important decisions; involvement and group discussions are encouraged.	Decisions are always made by the highest authority; there is little group discussion; members' involvement is minimal.
Structured controversy in which members advocate their views and challenge each other's information and reasoning is seen as the key to high quality and creative decision making and problem solving.	Disagreement among members is suppressed and avoided; quick compromises are sought to eliminate arguing; groupthink is prevalent.
Conflicts of interests are resolved through integrative negotiations and mediation so agreements are reached that maximize joint outcomes and leave all members satisfied.	Conflicts of interests are resolved through distributive negotiations or avoidance; some members win and some members lose or else conflict is ignored and everyone is unhappy.
Interpersonal, group, and intergroup skills are stressed; cohesion is advanced through high levels of inclusion, affection, acceptance, support, and trust; individuality is endorsed.	The functions of group members are stressed; individuality is deemphasized; cohesion is ignored; rigid conformity is promoted.

Guideline 4: Ensure the use of power is distributed among group members and patterns of influence vary according to the needs of the group as members strive to achieve their mutual goals. Members' power is based on expertise, ability, and access to information, not on authority or personality characteristics. Coalitions that help fulfill personal goals should be formed among group members on the basis of mutual influence and interdependence. Power is discussed in Chapter 6.

Guideline 5: Match decision-making procedures with the needs of the situation. There are many different ways groups can make decisions. There must be a balance between the availability of time and resources (such as members' skills) and the method of decision making used. Another balance must be struck among the size and seriousness of the decision, the commitment needed to put it into practice, and the method used for making the decision. The most effective way of making a decision is usually by consensus (unanimous agreement). Consensus promotes distributed participation, the equalization of power, productive controversy, cohesion, involvement, and commitment. Decision making is discussed in Chapter 7.

     Guideline 6: Engage in controversy by disagreeing and challenging each other's conclusions and reasoning, thus promoting creative decision making and problem solving. In order to make effective decisions, members must present the best case possible for each major alternative course of action and subject all other alternatives to critical analysis. **Controversies** (conflicts among opposing ideas and conclusions) promote involvement in the group's work, quality and creativity in decision making, and commitment to implementing the group's decisions. The controversy procedure ensures that minority opinions are accepted and used. Such intellectual conflict results in more creative, effective decisions. Controversy and creativity are discussed in Chapter 8.

     Guideline 7: Face your conflicts and resolve them in constructive ways. This guideline is for group members to face their conflicts of interests (conflicts promoted by incompatible needs or goals, scarce resources, and by competitiveness) and engage in problem-solving (integrative) negotiations to resolve them. There are five basic strategies to manage conflicts of interests: withdrawal, forcing (distributive, win-lose negotiations), smoothing, compromise, and problem solving (integrative negotiations). The more effective the group, the more frequently conflicts of interests will be valued for their potential constructive outcomes and resolved through problem-solving negotiations. Where problem-solving negotiations fail, another group member needs to mediate. Even in intergroup and cross-ethnic conflicts, problem-solving negotiations need to be used. When they are resolved constructively, conflicts are an important and indispensable aspect of increasing group effectiveness. Conflicts of interest are discussed in Chapter 9.

     If you follow the above guidelines, the groups to which you are a member will be effective. It will help, however, if you also know the answers to the following questions:

1. What is a group?
2. What are the types of groups?
3. What is the nature of group structure?
4. How do groups develop over time?
5. What is the field of group dynamics?

Exercise 1.4: What Is a Group?

There has been considerable controversy as to what a group is. The purpose of this exercise is to structure a critical examination of the different definitions. The procedure is as follows:

1. The class forms groups of seven members.
2. Each member receives a sheet containing one of the seven definitions that appear on the following pages. Without interacting with the other group members, each member is to:
   a. Study his or her definition until it is thoroughly understood.
   b. Plan how to teach the definition to the other members of the group.

c. Name three examples of groups that meet the criterion contained in the definition.

d. Name three examples of two or more people in close proximity who do not meet the criterion contained in the definition.

e. Explain in what way(s) his or her group (doing this exercise) meets the criterion contained in the definition.

Allow ten minutes for this phase of the exercise.

3. Each group meets to derive a single definition of the concept group. Up to twenty minutes are allowed for this phase.

4. Each group reads its definition to the entire class.

5. If there is substantial disagreement, the class forms new groups (composed of one member from each of the previous groups). The task of the new group is to arrive at one definition of the concept group, each member representing the definition of his or her former group.

6. Each group reads its definition to the entire class.

WHAT IS A GROUP?

Everyone knows groups exist. Lots of social scientists think they know exactly what a group is. The trouble is, they do not agree with each other. Given below are seven of the most common definitions of the concept, "group." Which one do you like best?

Goals

Groups exist for a reason. People join groups in order to achieve goals they are unable to achieve by themselves. A **group** may be defined as a number of individuals who join together to achieve a goal. It is questionable whether a group could exist unless there were a mutual goal that its members were trying to achieve. Freeman, as early as 1936, pointed out that people join groups in order to achieve common goals. Other social scientists who have defined *group* this way are Mills and Deutsch:

> To put it simply, they [small groups] are units composed of two or more persons who come into contact for a purpose and who consider the contact meaningful (Mills, 1967, p. 2).

> A psychological group exists (has unity) to the extent that the individuals composing it perceive themselves as pursuing promotively interdependent goals (Deutsch, 1949a, p. 136).

Interdependence

A **group** may be defined as a collection of individuals who are interdependent in some way. According to this definition, the individuals are not a group unless an event that affects one of them affects them all. Social scientists who have defined *group* in this way are Cartwright and Zander, Fiedler, and Lewin:

> A group is a collection of individuals who have relations to one another that make them interdependent to some significant degree. As so defined, the term group

refers to a class of social entities having in common the property of interdependence among their constituent members (Cartwright and Zander, 1968, p. 46).

By this term [group] we generally mean a set of individuals who share a common fate, that is, who are interdependent in the sense that an event which affects one member is likely to affect all (Fiedler, 1967, p. 6).

Conceiving of a group as a dynamic whole should include a definition of group which is based on interdependence of the members (or better, the subparts of the group) (Lewin, 1951, p. 146).

Interpersonal Interaction

A **group** may be defined as a number of individuals who are interacting with one another. According to this definition, a group does not exist unless the individuals are interacting with one another. Social scientists who have defined *group* in this way are Hare, Bonner, Stogdill, and Homans.

For a collection of individuals to be considered a group there must be some interaction (Hare, 1976, p. 4).

A group is a number of people in interaction with one another, and it is this interaction process that distinguishes the group from an aggregate (Bonner, 1959, p. 4).

A group may be regarded as an open interaction system in which actions determine the structure of the system and successive interactions exert coequal effects upon the identity of the system (Stodgill, 1959, p. 18).

We mean by a group a number of persons who communicate with one another often over a span of time, and who are few enough so that each person is able to communicate with all the others, not at secondhand, through other people, but face-to-face (Homans, 1950, p. 1).

Perceptions of Membership

A **group** may be defined as a social unit consisting of two or more persons who perceive themselves as belonging to a group. According to this definition, the persons are not a group unless they perceive themselves to be part of a group. Social scientists who have defined *group* in this way are Bales and Smith:

A small group is defined as any number of persons engaged in interaction with one another in a single face-to-face meeting or series of such meetings, in which each member receives some impression or perception of each other member distinct enough so that he can, either at the time or in later questioning, give some reaction to each of the others as an individual person, even though it be only to recall that the other was present (Bales, 1950, p. 33).

We may define a social group as a unit consisting of a plural number of separate organisms (agents) who have a collective perception of their unity and who have the ability to act and/or are acting in a unitary manner toward their environment (Smith, 1945, p. 227).

Structured Relationships

A **group** may be defined as a collection of individuals whose interactions are structured by a set of roles and norms. According to this definition, the individuals are not a group unless their interactions are structured by a set of role definitions and norms. Social scientists who have defined *group* in this way are McDavid and Harari and Sherif and Sherif:

> A social-psychological group is an organized system of two or more individuals who are interrelated so that the system performs some function, has a standard set of role relationships among its members, and has a set of norms that regulate the function of the group and each of its members (McDavid & Harari, 1968, p. 237).

> A group is a social unit which consists of a number of individuals who stand in (more or less) definite status and role relationships to one another and which possesses a set of values or norms of its own regulating the behavior of individual members, at least in matters of consequence to the group (Sherif & Sherif, 1956, p. 144).

Mutual Influence

A **group** may be defined as a collection of individuals who influence each other. Individuals are not a group unless they are affecting and being affected by each other and, therefore, the primary defining characteristic of a group is interpersonal influence. Shaw (1976, p. 11) stated, "A group is two or more persons who are interacting with one another in such a manner that each person influences and is influenced by each other person."

What Is the Best Way to Define a Group?

Given below are several definitions of the concept *group*. Rank them from most accurate (1) to least accurate (7). Write down your rationale for your ranking. Find a partner and share your ranking and rationale, listen to his or her ranking and rationale, and cooperatively create a new, improved ranking and rationale. Then find another pair and repeat the procedure in a group of four.

Rank	Definition
	A **group** is a number of individuals who join together to achieve a goal.
	A **group** is several individuals who are interdependent in some way.
	A **group** is a number of individuals who are interacting with one another.
	A **group** is a social unit consisting of two or more persons who perceive themselves as belonging to a group.
	A **group** is a collection of individuals whose interactions are structured by a set of roles and norms.
	A **group** is a collection of individuals who influence each other.
	A **group** is a collection of individuals who are trying to satisfy some personal need through their joint association.

Motivation

A **group** may be defined as a collection of individuals who are trying to satisfy some personal need through their joint association. According to this definition, the individuals are not a group unless they are motivated by some personal reason to be part of a group. Individuals belong to the group in order to obtain needed rewards or to satisfy personal needs. It is questionable that a group could exist without its members' needs being satisfied by their membership. Social scientists who have defined group in this way are Bass and Cattell:

> We define "group" as a collection of individuals whose existence as a collection is rewarding to the individuals (Bass, 1960, p. 39).

> The definition which seems most essential is that a group is a collection of organisms in which the existence of all (in their given relationships) is necessary to the satisfaction of certain individual needs in each (Cattell, 1951, p. 167).

THE NATURE OF GROUPS

It takes two flints to make a fire.

Louisa May Alcott

In a bus trapped in a traffic jam, six passengers begin to talk to each other, comparing reactions and sharing previous similar experiences. They start to develop a plan of action to get the bus out of the heavy traffic. Is this a group? In Yellowstone National Park it is deep winter. Several cross-country skiers glide through an isolated, snow-covered valley. They are studying winter ecology and photography. Periodically they cluster around a professional photographer as he explains the ways the winter scenes may be photographed. The vacationers admire and discuss the beautiful winter scenery as they photograph it. Is this a group? Do groups exist at all? How do you tell when you are a member of a group?

Not every collection of people can be considered a group. The *Oxford English Dictionary* (1989) defines **group** as a number of persons or things regarded as forming a unit on account of any kind of mutual or common relation, or classified together on account of a common degree of similarity. Groups may be contrasted with aggregates. An **aggregate** is a collection of individuals who are present at the same time and place but who do *not* form a unit or have a common degree of similarity. Individuals standing on a street corner, the members of an audience at a play, and students listening to a lecture are aggregates, not groups.

Despite the Oxford definition, there are many different definitions of the concept group. Whereas the definition of small groups usually includes member interaction, a group can involve large numbers of members who have some common characteristic without actually meeting each other (such as a reference group). A community can be a large group. Individuals with the same ethnic heritage can be considered a large group. The social scientists who have tried to define what a group is seem much like the blind men trying to describe an elephant. Each social scientist has taken some aspect of a group and assumed that aspect revealed the essence of a group. One solution to the profusion of definitions is to combine them all into one definition. A small group may be defined as two or more individuals who (a) pursue common goals, (b) are interdependent, (c) interact with each other, (d) share norms concerning matters of common interest and participate in a system of interlocking roles, (e) influence each other, (f) find the group rewarding, and (g) define themselves and are defined by others as belonging to the group. Not all of these characteristics are equally important, and although it is impossible to gain consensus among social scientists as to which characteristics are most important, the authors prefer the following definition: A **small group** is two or more individuals in face-to-face interaction, each aware of positive interdependence as they strive to achieve mutual goals, each aware of his or her membership in the group, and each aware of the others who belong to the group. Though there may be some groups that do not fully fit this definition, the most commonly recognized examples of groups do.

Based on the above definitions, how do you tell the difference between an aggregate and a group? Is an audience at a concert a group? Are the people traveling in the same airplane a group? Are the children waiting in the same line to talk to Santa Claus a group? Are all twenty-one-year-old males in our society a group?

Group Orientation	Individual Orientation
The **group orientation** focuses on the group as a whole. In explaining the actions of group members, social scientists focus on the influences of the group and the larger social systems of which it is part. Emile Durkhem (1898, p. 104), arguing that groups were entities different from individuals, stated, "If, then, we begin with the individual, we shall be able to understand nothing of what takes place in the group." He posited that small **primary groups** (small groups characterized by face-to-face interaction, interdependency, and strong group identification such as families and very close friends) were the building blocks of society and he worked upward from this level to an analysis of social systems in general. He was convinced that a group mind or collective consciousness dominated individual will in many situations. Le Bon (1897) believed that a group mind existed separate from the minds of individual members. Cartwright and Zander (1968) maintained that a group can be emotionally healthy or pathological. Cattell (1951) described groups as possessing different personalities. Lewin (1935), as a Gestalt psychologist, noted that a group cannot be understood by considering only the qualities and characteristics of each member. When individuals merge into a group something new is created that must be seen as an entity in and of itself. Changes in one aspect of a group will necessarily lead to changes in the other group features.	The **individualistic orientation** focuses on the individual in the group. In order to explain the functioning of the group, psychologists focus on the attitudes, cognitions, and personalities of the members. Floyd Allport (1924) argued that groups do not think, feel, or act (only people do) and, therefore, groups are not real and are not deserving of study. He used to say, "Groups have no nervous systems, only individuals have nervous systems." To Allport, groups were no more than (a) shared sets of values, ideas, thoughts, and habits that exist simultaneously in the minds of several persons; or (b) the sum of the actions of each member taken separately. His *coup de grace* was his observation, "You can't stumble over a group." Many social scientists have agreed with Allport and taken a rather cavalier approach to the definitive facts that determine whether or not a collection of people is a group. Groups have also been defined on the basis of individual perceptions of other members (Bales, 1950), individual reward (Bass, 1960), and individual purpose and meaning (Mills, 1967). Much of the research on groups, furthermore, has used individual members as the unit of analysis.

Because the concept group can be defined does not mean that everyone believes that groups exist. One of the more interesting social scientific debates centers on the nature of groups. There are two contrasting positions: the group orientation and the individual orientation.

Solomon Asch (1952) adopted a middle ground by comparing groups to water. He argued that in order to understand the properties of water, it is important to know the characteristics of its elements, hydrogen and oxygen. This knowledge alone, however, is not sufficient to understand water—the combination of hydrogen and oxygen must be examined as a unique entity. Similarly, groups must be studied as unique entities, even though it is important to know the characteristics of the individual members. There is evidence that groups evoke stronger reactions than an individual engaging in the same behavior, and actions by groups and individuals elicit differing preferences for

Barriers to Capitalizing on the Power of Groups

Directions: Consider the five sources of resistance to using cooperative learning given above. Rate yourself from 1 to 5 on each source.

The Causes of the Missed Opportunities to Capitalize on the Power of Groups

	1———2———3———4———5	
Low	**Middle**	**High**
Not a Concern of Mine	Somewhat a Concern	Consistently and Strongly a Concern

_____ **Belief that isolated work is the natural order of the world.** Such myopic focus blinds individuals to the realization that no one person could have built a cathedral, achieved America's independence from England, or created a supercomputer.

_____ **Resistance to taking responsibility for others.** Many individuals do not easily (a) take responsibility for the performance of colleagues or (b) let colleagues assume responsibility for their work.

_____ **Confusion about what makes groups work.** Many individuals may not know the difference between effective groups and traditional groups.

_____ **Fear that they cannot use groups effectively to enhance learning and improve teaching.** Not all groups work. Most adults have had personal experiences with very ineffective and inefficient committees, task forces, and clubs and know firsthand how bad groups can be. When many educators weigh the potential power of learning groups against the possibility of failure, they choose to play it safe and stick with the status quo of isolated work.

_____ **Concern about time and effort required to change.** Using groups requires individuals to apply what is known about effective groups in a disciplined way. Learning how to do so and engaging in such disciplined action may seem daunting.

redress (Abelson, Dasgupta, Park, & Banaji, 1998). When individuals are perceived to be part of a cohesive group (as opposed to an aggregate of unrelated individuals), observers express stereotypic judgments about the individuals and infer that their behavior was shaped by the presence of others (Oakes & Turner, 1986; Oakes, Turner, & Haslam, 1991; Wilder, 1977, 1978). A racial slur by an individual, for example, provokes a different reaction than a racial slur delivered by a group. Social scientists of both the individualistic and group persuasions have been productive in generating theories of group functioning and conducting research to validate or disconfirm the theories. They are both represented in this book.

ASPECTS OF GROUPS

In order to understand the nature of groups, it is necessary to understand:

1. The way you structure a group will determine how productive it will be.
2. The nature of group structure.
3. The ways groups develop over time.
4. How the dynamics of the group determine its effectiveness.

CREATING PRODUCTIVE GROUPS

There is nothing magical about working in a group. Some groups are highly effective and achieve amazing things. Some groups are highly ineffective and waste everyone's time. The authors have studied various types of groups for over thirty years. We have interviewed thousands of members in a wide variety of organizations in a number of different countries over four different decades to discover how groups are being used and where and how groups work best. On the basis of our findings and the findings of other researchers such as Katzenbach and Smith (1993), we have developed a group performance curve to clarify the difference between ineffective and effective groups (Figure 1.2). The group performance curve illustrates that how well any small group performs depends on how it is structured (Katzenbach & Smith, 1993). On the performance curve four types of groups are described. It begins with the individual members of the group and illustrates the relative performance of these members to pseudogroups, traditional work groups, effective groups, and high-performance groups.

A **pseudogroup** is a group whose members have been assigned to work together but they have no interest in doing so. They believe they will be evaluated by being ranked from the highest performer to the lowest performer. While on the surface members talk to each other, under the surface they are competing. They see each other as rivals who must be defeated, block or interfere with each other's performance, hide information from each other, attempt to mislead and confuse each other, and distrust each other. The result is that the sum of the whole is less than the potential of the individual members. Members would be more productive if they were working alone. The group does not mature because members have no interest in or commitment to each other or the group's future.

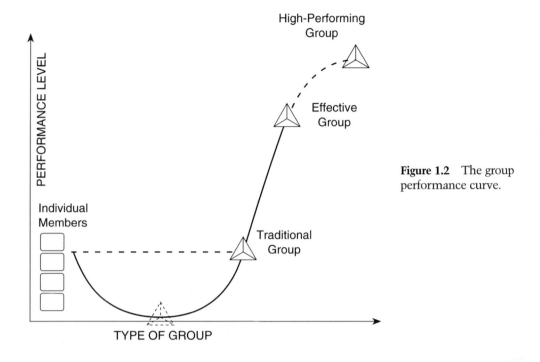

Figure 1.2 The group performance curve.

A **traditional work group** (see Figure 1.2) is a group whose members are assigned to work together and accept that they have to do so. Members believe that they will be evaluated and rewarded as individuals, not as members of the group. The work is structured so that very little joint work is required. Members interact primarily to clarify how the work is to be done. They seek each other's information but have no motivation to inform their group mates. Helping and sharing is minimized. Members are accountable as separate individuals, not as members of a team. Some members loaf, seeking a free ride on the efforts of their more conscientious groupmates. The conscientious members feel exploited and do less. The result is that the sum of the whole is more than the potential of some of the members, but the more hard-working and conscientious members would perform higher if they worked alone.

An **effective group** is more than a sum of its parts. It is a group whose members commit themselves to the common purposes of maximizing their own and each other's success. Members are assigned to work together and they are happy to do so. They believe that their success depends on the efforts of all group members. An effective group has a number of defining characteristics. They include positive interdependence that unites members together to achieve clear, operational goals, two-way communication, distributed leadership, power based on expertise, a decision-making procedure appropriate to the situation; to challenge each other's information and reasoning; and to resolve conflicts constructively. In addition, members hold each other accountable to do his or her fair share of the work, promote each other's success, appropriately engage in small group skills, and process how effectively they are working together.

Types of Groups

Demonstrate your understanding of the different types of groups by matching each definition with the appropriate group. Check your answers with your partner and explain why you believe your answers to be correct.

	Type of Group	Definition
_____	1. Pseudogroup	a. A group in which members work together to accomplish shared goals. Members perceive they can reach their goals if and only if the other group members also reach their goals.
_____	2. Traditional group	b. A group whose members have been assigned to work together but they have no interest in doing so. The structure promotes competition at close quarters.
_____	3. Effective group	c. A group that meets all the criteria for being an effective group and outperforms all reasonable expectations, given its membership.
_____	4. High-performance group	d. A group whose members agree to work together, but see little benefit from doing so. The structure promotes individualistic work with talking.

A **high-performance group** meets all the criteria for being an effective group and outperforms all reasonable expectations, given its membership. What differentiates the high-performance group from an effective group is the level of commitment members have to each other and the group's success. Jennifer Futernick, who is part of a high-performing, rapid response team at McKinsey & Company, calls the emotion binding her teammates together a form of love (Katzenbach & Smith, 1993). Ken Hoepner of the Burlington Northern Intermodal Team (also described by Katzenbach & Smith, 1993) stated: "Not only did we trust each other, not only did we respect each other, but we gave a damn about the rest of the people on this team. If we saw somebody vulnerable, we were there to help." Members' mutual concern for each other's personal growth enables high-performance groups to perform far above expectations and also to have lots of fun. The bad news about high-performance groups is that they are rare. Most groups never achieve this level of development.

Exercise 1.5: Developing an Effective Group

The purpose of this exercise is to give participants some practice in planning how to develop an effective group. The procedure for the exercise is as follows:

1. The class forms groups of four.

2. Groups read and discuss the paragraph below, and then answer the following questions about the situation:
   a. Which alternative would you choose if you were there?
   b. What kind of people would you want as companions in such a situation?
   c. What should the goals of the group be?
   d. How should leadership be managed?
   e. Who should have the most power in making decisions?
   f. What decision-making procedure should be used?
   g. How should conflicts be managed?
3. Each group decides whether its answers to the above questions are indicative of an effective or an ineffective group.
4. Each group shares its answers with the rest of the class.

SINKING BOAT SITUATION

On a dark summer night seven persons cling to a swamped and slowly sinking boat on a black tropical sea. They are not alone. A large shark glides below them, and soon, perhaps, there will be more. With fear thick in their salt-swollen throats, the seven are faced with a difficult choice. If they kick in unison, they may be able to fight the fierce current and tides driving them away from the shore and all make it to safety; if they stick together they have an equal chance to survive or drown. If they split up, each going it alone, one or two of the stronger swimmers might make it to safety, but the majority will certainly drown or be devoured by sharks.

1. Which alternative would you choose if you were there?
2. Which alternative would you want your companions to choose?
3. What are the characteristics the group would have to exhibit in order to ensure everyone survives?

GROUP STRUCTURE

Imagine you are an ecologist whose career has been dedicated to studying the seven corners of the world. In your studies of six of the corners you have encountered many diverse and unique habitats, from thick rain forests to severe deserts. They all, however, had a set of features in common: topography, weather patterns, plants, animals, and their interconnections. You have observed, for example, that plants and animals have certain territories that comprise an elaborate division of labor and broad symbioses, and that plants and animals adapt over time so that they are uniquely suited to survive and flourish within their habitat. Thus, you expect to find a basic ecological structure within the final, seventh corner of the world.

Now imagine you are studying small groups. Although there are many diverse types of groups, when you approach a new group you look for the basic features that characterize all groups: a purpose that defines the territory of the group and binds the members together, a definable pattern of communication among members, different members performing different functions that fit into an overall division of labor, procedures for managing conflicts, expectations concerning acceptable and unacceptable behavior by group members, and the adaptation of the group to the organization, society, and culture within which it is based. Once the basic structure has been identified, the nature of interpersonal relations in the group can be understood as clearly as the functioning of an ecosystem.

Just like ecosystems, groups have a structure. Observers of groups look beyond the unique features of the group to its basic structure. The **group structure** is a stable pattern of interaction among members. Groups function as members interact. Groups are networks of human relationships, and a group is effective only if members are effective in cooperating with each other. Whenever two or more individuals join together to achieve a goal, a group structure develops. Within any group, no matter which organization, society, or culture it is within, there are differentiated roles and integrating norms. The interaction among group members is structured by the group's roles and norms. Roles differentiate the responsibilities of group members whereas norms integrate members' efforts into a unified whole. Each is discussed briefly below.

Roles: Differentiation Within Groups

Think of one of the groups you have belonged to. Once you have a specific group in mind, answer this question: Did everyone in the group act in the same way or perform the same functions? In all likelihood, your answer is "no." Usually, a considerable degree of **differentiation** exists within groups so different members work on different tasks and are expected to accomplish different things for the group. In other words, different group members play different roles. Roles define the formal structure of the group and differentiate one position from another. Formally, a **role** may be defined as a set of expectations defining the appropriate behavior of an occupant of a position toward other related positions. Often such roles are assigned in a relatively formal manner, such as appointing a president, secretary, treasurer, and so on. Other times individuals drift into various roles on the basis of their interests and skills. Once a role is assumed, however, the member is expected (by other group members) to behave in certain ways and members who conform to their role requirements are rewarded, whereas those who deviate are punished. Roles ensure that the task behaviors of group members are appropriately interrelated so that the group's goals are achieved. The roles are complementary in that one cannot be performed without the other (e.g., the roles of "teacher" and "student").

Group Structure

	Definition	Example
Roles	Expectations defining the appropriate behavior of an occupant of a position toward other related positions.	President, vice president, secretary; summarizer, recorder
Norms	Common beliefs regarding group members' appropriate behavior, attitudes, and perceptions; rules, implicit or explicit, that regulate the behavior of group members.	Promptness, courtesy, reciprocity, responsibility

The expectations that define a role include both rights and obligations. The obligations of one role are the rights of other roles. One of the obligations of being a teacher, for example, includes structuring a learning situation; one of the rights of being a student is to have learning situations structured by the teacher. Within a group, expectations of the obligations of a role can conflict (i.e., role conflict). What a principal and what students expect from a teacher, for example, can be contradictory. Contradictory expectations can create one type of role conflict. There is also a second type.

Imagine that you are Pat Garrett and one of your best friends is Billy the Kid. You are appointed sheriff and your superiors expect you to fulfill your role by arresting Billy the Kid. Billy expects you to fulfill your role as friend by letting him alone. Which role would you want to fulfill if you were Pat Garrett? What would you actually do? Each person is required to fill multiple roles. When the demands of one role are incompatible with the demands of another, **role conflict** exists. Sometimes such role conflict can be great drama. What Sheriff Pat Garrett illustrated when he shot down his friend Billy the Kid was that roles can powerfully influence our actions, often leading us to act contrary to our private feelings or vested interests. Milgram (1974) provided another example with his famous studies on obedience to authority. In these studies, he placed paid adult subjects in the role of teacher and gave them the responsibility of giving "learners" an electric shock when they committed a memory error. Milgram intended to show that the teacher would refuse to comply with the requirements of his role, but although almost all teachers began to express reluctance and show signs of stress as the intensity of the shock increased and the learner cried out in pain, the majority of the teachers continued to administer the shocks. Over 60% of subjects administered the maximum shock voltage (450V) to the learner. Even when the teacher was compelled to hold the learner's hand to the shock plate, the figure dropped only to 30%. Milgram's results point out how a good number of people could be pressured into committing a variety of costly, harmful, and even immoral actions if role pressure is severe enough.

Different social roles are usually associated with different degrees of status. **Status** is generally a function of the degree to which an individual's contribution is crucial to the success (and prestige) of the group, how much power (control over outcomes) that individual has, and the extent to which the person embodies some idealized or admired characteristic (such as being physically attractive). In many subhuman groups (and some human ones) status is determined by physical dominance. Although status and power ordinarily go hand in hand, they need not. Johnson and Allen (1972) separated status and power experimentally. They found that having high status and high power in an organization results in an enhanced self-perception that leads to altruistic behavior but disdain for the worker. But when individuals have high status but low power in an organization that rewards high power, they engage in selfish behavior (they deviate from the prescribed norms in order to increase their own rewards) and respect for the worker.

Status differences have a number of important effects on group process. High-status individuals are likely to be valued by the group and treated more tolerantly. They are often less affected, therefore, by group norms and peer pressure than lower status members, in part because they are less likely to expect punishment for their actions (Johnson & Allen, 1972). High-status members, furthermore, have a disproportionately strong impact on group decisions and judgments, whereas those low in status tend to be ignored, even when they offer intelligent and creative advice. Torrance (1954) studied the decision making of B-26 combat crews, in which the pilot was the commanding officer, the navigator was a commissioned officer, and the tail gunner was an enlisted man inferior in status to the two officers. He found that when one of the men had the right answer and the other two were mistaken, the pilots were almost always successful in persuading the other two to accept their view (94%), the navigators not quite as successful (80%), and the tail gunners much less persuasive (63%). It is not uncommon in decision-making groups for a low-power person to have a critical insight or piece of information and be ignored. Sometimes the tail gunner's opinions were correct, but they were still ignored.

Norms: Integration of Members' Actions

Whereas roles differentiate members' rights and obligations from each other, norms integrate the actions of all group members. Norms are rules, implicit or explicit, established by groups to regulate the behavior of their members. Norms tell group members how to behave, or how *not* to behave, in various situations. The **norms** of a group are the group's common beliefs regarding appropriate behavior, attitudes, and perceptions for members. They are the prescribed modes of conduct and belief that not only guide the behavior of group members but also help group interaction by specifying the kinds of responses that are expected and acceptable in particular situations. All groups have norms, set either formally or informally. A group of students that often parties together, for example, will have common ideas about what is acceptable and unacceptable behavior at a party, about what is expected of everyone. More formally organized groups, such as classrooms, will have norms about absence, tardiness, accomplishment of assigned work, and appropriate times to speak. In any group some norms specify the behavior expected of all group members and others apply only to persons in specific roles. In the classroom, for instance, some norms govern both the teacher's and the students' behavior but others may apply only to the teacher or only to the students. Because norms refer to the expected behavior sanctioned (rewarded or punished) by a group, they have a specific "ought to" or "must" quality: Group members must not disrupt the group's work, group members ought to participate in discussions, and so on. The norms of any group vary in importance. Those that are less important for the objectives and values of the group usually allow for a greater range of behavior and bring less severe pressures for members to conform than do norms that are highly relevant to group functioning. Because most groups insist on adherence to their norms as a basic requirement for membership, it is hardly surprising that individuals wishing to join or remain in specific groups generally follow these "rules of the game." If they do not, they may soon find themselves on the outside looking in!

For a group norm to influence a person's behavior, the person must recognize that it exists, be aware that other group members accept and follow the regulation, and accept and follow it him or herself. At first a person may conform to a group norm because the group typically rewards conforming behavior and punishes nonconforming behavior. Later the person may internalize the norm and conform to it automatically, even when no other group members are present. A regulation that all members should be on time for group meetings, for example, becomes a norm only to the extent that the individual group member accepts it, sees other group members accepting it, and sees them enforcing the regulation among themselves.

Group norms help a group maintain behavioral consistency among its members. They provide a basis for predicting the behavior of other members and serve as a guide for a member's own behavior. Norms thus help each group member anticipate how the others are going to behave in repetitive situations, and they reduce ambiguity concerning appropriate behavior within the group. Norms are formed only with respect to matters that have some significance to the group. Norms may apply to all members or only to certain members. Norms vary in the degree to which they are accepted by the group members. Some norms allow for more deviation by members than others. Some norms require strict adherence to a rule; others permit a wide range of behavior that is regarded as acceptable.

Norms cannot be imposed on a group, but rather develop out of the interaction among members. Norms are social products. This was demonstrated ingeniously by Muzafer Sherif (1936a). When a fixed point of light is viewed in total darkness, it appears to move spontaneously: a perceptual phenomenon known as the autokinetic effect. Sherif utilized this phenomenon in studying how group norms develop and how group members come to form coherent, shared beliefs about novel events. Sherif led individuals to a totally dark room and turned on a tiny bulb. He asked participants, first individually and then in groups, to note how much the light moved. When tested in groups the participants coalesced in their judgments on the amount of movement. Sherif was able to increase or decrease subjects' estimates of movement dramatically if he paid confederates to offer particularly large or small estimates. Once a group decision was made about how much the light was moving, the norm persisted even when the group was not present. Individual participants used the group judgment as a frame of reference within which to evaluate the perceived movement of the light. Many of the judgments and values of individual group members that seem to be their own are shaped in part by the judgments of their fellow group members.

Another classic study on the impact of group norms on the beliefs and values of group members was conducted by Theodore Newcomb (1943). Born in 1903, Newcomb had studied with Goodwin Watson and Gardner Murphy at Columbia University. He was a pioneer of social psychology and a cofounder of the social psychology program at the University of Michigan. He conducted a number of studies on the impact of the college experience on students, the most famous of which was his classic study of group norms at Bennington College. The students, all females from mostly well-to-do and politically conservative families, lived in a community where most of the faculty and older students were somewhat materialistic and politically liberal. A majority of the Bennington students became progressively more liberal over their careers, but some did not. Newcomb was able to relate the student's ultimate political orientation to the group she identified with—liberal, if she thought of herself as foremost a member of the campus community, and conservative, if her primary identification was with her family. This study served as the basis on which the study of referenced groups began. A **reference group** is a group people identify with, compare their attitudes to, and use as a means to evaluate those attitudes.

THE DEVELOPMENT OF GROUPS OVER TIME

In addition to having a structure, groups change over time. The kinds of developmental changes seen in most groups have been described by well over one hundred theories. Most of these theories have taken one of two approaches (Hill & Gruner, 1973; Shambaugh, 1978). **Recurring-phase theories** specify the issues that dominate group interaction that recur again and again. Robert Freed Bales (1965), for example, stated that an equilibrium had to exist between task-oriented work and emotional expressions to build better relationships among group members. The group tends to oscillate between these two concerns, sometimes for more solidarity and sometimes for a more work-oriented focus. Bion (1961) stated that groups focus on the three basic themes of dependency on the leader, pairing among members for emotional support, and fight–flight reactions to a threat to the group. William Schultz (1958) proposed that group development occurs as members concern themselves with three issues—affection, inclusion, and control.

Sequential-stage theories specify the "typical" order of the phases of group development. Moreland and Levine (1982, 1988) suggested that group members go through predictable stages of membership: prospective member, new member, full member, marginal member, and ex-member. At each stage, the member is concerned about a different aspect of group life. For example, the new member attempts to change the group to meet his or her needs while the group attempts to mold the new member to fit group needs. The full member engages in role negotiation in order to find a niche that is most comfortable. Worchel, Coutant-Sassic, and Grossman (1992) proposed six stages to group development. There is a stage of discontent, when individuals feel that their present group(s) are not meeting their needs. A precipitating event brings members together. Members begin to identify with the group. Attention then turns to group productivity. Attention shifts to the individual group member who negotiates with the group to expand task efforts to meet personal goals. Finally, the group begins to disintegrate. Outside of group research, Levinger (1980) proposed there are five stages to close relationships, where there is initial attraction, building a relationship, continuation, deterioration, and ending the relationship. Hopper (1950) proposed that revolutions developed through a series of identifiable stages. There is a preliminary stage in which crime, suicide, travel, and emigration all increase; a popular stage in which the discontent spreads; and an institutional stage in which a new government is established. With all of these theories to choose from, the only conclusion may be that groups follow a pattern of development; there have been frequent attempts to define what those states are, but they still remain unclear.

Probably the most famous sequential-stage theory was formulated by Bruce W. Tuckman (1965; Tuckman & Jensen, 1977). Tuckman reviewed over fifty studies on group development conducted in a variety of settings (mostly therapy and training groups of limited duration). Although the description of the stages the groups went through varied widely on the surface (some studies identifying three stages and others identifying seven or eight), Tuckman found a surprising amount of agreement beneath the diversity. He identified five stages: forming, storming, norming, performing, and adjourning. At each stage groups focus on specific issues and this focus influences members' behaviors. During the **forming stage,** there is a period of uncertainty in which members try to determine their place in the group and the procedures and rules of the group. During the **storming stage,** conflicts begin to arise as members resist the influence of the group and rebel against accomplishing the task. Members often confront their various differences and the management of conflict becomes the focus of attention. During the **norming stage,** the group establishes some consensus regarding a role structure and a set of group norms for appropriate behavior. Cohesion and commitment increase. In the **performing stage** the group members become proficient in working together to achieve the group's goals and become more flexible in its patterns of working together. In the **adjourning stage** the group disbands. Of all the sequential-stage theories, Tuckman's emphasis on forming, storming, norming, performing, and adjourning still seems the most useful and creates the most interest.

Virtually all the studies that Tuckman reviewed, however, involved group leaders who were passive and nondirective and who made no attempt to intervene in the group process. In most groups there is a coordinator, team leader, or instructor who tries to ensure that the group functions productively. In applying Tuckman's conclusions to such groups, the authors (with the help of Roger Johnson and a number of other colleagues) identified seven stages of development:

1. Defining and structuring procedures.
2. Conforming to procedures and getting acquainted.
3. Recognizing mutuality and building trust.
4. Rebelling and differentiating.
5. Committing to and taking ownership for the goals, procedures, and other members.
6. Functioning maturely and productively.
7. Terminating.

Each of these stages is discussed in turn.

Defining and Structuring Procedures

When a group begins, the members are usually concerned about what is expected of them and the nature of the group's goals. Group members want to know what is going to happen; what is expected of them; whether or not they will be accepted, influential, and liked; how the group is going to function; and who the other group members are. Group members expect the coordinator to explain how the group is to function in a way that reassures them that their personal needs will be met. When a group first meets, therefore, the coordinator should define the procedures to be used, define the group's goals, establish the interdependence among members, and generally organize the group and announce the beginning of the group's work.

Conforming to Procedures and Getting Acquainted

As group members follow the prescribed procedures and interact around the task, they become acquainted with one another and familiarize themselves with the procedures until they can follow them easily. They learn the strengths and weaknesses of the other group members. During this stage the group members are dependent on the coordinator for direction and clarification of the goals and procedures of the group. It is also during this stage that the coordinator stresses the following group norms:

1. Taking responsibility for one's own performance and the performance of the other members of the group.
2. Providing help and assistance to other members.
3. Responding to other members in an accepting, supportive, and trustworthy way.
4. Making decisions through consensus.
5. Confronting and solving problems in group functioning. During this stage the goals and procedures of the group are the coordinator's. The group members conform to the prescribed procedures and interact with each other, but they are not personally committed to the group's goals and each other.

Recognizing Mutuality and Building Trust

The third stage of group development is marked by group members (a) recognizing their interdependence and (b) building trust. A sense of mutuality is built as group members recognize they "sink or swim together." Members begin to take responsibility for each other's performance and appropriate behavior. Trust is built through disclosing one's thoughts, ideas, conclusions, and feelings, and having the other group members respond with acceptance, support, and reciprocation of the disclosures. Trust is discussed at length in Chapter 3 and in Johnson (2000).

Rebelling and Differentiating

The fourth stage of group development is marked by group members (a) rebelling against the coordinator and the procedures and (b) differentiating themselves from each other through disagreements and conflicts. On the road to maturity a group will go through a period (sometimes short, sometimes long) of challenging the authority of the coordinator. It is an ordinary occurrence and should be expected. This swing toward independence contrasts sharply with the dependence demonstrated by members during stage 2. Many group members may have the attitude that participation is a passive process in which they can slip by without doing much work. Group members may wish to test and challenge the coordinator's sincerity and commitment to the procedures. Members may become "counterdependent" and attempt to establish their independence by doing just the opposite of what the group-learning procedures call for. Relationships among group members are often built through a cycle of becoming friendly, establishing independence through disagreement and conflict, and then committing oneself to a relationship. Differentiating is important for group members to establish boundaries and autonomy (Johnson, 1979, 1980a).

The coordinator can expect both rebelling against the group procedures and conflict among group members as a natural and expected stage of group development. The coordinator will want to deal with both in an open and accepting way. Some advice for doing so includes:

1. Do not tighten control and try to force conformity to prescribed procedures; reason and negotiate.

2. Confront and problem solve when members become counterdependent and rebellious.
3. Mediate conflicts among members helping the group establish members' autonomy and individuality.
4. Work towards members taking ownership of the procedures and committing themselves to each other's success.

Coordinating a group at this stage is like teaching a child to ride a bicycle: One runs alongside to prevent the child from falling, but one must let loose so the child can learn to balance on his or her own.

Committing to the Group's Goals and Procedures

During this stage, dependence on the coordinator and conformity to the prescribed procedures are replaced by dependence on the other members of the group and personal commitment to the collaborative nature of the experience. The "changing hands" from the coordinator's group to our group that began in the previous stage is finalized in this stage. The group becomes "ours" rather than "the coordinator's." Group norms become internalized and group members enforce the norms on themselves. Motivation becomes intrinsic rather than extrinsic. Members become committed to the procedures and accept responsibility for maximizing the performance of all group members. Group members also become concerned about each other's welfare, provide support and assistance (not because the coordinator wants them to but because they care about each other), believe that they can rely on the support and assistance of other group members, and truly become friends.

Functioning Maturely and Productively

As the group achieves maturity, autonomy, and productivity, a group identity emerges. Group members work together to achieve a variety of goals and deal with conflict in constructive ways. Group members clearly collaborate to achieve the group's goals while ensuring that their relationships with each other are maintained at a high-quality level. The coordinator becomes a consultant to the group rather than a directive leader. The relationships among group members continue to improve, as does the relationship between the coordinator and the members. In the maturely functioning group, all the criteria for effective groups are met. Many groups never reach this stage.

Terminating

The life of every group is finite. The group eventually ends and the members go their separate ways. The more mature and cohesive the group, and the stronger the emotional bonds that have been formed among group members, the more potentially upsetting is the termination period. Nevertheless, group members deal with the problems of separating so that they can leave the group experience behind them and move on to new experiences.

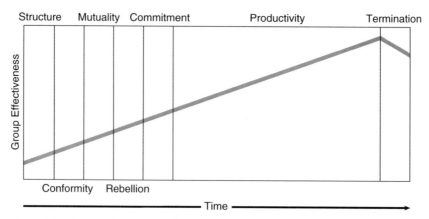

Figure 1.3   Stages of group development.

Length of Each Stage

Not all stages last the same amount of time. Many groups move very quickly through the first five stages, spend considerable time functioning maturely, and then terminate quickly. The average amount of time groups tend to spend in each stage is presented in Figure 1.3.

Conclusion

Both the sequential-stage and the recurring-phase perspectives are useful for understanding group development. They are not contradictory. A group may move through

Summary of Coordinator's Role

1. Introduce, define, and structure the group.
2. Clarify procedures, reinforce members for conforming to the procedures, and help members become acquainted.
3. Emphasize and highlight the cooperative interdependence among group members and encourage their engaging in both trusting and trustworthy behaviors.
4. Accept the rebellion by and differentiation among group members as a normal process and use confrontation and constructive negotiation to help members establish their independence from each other and the prescribed procedures.
5. Facilitate the members' committing themselves to and taking ownership for the group's goals and procedures.
6. Be a consultant to the group providing needed resources for the group to function effectively.
7. Signal termination and help the members move on to future groups.

various stages while dealing with basic themes that surface as they become relevant to the group's work. Because the issues underlying the themes are never completely resolved, they can recur later.

Exercise 1.6: Are Groups Beneficial or Harmful?

There has been some controversy over whether group membership is constructive or destructive. The purpose of this exercise is to structure a critical discussion of the issue.

1. **Assignment to Groups:** Assign participants to groups of four. Each group is to write a short statement summarizing and explaining its position on whether individual or group decision making is more effective.
2. **Assignment to Pairs and Positions:** Divide each group into two pairs:
   a. Pair One is assigned the position that individuals are superior to groups in making decisions and given Briefing Sheet One.
   b. Pair Two is assigned the position that groups are superior to individuals in making decisions and given Briefing Sheet Two.
3. The procedure and guidelines for constructive controversy may be reviewed (page 330).
4. Conduct the exercise and monitor participants to ensure the procedures are skillfully followed.
5. Have participants process their experience.

ARE GROUPS BENEFICIAL OR HARMFUL?

Tasks

1. Make the best case possible for your assigned position. Ensure that it gets a fair and complete hearing.
2. Critically analyze and challenge the opposing positions. Ensure that the information and logic stand up under critical scrutiny.
3. Reach consensus on the group's best reasoned judgment about the issue.

Procedure

1. **Prepare Positions:** Working with your partner, prepare a persuasive presentation that makes the best case possible for your assigned position. The presentation should have three parts: thesis statement (your position), rationale (your information organized in a logically compelling way), and conclusion (your position). In preparing your presentation, use the attached overview of social-psychological research, applicable text material, and what you know from other sources. You have ten minutes to prepare (a) a forceful and persuasive three-minute presentation and (b) your arguments for the open discussion. Both members of the pair have to be ready to give the presentation.
2. **Present Positions:** Meet with a person representing the opposing position. Give a three minute presentation of the best case possible for your position. Be persuasive. Listen to the other person's three-minute presentation; take notes and ask for clarification of anything that is not fully understood.
3. **Advocate, Attack and Defend Discussion:** Continue to advocate the best case possible for your position. Critically analyze and challenge the opposing position. Point out the shortcomings in its information and logic. Defend your position from the attacks of the

opponent. The discussion should focus on theory, research, and facts, not on opinions and impressions. You have ten minutes to discuss the issue.

4. **Reverse Perspectives:** Give a two-minute presentation of the best case possible for the opposing position. Summarize the opposing position (information and logic). The summary should be complete and accurate. Add any additional information you may have that supports the opposing position. Listen to the opponent's presentation of your position and correct anything that is incorrectly understood.

5. **Write Joint Report:** Drop all advocacy. Reach consensus as to the nature of your best reasoned judgment about the issue. Write one statement summarizing and explaining your joint conclusions on whether individual or group decision making is more effective. The best reasoning from both sides should be synthesized or integrated into your best reasoned judgment. Base your conclusions on theory, research, and facts.

RULES FOR CONSTRUCTIVE CONTROVERSY

1. I am critical of ideas, not individuals. I challenge and refute the ideas of the opposing pair, but I do not indicate that I personally reject the members of the pair.
2. I focus on coming to the best decision possible, not on "winning." I remember that we are all in this together.
3. I encourage everyone to participate and to master all the relevant information.
4. I listen to everyone's ideas, even if I don't agree.
5. I paraphrase or restate what someone has said if it is not clear to me.
6. I first bring out all the ideas and facts supporting both sides, and then I try to put them together in a way that makes sense.
7. I try to understand both sides of the issue.
8. I change my mind when the evidence indicates that I should do so.

BRIEFING SHEET ONE: GROUPS ARE GOOD FOR HUMANS

1. Under most conditions, the productivity of groups is higher than the productivity of individuals working alone.
2. Groups make more effective decisions and solve problems more effectively than individuals working alone.
3. It is through group memberships that the values of altruism, kindness, consideration for others, responsibility, and so forth, are socialized in us.
4. The quality of emotional life in terms of friendship, love, camaraderie, excitement, joy, fulfillment, and achievement is greater for members of groups than for individuals acting alone.
5. The quality of everyday life is greater in groups because of the advantages of specialization and division of labor. Our material standard of living, for example—our housing, food, clothing, transportation, entertainment, and so forth—would not be possible for a person living outside of a society.
6. Conflicts are managed more productively in groups. Social influence is better managed in groups. Without group standards, social values, and laws, civilization would be impossible.
7. A person's identity, self-esteem, and social competencies are shaped by the groups of significance to him or her.
8. Without cooperation, social organization, and groups of various kinds, humans would not survive. Humans have a basic social nature, and our survival and evolution are the results of the effectiveness of our groups.

9. Friendship, love, companionship, meaning, purpose, cooperation, and all that is good in life occur in groups.

BRIEFING SHEET TWO: GROUPS ARE NOT GOOD FOR HUMANS

1. People in groups are more likely to take greater risks than they would alone. Groups tend to take more extreme positions and indulge in more extreme behavior than their members would alone.
2. In groups there is sometimes a diffusion of responsibility such that members take less responsibility for providing assistance to someone in need or for rewarding good service.
3. In large groups individuals can become anonymous and therefore feel freer to engage in rowdy, shocking, and illegal behavior. When one member engages in impulsive and antisocial behavior, others may do likewise. Riots are often initiated and worsened by such modeling effects.
4. Being identified as part of a group may increase the tendency of nonmembers to treat one in impersonal and inhumane ways. It is easier, for example, to drop a bomb on the "enemy" than on a person.
5. Group contagion often gives rise to collective panic.
6. Millions of people have been swept into mass political movements only to become unhappy victims of the distorted visions of their leaders.
7. Groups often influence their members to conform. One type of conformity, obedience to authority, can cause a person to act in cruel and inhumane ways to others. The identity of the individual can be threatened when conformity is too extreme.
8. It is within groups that injustice, abuse, bullying, stereotypes, scapegoating, and all antisocial actions occur.

THE FIELD OF GROUP DYNAMICS

Close cooperation between theorists and practitioners can be accomplished . . . if the theorist does not look toward applied problems with highbrow aversion or with a fear of social problems, and if the applied psychologist realizes that there is nothing so practical as a good theory.

Kurt Lewin (1951, p. 169)

The Nature of Group Dynamics

The field of group dynamics is a combination of theory, research, and practice. Theory identifies the characteristics of effective groups, research validates or disconfirms the theories, and practical procedures based on the validated theory are implemented in the "real world" to see if they work. The theory, research, and practical applications of group dynamics all interact and enhance each other (see Figure 1.4). Theory both guides and summarizes research. Research validates or disconfirms theory, thereby leading to its refinement and modification. Practice is guided by validated theory, and applications of the theory reveal inadequacies that lead to refining of the theory, conducting new research studies, and modifying the application. This book emphasizes the interaction among theory, research, and practice.

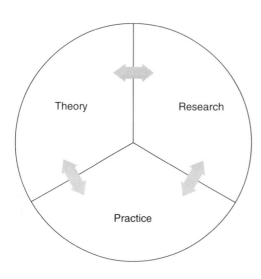

Figure 1.4   Relationship among theory, research, practice.
Source: D. W. Johnson & R. T. Johnson, *Cooperation and Competition: Theory and Research* (Edina, MN: Interaction Book Company, 1989). Used with permission of the authors.

Theory   Guides and summarizes research.
Research   Validates or disconfirms theory, thereby leading to its refinement and modification.
Practice   Guided by validated theory. Applications of the theory reveal inadequacies that lead to refining of the theory, conducting new research studies, and modifying the application.

Group dynamics is the scientific study of behavior in groups to advance our knowledge about the nature of groups, group development, and the interrelations between groups and individuals, other groups, and larger entities. What happens among group members is dynamic, not static. The interaction among group members is characterized by forces such as communication and leadership that are in constant motion and change. Social scientists interested in groups analyze the dynamics within groups by constructing theories and conducting research to test the theories. They then apply the validated theory to "real-world" situations to see if they work.

History of the Field of Group Dynamics

Group dynamics is a relatively young field, one that is rooted in a wide range of traditionally separate fields. Although the earliest existing philosophical literature contains a great deal of wisdom about the nature of groups, and although the basic assumptions that guide the field of group dynamics were discussed from the sixteenth through the nineteenth centuries, the field of group dynamics is strictly a twentieth-century development. Interested scientists come from many different disciplines and branches of the social sciences. The field of group dynamics, therefore, is the common property of all the social sciences.

Although its roots go back to the late 1800s, the field of group dynamics gained prominence in the early 1940s. After a worldwide depression, the rise of dictatorship in Europe, and the Second World War, most Americans were worried about the fate of their country and the future of democracy. There was general agreement that a better understanding was needed of how democratic organizations could be made to function more effectively. Scientists had helped win the war, many people said, and now research should improve democracy. The field of group dynamics was thought to have significant potential for doing so. The health of a democratic society was seen as depending on the effectiveness of its component groups. Strengthening the family, the community, and the multitude of groups within our society was viewed as the primary means of ensuring the vitality of our democracy. The scientific study of the functioning of groups was viewed by the public as the means for maintaining a democratic form of government and solving current social problems.

The drive to strengthen democracy by using the scientific method to strengthen groups resulted in two interrelated movements within psychology. The *first* was the scientific study of group dynamics. Searching for ways to strengthen democracy, social psychologists (a newly arrived group of specialists) (a) developed experimental methods of studying group dynamics and (b) began to conduct studies of group discussion, group productivity, attitude change, and leadership. The *second* movement was the application of group dynamics theory and research to deriving methods for training leaders and group members in the social skills needed to promote effective functioning of democratic groups. At the heart of both movements was Kurt Lewin, perhaps the greatest social psychologist who ever lived. He was not the first person, however, to develop theory and conduct research on group dynamics.

In the late nineteenth century, early researchers on group dynamics focused on the question, "What change in an individual's normal solitary performance occurs when other people are present?" Norman Triplett, an Indiana University psychologist, studied the records of the Racing Board of the League of American Wheelmen. Triplett observed that cyclists' times were faster when they were racing against each other than when the cyclists simply raced against the clock. He hypothesized that the presence of other people (i.e., competitors) acts as a stimulant to the performer. If the hypothesis were valid, Triplett reasoned, it would hold for activities other than bicycle racing. Creating an analogy to bicycle racing, Triplett (1898) asked children to wind fishing reels and compared their performance when alone with their performance when another child was present. They performed faster when the audience was present. This experiment was the first attempt to investigate the impact of social interdependence (i.e., competitive versus individualistic efforts) of achievement of a motor performance task.

Triplett's work later resulted in research on social facilitation–impairment (Zajonc, 1965), social interdependence (Johnson & Johnson, 1989), and social loafing (Harkins & Szymanski, 1987). Social facilitation researchers, for example, were interested in the question "Does the impact of an audience differ on simple versus complex tasks?" If you were running a mile, would an audience make you run faster or slower? If you were asked to assemble a complex new machine you had never seen before, would an audience increase or decrease the speed with which you assembled the machine? Allport (1924), Moede (1920), and others found that on simple tasks an audience increased speed of performance, whereas on complex tasks an audience decreased the speed of performance.

The second line of research, which became prominent in the late 1920s and 1930s, focused on the question "Are individuals or groups more productive on problem-solving and decision-making tasks?" (Gordon, 1924; Shaw, 1932; Watson, 1928). Overall, the results indicated that groups are more productive than are individuals. The descendants of this tradition are the research on social interdependence (Deutsch, 1962; Johnson & Johnson, 1989), jury decision making (e.g., Kerr et al., 1976), minority influence in groups (e.g., Moscovici, 1985a), conformity (e.g., Asch, 1951), and group polarization (e.g., Myers, 1978).

At the end of the 1930s the field of group dynamics advanced rapidly, due largely to the efforts of Kurt Lewin and three sociologists. In the 1930s and 1940s research on groups was popularized by the pioneering work of Kurt Lewin, who maintained that the behavior of individuals should be understood in terms of the nature of the groups to which they belong (Lewin, 1943, 1948). Sherif (1936) studied the impact of group norms on perception of an ambiguous stimulus. In an ingenious experiment he demonstrated that the judgments made by individuals were influenced by the judgments of their fellow group members. During the years 1935 to 1939, Newcomb (1943) conducted his famous field study investigating the impact of social norms concerning political issues on the students at Bennington College. As a result of their interaction, students tended to change their politically conservative attitudes to politically liberal ones. In 1937, W. F. Whyte moved into one of the slums of Boston and began a three-and-a-half-year study of social clubs, political organizations, and racketeering. Whyte (1943) reported in vivid detail the structure, culture, and functioning of the Norton Street gang and the Italian Community Club. His study dramatized the great significance of groups in the lives of individuals and in the functioning of larger social systems.

It was Kurt Lewin more than anyone else who stressed the importance of applying existing knowledge to solving social issues. In 1942, the Second World War had just begun for America, and travel was restricted. The Society for the Psychological Study of Social Issues had canceled its annual convention and was holding a dinner for members who lived in or near Washington, D.C. On that September evening, Kurt Lewin spoke to an audience deeply concerned about the fate of their country and the future of democracy. He made the brave prediction (Lewin, 1943):

> Although the scientific investigations of group work are but a few years old, I don't hesitate to predict that group work—that is, the handling of human beings not as isolated individuals, but in the social setting of groups—will soon be one of the most important theoretical and practical fields. . . . There is no hope for creating a better world without a deeper scientific insight into the . . . essentials of group life.

Lewin's prediction came true. From 1890 to 1940 there had been a gradual growth in the number of published studies on group behavior from 1 per year to approximately 30 per year. By the late 1940s, 55 studies were being published annually, and by the end of the 1950s the rate had skyrocketed to about 150. During the 1960s and 1970s the rate of research studies on group dynamics persisted at about 125 per year. Primarily through the influence of Lewin and his associates and students, group dynamics became one of the dominant fields in the social sciences.

By far the most influential study of group dynamics in the late 1930s was that of three psychologists, Lewin, Lippitt, and White (1939). This study made it clear that important social issues could be produced in the laboratory and studied experimentally. The study focused on the influences of different leadership patterns on groups and group members. Groups of ten- and eleven-year-old children met regularly for several weeks under the leadership of an adult, who behaved in one of three ways: democratically, autocratically, or in a laissez-faire manner. The effects of these leadership styles on the behavior of group members were large and dramatic. Severe forms of scapegoating, for example, occurred in the autocratic groups, and at the end of the experiment the children in some of those groups destroyed the things they had constructed.

Following this study, Lewin and his associates began a number of research studies aimed at developing a theory of group dynamics. French (1941) conducted a laboratory experiment comparing the effects of fear and frustration on organized versus unorganized groups. Bavelas (1942) conducted an experiment to determine whether the behavior of leaders of youth groups could be significantly modified through training. With the entry of the United States into the Second World War, Lewin, French, and Marrow (Marrow, 1957) explored group-decision procedures as a means of improving industrial production; and Lewin, Radke, and others (Lewin, 1943; Radke and Klisurich, 1947) conducted a number of experiments on group decision as a means of changing eating habits related to wartime food shortages.

In the 1950s, Bales and his colleagues' research on small discussion groups generated insight into the patterning of group members' responses and the nature of roles within a group (Bales, 1950, 1953; Bales & Slater, 1955). Bavelas (1948) and Leavitt (1951) examined information exchange by imposing network structures on decision-making groups and observing their effects on subsequent productivity. Schachter (1951) researched group reactions to the opinions of deviates. Deutsch (1949b, 1962) investigated cooperation and competition and the nature of trust.

In the 1950s the seeds were planted that ended the group dynamics movement. Festinger's theories of informal social communication (1950) and social comparison (1954) focused social psychology on the individual (not the group) as the primary unit of analysis. Social psychology began to examine how attitudes, values, personality, and thoughts internal to an individual guided and influenced social behavior. This individualistic trend was accelerated by the emergence of several other theoretical perspectives during the late 1950s, such as attribution theory (Heider, 1958), cognitive dissonance (Festinger, 1957), and persuasion (Hovland, Janis, & Kelley, 1953).

In the 1960s and 1970s, to most social psychologists the individual appeared to be a simpler unit than the group on which to base the study of social interaction. Statistical and methodological difficulties in group research moved researchers towards research on individual variables. Psychologists were disposed to decompose social variables into smaller segments rather than integrating them into larger social structures. A preference developed for using single-factor explanations for behavior rather than multifactor explanations. Studies that involved the systematic observation of groups in naturalistic settings typically were too difficult and expensive to conduct, analyze, and interpret.

In the 1980s and 1990s, however, the investigation of group dynamics had a resurgence. Many of the pragmatic, methodological, and statistical difficulties that thwarted group research in the 1950s and 1960s were either ameliorated or largely overcome. The research on a number of group issues such as cooperation, conflict resolution, distributive justice, intergroup relations, and cross-cultural interaction became major foci of social psychology (Deutsch, 1985; Johnson & Johnson, 1989; Tjosvold, 1991a; Tjosvold &

Johnson, 1982). In industrial psychology the determinants of work-group productivity and modes of effective leadership were the focus of considerable research (Hackman & Oldham, 1980; Tjosvold, 1991b). Clinical psychologists emphasized the client-therapist dyad and treatment of families as dysfunctional systems (e.g., Johnson & Matross, 1977; Wolman & Strikcer, 1983). In sociology, research focused on the possession and use of power, dominance hierarchies, and group structure (e.g., Berger, Rosenholtz, & Zelditch, 1980). In Europe interest was focused on group issues such as minority influence (Moscovici, 1985) and intergroup relations (Tajfel, 1981).

As we move through the millennium, interest in group dynamics is on the rise.

KURT LEWIN AND THE FIELD OF GROUP DYNAMICS

At the head of both of the group dynamic movements in the 1940s was one of the most important psychologists of the twentieth century, Kurt Lewin. Lewin was born on September 9, 1890, in the tiny village of Mogilno in the Prussian province of Posen (now part of Poland), where his father owned and operated a general store. In 1910 Lewin began studying for a doctorate in philosophy and psychology at the University of Berlin. After finishing his doctoral work in 1914, he entered the kaiser's army as a private and fought for four years in World War I in the infantry. He left the army as a lieutenant with an Iron Cross and returned to the University of Berlin to teach. There he became part of the Psychological Institute, where Max Wertheimer, Kurt Koffka, and Wolfgang Kohler were formulating their Gestalt theory. Lewin became one of the Gestaltists, but he was never an orthodox follower of their early leaders. His interests were in the area of motivation, and his work was directed more to practical application than to understanding for its own sake. In 1933, as Hitler was rising to power, Lewin migrated to the United States. He subsequently worked at Cornell University, the University of Iowa (where he taught at the Child Welfare Research Station), and the Massachusetts Institute of Technology, where he set up and headed the famous Research Center for Group Dynamics (which later moved to the Institute for Social Research at the University of Michigan). On February 11, 1947, Lewin died unexpectedly of a heart attack.

In his advocacy of the study of group dynamics Lewin was noted for three things: his development of theory, his early championing of the use of experimental methodology, and his insistence that theory and research be relevant to social practice.

Kurt Lewin was above all a theorist. Throughout his career he was concerned primarily with the problem of constructing an empirically based theory of human behavior. Lewin believed that every field of science must be concerned primarily with theory, because it is theory that illuminates the causal structure of the empirical world. Lewin's contributions to theory in group dynamics included (a) an emphasis on building conceptual systems that explained the dynamics observed in groups and (b) creating a field theory analysis of the field (Lewin, 1943, 1948). Borrowing concepts and language from force field physics, Lewin theorized individuals locomote through different regions of their lifespace, being either impelled by forces or drawn by valences that exist along power vectors. Some of the strongest forces and valences an individual experiences stem from groups. From this theoretical orientation, he and his associates and students formulated a wide variety of theories and research programs that defined the field of group dynamics.

Kurt Lewin

Lewin had a genius for thinking of ways to study his ideas experimentally, and he inspired in his students something of this ability. It was Lewin's study of different leadership strategies that proved that complex social phenomena could be studied with experimental methods. Lewin was convinced that the use of experimental methods in researching the dynamics of groups would revolutionize the field, and he was right.

Lewin did not see his commitment to theory as irrelevant to, or in any way incompatible with, his concern for the solution of social problems. He was convinced that the interests of the theorist and the practitioner were inextricably interrelated. He believed that social science theory should do more than advance knowledge—it should also provide guidelines for action. Lewin coined the term **action research** for the use of the scientific method in solving research questions that have significant social value. He urged social scientists to develop theories that could be applied to important social problems.

Lewin saw clearly that practitioners and theorists share a common interest in understanding reality and acting competently. He viewed them as having interdependent tasks: Practitioners identify significant problems to be solved, theorists develop a valid view of reality that contains the keys for solving the problems, and practitioners apply the theory. Practitioners keep theorists in contact with social reality, and theorists provide practitioners with a deeper understanding of the social problems that confront them. Lewin believed that theorists have a special obligation: to provide the kind of theory that can be used in solving social problems. Lewin was a doer, and he wanted to conduct and inspire research that made a difference in the real world of human affairs. He was constantly suggesting ways to bridge the gap between theoretical science and public policies and practices. The particular applications he suggested were infused with democratic values. He had a profound faith in democracy, which to him was much more than just a political system. It was also a way of life, based on mutual participation and continual interaction in decision making for purposeful change.

Kurt Lewin was in his element with an informal seminar group. He was not at his best in a formal lecture, as he was not highly organized. But he had an enthusiasm for psychological analysis that was contagious. His contacts with his students were so strong that sometimes an afternoon discussion would last beyond midnight. Informal group discussions reflected not only Lewin's style of interacting with other people but also his beliefs in democracy. Given his style of working with groups, his interests in social action, and his concern for democratic decision making, it was not surprising that Lewin turned increasingly to the study of group dynamics in his years in America. Although Lewin did not create the field of group dynamics (it was the result of developments occurring over several decades and different disciplines), he was the major link between much of the theorizing and much of the practical application in the field. The contents of this book as well as the entire field of group dynamics are heavily influenced by Lewin and his work.

NATURE OF THIS BOOK AND HOW TO USE IT

This is not a book that you can read with detachment. It is written to involve you with its contents. By reading this book you will not only be able to learn the theoretical and empirical knowledge now available on group dynamics, but you will also learn to apply this knowledge in practical ways within the groups to which you belong. Often in the past, group dynamics practitioners did not pay attention to the research literature, and group dynamics researchers neglected to specify how their findings could be applied. Thus, the knowledge about effective groups and the learning of group skills was often divided. In this book we directly apply existing theory and research to the learning and application of effective group skills. As you participate in the exercises, use diagnostic procedures for assessing your current skill levels, and discuss the relevant theory and research provided, you will bridge the gap between theory and practice.

In selecting exercises to include in this book, we tried to include exercises that were original, short, relevant to the theory and research being discussed, clear and simple, and easy to prepare. We intended each exercise to be like a supporting actor; it should do its work effectively, unobtrusively, and without upstaging the theory and research being presented. Each exercise is also aimed at promoting the development of group skills. The book defines the skills needed for effective group functioning and provides opportunities for readers to practice the skills for themselves and to receive feedback on their performance.

The purpose of this book is to bring together the theory on group dynamics, the research testing that theory, and structured exercises aimed at building practical group skills and illuminating the meaning of the theory and research presented. The central aim of each chapter is to review the most important theory and research, analyze basic

Keeping a Personal Journal

As you read this book you will be well advised to keep a journal in which you record what you are learning about group dynamics and about how you behave in group situations. You may also wish to include specific information you have learned about the social psychology of groups, effective behavior in groups, and the extent to which you have developed the group skills you want. A **journal** is a personal collection of writing and thoughts that have value for the writer. It has to be kept up on a regular basis. Entries are evaluated by whether they are valuable to the author, have some possibilities for sharing with others, and reflect significant thinking. Such a journal will be of great interest to you after you have finished this book. You may also wish to include specific information you have learned about group dynamics. *The purposes of the journal are:*

1. To keep track of the activities related to group dynamics.

2. To answer in writing some of the questions that are important for a clear understanding of the book's content (these will often be suggested, but others can be selected by you).

3. To collect thoughts that are related to the book's content (the best thinking often occurs when you are driving to or from school, about to go to sleep at night, and so forth).

4. To collect newspaper and magazine articles and references that are relevant to the topics covered in each chapter.

5. To keep summaries of conversations and anecdotal material that are unique, interesting, or illustrate things related to group dynamics.

(Note: If you publish your journal as did John Holt, Hugh Prather, and others, all we ask is a modest 10 percent of the royalties.)

issues in group dynamics, and provide structured skill-building exercises and other instructional aids. The format of each chapter is based on sound pedagogy and the principles of experiential learning. Most chapters begin with a discussion task involving the concepts presented in the chapter. At the beginning of most chapters is a short diagnostic instrument that will help you become more aware of your current behavior in the area discussed in the chapter. Also in most chapters is a controversy in which you and your classmates argue different sides of one of the central issues of the chapter. Exercises aimed at developing skills and understanding in the topic of the chapter are then provided. The relevant theory and research are presented. At the end of many of the chapters there is a procedure for examining the changes in your knowledge and skills.

In using this book you should diagnose your present knowledge and skills in the areas that are covered, actively participate in the exercises, reflect on your experiences, read the chapters carefully, and integrate the information and experiences into action theories related to group dynamics. You should then plan how to continue your skill- and knowledge-building activities after you have finished the book.

Learning Contract

Before beginning the next chapter, we would like to propose a learning contract. The contract is as follows:

I understand that I will be taking an experiential approach to learning about group dynamics and to developing the skills needed to function effectively in groups. I willingly commit myself to the statements hereunder.

1. I will use the structured experiences in this book to learn from. This means I am willing to engage in specified behaviors, seek out feedback about the impact of my behavior on others, and analyze my interpersonal interactions with other class members in order to make the most of my learning.

2. I will make the most of my own learning by (a) engaging in specified behaviors and in being open about my feelings and reactions to what is taking place in order that others may have information to react to in giving me feedback and in building conclusions about the area of study; (b) setting personal learning goals that I will work actively to accomplish—which means that I will take responsibility for my own learning and not wait around for someone else to "make me grow"; (c) being willing to experiment with new behavior and to practice new skills; (d) seeking out and being receptive to feedback; and (e) building conclusions about the experiences highlighted in the exercises.

3. I will help others make the most of their learning by (a) providing feedback in constructive ways, (b) helping to build the conditions (such as openness, trust, acceptance, and support) under which others can experiment and take risks with their behavior, and (c) contributing to the formulation of conclusions about the experiences highlighted in the exercises.

4. I will use professional judgment in keeping what happens among group members in the exercises appropriately confidential.

Signed: _____

The journal is an important part of this book. It is not an easy part. The entries should be important to you in your effort to make this course useful to youself, and because this is a cooperative course, useful to your fellow participants. You may be surprised how writing sharpens and organizes your thoughts.

YOUR SKILL LEVEL

Before going on, it will be useful for you to assess your current group skill level. Answer the following questions, describing yourself as accurately as you can:

1. How do you see yourself as a group member? What is your style of functioning within groups?

2. What are your strengths in functioning in groups? How do they fit into how you see yourself as a group member?

3. What situations within groups do you have trouble with and why? How do you feel when faced with them? How do you handle them? How would you like to handle them?

4. In what group skills do you wish to grow and develop? What changes would you like to make in your present group behavior? What new strengths in group behavior would you care to develop? What new group skills would you like to acquire?

SUMMARY

Humans are small group beings. Groups are ubiquitous and it is inevitable that you now belong to many, many groups. As the effectiveness of your groups go, so goes the quality of your life. You, therefore, have to have a working knowledge of group dynamics and the small group skills required to put that knowledge to use in school, at work, during leisure activities, at home, in your neighborhood, and in every other arena of your life. To begin with, you must know what is and is not a group. That is harder than it seems, as social scientists have yet to agree on a single definition. Generally, however, a *small group* is two or more individuals in face-to-face interaction, each aware of positive interdependence as they strive to achieve mutual goals, each aware of his or her membership in the group, and each aware of the others who belong to the group. Group dynamics is the scientific study of behavior in groups. The study of group dynamics has about a one hundred-year history in North America. All groups have a basic structure that includes roles and norms. Groups develop over time and pass through stages, although there is little agreement as to what those stages are. Their productivity depends on five basic elements (positive interdependence, individual accountability, promotive interaction, appropriate use of social skills, group processing). Not all groups are effective. To be effective, group members have to (a) ensure each other's commitment to clear mutual goals that highlight members' interdependence, (b) ensure accurate and complete communication among members, (c) provide leadership and appropriate influence, (d) flexibly use decision-making procedures that ensure all alternative courses of action receive a fair and complete hearing and each other's reasoning and conclusions are challenged and critically analyzed, and (e) resolve their conflicts constructively. One of the most important figures in the field of group dynamics is Kurt Lewin. His work, more than anyone's, shows the interrelationships between knowledge about group dynamics and actual small group skills. The purpose of this book is to bring together the theory on group dynamics, the research testing it, and structured exercises aimed at helping readers master practical group skills. The experiential learning procedures used in creating this integration of theory, research, and practical skills are discussed in the next chapter.

2 *Experiential Learning*

Basic Concepts to Be Covered in This Chapter

In this chapter a number of concepts are defined and discussed. The major ones are listed below. The procedure for learning these concepts is as follows:

1. Divide into heterogeneous pairs.
2. The task for each pair is to:
   a. Define each concept, noting the page on which it is defined and discussed.
   b. Ensure that both members of the pair understand the meaning of each concept.
3. Combine into groups of four. Compare the answers of the two pairs. If there is disagreement, the members look up the concept in the chapter and clarify it until they all agree on the definition and understand it.

Concepts

1. Action theory
2. Experiential learning
3. Role playing
4. Process observation
5. Content
6. Process
7. Participant-observer
8. Feedback
9. Observation procedures
10. Procedural learning

PROCEDURAL LEARNING

Knowing is not enough; we must apply. Willing is not enough; we must do.

Goethe

One learns by doing the thing; for though you think you know it, you have no certainty until you try.

Sophocles

The hand is the cutting edge of the mind.

Jacob Bronowski, *Ascent of Man*

Increasing your expertise in group dynamics requires procedural learning. Learning how to implement group dynamics theory and research is very similar to learning how to play tennis or golf, how to perform brain surgery, or how to fly an airplane. It involves more than simply reading material for a recognition level or even a total-recall level of mastery. **Procedural learning** exists when you study group dynamics to:

1. Learn conceptually group dynamics theory and research.
2. Translate your conceptual understanding into a set of group skills.
3. Actually use your group skills.
4. Eliminate errors in using your group skills to move through the initial awkward and mechanical stages of mastery to attain a routine-use, automated level of mastery.

In other words, you must acquire an understanding of group dynamics theory and research, develop a conceptualization of group skills, engage in guided practice to enact the skills and eliminate implementation errors, and persevere in using the group skills so that you can appropriately use them in a more and more automated fashion.

Procedural learning differs from simply learning facts and acquiring knowledge due to a heavier reliance on feedback about performance and the modification of implementation efforts until the errors of performance are eliminated. Procedural learning involves a progressive refinement of knowledge and skill as the procedures are practiced, practiced, and practiced.

It is the procedural nature of mastering group dynamics that makes this book different from most other textbooks. This may seem strange at first. Traditionally, in the United States, we have made a separation between "head" learning and "hand" learning. "Real" classes are supposed to be head learning whereas "vocational" classes are supposed to be hand learning. Thus, there is a focus on the head and a denial that the hand is present and important. In learning group dynamics, however, you should remember Jacob Bronowski's (1973) observation that it is the "hand" that drives the subsequent evolution of conceptual understanding. The "hand" becomes an instrument of vision, revealing the conceptual nature of the procedure being used. To "understand" you have to "do." True understanding results only from doing. **It is from using group skills that you will gain an understanding of what group dynamics is and how useful it can be.**

Procedural learning is based on experiential learning. The Russian cognitive theorist L. S. Vygotsky stated that learning from experience is the process whereby human development occurs. Your development and continual improvement of group skills depends on your participation in the skill-building exercises included in this book. Those exercises, and the links they provide with the theory and research discussed, are based on experiential learning. In experiential learning the responsibility for your learning lies with you, not with the teacher or instructor. Experiential exercises are structured so that you can experiment with your behavior, try things out, see what works, build skills, and develop action theories out of your own experiences. Appropriate theory is then presented so that you can summarize your learning and build conceptual frameworks within which you can organize what you know. Although experiential learning is a stimulating and involving activity, it is important to remember always that experience alone is not beneficial. You learn from the combination of experience and the conceptualization of your experiences.

In this chapter the nature of action theories and experiential learning is discussed. The procedures through which group skills are learned are presented. In addition, directions for how to conduct a skill-training experience and the ethics of doing so are discussed. First of all, to understand experiential learning you must first know what an action theory is.

ACTION THEORIES

Change and growth take place when a person has risked himself and dares to become involved with experimenting with his own life.

Herbert Otto

All humans need to become competent in taking action and simultaneously reflecting on their action in order to learn from it. Integrating thought with action requires that we plan our behavior, engage in it, and then reflect on how effective we were. When we learn a pattern of behavior that effectively deals with a recurrent situation, we tend to repeat it over and over until it functions automatically. Such habitual behavioral patterns are based on theories of action. An **action theory** is a theory as to what actions are needed to achieve a desired consequence in a given situation. All theories have an "if . . . then . . . " form. An action theory states that in a given situation if we do *x*, then *y* will result. Our theories of action are normative. They state what we ought to do if we wish to achieve certain results. Examples of action theories can be found in almost everything we do. If we smile and say hello, then others will return our smile and greeting. If we apologize, then the other person will excuse us. If we steal, then we will be punished. If a person shoves us, then we should shove back. All our behavior is based on theories that connect our actions with certain consequences.

In essence we build an action theory. As our behavior becomes habitual and automatic, our action theories become tacit (we are not able to put them into words). When our behavior becomes ineffective, we become aware of our action theories and modify them.

As children we are taught action theories by parents and other socializing agents. As we grow older we learn how to modify our action theories and develop new ones. We learn to try to anticipate what actions will lead to what consequences, to try out and experiment with new behaviors, to experience the consequences, and then to reflect on our experiences to determine whether our action theory is valid or needs modification. Experiential learning is a procedure based on the systematic development and modification of action theories.

Kurt Lewin and Experiential Learning

The use of experiential procedures to learn about behavior in groups was greatly influenced by Kurt Lewin. When Lee Bradford and Ken Benne were looking for help in training community leaders in leadership and group decision-making skills, they approached Kurt Lewin. What resulted was the experiential learning method. One of Lewin's characteristics was to discover valuable concepts and principles by observing his own and other people's experiences. The most trivial event, the most casual comment might spark a thought in Lewin's mind that would result in a new theoretical breakthrough in the social psychology of groups. Those associating with Lewin never knew when he might make an important discovery, and this produced an excitement rare in a relationship with a colleague or teacher. Students and colleagues learned from Lewin how important it is to examine one's own experiences for potential principles about the way in which groups develop and work. Thus, Lewin's personal style focused on experiential learning.

Much of Lewin's research highlighted the importance of active participation in groups in order to learn new skills, develop new attitudes, and obtain new knowledge about groups. His research demonstrated that learning is achieved most productively in groups whose members interact and then reflect on their mutual experiences. In this way members are able to spark one another's insights and creativity in deriving conclusions about group dynamics. From Lewin, therefore, came an emphasis on studying one's own experiences in order to learn about group dynamics, on discussing mutual experiences to increase mutual learning and creativity, and on behaving democratically in structuring learning situations.

We all have many action theories, one for every type of situation we regularly find ourselves in. This does not mean that we are aware of our action theories. An action is usually based on tacit knowledge—knowledge that we are not always able to put into words. Because most of our action theories function automatically, we are rarely conscious of our assumed connections between actions and their consequences. One of the purposes of this book is to help you become more conscious of the action theories that guide how you behave in small group situations, test these theories against reality, and modify them to make them more effective.

GAINING EXPERTISE THROUGH EXPERIENTIAL LEARNING

We shall not cease from exploration
And the end of all our exploring
Will be to arrive where we started
And know the place for the first time.

      T. S. Eliot, "Four Quartets"

Aesop tells the story of the lion, the bear, and the fox. The bear was about to seize a stray goat when the lion leaped from another direction on the same prey. The bear and the lion then fought furiously for the goat until they had received so many wounds that both sank down unable to continue the battle. Just then the fox dashed up, seized the goat, and made off with it as fast as he could go, while the lion and the bear looked on in helpless rage. "How much better it would have been," they said, "to have shared in a friendly spirit." The bear and the lion had learned from their direct experience an important lesson in the advantages of cooperation over competition.

We all learn from our experiences. From touching a hot stove we learn to avoid heated objects. By dating we learn about male–female relationships. Every day we have experiences we learn from. Many aspects of group dynamics can be learned only by experience. Hearing a lecture on resisting group pressure is not the same as actually experiencing group pressure. Seeing a movie on how to manage conflict is not the same as facing an angry neighbor who is yelling in your face. Reading a description of leadership is not the same as leading the charge up San Juan Hill. It takes more than listening to explanations to learn group skills.

Experiential learning may be defined as generating an action theory from your own experiences and then continually modifying it to improve your effectiveness. The purpose of experiential learning is to affect the learner in three ways: (1) The learner's cognitive structures are altered, (2) the learner's attitudes are modified, and (3) the learner's repertoire of behavioral skills is expanded. These three elements are interconnected and change as a whole, not as separate parts. Working on any one part in the absence of the other two will be ineffective:

1. Information and knowledge can generate interest in changing, but will not bring about change. Knowing a rationale for change is not sufficient for motivating a person to change.
2. Firsthand experience alone will not generate valid knowledge. For hundreds of years, for example, scientists believed that there were four elements in the world—earth, air, fire, and water. Experience with different types of gases and different types of matter did not generate a correct theory of physics. Besides experience there must be a theoretical system that the experience tests out, and reflection on the meaning of the experience.
3. It takes more than engaging in a new behavior to result in permanent change. New skills may be practiced and mastered but will fade away unless action theories and attitudes also change.

The process of experiential learning is shown in Figure 2.1. When you generate an action theory from your own experiences and then continually modify it to improve its effectiveness, you are learning experientially. Experiential learning can be conceived of in a simplified way as a four-stage cycle: (1) Take action on the basis of one's current action theory, (2) assess consequences and obtain feedback, (3) reflect on how effective actions were and reformulate/refine the action theory, and (4) implement the revised action theory by taking modified action. As learners engage in these four steps, they must perceive themselves as being capable of implementing the procedures and strategies contained in the theory, perceive these procedures and strategies as being appropriate to their social world, and develop positive attitudes toward the theories and their implementation. This process of continuous improvement is repeated over and over again until expertise in the use of group skills is developed.

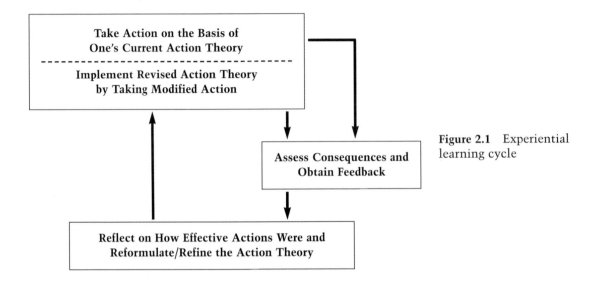

Take Action on the Basis of
One's Current Action Theory
- -
Implement Revised Action Theory
by Taking Modified Action

Assess Consequences and
Obtain Feedback

Reflect on How Effective Actions Were and
Reformulate/Refine the Action Theory

Figure 2.1 Experiential learning cycle

The experiential learning process of formulating an action theory, testing it out behaviorally, assessing consequences and obtaining feedback, reflecting, and modifying and refining the theory is based on a number of principles that need to be understood and followed. These principles are based on the theorizing of Kurt Lewin (Lewin, 1935; Lewin & Grabbe, 1945).

Principle 1: Effective experiential learning will affect the learner's cognitive structures (action theories), attitudes and values, perceptions, and behavioral patterns. To learn to be a more effective decision-maker, for example, the learner must develop (a) a concept of what decision making is (knowledge), (b) an action theory concerning what decision-making behaviors will lead to effective group decision making, (c) positive attitudes towards new decision-making procedures, (d) perceptions that the new decision-making actions are situationally appropriate and that one is capable of performing them, and (e) the behavioral skills needed to perform the new decision-making actions.

Principle 2: People will believe more in knowledge they have discovered themselves than in knowledge presented by others. Lewin was a great believer in experimental procedures whereby a person behaviorally validates or disproves a theory. He believed that such procedures needed to be introduced into the educational process so that students could test

alternative behavioral patterns within controlled conditions. An approach to learning based on inquiry and discovery has been found to increase students' motivation to learn and their commitment to implement their conclusions in the future.

Principle 3: Learning is more effective when it is an active rather than a passive process. When a learner can take a theory, concept, or practice and "try it on for size," he or she will understand it more completely, integrate it more effectively with past learning, and retain it longer. Many concepts (such as mathematical procedures) are never really learned until one uses them.

Principle 4: Acceptance of new action theories, attitudes, and behavioral patterns cannot be brought about by a piecemeal approach—one's whole cognitive-affective behavioral system has to change. The three elements are interconnected, and they change as a whole rather than as separate parts. Like any system, a cognitive-affective behavioral system demands coherence, consistency, orderliness, and simplicity. Trying to change part of the system will not be effective. The need for consistency creates resistance to the item-by-item approach to new learning. Only when the whole system changes will the new learning be fully accepted and integrated.

Principle 5: It takes more than information to change action theories, attitudes, and behavioral patterns. Telling people about the desirability of change does not mean that they will change. Providing a rationale for change is not sufficient to motivate people to change. Reading a book or listening to a lecture does not result in mastery and retention of the material, does not promote attitude change, and does not increase social skills. Information does generate interest in learning more about the desired changes.

Principle 6: It takes more than firsthand experience to generate valid knowledge. Lewin used to state that thousands of years of human experience with falling bodies did not bring humans to a correct theory of gravity. Besides experience, there needs to be a theoretical system that the experience tests out, and reflection on the meaning of the experience.

Principle 7: Behavior changes will be temporary unless the action theories and attitudes underlying them are changed. New behavioral skills may be practiced and mastered, but without changes in the person's action theories and attitudes, the new behavior patterns will fade away.

Principle 8: Changes in perceptions of oneself and one's social environment are necessary before changes in action theories, attitudes, and behavior will take place. Learners must perceive themselves as capable of doing the needed behaviors and must see the behaviors as being appropriate to the situation before they will engage in them. Lewin believed that behavior, action theories, and attitudes are all steered by perception. Your perceptions of yourself and your immediate situation affect how you behave, what you believe, and how you feel.

Principle 9: The more supportive, accepting, and caring the social environment, the freer a person is to experiment with new behaviors, attitudes, and action theories. As the need to justify oneself and protect oneself against rejection decreases, it becomes easier to experiment with new ways of behaving, thinking, and valuing.

Principle 10: In order for changes in behavior patterns, attitudes, and action theories to be permanent, both the person and the social environment have to change. The person's role definitions, the expectations of the person held by colleagues and friends, and the general values of career and social settings all must change if the person is to maintain these changed behaviors, attitudes, and action theories. Team training is more effective than individual training because it changes both individuals and their social environment at the same time.

Principle 11: It is easier to change a person's action theories, attitudes, and behavioral patterns in a group context than in an individual context. The discussion and consensual validation that takes place within a group provides a personal commitment and encouragement for change that is not present when only one person is being changed.

Principle 12: A person accepts a new system of action theories, attitudes, and behavioral patterns when he or she accepts membership in a new group. New groups with new role definitions and expectations for appropriate behavior are helpful in educational efforts. A person becomes socialized by internalizing the normative culture of the groups to which one belongs. As the person gains membership in a new group, a new normative culture is accepted and internalized.

Experiential learning procedures are especially useful when you want to learn new skills. In the next section we shall review how skills are learned.

LEARNING GROUP SKILLS

For things we have to learn before we can do them, we learn by doing them.

Aristotle

You are not born with group skills, nor do they magically appear when you need them. You have to learn them. Group skills are learned just as any other skill is learned. Learning how to lead a group is no different from learning how to play the piano or throw a football. All skills are learned the same way, according to the following steps:

1. **Understand why the skill is important and how it will be of value to you.** To want to learn a skill, you must see a need for it. You need to know that you will be better off with the skill than without the skill.

2. **Understand what the skill is, what are the component behaviors you have to engage in to perform the skill, and when it should be used.** To learn a skill, you must have a clear idea of what the skill is and you must know how to perform it. Often it is helpful to observe someone who has already mastered the skill perform it several times while describing it step by step. Apprentices, for example, watch masters of their craft perform the skill over and over again.

3. **Find situations in which you can practice the skill over and over**

and over again while a "coach" watches and tells you how well you are performing the skill. There are four levels of guided practice. The first level of guided practice consists of practicing successive approximations of the group skill while others provide scaffolding on how to do so. **Scaffolding** is support, in the form of reminders, prompts, and help, that you require to approximate the expert use of the group skills. As you practice the skills again and again, the scaffolding gradually fades until you use the skill by yourself, which is called soloing. The *second* level of guided practice consists of using the group skills while articulating and explaining out loud how to do so to your "coach." This ensures that the scaffolding is internalized and self-monitoring and self-correcting on how to engage in the skill take place. The *third* level is independent practice. You engage in the skill while self-monitoring and self-correcting your efforts. In effect, you give yourself feedback. This solidifies your sense of self-efficacy and commitment to use the skills. *Finally,* you decontextualize your use of the skills by using them in a variety of groups and in a variety of different situations. Try practicing the skill for a short time each day for several days until you are sure you have mastered it completely.

4. **Assess how well the group skills are being implemented.** The key to assessing how well you engage in the skill is to realize that you can never fail. Rather, your behavior approximates what you ideally wish and, through practice and the process of experiential learning (i.e., progressive refinement), the approximations get successively closer and closer to the ideal. You have to sweat in practice before you can perform in concert! Short-term failure is part of the process of gaining expertise, and long-term success is inevitable when short-term failure is followed by persistent practice, obtaining feedback, and reflecting on how to implement the group skills more competently. Receiving feedback, furthermore, is necessary for correcting mistakes in learning a skill and for identifying problems you are having in mastering the skill. Through feedback you find out how much progress you are making in mastering the skill. Feedback lets you compare how well you are doing with how well you want to do.

5. **Keep practicing until the skill feels real and it becomes an automatic habit pattern!** Most skill development goes through the following steps:
   a. Self-conscious, awkward engagement in the skill. Practicing any new skill feels awkward and group skills are no exception. The first few times someone throws a football, plays a violin, or paraphrases, it feels strange.
   b. Feelings of phoniness while engaging in the new skill. After a while the awkwardness passes and enacting the skill becomes more smooth. Many individuals, however, feel that the skill is unauthentic or phony. Encouragement is needed to move the members through this stage.
   c. Skilled but mechanical use of the skill.
   d. Automatic, routine use where the skill is fully integrated into your behavioral repertoire and seems like a natural action to engage in. You have to practice the skills long enough to go through the stages of skill development. The more you use a skill, the more natural it feels. It is then, when you apply the skills to real situations, that the skills will gain the fire and life that may sometimes be lacking when you practice.

6. **Load your practice toward success.** Set up practice units that you can easily master. It always helps to feel like a success as you practice a skill.
7. **Get friends to encourage you to use the skill.** Your friends can help you learn by giving you encouragement to do so. The more encouragement you receive, the easier it will be for you to practice the skill.
8. **Help others learn the group skills.** Harvey S. Firestone said, "It is only when we develop others that we permanently succeed." Nothing is completely learned until it is taught to someone else. By helping others learn group skills, you will enhance your own expertise.

In the learning of most skills there is a period of slow learning, then a period of rapid improvement, then a period where performance remains about the same (a plateau), then another period of rapid improvement, then another plateau, and so forth. Plateaus are quite common in skill learning. You have to persevere in practicing the skill until the next period of rapid improvement begins.

In order for you to move from awkwardness to the automatic use of the skills, sustained practice of the skills over a long period of time has to be encouraged. The goal for all skill learning is to reach the state where you automatically and naturally engage the small group skills while working with others to achieve mutual goals.

This book is designed to provide you with information about the nature of and the need for the group skills discussed. The behaviors needed to engage in the skills are specified. Questions that test your comprehension and understanding of the material presented are included in most chapters. You are given instructions for participating in exercises that provide you with a chance to practice the skills and receive feedback on how well you are mastering them. It is up to you, after engaging in the exercises, to practice the skills until you feel comfortable performing them. At the end of most chapters you will be asked to evaluate the extent to which you have mastered the skills presented in the chapter.

In short, this book provides you with guidance for increasing your group skills. It is up to you to take advantage of the material and exercises presented and use them in ways that will increase your group skills. The extent of your learning and skill development rests entirely on your commitment to use this book in fruitful ways.

EXPERIENTIAL LEARNING AND MOTIVATION

All men by nature desire to learn.

        Aristotle

What motivates you to learn concepts and skills? If someone offered you the opportunity either to earn a great deal of money or to experience a basic sense of accomplishment and satisfaction from learning a skill, which would you choose? Some educators seem to believe that students must be forced or persuaded into learning; others seem to believe that learning is fun and enjoyable in its own right. What do you believe? Experiential learning stresses the intrinsic sense of success of accomplishment in learning. Motivation is based upon what you see as desirable learning goals and the method you choose to accomplish them. The goal-directed aspect of motivation places an emphasis upon your feelings of success or failure in the learning situation. What leads to a psychological feeling of success in a learning situation? Kurt Lewin and his associates (1944) came up with four factors. They found evidence that you will experience psychological success (as opposed to psychological failure) if:

1. You are able to define your own goals.
2. The goals are related to your central needs and values.
3. You are able to define the paths that lead to the accomplishment of the goals.
4. The goals represent a realistic level of aspiration for you—neither too high nor too low, but high enough to test your capabilities.

Feelings of success will be promoted when you are encouraged to take as much responsibility for your own behavior as you can handle. You must believe that you are in control of (or at least have some influence over) your learning in order to feel psychological success. Experiential learning offers the opportunity for experiencing success by allowing you freedom to decide what aspects of your experience you wish to focus upon, what skills you wish to develop, and how you conceptualize the conclusions drawn from your experience. This is quite different from the traditional lecture approach to learning, in which you are a passive listener and the control of the material being presented is in the hands of the instructor. When an instructor decides what material will be presented and how it will be presented without letting learners have any influence over the decision, learners will experience psychological failure no matter how entertaining the presentation is.

Although the primary motivation for learning in experiential situations is psychological success, there are extrinsic factors that will encourage further learning. The approval and support of other learners is an example of extrinsic motivators that facilitate learning without interfering with intrinsic motivators, such as a sense of accomplishment. As you participate in the exercises in this book, your learning will accelerate if other participants give you approval and recognition for successful learning. You should consciously try to give approval to other readers who are seriously trying to increase their group skills. Few influences on our behavior are more powerful than the support and approval of a group of friends or acquaintances. Using such group influences to help individuals learn is one of the most constructive ways of assuring the development of group skills and knowledge.

ROLE PLAYING

Role playing is a tool for bringing patterns of behavior and their consequences into focus by allowing participants to:

1. Experience the situation concretely.
2. Identify effective and ineffective behavior.
3. Gain insight into their behavior.
4. Practice the skills required to manage the situation constructively.

Role playing is a vital training tool for mastering new skills. It can simulate real-life situations, making it possible to try new ways of handling situations without your suffering any serious consequences if the methods fail. Within a role-playing situation an imaginary situation is set up in which individuals act and react in terms of the assumptions they are asked to adopt, the beliefs they are asked to hold, and the characters they are asked to play. The outcome of a role-playing situation is not determined in advance, and the situation is not rehearsed. Initial instructions are given and the actors determine what happens.

When participating in a role-playing exercise, remain yourself and act as you would in the situation described. You do not have to be a good actor to play a role. You only need to accept the initial assumptions, beliefs, background, or assigned behaviors and then let your feelings, attitudes, and behavior change as circumstances seem to require. The role-play instructions describe the point of departure and the beginning frame of reference. You and the situation then take over.

Your experiences in participating in the role play may lead you to change your attitudes and future behavior. You may have emotional experiences that were not expected when the role playing began. The more real the role playing and the more effective the exercise, the more emotional involvement you will feel and the more you will learn.

In role playing, questions may be raised that are not answered in your briefing sheet. When this happens, you are free to make up facts or experiences that apply to the circumstances. Do not make up experiences or facts that do not fit the role. In participating in role playing, you should not consult or look at your role instructions. Once they are used to start the action, you should be yourself. A role player should not act the way he or she feels a person described in the instructions should behave. The role player should act as naturally as possible, given the initial instructions of the role.

In conducting role plays, there are three important points to remember. *First*, help the participants get into the situation and their roles by introducing them in such a way that the players are emotionally involved. Introduce the scene to the role players. *Second*, always discuss the role play when it is finished. How could the conflict have been prevented? How did the characters feel in the situation? Was it a satisfactory solution? What other solutions might have worked? *Third*, be sure to "de-role" after the role playing has ended. Some participants will have trouble "getting into their role" and other participants will have trouble "getting out of their role." Announce clearly that the role play is over and participants should reflect on and analyze the role play, not continue it.

LEARNING HOW TO BE A PARTICIPANT-OBSERVER

What is a Participant-Observer?

A **participant-observer** is a person who is skilled enough to both participate in group work and observe group process at the same time (see Figure 2.2). While a group is working, a distinction is commonly made between:

1. **Content**: What is being discussed in order to achieve the group's goals.
2. **Process**: The sequence of group members' actions that take place over time and are aimed at achieving the group's goal.

Ideally, a competent group member actively participates in the group's work while also observing the process being used to achieve the group's goals. To do so, a group member must function on two levels—as participant and as observer. Periodically, the group should stop its taskwork and discuss the process being used. Members continuously improve the group by (a) discussing the quality of the process being used, (b) reflecting on its effec-

Group Processing

> Receive feedback
> Analyze and reflect
> Set improvement goals
> Celebrate

tiveness in achieving the group's goals and maintaining effective working relationships among members, and (c) setting goals for improving the process. Such reflection and discussion are aimed at (a) streamlining the group's process to make it simpler (reducing complexity) and (b) eliminating unskilled and inappropriate actions (error-proofing the process). The process a group uses to achieve its goals includes setting clear goals that create positive interdependence, communicating effectively, providing leadership, using appropriate decision-making procedures, resolving conflicts constructively, and so forth. A person highly skilled in process observation can participate in group work and observe group process at the same time, thus becoming a participant-observer. The steps in developing competence in being a participant observer are:

1. Observing.
2. Giving and receiving feedback.
3. Reflecting and setting goals for improvement.
4. Modifing behavior in the next group meeting.
5. Repeating the cycle over and over again automatically in every group of which you are a member.

Learning How to Observe

Learning how to be a participant-observer begins with learning how to observe the process the group is using to achieve its goals. The process includes goal setting, communication, leadership, use of power, decision making, and conflict resolution. Gaining competence in observing involves consciously engaging in formal observation with a wide variety of observation schedules, for hundreds of times until the observation procedures become internalized and become an automatic habit pattern. Such automaticity is developed by repetition and the use of a variety of procedures.

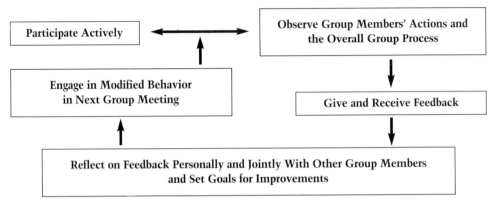

Figure 2.2 Participant observer.

Observing is aimed at describing and recording behavior as it occurs. From the behavior of group members an observer can make inferences about the group process—the way in which the group is functioning. The problem with observation of groups is the potential for lack of objectivity by the observers (Hastorf & Cantril, 1954). Each group member is biased in ways that may affect his or her perception and assessment of what is taking place in the group. A solution to the problem of bias is the use of structured coding systems, which require observers to categorize each group behavior into an objectively definable category.

Four steps are usually involved in observation. The first step is to prepare for observing. You must decide which member behaviors, actions, and skills are to be observed (the guidelines for creating effective groups in Table 1.1 detail the aspects of group process to be observed). You choose a member to be an observer. If you are observing more than one group, you must make a sampling plan (how long you will observe each group, in what order you will observe the groups). You next find or construct an observation form or checklist that specifies observable and countable behaviors reflecting the aspect of group process to be studied. Numerous observation sheets are included in this book. You train the observers to use the selected or created form. You may also use an unstructured procedure to record the frequencies of targeted actions.

Second you observe and record how often each member performs the specified behaviors. When there is more than one observer, you may be able to focus only on some of the group members. Third, you look at the frequency with which group members are engaged in the specified behaviors and then infer how well the group is functioning in that aspect of the group process under observation. The final step is to summarize the observations in a clear and useful manner and then present the summary to the group as feedback. The group can discuss the observations and revise the group process to make it more effective.

You report the results of your observations to the other group members as feedback. **Feedback** is information on actual performance that individuals compare with criteria for ideal performance. When feedback is given skillfully, it generates energy, directs the energy toward constructive action, and transforms the energy into action towards im-

Feedback Checklist

Feedback	Yes	No, Start Over
Is feedback given?		Was not given or received; start over.
Is feedback generating energy in students?		Students are indifferent; start over.
Is energy directed towards identifying and solving problems so performance is improved?		Energy used to resist, deny, avoid feedback; start over.
Do students have opportunities to take action to improve performance?		No, students are frustrated and feel like failures; start over.

proving the performance of the teamwork skills. Member performance improves and the discrepancy between actual and real performance decreases. Increased self-efficacy tends to result. Members tend to feel empowered to be even more effective next time. The following checklist may help in assessing the effectiveness of feedback.

Constructing an Observation Procedure

Observation forms are used to answer the question "How often are certain actions or events happening?" Observation forms are used to tally and count the number of times a behavior, action, or event is observed in a specified time period. An example is given below. The form has to be designed so that all potential observers can use it (i.e., age appropriate). **A structured (formal) observation form is created in the following way.**

1. Define exactly what behaviors, actions, skills, or events are being observed (such as contributes ideas, encourages participation, checks for understanding, gives group direction). All observers have to be looking for the same thing.

2. Determine time period during which data will be collected. One group may be observed for fifty minutes or each group may be observed for two minutes. Observations may be summarized after one class session or after several class sessions.

3. Enter the actions to be observed in the first column (each action or skill is placed in a separate row, the final row is reserved for the total of the columns).

4. Make an additional column for each member of the group and making a final column to record the total for each row on the form.

5. Make sure all columns are clearly labeled and wide enough to enter data.

The purpose of process observation is to clarify and improve the ways in which the group is presently functioning through an objective assessment of the interaction among members. Information about group process is collected and then openly discussed so that modifications in group procedures and members' behavior can be made in order to improve the group's effectiveness.

By the time you finish this book you will have developed skills in observing group process. At first the observation tasks specified in the exercises will seem difficult, but gradually you will find them easier and more helpful as your skills develop. As effective future behavior depends upon awareness of the nature and consequences of current behavior, there is no substitute for direct observation in skill development and in the facilitation of group effectiveness. Any effective group member must be aware of group process while participating in the group, and it is through observation practice that such skills are developed.

CONDUCTING SKILL-TRAINING EXERCISES

A Typical Skill-Training Session

Before discussing how to conduct a skill-training session it may be helpful to review the overall structure of a group exercise. A typical session would involve the following procedures:

1. Participants are presented with an introduction by a coordinator, who then conducts a warm-up discussion. The introduction should include the objectives of the session, an outline of what will happen, and a description of the specific skills with which the participants will be concerned during the exercise: The warm-up discussion sets the stage for the exercise, engenders participant involvement, and promotes some sort of emotional connection among participants. The warm-up could take the form of a brief exchange of current feelings among participants or an interesting anecdote about group skills told by the coordinator. The expectations of the participants should be set at this point.
2. The exercise is then conducted.
3. After the exercise is completed, the participants are asked to conceptualize, analyze, and summarize their experience. This step may be structured through discussion questions or data feedback about how each person and the group behaved. The personal learnings of each participant, their application to his or her life, and the theoretical principles into which the participants gained insight as a result of their experience can be focused upon.
4. In a general session participants should talk over the experience and summarize their ideas about their experience. The coordinator should integrate appropriate theory and cognitive frameworks into the participants' statements. The emphasis at this point is upon integrating the important learnings, theory, and research with their experiences.
5. The coordinator should then discuss the issues of applying the learnings and skills to the participants' specific life situations.

6. An evaluation of the success of the session in accomplishing its objectives should be made.
7. At the end of the session a sense of closure needs to be provided by the coordinator. This may be achieved by a short, fun, involving experience. Or the coordinator may simply say that the training exercise is over.

Designing a Skill-Training Session

A skill-training program could involve any number and combination of the exercises presented in this book. It could consist of a single exercise or of several exercises drawn from different chapters. It could last a few minutes or several days. Whatever the length of the session and the number of exercises used, the basic design of the training process is the same. The following elements need to be considered when the coordinator designs a skill-training session:

1. The coordinator–participant relationship must be examined. Useful questions to be cleared up include: What is the purpose of the session? Why is the coordinator conducting it? What is the contract between the coordinator and the participants? What is the relationship between the coordinator and the participants? Your motivation as coordinator, hidden agendas (if any), explicit and implicit assumptions about the session and the participants, and your limitations and competencies should be reviewed. It is also helpful to know the following information about the participants:
    a. *Expectations:* What do the participants hope, believe, or fear will happen or not happen?
    b. *Experience:* What kind of previous training have the participants had?
    c. *Relevance:* How might the learnings be used after the session?
    d. *Relationships:* What are the participants' past and future relationships with each other?
    e. *Needs:* What specific learnings, and what general kinds of learnings, do the participants want or need?
    f. *Vital data:* Sex, age, marital status, general attitudes, physical or emotional problems and pressures, back-home support possibilities, and so on.
    g. *Motivation:* What is the level of the participants' motivation?
    h. *Recruitment:* How were the participants recruited? Did they all voluntarily agree to attend the session?
2. The desired outcomes of the session should be specified; they are usually discussed as objectives or goals. They should specify who is to be trained and what is to be the direction and magnitude of the desired learning. Clearly specified goals are useful when you are deciding upon the components of the session and its evaluation. All the criteria for clear goals given in Chapter 4 are of importance when you are stating the session's objectives. Participants should be able to spell out the learnings they will try to achieve.
3. Detail the constraints on the session. These include the time periods available, the location, the facilities, and your range of competencies.

4. Generate a list of alternative exercises and activities that can be used in the skill-training session. These alternatives may include a variety of exercises and theory sessions. This list can be put together from two sources: the desired outcomes of the session and the resources and preferences of the coordinator(s). All the exercises in this book and in *Reaching Out* are possibilities.

5. Make a tentative design for the session. Evaluate it in terms of these questions:
   a. Is it appropriate for accomplishing the desired outcomes?
   b. Are the activities within your range of competencies?
   c. Is there an opportunity for participants to express their needs or expectations or both?
   d. Does it enable the participants to make the transition from the "outside" world to the session and back to the "outside" world?
   e. Does it encourage the transfer of learnings?
   f. Does it have high personal relevance for the participants, and will it enable them to function better in their day-to-day life?
   g. If there is more than one coordinator, does it allow time for you to check signals with each other?
   h. Are high- and low-tension activities appropriately placed within the design?
   i. Are the assumptions about the skill and background of the participants appropriate?
   j. Does the overall design provide a sense of continuity, appropriate transitions among activities, a good "flow"?
   k. Are participants able to see the relationship between the exercises and the desired outcomes of the session?
   l. Does it allow for a logical flow of experiences?
   m. Does it offer flexibility in case of unexpected and emerging needs?
   n. Is it consistent with the principles of experiential learning?
   o. Is there opportunity for ongoing participant feedback and evaluation?
   p. Are you prepared to recognize and deal with unanticipated learning outcomes?
   q. Are all the necessary materials and facilities available?

6. Make sure you are highly committed to the final design. If there is more than one coordinator, assign responsibilities. Arrange for the materials and facilities.

7. If there is more than one coordinator, assess how you function as a staff. See if any team development needs to take place among the staff before the skill-training sessions begin.

Evaluation

Evaluation is the process of determining how successful—or unsuccessful—a group was in achieving its goal or objective. In the case of a skill-training session, it is the process by which evidence is gathered about whether the desired outcomes of the session were accomplished, what unanticipated learnings were accomplished, how the activities involved in the session contributed to its success or failure, and what the coordinator(s) could do to improve their competencies. In an evaluation there must be a clear, operational statement of the desired outcomes, ways to measure how nearly the desired outcomes were achieved and what activities and coordinator behaviors contributed to the session's success or failure, time for the participants to give feedback on the effectiveness of the session, and time following the session for the data to be analyzed and conclusions drawn.

In evaluation it is helpful to know such things as the emotional reactions of the participants (how they feel now), the specific or significant learnings the participants have obviously achieved, the amount of increased participant competence in performing the skills, what sort of future experiences the participants now see the need for, the degree to which the desired outcomes were accomplished, the participants' reactions to various parts of the session, and what the coordinator(s) did that was helpful or unhelpful to the participants.

A variety of data-collection procedures can be used by the coordinator(s) to evaluate a session: interviews, general statements made by the participants, questionnaire responses, observation of how skills were applied, and so on. All sessions do not have to be evaluated at a high level of proficiency, but more than the general impressions of the coordinator(s) should be used. At the very least, the coordinator(s) should be able to direct the same session in the future in a more effective and efficient way.

Helpful Guidelines

In conducting the exercises in this book the coordinator will have a set of general responsibilities. These include:

1. Organizing the materials, procedures, facilities she will need in order to manage the exercise.
2. Introducing, ending, and tying together the experiences involved in the exercise.
3. Keeping time in a task-oriented way in order to prevent the participants from getting sidetracked.
4. Restating and calling attention to the main learnings of the exercise, which include relating the experiences to the theory.
5. Setting a climate of experimentation, acceptance, openness, and warmth so that participants will be encouraged to try out new skills and improve their competencies.
6. Serving as an anchor point by being reliable, knowledgeable, trustworthy, and responsible.
7. Modeling the skills he wishes to teach.
8. Following the general outlines of experiential learning.
9. Being enthusiastic about the value of the exercise.
10. Knowing and understanding the material well.
11. Making sure everyone understands her instructions and responsibilities.
12. Being sensitive to the differences in participation, needs, and styles of the participants.

13. Remaining flexible so that the preplanned procedures do not interfere with the participants' learning.
14. Enjoying himself and making sure that he also learns and benefits from the exercises.

ETHICS OF EXPERIENTIAL LEARNING

All learning activities require a code of ethics, either implicit or explicit. A great deal of attention has been paid to the ethics of growth-group leaders, but little consideration has been given to the ethics of conducting experiential-learning activities. Some of the ethical issues relevant to the type of skill-training exercises included in this book are as follows.

The most serious ethical issue involved in teaching group skills is determining the value and necessity of such cognitive and behavioral changes for the participants. Attempting to teach another person carries with it a responsibility not to work against that person's best interests and needs. It should also be noted that the only way to promote ethical standards in teaching–learning relationships is for the teachers to enforce their code of ethics on themselves and to use good judgment in what they do. As long as a teacher's behavior is based on care, respect, and regard for participants, ethical violations will be minimized. Persons leading experiential-learning activities must therefore develop a personal code of ethics to which they hold themselves accountable. The following points should provoke some thought as to what that personal code of ethics might include.

The Contract: Informed Consent and Mutual Agreement

1. The coordinator's intentions and objectives should be clearly communicated to the participants. The participants should understand that they are going to participate in an experiential exercise in which they will be expected to examine their own behavior and the behavior of others, and analyze the behaviors for purposes of learning.
2. The nature of the contract should be easily understood by the coordinator and the participants. The number of experiences, the length of each session, and the appropriateness and the objectives of each exercise should be agreed upon.
3. The point at which the contract is terminated should be clear to both the coordinator and the participants.

The Activities

1. Respect Participants' Freedom of Choice: Participation should be voluntary. Advise participants that they can say "no" and sit on the sidelines as the exercise is being conducted.
2. Explain the Reason and Objectives of the Exercise: The coordinator should have an explicit reason for conducting the exercise and be prepared to explain the reason clearly.

3. Know Your Limitations: Only exercises the coordinator is competent to direct should be conducted.

4. The coordinator should present relevant theory and research when it is appropriate to the participants' learning and increased effectiveness.

5. The coordinator should be constantly aware of his or her behavior styles and personal needs, and deal with them productively in the performance of his or her role. The coordinator should also be aware of the impact of his or her needs and style on the participants.

6. The coordinator should assess all experiences by discussing the participants' feelings and reactions to them and by asking the participants what can be learned from the experiences. Adequate time must be programmed into the design of the session for this purpose.

7. The coordinator should not initiate confrontations between participants, which may damage their future relationship. This does not mean that coordinators should discourage risk taking in giving feedback, the making of honest disclosures, or attempts to face conflicts and improve the relationship. It simply means that confrontations should originate with the participants, not the coordinator.

8. If any personal information is revealed, the coordinator should make sure that the possibility of it being used in any way to damage the participants is minimized.

9. Ideally, the coordinator should be able to recognize symptoms of serious psychological stress and be able to make responsible decisions when such problems arise. At the very least, the coordinator should know where emergency psychological services are available.

10. Sessions should be evaluated in such a way that the coordinator receives feedback that will improve his or her performance. The sessions should be open to scrutiny by competent professionals interested in the effectiveness of experiential learning.

11. The coordinator conducts follow-up interviews with participants to determine the impact of the sessions on them and to assess their feelings and reactions to the sessions.

The Coordinator's Knowledge, Skills, and Needs

1. **Knowledge:** The coordinator's actions need to be based on empirically validated theory. Folklore, superstition, common sense, fads, popular gimmicks, and personal experiences are not adequate bases for teaching others. The coordinator should thoroughly understand the principles of experiential learning, the steps of skill development, and the knowledge the exercise is designed to teach.

2. **Experience:** The coordinator should have some experience and skill in conducting exercises and helping participants reflect on their own and other's behavior. Knowing the steps of experiential learning is not enough: The coordinator should also have some skills and competencies in applying the principles of experiential learning.

3. **Clear Explanations:** At any time during the exercises the coordinator should be able to explain the relevant theory and the way in which current activities relate to the theory. This does not mean that the coordinator will not use intuition when conducting an exercise, but the coordinator should be able to reconstruct the theory behind his or her intuitive actions.

4. **Self-Awareness:** The coordinator should be aware of his or her personal needs and deal with them productively. The coordinator should also be aware of the impact of his or her personal needs and styles on the participants and the instructional activities.

Final Notes

Your ability to conduct and coordinate experiential-learning exercises will improve as you apply the material in this book with intelligence and caution. If you are interested in other skill-building exercises, see Johnson (1991, 2000) and Johnson & Johnson (1997). You do not have to be a skilled teacher to conduct the exercises contained in this book, but constant concern for increasing your knowledge and skills in experiential learning is helpful.

The preceding statements are meant to be guidelines, not rigid rules. The only effective way to enforce ethical standards in educational activities is for the persons conducting the educational problems to enforce their code of ethics on themselves and use good judgment in what they do. Again, as long as a coordinator's behavior is based on care, respect, and regard for the participants, ethical violations will probably be avoided. It is hoped that the above guidelines will be provocative in helping the users of this book build a personal code of ethical conduct.

SUMMARY

To master the field of group dynamics you must conceptually learn the relevant theory and research and master the skills that put that knowledge into action. Such procedural learning results from skill-building experiences as well as academic study. Procedural learning involves a progressive refinement of knowledge and skill as the procedures are practiced, practiced, and practiced. In other words, this book focuses on both "head" and "hand" learning.

Experiential learning begins with the formulation of an action theory. Action theories specify what actions are needed to achieve a desired consequence in a given situation. The next step is to take action and engage in the relevant group skills. The success or failure of the actions is assessed. Upon reflection, the action theory is refined and reformulated. Then the group skills are used again in a modified and improved way. This cycle is repeated over and over again as the skills are refined and continuously improved upon. This continuous improvement process eventually results in expertise in the use of group skills as changes in cognitive understanding, attitudes, and behavioral patterns result. While learning experientially, you experience psychological success. While mastering group skills, furthermore, you need to observe how they are being used by other group members while you fully participate in the group. Such participant-observation enables you to know when to use various group skills and how to help others to do so in order to improve the ways in which the group is functioning. In order to learn the group skills discussed in this book, the skill-building exercises need to be conducted competently and ethically.

3

Group Goals, Social Interdependence, and Trust

INTRODUCTION

The honor of one is the honor of all.
The hurt of one is the hurt of all.

> Creek Indian Creed

Groups form for a cooperative purpose. Since our beginnings, humans have joined together to cooperate to achieve goals that each individual member could not achieve alone. Whereas elephants have size and cheetahs have speed, it is our ability to engage in cooperative enterprises to achieve group goals that distinguishes us as a species. Social interdependence defines the ways in which the goals of individuals are related. Social interdependence is the heart of all human interaction, and cooperation is the heart of all small group efforts. To be effective, groups must set group goals that all members commit themselves to cooperate in achieving. There are two steps to do so:

1. Operational goals and the paths to achieving the goals are clearly specified and measurable.
2. Cooperative interdependence is structured among group members.

Exercise 3.1: Orientations Toward Social Interdependence

This exercise has two purposes: (1) to make you more aware of your orientation towards goal interdependence with others and (2) to make your group more aware of members' orientations towards social interdependence. The procedure is as follows:

1. Working by yourself, complete the following questionnaire.
2. Using the scoring table that follows the questionnaire, determine your score and then determine the group average for each scale.
3. Have a group discussion concerning the orientations towards social interdependence of group members.

SOCIAL INTERDEPENDENCE QUESTIONNAIRE

For each item below, indicate your **general** perceptions about each statement. In the appropriate space, write down the number that most accurately describes your actions.

> 1 = never
> 2 = seldom
> 3 = sometimes
> 4 = mostly
> 5 = always

1. I like to compare myself with others to see who is best.
2. In my situation, people spend a lot of time working by themselves.
3. In my situation, people share their ideas and resources with each other.
4. In my situation, people are motivated to see who can do the best job.
5. In my situation, individuals like to work by themselves.
6. In my situation, individuals learn lots of important things from each other.
7. In my situation, individuals want to do better than others.
8. In my situation, it bothers individuals when they have to work with each other.

9. In my situation, individuals help each other do a good job.
10. In my situation, individuals are encouraged to outperform each other.
11. In my situation, individuals would rather work alone than work together.
12. In my situation, individuals believe that they are more productive when they work with each other.

Competitive	*Individualistic*	*Cooperative*
1. _____	2. _____	3. _____
4. _____	5. _____	6. _____
7. _____	8. _____	9. _____
10. _____	11. _____	12. _____
Total _____	Total _____	Total _____

Exercise 3.2: Are Group Goals Necessary?

There has been some controversy over whether group goals are necessary. The purpose of this exercise is to structure a critical discussion of the issue. The procedure is as follows.

1. **Assignment of Positions:** The class forms groups of four. Each group is ultimately to write a report summarizing its position on whether:
   a. Groups cannot function without goals.
   b. Group goals are of no use.
   The report is to contain the group's overall conclusions and the facts and rationale supporting its position. The supporting facts and rationale may be obtained from this chapter, the entire book, and outside reading.
2. **Preparation Pairs:** Each group divides into pairs. One pair is assigned the position that groups cannot function without goals and the other pair the position that group goals are of no use. The pairs review the supporting sections of this chapter, the procedure for the exercise, and the guidelines for constructive controversy (pp. 330). Each pair prepares a persuasive "best case" rationale for its assigned position that includes as many facts and research findings as possible. Ten minutes are allowed for this phase.
3. **Presentations:** One member of each pair changes chairs. A "group goals are necessary" person should be seated with a "group goals are unnecessary" person. The "group goals are necessary" person has up to three minutes to present the best case possible for the position, being as forceful and persuasive as possible. The "group goals are unnecessary" person takes notes and asks for clarification of anything that is not fully understood. The "group goals are unnecessary" person then presents.
4. **Open Discussion** (Refute and Rebut): There is an open discussion of whether or not group goals are necessary. Each side presents as many facts and research findings as it can to support its point of view. Members listen critically to the opposing position and ask for supporting facts for any conclusions made by the opponent. Participants should ensure that all the facts supporting both sides are brought out and discussed. The guidelines for constructive controversy should be followed. About ten minutes are allowed for this phase.
5. **Perspective Reversal:** Members of each pair change chairs. The "group goals are necessary" person presents in three minutes the best case possible for the "group goals are unnecessary" position. He or she should be as forceful and persuasive as he or she can and add new arguments or facts if possible. The "group goals are unnecessary" person then similarly presents the best case possible for the "group goals are necessary" position.

6. **Synthesis and Integration:** Participants drop all advocacy and come to their best reasoned judgment as to whether group goals are necessary. The pair of members summarize the information and arguments for each position and come to an agreement. Each pair prepares a short presentation on its conclusion to the rest of the class. Because other groups will have other conclusions, each group may need to explain the validity of its position to the class. About ten minutes are allowed for this phase.

7. **Whole Class Discussion:** The coordinator samples the decisions made by the groups of four by having several of them present their position to the class. The class then discusses similarities and differences among the positions and the coordinator summarizes what the participants have learned about group goals.

BRIEFING SHEET: GROUPS CANNOT FUNCTION WITHOUT GOALS

Your position is that a group cannot function without having at least one goal that is understood and accepted by several of its members. To support your position, use the rationale given below, any material from this chapter that is applicable, and your outside reading.

Group goals guide the actions of members and allow them to plan and coordinate their efforts. Group goals direct, channel, guide, energize, motivate, and coordinate the behavior of group members. Groups cannot exist unless the activities of their members are directed towards achieving something (a goal). It is the power of goals to influence members to engage in needed behaviors that makes goals essential to an effective group. All in all, groups cannot function effectively or even exist without goals.

BRIEFING SHEET: GROUP GOALS ARE OF NO USE

Your position is that a goal is not useful to a group and is a concept that has no basis in reality. To support your position, use the rationale given below, any material from this chapter that is applicable, and your outside reading.

Group goals are often stated in such vague terms that they could not possibly be effective guides for the actions of members. When asked, many group members cannot accurately describe the group's goals and thus the goals can have no impact on these persons. Often goals do not determine members' efforts because the goals seem unrelated to what group members actually do. Appraisals of group process, moreover, usually reveal that groups have not achieved their goals, which suggests that the goals are not the true motivators of members' actions. It may even be that groups do not try to accomplish anything; they just exist. All in all, goals are of no use to a group.

Why Goals Are Important

1. **Goals are guides for action.** They direct, channel, and determine what members and teachers do.
2. **Goals motivate behavior.** Goals are motivators and energizers. No goals, no motivation.
3. **Goals provide the basis for resolving conflicts.** Conflicts among group members are resolved on the basis of what members want to accomplish.
4. **Goals are a prerequisite for assessment and evaluation.** Without knowing what the purpose of the activity is, no assessment can be conducted.

WHAT IS A GOAL?

*No wind favors him who
has no destined port.*

Montaigne

On September 17, 1868, Major George A. Forsyth and fifty handpicked scouts were camped on Beecher's Island (a small island in the dry bed of the Arikaree River) in eastern Colorado Territory. Full-scale war had just erupted with the Indian tribes of the Great Plains. Forsyth and his scouts had left Fort Hays in Kansas to find the enemy, but the Native Americans found Forsyth first. On that morning, the Cheyenne war chief known as Roman Nose led over seven hundred Cheyenne and Oglala warriors in a dawn attack on Forsyth's camp. Many of Forsyth's men and all his horses were killed or wounded. Forsyth was shot in both legs and a bullet creased his skull. They were trapped on the island. By September 25, as a result of stealthy sniping and repeated charges, half of Forsyth's men were casualties. Wondering whether he would live to see another morning, Forsyth lay stretched out beside the rotting carcass of his dead horse. A horrific stench rose from the dead men and animals all around him. The overall goal of Forsyth and his scouts was to survive. They did have, however, a number of short-term goals. They had to construct a barrier to protect them from enemy fire. They used the dead horses. Maintaining group unity and support was essential for morale, hope, and an effective defense. Water, shelter, food, and caring for the wounded were problems. Luckily, the weather was mild enough that shelter was not a necessity. They had enough water on the island to survive. After several days, however, the scouts began to eat their horses' decaying flesh.

The situation seemed hopeless. Suddenly, the Indians withdrew. Puzzled, the survivors soon saw why. A company of cavalry was galloping toward the island. Unknown to Forsyth, two of his scouts had slipped through the besieging Indians and traveled to Fort Wallace in Kansas. Captain Louis H. Carpenter, a Civil War comrade of Forsyth's, immediately mounted a company of cavalry for a rescue expedition. Carpenter's troopers were officially known as Company H of the 10th Calvary, but to their Indian foes they were the "buffalo soldiers." Rather than fight these soldiers, Roman Nose decided to withdraw. Over the course of three decades, the buffalo soldiers gained a reputation of being the most professional, experienced, and effective troops on the frontier.

Groups exist for a reason. People join groups in order to achieve goals they are unable to achieve by themselves. The goal may be to build a better mousetrap, to climb a mountain, to get the most pay for the least amount of work, or to apply the material being presented in this book. The essence of a **goal** is that it is an ideal. It is a desired place towards which people are working, a state of affairs that people value. **The goals of individuals are related through social interdependence.** There may be a positive correlation among individuals' goal attainment (i.e., cooperation), a negative correlation among individuals' goal attainments (i.e., competition), or no correlation among individuals' goal attainments (i.e., individualistic efforts). Such **goal structures** specify the type of social interdependence among individuals as they strive to accomplish their goals. They specify the ways in which individuals will interact with each other. Social interdependence is discussed in depth in a later section of this chapter. When a positive correlation exists among individuals' goal attainments, a group goal results. A **group goal** is a future state of affairs desired by enough members of a group to motivate the group to work towards its achievement. Ever since there were two humans on earth, we have joined together to achieve mutual goals and to maximize our joint welfare.

A Joint Vision

Goals are not intellectual, cold, or analytical. Goals enlist the emotions of group members and point them towards coordinated efforts. The more the goal elicits emotions the more it is a vision. Group members share a vision as to what they can accomplish when they work together. A **vision** is an ideal and unique image of the future. The vision clarifies the mission and goals of the group. Stephen Wozniak and Stephen Jobs shared a vision as they invented the Apple computer in a garage. They took their dream from a garage to a multinational computer company. To end world hunger, to prevent the pain and anguish of children dying of cancer, to allow the deaf to hear with an artificial ear, to allow people to live with an artificial heart, to find a drug to prevent the body's rejection of transplanted organs—all are visions that bring tears, laughter, bitter disappointment, determination, hope, depression, enthusiasm, and joy. The vision tells group members what is uniquely possible if all work together for a common purpose. It shows members how their values and interests will be served by the accomplishments they are striving for. The goals of the group create a compelling vision that focuses the passion of members and ignites the flame of inspired work. The vision binds members through a shared, *emotional* commitment. Group goals breathe life into group members' hopes and dreams and enable them to see the exciting possibilities of their joint efforts.

Do Group Goals Exist?

Do groups have goals? Or are there only the various individual goals of the group's members? As dry as these questions may seem, social psychologists have hotly debated this issue for decades. Emmy Pepitone (1980), for example, insists that group goals can be identified, that they function as an important source of member interdependence in groups, and that they denote a common, central focus that is present most of the time and is readily identifiable as an objective reality. She states that group goals provide an aspect of unity, of a common fate, that one cannot readily convey simply by noting the individual goals of group members. Lewin (1944) said that there are situations in which group members do seem to act to maximize joint outcomes or accomplish group goals rather than to maximize their individual outcomes or achieve their individual goals.

Both Horwitz (1954) and Pepitone (1952) conducted studies that indicated that group members become motivated to have their group achieve its goal and are personally satisfied when the group does so. The success of the group, rather than their personal gain, seems to be the major source of their satisfaction. More recent studies (Matsui, Kakuyama, & Onglateo, 1987; Mitchell & Silver, 1990) indicate that group goals, compared with individual goals, result in higher group performance, greater goal acceptance, and more cooperation among group members. Numerous other studies have demonstrated that individuals do focus on joint outcomes rather than individual outcomes when they are placed in situations requiring cooperation with others.

Many social scientists, however, believe that a group goal is a combination of the individual goals of all group members. People, therefore, become group members because they have certain goals and motives that they wish to express or fulfill through group membership. Each person brings to the group a wish to satisfy personal goals. These goals are not always clearly known to the member—he or she may be completely aware, partially aware, or totally unaware of his or her goals and motives during a group meeting.

There is no definitive answer to whether group goals exist in and of themselves or are simply a reflection of the overlap among the personal goals of the group's members. It is safe to conclude, however, that both group and individual goals exist, and the group goals must be relevant to the individual needs of the members. Group members try usually to achieve both individual and group goals, and the degree to which they can accomplish this through the same activities determines how effective the group will be in attaining its goals. The situation is further complicated by the fact that most groups and individuals have several goals and different members value different goals at different times and even the same member places different values on the same goal at different times.

Whether group goals are entities in and of themselves or simply a combination of the individual goals of members, they are important for numerous reasons.

Exercise 3.3: Your Goal-Related Behavior

This exercise examines goal-related behavior in problem-solving groups. Working by yourself, answer the following three questions. Be honest. Check as many responses to each question as are characteristic of your usual behavior. Then form a triad with two of your classmates, and discuss your answers and why you answered them as you did. Develop as much awareness of your behavior in goal-related situations as possible.

1. When I am a member of a group that does not seem to have a clear awareness of what its goals are or how they are to be achieved, I usually:

   _____ Feel disinterested and refuse to attend meetings.

   _____ Ask the designated leader to stop messing around and tell the group what it is supposed to be doing.

   _____ Ignore the situation and be extra nice to the other members.

   _____ (Take over the conversation and tell the other group members what the group's goals are.) Propose that members review the group's goals and in return they will be told what to do to achieve the goals.

_____ Initiate a group discussion to clarify each member's understanding of the group goals until all group members clearly understand what they are and what actions the group needs to take to accomplish them.

2. When a member of a group that has a clear understanding of its goals but seems to have little commitment to accomplishing them, I usually:

_____ Refuse to have anything to do with the other member and avoid him or her.

_____ Make fun of the other group member until he or she becomes more committed.

_____ Pretend that there is nothing wrong and be nice to the other person.

_____ Propose a compromise in which the person works harder and the group expects less.

_____ Initiate a group discussion in which the group goals are considered and reformulated to make them more relevant to each member's goals.

3. When I am a member of a group that has conflicting opinions on what its goals should be, or that has members with conflicting needs and motives, I usually:

_____ Simply withdraw and wait for them to work out their differences.

_____ Tell the leader to decide who is right and who is wrong and tell the losers to shut up.

_____ Try to smooth over the differences and ask everyone to be nice and keep their differences to themselves.

_____ Propose a 50/50 compromise where everyone gets half of what he or she wants.

_____ Figure out how much cooperative and competitive behavior exists in the group and give the group feedback based on my observations in an attempt to increase cooperativeness among its members.

_____ Start a group discussion on the different positions, goals, and motives of group members and seek a solution that is acceptable to everyone.

START WITH GOALS

If a man does not know to which port he is sailing, no wind is favorable.

Seneca

There are two aspects of ensuring member commitment to the group's goals. The *first* is to ensure that the goals meet the START criteria (see Table 3.1). To be effective, goals need to be specific (so it is clear what needs to be done next), measurable (so progress can be tracked), challenging but achievable, relevant, and aimed at competencies that will be transferred to other situations. The *second* way to ensure member commitment is to involve group members in the process of forming the goals. When group members participate in setting goals, there tends to be a better match between the group goals and the motives of members and a better understanding of the actions needed to achieve the goals. In addition, involvement leads to ownership of the goals, which leads to commitment. While indifferent to others' goals, individuals seek out opportunities to achieve their own goals and commit considerable energy to doing so. Other factors influencing commitment are how desirable the goal seems (the benefits group members will receive if the goal is accomplished) and the ways in which members will relate to each other in working toward the accomplishment of the goal (some ways of relating are more fun and involving than others).

Table 3.1   **START with Goals**

Goal Characteristic	Definition of Characteristic
S Specific	Goals have to be specific enough so that they are clearly understood and a plan to achieve them can be developed. Specific goals indicate what needs to be done next.
T Measurable and Trackable	Members must be able to determine the extent to which they have reached the goals. Goals must be operationalized so that the steps to achieving them are clear and understandable.
A Challenging but Achievable	Goals must be challenging enough so that the group has a 50/50 percent chance of achieving them. Group must be able to achieve the goals if they work hard enough and have sufficient teamwork.
R Relevant	Goals must be relevant to the member's interests and the interests of other stakeholders in the group. Members must see the goals as meaningful and be personally committed to achieving them.
T Transfer	Goals must be aimed at having members take what is learned and transfer it to other situations. Whatever skills members master today, they should be able to use in other situations tomorrow.

Exercise 3.4: Clear and Unclear Goals

This exercise constructs the behavioral consequences of having clear and unclear goals. Approximately one hour is needed to complete it. The procedure is as follows:

1. Seat the participants in groups of six to eight, formed into circles.
2. Introduce the exercise as focusing upon clear and unclear group goals.
3. Have each group select an observer, who reports to a designated place for instructions. While the observers are being briefed, urge the group members to get acquainted with one another.
4. Give each observer a copy of the observation guide and tell observers that the groups will work on two tasks. The first task will be unclear, the second clear. Their job is to make careful observations of group behavior on the two tasks. The observers then return to their groups, but sit outside the circle.
5. Brief all groups as follows: "We are going to study group behavior by working on two brief tasks. Your observer will not participate, but will report to you at the end of the second task. Your first task will take about eight minutes. I will give you a warning a minute before the time is up. The task is: List the most appropriate goals to govern the best developmental group experiences in order to maximize social development in a democratic society."
6. While the groups work on the task, the observers should take notes. After seven minutes give the warning and after eight minutes end the discussion.
7. Give Task 2: "List as many of the formally organized clubs or organizations that exist in a typical community as you can." State that the groups will have six minutes to work on the task. At the end of five minutes give a one-minute warning and after six minutes end the discussion.
8. Give a copy of the observation guide to all participants. Then have each group discuss its experience, using the information obtained by the observers as its major resource. This discussion should last ten to fifteen minutes.

9. Form clusters by asking one group to pull its chairs in a circle around another group. The inner group becomes group A and the outer group becomes group B. Instruct group A to produce a list of characteristics of clear and unclear goals with one person recording them on newsprint in two columns. Allow six minutes for this task. Group B is to listen to group A, take notes, and be ready to add to the list. After six minutes instruct group B to comment on the list and have both groups jointly select the four or five most important characteristics of clear and unclear goals from the list. Give them nine minutes to do so.
10. Groups A and B then change places, with group B now in the center. Group B is told to list behavioral symptoms of each of the characteristics of clear and unclear goals listed on the newsprint, beginning with the most important characteristics. After nine minutes group A joins the discussion, which should take another six minutes.
11. Each cluster presents its work to the other group. Hold a general discussion on the nature of group goals and their consequences in feeling and behavior, using the material in the following section.

CLEAR AND UNCLEAR GOALS EXERCISE: OBSERVATION GUIDE

During this exercise the groups will work on two tasks. The first task will be unclear, and the second will be clear. Your job as an observer is to make careful notations of group behavior on the two tasks. When you understand the form, return to your group but sit outside the circle.

	First Task	Second Task
1. Number of times a member clarified the goal or asked that it be clarified.		
2. Assessment of "working" climate of the group: Was it cooperative, hostile, pleasant, critical, accepting, and so forth? At the beginning?		
At the middle?		
At the end?		
3. Frequency of verbal behavior not directly related to getting the job done (side conversation, jokes, comments).		
4. Frequency of nonverbal behavior not related to getting the task done (looking around the room, horseplay, bored withdrawal, hostility).		
5. How much progress did the group make in getting the task done? (Make an estimate.)		

CLARITY OF GOALS

To be useful, goals have to be clear. If you have done the preceding exercise, you will have a list of both the characteristics of clear and unclear goals and the behavioral symptoms of groups with clear and unclear goals. Some of the symptoms of unclear goals are a high level of group tension, joking or horseplay, distraction into side issues, and the failure to use good ideas. The importance of clear goals may be seen when groups lose their direction. John DeLorean (Wright, 1979) describes how highly qualified executives in General Motors held numerous pointless meetings where trivial issues were discussed at length. These highly paid executives forgot their true goal of planning for the corporation's future. Latham and Baldes (1975) report the beneficial effects of clear goals. When truck drivers who hauled logs from the woods to the mill were told to "do their best" when loading the logs they carried about 60% of what they could legally haul. When they were later encouraged to reach a goal of 94% of the legal limit, they met this specific goal. In financial terms, this clarification of goals earned the company more than a quarter of a million dollars. Goal accomplishment depends on members' coordinating and synchronizing their actions. To do so, the goal and the actions required to achieve the goal must be clear. Goals become clarified as they are made more specific, operational, workable, measurable, and observable.

OPERATIONAL GOALS

The secret of success is constancy of purpose.

   Benjamin Disraeli

Operational goals are goals for which specific steps to achievement are clear and identifiable. **Nonoperational goals** are abstract and ambiguous—the specific steps required to achieve them are not discernable. Broad, long-range goals are often nonoperational and can be related to specific actions only through the formation of subgoals. An example of an operational goal is "Name three qualities of a good group member." An example of a nonoperational goal is "Make conclusions about the theoretical and empirical findings of qualities of effective actions by a group member."

   An operational goal has indicators that will make it evident when it has been achieved. There is no sense in going somewhere if you do not know when you have arrived. The goal "Name three qualities of a good group member" is operational in that when you have listed three items, and if they refer to group membership, you will know the goal has been reached. The goal "Make conclusions about the theoretical and empirical findings of qualities of effective actions by a group member" is nonoperational in that it may be difficult to tell when such a goal has been achieved. Whatever indicators are used to tell when a group has accomplished its goals, several of them are better than one, and indicators that are observable, countable, and specific are better than those that are nonobservable, noncountable, and ambiguous. Usually the goal of a problem-solving group will have indicators that reflect both the accomplishment of the goal (profit, new members gained, problems solved) and maintaining working relationships among group members (group cohesion, effective communication, effective decision making, high level of trust among members).

   There are several advantages for a group in having operational goals. The *first* advantage is in facilitating communication among its members and between the group and other groups. A goal must be stated in such a way that it succeeds in telling what the group intends to accomplish, and this communication is successful when any knowledgeable person can look at the group's behavior or products and decide whether or not the goal has been reached. *Second,* operational goals help guide the group in planning and carrying out its tasks. Operational goals help a group to select and to organize the appropriate resources and methods it will need in working on its tasks. *Third,* operational goals help the group evaluate both the group process and the group product. By specifying the criteria for goal accomplishment, the group can evaluate its progress. Fourth, when goals are operational, conflicts about what actions the group members should take are more likely to be decided by rational, analytic processes.

How are clear, operational goals developed? It must be recognized that for most groups clear goals cannot always be determined in advance, especially if they are to be acceptable to all or most of the members. The first job of any group, therefore, is to modify any stated goal until all the group members understand it and a consensus exists concerning how it is to be operationalized or put into practice. Through such discussions, commitment to goals is built and the goals become acceptable to the group members. The more time a group spends establishing agreement on clear goals, the less time it needs in achieving them—and the more likely it will be that the members will work effectively for the common outcome.

GROUP GOALS AND LEVEL OF ASPIRATION

Kurt Lewin and his associates developed a theory of level of aspiration to explain how people set goals for themselves and their groups (Lewin, Dembo, Festinger, & Sears, 1944). **Level of aspiration (LOA)** may be defined as the compromise between ideal goals and more realistic expectations. The theory generally predicts that individuals enter situations with an ideal outcome in mind (for example, earning a B in this course) but revise their goals upward after success and downward after failure (if they get A's on the first two tests, they change their LOA to aspire for an A, but if they get C's on the first two tests, they change their LOA to aspire for a C). As they gain experience, individuals revise their ideal expectations to match the reality of the situation.

Groups, like individuals, develop levels of aspirations. Alvin Zander conducted a series of studies with populations as diverse as high school boys batting a ball down a runway as a team (Zander & Medow, 1963) and United Fund chapters setting their fundraising goals (Zander, 1971). He demonstrated that groups set goals that are slightly optimistic and revised their goals as feedback about performance levels became available. Groups tended to lower their level of aspiration somewhat less after failure than they raised it after success. In the United Fund study, for example, of the chapters that failed to reach their goal, only 40% lowered their goal for the next year. Of the chapters that succeeded in reaching their goal, 80% raised their goal. Although this optimistic bias is constructive in most circumstances, there are times when it leads to a cycle of failure. When unsuccessful United Fund chapters set overoptimistic goals year after year, the continued failure decreased morale, work enjoyment, and group efficiency. Whereas optimistic goal setting challenges members to work hard to improve performance, the refusal to revise overly idealistic goals in unsuccessful groups can set the stage for future failure and its consequences.

DEALING WITH HIDDEN AGENDAS

The personal goals of the group members can be homogeneous (alike) or heterogeneous (different). Homogeneity of individual members' goals (or consensus about what the group's goals should be) usually helps group functioning, whereas heterogeneity of in-

dividual members' goals (or disagreement about what the group's goals should be) usually interferes with group functioning. Individual group members with homogeneous goals are usually happier with the group and its tasks than are members of groups with heterogeneous individual goals. Heterogeneous goals may easily become **hidden agendas**—personal goals that are unknown to all the other group members and are at cross-purposes with the dominant group goals. Hidden agendas can greatly hinder, and even destroy, group effectiveness. Yet they are present in almost every group. A group, therefore, must both increase consensus among group members on what the group's goals should be and decrease disagreement among different members' goals. Some procedures for doing this are as follows:

1. When you first form a group, thoroughly discuss its goals, even when they are prescribed by superiors or by the constitution of the group. Such a discussion will clarify the members' understanding of the goals and help clear away any misunderstandings concerning the tasks necessary to reach them. During the discussion the group should reword, reorganize, and review the goals until the majority of members feel a sense of "ownership" towards them.

2. As the group progresses in its activities, remember that it is continuously working on two levels at once: towards the achievement of the group's goals and towards the achievement and satisfaction of the individual members' goals and motives. Look for hidden agendas. The recognition of a group problem is the first step in diagnosing and solving it.

3. Bear in mind that there are conditions under which hidden agendas should be brought to the surface and rectified, and conditions under which they should be left undisturbed. A judgment must be made about the consequences of bringing hidden agendas to the attention of the entire group. One way in which to tell how willing other group members are to deal with hidden agendas is to initiate a discussion on the subject, taking care not to force anyone to admit his or her own hidden agenda. A statement like this one may be helpful: "I wonder if we've

said all that we feel like saying about the issue. Maybe we should take time to go around the table so that any further thoughts can be brought up."

4. Do not scold or pressure the other group members when hidden agendas are recognized. They are present and legitimate and must be worked on in much the same manner that group tasks are. Hidden agendas should be given different amounts of attention at different times, depending upon their influence on the group's effectiveness and upon the nature of the group and its members.

5. Spend some time evaluating the ability of the group to deal productively with hidden agendas. Each experience the group has should reveal better ways in which to handle agendas more openly. As groups mature, hidden agendas are reduced.

HELPING GROUPS SET EFFECTIVE GOALS

Still the question recurs, "Can we do better?" The dogmas of the quiet past are inadequate to the stormy present. The occasion is piled high with difficulty, and we must rise with the occasion. As our case is new, so we must think anew, and act anew.

Abraham Lincoln, Annual Message to Congress, December 1, 1862

Two methods of helping groups set effective goals are the survey-feedback method and program evaluation and review. The **survey-feedback method** begins with the consultant or leader interviewing the individual members of the group about group goals and the priorities of the group as they see them. These interviews are conducted before a periodic meeting of the group (such as annually or semiannually). On the basis of the in-

Effective Group Goals

1. The extent to which the goals are operationally defined so they are measurable and observable. Members need to know what they are supposed to do.

2. The extent to which group members see the goals as being meaningful, relevant, realistic, acceptable, and attainable.

3. The extent to which the goals create positive interdependence among group members.

4. The degree to which both group goals and individual members' goals can be achieved by the same tasks and activities.

5. The extent to which the goals are challenging and offer a moderate risk of failure.

6. How easily the goals can be modified and clarified.

7. How long a group has to attain its goals.

formation collected, and working within the organizational goals, the consultant conducts a group session in which the group sets its goals and priorities for the next six months or year. During this meeting the group plans its short-term goals, defines specific responsibilities for working on the tasks, ranks the tasks and goals in terms of priority to the group, and sets group-development goals for more effective group work. Special attention is paid to specifying the leadership and membership-role relationships necessary not only for working on the tasks but also for developing ways in which to identify and solve group-relationship problems that might hinder goal achievement.

In program evaluation and review—or the **critical path method**—groups are helped by a consultant to set effective goals by first specifying the end state they want to achieve. Working backward from this final goal, the group then details what must happen immediately before it is achieved, and the tasks and subgoals needed to accomplish it are all spelled out. The group decides which of the activities and subgoals are most critical for final goal accomplishment and allocates resources accordingly. A timetable for accomplishing each subgoal is set. The whole process is then reviewed and responsibilities assigned.

Exercise 3.5: Plane Wreck

The purpose of this exercise is to provide participants with an opportunity to experience co-operation based on a division of labor as well as a joint goal. The procedure is as follows:

1. The class forms groups of three. One member plays the role of observer, another member the role of A, and the third member B.
2. Each group of three needs the following materials:
   a. a blindfold
   b. five or six odd-sized pieces of cardboard
   c. a roll of cellophane tape or masking tape
   d. a piece of rope at least three feet long
3. *The situation:* A and B were flying a plane that suddenly developed engine trouble and crashed on a desert island with no water. They will be rescued in a few days, but they must have water if they are to survive. They have some materials for making a container to hold rainwater. The only problem is that B received a heavy blow on her head and is now both blind and mute. A has badly burned both hands and is not able to use them at all. But they must build the container if they are to live. A rain cloud is quickly approaching, and they must have the container finished before it reaches the island. A few drops are already beginning to fall.
4. The observer ties A's hands behind his back and blindfolds B. B is not to say a word during the entire building process.
5. The observer takes notes on how well the two persons work together. How good are the directions? How well are they carried out? How cooperative are the two persons? What communication problems exist? What could they have done differently?
6. If the container is not finished in twenty minutes, the two persons stop. The group then combines with another group of three and the two groups discuss the following questions:
   a. How did the person playing A feel?
   b. How did the person playing B feel?

c. What does the container look like? If it were made of wood and nails instead of cardboard and tape, would it hold water? (If there is a hole in the bottom, the answer is "no.")
d. What would have improved the cooperation between A and B?
e. What did you learn about the division of labor in a cooperative task?

7. Each group of six shares its major conclusions and experiences with the rest of the class.

Exercise 3.6: Broken Squares

The purpose of this exercise is to explore the results of cooperation and competition among group members in solving a group problem. The exercise is done in groups of five participants and two observers. Tables that seat five should be used. At least four groups are recommended, but two may do in a pinch. Place the tables far enough apart so that members of one group cannot observe the activities of the other groups. One set of squares is needed for each group of five. (Instructions for making a set of squares may be found in the Appendix on page 579.) Approximately one hour is needed for the exercise. The procedures for the coordinator are as follows:

1. Introduce the exercise as one that focuses upon the way in which goals are defined by members of a group. State that it will consist of completing a group task involving a puzzle.
2. Hand out the observation instructions to the observers. Within each group give each participant an instruction sheet and an envelope containing pieces of the puzzle (see the directions for making a set of squares). Half of the groups should receive instructions that they are to act cooperatively, and half instructions that they are to act competitively. State that the envelopes are not to be opened until the signal is given. Review the instructions with each group in such a way that cooperative groups do not hear the instructions to the competitive groups, and vice versa. Ask if the observers understand their role.
3. Give the signal to begin. The groups are to work until all of them have solved the puzzle. Each group should be carefully timed by its observers. If a group becomes deadlocked for more than twenty-five minutes, this phase of the exercise should be ended.
4. Collect the observation sheets and record the information in the table below. While you are doing this the groups should pair off, a cooperative group with a competitive group, and share and discuss their instructions and experiences with each other. Group observers are to participate fully in this discussion. By the end of the discussion the groups should have recorded their conclusions about the differences between working in a cooperatively oriented and a competitively oriented problem-solving group.
5. Share the results of the discussions among all the groups. Then present the information gathered by the observers. Using the material in the following section on goal structures, define cooperation and competition and discuss the impact of goal structures on group functioning and effectiveness.

You may conduct this exercise with only one group by leaving out the instructions about cooperative and competitive orientations and the comparison between cooperative and competitive groups. The issue of goal structure can still be discussed profitably.

**BROKEN SQUARES EXERCISE: INSTRUCTIONS TO EACH MEMBER
OF THE COOPERATIVE GROUP**

Each member of your group has an envelope containing pieces of cardboard for forming squares. When the signal is given to begin, the task of the group is to form one square in front of each member. Only parts of the pieces for forming the five squares are in each envelope. The exercise has two goals: your individual goal of forming a square in front of yourself as fast as possible and the group's goal of having squares formed in front of every member as fast as possible. The individual goal is accomplished when you have a completed square in front of you. The group goal is accomplished when all group members have completed squares in front of them.

You are to role play a member of a group whose members are all highly cooperative. To you the group goal is far more important than the individual goal. Your job is to cooperate with the other group members as much as possible in order to accomplish the group goal in the shortest period of time possible. To you the other group members are your partners, and you are concerned with helping them put together a completed square. All members of your group have received the same instructions.

The specific rules for the exercise are as follows:

1. No talking, pointing, or any other kind of communication is allowed among the five members of your group.
2. No person may ask another member for a piece of the puzzle or in any way signal that another person is to give her a puzzle piece.
3. Members may give puzzle pieces to other members.
4. Members may not throw their pieces into the center for others to take; they have to give the pieces directly to one person.
5. Anyone may give away all the pieces of his puzzle, even if he or she has already formed a square.
6. Part of the role of the observers is to enforce these rules.

BROKEN SQUARES EXERCISE: INSTRUCTIONS TO EACH MEMBER OF THE COMPETITIVE GROUP

Every person in this group has an envelope that contains pieces of cardboard for forming squares. When the signal is given to begin, your task is to form a square in front of you. Only parts of the pieces for forming the five squares are in each envelope. The exercise has two goals: your individual goal of forming a square in front of you as fast as possible and the group's goal of forming squares in front of every member as fast as possible. The individual goal is accomplished when you have a completed square in front of you. The group goal is accomplished when all group members have completed squares in front of them.

Data from Observation Sheets

	Cooperative	Competitive
Number of groups completing the task		
Time for task completion		
Number of times a member gave away a puzzle piece		
Number of times a member took a puzzle piece		
Number of members who cut themselves off from others		
Cooperative behaviors		
Competitive behaviors		

You are to role play a member of a group whose members are all highly competitive. To you the individual goal is far more important than the group goal. Your job is to compete with the other group members to see who can get a complete square in front of himself first. At the end of the exercise group members will be ranked on the basis of their speed in completing their square. The member finishing first will be labeled the best person in the group, the person finishing second will be labeled the second best person in the group, and so on, with the last person finishing being labeled the worst person in the group. The other group members are your competitors, and you are concerned with completing your square before they do. If you complete your square and then decide to give a piece of it away, you lose your previous rank in terms of the order of members completing their squares and must start over. All members of your group have received the same instructions.

The specific rules for the exercise are as follows:

1. No talking, pointing, or any other kind of communicating is allowed among the five members of your group.
2. No person may ask another member for a piece of the puzzle or in any way signal that another person is to give him or her a puzzle piece.
3. Members may give puzzle pieces to other members.
4. Members may not throw their pieces into the center for others to take; they have to give the pieces directly to one person.
5. Part of the role of the observers is to enforce these rules.

BROKEN SQUARES EXERCISE: INSTRUCTIONS FOR OBSERVERS

Your job is part observer, part recorder, and part rule enforcer. Do your best to strictly enforce the rules on the instruction sheet for participants. Then observe and record as accurately as possible the items listed below. The information you record will be used in a discussion of the results of the exercise.

1. Did the group complete the task? _____ Yes _____ No
2. How long did it take the group to complete the task? _____ minutes, _____ seconds
3.

Number of times a group member took a puzzle piece from another member:	Number of times a group member gave a puzzle piece to another member:

4. Number of members who finished their square and then divorced themselves from the struggles of the rest of the group: _____
5. Were there any critical turning points at which cooperation or competition increased?

_____

_____

_____

_____

6. What behaviors in the group showed cooperativeness or competitiveness?

_____

_____

_____

_____

Exercise 3.7: *Cooperative, Competitive, and Individualistic Goal Structures*

The purposes of this exercise are (a) to provide an experiential definition of the three goal structures and (b) to direct participants' attention to the contrasting patterns of interaction created by these three structures. (The correct answers are in the Appendix on page 579.) The procedure for the coordinator is as follows:

1. Assign participants to heterogeneous groups of three.
2. Conduct a competitive task experience as follows:
   a. State that the members of each triad are to compete to see who is best in identifying how many squares are in a certain geometric figure. The criterion for winning is simply to identify more correct squares than the other two triad members. Ask the participants to turn their square figure right side up, and tell them to begin.
   b. At the end of four or five minutes instruct the participants to stop. Ask them to determine who is the winner of each triad, ask the winners to stand, and then have everyone applaud.
   c. Tell the participants to turn away from their triad and, working by themselves, write down (1) how they felt during the competition and (2) what they noticed during the competition. Give them another three or four minutes to do this.
3. Conduct an individualistic task experience as follows:
   a. State that participants are to work individualistically to find as many two-sided figures in a geometric figure as they can. All participants who find 95% of the biangles will receive an evaluation of excellent, all those who find 90% will receive an evaluation of good, and so forth. Tell the participants to turn their biangles figure right side up and begin.

Goal Structure and Interaction Among Group Members

	Goal Structures		
	Cooperative	Competitive	Individualistic
Interaction			
Communication			
Facilitation of others' efforts			
Peer influence			
Utilization of others' resources			
Divergent thinking			
Emotional involvement in task			
Acceptance and support among members			
Trust among members			
Conflict management			
Division of labor			
Fear of failure			

In the spaces provided, summarize your observations of the three types of task situations.

      b. At the end of four or five minutes ask the participants to stop. Then announce the number of biangles in the figure. Ask the participants to leave their triad and, working by themselves, describe (1) how they felt and (2) what they noticed during this task. Give them another three or four minutes to do this.

4. Conduct a cooperative task experience as follows:

      a. State that the participants are to re-form their triads and work as a group to identify as many triangles in a geometric figure as they can, making sure that all members of the triad can correctly identify all the triangles. When they are finished, the members of each triad should sign the group's paper to indicate their agreement with the group's answer. All members of the groups finding 95% of the triangles will receive an evaluation of excellent, all members of the groups finding 90% of the triangles will receive an evaluation of good, and so forth. Tell the participants to turn their triangles figure right side up and begin.

      b. At the end of nine or ten minutes tell the participants to stop. Inform them of the number of triangles in the figure. Then ask them to turn away from their triad and, working by themselves, write down (1) how they felt and (2) what they noticed during the cooperative task. Give the participants four minutes to do this.

5. Instruct the participants to share their reactions to the three types of task situations with the other members of their triad. Give them ten or twelve minutes to do so. Then sample the reactions of the triads in a class discussion. Ask the participants to make conclusions about the reactions of the triads to the three task experiences.

6. Instruct the triads to fill out the table on page 91 on the basis of their experiences in the three goal structures and the comments made by the other triads. In the spaces provided, they should summarize their observations of the interaction that occurred in three task situations.

7. Review with the entire class the conceptual definitions of the three goal structures and discuss their views of the impact of each of these structures on group functioning and productivity.

Goal Structure Exercise: Squares

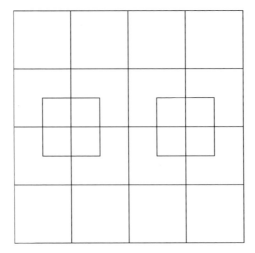

How did I feel?

What did I notice?

Goal Structure Exercise: Biangles

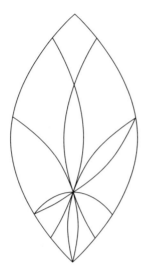

How did I feel?
What did I notice?

Goal Structure Exercise: Triangles

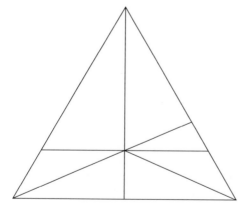

How did I feel?
What did I notice?

Exercise 3.8: Subsistence

The purpose of this exercise is to observe the effect of unequal resources on the development of cooperation or competition within a group. The exercise simulates the effects of poverty and affluence in a life and death situation. The procedure is as follows:

1. Form groups of seven. One member should volunteer to be the recorder and another member should volunteer to be the observer. Each group should have five participants, one recorder, and one observer.
2. To play the game contained in this exercise the group needs a pack of blank 3 × 5-inch index cards to serve as food cards. The group also needs a pack of hunting and gathering cards. Each card should have one of the statements listed on pages 96–97 written on it.
3. The basic procedure of the game is as follows:
   a. Each participant receives three food cards.
   b. The recorder shuffles the hunting and gathering cards and places them in the center of the group.
   c. Each participant draws a card in turn (going counterclockwise), reads it to the group, and receives from or gives to the recorder the required number of food cards.
   d. The day's hunting and gathering is over when every participant has drawn one card. Participants may give any number of food cards to each other. At the end of the day they must give one food card to the recorder. Failure to do so results in death by starvation and dropping out of the game.
   e. After seven rounds the week's hunting and gathering is over. Points are awarded to group members.
   f. The game is played for a minimum of two weeks.
4. The role of the observer is to record the frequency of the behaviors listed on the observation sheet. The frequencies are reported to the group during the concluding group discussion.
5. The role of the recorder is to
   a. Read the Subsistence Instruction Sheet to the group.
   b. Review the rules with participants.
   c. Give each participant three food cards.
   d. Shuffle the hunting and gathering cards and place them in the center of the group.
   e. Distribute and collect food cards on the basis of the cards drawn.
   f. At the end of each round collect one food card from each participant.
   g. Ensure that each participant announces how many food cards he or she has at the end of each round.
   h. Announce how many participants starved to death and who has the most food cards at the end of each week (seven rounds).
6. When the game is over, discuss the following questions:
   a. Who survived and who died?
   b. How was a cooperative or a competitive strategy decided on?
   c. How did participants feel about the impending death by starvation?
   d. How did the dead feel when they knew others could have saved them?
   e. How did the survivors feel when others died when they had extra food cards?
   f. Who organized the group to create a just distribution of food?
   g. What real-life situations parallel this exercise?

SUBSISTENCE INSTRUCTION SHEET

A severe drought has devastated your world. Because food is so scarce, you have banded together into a hunting and gathering group. It is more efficient for several people to coordinate their hunting and gathering so that more territory may be covered in any one day. There are five members of your hunting and gathering group. The food cards in your hands represent all you have left of your dwindling food supply. Because you are already weakened by hunger, you must eat at the end of each day (round) or die. At that time, you must give up one food card. When you are out of cards, you will die of starvation. A member who does not have one food card at the end of a day (round) is considered to be dead and can no longer participate in the group. Members with only one food card may not talk. Only members with two or more food cards may discuss their situation and converse with each other. You may give food cards to each other whenever you wish to do so.

RULES FOR SUBSISTENCE EXERCISE

1. The game begins when the recorder gives all participants three food cards, shuffles the hunting and gathering cards, and places them in the center of the group.
2. The purpose of the game is to gain points. You receive eight points if at the end of the week of hunting and gathering (seven rounds) you have more food cards than does any other participant in your group. If no one in your group has starved at the end of the week of hunting and gathering, all participants receive five points.
3. The game is played for a minimum of two weeks. At the beginning of each week all participants begin with three food cards and with all five participants alive.
4. You draw one card during each round. You read it aloud to the group and receive from or give to the recorder the number of food cards indicated.
5. During a round you may give food cards to other participants if you wish to.
6. All participants read the hunting and gathering cards aloud. Only those with two or more food cards, however, may discuss the game with each other. Participants with one or no food cards must be silent.
7. At the end of each round participants hold up their food cards and announce to the group how many food cards they have.
8. At the end of each round participants give one food card each to the recorder. This symbolizes the food eaten during the day to stay alive.
9. If a participant cannot give a food card to the recorder at the end of a round, the participant dies of starvation and is excluded from further rounds during that week.
10. At the end of each week of hunting and gathering (seven rounds) the recorder announces who has the most food cards and how many participants starved to death. Points are then awarded.

Subsistence Record Sheet

Name	Round 1	Round 2	Round 3	Round 4	Round 5	Round 6	Round 7

Subsistence Observation Sheet

	Round 1	Round 2	Round 3	Round 4	Round 5	Round 6	Round 7
Number of cards given away							
Number of cards taken away							
Number of people starved							
Cooperative strategy suggested							
Competitive comment							
Other							
Other							

SUBSISTENCE EXERCISE: HUNTING AND GATHERING CARDS

You found no food today.

You made a beautiful shot at what looked like a deer, but it turned out to be a strangely shaped rock. You got no food today.

You shot a bird. You get one food card from the recorder.

Wild dogs chased you and to get away you threw them one day's food. Give the recorder one food card. If you do not have a food card, and if no one will give you one, you die of starvation.

You fell asleep and slept all day. You got no food today.

Excellent shot. You killed a deer worth two days' food. You get two food cards from the recorder.

You met a member of another group and fell in love. To impress your new love you gave him or her one day's food. Give the recorder one food card. If you do not have a food card, and no one will give you one, you die of starvation.

You shot a snake. You get a food card from the recorder.

Army ants chased you and to get away you threw them one day's food. Give the recorder one food card. If you do not have a food card, and if no one will give you one, you die of starvation.

You shot a lizard. You get one food card from the recorder.

While running away from a lion, you took refuge in a peach tree. You receive one food card from the recorder.

You shot a deer but missed. You got no food today.

Lucky fluke! You shot at a deer and hit a rabbit. You get one food card from the recorder.

While you were hunting, a skunk broke into your hut and ate two days' worth of food. Give two food cards to the recorder. If you do not have two food cards, and if no one will give you any, you die of starvation.

While you were hunting, a lion ate you and all your food. Give all your food cards to the recorder and drop out of the game. Since you did not starve, your group's points are not affected. You are reborn the next week.

You found a nest of field mice and bopped them on their heads. You get one food card from the recorder.

You found no food today.

You shot a bird. You get one food card from the recorder.

You found a berry bush. Berries are in season. You get one food card from the recorder.

Lucky fluke! You shot at a wild pig and hit a rabbit. You get one food card from the recorder.

Excellent shot. You aimed at a bird you thought was standing on a rock. Your arrow hit the rock, which turned out to be a wild pig. You get two food cards from the recorder.

You found a deer, but a bear scared it away before you could shoot at it. You got no food today.

Excellent shot. Just as you shot at a deer, a wild pig ran in the way and got killed. You receive two food cards from the recorder.

You shot a rabbit. You get one food card from the recorder.

You found no food today. Probably too hot for anything to be out and around.

You found some wild carrots. You get one food card from the recorder.

You found an apple tree. Birds had eaten almost all of them. You get one food card from the recorder.

Excellent shot. You killed a wild pig. You get two food cards from the recorder.

While hunting, you accidentally stepped on a snake and killed it. You receive one food card from the recorder.

On your way home you fell into a swamp. You lost two days' worth of food to a hungry crocodile. Give two food cards to the recorder. If you do not have them, and if no one will give them to you, you die of starvation.

Excellent shot. You killed a deer. You get two food cards from the recorder.

You found some wild lettuce. You get one food card from the recorder.

You shot a rabbit. You get one food card from the recorder.

You shot a bird. You get one food card from the recorder.

You shot an aardvark. You get one food card from the recorder.

While hunting, you found a berry bush. Berries are in season. You get one food card from the recorder.

Best of luck! You found a deer with a broken leg. You killed it with your stone club. You get two food cards from the recorder.

You looked and looked and looked but found no food today.

You shot at a rabbit but it zigged instead of zagged. You got no food today.

You walked for miles and found nothing to gather or shoot at. You got no food today.

GROUP GOALS AND SOCIAL INTERDEPENDENCE AMONG MEMBERS

Theoretical Orientations

Two are better than one, because they have a good reward for their toil. For if they fall, one will lift up his fellow; but woe to him who is alone when he falls and has not another to lift him up. . . . And though a man might prevail against one who is alone, two will withstand him. A threefold cord is not quickly broken.

Ecclesiastes 4:9–12

Sandy Koufax was one of the greatest pitchers in the history of baseball. He was perhaps the only major-league pitcher whose fastball could be heard to hum. Opposing batters, instead of talking and joking in the dugout, would sit quietly and listen for Koufax's fastball to hum. When it was their turn to bat, they were already intimidated. There was, however, a simple way for Koufax's genius to have been negated. By making the first author of this book his catcher. To be great, a pitcher needs an outstanding catcher (Koufax's great partner was Johnny Roseboro). David is such an unskilled catcher that Koufax would have had to have thrown the ball much slower in order for David to catch it. This would have deprived Koufax of his greatest weapon. Placing Frank at a key defensive position in the infield or outfield, furthermore, would have seriously affected Koufax's success. Sandy Koufax was not a great pitcher on his own. Only as part of a team could Koufax achieve greatness. In baseball and in every other group, it takes a cooperative effort. Extraordinary achievement comes from a cooperative group, not from the individualistic or competitive efforts of isolated individuals.

Understanding the nature of cooperative, competitive, and individualistic efforts begins with theory. At least three general theoretical perspectives have guided research on cooperation—cognitive-developmental, behavioral, and social interdependence (see Figure 3.1). The **cognitive developmental perspective** is largely based on the theories of Piaget and Vygotsky. The work of Piaget and related theorists is based on the premise that when individuals cooperate on the environment, sociocognitive conflict occurs that creates cognitive disequilibrium, which in turn stimulates perspective-taking ability and cognitive development. The work of Vygotsky and related theorists is based on the premise that knowledge is social, constructed from cooperative efforts to learn, understand, and solve problems. The **behavioral theory perspective** focuses on the impact of group reinforcers and rewards on productivity. Skinner focused on group contingencies, Bandura focused on imitation, and Homans as well as Thibaut and Kelley focused on the balance of rewards and costs in social exchange among interdependent individ-

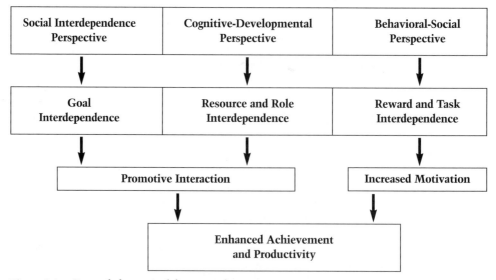

Figure 3.1 General theoretical framework.
Source: Reprinted with permission from D. W. Johnson and R. Johnson, *Cooperation and Competition: Theory and Research* (Edina, MN: Interaction Book Company, 1989).

uals. Although the cognitive-developmental and behavioral theoretical orientations have their followings, by far the most important theory dealing with cooperation and competition is **social interdependence theory.**

Social Interdependence Theory

Theorizing on **social interdependence** began in the early 1900s, when one of the founders of the Gestalt school of psychology, Kurt Koffka, proposed that groups were dynamic wholes in which the interdependence among members could vary. One of his colleagues, Kurt Lewin, refined Koffka's notions in the 1920s and 1930s, stating that (a) the essence of a group is the interdependence among members (created by common goals) that results in the group being a "dynamic whole" so that a change in the state of any member or subgroup changes the state of any other member or subgroup, and (b) an intrinsic state of tension within group members motivates movement toward the accomplishment of the desired common goals.

Lewin's students and colleagues conducted research indicating that it is the drive for goal accomplishment that motivates cooperative and competitive behavior. Ovisankina (1928) demonstrated that interrupted tasks were almost always resumed when the subjects were left free to do as they wished. Lissner (1933), Mahler (1933), and many others investigated the conditions under which one activity can substitute for and, hence, release the tension connected with another, interrupted activity. The substitute value was measured by the amount of decrease in resumption or recall of the interrupted original activity after a substitute activity had been completed. Helen Block Lewis (Lewis, 1944; Lewis & Franklin, 1944) demonstrated that cooperative work that is interrupted and not completed can lead to a persisting force to recall that is not much different from the pressure to recall induced by interrupted individual work. In other words, if a collaborator completes the original activity his or her actions substitute for one's own, and the tension induced by being interrupted before the task was completed is released. From Lewin's field theory, and the research of these and other members and colleagues of Lewin, it may be concluded that it is the drive for goal accomplishment that motivates cooperative, competitive, and individualistic behavior.

In the late 1940s, one of Lewin's graduate students, Morton Deutsch, extended Lewin's reasoning about social interdependence and formulated a theory of cooperation and competition (Deutsch, 1949a, 1962). Deutsch conceptualized two types of social interdependence—cooperative and competitive—and individualistic efforts as the absence of interdependence. Deutsch was born in 1920, graduated from City College of New York in 1939, and obtained a master's degree from the University of Pennsylvania in 1940. After serving in the United States Air Force from 1942 to 1945, he entered the doctoral program in social psychology at MIT to study with Kurt Lewin. Deutsch has received a variety of professional rewards during his career, including the prestigious Kurt Lewin Memorial Award for contributions to the solution of social problems through theory and research and the Gordon Allport Memorial Award for contributions to constructive intergroup relations through theory and research. Following in Lewin's footsteps, Deutsch has become noted as an outstanding social psychologist because of his commitment to the development of theory about complex social issues, his ability to find ways to study these issues in a laboratory setting, and his dedication to the solution of social problems. Deutsch's (1949a) original theory has served as a major

Morton Deutsch

conceptual structure for this area of inquiry for the past forty-five years. His theory and research pioneered future work on social interdependence. Since his initial theorizing, Deutsch has extended his theory of social interdependence to include trust, conflict resolution, and systems of distributive justice. The progression of his theorizing over the past forty years is one of the seminal works in the history of psychology. Deutsch's theory was extended and applied to education by the authors at the University of Minnesota (Johnson, 1970; Johnson & Johnson, 1974, 1989). Our work has been extended and applied to business and industry (Tjosvold, 1986).

Social interdependence exists when individuals share common goals and each individual's outcomes are affected by the actions of the others (Deutsch, 1949a, 1962; Johnson & Johnson, 1989). It may be differentiated from **social dependence** (i.e., the outcomes of one person are affected by the actions of a second person but not vice versa) and **social independence** (i.e., individuals' outcomes are unaffected by each other's actions). There are two types of social interdependence: cooperative and competitive. The absence of social interdependence and dependence results in individualistic efforts.

When individuals take action there are three ways what they do may be related to the actions of others. One's actions may promote the success of others, obstruct the success of others, or not have any effect at all on the success or failure of others. In other words, individuals may be (Deutsch, 1949a, 1962; Johnson & Johnson, 1989):

1. Working together cooperatively to accomplish shared learning goals. When a situation is structured **cooperatively,** individuals' goal achievements are posi-

tively correlated; individuals perceive that they can reach their goals if and only if the others in the group also reach their goals. Thus, individuals seek outcomes that are beneficial to all those with whom they are cooperatively linked.

2. Working against each other to achieve a goal that only one or a few can attain. When a situation is structured **competitively,** individuals work against each other to achieve a goal that only one or a few can attain. Individuals' goal achievements are negatively correlated; each individual perceives that when one person achieves his or her goal, all others with whom he or she is competitively linked fail to achieve their goals. Thus, individuals seek an outcome that is personally beneficial but detrimental to all others in the situation.

3. Working by oneself to accomplish goals unrelated to the goals of others. When a situation is structured **individualistically,** there is no correlation among participants' goal attainments. Each individual perceives that he or she can reach his or her goal regardless of whether other individuals attain or do not attain their goals. Thus, individuals seek an outcome that is personally beneficial without concern for the outcomes of others.

The basic premise of social interdependence theory is that the type of interdependence structured in a situation determines how individuals interact with each other, which, in turn, determines outcomes (see Table 3.2). Positive interdependence tends to result in promotive interaction, negative interdependence tends to result in oppositional or contrient interaction, and no interdependence results in an absence of interaction. In cooperative situations the actions of participants substitute for each other, participants respond positively to each other's effective actions, and members are open to influence by each other. In competitive situations the actions of participants do not substitute for each other, participants respond negatively to each other's effective actions, and they refuse to be influenced by each other. When there is no interaction, there is little substitutability, emotional response, or influence. The relationship between the type of social interdependence and the interaction pattern it elicits is assumed to be bidirectional. Each may cause the other.

Social interdependence to humans is like water to fish. Because we are immersed in it, social interdependence can escape our notice. Whether it is quite personal or so impersonal that we are barely aware of it, we regularly underestimate the role that social interdependence plays in human life. Because we cannot imagine its absence, we often do not consider its presence.

Table 3.2 **Social Interdependence Theory**

Process	Cooperative	Competitive	Individualistic
Interdependence	Positive	Negative	None
Interaction pattern	Promotive	Oppositional	None
Outcome 1	High effort to achieve	Low effort to achieve	Low effort to achieve
Outcome 2	Positive relationships	Negative relationships	No relationships
Outcome 3	Psychological health	Psychological illness	Psychological pathology

Interaction Patterns

Between 1898 and 1989, over 575 experimental and 100 correlational studies were conducted by a wide variety of researchers in different decades with different age subjects, in different subject areas, and in different settings (see Johnson & Johnson, 1989, for a complete listing of these studies). One of the issues addressed by this research is the type of interaction patterns found within cooperative, competitive, and individualistic situations.

Positive interdependence creates promotive interaction. **Promotive interaction** occurs as individuals encourage and facilitate each other's efforts to reach the group's goals (such as maximizing each member's learning). Group members promote each other's success by (Johnson & Johnson, 1989):

1. Giving and receiving help and assistance (both task-related and personal).
2. Exchanging resources and information. Group members seek information and other resources from each other, comprehend information accurately and without bias, and make optimal use of the information provided. There are a number of beneficial results from (a) orally explaining, elaborating, and summarizing information, and (b) teaching one's knowledge to others. Explaining and teaching increase the degree to which group members cognitively process and organize information, engage in higher-level reasoning, attain insights, and become personally committed to achieving. Listening critically to the explanations of groupmates provides the opportunity to utilize other's resources.
3. Giving and receiving feedback on taskwork and teamwork behaviors. In cooperative groups, members monitor each other's efforts, give immediate feedback on performance, and, when needed, give each other help and assistance.
4. Challenging each other's reasoning. Intellectual controversy promotes curiosity, motivation to learn, reconceptualization of what one knows, higher quality decision making, greater insight into the problem being considered, and many other important benefits (Johnson & Johnson, 1979, 1995b).
5. Advocating increased efforts to achieve. Encouraging others to achieve increases one's own commitment to do so.
6. Mutually influencing each other's reasoning and behavior. Group members actively seek to influence and be influenced by each other. If a member has a better way to complete the task, groupmates usually quickly adopt it.
7. Engaging in the interpersonal and small group skills needed for effective teamwork.
8. Processing how effectively group members are working together and how the group's effectiveness can be continuously improved.

Negative interdependence typically results in oppositional interaction. **Oppositional interaction** occurs as individuals discourage and obstruct each other's efforts to achieve. Individuals focus both on increasing their own success and on preventing anyone else from being more successful than they are. **No interaction** exists when individuals work independently without any interaction or interchange with each other. Individuals focus only on increasing their own success and ignore as irrelevant the efforts of others. Each of these interaction patterns creates different outcomes.

Types of Positive Interdependence

Positive Goal Interdependence: Students perceive that they can achieve their learning goals if and only if all the members of their group also attain their goals. Members of a learning group have a mutual set of goals that they are all striving to accomplish.

Positive Celebration/Reward Interdependence: Group celebrates success. A joint reward is given for successful group work and members' efforts to achieve.

Positive Resource Interdependence: Each member has only a portion of the information, resources, or materials necessary for the task to be completed and the member's resources have to be combined in order for the group to achieve its goal.

Positive Role Interdependence: Each member is assigned complementary and interconnected roles that specify responsibilities that the group needs in order to complete a joint task.

Positive Identity Interdependence: The group establishes a mutual identity through a name, flag, motto, or song.

Environmental Interdependence: Group members are bound together by the physical environment in some way. An example is putting people in a specific area in which to work.

Positive Fantasy Interdependence: A task is given that requires members to imagine that they are in a life or death situation and must collaborate in order to survive.

Positive Task Interdependence: A division of labor is created so that the actions of one group member have to be completed if the next team member is to complete his or her responsibility.

Positive Outside Enemy Interdependence: Groups are placed in competition with each other. Group members then feel interdependent as they strive to beat the other groups and win the competition.

Promotive interaction tends to result in a wide variety of outcomes that may be subsumed into the categories of high effort to achieve, positive relationships, and psychological health. Oppositional interaction tends to result in low effort to achieve by most students, negative relationships, and low psychological health, and no interaction tends to result in low effort to achieve, an absence of relationships, and psychological pathology.

OUTCOMES OF SOCIAL INTERDEPENDENCE

The fundamental facts that brought about cooperation, society, and civilization and transformed the animal man into a human being are the facts that work performed under the division of labor is more productive than isolated work and that man's reason is capable of recognizing this truth. But for these facts men would have forever remained deadly foes of one another, irreconcilable rivals in their endeavors to secure a portion of the scarce supply of means of sustenance provided by Nature. Each man would have been forced to view all other men as his enemies; his craving for the satisfaction of his own appetites would have brought him into an implacable conflict with all his neighbors. No sympathy could possibly develop under such a state of affairs. . . .We may call consciousness of kind, sense of community, or sense of belonging together the acknowledgment of fact that all other human beings are potential collaborators in the struggle for survival because they are capable of recognizing the mutual benefits of cooperation.

Ludwig Von Mises (1949)

Within Yosemite National Park lies the famous Half Dome Mountain. The Half Dome is famous for its 2,000 feet of soaring, sheer cliff wall. Unusually beautiful to the observer, and considered unclimbable for years, the Half Dome's northwest face was first scaled in 1957 by Royal Robbins and two companions. This incredibly dangerous climb took five days, with Robbins and his companions spending four nights on the cliff, sleeping in ropes with nothing below their bodies but air. Even today, the northwest face is a death trap to all but the finest and most skilled rock climbers. Far above the ground, moving slowly up the rock face, are two climbers.

The two climbers are motivated by a shared vision of successfully climbing the northwest face. As they move up the cliff they are attached to each other by a rope **(the lifeline).** As one member climbs **(the lead climber),** the other **(the belayer)** ensures that the two have a safe anchor and that he or she can catch the climber if the climber falls. The lead climber does not begin climbing until the belayer says "go." Then the lead climber advances, puts in a piton, slips in the rope, and continues to advance. The pitons help the belayer catch the climber if the climber falls and they mark the path up the cliff. The lifeline (i.e., rope) goes from the belayer through the pitons up to the climber. When the lead climber has completed the first leg of the climb, he or she becomes the belayer and the other member of the team begins to climb. The pitons placed by the lead climber serve to guide and support the second member of the team up the rock face. The second member advances up the route marked out by the first member until the first leg is completed, and then leapfrogs and becomes the lead climber for the second leg of the climb. The roles of lead climber and belayer are alternated until the summit is reached.

All human life is like mountain climbing. The human species seems to have a **cooperation imperative:** We desire and seek out opportunities to operate jointly with others to achieve mutual goals. We are attached to others through a variety of "lifelines," and we alternate supporting and leading others to ensure a better life for ourselves, our colleagues and neighbors, our children, and all generations to follow. Cooperation is an inescapable fact of life. From cradle to grave we cooperate with others. Each day, from our first waking moment until sleep overtakes us again, we cooperate within family, work, leisure, and community by working jointly to achieve mutual goals. Throughout history, people have come together to (a) accomplish feats that any one of them could not achieve alone and (b) share their joys and sorrows. From conceiving a child to sending a rocket to the moon, our successes require cooperation among individuals. The cooperation may be less clear than it is in climbing up a cliff, but it exists none the less.

Considerable research based on Deutsch's classic work on cooperation and competition has been conducted during the past 30 years. Working together to get the job done can have profound effects. In trying to understand how cooperation works, and in continually refining our understanding of how to implement cooperation most effectively, we have (a) reviewed over 550 experimental and over 100 correlational research studies conducted during the last 100 years comparing cooperative, competitive, and individualistic efforts, and (b) conducted a 35-year program of research that has resulted in over 85 published studies. The numerous variables that are affected by cooperation may be subsumed within three broad and interrelated outcomes (see Figure 3.2) (Johnson & Johnson, 1989):

1. Effort exerted to achieve.
2. Quality of relationships among participants.
3. Participants' psychological adjustment and social competence.

If research is to have impact on theory and practice, it must be summarized and communicated in a complete, objective, impartial, and unbiased way. In an age of information explosion, there is considerable danger that theories will be formulated on

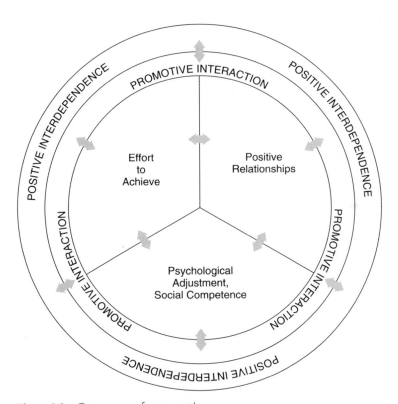

Figure 3.2 Outcomes of cooperation.
Source: D. W. Johnson & R. T. Johnson, *Cooperation and Competition: Theory and Research* (Edina, MN: Interaction Book Company, 1989). Used with permission of authors.

small and nonrepresentative samples of available knowledge, thereby resulting in falla-cious conclusions that in turn lead to mistaken practices. A quantitative reviewing pro-cedure, such as meta-analysis, allows for more definitive and robust conclusions. A **meta-analysis** is a method of statistically combining the results of a set of independent studies that test the same hypothesis and using inferential statistics to draw conclusions about the overall result of the studies. The essential purpose of a meta-analysis is to summarize a set of related research studies, so that the size of the effect of the inde-pendent variable on the dependent variable is known.

Effort to Achieve and Produce

Two heads are better than one.

John Heywood

The investigation of the relative impact of the three types of social interdependence on achievement is the longest standing research tradition within American social psy-chology. Between 1898 and 1989, researchers conducted over 375 experimental stud-ies with over 1,700 findings on social interdependence and productivity and achievement (Johnson & Johnson, 1989). That does not count the research on social fa-cilitation and other related areas where implicit competition may be found. Because research participants have varied widely as to sex, economic class, age, and cultural background, because a wide variety of research tasks and measures of the dependent variables have been used, and because the research has been conducted by many dif-ferent researchers with markedly different orientations working in different settings and in different decades, the overall body of research on social interdependence has considerable generalizability.

A meta-analysis of all studies (Johnson & Johnson, 1989) found that the average person cooperating performed at about two-thirds a standard deviation above the av-erage person learning within a competitive (effect size = 0.67) or individualistic situa-tion (effect size = 0.64) (see Table 3.3). Not all the research, however, has been carefully conducted. The methodological shortcomings found within many research studies may significantly reduce the certainty of the conclusion that cooperative efforts pro-duce higher achievement than do competitive or individualistic efforts. When only studies with high internal validity were included in the analysis, the effect sizes were 0.88 and 0.61, respectively. Further analyses revealed that the results held constant when group measures of productivity were included as well as individual measures, for short-term as well as long-term studies, and when symbolic as well as tangible rewards were used.

A number of the studies conducted operationally defined cooperation in a way that included elements of competition and individualistic work. The original jigsaw stud-ies, for example, operationalized cooperative learning as a combination of positive re-source interdependence and an individualistic reward structure (Aronson et al., 1978). Teams-Games-Tournaments (TGT; DeVries & Edwards, 1974) and Student-Team-Achievement-Divisions (STAD; Slavin, 1986) operationalized cooperative learning as a combination of in-group cooperation and intergroup competition, and Team-Assisted-Individualization (TAI; Slavin, 1986) is a mixture of cooperative and individualistic

Table 3.3 **Mean Effect Sizes for Impact of Social Interdependence on Dependent Variables**

Conditions	Achievement	Interpersonal Attraction	Social Support	Self-Esteem
Total Studies				
Coop vs. Comp	0.67	0.67	0.62	0.58
Coop vs. Ind	0.64	0.60	0.70	0.44
Comp vs. Ind	0.30	0.08	−0.13	−0.23
High-Quality Studies				
Coop vs. Comp	0.88	0.82	0.83	0.67
Coop vs. Ind	0.61	0.62	0.72	0.45
Comp vs. Ind	0.07	0.27	−0.13	−0.25
Mixed Operationalizations				
Coop vs. Comp	0.40	0.46	0.45	0.33
Coop vs. Ind	0.42	0.36	0.02	0.22
Pure Operationalizations				
Coop vs. Comp	0.71	0.79	0.73	0.74
Coop vs. Ind	0.65	0.66	0.77	0.51

Note: Coop = Cooperation, Comp = Competition, Ind = Individualistic

Source: D. W. Johnson and R. Johnson, *Cooperation and Competition: Theory and Research* (Edina, MN: Interaction Book Company, 1989).

learning. When such "mixed" operationalizations were compared with "pure" operationalizations, the effect sizes for the cooperative versus competitive comparison were 0.45 and 0.74, respectively, $t(37) = 1.60$, $p < 0.06$ (Johnson & Johnson, 1989). The effect sizes for the cooperative versus individualistic comparisons were 0.13 and 0.61, respectively, $t(10) = 1.64$, $p < 0.07$.

Besides higher achievement and greater retention, cooperation, compared with competitive or individualistic efforts, tends to result in more (Johnson & Johnson, 1989):

1. Willingness to take on difficult tasks and persist, despite difficulties, in working toward goal accomplishment. In addition, there is intrinsic motivation, high expectations for success, high incentive to achieve based on mutual benefit, high epistemic curiosity and continuing interest in learning, and high commitment to achieve.
2. Long-term retention of what is learned.
3. Higher-level reasoning, critical thinking, and metacognitive thought. Group members should be able to "sort sense from nonsense" and have the critical-thinking abilities of grasping information, examining it, evaluating it for soundness, and applying it appropriately. Cooperative situations promote a greater use of higher-level reasoning strategies and critical thinking than do competitive or individualistic situations. Cooperative experiences promote more

frequent insight into and use of higher-level cognitive and moral reasoning strategies than do competitive or individualistic experiences (effect sizes = 0.93 and 0.97 respectively).

4. Creative thinking (process gain). **Process gain** occurs when new ideas, solutions, or efforts are generated through group interaction that are not generated when persons work individually. In cooperative groups, members more frequently generate new ideas, strategies, and solutions than they would think of on their own.

5. Transfer of learning from one situation to another (group to individual transfer). **Group-to-individual transfer** occurs when individuals who learned within a cooperative group demonstrate mastery on a subsequent test taken individually. What individuals learn in a group today, they are able to do alone tomorrow.

6. Positive attitudes towards the tasks being completed. Cooperative efforts result in more positive attitudes towards the tasks being completed and greater continuing motivation to complete them. The positive attitudes extend to the work experience and the organization as a whole.

7. Time on task. Over thirty studies did in fact measure time on task. They found that cooperators spent more time on task than did competitors (effect size = 0.76) or students working individualistically (effect size = 1.17). Competitors spent more time on task than did students working individualistically (effect size = 0.64). These effect sizes are quite large, indicating that members of cooperative learning groups do seem to spend considerable more time on task than do students working competitively or individualistically.

Because the most credible studies (due to their high quality methodologically) and the "pure" operationalizations of cooperative learning produced stronger effects, considerable confidence can be placed in two conclusions about cooperative efforts: They promote more positive cross-ethnic relationships than do competitive or individualistic efforts, and they promote greater effort to achieve than do competitive or individualistic efforts.

Not all research supporting the use of a cooperative goal structure has been experimental. Balderston (1930) conducted a study of group-incentive plans by collecting written descriptions of such plans from a number of companies. In each instance, the pay of all members depended on the productivity of the group as a whole. Balderston found that this method of work doubled the efficiency of the workers, increased their pay about 25%, and reduced their costs substantially compared to the flat rate previously paid to each individual. The users of group-incentive methods stated that their plans were valuable because they increased cooperation and team spirit among members, reduced monotony on the job, and caused workers to focus on a common goal.

Kurt Lewin often stated, "I always found myself unable to think as a single person." Most efforts to achieve are a personal but social process that requires individuals to cooperate and to construct shared understandings and knowledge. Both competitive and individualistic structures, by isolating individuals from each other, tend to depress achievement and productivity.

Quality of Relationships

A faithful friend is a strong defense, and he that hath found him,
hath found a treasure.

Ecclesiastics 6:14

We are created, not for isolation, but for relationships. At heart, we are not a thousand points of separated light but, rather, part of a larger brightness. **Within organizations caring and committed relationships are not a luxury. They are a necessity.** Organizations increasingly have members who are isolated and unattached to family or peers and members from a variety of ethnic, historical, and cultural backgrounds. Recent national surveys indicate that it is feeling valued, loved, wanted, and respected by others that gives life meaning and purpose, and it is intimate relationships that create happiness. Organizations may focus on building positive relationships among heterogeneous members. There is considerable evidence comparing the impact of cooperative, competitive, and individualistic efforts on interpersonal attraction and social support.

Since 1940, over 180 studies have compared the impact of cooperative, competitive, and individualistic efforts on interpersonal attraction (Johnson & Johnson, 1989). Cooperative efforts, compared with competitive and individualistic experiences, promoted considerable more liking among individuals (effect sizes = 0.66 and 0.62 respectively) (see Table 3.3). The effects sizes were higher for (a) high-quality studies and (b) studies using pure operationalizations of cooperative learning than for studies using mixed operationalizations. The weighted effect sizes for cooperation versus competition and cooperation versus individualistic efforts are 0.65 and 0.64, respectively. When only the methodologically high-quality studies are examined, the effect sizes go up to 0.77 and 0.67. "Pure" cooperation results in greater effects than do mixtures of cooperative, competitive, and individualistic efforts (cooperative vs. competitive, pure = 0.75 and mixed = 0.48; cooperative vs. individualistic, pure = 0.67 and mixed = 0.36).

Much of the research on interpersonal relationships has been conducted on relationships between white and minority students and between students with and without disabilities (Johnson & Johnson, 1989). There have been over forty experimental studies comparing some combination of cooperative, competitive, and individualistic experiences on cross-ethnic relationships and over forty similar studies on mainstreaming of students with disabilities (Johnson & Johnson, 1989). Their results are consistent. Working cooperatively creates far more positive relationships among diverse and heterogeneous students than does learning competitively or individualistically.

An extension of social interdependence theory is **social judgment theory,** which focuses on relationships among diverse individuals (Johnson & Johnson, 1989). The social judgments individuals make about each other increase or decrease the liking they feel towards each other. Such social judgments are the result of either a process of acceptance or a process of rejection (Johnson & Johnson, 1989). The **process of acceptance** is based on the individuals promoting mutual goal accomplishment as a result of their perceived positive interdependence. The promotive interaction tends to result in frequent, accurate, and open communication; accurate understanding of each other's perspective; inducibility; differentiated, dynamic, and realistic views of each other; high self-esteem; success and productivity; and expectations for positive and productive future interaction. The **process of rejection** results from oppositional or no interaction based on perceptions of negative or no interdependence. Both lead to no or inaccurate communication; egocentrism; resistance to influence; monopolistic, stereotyped, and static views of others; low self-esteem; failure; and expectations of distasteful and unpleasant interaction with others. The processes of acceptance and rejection are self-perpetuating. Any part of the process tends to elicit all the other parts of the process.

The positive relationships among members promoted by cooperative efforts result in a high level of group cohesion. **Group cohesion** may be defined as the mutual attraction among members of a group and the resulting desire to remain in the group. Highly cohesive groups, where members like each other, are characterized by greater ease in setting goals (Festinger, Schachter & Back, 1950), greater likelihood in achieving those goals (Seashore, 1954; Wolfe & Box, 1988), and greater susceptibility to influence by groupmates (Schachter, Ellertson, McBride, & Gregory, 1951). The impact of group cohesiveness on group performance is stronger for small groups and real groups and seems to be driven predominantly by members' commitment to the successful task performance and regulate their behavior towards that end (Mullen & Cooper, 1994) (see Figure 3.3). Groups become cohesive by formulating and working together on issues that are specific, immediate, and realizable. As cohesiveness increases, absenteeism and turnover of membership decrease, and the following increase: member commitment to group goals, feelings of personal responsibility to the group, willingness to take on difficult tasks, motivation and persistence in working towards goal achievement, satisfaction and morale, willingness to endure pain and frustration on behalf of the group, willingness to defend the group against external criticism or attack, willingness to listen to and be influenced by colleagues, commitment to each other's professional growth and success, and productivity (Johnson & Johnson, 1989; Watson & Johnson, 1972). Cohesiveness within a group, team, department, business, classroom, or school is determined by how well members like each other as people and colleagues.

Positive peer relationships influence the social and cognitive development of students and such attitudes and behaviors as educational aspirations and staying in school (Johnson & Johnson, 1989). Relationships with peers influence what attitudes and values students adopt, whether students become prosocial or antisocial oriented, whether students learn to see situations from a variety of perspectives, the development of au-

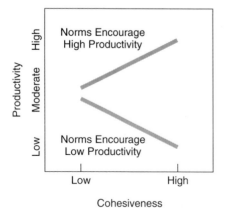

Figure 3.3   The hypothesized link between productivity and cohesiveness.

tonomy, aspirations for postsecondary education, and whether students learn how to cope with adversity and stress.

Besides liking each other, cooperators give and receive considerable social support, both personally and academically (Johnson & Johnson, 1989). Since the 1940s, more than 106 studies comparing the relative impact of cooperative, competitive, and individualistic efforts on social support have been conducted. Social support may be aimed at enhancing another person's success (task-related social support) or at providing support on a more personal level (personal social support). Cooperative experience promoted greater task-oriented and personal social support than did competitive (effect size = 0.62) or individualistic (effect size = 0.70) experiences. Social support tends to promote achievement and productivity, physical health, psychological health, and successful coping with stress and adversity.

Psychological Adjustment and Social Competence

All for one, one for all.

Alexandre Dumas

The third set of issues researched involve promoting psychological health, self-esteem, and social competencies. **Psychological health** is the ability to develop, maintain, and appropriately modify interdependent relationships with others to succeed in achieving

goals (Johnson & Johnson, 1989). To manage social interdependence, individuals must correctly perceive whether interdependence exists and whether it is positive or negative, be motivated accordingly, and act in ways consistent with normative expectations for appropriate behavior within the situation. Four studies have directly measured the relationship between social interdependence and psychological health. The samples studied included suburban high school seniors (Johnson & Norem-Heibeisen, 1977), juvenile and adult prisoners (N. James & Johnson, 1983), step-couples (S. James & Johnson, 1988), and Olympic hockey players (Johnson, Johnson, & Krotee, 1986). The results indicated that (a) working cooperatively with peers and valuing cooperation result in greater psychological health than does competing with peers or working independently; and (b) cooperative attitudes are highly correlated with a wide variety of indices of psychological health, competitiveness was in some cases positively and in some cases negatively related to psychological health, and individualistic attitudes were negatively related to a wide variety of indices of psychological health. Cooperativeness is positively related to a number of indices of psychological health, such as emotional maturity, well-adjusted social relations, strong personal identity, ability to cope with adversity, social competencies, and basic trust in and optimism about people. Personal ego strength, self-confidence, independence, and autonomy are all promoted by being involved in cooperative efforts. Individualistic attitudes tend to be related to a number of indices of psychological pathology, such as emotional immaturity, social maladjustment, delinquency, self-alienation, and self-rejection. Competitiveness is related to a mixture of healthy and unhealthy characteristics. Whereas inappropriate competitive and individualistic attitudes and efforts have resulted in alienating individuals from others, healthy and therapeutic growth depends on increasing individuals' understanding of how to cooperate more effectively with others. Cooperative experiences are not a luxury. They are absolutely necessary for healthy development.

Social interdependence theory has been extended to self-esteem. A **process of self-acceptance** is posited to be based on (a) internalizing perceptions that one is known, accepted, and liked as one is; (b) internalizing mutual success; and (c) evaluating oneself favorably in comparison with peers. A process of self-rejection may occur from (a) not wanting to be known, (b) low performance, (c) overgeneralization of self-evaluations, and (d) the disapproval of others. Since the 1950s, there have been over eighty studies comparing the relative impact of cooperative, competitive, and individualistic experiences on self-esteem (Johnson & Johnson, 1989). Cooperative experiences promote higher self-esteem than do competitive (effect size = 0.58) or individualistic (effect size = 0.44) experiences. Our research demonstrated that cooperative experiences tend to be related to beliefs that one is intrinsically worthwhile, others see one in positive ways, one's attributes compare favorably with those of one's peers, and one is a capable, competent, and successful person. In cooperative efforts, students (a) realize that they are accurately known, accepted, and liked by their peers; (b) know that they have contributed to own, others', and group success; and (c) perceive themselves and others in a differentiated and realistic way that allows for multidimensional comparisons based on complementarity of own and others' abilities. Competitive experiences tend to be related to conditional self-esteem based on whether one wins or loses. Individualistic experiences tend to be related to basic self-rejection.

A number of studies have related cooperative, competitive, and individualistic experiences to perspective-taking ability (the ability to understand how a situation appears to other people) (Johnson & Johnson, 1989). Cooperative experiences tend to increase perspective-taking ability whereas competitive and individualistic experiences tend to promote egocentrism (being unaware of other perspectives other than your own) (effect sizes of 0.61 and 0.44, respectively). Individuals, furthermore, who are part of a cooperative effort learn more social skills and become more socially competent than do persons competing or working individualistically. Finally, it is through cooperative efforts that many of the attitudes and values essential to psychological health (such as self-efficacy) are learned and adopted.

An important aspect of psychological health is social competence. **Social skills and competencies tend to increase more within cooperative than in competitive or individ-**

ualistic situations (Johnson & Johnson, 1989). Working together to get the job done increases students' abilities to provide leadership, build and maintain trust, communicate effectively, and manage conflicts constructively. Employability and career success depend largely on such social skills. Most modern work occurs within teams. Intelligence and technical expertise are of no use if individuals are not skillful group members. The social skills learned within cooperative learning groups, furthermore, provide the basis for building and maintaining lifelong friendships, loving and caring families, and cohesive neighborhoods.

The higher the level of an individual's psychological pathology (e.g., depression, anger, anxiety), the less able he or she is to develop and maintain caring and committed relationships. The association between antisocial behavior and rejection by the normal peer group, for example, is well documented (Cantrell & Prinz, 1985; Dodge, Coie, & Bakke, 1982; Roff & Wirt, 1984). Inappropriately aggressive behavior leads to rejection by peers (Coie & Kupersmidt, 1983; Dodge, 1983). Rejected children are also deficient in a number of social-cognitive skills, including peer group entry, perception of peer group norms, response to provocation, and interpretation of prosocial interactions (Asarnow & Callan, 1985; Dodge, 1983; Putallaz, 1983). Among children referred to child guidance clinics, 30% to 75% (depending on age) are reported by their parents to experience peer difficulties (Achenbach & Edelbrock, 1981). These difficulties are roughly twice as common among clinic children as among nonreferred youngsters. Moreover, referred children have fewer friends and less contact with them than nonreferred children, their friendships are significantly less stable over time, and their understanding of the reciprocities and intimacies involved in friendships is less mature (Selman, 1981).

RECIPROCAL RELATIONSHIPS AMONG THE THREE OUTCOMES

The reason we were so good, and continued to be so good, was because he (Joe Paterno) forces you to develop an inner love among the players. It is much harder to give up on your buddy, than it is to give up on your coach. I really believe that over the years the teams I played on were almost unbeatable in tight situations. When we needed to get that six inches we got it because of our love for each other. Our camaraderie existed because of the kind of coach and kind of person Joe was.

David Joyner

Each of the outcomes of cooperative efforts (effort to achieve, quality of relationships, and psychological health) influences the others and, therefore, they are likely to be found together (Johnson & Johnson, 1989). *First,* caring and committed friendships come from a sense of mutual accomplishment, mutual pride in joint work, and the bonding that results from joint efforts. The more individuals care about each other, the harder they will work to achieve mutual goals. *Second,* joint efforts to achieve mutual goals promote higher self-esteem, self-efficacy, personal control, and confidence in one's competencies. The healthier psychologically individuals are, the better able they are to work with others to achieve mutual goals. *Third,* psychological health is built on the internalization of the caring and respect received from loved ones. Friendships are developmental advantages that promote self-esteem, self-efficacy, and general psychological adjustment. The healthier people are psychologically (i.e., free of psychological pathology such as depression, paranoia, anxiety, fear of failure, repressed anger, hopelessness, and meaninglessness), the more caring and committed their relationships. Because each outcome can induce the others, you are likely to find them together. They are a package with each outcome a door into all three. Together they induce positive interdependence and promotive interaction.

Competitive and Individualistic Efforts

The basic social psychological query is "Under what conditions are cooperative, competitive, and individualistic efforts effective?" The hundreds of studies that have been conducted to try to answer this question indicate that under most conditions, cooperation has more powerful effects on the variables studied than do competitive or individualistic efforts. Under most conditions, cooperative efforts are more effective than are competitive and individualistic efforts.

There are conditions under which competition may be used effectively (Johnson, Johnson, & Holubec, 1998b; Stanne, Johnson, & Johnson, 1999). First, competition has to take place within the broader context of positive interdependence. The location, boundaries, criteria for winning, and rules of conduct have to all be agreed upon and followed if a competition is to be constructive. Second, the competition should be between groups not individuals. Third, the task has to be appropriate. The task should require well-learned skills to be practiced; well-learned material to be reviewed; or simple, unitary/nondivisible, overlearned tasks to be performed. When tasks are new and/or complex, competition is inappropriate. Fourth, competition is appropriate only when competitors are evenly matched in terms of previous performance so they will believe that they have a reasonable chance of winning. If they believe they have no chance of winning or can win with no effort, they exert little effort. Finally, competition is appropriate only when it does not matter who wins and who loses. When competition is engaged in for fun and enjoyment, winning is incidental. When winning is considered of great importance, it generates high levels of anxiety that interfere with performance, especially when tasks are new and complex. There is some evidence that on very simple, overlearned, repetitive motor tasks, competition may produce higher achievement than does cooperation (Johnson & Johnson, 1989).

It is unclear whether individualistic efforts have any advantage over cooperative efforts. There is considerably more research needed to clarify the conditions under which competitive or individualistic efforts may have more powerful effects than cooperation.

MEDIATING VARIABLES: THE BASIC ELEMENTS OF COOPERATION

The truly committed cooperative learning group is probably the most productive tool humans have. Creating and maintaining truly committed cooperative groups, however, are far from easy. Individuals fool themselves if they think well-meaning directives to "work together," "cooperate," and "be a team" will be enough to create cooperative efforts among members. **There is a discipline to creating cooperation.** Making teams work is like being on a diet. It does no good to diet one or two days a week. If you wish to lose weight, you have to control what you eat every day. Similarly, it does no good to structure a team carefully every fourth or fifth meeting. The basic elements are a regimen that, if followed rigorously, will produce the conditions for effective cooperation. The **basic components of effective cooperative efforts** are positive interdependence, individual and group accountability, face-to-face promotive interaction, appropriate use of social skills, and group processing.

Positive Interdependence: We Instead of Me

Within a football game, the quarterback who throws the pass and the receiver who catches the pass are positively interdependent. The success of one depends on the success of the other. It takes two to complete a pass. One player cannot succeed without the other. Both have to perform competently to assure their mutual success. If one fails, they both fail.

Positive group interdependence exists when one perceives that one is linked with others in a way so that one cannot succeed unless they do (and vice versa) and/or that one must coordinate one's efforts with the efforts of others to complete a task (Johnson & Johnson, 1989). The discipline of using cooperative groups begins with structuring positive interdependence. Group members have to know that they "sink or swim together", that is, they have two responsibilities: to maximize their own productivity and to maximize the productivity of all other group members. There are two major categories of interdependence: outcome interdependence and means interdependence (Johnson & Johnson, 1989; Johnson, Johnson, & Holubec, 1998a). When persons are in a cooperative or competitive situation, they are oriented towards a desired outcome, end state, goal, or reward. If there is no outcome interdependence (goal and reward interdependence), there is no cooperation or competition. In addition, the means through which the mutual goals or rewards are to be accomplished specify the actions required on the part of group members. Means interdependence includes resource, role, and task interdependence (which are overlapping and not independent of each other).

Positive interdependence has numerous effects on individuals' motivation and productivity, not the least of which is to highlight the fact that the efforts of all group members are needed for group success. When members of a group see their efforts as dispensable for the group's success, they may reduce their efforts (Kerr, 1983; Kerr & Bruun, 1983; Sweeney, 1973). When group members perceive their potential contribution to the group as being unique, they increase their efforts (Harkins & Petty, 1982). When goal, task, resource, and role interdependence are clearly understood, individuals realize that their efforts are required in order for the group to succeed (i.e., there can be no "free riders") and that their contributions are often unique. In addition, reward interdependence needs to be structured to ensure that one member's efforts do not make the efforts of other members unnecessary. If the highest score in the group determined the group grade, for example, low-ability members might see their efforts as unnecessary and contribute minimally, and high ability members might feel exploited and become demoralized and, therefore, decrease their efforts so as not to provide undeserved rewards for irresponsible and ungrateful "free riders" (Kerr, 1983).

A series of research studies was conducted to clarify the impact of positive interdependence on achievement. The results indicated the following:

1. Group membership in and of itself does not seem sufficient to produce higher achievement and productivity—positive interdependence is also required (Hwong, Caswell, Johnson, & Johnson, 1993). Knowing that one's performance affects the success of groupmates seems to create "responsibility forces" that increase one's efforts to achieve.

2. Interpersonal interaction is insufficient to increase productivity—positive interdependence is also required (Lew, Mesch, Johnson, & Johnson, 1986a, 1986b; Mesch, Johnson, & Johnson, 1988; Mesch, Lew, Johnson, & Johnson, 1986). Individuals achieved higher under positive goal interdependence than when they worked individualistically but had the opportunity to interact with classmates.

3. Goal and reward interdependence seem to be additive (Lew, Mesch, Johnson, & Johnson, 1986a, 1986b; Mesch, Johnson, & Johnson, 1988; Mesch, Lew, Johnson, & Johnson, 1986). Whereas positive goal interdependence is sufficient to produce higher achievement and productivity than do individualistic efforts, the combination of goal and reward interdependence is even more effective.

4. Both working to achieve a reward and working to avoid the loss of a reward produced higher achievement than did individualistic efforts (Frank, 1984). There is no significant difference between working to achieve a reward and working to avoid a loss.

5. Goal interdependence promotes higher achievement and greater productivity than does resource interdependence (Johnson, Johnson, Ortiz, & Stanne, 1991).

6. Resource interdependence by itself may decrease achievement and productivity compared with individualistic efforts (Johnson, Johnson, Stanne, & Garibaldi, 1990; Ortiz, Johnson, & Johnson, 1996).

7. The combination of goal and resource interdependence increased achievement more than goal interdependence alone or individualistic efforts (Johnson, Johnson, Stanne, & Garibaldi, 1990; Ortiz, Johnson, & Johnson, 1996).

8. Positive interdependence does more than simply motivate individuals to try harder; it facilitates the development of new insights and discoveries through promotive interaction (Gabbert, Johnson, & Johnson, 1986; Johnson & Johnson, 1981; D. Johnson, Skon, & Johnson, 1980; Skon, Johnson, & Johnson, 1981). Members of cooperative groups use higher-level reasoning strategies more frequently than do individuals working individualistically or competitively.

9. The more complex the procedures involved in interdependence, the longer it will take group members to reach their full levels of productivity (Ortiz, Johnson, & Johnson, 1996). The more complex the teamwork procedures, the more members have to attend to teamwork and the less time they have to attend to taskwork. Once the teamwork procedures are mastered, however, members concentrate on taskwork and outperform individuals working alone.

The constructive effects that positive interdependence contribute to cooperative efforts do not mean that it is always advantageous. There are conditions under which positive interdependence may have negative effects on cooperation. Further research is needed to clarify the conditions under which positive interdependence does and does not contribute to cooperation's effectiveness.

Individual Accountability/Personal Responsibility

After positive interdependence, a key variable mediating the effectiveness of cooperation is a sense of personal responsibility for contributing one's efforts to accomplish the group's goals. This involves being responsible for (a) completing one's share of the work and (b) facilitating the work of other group members and minimally hindering their efforts. Personal responsibility is promoted by individual accountability. Certainly lack of individual accountability reduces feelings of personal responsibility. Members will reduce their contributions to goal achievement when the group works on tasks where it is difficult to identify members' contributions, when there is an increased likelihood of redundant efforts, when there is a lack of group cohesiveness, and when there is lessened responsibility for the final outcome (Harkins & Petty, 1982; Ingham, Levinger, Graves, & Peckham, 1974; Kerr & Bruun, 1981; Latane, Williams & Harkins, 1979; Moede, 1927; Petty, Harkins, Williams, & Latane, 1977; Williams, 1981; Williams, Harkins, & Latane, 1981). If, however, there is high individual accountability and it is clear how much effort each member is contributing, if redundant efforts are avoided, if every member is responsible for the final outcome, and if the group is cohesive, then the social loafing effect vanishes. The smaller the size of the group, in addition, the greater the individual accountability may be (Messick & Brewer, 1983).

Archer-Kath, Johnson, and Johnson (1994) investigated whether or not positive interdependence and individual accountability are two separate and independent dimensions. They compared the impact of feedback to the learning group as a whole with the individual feedback to each member on achievement, attitudes, and behavior in cooperative learning groups. Students received either individual or group feedback in written graph/chart form only on how frequently members engaged in the targeted behaviors. If individual accountability and positive interdependence are unrelated, no differences should be found in perceived positive interdependence between conditions. If they are related, students in the individual feedback condition should perceive more positive interdependence than students in the group feedback condition. Individual feedback resulted in greater perceptions of cooperation, goal interdependence, and resource interdependence than did group feedback, indicating that positive interdependence and individual accountability are related and by increasing individual accountability perceived interdependence among group members may also be increased.

The results of these studies indicated that individual accountability does increase the effectiveness of a group in ensuring that all members achieve and contribute to the achievement of their groupmates.

Promotive (Face-to-Face) Interaction

Promotive interaction may be defined as individuals encouraging and facilitating each other's efforts to complete tasks and to achieve in order to reach the group's goals. Promotive interaction is characterized by students (a) providing others with efficient and effective help and assistance, (b) exchanging needed resources such as information and materials and processing information more efficiently and effectively, (c) providing each other with feedback in order to improve their subsequent performance on assigned tasks and responsibilities, (d) challenging each other's conclusions and reasoning in order to promote higher-quality decision making and greater insight into the problems being considered, (e) advocating exerting efforts to achieve mutual goals, (f) influencing each other's efforts to achieve mutual goals, (g) acting in trusting and trustworthy ways, (h) being motivated to strive for mutual benefit, and (i) feeling less anxiety and stress (Johnson & Johnson, 1989). The amount of research documenting the impact of promotive interaction on achievement is too voluminous to review here. Interested readers are referred to Johnson and Johnson (1989).

Social Skills

Placing socially unskilled students in a learning group and telling them to cooperate will obviously not be successful. Students must be taught the interpersonal and small group skills needed for high-quality cooperation, and be motivated to use them. To coordinate efforts to achieve mutual goals students must (a) get to know and trust each other, (b) communicate accurately and unambiguously, (c) accept and support each other, and (d) resolve conflicts constructively (Johnson, 2000; Johnson & Johnson, 1997). Interpersonal and small group skills form the basic nexus among individuals, and if individuals are to work together productively and cope with the stresses and strains of doing so, they must have a modicum of these skills. Students need to master and use interpersonal and small group skills to capitalize on the opportunities presented by a cooperative learning situation. Especially when learning groups function on a long-term basis and engage in complex, free exploratory activities over a prolonged period, the interpersonal and small group skills of the members may determine the level of members' achievement and productivity.

In their studies on the long-term implementation of cooperative learning, Marvin Lew and Debra Mesch (Lew, Mesch, Johnson, & Johnson, 1986a, 1986b; Mesch, Johnson, & Johnson, 1988; Mesch, Lew, Johnson, & Johnson, 1986) investigated the impact of a reward contingency for using social skills as well as positive interdependence and a contingency for academic achievement on performance within cooperative learning groups. In the cooperative skills conditions students were trained weekly in four social skills, and each member of a cooperative group was given two bonus points towards the quiz grade if all group members were observed by the teacher to demonstrate three out of four cooperative skills. The results indicated that the combination of positive goal interdependence, an academic contingency for high performance by all group members, and a social skills contingency promoted the highest achievement. Archer-Kath, Johnson, and Johnson (1994) trained students in the social skills of praising, supporting, asking for information, giving information, asking for help, and giving help. Students received either individual or group feedback in written graph/chart form on how frequently members engaged in the targeted behaviors. The researchers found that giving students individual feedback on how frequently they engaged in targeted social skills was more effective in increasing students' achievement than was group feedback. The more socially skillful students are, the more attention teachers pay to teaching and rewarding the use of social skills, and the more individual feedback students receive on their use of the skills, the higher the achievement that can be expected within cooperative learning groups.

Not only do social skills promote higher achievement, they contribute to building more positive relationships among group members. Putnam, Rynders, Johnson, and

Johnson (1989) demonstrated that, when students were taught social skills, observed by the teacher, and given individual feedback as to how frequently they engaged in the skills, their relationships became more positive.

Group Processing

In order to achieve, students in cooperative learning groups have to work together effectively. Effective group work is influenced by whether or not groups periodically reflect on how well they are functioning and plan how to improve their work processes. A **process** is an identifiable sequence of events taking place over time, and **process goals** refer to the sequence of events instrumental in achieving outcome goals. **Group processing** may be defined as reflecting on a group session to (a) describe what member actions were helpful and unhelpful and (b) make decisions about what actions to continue or change. The purpose of group processing is to clarify and improve the effectiveness of the members in contributing to the joint efforts to achieve the group's goals.

Yager, Johnson, and Johnson (1985) examined the impact on achievement of (a) cooperative learning in which members discussed how well their group was functioning and how they could improve its effectiveness, (b) cooperative learning without any group processing, and (c) individualistic learning. The results indicate that the high-, medium-, and low-achieving students in the cooperation with group processing condition achieved higher on daily achievement, post-instructional achievement, and retention measures than did the students in the other two conditions. Students in the cooperation without group processing condition, furthermore, achieved higher on all three measures than did the students in the individualistic condition.

Putnam, Rynders, Johnson, and Johnson (1989) conducted a study in which there were two conditions: cooperative learning with social skills training and group processing and cooperative learning without social skills training and group processing. Forty-eight fifth-grade students (32 nonhandicapped and 16 students with IQs ranging from 35 to 52) participated in the study. In the cooperative learning with social skills training condition, the teacher gave students examples of specific cooperative behaviors to engage in, observed how frequently students engaged in the skills, gave students feedback as to how well they worked together, and had students discuss for five minutes how to use the skills more effectively in the future. In the uninstructed cooperative groups condition, students were placed in cooperative groups and worked together for the same period of time with the same amount of teacher intervention (aimed at the academic lesson and unrelated to working together skillfully). Students both with and without disabilities were randomly assigned to each condition. They found more positive relationships developed between those with and without disabilities in the cooperative skills condition and that these positive relationships carried over to postinstructional free-time situations.

Johnson, Johnson, Stanne, and Garibaldi (1990) conducted a study comparing cooperative learning with no processing, cooperative learning with teacher processing (teacher specified cooperative skills to use, observed, and gave whole class feedback as to how well students were using the skills), cooperative learning with teacher and student processing (teacher specified cooperative skills to use, observed, gave whole class feedback as to how well students were using the skills, and had learning groups discuss how well they interacted as a group), and individualistic learning. Forty-nine high-ability black American high school seniors and entering college freshmen at Xavier University participated in the study. A complex computer-assisted problem-solving assignment was given to all students. All three cooperative conditions performed higher than did the individualistic condition. The combination of teacher and student processing resulted in greater problem-solving success than did the other cooperative conditions.

Archer-Kath, Johnson, and Johnson (1994) provided learning groups with either individual or group feedback on how frequently members had engaged in targeted social skills. Each group had five minutes at the beginning of each session to discuss how well the group was functioning and what could be done to improve the group's effectiveness. Group processing with individual feedback was more effective than was group processing with whole group feedback in increasing students' (a) achievement motivation, actual achievement, uniformity of achievement among group members, and influence toward higher achievement within cooperative learning groups; (b) positive relationships among group members and between students and the teacher; and (c) self-esteem and positive attitudes towards the subject area.

The results of these studies indicated that engaging in group processing clarifies and improves the effectiveness of the members in contributing to the joint efforts to achieve the group's goals, especially when specific social skills are targeted and students receive individual feedback as to how frequently and how well they engaged in the skills.

Summary

There is nothing magical about telling individuals to work together as a team. The basic elements that both (a) create cooperative efforts and (b) mediate the relationship between cooperation and outcomes must be vigilantly structured into every group session. The basic elements are positive interdependence, individual accountability, promotive interaction, appropriate use of social skills, and group processing. These elements are a regimen that, if followed rigorously, will produce the conditions for effective cooperation.

THE EVOLUTION OF COOPERATION

Within group efforts cooperation has to evolve (Axelrod, 1984). The pursuit of self-interest by each group member leads to a poor outcome for all. The problem is that although an individual can benefit from mutual cooperation, each one can also do even better by exploiting the cooperative efforts of others. But when the interactions are repeated, both participants attempt to exploit the other, leading to mutual poor outcomes. Exploiting the cooperative efforts of others may pay off when there is a known and limited number of interactions between yourself and the other group members and when you can remain lost in a sea of anonymous others and, therefore, other individuals cannot retaliate effectively. Cooperation, however, pays off when:

1. The number of interactions are not fixed in advance. Cooperation requires that individuals have a sufficiently large chance to meet again so that they have a stake in their future interaction. Cooperation is very difficult to establish in

one-time encounters. An important way to promote cooperation is to arrange that the same two people meet each other again, be able to recognize each other from the past, and each recall how the other has behaved until now. This continuing interaction is what makes it possible for cooperation based on reciprocity to be stable. In other words, make the future more important relative to the present. Enlarge the shadow of the future. There are two ways of doing this. First, by making the interactions more durable. Prolonged interaction allows patterns of cooperation that are based on reciprocity to be worth trying and allows them to become established. Second, by making the interactions more frequent. The more frequent the interactions, the more important future cooperation is. One way to increase the frequency of interactions is to keep others away. By breaking cooperation into small pieces, the potential gain from competition in any one interaction is small compared to the future gains from continued cooperation.

2. You and the other group members are easily identifiable to each other. That is, because of continuing contact and other factors such as a fixed meeting place, each group member must realize that retaliation is possible. When interaction among group members is durable and frequent cooperation is the only behavior that makes sense. Improve recognition abilities. The ability to recognize the other people from past interactions, and to remember the relevant features of those interactions, is necessary to sustain cooperation. Exploitative behavior must be recognized when it occurs. The scope of sustainable cooperation can be expanded by any improvements in the individuals' ability to recognize each other from the past, and to be confident about the prior actions that have actually been taken.

3. Group members emotionally identify with the other and with the group so that they value each other's well-being and want to promote each other's long-term welfare and the long-term success of the group. Group members need to care about each other and about the group. An excellent way to promote cooperation is to teach people to care about the welfare of others. The greater the altruistic motives of the individuals involved, the more stable the cooperation.

4. Group members understand the value of reciprocity and are able and willing to reciprocate both cooperation and competition. One of the basic principles of cooperation is reciprocation. Practice reciprocity. Follow a tit-for-tat strategy so that both cooperation and competition are reciprocated.

5. The temptation to exploit the cooperative efforts of group members is reduced by:

   a. Changing the payoffs so that competition is too costly to be considered. The short-term incentive for cooperation should ideally be greater than the short-term incentive for competition.

   b. Not being envious. You should be more concerned as to how you are doing relative to individualistic and competitive alternatives than whether another group member is benefiting more than you from the collaboration.

   c. Not being the first to exploit another members' cooperative efforts. It pays to cooperate as long as the other group members are doing so. You will avoid much unnecessary conflict by keeping a clear cooperative orientation.

GOAL STRUCTURES AND THE ALLOCATION
OF REWARDS AMONG GROUP MEMBERS

*I am in Birmingham because injustice is here. . . . Injustice anywhere is a
threat to justice everywhere. We are caught in an inescapable network of
mutuality, tied in a single garment of destiny.*

Martin Luther King, Letter from the *Birmingham Jail*

Aesop tells a story of a man who had four sons. The father loved them very much, but they troubled him greatly, because they were always fighting with each other. Nothing the father said stopped their quarreling. "What can I do to show my sons how wrong it is to act this way?" the father thought. One day he called his sons to him and showed them a bundle of sticks. "Which of you, my sons, can break this bundle of sticks?" he asked them. All the boys tried in turn, but not one of them could do it. Then the father untied the bundle and gave each son a single stick. "See if you can break that," he said. Of course, they could easily do it. "My sons," the father said, "each of you alone is weak. He is as easy to injure as one of these sticks. But if you will be friends and stick together, you will be as strong as the bundle of sticks."

Individuals join groups because in the long run they are better off being part of the group than not. The better the group functions, the better off the individual members are; the better off the individual members are, the more they can contribute to the group's efforts; and therefore the better the group functions. Part of the process whereby effective cooperation among members is promoted in order to ensure their individual well-being is the distribution of rewards. The way in which rewards are distributed among group members can have a marked effect on how members behave towards one another in the future and how effective the group is (Deutsch, 1975, 1979). Depending on the circumstances, rewards may be distributed according to merit, equality, or need.

The **equity or merit view of distributing rewards** has been presented by Homans (1961) as a basic rule of distributive justice and equity theory—in a just distribution, rewards will be distributed among individuals in proportion to their contributions. In other words, those members who contribute the most to the group's success should receive the greatest benefits. It is commonly assumed that when rewards (for example, bonuses, salaries, advancement, grades) are contingent on performance, productivity will increase. Individual incentive plans, however, sometimes run into problems as individuals restrict output out of fear of being rejected by colleagues, intrinsic motivation is replaced with extrinsic motivation, and the negative consequences of competition may surface within the group. There are a number of other problems with the merit approach to distributing rewards within a group. One is that the economic values upon which equity theory is based can have unfortunate effects on group members' views of themselves and each other as well as on the relationships among members. From a utilitarian, economic point of view, group members are of value only to the extent that they contribute to the group's success. Such a view results in a depersonalization of both self and others and the attitude that different members have different value. Depersonalization of differential value undermine respect for self and other group members. Members may view their self-worth as being related to the rewards they receive, which in turn are related to the contributions they make to group goal accomplishment. Other members are viewed in the same way. Thus, if a member contributes little to group success and receives disproportionately small rewards, he or she is viewed as having little personal worth. Diesing (1962) describes such a situation as being alienated from oneself and others.

From the equity point of view, rewards have value only because they are a scarce commodity that one competes with others to obtain. Any intrinsic value is ignored. The utilitarian value of a reward increases with the number of persons who want the reward; the reward becomes a scarce commodity when its supply is far less than the demand for it. The symbolic meaning of the reward may become far more important than the intrinsic value of the reward. Children fight over being first in line not because of the intrinsic value of the position but rather because it symbolizes that they are a winner, superior to those who are positioned behind them. Diesing (1962) describes such a situation as being alienated from one's possessions and creations. Thus, the competition among group members that is fostered by rewards being proportionate to members' contributions may seriously reduce the cohesiveness of the group, cause morale problems, and undermine group effectiveness as trust and communication among members deteriorate.

Group members who are successful under a merit system of distributive justice often misattribute their success to their efforts rather than to their talents. Certain group members will have more resource attractors than others. A **resource attractor** is an attribute that tends to attract other resources because it gives the possessor an advantage in a competition for these other resources. Examples of resource attractors are ability, training, previous experience, drive, and character. Group members with a high number of resource attractors often get higher rewards than members with few resource attractors and may attribute their success to their worthiness and effort (implying that those who have fewer resource attractors are less worthy and more lazy).

Finally, a merit system often results in a situation in which the group members who are rewarded the most are given the power to distribute future rewards on the basis of their assessment of how much each member is contributing to the group effort. Deutsch (1975, 1979) notes that this allows those who are in power to bias the system of allocation to perpetuate their disproportionate rewards and power even when they are no longer making relatively large contributions to the group's well-being.

An **equality system of distributive justice** rewards all group members equally. If a football team wins the Super Bowl, all members receive a Super Bowl ring. If a learning group completes an assignment at an A level, all members of the group receive an A. To prevent the problems of the merit system, group incentive systems may be used. In most stores, for example, salesclerks are on individual commission systems. What happens when they are switched to a group commission system? Babchuk and Good (1951) decided to find out. Sales were good with the individual incentive program, but the clerks avoided maintenance duties, competed with one another for customers, and suffered low morale. Under the group plan a sense of teamwork developed and the salesclerks reported greater feelings of satisfaction. Blau (1954) compared two groups of interviewers in an employment agency. In one, there was fierce competition to fill job openings. In the other, the interviewers worked cooperatively. Members of the competitive group, who were personally ambitious and extremely concerned about productivity, hoarded job notifications rather than posting them so everyone could see them, as they were supposed to do. This practice eventually was used defensively and so became self-perpetuating. Members of the cooperative group, by contrast, told each other about vacancies and encouraged each other to fill them. The cooperators ended up filling significantly more jobs. Deutsch (1975, 1979) notes that consequences of an equality system of distributive justice are mutual esteem, equal status, and mutual respect among members. He states that the principle of equality is more congenial to the fostering of enjoyable personal relationships, group loyalty, and cooperativeness.

The **distribution of rewards according to need** results in a situation in which the group members who are most in need of the rewards receive a disproportionate amount of them. The member who has the largest family may receive the highest monetary bonus, the member who is grieving for the death of her parents may be asked to do the least work, or the member who has the least ability will be given the most support and assistance for completing his assigned tasks. A student who has never received an A might be given the highest grade in the group. Rawls (1971) pointed out that one of the natural duties of members of a group is to help another member who is in need or in jeopardy, providing one can do so without excessive loss or risk to oneself. The gain to the member who needs help is seen as far outweighing the loss or risk to oneself as well as the loss of that required to assist that person. Such a system of distributive justice emphasizes the confidence and trust members may have in their colleagues' good intentions. Deutsch (1975, 1979) notes that a caring-oriented group will stress responsibility for each other, permissiveness toward members expressing their needs, heightened sensitivity to each other's needs, and support and nurturance of each other's legitimate needs.

Whatever system of distributing rewards a group uses, it has to be perceived as "just" by group members. When rewards are distributed unjustly the group may be characterized by low morale and high conflict among its members, which in turn may decrease productivity. The evidence indicates that before a task is performed, there is a general perception that an equity or competitive reward system is fairest, but after a task is completed, an equality of cooperative reward system in which all group members receive the same reward is viewed as the fairest (Deutsch, 1979, 1985; Johnson & Johnson, 1983; Johnson, Johnson, Buckman, & Richards, 1986; Wheeler & Ryan, 1973).

SOCIAL INTERDEPENDENCE AND THE REAL WORLD

In real life all three types of interdependence exist simultaneously and continuously. All individuals within a modern industrial/information-based society need to be able to work cooperatively with peers, superiors, and subordinates; compete for fun and enjoyment; and work autonomously on their own. In most situations, group members will usually have a mixture of cooperative, competitive, and individualistic motives. They may be committed to group goals and work to maximize joint outcomes while at the same time seeking to outperform a peer and to meet personal needs unrelated to the concerns of other members. Frank Pierce, for example, as a division chief for Skidmore Corporation, has cooperative interests in ensuring a high level of productivity for his division, competitive interests in being seen as the most productive division head within the company, and individualistic interests in keeping blocks of time free to write a book on successful management. Within a basketball team a player may be focused on the cooperative goal of ensuring the team wins, a competitive goal of being the best player on the team, and an individualistic goal of perfecting a jump shot. Mixtures of the three types of social interdependence are continually present in any situation. Which one dominates the situation, however, has important implications for individual, group, and organization productivity, morale, and well-being.

The effectiveness of a group can be easily damaged when an individual dominated by competitiveness joins the group. Kelley and Stahelski (1970) found that several things happen in such a situation. First, the cooperative members begin behaving in competitive ways, violating trust, hiding information, and cutting off communication. Second, the competitive person sees the formerly cooperative members as having always been competitive. Third, the cooperative members are aware that their behavior is being determined by the other's competitive behavior, but the competitive person is not aware of his or her impact on cooperative members. Cooperativeness needs to dominate group life. Effective patterns of interaction among members are usually far easier to destroy than to build.

Exercise 3.9: Your Cohesion Behavior

How does your behavior affect group cohesion? When you want to increase group cohesion what do you do? How would you describe your behavior in influencing group cohesion?

The following questions should help you reflect upon how your behavior influences the cohesion of the groups to which you belong. Answer each question as honestly as possible.

1. I try to make sure that everyone enjoys being a member of the group.
   Never   1 : 2 : 3 : 4 : 5 : 6 : 7 : 8 : 9   Always
2. I discuss my ideas, feelings, and reactions to what is currently taking place within the group.
   Never   1 : 2 : 3 : 4 : 5 : 6 : 7 : 8 : 9   Always
3. I express acceptance and support when other members disclose their ideas, feelings, and reactions to what is currently taking place in the group.
   Never   1 : 2 : 3 : 4 : 5 : 6 : 7 : 8 : 9   Always
4. I try to make all members feel valued and appreciated.
   Never   1 : 2 : 3 : 4 : 5 : 6 : 7 : 8 : 9   Always
5. I try to include other members in group activities.
   Never   1 : 2 : 3 : 4 : 5 : 6 : 7 : 8 : 9   Always
6. I am influenced by other group members.
   Never   1 : 2 : 3 : 4 : 5 : 6 : 7 : 8 : 9   Always
7. I take risks in expressing new ideas and my current feelings.
   Never   1 : 2 : 3 : 4 : 5 : 6 : 7 : 8 : 9   Always
8. I express liking, affection, and concern for other members.
   Never   1 : 2 : 3 : 4 : 5 : 6 : 7 : 8 : 9   Always
9. I encourage group norms that support individuality and personal expression.
   Never   1 : 2 : 3 : 4 : 5 : 6 : 7 : 8 : 9   Always

These questions focus upon several ways of increasing group cohesion. The first question describes a general attempt to keep cohesion high. Questions 2 and 3 pertain to the expression of ideas and feelings and the support for others expressing ideas and feelings; such personal participation is essential for cohesiveness and for the development of trust. Questions 4 and 8 also focus upon support for, and liking of, other group members. Question 5 refers to the inclusion of other members, and question 6 takes up one's willingness to be influenced by other members. Questions 7 and 9 center on the acceptance of individuality within the group. All these factors are important for group cohesion. Discuss your answers with another group member. Then add all your answers together to get a total cohesion score. Keep your responses to these questions in mind as you proceed through this chapter.

Exercise 3.10: The Level of Acceptance in Your Group

What is the level of acceptance in your group? The purpose of this exercise is to provide a way in which the level of acceptance in your group may be assessed and discussed. The procedure is as follows:

1. With the other members of your group, fill out the questionnaire below. Questionnaires should be unsigned so that no one's responses can be identified.
2. Tabulate the results in the summary table that follows the questionnaire.
3. Discuss the conclusions that can be drawn from the results. Consider these two questions:
   a. What is contributing to the present high or low level of acceptance in the group?
   b. How may the level of acceptance in the group be increased?

QUESTIONNAIRE: LEVEL OF ACCEPTANCE

Think about the ways in which the members of your group normally behave toward you. In the parentheses in front of the statements below, place the number corresponding to your perceptions of the group as a whole, using the following scale:

> 5 = they *always* behave this way
> 4 = they *typically* behave this way
> 3 = they *usually* behave this way
> 2 = they *seldom* behave this way
> 1 = they *rarely* behave this way
> 0 = they *never* behave this way

My fellow group members:

1. (——) .... are completely honest with me.
2. .... (——) .... understand what I am trying to communicate.
3. .... (——) .... interrupt and ignore my comments.
4. .... (——) accept me just the way I am.
5. (——) .... tell me when I bother them.
6. .... (——) .... don't understand things I say or do.
7. .... (——) .... are interested in me.
8. .... (——) make it easy for me to be myself.
9. (——) .... don't tell me things that would hurt my feelings.
10. .... (——) .... understand who I really am.
11. .... (——) .... include me in what they are doing.
12. .... (——) evaluate whether I am acceptable or unacceptable.
13. (——) .... are completely open with me.
14. .... (——) .... immediately know when something is bothering me.
15. .... (——) .... value me as a person, apart from my skills or status.
16. .... (——) accept my differences or peculiarities.
    (——) Authenticity with me
        (——) Understanding of me
            (——) Valuing of me
                (——) Accepting of me

Total the number of points in each column. Statements 3, 6, 9, and 12 are reversed in the scoring—subtract from 5 the rating given to each before placing the remainder in each column.

Summary Table: Level of Acceptance

Score	Authenticity	Understanding	Valuing	Accepting
0–4	_____	_____	_____	_____
5–8	_____	_____	_____	_____
9–12	_____	_____	_____	_____
13–16	_____	_____	_____	_____
17–20	_____	_____	_____	_____

Exercise 3.11: How Trusting and Trustworthy Am I?

When you are attempting to build a relationship with someone there is always the risk that the person will react in a rejecting and competitive way. In order for two group members to trust each other, each has to expect the other to be trustworthy and each has to engage in trusting behavior. This exercise allows you to compare the way you see your trust-building behavior in the group with the way other members see it. The procedure is as follows:

1. Complete the questionnaire below. Score your responses.
2. Then make a slip of paper for each member of your group. Fill out each slip as shown below, rating the member from 1 (low) to 7 (high) on how open and accepting you perceive him or her to be.

> **Member receiving feedback: Edythe**
> 1. Openness and sharing: 3
> 2. Acceptance, support, and cooperativeness: 6

Base your rating on how you think the person has behaved during the entire time your group has met together.

3. Hand each member his or her slip. If there are six members in your group, you should receive five ratings of yourself, and each of the other members should likewise end up with five slips. Compute an average of how the other members see your behavior by adding all your ratings for openness and dividing up the number of slips and then doing the same with your ratings for acceptance.
4. In the diagram at the end of the exercise, you average openness and acceptance by (a) drawing a dotted line for the results of the feedback slips you received and (b) drawing a solid line for the results of your questionnaire.
5. Discuss with the other group members how similar your perception and their perceptions of your openness and acceptance are. If there is a difference between the two, ask the group to give you more specific feedback about your trust-building behavior in the group. Then discuss how to build trust with others in situations outside the group.

UNDERSTANDING YOUR TRUST ACTIONS QUESTIONNAIRE

The following is a series of statements that describe behavior in a group. Rate each statement as honestly as you can. There are no right or wrong answers. It is important for you to describe your behavior as accurately as possible. Answer between 1 (I never behave that way) and 7 (I always behave that way).

7 = I always behave that way   **3** = I occasionally behave that way
6 = I almost always behave that way   **2** = I seldom behave that way
5 = I frequently behave that way   **1** = I never behave that way
4 = I behave that way as frequently as not

When I Am a Member of a Group:

_____ 1. I offer facts, give my opinions and ideas, provide suggestions and relevant information to help the group discussion.

_____ 2. I express my willingness to cooperate with other group members and my expectations that they will also be cooperative.

_____ 3. I am open and candid in my dealings with the entire group.

_____ 4. I give support to group members who are on the spot and struggling to express themselves intellectually or emotionally.

_____ 5. I keep my thoughts, ideas, feelings, and reactions to myself during group discussions.

_____ 6. I evaluate the contributions of other group members in terms of whether their contributions are useful to me and whether they are right or wrong.

_____ 7. I take risks in expressing new ideas and current feelings during a group discussion.

_____ 8. I communicate to other group members that I am aware of and appreciate their abilities, talents, capabilities, skills, and resources.

_____ 9. I offer help and assistance to anyone in the group in order to bring up the performance of everyone.

_____ 10. I accept and support the openness of other group members, supporting them for taking risks, and encouraging individuality in group members.

_____ 11. I share any materials, books, sources of information, or other resources I have with the other group members in order to promote the success of all members and the group as a whole.

_____ 12. I often paraphrase or summarize what other members have said before I respond or comment.

_____ 13. I level with other group members.

_____ 14. I warmly encourage all members to participate, giving them recognition for their contributions, demonstrating acceptance and openness to their ideas, and generally being friendly and responsive.

SCORING THE TRUST QUESTIONNAIRE

In order to obtain a total score for trusting actions and trustworthy actions, write the score for each item in the appropriate column and then total the scores for each column. Reverse the scoring for the starred questions (If you circled 2, write 6; if you circled 1, write 7; 4 remains the same).

Trusting (Openness   *Trustworthy (Acceptance*
and Sharing) Actions   *and Support) Actions*

     _____ 1.   _____ 2.
     _____ 3.   _____ 4.

_____ 5.*   _____ 6.*

_____ 7.   _____ 8.

_____ 9.   _____ 10.

_____ 11.   _____ 12.

_____ 13   _____ 14.

_____ **Total**   _____ **Total**

If you have a score of 35 or over, classify yourself as being trusting or trustworthy, whichever the case might be. If you have a score of under 35, classify yourself as being distrustful or untrustworthy, whichever the case may be.

Plot the total scores in the Johnson Trust Diagram: Part One. Plot an *x* on the horizontal axis at the point representing your "trusting" total score. Plot an *x* on the vertical axis at the point representing your "trustworthy" total score. Then place an *x* at the point on the graph where the two scores intersect. This represents your level of trust. You may wish to plot the scores of all group members and compare how the trusting and trustworthy scores match.

Exercise 3.12: Practicing Trust-Building Skills

This exercise provides an opportunity to practice the trust-building skills. Form a group of six members. Choose one member to be an observer. Complete the following task. Then listen carefully to the report of the observer on the interaction among group members and analyze the dynamics of building trust.

GENETIC TRAITS TASK

Working as a group, estimate the number of people in your school who possess each of the following genetic traits. Establish the frequency of occurrence of each genetic trait, first in your group, then in the entire class. On the percentage of occurrence in your group and the class, estimate the number of people in your school who possess each trait.

Trait	Group	Class	School
1. Dimples in the cheeks versus no dimples.			
2. Brown (or hazel) eyes vs. blue, gray, or green eyes.			
3. Attached vs. free earlobes (an earlobe is free if it dips below the point where it is attached).			
4. Little-finger bend versus no bend (place your little fingers together with your palms toward you—if your little fingers bend away from each other at the tips, you have the famous "little finger bend").			
5. Tongue roll versus no tongue roll (if you can curl up both sides of your tongue to make a trough, you have it, and it's not contagious).			
6. Hairy versus nonhairy middle fingers (examine the backs of the middle two fingers on your hands and look for hair between the first and second knuckle).			
7. Widow's peak versus straight or curved hairline (examine the hairline across your forehead and look for a definite dip or point of hair extending down toward your nose).			

Observation Sheet

	1	2	3	4	5	Total
1. Contributes ideas						
2. Describes feelings						
3. Paraphrases						
4. Expresses acceptance and support						
5. Expresses warmth and liking						
Total						

Trusting Behaviors = 1 and 2; Trustworthy Behaviors = 3, 4, and 5

Exercise 3.13: Open Versus Closed Relationships

Are the relationships among group members open or closed? This exercise provides participants with an opportunity to reflect on and to discuss this question. The procedure is as follows:

1. Read carefully the information in Table 3.4 on open and closed relationships.
2. Working by yourself, write down the answers to the following questions:
   a. On a scale of 1 (*very closed*) to 10 (*very open*), how open are your relationships with other group members?
   b. Are there relationships in the group you wish to make more open?
   c. Are there relationships in the group you wish to make more closed?
   d. What actions are needed to make a relationship more open?
   e. What actions are needed to make a relationship more closed?
3. Meet as a group and discuss each of the questions. Arrive at a group consensus on the answers to questions (d) and (e).
4. Each group shares its conclusions about open and closed relationships with the rest of the class.

DEVELOPING AND MAINTAINING TRUST

I am afraid to tell you who I am, because, if I tell you who I am,
you may not like who I am, and it's all that I have.

John Powell

An essential aspect of group effectiveness is developing and maintaining a high level of trust among group members. The more members trust each other, the more effectively they will work together (Deutsch, 1962, 1973; Johnson, 1974). Group effectiveness rests on every member's sharing resources, giving and receiving help, dividing the work, and contributing to the accomplishment of mutual goals. Such behaviors will occur when there is trust that everyone else is contributing to the group's progress and not using members' openness and sharing of resources for personal rather than group gain. Group members will more openly express their thoughts, feelings, reactions, opinions, information, and ideas when the trust level is high. When the trust level is low, group

Table 3.4 Open and Closed Relationships

Closed ➤ ———————————————————————————————— ➤ Open

	Closed		Open	
Content being discussed	The content is of concern to no one (weather talk).	The content consists of technical aspects of work.	The content consists of the ideas and feelings of one person.	The content consists of the relationship between the two persons.
Time reference	No time reference (jokes and generalizations).	Distant past or future being discussed.	Recent past or future being discussed.	The immediate "here and now" being discussed.
Awareness of your sensing, interpreting, feeling, intending	You never listen to yourself and try to ignore, repress, and deny feelings and reactions.		You are constantly aware of what you are sensing, the interpretations you are making, your feelings, and your intentions about acting on your feelings.	
Openness with own ideas, feelings, reactions	Your statements are generalizations, abstract ideas, intellectualizations; feelings are excluded as irrelevant, inappropriate, and nonexistent.		Your personal reactions such as attitudes, values, preferences, feelings, experiences, and observations of the present are stated and focused upon; feelings are included as helpful information about the present.	
Feedback from other people	Feedback from others is avoided, ignored, not listened to, and perceived as being hostile attacks on your personality.		Feedback from others is asked for, sought out, listened to and used to increase your self-awareness; it is perceived as being a helpful attempt to add to your growth and effectiveness.	
Acceptance of yourself	You believe that once you are known you will be disliked and rejected and, therefore, you hide your real self and try to make the impression you think will be most appreciated by other people.		You express confidence in your abilities and skills; can discuss your positive qualities without bragging and without false modesty; you understand how you have used your strengths in the past to achieve your goals and are confident you will do so again in the future.	
Openness to others' ideas, feelings, reactions	You avoid and disregard others' reactions, ideas and feelings; you are embarrassed and put off by others' expressions of feelings; you reject other people and try to one-up and better them; you refuse to hear their feedback on their reactions to your behavior.		You listen to and solicit others' reactions, ideas, and feelings; you are interested and receptive to what others are saying and feeling; you express desire to cooperate fully with them; you make it clear that you see their value and strengths even when you disagree with them; you ask others for feedback on their perceptions of your behavior.	
Acceptance of other people	You evaluate the other person's actions, communicate that the other is unacceptable, show disregard for the other as a person.		You react without evaluation to other's actions, communicate that the other is acceptable, value the other as a person.	

The Elements of Trust

1. You are in a situation where a choice to trust another person can lead to either beneficial or harmful consequences for your needs and goals. Thus, you realize there is a risk involved in trusting.

2. You realize that whether beneficial consequences or harmful consequences result depends on the actions of another person.

3. You expect to suffer more if the harmful consequences result than you will gain if the beneficial consequences result.

4. You feel relatively confident that the other person will behave in such a way that the beneficial consequences will result.

members will be evasive, dishonest, and inconsiderate in their communications. The development and maintenance of trust is discussed at length in Johnson (2000).

Trust is essential for relationships to grow and develop among group members. In order to build a productive group, members must create a climate of trust that reduces their own and other members' fears of betrayal and rejection and promotes the hope of acceptance, support, and confirmation. Trust is not a stable and unchanging personality trait. Trust is dynamic. It is an aspect of relationships and constantly changes and varies. Every action each member takes increases or decreases the trust level in the group.

What is trust and how do you create it? Trust is a word everyone uses, yet it is a complex concept and difficult to define. Deutsch (1962) may have developed the best definition. He defined *trust* as including the following elements.

Making a choice to trust another member involves the perception that (a) the choice can lead to gains or losses, (b) whether you will gain or lose depends on the behavior of the other member, (c) the loss will be greater than the gain, and (d) the other member will probably behave in such a way that you will gain rather than lose. Sounds complicated, doesn't it? In fact, there is nothing simple about trust; it is a complex concept and difficult to explain. An example may help. Imagine you are a part of a group analyzing *Hamlet*. You begin to contribute to the discussion, knowing you will gain if you contribute good ideas that other members accept but lose if your ideas are laughed at and belittled. Whether you gain or lose depends on the behavior of other group members. You will feel more hurt if you are laughed at than you will feel satisfaction if your ideas are appreciated. Yet you expect the other group members to consider your ideas and accept them. The issue of trust is captured in the question every group member asks: "If I openly express myself, will what I say be used against me?"

Another example may help. Trust is when you lend your older brother your bicycle. You can gain his appreciation or lose your bike; which one happens depends on him. You will suffer more if your bike is wrecked than you will gain by his appreciation, yet you really expect him to take care of your bike. (Sad experience has led an unnamed person to recommend that you never lend your bike to your older brother!)

Building Interpersonal Trust

In order to work together effectively to achieve a mutual goal, individuals must establish mutual trust. Trust is established through a sequence of trusting and trustworthy actions (see Figure 3.4). If person A takes the risk of being self-disclosing, he may be either confirmed or disconfirmed, depending on whether person B responds with acceptance or rejection. If person B takes the risk of being accepting, supportive, and cooperative, she may be confirmed or disconfirmed, depending on whether person A is disclosing or nondisclosing. To complete tasks and achieve goals, group members are required to disclose more and more of their ideas, thoughts, conclusions, feelings, and reactions to the immediate situations and to each other. Once they do, other group members are required to respond, hopefully with acceptance, support, and cooperativeness. If group members express an opinion and do not get the acceptance they need, they may withdraw from the group. If they are accepted, they will continue to risk disclosing their thoughts and observations and continue to develop their relationships with other members.

Interpersonal trust is *built* through risk and confirmation and is *destroyed* through risk and disconfirmation. Without risk there is no trust, and the relationship cannot move forward. The steps in building trust are:

1. Person A takes a risk by disclosing his thoughts, information, conclusions, feelings, and reactions to the immediate situation and to person B.
2. Person B responds with acceptance, support, and cooperativeness and reciprocates person A's openness by disclosing her own thoughts, information, conclusions, feelings, and reactions to the immediate situation and to person A.

An alternative way in which trust is built is:

1. Person B communicates acceptance, support, cooperativeness towards person A.
2. Person A responds by disclosing his thoughts, information, conclusions, feelings, and reactions to the immediate situation and to person B.

		High Acceptance, Support, and Cooperativeness		Low Acceptance, Support, and Cooperativeness	
High Openness and Sharing	Person A	Trusting	Confirmed	Person A	Trusting Disconfirmed
	Person B	Trustworthy	Confirmed	Person B	Untrustworthy No risk
Low Openness and Sharing	Person A	Distrusting	No risk	Person A	Distrusting No risk
	Person B	Trustworthy	Disconfirmed	Person B	Untrustworthy No risk

Figure 3.4 The dynamics of interpersonal trust.

Being Trusting and Trustworthy

In a cooperative group, the crucial elements of trust are openness and sharing on the one hand and acceptance, support, and cooperative intentions on the other. Working cooperatively with others requires openness and sharing, which in turn are determined by the expression of acceptance, support, and cooperative intentions in the group. **Openness** is the sharing of information, ideas, thoughts, feelings, and reactions to the issue the group is pursuing. **Sharing** is the offering of your materials and resources to others in order to help them move the group towards goal accomplishment. **Acceptance** is the communication of high regard towards others and their contributions to the group's work. **Support** is the communication to others that you recognize their strengths and believe in their capability to manage productively the situation they are in. **Cooperative intentions** are the expectations that you are going to behave cooperatively and that every group member will also cooperate in achieving the group's goals.

The level of trust within a group is constantly changing according to members' ability and willingness to be trusting and trustworthy. **Trusting behavior** may be defined as the willingness to risk beneficial or harmful consequences by making oneself vulnerable to other group members. More specifically, trusting behavior involves your being self-disclosing and willing to be openly accepting and supportive of others. **Trustworthy behavior** may be defined as the willingness to respond to another person's risk-taking in a way that ensures that the other person will experience beneficial consequences. This involves your acceptance of another person's trust in you. Expressing acceptance, support, and cooperativeness as well as reciprocating disclosures appropriately are key aspects of being trustworthy in relationships with other group members. In considering members' trustworthy behavior, you should remember that **accepting and supporting the contributions of other group members does not mean that you agree with everything they say.** You can express acceptance and support for the openness and sharing of other members and at the same time express different ideas and opposing points of view.

Acceptance is probably the first and deepest concern to arise in a group. Acceptance of others usually begins with acceptance of oneself. Group members need to accept themselves before they can fully accept others. **Acceptance is the key to reducing anxiety and fears about being vulnerable.** Defensive feelings of fear and distrust are common blocks to the functioning of a person and to the development of constructive relationships. Certainly, if a person does not feel accepted, the frequency and depth of participation in the group will decrease. To build trust and to deepen relationships among group members, each member needs to be able to communicate acceptance, support, and cooperativeness.

The key to building and maintaining trust is being trustworthy. The more accepting and supportive you are of others, the more likely they will disclose their thoughts, ideas, theories, conclusions, feelings, and reactions to you. The more trustworthy you are in response to such disclosures, the deeper and more personal the thoughts a person will share with you. When you want to increase trust, increase your trustworthiness.

The major skills necessary for communicating acceptance, support, and cooperativeness involve the expression of warmth, accurate understanding, and cooperative intentions. There is considerable evidence that the expression of warmth, accurate understanding, and cooperative intentions increase trust in a relationship, even when there are unresolved conflicts between the individuals involved (Johnson, 1971; Johnson & Matross, 1977; Johnson & Noonan, 1972). The procedures for communicating feelings such as warmth and in communicating that one is listening and accurately understands what the other is saying are covered in the chapter on communication skills. Cooperative intentions are expressed by comments indicating that you want to work together to achieve a mutual goal.

When you reciprocate self-disclosures, you increase trust and influence the other person to be even more self-disclosing. Reciprocating self-disclosures makes oneself vulnerable to rejection, and the mutual vulnerability resulting when all members actively participate in a group increases members' trust that all other members will be accepting and supportive of the others.

Destroying Trust

For trust to develop, one person has to let down his or her guard and become vulnerable to see whether the other person abuses that vulnerability. Many such tests are necessary before the trust level between two people becomes very high. A series of positive encounters may be necessary before trust is high. **It often takes, however, just one betrayal to establish distrust and, once established, distrust is extremely resistive to change.** Distrust is difficult to change because it leads to the perception that despite the other person's attempts to "make up," betrayal will recur in the future.

Creating distrust is not a good idea for several reasons. *First*, when group members distrust other members to do their share of the work, for example, they will loaf themselves rather than risk looking like a "sucker" who did the bulk of the work (Kerr, 1983). *Second*, when group members cannot trust each other, they often compete simply to defend their own best interests. Such competition is self-defeating in the long run, because it initiates a negative cycle. Distrust creates competition, which creates greater distrust, which creates greater competition. *Third*, distrust creates destructive conflict among group members. But to know how to maintain trust in a relationship it is important to be aware of the actions that make you look untrustworthy.

There are three types of behavior that will decrease trust in a relationship. The *first* is the use of rejection, ridicule, or disrespect as a response to the other's openness. Making a joke at the expense of the other person, laughing at his disclosures, moralizing about her behavior, being evaluative in your response, or being silent and poker-faced all communicate rejection and will effectively silence the other person and destroy some of the trust in the relationship. The *second* is the nonreciprocation of openness. To the extent that you are closed and the other members are open, they will not trust you. If a group member is open and you do not reciprocate, she will often feel overexposed and vulnerable. The *third* type of behavior that will decrease trust in a relationship is the refusal to disclose your thoughts, information, conclusions, feelings, and reactions after the other person has indicated considerable acceptance, support, and cooperativeness. If a group member indicates acceptance and you are closed and guarded in response, he will feel discounted and rejected.

Definitions Exercise

Given below are concepts and definitions. Match the correct definition with the correct concept. Find a partner and (a) compare answers and (b) explain your reasoning for each answer.

_____	**1. Openness**	a. The willingness to risk beneficial or harmful consequences by making oneself vulnerable to other group members.
_____	**2. Sharing**	b. The communication to another person that you recognize her strengths and believe she has the capabilities she needs to manage productively the situation she is in.
_____	**3. Acceptance**	c. The expectations that you are going to behave cooperatively and that every group member will also cooperate in achieving the group's goals.
_____	**4. Support**	d. The sharing of information, ideas, thoughts, feelings, and reactions to the issue the group is pursuing.
_____	**5. Cooperative Intentions**	e. The willingness to respond to another person's risk-taking in a way that ensures that the other person will experience beneficial consequences.
_____	**6. Trustworthy Behavior**	f. The communication of high regard for another person and his contributions to the group's work.
_____	**7. Trusting Behavior**	g. The offering of your materials and resources to others in order to help them move the group towards goal accomplishment.

Reestablishing Trust After It Has Been Broken

How can trust, once lost, be regained? The following guidelines may help. To reestablish trust, group members should:

1. Increase positive outcome interdependence by establishing cooperative goals that are so compelling that everyone will join in to achieve them. Such goals are often referred to as superordinate goals.
2. Increase their resource interdependence so that it is clear that no one person has a chance for succeeding on his or her own.
3. Openly and consistently express their cooperative intentions.
4. Reestablish credibility by making certain that their actions match their announced intentions. They must always follow up on their word.
5. Be absolutely and consistently trustworthy in their dealing with each other. Acceptance and support of other members are critical.
6. Periodically "test the waters" by engaging in trusting actions and making themselves vulnerable to the other members.
7. Apologize sincerely and immediately when they inadvertently engage in untrustworthy actions.
8. Strive to build a "tough but fair" reputation by:
   a. Initially and periodically responding cooperatively to other members who act competitively (even when they know in advance that the others plan to compete).
   b. Using a tit-for-tat strategy that matches the other person's behavior if the others continue to compete. When the competitors realize that their competitiveness is self-defeating and the best they can hope for is mutual failure, they may start cooperating.

Trusting Appropriately

Trust no one.

The X Files

Trust is not always appropriate. There are times when you will think it inadvisable to disclose your thoughts, feelings, or reactions to another person. There are people you undoubtedly know who would behave in very untrustworthy ways if you made yourself vulnerable to them. To master the skills in building and maintaining trust, therefore, you need to be able to tell when it is appropriate to be trusting and when it is not. A person must develop the capacity to size up situations and make an enlightened decision about whom to trust and when, and how much to trust others. Remember not to reveal yourself so fast to another person that he is overpowered and bewildered. Remember also that there are situations in which trust is inappropriate and destructive to your interests.

Never trusting and *always* trusting are inappropriate. Trust is appropriate only when you are relatively confident that the other person will behave in such a way that you will benefit rather than be harmed by your risk, or when you are relatively sure the other person will not exploit your vulnerability. In some situations, such as competitive ones, trust is not appropriate. When you have a mean, vicious, hostile boss who has taken advantage of your openness in the past, it is inappropriate to engage in trusting behavior in the present.

Trusting as a Self-Fulfilling Prophecy

Tom joins a new group expecting the members to dislike and reject him. He behaves, therefore, in a very guarded and suspicious way towards the other group members. His actions cause them to withdraw and look elsewhere for a friendly companion. "See," he then says, "I was right. I knew they would reject me." Sue, who joins the same group at the same time Tom does, expects the members to be congenial, friendly, and trustworthy. She initiates warmth and friendliness, openly discloses her thoughts and feelings, and generally is accepting and supportive of the other members. Consequently, she finds

her fellow members to be all that she expected. Both Tom and Sue have made a self-fulfilling prophecy.

A **self-fulfilling prophecy** is, in the beginning, a false definition of a situation that evokes a new behavior, one that makes it possible for the originally false impression to come true. The assumptions you make about other people and the way in which you then behave often influence how other people respond to you, thus creating self-fulfilling prophecies in your relationships. People usually conform to the expectations others have for them. If other people feel that you do not trust them and expect them to violate your trust, they will often do so. If they believe that you trust them and expect them to be trustworthy, they will often behave that way. The perceptions of others as untrustworthy is probably a major source of tensions leading to conflict. The history of labor–management strife, interracial violence, war, and revolution demonstrates the power of distrust. The lack of trust helps create conflict, and conflict can lead to increased distrust. There can be a vicious circle of distrust causing conflict that increases distrust that increases conflict.

In building trust in a relationship, your expectations about the other person may influence how you act toward that person, thus setting up the possibility of a self-fulfilling prophecy. There is a lot to be said for assuming that other people are trustworthy.

Personal Proclivity to Trust

Although trust exists in relationships, not in people, there has been some attempt to measure individual differences in willingness to trust others. Rotter (1971) developed the **Interpersonal Trust Scale** to distinguish between people who have a tendency to

Helpful Hints About Trust

1. **Trust is a very complex concept to understand and teach to your students.** It may take a while before they fully understand it.

2. **Trust exists in relationships, not in someone's personality.** Although some people are more naturally trusting than others, and it is easier for some people to be trustworthy than others, trust is something that occurs **between** people, not **within** people.

3. **Trust is constantly changing as two people interact.** Everything you do affects the trust level between you and the other person to some extent.

4. **Trust is hard to build and easy to destroy.** It may take years to build up a high level of trust in a relationship; then one destructive act can destroy it all.

5. **The key to building and maintaining trust is being trustworthy.** The more accepting and supportive you are of others, the more likely they will disclose their thoughts, ideas, theories, conclusions, feelings, and reactions to you. The more trustworthy you are in response to such disclosures, the deeper and more personal the thoughts a person will share with you. When you want to increase trust, increase your trustworthiness.

6. **Trust needs to be appropriate. Never** trusting and **always** trusting are inappropriate.

7. **Cooperation increases trust; competition decreases trust.** Trust generally is higher among collaborators than among competitors.

8. **Initial trusting and trustworthy actions within a group can create a self-fulfilling prophecy.** The expectations you project about trust often influence the actions of other group members toward you.

trust others and those who tend to distrust. A high truster tends to say, "I will trust a person until I have clear evidence that he or she cannot be trusted." A low truster tends to say, "I will not trust a person until there is clear evidence that he or she can be trusted." High trusters tend to be more trustworthy than will low trusters. High trusters, compared with low trusters, are (a) more likely to give others a second chance, respect the rights of others, and be liked and sought out as friends (by both low- and high-trust people); and (b) less likely to lie and be unhappy, conflicted, or maladjusted.

SUMMARY

Groups exist for a reason. People join groups to achieve goals they are unable to achieve by themselves. The personal goals of individual group members are linked together by positive interdependence. Group goals result. Group goals direct, channel, motivate, co-ordinate, energize, and guide the behavior of group members. To be useful, however, group goals have to be clear and operational. The group level of aspiration is continually being revised on the basis of success and failure.

The basis for the group goals is the positive interdependence among group members. Social interdependence theory originated from Kurt Lewin's field theory and was formalized by Morton Deutsch. In the past ninety years over six hundred studies have been conducted. The numerous variables that are affected by cooperation may be subsumed within three broad and interrelated outcomes: effort to achieve, quality of relationships among participants, and psychological health and social competence. Within cooperative groups, as opposed to competitive and individualistic efforts, achievement is higher, committed and caring relationships form, and the self-esteem and social competence required to cope with stress and adversity develop. Each of these outcomes affects the others. The more group members work together to get the job done, the more members care about each other. The more members care about each other, the harder they work to get the job done. The more group members work together to get the job done, the greater their social competencies and psychological health become. The healthier they are psychologically, the harder they will work to get the job done. The more caring and supportive the relationships, the greater the psychological health and the greater the psychological health the more caring and support individuals can give to each other. When individuals join into a cooperative effort, the whole gestalt results. The key elements that power cooperation are positive interdependence, individual accountability, promotive interaction, social skills, and group processing. Finally, there are conditions under which competitive and individualistic efforts are productive. Group members will often have a mixture of cooperative, competitive, and individualistic goals. In both cases, the cooperative goals must dominate.

An essential aspect of ongoing cooperation is the level of trust among members. Trust consists of two parts: being trusting and being trustworthy. Trust is built when a person takes a risk and acts in a trusting way and the other person responds supportively in a trustworthy way. The key to trust, therefore, is being trustworthy.

The cooperative effort to achieve group goals requires frequent, clear, and accurate communication. Group members must be able to communicate and listen clearly and effectively. You will learn how to do this in the next chapter.

4

Communication Within Groups

Basic Concepts to Be Covered in This Chapter

In this chapter a number of concepts are defined and discussed. The major ones are listed below. The procedure for learning these concepts is as follows:

1. The class forms heterogeneous groups of four.
2. Each group divides into two pairs.
3. The task for each pair is to:
   a. Define each concept, noting the page on which it is defined and discussed.
   b. Make sure that both members of the pair understand the meaning of each concept.
4. In each group, members compare the answers of the two pairs. If there is disagreement, the members look up the concept in the chapter and clarify it until they all agree on the definition and understand it.

Concepts

1. Interpersonal communication
2. Effective communication
3. Sender
4. Receiver
5. Message
6. Channel
7. Defensive behavior
8. One-way communication
9. Two-way communication
10. Communication network
11. Information gatekeepers
12. Leveling
13. Sharpening
14. Assimilation

INTRODUCTION AND DEFINITIONS

Communication is the basis for all human interaction and for all group functioning. Every group must take in and use information. The very existence of a group depends on communication, on exchanging information and transmitting meaning. All cooperative action is contingent upon effective communication, and our daily lives are filled with one communication experience after another. Through communication members of groups reach some understanding of one another, build trust, coordinate their actions, plan strategies for a goal accomplishment, agree upon a division of labor, conduct all group activity—even exchange insults. It is through communication that the members interact, and effective communication is a prerequisite for every aspect of group functioning.

One primary difficulty in discussing communication within groups is that there are so many definitions of communication and so little agreement about which definition is the most useful. Dance (1970), for example, did a content analysis of ninety-five definitions of communication that he found published in several different academic fields. Among these definitions were several distinct concepts of communication. He noted that this variety of definitions has taken different theorists and researchers in different and sometimes contradictory directions. Dance concluded that the concept of communication is overburdened and that a family of concepts needs to be developed to replace it. Despite the difficulties in defining communication, however, there are ways to view the process of transmitting information that are helpful in discussing interpersonal and group communication skills.

Two persons seeing each other have a continuous effect on each other's perceptions and expectations of what the other is going to do. Interpersonal communication, then, can be defined broadly as any verbal or nonverbal behavior that is perceived by another person (Johnson, 1973, 2000). Communication, in other words, is much more than just the exchange of words: All behavior conveys some message and is, therefore, a form of communication. **Interpersonal communication,** however, is more commonly defined as a message sent by a person to a receiver (or receivers) with the conscious intent of affecting the receiver's behavior. A person sends the message "How are you?" to evoke the response "Fine." A teacher shakes his head to get two students to stop throwing erasers at him. Under this more limited definition, any signal aimed at influencing the receiver's behavior in any way is communication.

This definition of communication does not mean that there is always a sequence of events in which a person thinks up a message, sends it, and someone else receives it. Communication among persons is a process in which everyone receives, sends, interprets, and infers all at the same time. There is no beginning and no end; all communication involves persons sending one another symbols to which certain meanings are attached. These symbols can be either verbal (all words are symbols) or nonverbal (all expressions and gestures are symbols). The exchange of ideas and experiences between two persons is possible only when both have adopted the same ways of relating a particular nonverbal, spoken, written, or pictorial symbol to a particular experience.

How do you tell when communication is working effectively and when it is not? What is effective communication? What is ineffective communication? **Effective com-**

munication exists between two persons when the receiver interprets the sender's message in the same way the sender intended it. If John tries to communicate to Jane that it is a wonderful day and he is feeling great by saying "Hi" with a warm smile, and if Jane interprets John's "Hi" as meaning John thinks it is a beautiful day and he is feeling well, then effective communication has taken place. If Jane interprets John's "Hi" as meaning he wants to stop and talk with her, then ineffective communication has taken place.

The model of communication presented by Johnson (2000) is typical of the applied approaches to interpersonal communication. In this model (Figure 4.1) the communicator is referred to as the **sender** and the person at whom the message is aimed is the **receiver.** The **message** is any verbal or nonverbal symbol that one person transmits to another; it is subject matter being referred to in a symbolic way (all words are symbols). A **channel** can be defined as the means of sending a message to another person: the sound waves of the voice, the light waves that make possible the seeing of words on a printed page. Because communication is a process, sending and receiving messages often take place simultaneously: A person can be speaking and at the same time paying close attention to the receiver's nonverbal responses.

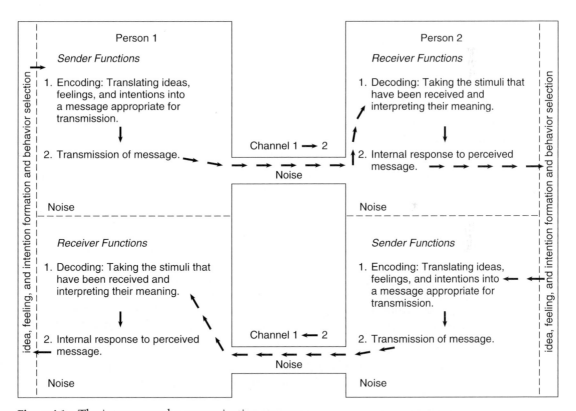

Figure 4.1 The interpersonal communication process.
From David W. Johnson, *Reaching Out*, 6th ed. (Needham Heights, MA: Allyn & Bacon, 2000), p. 108.

Figure 4.1 represents a model of the process of communication between two persons. The model has seven basic elements:

1. The ideas, feelings, and intentions of the sender and the way he or she decides to behave lead him or her to send a message.
2. The sender encodes a message by translating ideas, feelings, and intentions into a message appropriate for sending.
3. The sender sends the message to the receiver.
4. The message is sent through a channel.
5. The receiver decodes the message by interpreting its meaning. The receiver's interpretation depends on how well he or she understands the content of the message and the intentions of the sender.
6. The receiver responds internally to this interpretation of the message.
7. Noise is any element that interferes with the communication process. In the sender, noise refers to such things as his or her attitudes and frame of reference and the appropriateness of his or her language or other expression of the message. In the receiver, noise refers to such things as attitudes, background, and experiences that affect the decoding process. In the channel, noise refers to (a) environmental sounds, such as static or traffic, (b) speech problems, such as stammering, and (c) annoying or distracting mannerisms, such as a tendency to mumble. To a large extent, the success of communication is determined by the degree to which noise is overcome or controlled.

Exercise 4.1: Your Communication Behavior (I)

What is your communication behavior like in a group? How would you describe your communication actions? Begin a discussion of communication within groups by answering the following questions as honestly as possible:

1. If I as group chairperson were giving a set of instructions and the other group members sat quietly with blank faces, I would
   _____ State the instructions clearly and precisely and then move on.
   _____ Encourage members to ask questions until I was sure that everyone understood what he or she was supposed to do.
2. If the group chairperson gave a set of instructions to the group that I did not understand, I would
   _____ Keep silent and later ask another group member what he or she meant.
   _____ Immediately ask the chairperson to repeat the instructions and answer my questions until I was sure I understood what he or she wanted me to do.
3. How often do you let other group members know when you like or approve of something they say or do?
   Never 1 : 2 : 3 : 4 : 5 : 6 : 7 : 8 : 9 Always
4. How often do you let other group members know when you are irritated or impatient with, embarrassed by, or opposed to something they say or do?
   Never 1 : 2 : 3 : 4 : 5 : 6 : 7 : 8 : 9 Always
5. How often do you check out what other group members are feeling and how they are reacting rather than assuming that you know?
   Never 1 : 2 : 3 : 4 : 5 : 6 : 7 : 8 : 9 Always

6. How often do you encourage other group members to let you know how they are re-acting to your behavior and actions in the group?
Never 1 : 2 : 3 : 4 : 5 : 6 : 7 : 8 : 9 Always

7. How often do you check to make sure you understand what other group members mean before agreeing or disagreeing?
Never 1 : 2 : 3 : 4 : 5 : 6 : 7 : 8 : 9 Always

8. How often do you paraphrase or restate what other members have said before responding?
Never 1 : 2 : 3 : 4 : 5 : 6 : 7 : 8 : 9 Always

9. How often do you keep your thoughts, ideas, feelings, and reactions to yourself in group sessions?
Never 1 : 2 : 3 : 4 : 5 : 6 : 7 : 8 : 9 Always

10. How often do you make sure that all information you have about the current topic of discussion is known to the rest of the group?
Never 1 : 2 : 3 : 4 : 5 : 6 : 7 : 8 : 9 Always

These questions deal with several aspects of communication in groups that will be discussed in this chapter. The first two questions refer to whether communication is one-way (from the chairperson to the rest of the group members) or two-way. The third and fourth questions focus on your willingness to give feedback to other group members on how you are receiving and reacting to their messages. Questions 5 and 6 refer to your willingness to ask for feedback about how other group members are receiving and reacting to your messages. Questions 7 and 8 focus on receiving skills, and the final two questions relate to your willingness to contribute (send) relevant messages about the group's work. Review your answers to these questions and summarize your present communication behavior in a group.

EFFECTIVE INTERPERSONAL COMMUNICATION

All communication within groups is between individuals and is, therefore, interpersonal communication. There are many discussions of the skills needed for effective interpersonal communication. One of the authors, for example, has published a training program for interpersonal skill development that includes communication skills (Johnson, 2000). The focus in this chapter is on the unique aspects of communication among members of a problem-solving group, including the communication of task-relevant information among group members and the passage of messages through several authority levels. An example of the latter would be the passage of a chairperson's message to a vice-chairperson, who sends it to a committee chairperson, who sends it to the rest of the group.

Sending Messages Effectively

The first aspect of effective communication is the sending of a message. The three basic requirements for sending a message so that it will be understood are to phrase the message so it may be comprehended, have credibility as a sender, and ask for feedback on how the message is affecting the receiver. Research supports the following conclusions about the sending of messages (Johnson, 1974):

1. *Clearly own your messages by using first-person singular pronouns (I, my).* Personal ownership includes clearly taking responsibility for the ideas and feelings that one expresses. People disown their messages when they use phrases such as

"most people," "some of our friends," and "our group." Such language makes it difficult for listeners to tell whether the individuals really think and feel what they are saying or whether they are repeating the thoughts and feelings of others.

2. *Make your messages complete and specific.* Include clear statements of all necessary information the receiver needs to comprehend the message. Being complete and specific seems too obvious, but often people do not communicate the frame of reference they are using, the assumptions they are making, the intentions they have in communicating, or the leaps in thinking they are making.

3. *Make your verbal and nonverbal messages congruent.* Every face-to-face communication involves both verbal and nonverbal messages. Usually these messages are congruent. The person who is saying that he appreciates your help is smiling and expressing warmth in other nonverbal ways. Communication problems arise when a person's verbal and nonverbal messages are contradictory. If a person says, "Here is some information that may be of help to you" with a sneer on his face and a mocking tone of voice, the meaning you receive is confused by the two different messages being sent.

4. *Be redundant.* Sending the same message more than once and using more than one channel of communication (such as pictures and written messages as well as verbal and nonverbal cues) will help the receiver understand your messages.

5. *Ask for feedback concerning the way your messages are being received.* To communicate effectively you must be aware of how the receiver is interpreting and processing your messages. The only way to be sure is to continually seek feedback as to what meanings the receiver is attaching to your messages.

6. *Make the message appropriate to the receiver's frame of reference.* Explain the same information differently to an expert in the field and a novice, to a child and an adult, to your boss and your co-worker.

7. *Describe your feelings by name, action, or figure of speech.* When communicating your feelings it is especially important to be descriptive. You may describe your feelings by name ("I feel sad"), by actions ("I feel like crying"), or by figures of speech ("I feel down in the dumps"). Description will help communicate your feelings clearly and unambiguously.

8. *Describe others' behavior without evaluating or interpreting.* When reacting to the behavior of others be sure to describe their behavior ("You keep interrupting me") rather than evaluating it ("You're a rotten, self-centered egotist who won't listen to anyone else's ideas").

One of the most important elements in interpersonal communication is the credibility of the sender. **Sender credibility** refers to the attitude the receiver has towards the perceived trustworthiness of the sender's statements. Sender credibility has several dimensions:

1. The reliability of the sender as an information source—the sender's dependability, predictability, and consistency.

2. The sender's motives. The sender should be open as to the effect she or he wants the message to have upon the receiver.

3. The expression of warmth and friendliness.

4. The majority opinion of others concerning the trustworthiness of the sender. If most of our friends tell us the sender is trustworthy, we tend to believe it.
5. The sender's expertise on the topic under discussion.
6. The dynamism of the sender. A dynamic sender is seen as aggressive, emphatic, and forceful and tends to be viewed as more credible than a passive sender.

There is little evidence from the studies on sender credibility to suggest which of these dimensions is the most important. It seems that a highly credible sender is one who is perceived in a favorable light in *all* of these dimensions. A sender low in credibility, on the other hand, is one who is perceived in a negative light in *any one* of the dimensions. Unless we appear credible to a receiver, he or she will discount our message and we will not be able to communicate effectively with that person. Sender credibility, in short, might be defined as the perceived trustworthiness of the sender.

Effective message-sending skills are prerequisite to the skills covered in this chapter. Sending skills are examined in detail in Johnson (2000), which discusses the basic theory behind sending effective verbal and nonverbal messages and includes specific exercises for developing these skills. You should learn and review these skills before (or in combination with) the skills presented in this chapter.

Receiving Messages Effectively

Developing sending skills meets only half the requirements for communicating effectively; you must also have receiving skills. The skills involved in receiving messages are based on giving feedback about the reception and the message in ways that clarify and aid continued discussion. Receiving skills have two basic parts: (1) communicating the *intention* of wanting to understand the ideas and feelings of the sender and (2) understanding and interpreting the sender's ideas and feelings. Of the two, many theorists consider the first—communicating the intention to understand correctly, but not evaluate, a message—to be the more important. The principal barrier to building effective communication is the tendency of most persons to judge or evaluate the message they are receiving: The sender makes a statement and the receiver responds inwardly or openly with "I think you're wrong," "I don't like what you said," "I think you're right," or "That is the greatest (or worst) idea I have ever heard!" Such evaluative receiving will make the sender defensive and cautious and thereby decrease the openness of the communication. Though the tendency to give evaluative responses is common in almost all conversations, it is accentuated in situations where emotions are deeply involved. The stronger the feelings, the more likely two group members will evaluate each other's statements from their own point of view only. Thus it is highly important for the receiver to indicate that he or she wants to understand the sender fully before making an evaluation.

The specific receiving skills are paraphrasing, checking one's perception of the sender's feelings, and negotiating for meaning. Let's look at each of these skills in turn.

1. *Paraphrase accurately and nonevaluatively the content of the message and the feelings of the sender.* The most basic and important skill in receiving messages is paraphrasing—restating the words of the sender. Paraphrasing should be done in a way that indicates an understanding of the sender's frame of reference. The basic rule to follow

in paraphrasing is this: *Speak for yourself only after you have first restated the ideas and feelings of the sender accurately and to the sender's satisfaction.* When paraphrasing, it is helpful to restate the sender's expressed ideas and feelings in your own words rather than repeating his or her words exactly, avoid any indication of approval or disapproval, neither add nor subtract from her message, and try to place yourself in her shoes to understand what she is feeling and what her message means.

2. *Describe what you perceive to be the sender's feelings.* Sometimes it is difficult to paraphrase the feelings of the sender if they are not described in words in the message. Thus a second receiving skill is to check your perception of the sender's feelings simply by describing that perception. This description should tentatively identify those feelings without expressing approval or disapproval and without attempting to interpret them or explain their causes. It is simply saying, "Here is what I understand your feelings to be; am I accurate?"

3. *State your interpretation of the sender's message and negotiate with the sender until there is agreement as to the message's meaning.* Often the words contained in a message do not carry the actual meaning. A person may ask, "Do you always shout like this?" and mean "Please quiet down." Sometimes, therefore, paraphrasing the content of a message will do little to communicate your understanding of it. In such a case, you must negotiate the meaning of the message. You may wish to preface your negotiation for meaning with "What I think you mean is . . . ." If you are accurate, you then make your reply; if you are inaccurate, the sender restates the message until you can state what its essential meaning is. Keep in mind that it is the process that is important in negotiating meaning, not the actual phrasing you use. After the process becomes natural a variety of introductory phrases will be used. Be tolerant of others who are using the same phrases over and over as they are developing their skill.

A complete treatment of these basic receiving skills, so important to effective communication, can be found in Johnson (2000), which also contains exercises for developing verbal and nonverbal competence in them. These skills should also be learned and reviewed as a prerequisite for the skills discussed in this chapter.

One of the major influences upon the reception of a message is the usefulness of its content in accomplishing the receiver's goals and tasks. All messages may be evaluated in terms of whether they help or hinder the receiver's task performance within the group, and messages that are seen as helping goal and task accomplishment are comprehended most accurately and easily. Of course, it is quite common for group members to misunderstand the usefulness of certain messages. Opposition and disagreement, for example, are often seen as short-term obstructions instead of the long-term aids they might be by generating new and better ways of accomplishing tasks and goals.

Exercise 4.2: Bewise College

The purpose of this exercise is to examine the communication patterns within a task-oriented group. Our objectives are to see how task-relevant information is shared within a work group and to explore the effects of collaboration and competition in group problem solving. The materials to be used in the exercise are a briefing sheet, a series of data sheets, a candidate summary sheet, and an observer frequency chart. The exercise takes about two hours. Participants are organized into groups of five role players and two observers. An unlimited number of groups may be directed at the same time. The procedure for the coordinator is as follows:

1. Introduce the exercise as focusing upon communication within a problem-solving situation. Set the stage for the role playing by reviewing the briefing sheet in a realistic manner.
2. Divide the class into groups of seven—five participants plus two observers. Instruct the groups to choose the correct president based upon the data they will receive. Suggest that there is one correct solution to their problem and caution them that they must reach their solution independent of the other groups. Then distribute a briefing sheet, a candidate summary sheet, and one data sheet to each participant. Ensure that the five differently coded data sheets are distributed to different members in each group. Each sheet is coded by the number of dots, ranging from one to five, following the second sentence in the first paragraph. Part of each sheet contains data unique to that sheet. Tell the participants not to let other group members read their sheets.
3. While the five role players are studying their sheets, meet with the observers. Distribute copies of the frequency chart and brief observers on how they are used. All observers will need several copies of the chart, so time should be given for them to make their extra copies.

OBSERVER FREQUENCY CHART: PATTERNS OF COMMUNICATION

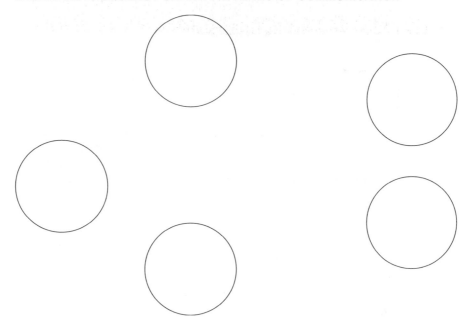

4. Give the signal to begin the group meeting. You may introduce an element of competition by posting groups' solutions in order of completion and by posting the number of minutes used by each group in solving the problem.
5. After all the groups have submitted their solution to the problem, review the answers and compare them with the correct answer, which appears on page 580 in the Appendix. Then ask the group to discuss their experience, using the observations of the observers. Here are some relevant questions for discussion.
   a. What were the patterns of communication within the group? Who spoke to whom? Who talked, how often did they talk, and for how long? Who triggered whom in what ways? How did members feel about the amount of their participation? What could have been done to gain wider participation?
   b. Was the needed information easily obtained by all the group members? Did group members share their information appropriately, request each other's information, and create the conditions under which the information could be shared?
   c. Were the resources of all group members used? Was everyone listened to?
   d. How cooperative or competitive were the group members?
   e. How did the group make decisions?
   f. What problems did the group have in working together?
   g. What conclusions about communication can be made from the group's experience?
6. Have all the groups share their conclusions with one another. Review the observation sheets and discuss the nature of communication within goal-oriented groups.

Interval _____ (Use one sheet for each five-minute interval.) Label the circles with the names of the group members. Indicate a message from a sender to a receiver with an arrow; when someone sends a message to the entire group, indicate this with an arrow to the center. Indicate frequency of message sending with tally marks (卌 II). Place an *x* in the member's circle every time he or she interrupts or overrides another group member; place a check ✓ in the member's circle every time he or she encourages another member to participate. See the example at the top of the page.

BEWISE COLLEGE BRIEFING SHEET

1. This is the first meeting of your group.
2. Basically, the data you bring with you are in your head.
3. Assume there is one solution.
4. Assume that all information in your data sheet is correct.
5. There must be substantial agreement within the group when the problem has been solved.
6. You must work on the problem as a group.

BEWISE COLLEGE DATA SHEET

Your group is a committee consisting of board members, administrators, faculty, and students of Bewise College. Your group has been authorized by the Board of Regents to select a new president of the college from the list of candidates.

Each of the represented groups (Board of Regents, administrators, faculty, students) has its own list of requirements for the new president. Insofar as possible, your group is pledged to select a candidate who meets these requirements.

Bewise College was established in 1969. It is located in the heart of an industrial city with a population of about 100,000. In addition to a standard liberal arts curriculum, Bewise College offers a curriculum in which students can receive college credit for work and learning experiences outside the college. There is only one other college in the same city; it is the smallest college in the state, and until 1954 all students attending it were African Americans.

The new president faces a series of challenges. The Board of Regents wants a president who can raise money for the college, as the college is now in a desperate financial position. The college administration is very much afraid of a president who will not be a competent administrator. Students are dissatisfied with faculty teaching, and faculty members are dissatisfied with student unresponsiveness to their teaching. Both students and faculty see the necessity of having a president who comes from a background that would provide insights into the type of student attending Bewise.

BEWISE COLLEGE DATA SHEET

Your group is a committee consisting of board members, administrators, faculty, and students of Bewise College. Your group has been authorized by the Board of Regents to select a new president of the college from the list of candidates. . . .

Each of the represented groups (Board of Regents, administrators, faculty, students) has its own list of requirements for the new president. Insofar as possible, your group is pledged to select a candidate who meets these requirements.

Bewise College was established in 1969. It is located in the heart of an industrial city with a population of about 100,000. In addition to a standard liberal arts curriculum, Bewise College offers a curriculum in which students can receive college credit for work and learning experiences outside the college. Within the state, only Brown College, Samuels College, and Holubec College are larger, which makes Bewise one of the largest colleges in the state; Andrews is the smallest.

The new president faces a series of challenges. The Board of Regents wants a president who can raise money for the college. The college administration will not accept a new president who does not have administrative experience. The faculty is upset about the difficulty in teaching the students and, therefore, wants a president with experience in teaching the type of student who attends Bewise. Teaching experience is also considered crucial because it would make the president sympathetic to the problems of the faculty.

BEWISE COLLEGE DATA SHEET

Your group is a committee consisting of board members, administrators, faculty, and students of Bewise College. Your group has been authorized by the Board of Regents to select a new president of the college from the list of candidates. . . .

Each of the represented groups (Board of Regents, administrators, faculty, students) has its own list of requirements for the new president. Insofar as possible, your group is pledged to select a candidate who meets these requirements.

Bewise College was established in 1969. It is located in the heart of an industrial city with a population of about 100,000. In addition to a standard liberal arts curriculum, Bewise College offers a curriculum in which students can receive college credit for work and learning experiences outside the college. Because universities are always larger than colleges, Bewise is smaller than the State University, but it is growing rapidly.

The new president faces a series of challenges. The students are dissatisfied with the faculty's teaching and have stated that the only qualification they will recognize as valid for judging faculty teaching ability is for the president to have an education degree. The faculty, on the other hand, demands that the new president have experience in working with the type of student attending Bewise. The Board of Regents sees the need for a president who can raise money to support the college.

BEWISE COLLEGE DATA SHEET

Your group is a committee consisting of board members, administrators, faculty, and students of Bewise College. Your group has been authorized by the Board of Regents to select a new president of the college from among the list of candidates. . . .

Each of the represented groups (Board of Regents, administrators, faculty, students) has its own list of requirements for the new president. Insofar as possible, your group is pledged to select a candidate who meets these requirements.

Bewise College was established in 1969. It is located in the heart of an industrial city with a population of about 100,000. In addition to a standard liberal arts curriculum, Bewise College offers a curriculum in which students can receive college credit for work and learning experiences outside the college. The faculty at Bewise College is made up primarily of young and dedicated but not highly experienced teachers.

The new president faces a series of challenges. The Board of Regents is most concerned about the ability of the president to be a public relations person for the college and raise money. The college has been in the red for the past two years and may have to close if it cannot balance its budget. The new president will be expected to make many public speeches to raise money from the community. The students are angry about the quality of teaching and want a president who can judge the teaching ability of faculty. Members of the college administration have nightmares about getting a president who is an incompetent administrator.

BEWISE COLLEGE DATA SHEET

Your group is a committee consisting of board members, administrators, faculty, and students of Bewise College. Your group has been authorized by the Board of Regents to select a new president of the college from among the list of candidates. . . .

Each of the represented groups (Board of Regents, administrators, faculty, students) has its own list of requirements for the new president. Insofar as possible, your group is pledged to select a candidate who meets these requirements.

Bewise College was established in 1969. It is located in the heart of an industrial city with a population of about 100,000. In addition to a standard liberal arts curriculum, Bewise College offers a curriculum in which students can receive college credit for work and learning experiences outside of the college. Bewise College was established to provide higher education for persons such as minority group members, working-class and lower-income students, the elderly, and dropouts from other colleges and universities.

The new president faces a series of challenges. The Board of Regents is most concerned about the ability of the president to be a public relations person for the college and raise money. The college has been losing money for the past two years. The college administration is very much afraid of a president who will not be a competent administrator. Students are dissatisfied with the quality of teaching. Faculty members are having a very difficult time in the classroom and want to make sure the new president has a background that includes experience in working with the type of students attending Bewise College.

BEWISE COLLEGE CANDIDATE SUMMARY SHEET

Name: David Wolcott
Education: Graduated from Andrews College in liberal arts in 1972; Master of Education from Winfield University in English in 1974; doctorate in political science from Winfield University in 1983.
Employment: Instructor in English at Winfield University, 1974–1978; taught political science at James University, 1978–1987; representative in state legislature, 1980–1982; chairman of the department of political science at James University, 1985–1992; dean of students at James University, 1992 to the present.
Other: Is well-known for his scholarship and intelligence.

Name: Roger Thornton
Education: Graduated from Samuels College in industrial arts in 1965; Master of Education in chemistry from Smith University in 1972; doctorate in administration from Smith University in 1986.
Employment: High school chemistry teacher, 1972–1979; high school principal, 1979–1986, school superintendent, 1986 to the present.
Other: Very innovative and efficient administrator; very successful political speaker (the superintendent of schools is elected in his district); his father is vice president of a large bank.

Name: Edythe Holubec
Education: Graduated from Brown College in liberal arts in 1975; Master's in accounting from Smith University in 1980; doctorate in administration in 1988 from Smith University.
Employment: Insurance agent, 1975–1980; certified public accountant, 1980–1988; vice president of finance, Williams College, 1988 to the present.
Other: Taught accounting in night school for eight years; volunteer director of a community center in a lower-class neighborhood for four years; has a competing job offer from a public relations firm for which she has worked part time for two years.

Name: Frank Pierce
Education: Graduated from Smith University in liberal arts in 1978; Master of Education in mathematics in 1981 from Smith University; doctorate in administration from Johnson Institute in 1987.
Employment: Neighborhood worker, 1978–1981; coordinator of parent-volunteer program for school system, 1981–1985; assistant superintendent for community relations, 1985 to the present.
Other: Has written a training program for industrial education.

Name:	Helen Johnson
Education:	Graduated from Brown College in social studies education in 1976; Master of Education in social studies in 1980 from Brown College.
Employment:	Teacher of basic skills in a neighborhood center run by school system, 1976–1980; chairwoman of student teaching program, Smith University, 1980–1984; dean of students, Smith University, 1986–1990; vice president for community relations and scholarship fund development, Smith University, 1990 to the present.
Other:	Grew up in one of the worst slums in the state; has written one book and several scholarly articles. Given award for fund-raising effectiveness.
Name:	Keith Clement
Education:	Graduated in biology education from Mulholland College in 1977; Master's in administration from Mulholland College in 1979.
Employment:	Biology teacher in a high school, 1976–1982; consultant in fund-raising, public relations firm, 1982 to the present.
Other:	Is recognized as one of the best fund-raisers in the state; has written a book on teaching working-class students; extensive volunteer work in adult education.

Exercise 4.3: Solstice-Shenanigans Mystery

The purpose of this exercise is to study the way in which information is communicated in problem-solving groups. A mystery situation is used. Each of the accompanying clues should be written on a separate card. (The answers appear on page 580 in the Appendix.) The procedure is as follows:

1. The class forms heterogeneous groups of six. One member should volunteer to be an observer. The observer's task is to record the communication patterns of the group, using the observation chart from the previous exercise.
2. The task of each group is to work cooperatively to solve a mystery. Each group is to decide
   a. What was stolen
   b. How it was stolen
   c. Who the thief was
   d. What the thief's motive was
   e. What time the crime took place
3. Each group receives a deck of cards. On each card is written a clue to the mystery. Keeping the cards face down so that the clues cannot be read, one member deals them all out so that each member has several clues.
4. Each group member is to read aloud the clues on his or her cards, but not show them to anyone else. Members may take notes, but may not show them to other members. All communication in the group is to be verbal.
5. When a group has answered the five questions above, it may wish to answer the following two questions if the other groups are not yet done:
   a. What happened to the other items?
   b. Who was present at the party?

6. Each group is to discuss the communication patterns they used in solving the mystery. Members may use the following questions to structure the discussion:
   a. What were the patterns of communication within the group? Who spoke to whom? Who talked, how often did they talk, and for how long? Who triggered whom in what ways? How did members feel about the amount of their participation? What could have been done to gain wider participation?
   b. Was the needed information easily obtained by all the group members? Did group members share their information appropriately, request each other's information, and create the conditions under which the information could be shared?
   c. Were the resources of all group members used? Was everyone listened to?
   d. How did the group make decisions?
   e. What problems did the group have in working together?
   f. What conclusions about communication can be made from the group's experience?
7. Each group shares its conclusions with the rest of the class.

SOLSTICE-SHENANIGANS MYSTERY CLUES

Mr. Purloin showed great interest in Mrs. Klutz's expensive diamond ring.
Mr. Purloin danced all evening with Ms. Beautiful.
Mrs. Klutz was always losing things.
Mrs. Klutz could not find her diamond ring after leaving the party.
The Hosts had a big party to celebrate the summer solstice.
The Hosts had a painting by Artisimisso.
Artisimisso was a sixteenth-century Italian artist.
Paintings by sixteenth-century Italian artists are quite valuable.
Mr. Avarice was heard to say that he would do anything for a valuable painting.
Mr. Klutz is a dealer in fine art.
Mr. Klutz needed money badly to keep his business from failing.
Mr. Klutz always carried his briefcase with him.
Mr. Avarice is known to be very rich.
All of Artisimisso's paintings are small.
Mrs. Klutz spent most of the evening in a dark corner of the patio with Mr. Handsome.
Ms. Perceptive saw something glitter in a corner of the patio as she was getting ready to leave the party.
Ms. Perceptive admired a painting by Artisimisso when she arrived at the party.
Ms. Perceptive noticed that the picture she admired was not there when she left the party.
Ms. Perceptive left the party at 10:00.
Ms. Wealthy brought her dog to the party.
Ms. Wealthy could not find what she had brought to the party.
The Neighbors owned three dogs.
The Neighbors found four dogs in their backyard after the party.
Mrs. Klutz admired the painting by Artisimisso when she left the party.
Mrs. Klutz left about 9:30.
Mr. Handsome was a kleptomaniac.
Mr. Handsome left the party twenty minutes after Mrs. Klutz.
Mr. and Mrs. Klutz left the party together.
Mr. Purloin was a jewel thief.
Ms. Beautiful noticed the painting when she left the party at 9:45.
Ms. Beautiful left the party with Mr. Purloin.
Ms. Wealthy and Mr. Avarice left the party together.
Ms. Wealthy left the party about the time Mr. Klutz did.

Exercise 4.4: Liepz and Bounz

The following exercise is based on the same principle as the mystery exercise. It may be conducted in forty-five minutes. Use the same procedures, observation tasks, and discussion tasks as used in the mystery exercise. Use six group members (including one observer). The solution is on page 580 in the Appendix.

The instructions for the exercise are as follows:

Pretend that liepz and bounz are new ways of measuring distance and that hobz, skibz, and jumpz represent a new way of measuring time. David jogs from Farmland through Parker and Selma to Muncie. The task of your group is to determine how many jumpz the entire trip took. You will be given cards containing information related to the task of the group. You may share this information orally, but do not show your cards to anyone. You have twenty minutes for the task. The information for individual group members is as follows:

Each of the following pieces of information is to be placed on a card. The cards are randomly distributed among the five group members.

It is five liepz from Farmland to Parker.
It is eight liepz from Parker to Selma.
It is nine liepz from Selma to Muncie.
A liepz is ten bounz.
A liepz is a way of measuring distance.
There are four bounz in a mile.
A hobz is ten skibz.
A skibz is ten jumpz.
A jumpz is a way of measuring time.
There are four jumpz in an hour.
A hobz is a way of measuring time.
A skibz is a way of measuring time.
David jogs from Farmland to Parker at the rate of twenty-five liepz per jumpz.
David jogs from Parker to Selma at the rate of twenty liepz per jumpz.
David jogs from Selma to Muncie at the rate of fifteen liepz per jumpz.

COMMUNICATING INFORMATION IN A PROBLEM-SOLVING GROUP

For any problem-solving group to be effective, the members have to obtain the information they need to solve the problem and they have to put it together in such a way that an accurate or creative solution results. The previous exercises focused on the communication of information within a group. The situation in each exercise can be seen in Figure 4.2.

In most problem-solving groups, some information is shared by everyone, some information is known only to a few members, and each member has information that no one else in the group knows. Each member is responsible for communicating what he or she knows to the other members of the group. Each member is also responsible for seeking out the information known by the other members but not by that person. Thus, effective sending and receiving skills are both essential for all group members. What makes the exchange of information problematic is the **noise** that is usually present in problem-solving groups. Noise is defined as anything that gets in the way of effective communication. Determinants of noise include how a group member is perceived, how

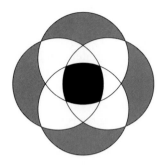

Figure 4.2 Communication of information. The black area represents information known to all group members; the gray area represents information known to only one group member; the white area represents information known to two or more members of the group.

much information a group member thinks each of the others has, how trustworthy a member has been in the past, how the messages are formulated and sent, what receiving skills are used, how cooperative the group is, and whether the member believes his or her information will contribute to the group's efforts.

The coordination of information, ideas, experiences, and opinions is an essential part of problem solving in a group. How successful a group is with such coordination depends on the skills of the group members in sending and receiving messages and on the group norms about and procedures for communicating.

PATTERNS OF COMMUNICATION AMONG GROUP MEMBERS

The patterns of communication among group members are an important aspect of group process to observe and discuss. There are several patterns of communication within a group that are often helpful to observe. (The frequency chart in the Bewise College exercise is one means of distinguishing them.) One of these patterns is the relative frequency and length of communication acts—who talked, how often he or she talked, and how much of the total available time that person used. A second pattern to figure out is who communicates to whom. Some persons speak to those they are trying to impress, others to those from whom they want support, and still others to those from whom they expect opposition. Information on this pattern of communication among group members is often helpful in pinpointing conflicts that must be resolved and increasing the group members' understanding of how they are relating to one another.

A third pattern of communication to observe is who triggers whom and in what ways. There are clear patterns of triggering. For example, whenever one member speaks another may always speak next, even if the remarks are not initially directed to him. This kind of triggering may reflect either support ("Attaboy") or a desire to undo the point ("Yeahbut") that has just been made. Schein (1969) quotes a businessman as saying that in group discussions in his company it takes at least three "attaboys" to undo the damage of one "yeahbut." Another type of triggering is when one member of a group interrupts other members. Knowing who interrupts whom gives the observer clues as to how members see their own status or power in the group relative to that of other members. Generally, high-authority members feel freer to interrupt low-authority members than vice versa. Interrupting others is one of the more common and more destructive kinds of communication behavior, and observing the patterns of interruption often reveals a great deal about relationships among members.

EFFECTS OF COMPETITION ON COMMUNICATION

A considerable body of research shows that when a situation within a group is cooperatively structured, relevant information is communicated openly, accurately, and honestly; in a competitively structured situation, communication is either lacking or misleading. With a cooperative structure each group member is interested in informing as well as being informed by others. Competition, on the other hand, gives rise to (a) espionage or other techniques for getting information another group member is unwilling to communicate and (b) tactics for misleading other group members about oneself. The more intense the competition, the more likely communication will be blocked or, if group members have to communicate with one another, the more likely they will communicate only lies and threats. The very nature of competition, in which one works to gain an edge toward winning and fears the possibility of losing, promotes a great deal of defensiveness among group members.

Defensive behavior in a group is behavior that occurs when a person feels threatened or anticipates a threat. Competition is inevitably accompanied by defensive behavior, and defensive individuals, even if they work on the group's tasks, devote a lot of energy just to defending themselves. They think about how they look to others, how they may win over or dominate their peers, how they may impress their superiors, how they may keep from losing, and how they may protect themselves from anticipated attacks. As a person becomes more and more defensive, furthermore, he or she becomes less and less able to see correctly the motives, values, emotions, and content involved in messages of other group members. Gibb (1961) demonstrated that defensive behavior is correlated positively with losses in efficiency and effectiveness of communication. Thus as people become less defensive their communication behavior becomes more efficient and effective. Competitiveness in one group member breeds competition in all group members, and defensiveness will continue to spiral as long as competition thrives among members.

The arousal of defensiveness makes it difficult, if not impossible, to communicate ideas clearly and move purposefully toward accomplishing the group's goals. In an eight-year study of communication behavior in groups, Gibb (1961) found several behaviors that prompt defensiveness among group members as well as other behaviors that lessen defensiveness. For example, if one group member sends messages that she is evaluating or judging other group members, they will become defensive. Descriptive messages, on the contrary, tend to arouse little uneasiness. Messages that try to control other group members increase their defensiveness, especially if the control attempts are subtle and denied. Yet if the sender is oriented toward the group problem; communicates a desire to help in defining and solving it; and implies that he has no predetermined solution, attitude, or method to impose upon the other group members; the same problem orientation tends to be created in the receivers. When the sender is seen as being engaged in a strategy involving many ambiguous motives, the receivers again tend to become defensive: No one likes to be the victim of some hidden motivation, and most groups dislike deceit. Behavior that seems to be spontaneous and free of deception reduces defensiveness in the receivers.

Gibb also found that when neutrality in communication appears to the receiver to evidence lack of concern for one's welfare, that person becomes defensive. Communications that are particularly persuasive in reducing defensiveness are those that show empathy with the feelings of the receiver and respect for the receiver's worth. When a person communicates that he or she feels superior in some way to the receiver, defensiveness is aroused. When the sender communicates a willingness to enter into participative planning with others in mutual trust and respect, on the other hand, defensiveness is lessened. Finally, those who seem to know the answers, who need no additional information, and who see themselves as teachers rather than co-workers tend to arouse defensiveness in others. A person minimizes that defensiveness of receivers by communicating that he or she is willing to experiment with his or her own behavior, attitudes, and ideas. These behaviors, which are characteristic of either a competitive or a cooperative orientation in a group, are summarized below.

Competitive orientation	*Cooperative orientation*
evaluation	description
control	problem orientation
strategy	spontaneity
neutrality	empathy
superiority	equality
certainty	provisionalism

Groups that display a highly cooperative orientation, groups whose members are good listeners, more accepting of the ideas of others, and less possessive of their own, generally demonstrate greater sending and receiving skills. Achievement will be higher in a cooperative group than in a competitive one, more attentiveness will be paid to members' ideas, and a friendlier climate will prevail. A cooperative orientation leads to increased cohesiveness and greater group productivity. One sound means of improving the communication among group members is to increase their cooperativeness and decrease their competitiveness.

PHYSICAL BARRIERS TO COMMUNICATION

Physical factors can also block effective communication within a group. Group members should pay attention to the acoustics of the room in which they are meeting; how members are seated; the duration of the meeting; the ventilation, temperature, and lighting in the room; and what time of day it is. All these are potential physical barriers to effective communication among members. Once noted, of course, they can usually be changed or compensated for.

Exercise 4.5: Transmission of Information

The objective of this exercise is to show the effects of using one-way and two-way communication to pass information through a series of group members. At least ten persons and two observers are required. The time needed to complete the exercise is approximately one hour, and the procedure for the coordinator is as follows:

1. Introduce the exercise as an example of information being passed from member to member within a group.
2. Ask ten persons to leave the room. They are to constitute two groups of five members each. The first group is to demonstrate *one-way communication*. Entering the room one

by one, each is to listen to a brief story and repeat it to the next person in his or her own way without help from other participants or the group's observer. The receiver cannot ask questions or comment: He or she must simply listen to the story and then repeat it to the next person. The second group is to demonstrate *two-way communication.* Entering the room one by one, each is to listen to the story and ask questions about it to clarify its meaning and to make sure that he or she knows what the story is about. The person then repeats the story to the next person in the group in his or her own way without help from other participants or the group's observer; the receiver can ask as many questions as he or she wants. You may wish to record the whole experience so that it can be played back for the participants' benefit.

3. After the ten participants have left the room, pass out copies of the accompanying observation sheets and a copy of "The Story" to the observers. Discuss the use of the observation sheet and read the story aloud. Explain the basic concepts of leveling, sharpening, and assimilation (these are discussed in the section on the effects of one-way communication on a message).

4. Begin the demonstration of one-way communication. Ask the first person to enter the room, read the story once, ask the second person to enter, have the first person repeat the story to the second person, and so on until the fifth person repeats the story to the observers.

5. Begin the demonstration of two-way communication. Ask the first person to enter the room, read the story once, answer all questions he or she has about the story, ask the second person to enter, have the first person repeat the story to the second person and answer all of the second person's questions, and so on until the fifth person repeats the story to the observers.

6. Reread the original story out loud. Using the results recorded by the observers and the following summary tables and summary graph, chart the percentages of original details

Summary Table: One-Way Communication

Person	Details Correct		Details Incorrect		Details Left Out		Total Details
	Number	Percentage	Number	Percentage	Number	Percentage	
1							20
2							20
3							20
4							20
5							20

Summary Table: Two-Way Communication

Person	Details Correct		Details Incorrect		Details Left Out		Total Details
	Number	Percentage	Number	Percentage	Number	Percentage	
1							20
2							20
3							20
4							20
5							20

retained correctly in the successive reproductions and compare the one-way and two-way communications. Discuss the results, incorporating the material in the sections on the characteristics of communication within an authority hierarchy and the effects of one-way communication on a message. Ask the group for further evidence that leveling, sharpening, and assimilation occurred. Then ask what conclusions about one-way and two-way communication can be made on the basis of the results of the demonstration. Finally, ask the group what conclusions can be made about communication in authority hierarchies.

Other stories can be used in this exercise. Often, the more the cultural background of the story differs from the listener's culture, the more the story is taken in. A story from the Eskimo culture that might be used in this exercise appears below "The Story."

SUMMARY GRAPH

On this graph plot the percentages of original details retained correctly in one-way and two-way communication. Connect the one-way results with a solid line and the two-way results with a broken line.

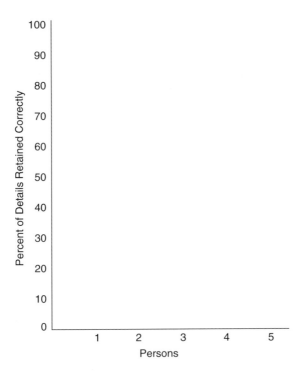

THE STORY*

A *farmer* in *western Kansas* put a *tin roof on his barn.* Then a *small tornado blew* the roof off, and when the farmer found it *two counties away,* it was *twisted and mangled* beyond repair.

A *friend and a lawyer* advised him that the *Ford Motor Company* would pay him a *good price* for the scrap tin, and the farmer decided he would *ship the roof* up to the company to see *how much he could get for it.* He crated it up in a *very big wooden box* and sent it off

*This story by Samuel J. Sackett, the actual title of which is "Tin Lizzie," is included in Botkin (1957). This title should not be mentioned until the end of the exercise.

to *Dearborn, Michigan,* marking it plainly with his *return address* so that the Ford Company would know where to *send the check.*

Twelve weeks passed, and the farmer didn't hear from the Ford Company. Finally, he was just on the *verge of writing them* to find out what was the matter, when he *received an envelope* from them. It said, "We don't know *what hit your car,* mister, but we'll have it fixed for you by the *fifteenth of next month.*"

THE WAR OF THE GHOSTS

One night two young men from Egulac went down to the river to hunt seals, and while they were there it became foggy and calm. Then they heard war cries, and they thought: "Maybe this is a war party." They escaped to the shore and hid behind a log. Now canoes came up, and they heard the noise of paddles, and they saw one canoe coming up to them. There were five men in the canoe and they said:

"What do you think? We wish to take you along. We are going up the river to make war on the people."

One of the young men said: "I have no arrows."

"Arrows are in the canoe," they said.

"I will not go along. I might be killed. My relatives do not know where I have gone. But you," he said, turning to the other, "may go with them."

So one of the young men went, but the other returned home.

The warriors went on up the river to a town on the other side of Kalama. The people came down to the water and they began to fight, and many were killed. Presently the young man heard one of the warriors say: "Quick, let us go home. That Indian has been hit." Now he thought, "Oh, they are ghosts." He did not feel sick, but they said he had been shot.

So the canoes went back to Egulac, and the young man went ashore to his house and made a fire. And he told everybody: "Behold, I accompanied ghosts, and we went to fight. Many of our fellows were killed, and many of those who attacked us were killed. They said I was hit, but I did not feel sick."

He told it all, and then he became quiet. When the sun rose he fell down. Something black came out of his mouth. His face became contorted. The people jumped up and cried.

He was dead.

OBSERVATION SHEET: ONE-WAY COMMUNICATION (see page 163)

List in the first column the twenty specific details of the story (these appear in italics in the story). Verify the list when the coordinator reads the story to the first person. As person 1 repeats the story to person 2, note the mistakes in person 1's version by writing the wrong words or phrases in the proper row and column. To help in scoring, use a check mark for details correctly reported and a zero for details left out. Repeat this procedure for the rest of the participants.

OBSERVATION SHEET: TWO-WAY COMMUNICATION (see page 163)

List in the first column the twenty specific details of the story (these appear in italics in the story). Verify the list when the coordinator reads the story to the first person. As person 1 repeats the story to person 2, note the mistakes in person 1's version by writing the wrong words or phrases in the proper row and column. To help in scoring, use a check mark for details correctly reported and a zero for details left out. Repeat this procedure for the rest of the participants.

Detail	Original Story	Version 1	Version 2	Version 3	Version 4	Version 5
1						
2						
3						
4						
5						
6						
7						
8						
9						
10						
11						
12						
13						
14						
15						
16						
17						
18						
19						
20						

Detail	Original Story	Version 1	Version 2	Version 3	Version 4	Version 5
1						
2						
3						
4						
5						
6						
7						
8						
9						
10						
11						
12						
13						
14						
15						
16						
17						
18						
19						
20						

Exercise 4.6: One- and Two-Way Communication

This is another exercise that contrasts the impact of one-way and two-way communication on communication effectiveness. For this exercise each participant needs two sheets of paper and a pencil. The coordinator needs copies of the accompanying square arrangements, which are given on page 580 in the Appendix. The coordinator may wish to copy the three summary tables below onto a blackboard or a large sheet of paper. The procedure for the coordinator is as follows:

1. Select a sender and two observers (if the group has less than seven members, select only one observer). The sender should be a person who communicates well and who speaks clearly and loudly enough to be heard.
2. Have the sender sit either with her back to the group of receivers or behind a screen. Give her the first square arrangement, being careful that the group members do not see it. Tell her to study the arrangement of squares carefully for two minutes in order to be prepared to instruct the group members on how to draw a similar set of squares on their paper.
3. Ask the first observer to note the behavior and reactions of the sender during the exercise and to make notes for later comments. Ask the second observer to make notes on the behavior and reactions of the group members. Facial reactions, gestures, posture, and other nonverbal behaviors may be observed.

Table A: Medians for Trials I and II

Medians	I	II
Time elapsed:		
Guess accuracy:		
Actual accuracy:		

Table B: First Trial

Number Correct	Guess	Actual
5		
4		
3		
2		
1		
0		

Table C: Second Trial

Number Correct	Guess	Actual
5		
4		
3		
2		
1		
0		

4. Give the group these instructions: "The sender is going to describe a drawing to you. You are to listen carefully to her instructions and draw what she describes as accurately as you can. You will be timed, but there is no time limit. *You may ask no questions of the sender and give no audible response.* You are asked to work independently."

5. Display the three summary tables in the front of the room. Then tell the sender to proceed to give the instructions for drawing the first arrangement of squares as quickly and accurately as she can. Make sure that there are no questions or audible reactions from the group members.

6. When the sender has completed giving the instructions for the first square arrangement, record the time it took her to do so in the proper space in the first table. Ask all members of the group to write down the number of squares they think they have drawn correctly in relation to the preceding square.

7. Instruct the sender to face the group members. Give her the second square arrangement and tell her to study the relationship of the squares in this new diagram for two minutes in preparation for instructing the group members on how to draw it.

8. Give the group these instructions: "The sender is going to describe another drawing to you. This time she will be in full view of you and you may ask as many questions as you wish. She is free to reply to your questions or amplify her statements as she sees fit. She is not, however, allowed to make any hand signals while describing the drawing. You will be timed, but there is no time limit. Work as accurately and rapidly as you can."

9. Tell the sender to proceed.

10. When the sender has completed giving instructions for the second figure, record the time in the appropriate space in Table A. Ask the group members to guess the number of squares they have drawn correctly and to record the number on their papers.

11. Obtain a median for guessed accuracy on the first drawing by recording the number of group members who guessed zero, the number who guessed one, and so on in Table B. Find the median guessed number by counting from zero the number of group members guessing each number until you reach half the members of the group. Then record the median in Table A.

12. Repeat this method to get the median of accurate guesses for the second drawing.

13. Show the group members the master drawing for the first set of squares, and point out the relationship of each square to the preceding one. Each square must be in the exact relationship to the preceding one as it appears on the master drawing in order to be counted as correct. When this step has been completed, ask the members to count and record the actual number right. Have them make a similar count for the second square arrangement.

14. Obtain the median for accuracy for the first and second arrangements and place them in Table A.

15. Discuss the following questions with the class:
    a. What may be concluded from the results in terms of time, accuracy, and level of confidence?
    b. What did the observers record during the exercise? How did the behavior of the sender and the group members vary from one situation to the other? What were the group members and the sender feeling during the two situations?
    c. How does this exercise compare with situations you find yourself in at work, school, or home? How might you change your behavior in relating to your friends and acquaintances as a result of what you have experienced during this exercise?

COMMUNICATION WITHIN AN AUTHORITY HIERARCHY

Within every organization and in many groups there is an authority hierarchy. An authority hierarchy exists when role requirements are established in such a way that different members perform different roles and members performing particular roles supervise the other members to make sure they fulfill their role requirements. If a group, for example, is divided into several committees, each responsible for a different aspect of the group's work, its role structure would look like Figure 4.3. The members are supervised by the committee chairpersons, and the committee chairpersons are supervised by the group chairperson. Within an authority hierarchy a system of rewards and punishments is usually established so that a supervisor will have some power over the persons he or she is supervising. Although authority hierarchies are established to facilitate the effectiveness of the group, they can often interfere with its effectiveness by undermining necessary processes such as distributed participation and leadership, equalization of power, controversy procedures, and communication. In this chapter we will focus on the effect of authority hierarchies upon communication within a group and thus elaborate on the conclusions resulting from the previous exercises.

To organize itself to accomplish its goals, maintain itself in good working order, and adapt to a changing world, a group must structure its communication. Meetings will be scheduled; reports from group members will be requested; conferences among members will be set up; summaries of group progress may be written and sent to all members. All these activities are structured communication opportunities. The **communication network** thus created determines the amount and type of information a group member will receive from the other members. The very nature of a group implies that communication is selective, that a communication network exists, that incentives to use it properly are present, and that members must use certain procedures for communicating with each other. Thus, a college seminar will schedule meetings and teacher–student conferences as the communication network, be selective in the material upon which communication will be based, use learning and grades as incentives for participating in the network, and encourage certain procedures (for example, when the teacher talks, students listen). The formal network, incentives, and procedures are established to coordinate members' efforts to accomplish goals. In addition to the formal commu-

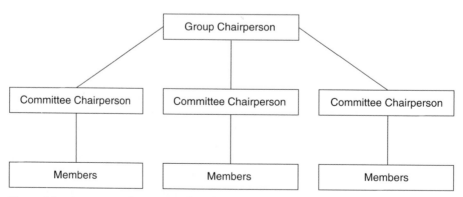

Figure 4.3   A group and its internal authority hierarchy.

nication network, in many groups there is an informal network, which includes patterns of friendship and social contact among group members.

The procedures used within the formal communication network of a group can be examined in several different ways; the approach most relevant to a discussion of authority hierarchies focuses on three types: one-way, one-way-with-feedback, and two-way. In an authority hierarchy a one-way communication procedure is characterized by a group chairperson giving instructions or making announcements to the other group members, who are not allowed to communicate with her. The listeners, then, are entirely passive, and communication effectiveness is determined by how the messages are created and presented. Usually there is someone higher in the authority hierarchy who communicates messages to the chairperson, who then communicates them to the group members. One-way communication takes little time compared with the other two procedures, but it is less effective. Though it is less frustrating for the sender, it is far more unsatisfactory for the receivers.

One-way-with-feedback communication is often called *directive* or *coercive communication* (McGregor, 1967). In this communication procedure within an authority hierarchy, the chairperson presents the message and the group members give feedback on how well they understand it. The exchange is completed when the group members indicate to the chairperson that they have received the message correctly. This procedure is called coercive because no provision exists for mutual influence or exchange: Communication begins with the belief that the chairperson's position is correct and that the only information he or she needs from the group members is that they correctly understand and accept the message. The chairperson influences, while the group members merely understand. This second procedure is, in the short run, faster than two-way communication and less frustrating for the chairperson, but also less accurate and more frustrating for the group members.

When one-way and one-way-with-feedback communication procedures are used in groups, communication can be so poor that informal communication among group members is necessary in order for them to complete the group's tasks adequately. This reduces the long-term effectiveness of these procedures. The original messages can become distorted as they pass through the informal network, and this can hinder the coordination of member behavior. Such distortion and misunderstanding are most frequent when the most influential members of the informal network disagree with the decisions and points of view of the chairperson and his or her superiors (if he or she has them), or when distrust and competition exist among group members or between the chairperson and the group members. Unless group members have the opportunity to communicate freely with the chairperson, the informal network may become more influential, powerful, important, and effective than the group's formal network.

Two-way communication is a reciprocal process in which each member starts messages and tries to understand the other members' messages. In a two-way communication procedure, the chairperson and the other group members freely exchange ideas and information in a productive discussion. Both sending and receiving skills are needed. All members are able to participate at will, and minority opinions are encouraged and more apt to be expressed. Feelings of resistance or doubt can be discussed and resolved at the time they are experienced so that they are not potential barriers to commitment. Two-way communication encourages open and candid member interaction,

distributed participation and leadership, consensual decision making, and other elements of group effectiveness. Although two-way communication is much more time-consuming than the one-way procedures and more frustrating for the chairperson, it is less frustrating for the group members and much more effective in the long run. Any goal-directed, problem-solving group that hopes to be effective must use two-way communication procedures.

Even when a two-way communication procedure is encouraged, the authority hierarchy will influence communication among group members. High-authority group members usually do most of the talking, and most of the messages are directed at them. Low-authority members often do not communicate very much with each other during a group meeting, preferring to address their remarks to high-authority members. Because they generally fear evaluation by those with power, members without power can be expected to take few risks, speak inconsequentially, and avoid frankness in their remarks. High-authority members often hesitate to reveal any of their own limitations or vulnerability, a tendency that also decreases open and effective communication among group members. Thus, several influences push the group's use of communication procedures toward practices that thwart the kind of discussion and problem solving needed for it to function effectively.

How can these tendencies be avoided so that communication within a group is effective? There are two answers to this question. The first is to establish a cooperative group climate that encourages the equal participation of all members. The second is to promote group norms that foster the feeling that a member's ideas and views, no matter what his or her authority level, are of real interest to other group members. If a group is to function effectively, it must adopt a two-way communication procedure and develop a cooperative group climate and group norms that facilitate interaction among members. Because communication is an interpersonal phenomenon, furthermore, anything that interferes with the relationships among group members interferes with their communication. Much attention, therefore, must be paid to the interpersonal relationships of group members.

INFORMAL COMMUNICATION NETWORKS AND OPINION LEADERS

When one-way communication procedures are used in a group, comprehension of messages is often so poor that group members turn to the informal communication network to clarify what has been communicated. Often certain group members will be better able to interpret messages from higher-ups. In such cases other members will seek them out and ask them what the higher-ups meant by the latest communication. Such members are called **opinion leaders** or **gatekeepers** because they have more influence over members' comprehension of messages than do the persons in higher-authority positions who originated the messages. There are two common types of opinion leaders: **information gatekeepers,** who receive messages from superiors and outside sources or who read, listen, and reflect upon written reports and verbal messages to a greater extent than other group members, and **technological gatekeepers,** who read more of the theory and research literature in their field and consult more with outside sources than do the other group members.

Opinion leaders frequently serve as *translators* by taking messages from superiors and rephrasing them into more understandable form and into the specific meanings they have for different group members. When one-way communication procedures are being used, the original source is often not available for questioning and clarification of messages; group members, therefore, must rely on the opinion leaders to clarify the messages and what meanings they have for the specific group members. Group members, furthermore, may remember an opinion leader's interpretation of a message better than the original message! Research on testimony in court cases indicates that people remember initial reports of events they witnessed better than the events themselves (Jones & Gerard, 1967). If the opinion leader misconstrues the message, errors in understanding are amplified as interpretations are passed from member to member. Even within a two-way communication procedure, group members will at times be unable to clarify a message and will use opinion leaders to help them do so.

EFFECTS ON THE MESSAGE OF A ONE-WAY COMMUNICATION PROCEDURE

Some basic research has been conducted on what happens to information when it is passed through several persons with little or no clarification. The more the message is passed from person to person, the more distorted and changed it will become. Three psychological processes characterize the communication between persons who are unable to communicate directly with the original source of a message (Allport & Postman, 1945; Bartlett, 1932). These three processes are attempts to reduce the message to a simple one that has significance for the receiver in terms of his or her own interests, experience, frame of reference, and tasks. The three processes are as follows:

Leveling.   The receiver tends to reduce the amount of information he or she receives by remembering much less of the message than was presented by the sender. The message tends to grow shorter, more concise, and more easily grasped and told. In successive versions, fewer words are used and fewer details are mentioned.

Sharpening.   The receiver sharpens certain parts of the information so that a few high points are readily remembered while most of the message is forgotten. Sharpening, then, is the selective retaining, perceiving, and reporting of a limited number of details from a larger context. It is the reciprocal of leveling: One cannot exist without the other. Certain points become dominant, and all the others are grouped about them.

Assimilation.   The receiver takes much of the message into his own frame of reference and personality. Thus, his interpretations and memories of what he heard are affected by his own thoughts and feelings. This process involves not only changing the unfamiliar to some known context, but also leaving out material that seems irrelevant and substituting material that gives meaning in the person's own frame of reference.

Because these three processes are at work whenever one-way procedures are being used, inefficient and ineffective communication usually results. This is true even when opinion leaders supplement the procedure.

Exercise 4.7: Group Observation

Review the material in the last three sections by taking the frequency chart used in the Bewise College exercise and observing at least two groups of which you are a member—one group in which there is a chairperson (such as a teacher) who dominates the meeting and another group in which free and open discussions are held among members. Observe the communication patterns in both groups and compare them. Write a description of the communication patterns in each group and discuss them with other members of your class.

Exercise 4.8: Norms and Communication

This exercise should develop participants' awareness of how group norms affect communication among group members. The participating groups must be groups that have worked together for several hours. Observation sheets similar to the frequency chart used in the Bewise College exercise are needed; participants can construct their own. The exercise will take approximately one hour to complete. The procedure for the coordinator is as follows:

1. Introduce the exercise as a structured experience in learning how group norms affect communication among group members.
2. Have each group select two observers. The observers need to construct six observation sheets, making the number of circles on the sheets equal to the number of members in the group they are observing. Explain the use of these sheets.
3. Give each group a copy of the accompanying discussion sheet and state that the groups have thirty minutes to discuss the topic. Give the signal to begin.
4. At the end of thirty minutes ask the observers to report to their groups. Groups are to discuss the communication pattern among their members and how it relates to the group norms they have been listing. Each group should also discuss how its members feel about the amount of their participation and how it could change group norms so as to gain more widespread participation and more effective communication among members. Each group should then revise its list of group norms in light of the discussion. Allow twenty minutes for this discussion.
5. Have the groups share their conclusions in a general discussion.

DISCUSSION SHEET: WHAT IS NORM?

Norms develop in groups so that members will know how they are expected to behave and what is appropriate member behavior. They are common rules or customs followed by group members. In some groups, for example, members address each other by their last names; in other groups, first names are used. All groups have norms, and usually these norms are eventually followed without conscious thought. Norms can develop so that every member does the same thing (dressing formally for a group meeting) or something different (dressing differently for a group meeting).

Norms are not built from scratch, but develop from the values, expectations, and learned habits that the members bring with them when the group is first formed. "Don't interrupt the chairperson," an expression of respect for authority, is a norm that most persons bring with them into new groups. Norms can also be implied by the setting in which the group meets. Most persons do not sit on the floor in a room that appears to be arranged formally. Most persons do not remain standing when their group is meeting at a beach.

Norms have a powerful influence upon communication within a group. Such influences are seldom examined. It is even rarer that a group attempts to change its norms so as to facilitate goal accomplishment. Usually group members simply follow norms without question. This does not mean that norms do not change. Norms do change as expectations of appropriate member behavior change, but this is commonly an unobtrusive process.

What norms have developed in your group? Do you all sense where you are supposed to sit? Do you all sense who should be listened to and who should be ignored? Do you interrupt each other, or is politeness a group norm? Are jokes allowed, or is the tone of the group serious? How do discussions usually start? How are boredom and frustration generally expressed, if at all? Are certain topics permissible to talk about and others avoided? Is the emotional involvement of members supposed to be high or low? In answering these questions you will become more conscious of the norms that are present in your group.

Spend the next thirty minutes discussing your group norms and making a list of what they are.

Exercise 4.9: *Sitting in a Circle*

How a group sits has a great deal of influence on how its members communicate. This exercise focuses upon the effects of sitting in a circle. The procedure for each group is to engage in three five-minute discussions. After each one, each member writes down several adjectives to describe his or her reactions to the discussion. A different position is to be used for each discussion: (a) circle in which everyone's back is to the center, (b) circle with members face to face and a large rectangular table between them, and (c) circle with members face to face and nothing between them.

After the fifteen minutes of discussion, members compare their reactions to the three positions. What were the differences in feelings? Was there any difference in how productive the discussion was? What effects did the different positions have upon the discussion? How was communication affected? The advantage of sitting close together in a circle with nothing between members is that their unobstructed view of one another increases their opportunities to receive and send nonverbal messages. This type of circular seating arrangement also encourages more equal participation because there is no podium or seat at the head of a table to suggest that a particular member should assume leadership.

Exercise 4.10: *Communication Networks*

The purpose of this exercise is to compare the impact of four different communication patterns on productivity and morale. The procedure is as follows:

1. The class forms heterogeneous groups of six. One member needs to volunteer to be an observer. The task of the observer is to time how long it takes the group to

complete its task and to make notes about the behavior and apparent feelings of the participants.

2. The five participants in each group place themselves in a straight line with everyone facing the same way. Each member receives five cards from a regular deck of playing cards. No verbal communication is allowed, but members may write notes to the person in front of or behind them. Members may pass cards to the person in front of or behind them. The *group task* is to select one card from each member's hand in order to make the highest-ranking poker hand possible. After the group has decided on a poker hand each member should write an answer to the following questions:
   a. How satisfied are you with the group and its work?
   b. How did you feel?
   c. What did you observe?

3. The same task with the same rules is repeated, but this time the group members arrange themselves in a circle. Members may pass notes and cards only to the person on their left or right. No verbal communication is allowed. After the group has completed the task each member writes answers to the same three questions.

4. The same task with the same rules is repeated, but this time the group members arrange themselves in a wheel, as in Figure 4.4. Members on the outside may pass notes and cards only to the person in the middle; the member in the middle may pass notes and cards to anyone. No verbal communication is allowed. After the group has decided on a poker hand each member answers the same three questions.

5. The same task is repeated, this time with the members sitting in a circle. Any member may communicate with anyone else in the group. Members may pass cards and notes and may speak to whomever they wish in the group. After the group has decided on a poker hand each member answers the same three questions.

6. Using the reactions of the group members and the observer's impressions, the group should discuss the advantages and disadvantages of each communication pattern. Here are some questions the group may wish to talk about:
   a. What were the feelings of the members in the middle of a communication pattern? What were the feelings of those on the fringe?
   b. In what communication pattern was the shortest amount of time needed to arrive at a group poker hand?
   c. If you were in charge of a company, which communication pattern would you try to use?
   d. How many messages were sent in each type of communication pattern?
   e. Did each pattern have a leader? For those patterns that did, what position did the leader occupy?

7. Each group shares its conclusions with the rest of the class.

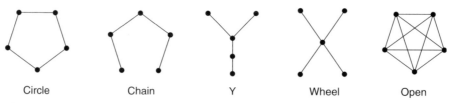

Circle   Chain   Y   Wheel   Open

Figure 4.4   Communication networks.

COMMUNICATION STRUCTURES AND NETWORKS

If a group is to function effectively, its members must be able to communicate easily and efficiently. Communication within the group needs to be arranged so that ideas, knowledge, and other information may flow freely among group members. To this end a number of studies has been conducted on the physical arrangement of communication networks—that is, who can communicate with whom and whether the communication is direct or via another group member. Typically, these studies imposed various communication networks on groups in order to determine their effects on group process. Some of the networks that have been investigated are diagrammed in Figure 4.4. The dots represent individual group members and the lines represent links in the communication network. The most common procedure for imposing communication networks was first formulated by Alex Bavelas (1948). He suggested placing group members in cubicles connected by slots in their walls, through which written messages could be passed. When all slots are open every group member can communicate directly with every other member. Other patterns are formed merely by selection of the appropriate slots.

Communication networks have been found to influence the emergence of leadership, the development of organization, the morale of group members, and the efficiency of problem solving (Leavitt, 1951; Shaw, 1964). The group member who occupies a central physical position in a communication network usually emerges as the leader of the group. Because the central member has more information, he or she can coordinate group activities.

A group becomes organized when it follows a consistent pattern of information exchange during the course of a problem solution. Research has found two basic patterns of organization in communication networks: *centralized* and *each-to-all.* In the centralized pattern all information is funneled to one person, who solves the problem and distributes the answer to the other group members. In the each-to-all pattern all available information is communicated to all group members, each of whom solves the problem independently. When a centralized communication network is imposed on a group, the group adopts a centralized organization. When a decentralized communication network is imposed on a group, each-to-all organization tends to develop.

Members who occupy a central position in a communication network are usually more satisfied with the group's work than members who occupy fringe positions. Typically, the morale of a group is higher in decentralized (circle, open) communication networks than in centralized ones (chain, Y, wheel).

Finally, when a task is simple and requires only the collection of information, a centralized network is more efficient in terms of speed and lack of errors. But when the task is complex and requires the analysis of information, the decentralized networks are more efficient, as we can see in Table 4.1. The problem with centralized communication networks is that the members in the centralized positions may easily receive more messages than they can handle. Furthermore, any extra demands that must be addressed by a member in a centralized position are likely to interfere with the efficiency of the network.

Table 4.1 **Differences Between Centralized (wheel, chain, Y) and Decentralized (circle, open) Communication Networks as a Function of Task Complexity**

	Simple Problems*	Complex Problems[†]	Total
Time			
Centralized faster	14	0	14
Decentralized faster	4	18	22
Messages			
Centralized sent more	0	1	1
Decentralized sent more	18	17	35
Errors			
Centralized made more	0	6	6
Decentralized made more	9	1	10
No difference	1	3	4
Satisfaction			
Centralized higher	1	1	2
Decentralized higher	7	10	17

* Simple problems: symbol, letter, number, and color identification tasks.

[†] Complex problems: arithmetic, word arrangement, sentence construction, and discussion problems.

Source: M. E. Shaw, "Communication Networks," in L. Berkowitz (Ed.), *Advances in Experimental Social Psychology*, Vol. 1 (New York: Academic Press, 1964). Reprinted with permission.

SEATING ARRANGEMENTS

The way in which group members seat themselves in relation to each other exerts significant influences on their perceptions of status, patterns of participation, leadership activities, and affective reactions (Gardin, Kaplan, Firestone, & Cowan, 1973; Howells & Becker, 1962; R. Myers, 1969; Steinzor, 1950; Strodtbeck & Hook, 1961). Members who perceive themselves to have relatively high status in the group select positions (such as the head of the table) that are in accord with this perception. Members sitting at the end positions of a rectangular arrangement participate more in the group and are seen as having more influence on the group decision than members seated at the sides. There is a strong tendency for members to communicate with members facing them rather than with members adjacent to them. Easy eye contact among members enhances frequency of interaction, friendliness, cooperativeness, and liking for the group and its work. The more formal a seating arrangement, the more anxious members may feel. The group's formal leader usually sits at the head of the table, and the member sitting at the head of the table is usually perceived to be the leader.

TAKING A SURVEY

Group effectiveness is always improved when members have clear expectations of the kinds of behaviors expected of them. One way to clarify such expectations is the survey method. In this method any member may ask for the opinion of all the others at any time. Each member then states in two or three sentences his or her current position on the topic under discussion. A survey is not a vote, and it does not bind the group members to a fixed position; it is a device to help communication and problem solving within a group.

IMPROVING COMMUNICATION AMONG GROUP MEMBERS

To improve communication among group members, one must observe their communication behavior in order to diagnose possible sources of difficulty. Once a diagnosis has been made and enough data have been gathered to confirm existing problems, both communication skills and the group's awareness of its present behavior need to be examined. If certain members—or all of them—lack some basic skills, this situation can easily be corrected by a training program. If members have the skills but are not fully aware that they are not using them, an analysis of the communication behavior in the group can be a great help. After examining member self-awareness and skills, one may analyze the effect of group norms and traditional practices to find out if they are suppressing effective communication behaviors and promoting ineffective ones. Group norms can then be adjusted so that communication effectiveness among members will increase.

Because communication is interpersonal, whatever interferes with the relationships among group members interferes with their communication. Changes in the relationships in a group can result in basic improvements in communication. And as we have noted before, perhaps the most powerful influence on the relationships among members and on communication in a group is the members' orientation toward participation in the group and toward its goal structure. Cooperativeness helps a group's effectiveness. Competitiveness, either in goal structure or member orientation, is highly destructive of communication and relationships.

Exercise 4.11: Your Communication Behavior (II)

How would you now describe your communication behavior in a problem-solving group? What are your strengths in communicating, and in what areas do you still wish to build skills? After completing the exercises in this chapter, take twenty minutes or so to write a description of how you see your communication behavior in problem-solving groups. Include a description of the way you formulate and send messages, the receiving skills you use, the way in which you contribute your information and ideas to the group, the way in which you receive information about group meetings and group business, and so on.

After you have written your description, meet with two persons who know you well and discuss it with them. Is it accurate? Can they add anything? Do they have other ideas that might help clarify your communication behavior?

SUMMARY

Now you are aware of the problems of communicating within a group and have had an opportunity to diagnose and practice effective and ineffective communication patterns. The next chapter will discuss the nature of leadership within groups.

5 *Leadership*

Basic Concepts to Be Covered in This Chapter

In this chapter a number of concepts are defined and discussed. The major ones are listed below. Divide into heterogeneous pairs. Each pair is to (a) define each concept, noting the page on which it is defined and discussed, and (b) ensure that both members of the pair understand the meaning of each concept. Then combine into groups of four. Compare the answers of the two pairs. If there is disagreement, look up the concept in the chapter and clarify it until all the members agree on and understand the definition.

Concepts

1. Trait approach to leadership
2. Charismatic leadership
3. Machiavellian leadership
4. Leadership styles
5. Initiating structure
6. Influence leadership
7. Role position approach to leadership
8. Distributed-actions approach to leadership
9. Task actions
10. Relationship actions
11. Member maturity
12. Telling
13. Selling
14. Participating
15. Delegating

WHAT IS LEADERSHIP?

Who built the seven towers of Thebes?
The books are filled with the names of kings.
Was it kings who hauled the craggy blocks of stone?
In the evening when the Chinese wall was finished,
Where did the masons go?

Bertolt Brecht

What is a leader? What is leadership? Are leaders born, or are they made? Does effective leadership originate in a person or in a set of actions and behaviors? All cooperative efforts take leadership. All during your life you will lead others and be led by others. Providing leadership and following someone else's leadership pervade all aspects of life, including work, school, play, and citizenship.

The English word *lead* is more than a thousand years old. Its meaning has changed little from its Anglo-Saxon root *laedare,* meaning "to lead people on a journey." To lead is to guide by influencing the destination and the direction for the group to go. The *Ox-*

Example of a Leader: Benjamin Franklin

Before Benjamin Franklin reached thirty years of age he had been chosen public printer for the colony of Pennsylvania, founded the famous and influential Junto Club, created and published Poor Richard's Almanac (the most widely read publication in America), founded the first circulating library, and been elected grand master of the Freemasons Lodge of Pennsylvania. The next year he inaugurated the first fire-fighting company in Pennsylvania and was chosen clerk of the Pennsylvania Assembly. He was one of the most successful businessmen in the colonies, but had enough interest in scholarship and research to be the founder (at age thirty-seven) of the American Philosophical Society. He continued to serve in a variety of leadership posts in politics, the army, science, diplomacy, and education (founding the academy that became the University of Pennsylvania). At eighty he led the group enterprise of writing the Constitution of the United States. A biographer noted, "Nobody could approach him without being charmed by his conversation, humor, wisdom, and kindness" (Fay, 1929).

How would you explain Benjamin Franklin's success as a leader? Was it due to his (pick only one):

_____ **1.** Inborn, genetic traits?

_____ **2.** Style of leadership?

_____ **3.** Ability to influence others?

_____ **4.** Occupation of positions of authority?

_____ **5.** Ability to provide helpful behaviors in diverse situations?

In selecting one of these alternatives, you have decided on a theory of leadership. In this chapter we shall review each of these theories.

ford English Dictionary notes the appearance of the word *leader* in the English language as early as 1300. The word *leadership,* however, did not appear until about 1800. A **leader** is a person who can influence others to be more effective in working to achieve their mutual goals and maintain effective working relationships among members. Individuals may become leaders through a wide variety of activities, such as winning supporters, solving problems, negotiating deals, building coalitions, mending fences among members, uniting rivals, or stirring emotions. Whatever the actions taken, leadership involves social influence. **Leadership** is the process through which leaders exert such influence on other group members. By comparison, the root origin of *manage* is a Latin word meaning "hand" and managers are individuals who "handle" the status quo.

Being a leader, exerting leadership, takes skill. In work, school, or play, you use leadership skills. **Leadership skills** are the sum total of your ability to help the group achieve its goals and maintain an effective working relationship among members. Just as you learn the skills for doing math or science, you learn how to provide leadership. Anyone can learn leadership skills. All it takes is practice, practice, practice. Once learned, leadership skills can be used your whole life.

Exercise 5.1: Who Are Your Heros?

Who is your ideal leader? Who does our society consider to be ideal leaders? Everyone has heroes whom they would like to imitate and be like. The strength and dedication of George Washington, the intellect and commitment of Thomas Jefferson, the courage of Harriet Tubman, the values and determination of Martin Luther King, may inspire us to wish to be like them. Who is your ideal leader? What qualities does our society believe the ideal leader must have?

Every society has a vision of what constitutes a leader. The *ancient Egyptians,* for example, attributed three qualities of divinity to their king (Frankfort, Frankfort, Wilson, & Jacobsen, 1949): "Authoritative utterance is in thy mouth, perception is in thy heart, and thy tongue is the shrine of justice." An analysis of leaders in Homer's *Iliad* resulted in four sets of ideal leadership qualities admired by *ancient Greeks* (Sarachek, 1968): (1) justice and judgment (Agamemnon), (2) wisdom and counsel (Nestor), (3) shrewdness and cunning (Odysseus), and (4) valor and action (Achilles).

1. Working by yourself, complete the following two tables.
2. Form a group of four. Compare answers and reach consensus about society's views of who are leaders and what characteristics they have.

Who Are Ideal Leaders?

Leaders Society Admires	*Leaders I Admire*	*Leaders We Admire*
1.	1.	1.
2.	2.	2.
3.	3.	3.
4.	4.	4.

What Are Qualities of Ideal Leaders?

Qualities Society Admires	Qualities I Admire	Qualities We Admire
1.	1.	1.
2.	2.	2.
3.	3.	3.
4.	4.	4.
5.	5.	5.
6.	6.	6.

EXAMPLE OF A HERO KING

Alfred is the only king in English history who is given the title "the Great." Alfred became king of Wessex in England in 849, a time when the Vikings had conquered the North and the Danes had conquered the East. It appeared that the Vikings and Danes might conquer all of England. Alfred, however, drove the Danes out of the south and west of England and united that part of England as never before. He became famous for courage and skill as a warrior who fought "like a wild boar." He built an efficient army and a navy that patrolled the English Channel, discouraging further invasions and turned the attention of the Vikings and Danes towards the north of France. He then proceeded to repair the ravages of the Danish incursions. He rebuilt churches, imported foreign scholars, founded schools, began the compilation of the English Chronicle, and personally translated a number of books from the Latin including *Bede's History* (which celebrates the glory of the English people). He is known as a lawgiver and educator who was devoted to the welfare of his people. His code of law was the first to survive in its original form. He hoped for a day when all the youth in England would be devoted to learning. Alfred was the first great statesman to emerge clearly from the mists of early English history. He died in 900 and, largely due to his work, most of the tenth century in England was a golden age of peace and prosperity. Never again was England to have such a king.

Exercise 5.2: Personal Leadership Experience Task

Write a description of a time in your life when you engaged in your most significant and effective leadership performance that represents your personal standard of excellence as a leader. Describe the details of the situation, including the place where it occurred, when it took place, who was involved, what was your role, what were the results, and what recognition (if any) you received. Also include what you learned about leadership from this experience.

_____

_____

_____

_____

_____

Form a group of four. Compare your descriptions. Write down four conclusions about leadership excellence. Be ready to share your conclusions with the entire class.

OUR CONCLUSIONS ABOUT OUR LEADERSHIP EXPERIENCES

1. _____

2. _____

3. _____

4. _____

Exercise 5.3: Controversy: What Is the Nature of Leadership?

The five views of leadership can be the basis for an academic controversy. The purpose of the controversy is to analyze the five views of leadership critically. The procedure is as follows:

Step 1   Forming Leadership Groups: Form leadership groups of five. The goals of the group are to:

a. Learn all five views of leadership.

b. Critically analyze each view of leadership.

c. Come to consensus about the nature of leadership based on group members' best reasoned judgment.

d. Write a summary of the group's conclusions about the nature of leadership.

To achieve these goals, group members need to participate in a structured controversy.

Step 2   Forming Preparation Pairs: In each group members count off from 1 to 5. Each group pairs up with another group. Members of the two groups form preparation pairs. The 1s become a pair, the 2s become a pair, and so forth. Each preparation pair adopts one of the leadership theories.

1s	Genetic Traits View of Leadership
2s	Style View of Leadership
3s	Influence View of Leadership
4s	Position View of Leadership
5s	Distributed-Actions View of Leadership

The pairs meet separately to (a) learn their position and (b) prepare a forceful three-minute presentation of their position. Both members must contribute to building a persuasive case for their view of leadership. The **purpose of the presentation** is to persuade the other members of their leadership group to adopt the recommended view as the most valid and reasonable view of leadership. The presentation should include (a) a position statement: "Our view is that a leader is someone who . . . "; (b) a rationale supporting the position containing as many facts and research findings as possible, arranged in logical order to maximize their persuasiveness, and illustrated with a visual drawing: "Because of a, b, and c, you must conclude that . . . "; and (c) a conclusion that is a restatement of the position statement: "Therefore, the most valid view of leadership is . . . ."

Each person needs his or her own copy of the presentation. The pairs have about ten minutes for this phase of the exercise.

Step 3   Practicing as Pairs: Each person finds a new partner who has the same number and is prepared to present the same view. A number 1 finds another 1, a number 2 finds another 2, and so forth. The pair members share their presentation plan and their visual. Each person takes something from the other's preparation and adds it to his or her own in order to strengthen the presentation.

PREPARATION FORM

1. "The most valid theory of leadership is:" (the theory assigned to me is):

_____

2. Because of: (List the reasons why your theory is the most valid view of leadership and then arrange the reasons in the most persuasive order.)

	Reason	*Most Persuasive Order*
a.		
b.		
c.		
d.		
e.		
f.		

3. Therefore, I have to conclude that the most valid theory of leadership is:

_____

Step 4 Presenting the Best Case Possible for the Assigned Position: The leadership group of five meets. Each member presents the best case possible for his or her assigned position. The presentation is aimed at persuading the other members to adopt the position as the most valid view of leadership. The other group members should listen carefully, take notes, and ask for clarification of anything that is not fully understood. Each person has about three minutes to present his or her position (fifteen minutes total for a group of five).

MY PRESENTATION

_____ I will give a strong, enthusiastic, sincere appeal for the listeners to agree with me.

_____ I will make eye contact, speak clearly, and use appropriate gestures.

_____ I will keep my presentation within the time limits.

_____ I will create a visual to illustrate my points.

Step 5 Challenging the Validity of Each Position: The group of five has an open discussion (anyone can speak at any time) in which members:

a. Continue to advocate the best case for their assigned position.
b. Continue to learn the other positions.
c. Challenge the validity of each of the other positions (give them a trial-by-fire) by critically analyzing (1) the theory, research, and assumptions of each position and (2) the logic of the presentation. ("Your position has the following flaws. . . . ")
d. Defend their own position from the challenges of the other group members. ("You are mistaken—my position is valid because. . . .)

Each member should present as many facts and research findings as possible to support the group's position. Members should listen critically to the opposing position, asking for

MY ANALYSIS OF THE THEORIES

Persuasive Points	*Criticisms*
Theory 1:	
Theory 2:	
Theory 3:	
Theory 4:	
Theory 5:	

facts to support any conclusions made by the opposing pair. Participants should ensure that all the facts supporting both sides are brought out and discussed. The rules for constructive controversy should be followed. About ten minutes should be allowed for this phase.

Step 6 Reversing Perspectives: Each person presents the best case possible for the position of the next higher number. (The number 1 presents the 2 position, 2 presents the 3 position, 3 presents the 4 position, 4 presents the 5 position, 5 presents the 1 position.) Group members need to be as forceful and persuasive as possible in arguing for the opposing position. They expand on the other position, adding new arguments or facts that the advocate did not present. Each member has about two minutes for the presentation (ten minutes total for the group of five).

Step 7 Synthesizing and Integrating the Five Positions: Group members drop all advocacy, synthesize and integrate the best information and reasoning from all five positions, and come to a consensus as to their view of leadership. Each writes down his or her best reasoned judgment as to the nature of leadership: (a) the group position, (b) the rationale arranged in a logical order, and (c) a conclusion that is the same as the position. About ten minutes should be allowed for each group for this phase.

OUR GROUP POSITION

1. Our group position is: _____

_____

_____

_____

2. Because of:

a. _____

b. _____

c. _____

d. _____

3. Therefore, you have to conclude that our conclusions are valid.

Step 8   Groups Present Their Positions to Entire Class: Each leadership group presents its final position to the entire class. Because other groups will have other conclusions, each group may explain the validity of its position to the class.

Step 9   Group Processing: Each leadership group discusses the following:

1. What leadership actions did each member take to help the group effectively advocate and challenge each of the leadership theories?

a. _____

b. _____

c. _____

d. _____

e. _____

2. What can each member do to be even more effective next time?

a. _____

b. _____

c. _____

d. _____

e. _____

3. What were the most fun parts of arguing about leadership?

a. _____

b. _____

c. _____

4. What did I learn about myself as an arguer?

a. _____

b. _____

c. _____

WHAT IS LEADERSHIP?

There are several different views of leadership. The following questionnaire measures your view. The procedure is:

1. Working by yourself, complete the following questionnaire.
2. Determine your score.
3. Form a group of four members. Compare your scores. Then read the following sections of this chapter.

The statements listed below reflect various theories of leadership. Read each statement carefully. Using the following scale, indicate the degree to which you agree or disagree with each statement.

1 = strongly disagree
2 = disagree
3 = neither disagree or agree
4 = agree
5 = strongly agree

1. Leaders are born, not made.
   Strongly Disagree   1———2———3———4———5   Strongly Agree
2. Each leader has his or her own style.
   Strongly Disagree   1———2———3———4———5   Strongly Agree
3. The leader in a group is the person who is most able to influence the others.
   Strongly Disagree   1———2———3———4———5   Strongly Agree
4. Whoever has the most authority (power invested in a position) is the leader.
   Strongly Disagree   1———2———3———4———5   Strongly Agree
5. With training, anyone can learn to be a leader.
   Strongly Disagree   1———2———3———4———5   Strongly Agree
6. Great leaders with unique and inborn traits are discovered, not developed.
   Strongly Disagree   1———2———3———4———5   Strongly Agree
7. If you want to be a leader, know your style and go with it.
   Strongly Disagree   1———2———3———4———5   Strongly Agree
8. If you are appointed leader, then you are the leader, because subordinates are supposed to obey their superiors.
   Strongly Disagree   1———2———3———4———5   Strongly Agree
9. A leader persuades and inspires members to follow the leader's views of what needs to be done.
   Strongly Disagree   1———2———3———4———5   Strongly Agree
10. Leadership is acting in a way that helps the group achieve its goals and maintain good working relationships among members.
    Strongly Disagree   1———2———3———4———5   Strongly Agree
11. A good predictor of leadership ability is whether or not the person comes from a family of leaders.
    Strongly Disagree   1———2———3———4———5   Strongly Agree
12. To choose who should lead, decide which style of leadership is most effective.
    Strongly Disagree   1———2———3———4———5   Strongly Agree
13. The leader is the person who influences others to do what is best.
    Strongly Disagree   1———2———3———4———5   Strongly Agree
14. A leader makes sure that subordinates do their jobs.
    Strongly Disagree   1———2———3———4———5   Strongly Agree

15. Any member of a group may become a leader by taking actions that help the group complete its goal and maintain effective working relationships.

Strongly Disagree   1———2———3———4———5   Strongly Agree

16. Leaders are "great persons" who become (or who are) members of elite social groups because of their outstanding inborn traits.

Strongly Disagree   1———2———3———4———5   Strongly Agree

17. Some leaders are democratic. Some leaders are authoritarian. Every leader has his or her own style.

Strongly Disagree   1———2———3———4———5   Strongly Agree

18. Leaders are leaders because they influence group members more than group members influence them.

Strongly Disagree   1———2———3———4———5   Strongly Agree

19. Leaders are given the authority and power to punish and reward group members.

Strongly Disagree   1———2———3———4———5   Strongly Agree

20. A leader varies his or her behavior from situation to situation to provide the appropriate leadership actions at the appropriate time.

Strongly Disagree   1———2———3———4———5   Strongly Agree

What Is Leadership: Scoring

Genetic Traits	Style	Influence	Authority	Needed Functions
___ 1	___ 2	___ 3	___ 4	___ 5
___ 6	___ 7	___ 8	___ 9	___ 10
___ 11	___ 12	___ 13	___ 14	___ 15
___ 16	___ 17	___ 18	___ 19	___ 20
___ **Total**	___ **Total**	___ **Total**	___ **Total**	___ **Total**

The higher the total score for each category, the more strongly you tend to believe in that explanation of leadership. The lower the total score in a category, the less strongly you tend to believe in that explanation of leadership.

TRAIT THEORIES OF LEADERSHIP

Perhaps Benjamin Franklin was one of the greatest leaders of the eighteenth century because he was genetically superior to his contemporaries. Throughout history many people have believed that leaders are born, not made, and that great leaders are discovered, not developed. Especially in times of great social upheaval and trouble many people have looked for a great leader who has unique, inborn traits. This is the "great-man" or "great-woman" theory of leadership. Royalty, members of elite social classes, older siblings, and early maturers are likely to believe in this approach to leadership. One of the strongest advocates of this theory of leadership was Aristotle, who once stated, "From the moment of their birth, some are marked for subjugation and others for command." There do seem to be individuals who dominate others through the force of their personality, their charisma, what they stand for, or their ability to manipulate others. There also have been historical periods when the prevailing ideology was that leaders are superior to other human beings.

In the early twentieth century there were many strong advocates of the trait theories of leadership. Wiggam (1931), for example, concluded that the survival of the fittest and marriage among them produce an aristocratic class that differs biologically from the lower classes. Advocating the social Darwinism that was popular at that time, Wiggam took the position that an adequate supply of superior leaders depended on a proportionately high birthrate among the abler classes. Henry Ford remarked, "The question 'Who should be boss?' is like asking 'Who ought to be the tenor in the quarter?' Obviously, the man who can sing tenor." He was suggesting the boss is a person who has the natural ability to lead. The historian Thomas Carlyle believed that genius would exert its influence wherever it were found.

Hundreds of research studies have been conducted to identify the personal attributes of leaders. In one of the more interesting ones, Frederick Adams Wood (1913), an early twentieth-century American historian, examined 386 rulers in 14 countries in Western Europe who lived between A.D. 1000 and the French Revolution. All of these rulers had absolute power over their kingdoms. Each was classified as strong, weak, or mediocre on the basis of knowledge about his or her intellectual and personal characteristics (which were presumably independent of the strength or weakness of the nation at that time). The condition of each country was also classified as prosperous, declining, or lacking a clear indication of either. (This classification was based on the country's economic and political status, not on its artistic, educational, and scientific development.) Wood found a relationship between the monarchs' personalities and the state of the countries. He summarized his results as follows: "Strong, mediocre, and weak monarchs are associated with strong, mediocre, and weak periods respectively" (p. 246). Although the correlation coefficient was reasonably strong (between +0.60 and +0.70), as with any correlation we cannot infer a direct relationship between cause and effect. However, Wood clearly favored the interpretations that strong leaders cause their countries to flourish.

The typical research studies on trait theories have compared the characteristics of a leader (defined as an individual holding a position of authority, such as the president of the United States) with the characteristics of a follower (defined as an individual not holding a position of authority, such as a low-level government employee). The findings of these studies are somewhat contradictory and inconclusive. Bird (1940) analyzed the results of 20 studies that had considered 79 leadership traits. He found little consistency in the results from one study to another. Of the 79 traits, 51 made a difference in only one study each. High degrees of 4 traits—intelligence, initiative, sense of humor, and extroversion—were identified often enough in leaders for Bird to consider them "general traits of leadership." Mann (1959) reviewed 125 studies of leadership and personality characteristics representing over 700 findings (see Table 5.1). He concluded that intelligence and personal adjustment seem to be correlated with leadership.

There may be leaders who are more intelligent than nonleaders, yet it is evident that many of the most intelligent people never obtain positions of leadership. Intelligence may have been a prerequisite for Benjamin Franklin's type of leadership, but it is doubtful whether Franklin or John Adams or George Washington possessed the highest IQ of their period (Cox, 1926). A follow-up study of one thousand highly intelligent children from California showed that in twenty-five years relatively few of them had reached the roster of famous leaders (Terman & Odor, 1947). None had attained high

Table 5.1   **Percentage of Significant Relationships Reported in a Positive or Negative Direction for 125 Studies, Representing 751 Findings on the Relationship of Various Personality Characteristics and Leadership**

Personality Factors and Number of Studies of Each	Number of Findings	Percent Yielding Sig. Positive Relationship	Percent Yielding Sig. Negative Relationship	Percent Yielding Neither
Intelligence, 28	(196)	46% (91)	1%* (1)	53% (104)
Adjustment, 22	(164)	30% (50)	2%* (2)	68% (112)
Extroversion, 22	(119)	31% (37)	5% (6)	64% (76)
Dominance, 12	(39)	38% (15)	15% (6)	46% (18)
Masculinity, 9	(70)	16% (11)	1%* (1)	83% (58)
Conservatism, 17	(62)	5% (3)	27% (17)	68% (42)
Sensitivity, 15	(101)	15% (15)	1%* (1)	84% (85)

*Rounded upward.

Source: R. Mann, "A Review of the Relationship Between Personality and Performance in Small Groups," *Psychological Bulletin,* 1959, 56, 241–270. Reprinted by permission.

political office or the presidency of a corporation or college. Only 5% were in *Who's Who* and only 13% were in *American Men of Science.* Despite the findings that leaders are better adjusted psychologically than nonleaders, many leaders (such as Adolf Hitler) have showed signs of being emotionally disturbed.

Stimulated by the personnel testing and selection programs begun during the First World War, social scientists attempted to identify the distinguishing traits of leaders. On these tests leaders were found to score higher than followers on a wide variety of characteristics, including intelligence and aptitude, personality, task motivation and performance, and social competence (Stogdill, 1974). Despite the great ingenuity displayed in the development of tests to measure these characteristics, however, such instruments have not proved reliably useful in the selection of leaders.

Although the correlations between individual traits and leadership measures are not large, some conclusions may be made. Stogdill (1974) divided the research on this subject into two periods: studies conducted between 1904 and 1947 and studies conducted between 1948 and 1970. The former body of research, he noted, revealed that leaders who participated actively in organizing cooperative tasks and carrying them through to completion were characterized by intelligence, alertness to the needs and motives of others, insight into situations, and such habits as responsibility, initiative, persistence, and self-confidence. The trait studies conducted between 1948 and 1970 indicated that leaders who have the capacity for organizing and expediting cooperative effort are characterized by a strong drive for responsibility and task completion, vigor and persistence in pursuit of goals, venturesomeness and originality in problem solving, a drive to exercise initiative in social situations, self-confidence and a sense of personal identity, willingness to accept the consequences of decisions and actions, readiness to absorb interpersonal stress, readiness to tolerate frustration and delay, ability to influence the behavior of others, and the capacity to structure social systems according to the purpose at hand.

These characteristics seem to differentiate (a) leaders from nonleaders, (b) effective from ineffective leaders, and (c) higher-echelon from lower-echelon leaders. Stogdill (1974) added, however, that when these characteristics are considered singly they hold little diagnostic or predictive significance. In combination they appear to be advantageous to the person seeking the responsibilities of leadership. Stogdill also noted that whether any one person with these characteristics rises to a leadership position depends considerably on chance: One must not only have the traits but also be in the right place at the right time. Perhaps the safest conclusion to draw from the trait and personality studies of leadership is that individuals who have the energy, drive, self-confidence, and determination to succeed will become leaders, because they work hard to get leadership positions.

Simon Bolivar once said, "Man is the weak toy of fortune." The trait theory of leadership gains some support when it is combined with social determinism. The **social determinism** or Zeitgeist theory of history states that historic events are determined by social forces, social movements, and changing social values. **Zeitgeist** means "spirit of the times" or "temper of the times." Leaders simply play out roles designed for them by broad social forces. As Victor Hugo wrote, "there is nothing in this world so powerful as an idea whose time has come." Dean Simonton (1979), for example, analyzed why certain scientists rise notably above their peers and suggested that sheer chance and the influence of the Zeitgeist and previous technological discoveries are more important determinants of scientific eminence than personal traits. The trait and social determinism views are combined in the view that the great person plays a unique and decisive role only when the historical situation permits major alternative paths of development (Hook, 1955). Only when choices exist does the great person influence history.

What makes one person a successful leader whereas another person fails in the same position? Some leaders (Napoleon, Hitler, Mao Tse-tung) have been able to control the destinies of millions of people. There are, however, at least four problems with trying to identify the traits of leaders: (1) An unlimited number of leadership traits may be identified; (2) different traits may be needed under different conditions; (3) "great" leaders are identified after the fact, but who will become a great leader cannot be predicted ahead of time; and (4) a match between the Zeitgeist and the great person may be required for great leadership to occur. In addition, there has been a biased focus on "great men" as leaders and a relative inattention to "great women." Perhaps the best predictor of leadership success is prior success in leadership roles (Stogdill, 1974).

Besides the extensive research trying to differentiate leaders from nonleaders on the basis of personal attributes, there has been considerable discussion and research on two major traits of some leaders: charisma and Machiavellianism.

Charismatic Leaders

One of the dictionary definitions of **charisma** is "an extraordinary power, as of working miracles." Sometimes charismatic leaders seem to inspire their followers to love and be passionately devoted to them. Other times charismatic leaders offer their followers the promise and hope of deliverance from distress. Charismatic leaders are saviors who say in essence, "I will make you safe," "I will give you identity," or "I will give your life significance and meaning."

Charisma does not seem to be correlated with any one personality type. The personalities of Alexander, Julius Caesar, George Washington, Robespierre, Bolivar, Sun Yat-sen, and Gandhi were widely different, yet all of these individuals were able to inspire confidence in their followers and to demand from them the sacrifice even of life itself. Garibaldi won the loyalty of his Roman soldiers with an unusual appeal: "What I have to offer you is fatigue, danger, struggle, and death; the chill of the cold night in the fall air, and heat under the burning sun; no lodgings, no provisions, but forced marches, dangerous watchposts, and the continual struggle with the bayonet against batteries—those who love freedom and their country may follow me!" Winston Churchill offered "blood, sweat, and tears," but sustained the faith and courage of millions.

Attempts to define charisma specifically and to measure the degree of charisma possessed by various leaders have failed. In general, however, a **charismatic leader** has (1) an extraordinary power or vision and is able to communicate it to others or (2) unusual powers of practical leadership that will enable him or her to achieve the goals that will alleviate followers' distress. The charismatic leader has a sense of mission, a belief in the social-change movement he or she leads, and confidence in him- or herself as the chosen instrument to lead the movement to its destination. The leader appears extremely self-confident in order to inspire others with the faith that the movement he or she leads will prevail and ultimately reduce their distress.

Machiavellianism

Current theories of leadership ignore not only the irrational aspects of leadership and followership reflected in charisma but also the realities of how power is often handled. If charismatic leaders found social movements and bring them to power, it is the Machiavellian leaders who consolidate and wield the power the charismatic leaders obtain. The essence of **Machiavellian leadership** is believing that (1) people are basically weak, fallible, and gullible, and not particularly trustworthy; (2) others are impersonal objects; and (3) one should manipulate others whenever necessary in order to achieve one's ends.

Niccolo Machiavelli (1469–1527) was a Florentine statesman whose treatise *The Prince* advocated the use of craft, duplicity, and cunning by rulers as political principles for increasing their power and success. He did not originate such an approach. Throughout history there have been theorists who conceived of leadership essentially in terms of

Trait Theory of Leadership

Strengths	*Weaknesses*

the possession and exercise of power for self-enhancement. After analyzing the historical literature on how political leaders should govern, Richard Christie (Christie & Geis, 1970) concluded that Machiavellian leaders who manipulate their followers for political and personal reasons have four characteristics. First, they have little emotional involvement in their interpersonal relationships, because it is easier to manipulate others if they are viewed as objects rather than as fellow humans. Second, because they take a utilitarian rather than a moral view of their interactions with others, they are not concerned with conventional morality. Third, because successful manipulation of followers depends on an accurate perception of their needs and of "reality" in general, they will not be grossly psychopathological. Finally, because the essence of successful manipulation is a focus on getting things done rather than on achieving long-term ideological goals, Machiavellian leaders will have a low degree of ideological commitment.

Exercise 5.4: Interpersonal Patterns

This exercise focuses on your interaction with other members of your group. It may help you think about how you conduct yourself in a group. The procedure for the exercise is as follows:

1. The class divides into groups of three. Each person fills out the checklist below.
2. Analyze the meaning of the verbs you checked by following the instructions below the checklist.
3. Share with the other two members of your triad the results of the exercise, and ask for their comments on whether they perceive you in the same way or differently.

The twenty verbs listed below describe some of the ways people feel and act from time to time. Think of your behavior in groups. How do you feel and act in groups? Check the five verbs that best describe your behavior in groups as you see it.

_____ acquiesce	_____ coordinate	_____ lead
_____ advise	_____ criticize	_____ oblige
_____ agree	_____ direct	_____ relinquish
_____ analyze	_____ disapprove	_____ resist
_____ assist	_____ evade	_____ retreat
_____ concede	_____ initiate	_____ withdraw
_____ concur	_____ judge	

	High dominance	Low dominance
High sociability	advises coordinates directs initiates leads	acquiesces agrees assists concurs obliges
Low sociability	analyzes criticizes disapproves judges resists	concedes evades relinquishes retreats withdraws

There are two underlying patterns of interpersonal behavior represented in the list of objectives: *dominance* (authority or control) and *sociability* (intimacy or friendliness). Most individuals tend either to like to control things (high dominance) or to let others control things (low dominance). Similarly, most persons tend either to be warm and personal (high sociability) or to be somewhat cold and impersonal (low sociability). In the diagram above, circle the five verbs you used to describe yourself in group activities. The set of ten verbs—horizontal for the dominance dimension and vertical for the sociability dimension—in which three or more are circled represents your tendency in that pattern of interpersonal behavior.

LEADERSHIP STYLES

Perhaps Benjamin Franklin became a leader through his style of relating to others. Franklin was noted for his charm, conversational skills, humor, wisdom, and kindness. But was Franklin's leadership style the same as George Washington's or Thomas Jefferson's? Even casual observation of leaders in action reveals marked differences in their styles of leadership. **Style** refers to the way in which something is said or done. It is usually contrasted with the **substance** of the statements and actions. The style with which an action is taken carries messages as well as the substance of the action. Style affects its legitimacy, credibility, and believability. Leadership may be defined as a style of behavior. Even casual observations of leaders in action reveal marked differences in their styles of leadership. Some leaders seem **autocratic:** They dictate orders and determine all policy without involving group members in decision making. Some leaders seem **democratic:** They set policies through group discussion and decision, encouraging and helping group members to interact, requesting the cooperation of others, and being considerate of members' feelings and needs. Finally, some leaders take a **laissez-faire** approach: They do not participate in their group's decision making at all. It seems obvious that such differences in leadership style should affect group productivity and the attitudes of group members.

The pioneering study of whether leadership styles do in fact make a difference in group functioning was conducted by Lewin, Lippitt, and White (1939). Although the study has many shortcomings, it demonstrated strikingly that the same group of individuals will behave in markedly different ways under leaders who behave differently. As we have seen in Chapter 1, groups of ten- and eleven-year-olds were run by three adult leaders who adopted each of three leadership styles for a specified period: autocratic, democratic, or laissez-faire. When the groups were under an autocratic leader, they were more dependent on the leader and more egocentric in their peer relationships. When rotated to a democratic style of leadership, the same children evidenced more initiative, friendliness, and responsibility, and continued to work even when the leader was out of the room. Their interest in their work and in the quality of their product was higher. Aggressive acts were more frequent under autocratic and laissez-faire leaders than they were under a democratic leader. Hostility was thirty times as great in the autocratic groups than in either of the other two: Frequently one group member was made the target of hostility and aggression until he or she left the group, and then another member would be chosen to perform the same function. Nineteen of twenty members liked the democratic leader better than the autocrat, and seven of ten liked the laissez-faire leader better than the autocrat.

Since this classic study a number of researchers have investigated the relative impact of democratic and autocratic leaders on group functioning. In reviewing these studies, Stogdill (1974) noted that neither democratic nor autocratic leadership can be advocated as a method for increasing productivity, but that member satisfaction is associated with a democratic style of leadership. Satisfaction with democratic leadership tends to be highest in small, interaction-oriented groups. Other studies have compared permissive, follower-oriented, participative, and considerate leadership styles with restrictive, task-oriented, directive, socially distant, and structured leadership styles. After reviewing the studies in each of these areas, Stogdill (1974) made the following conclusions:

1. Person-oriented styles of leadership are not consistently related to productivity.
2. Among the work-oriented leadership styles, socially distant, directive, and structured leader behaviors that tend to maintain role differentiation and let members know what to expect are consistently related to group productivity.
3. Among the person-oriented leadership styles, only those providing for member participation in decision making and showing concern for members' welfare and comfort are consistently related to group cohesiveness.
4. Among the work-oriented leadership styles, only the structuring of member expectations is uniformly related to group cohesiveness.
5. All of the person-oriented leadership styles tend to be related to member satisfaction.
6. Only the structuring of member expectations is related positively to member satisfaction among the work-oriented leadership styles.

Initiating structure by clearly defining one's role as a leader and what one expects from the other members of the group is the single style of leadership that contributes positively to group productivity, cohesiveness, and satisfaction. The most effective leaders may be those who show concern for the well-being and contributions of group members and at the same time structure members' role responsibilities.

The Lewin, Lippitt, and White (1939) study, along with other research conducted by Lewin and his colleagues, helped inspire and initiate the training programs in applied group dynamics conducted for the past thirty years at Bethel, Maine, by the National Training Laboratories Institute of Applied Behavioral Science. Immediately after the

Second World War a group of adult educators and Kurt Lewin and his associates began conducting workshops aimed at developing the leadership competencies of participants. These workshops formed the basis for the explosion of small group methods for personal and organizational change that took place during the 1960s and the growth in the number of consultants concerned with improving the development and planned change of organizations.

The major shortcomings of the style approach to leadership are that (a) different styles are effective under different conditions and (b) an unlimited number of styles may be identified. Certain conditions exist, for example, under which autocratic leadership seems more effective (such as when an urgent decision has to be made). In other conditions a democratic style may be most effective (such as when considerable member commitment to the implementation of the decision needs to be built). There are even conditions in which the laissez-faire style seems best (such as when the group is committed to a decision, has the resources to implement it, and needs a minimum of interference to work effectively). Because different leadership styles seem to be required in different situations, even with the same group, the attention of many social scientists has moved to situational approaches to leadership. But before considering such approaches, two other theories of leadership are briefly discussed.

Style Theory of Leadership

Strengths	Weaknesses

INFLUENCE THEORY OF LEADERSHIP

A leader is a man who has the ability to get other people to do what they don't want to do, and like it.

Harry S. Truman

Leadership is the ability to decide what is to be done, and then to get others to want to do it.

Dwight D. Eisenhower

Leadership appears to be the art of getting others to want to do something that you are convinced should be done.

Vance Packard, *The Pyramid Climbers*

Benjamin Franklin may have been an outstanding leader because he knew how to influence people. Leadership is influencing other group members. A leader may be defined as a group member who exerts more influence on other members than they exert on him or her. A number of studies have examined the factors affecting the amount of influence a leader has on the attitudes and behaviors of groupmates. Michener and Burt (1975), for example, found that the compliance of members is greater when a leader justifies his demands as being good for the group, has the power to punish members who do not do as he has asked, and has a legitimate right to make demands of subordinates. The success or failure of the group does not seem to affect a leader's ability to influence, nor does approval of him by subordinates.

An influence approach to leadership implies that there is a reciprocal role relationship between leaders and followers in which an exchange, or transaction, takes place. Without followers there can be no leader, and without a leader there can be no followers. The leader and the followers both give something to and receive something from each other. As Homans stated, "Influence over others is purchased at the price of allowing oneself to be influenced by others" (1961, p. 286). Although leadership may be defined as the successful influencing of other group members, the followers also influence the leader. The leader receives status, recognition, esteem, and other reinforcement for contributing his or her resources to the accomplishment of the group's goals. The followers obtain the leader's resources and ability to structure the group's activities towards the attainment of a goal. The leader provides structure, direction, and resources. The followers provide deference and reinforcement. Because both the leader and the followers control resources that the other desires, they can each influence the other's behavior.

The interdependence of leader and followers has been demonstrated by a number of studies. Leaders tend both to talk more than other group members and to receive more

Influence Theory of Leadership

Strengths	Weaknesses

communications than do other group members (Zander, 1979). When a person is reinforced and encouraged by other group members to engage in active leadership behaviors, the person's proportion of talking time increases as one's perceived leadership status increases (Bavelas, Hostort, Gross, and Kite, 1965; Zdep and Oakes, 1967). Pepinsky and his associates (1958) demonstrated that individuals who have previously exhibited few leadership behaviors were influenced to behave far more actively in such behaviors by the group's evident support for their assertions; individuals who had previously exhibited many leadership behaviors in earlier situations were affected in precisely the opposite way by the group's evident disagreement with their statements. From these and other studies it may be concluded that (a) the amount of participation and influence by a leader affects members' perceptions of his or her leadership, and (b) the amount of encouragement and support by followers affects the amount of a person's participation and perceived leadership status.

Viewing leadership as a reciprocal influence between a leader and a set of followers does not necessarily mean that leadership is based on domination. Hitler, for example, defined leadership as the ability to move the masses (either through persuasion or violence). Ho Chi Minh believed a good leader must learn to mold, shape, and change the people just as a woodworker must learn to use wood. Both views are erroneous. Leaders do not influence through domination and coercion. The influence of leaders is directed towards persuading group members to cooperate in setting and achieving goals. Leadership is thus the art of ensuring that group members work together with the least friction and the most cooperation. This often means that leaders need to persuade and inspire members to follow their views of what needs to be done in order to achieve a group's goals.

ROLE POSITION/APPROACH TO LEADERSHIP

Perhaps Benjamin Franklin was known as a leader simply because he was appointed to various leadership positions. A leader may be defined as a person who holds a position of authority. Leadership in organizations begins with the formal role structure that defines the hierarchy of authority. **Authority** is legitimate power vested in a particular position to ensure that individuals in subordinate positions meet the requirements of their organizational role. Because organizational law demands that subordinates obey their superiors in matters of role performance, a person with authority will influence his or

Authority–Position Theory of Leadership

Strengths	Weaknesses

her subordinates. A person who is directly above you in the authority hierarchy, therefore, is your leader.

There are at least three problems with the role position approach to leadership. First, it is unclear how individuals are appointed to high-authority positions. It does not have to be for leadership ability. Second, it does not explain how the leader can engage in nonleadership behaviors and the subordinates can engage in leadership actions. Not all of the appointed leader's actions are leadership behavior. In addition, subordinates can provide leadership. Third, the role behavior of subordinates is influenced by outsiders who have no direct authority over them.

Exercise 5.5: Understanding Your Leadership Actions Questionnaire

Each of the following statements describes a leadership action. For each statement mark:

5 = I always behave that way   2 = I seldom behave that way
4 = I frequently behave that way   1 = I never behave that way
3 = I occasionally behave that way

WHEN I AM A MEMBER OF A GROUP:

_____ 1. I offer facts and give my opinions, ideas, feelings, and information in order to help the group discussion.

_____ 2. I make sure I understand what other group members say by restating it in my own words. I use good communication skills and help facilitate effective communication among group members.

_____ 3. I give direction to the group by calling attention to the tasks that need to be done and suggesting procedures for completing them. I organize role responsibilities for group members.

_____ 4. I promote the open discussion of conflicts among group members in order to resolve disagreements and mediate when the members seem unable to resolve the conflicts directly.

_____ 5. I tell jokes and make amusing comments in order to make members laugh and to increase the fun we have working together.

_____ 6. I summarize the contributions of group members into one condensed statement and integrate all the diverse actions of members into a unified whole.

_____ 7. I express support, acceptance, and liking for other members of the group and give appropriate recognition and praise when another member has taken a constructive action in the group.

_____ 8. I ask for facts, information, opinions, ideas, and feelings from the other group members in order to use all the group's resources to complete the task.

_____ 9. I encourage all members of the group to participate. I try to give them the confidence to contribute actively to the group effort. I let them know I value their contributions.

_____ 10. I ask others to explain the group's answers and conclusions to ensure that they comprehend and understand the material being discussed by the group.

_____ 11. I give the group energy. I try to get group members excited about achieving our goals.

_____ 12. I observe the way the group is working and use my observations to help discuss how group members can work together better.

SCORING THE LEADERSHIP QUESTIONNAIRE

In order to obtain a total score for task actions and maintenance actions, write the score for each item in the appropriate column and then total the scores for each column (see Figure 5.1).

Task Actions

_____ 1. Information and opinion giver

_____ 3. Direction and role definer

_____ 6. Summarizer

_____ 8. Information and opinion seeker

_____ 10. Checker for understanding

_____ 11. Energizer

_____ **Total for Task Actions**

Maintenance Actions

_____ 2. Communication facilitator

_____ 4. Interpersonal problem solver

_____ 5. Tension reliever

_____ 7. Supporter and praiser

_____ 9. Encourager of participation

_____ 12. Process observer

_____ **Total for Maintenance Actions**

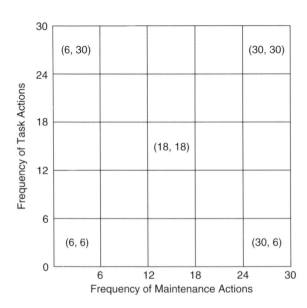

Figure 5.1 Task-maintenance grid.

TASK–MAINTENANCE PATTERNS

(6, 6) Only a minimum effort is given to getting the required work done. There is general noninvolvement with other group members. The person with this score may well be saying: "To hell with it all!" Or he or she may be so inactive in the group as to have no influence whatsoever on other group members.

(6, 30) High value is placed on keeping good relationships within the group. Thoughtful attention is given to the needs of other members. The person with the score helps create a comfortable, friendly atmosphere and work tempo. However, he or she may never help the group get any work accomplished.

(30, 6) Getting the job done is emphasized in a way that shows very little concern with group maintenance. Work is seen as important, and relationships among group members are ignored. The person with this score may take an army-drillmaster approach to leadership.

(18, 18) The task and maintenance needs of the group are balanced. The person with this score continually makes compromises between task needs and maintenance needs. Though a great compromiser, this person does not look for or find ways to creatively integrate task and maintenance activities for optimal productivity.

(30, 30) When everyone plans and makes decisions together, all the members become committed to getting the task done as they build relationships of trust and respect.

MATCHING EXERCISE 1

To help you learn the task and maintenance actions, match the following terms with their definitions (answers on page 227).

Task Actions

_____ 1.	Information and opinion giver
_____ 2.	Information and opinion seeker
_____ 3.	Direction and role definer
_____ 4.	Summarizer
_____ 5.	Energizer
_____ 6.	Comprehension checker

Maintenance Actions

_____ 7.	Encourager of participation
_____ 8.	Communication facilitator
_____ 9.	Tension reliever
_____ 10.	Process observer
_____ 11.	Interpersonal problem solver
_____ 12.	Supporter and praiser

a. Makes sure all group members understand what each other says.

b. Pulls together related ideas or suggestions and restates them.

c. Offers facts, opinions, ideas, feelings, and information.

d. Expresses acceptance and liking for group members.

e. Uses observations of how the group is working to help discuss how the group can improve.

f. Lets members know their contributions are valued.

g. Asks for facts, opinions, ideas, feelings, and information.

h. Asks others to summarize discussion to make sure they understand.

i. Encourages group members to work hard to achieve goals.

j. Calls attention to tasks that need to be done and assigns responsibilities.

k. Helps resolve and mediate conflicts.

l. Tells jokes and increases the group fun.

MATCHING EXERCISE 2

How Well Do I Understand Functioning (Leadership) Skills?

Match the following statements with goal relationship leadership action they best seem to fill (answers on page 227).

Goal Actions

_____ 1. Information and opinion giver
_____ 2. Information and opinion seeker.
_____ 3. Direction and role definer
_____ 4. Summarizer
_____ 5. Energizer
_____ 6. Comprehension

Relationship Actions

_____ 7. Encourager of participation
_____ 8. Communication facilitator
_____ 9. Tension reliever
_____ 10. Process observer
_____ 11. Interpersonal problem solver
_____ 12. Supporter and praiser

a. "Helen, my understanding is that you are suggesting that we define the problem before we try to solve it."

b. "How about giving our report on yoga while standing on our heads?"

c. "Three ideas have been suggested. Dale thinks we should play football, Jose thinks we should go to lunch, and Tai believes we should write a story about what we are doing."

d. "I think we should help resolve the conflict between David and Linda."

e. "George Washington was the first president of the United States and, in my opinion, the best one."

f. "Francene has not said anything for the past five minutes. Is there a problem?"

g. "That is an important insight, Roger. It indicates you have really worked hard on the homework."

h. "Fire up! We can find a good solution. Let's put a little more effort into it."

i. "Frank, explain to us step-by-step how to solve question 12."

j. "We should first define the problem and second suggest solutions. We can then decide which solution to adopt."

k. "Roger, do you know who the fourth president of the United States was and what he is famous for?"

l. "Helen, I would like to hear what you think about this; you have good ideas."

SITUATIONAL THEORIES OF LEADERSHIP

Perhaps Benjamin Franklin became a renowned leader because he was able to vary his behavior systematically from situation to situation so as to provide the appropriate leadership actions at the appropriate time. There is currently a consensus among social scientists that leadership skills and competencies are not inherited from one's ancestors, that they do not magically appear when a person is assigned to a leadership position, and that the same style will not provide adequate leadership in every situation. Different situations require different approaches to leadership. To be a leader, you must be able to vary your behavior to provide the functions a group needs at that specific time. In other words, **leadership is actions performed by many, not a position held by one.** You are not the leader, I am not the leader, what we do provides leadership! We shall discuss five situational theories in this chapter: the distributed-actions theory, Bale's interaction-process analysis, Fiedler's situational theory, and Hersey and Blanchard's situational theory.

The Distributed-Actions Theory of Leadership

Not the cry, but the flight of the wild duck, leads the flock to fly and follow.

Chinese proverb

The **distributed-actions theory of leadership** emphasizes that certain functions need to be done if a group is to achieve its goals and maintain effective working relationships among members. A *function* is an action that must take place in order for a group to be effective. At different times, different functions are needed. At one time, information may need to be contributed. At another time, the contributions of members may need to be summarized and integrated. Leadership is the performance of acts that help the group complete its goals and maintain effective working relationships among its members. Members must engage in the **goal-leadership actions** of contributing, asking for, summarizing, and coordinating information. Members have to structure and give direction to the group's efforts and provide the energy to motivate efforts to make the decision.

It does no good to achieve goals successfully if the manner of doing so alienates group members. Members must pay attention to maintaining good working relationships while working to achieve goals. Goals must be achieved in ways that increase the ability of group members to work together effectively in the future. Members engage in **relationship-leadership actions** when they encourage each other to participate, facilitate communication among themselves, relieve tension when it gets too high, and evaluate the emotional climate of the group. They have to discuss how the group's work can be improved, and they have to listen carefully and respectfully to one another.

The distributed-actions theory of leadership includes two basic ideas: (1) Any member of a group may become a leader by taking actions that help the group complete its goals and maintain effective working relationships; (2) any leadership function may be fulfilled by different members performing a variety of relevant behaviors. Leadership, therefore, is specific to a particular group in a particular situation. Under one set of circumstances an action may be helpful whereas under other circumstances the same action may be unhelpful. When a group is trying to define a problem, for example, providing information about the nature of the problem may be helpful, but when the group is deciding which solution to the problem to adopt, giving more information about the nature of the problem may be unhelpful.

To provide leadership, you must have:

1. The flexibility to engage in a wide variety of actions.
2. The ability to diagnose what behaviors are needed at a particular time in order for the group to function most efficiently.
3. The ability to fulfill these behaviors or to get other members to fulfill them.

To be a skilled leader, therefore, you have to have the diagnostic skills to be aware that a given function is needed, be sufficiently flexible to provide the diverse types of actions needed for different situations, and be able to utilize the abilities of other group members in providing the actions needed by the group.

For at least three reasons, it is usually considered necessary for the behaviors that fulfill group functions to be distributed among group members. *First,* if members do not participate, then their ideas, skills, and information are not being utilized. This hurts the group's effectiveness. *Second,* members become committed to what they help build. Members who participate become more committed to the group than do members who remain silent. *Third,* active members often become worried or annoyed about the silent members and view them as unconcerned about goal achievement. Unequal patterns of participation can create relationship problems within the group.

When you help the group achieve its goals and maintain good working relationships among members, you sometimes help yourself at the same time. Helping the group can clarify your personal identity (Who am I in this group? Where do I fit in?), fulfill personal goals (I am better off when I am a member of a successful group), increase your power and influence (How much power and influence do I have?), and build better relationships with others (How close will we get to each other? Who are my friends?).

The distributed-actions theory of leadership is one of the most concrete and direct approaches available for improving your leadership skills and for improving the effectiveness of the groups to which you belong. You can be taught the diagnostic skills and behaviors that help a group accomplish its goal and maintain effective working relationships among members. There is, however, some criticism of the approach. There are so many different actions members can take to help in goal achievement and maintaining relationships that specific ones are hard to pin down. What constitutes leadership then depends on the view of the person who is listing the leadership behaviors.

Interaction-Process Analysis

If you put five strangers together and assign them a task that requires them to cooperate, something quite remarkable but very predictable happens: The social interaction among them becomes patterned and a leadership structure emerges. One variable that is consistently related to the emergence of leadership is the amount of talking a group member does. The person who talks the most in the group is the most likely to emerge as leader (Burke, 1974; Stein & Heller, 1979). The average correlation between participation and leadership is 0.65. Group members attribute leadership qualities to certain behaviors they observe in the group: quantity of participation attributed to be a sign of motivation, involvement, willingness to share resources with the group, and seriously trying to contribute to the group's goals (Sorrentino & Boutiller, 1975).

Whether it is a work group, discussion group, learning group, or recreation group, one of the common forms this leadership structure takes is for one person to assume a **task-leadership role** that includes behaviors oriented primarily to task achievement (such as directing, summarizing, and providing ideas) and another person to assume a **social-emotional-leadership role** that includes behaviors oriented primarily to the expressive, interpersonal affairs of the group (such as alleviating frustrations, resolving tensions, and mediating conflicts).

Robert Bales (1950, 1952, 1955), in a series of studies in the late 1940s and early 1950s, was among the first to focus on task and social-emotional leadership. His work

Example of a Leader: Harriet Tubman

Harriet Tubman was born a slave about 1820 in Bucktown, Maryland. Her grandparents had been brought from Africa to America sometime after 1725. Very early in life, Harriet developed a rebellious nature, perhaps from the hard work and many beatings she endured. She was determined to be free. At age fifteen she was beaten nearly to death with a two-pound iron counterweight for helping another slave to escape. She never completely recovered, having a dent in her skull and seizures during which she would suddenly fall asleep. In 1849, Harriet escaped to Delaware and then to Pennsylvania. While working in Philadelphia, Harriet became involved with the Underground Railroad, a network of routes, guides, and hiding places that helped runaway slaves reach freedom in the northern states. As early as 1850 she began working as a guide or "conductor" for the railroad, risking her life over and over again to help others gain their freedom. She was given the name Moses for the frequency with which she conducted runaways to the North and was so successful that a reward of $40,000 was offered for her capture. She helped at least three hundred slaves escape in all. After the Fugitive Slave Law was passed in 1850, Harriet conducted escaped slaves all the way to Canada. During the Civil War she worked as a nurse, laundress, cook, and spy for the Union army in South Carolina. She spent the rest of her life working to feed and house needy blacks and to gain full freedom for them. She died at about the age of ninety-three on March 10, 1913. She embodies a leader whose actions spoke louder than words.

has been corroborated and extended by Burke (1972). The basic interaction-process theory consists of the following points:

1. When a group has a task to complete, its members engage in task-related behaviors on an unequal basis.
2. The members who are high on task behaviors tend to create some tension and hostility on the part of members who are less committed to the task.
3. There is a need for actions that help maintain effective working relationships among members.
4. Social-emotional actions are engaged in by members other than those high on task actions.
5. These differentiated roles (task and social-emotional) are stabilized and synchronized as the task and social-emotional leaders reinforce and support each other.

When the group has no task to achieve, or no commitment to achieve its assigned task, a task leader is not needed and will not appear. Correspondingly, with no commitment to a goal there is no need to maintain relationships among members, and a social-emotional leader will not evolve.

In his research Bales developed an observational instrument for identifying task and social-emotional behaviors within a small group (Figures 5.2 and 5.3). The instrument consists of several categories that are designed to allow a systematic classification of all the acts of participation in a group. As you can see in Figure 5.2, the categories are polarized: Category 1 is the opposite of category 12, 2 is the opposite of 11, and so on. The first three categories are positive emotions, the last three negative emotions. Categories 7, 8, and 9 request aid, whereas categories 4, 5, and 6 offer it.

Social-Emotional Area: Positive

1. Shows solidarity, raises others' status, gives help, rewards.

2. Shows tension release, jokes, laughs, shows satisfaction.

3. Agrees, shows passive acceptance, understands, concurs, complies.

Task Area: Neutral

4. Gives suggestions, directions, implying autonomy for others.

5. Gives opinions, evaluation, analysis; expresses feelings, wishes.

6. Gives orientation, information, repeats, clarifies, confirms.

Task Area: Neutral

7. Asks for orientation, information, repetition, confirmation.

8. Asks for opinions, evaluation, analysis, expressions of feeling.

9. Asks for suggestions, direction, possible ways of action.

Social-Emotional Area: Negative

10. Disagrees, shows passive rejection, formality, withholds help.

11. Shows tension, asks for help, withdraws, leaves the field.

12. Shows antagonism, deflates others' status, defends or asserts self.

Figure 5.2   Bales' system of categories used in observation.
Source: R. Bales, *Interaction Process Analysis* (Reading, MA: Addison-Wesley, 1950).

Bales' research indicates that positive emotions (categories 1, 2, and 3) are usually expressed more than twice as often as negative emotions (10, 11, and 12). Opinions and information are volunteered much more often (46% of all participant behaviors observed) than asked for (7%). Problem-solving groups tend to progress through three stages: orientation (What is the problem?), evaluation (How do we feel about it?), and control (What should we do about it?). As the discussion moves from the intellectual examination of the problem (the orientation phase) to evaluation and decision (the control phase), emotions are expressed more often.

Bales' observation form may be found in Figure 5.4. Why not try using it to observe a number of group meetings?

Fiedler's Situational Theory of Leadership

Social psychologist Fred Fiedler did a series of studies on leadership (1964, 1967, 1969) in many different situations and groups. Defining a leader's effectiveness in terms of the group's performance in achieving its goals, Fiedler divided leaders into those who were task oriented and those who were maintenance-oriented. He found no consistent relationship between group effectiveness and leadership behaviors, the reason being that maintenance oriented leaders were more effective in certain situations and task-oriented leaders more effective in other situations.

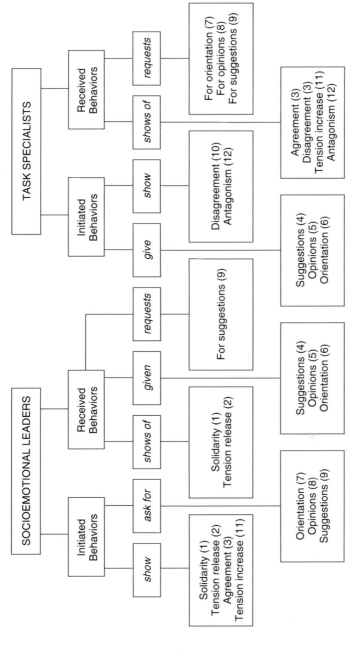

Figure 5.3 How behaviors differ for socioemotional leaders and task specialists. (Numbers in parentheses indicate category number from Bales' interaction-process analysis.)

Date ________ Group ________ Time: __________ to __________ Observer ________________________

	BEHAVIOR	Members												TOTALS
POSITIVE EMOTIONS	Shows solidarity													
	Shows tension release													
	Agrees													
TASK	Gives suggestions													
	Gives opinions													
	Gives orientation													
	Asks for orientation													
	Asks for opinions													
	Asks for suggestions													
NEGATIVE EMOTIONS	Disagrees													
	Shows tension													
	Shows antagonism													
	TOTALS													

Figure 5.4 Cumulative interaction form.

A **task-oriented leader** is effective under two sets of conditions. Under the first, he or she is on very good terms with the group members, the task is clearly structured, and the leader has a position of high authority and power. Under such conditions the group is ready to be directed and is willing to be told what to do. Under the second set of conditions, the leader is on poor terms with group members, the task is ambiguous, and he or she has a position of low authority and power. Under these conditions the leader can also be effective in taking responsibility for making decisions and directing group members. When moderately good or poor relations exist between the leader and the group members, when the leader has a position of moderate authority and power, and when the task is moderately clear, the **maintenance-oriented leader** who emphasizes member participation in decision making seems to be the most effective type of leader.

Fiedler's results imply that the distributed-functions theory of leadership needs to be modified to take into account the situational conditions influencing the impact of leadership style upon a group. There are some difficulties with this theory, however. For example, how can a person tell if the situational conditions of leader–member relations, task clarity, and leader power are high, moderate, or low? Almost all group situations fall into the moderate range; in only the most extreme cases are the sets of conditions in the high or low categories. A second difficulty is that although the theory is more complex than the outdated leadership-style theory, which held that a leader should always be democratic, it may not be complex enough. A good leader is always paying attention to the situational conditions that influence the group, modifying his or her behavior to make it effective. Moreover, leader-member relations, task clarity, and leader power may be only three of many different situational factors that group leaders should be aware of.

Exercise 5.6: The Least Preferred Co-worker Scale

Fiedler (1978) developed an indirect measure of leadership style known as the *Least Preferred Co-worker Scale* (LPC). See Figure 5.5. Think of a person with whom you can work least well. The person may be someone you work with now or someone you knew in the past. This person need not be the person you liked least well, but should be the person with whom you have had the most difficulty working to get the job done.

Your score will fall somewhere in between 16 and 128. To calculate your score, add up the numbers you have circled for each of the adjective pairs. If your score is 56 or less, then you are a low-LPC leader. The lower your score, the more task oriented you are. If your score is 63 or above, then you are a high-LPC leader. The higher your LPC score, the more "relationship oriented" you are. If your score falls between 56 and 63, then you do not fit easily into either category and may call yourself "socioindependent."

According to Fiedler (1978), people who describe their least preferred co-worker in very negative, rejecting terms are so oriented toward completing the task that it completely determines their perception of co-workers whom they have trouble working with. In effect, they say, "If I cannot work with you, if you frustrate my need to get the job done, then you cannot be any good in other respects. You are unfriendly, unpleasant, cold, and nasty." People who describe their least preferred co-workers in positive terms are relationship oriented. In effect, they say, "Even though I cannot work with you, getting the job done is not everything, and I can still see you as friendly, relaxed, and interesting."

Pleasant	: 8 7 6 5 4 3 2 1 :	Unpleasant
Friendly	: 8 7 6 5 4 3 2 1 :	Unfriendly
Rejecting	: 1 2 3 4 5 6 7 8 :	Accepting
Tense	: 1 2 3 4 5 6 7 8 :	Relaxed
Distant	: 1 2 3 4 5 6 7 8 :	Close
Cold	: 1 2 3 4 5 6 7 8 :	Warm
Supportive	: 8 7 6 5 4 3 2 1 :	Hostile
Boring	: 1 2 3 4 5 6 7 8 :	Interesting
Quarrelsome	: 1 2 3 4 5 6 7 8 :	Harmonious
Gloomy	: 1 2 3 4 5 6 7 8 :	Cheerful
Open	: 8 7 6 5 4 3 2 1 :	Guarded
Backbiting	: 1 2 3 4 5 6 7 8 :	Loyal
Untrustworthy	: 1 2 3 4 5 6 7 8 :	Trustworthy
Considerate	: 8 7 6 5 4 3 2 1 :	Inconsiderate
Nasty	: 1 2 3 4 5 6 7 8 :	Nice
Agreeable	: 8 7 6 5 4 3 2 1 :	Disagreeable
Insincere	: 1 2 3 4 5 6 7 8 :	Sincere
Kind	: 8 7 6 5 4 3 2 1 :	Unkind

Figure 5.5 The LPC Scale.
Source: F. Fiedler, "Recent Developments in Research on the Contingency Model," in L. Berkowitz (Ed.), *Group Processes* (New York: Academic Press, 1978).

Hersey and Blanchard's Theory of Situational Leadership

On the basis of studies of leadership conducted at Ohio State University, Paul Hersey and Kenneth Blanchard (1977) concluded that they can classify most of the activities of leaders into two distinct behavioral dimensions: initiation of structure (task actions) and consideration of group members (relationship of maintenance actions). They define **task behavior** as the extent to which a leader engages in one-way communication by explaining what each follower is to do as well as when, where, and how tasks are to be accomplished. They define **relationship behavior** as the extent to which a leader engages in two-way communication by providing emotional support and facilitating behaviors. According to Hersey and Blanchard, the Ohio State University studies found that some leaders focus mainly on directing task-accomplishment-related activities for their followers, whereas other leaders concentrate on providing emotional support through relationships with their followers. Still other leaders engage in both task and relationship behaviors, or in neither. Hersey and Blanchard determined that task and relationship behaviors are two separate dimensions, which can be portrayed as in Figure 5.6.

Hersey and Blanchard's situational-leadership theory assumes that any of the four combinations of leadership behaviors shown in Figure 5.6 may be ineffective or effective depending on the situation. Which combination of behaviors is appropriate depends on the level of maturity of the group. They define **maturity** as the capacity to set high but attainable goals (achievement motivation), willingness and ability to take responsi-

STYLE OF LEADER

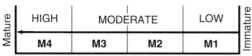

Figure 5.6   Situational leadership.
Source: P. Hersey and K. Blanchard, *Management of Organizational Behavior: Utilizing Human Resources,* 3rd ed. (Englewood Cliffs, NJ: Prentice Hall, 1977). Reprinted by permission.

bility, and the education and/or experience of group members. Maturity is determined only in relation to a specific task to be performed. On one task a member may have high maturity, on another task low maturity.

The essence of Hersey and Blanchard's theory is that when group members have low maturity in terms of accomplishing a specific task, the leader should engage in high-task and low-relationship behaviors. When members are moderately mature, the leader moves to high-task and high-relationship behaviors and then to high-relationship and low-task behaviors. When group members are highly mature in terms of accomplishing a specific task, then low-task and low-relationship behaviors are needed. Hersey and Blanchard refer to high-task/low-relationship leadership behavior as *telling,* because it is characterized by one-way communication in which the leader defines the roles of group members and tells them how, when, and where to do various tasks. As the members' experience and understanding of the task goes up, so does their task maturity. High-task/high-relationship leadership behavior is referred to as *selling,* because while providing clear direction as to role responsibilities the leader also attempts through two-way communication and socioemotional support to get the group members to psychologically buy into decisions that have to be made. As group members' commitment to the task increases, so does their maturity. Low-task/high-relationship leadership behavior is referred to as *participating,* because the leader and group members share in decision making through two-way communication and considerable facilitating behavior from the leader, because the group members have the ability and knowledge to complete the task. Finally, low-task/low-relationship leadership behavior is referred to as *delegating,* because the leader allows group members considerable autonomy in completing the task, because they are both willing and able to take responsibility for directing their own task behavior.

ORGANIZATIONAL LEADERSHIP

Whenever anyone asks me (how to be a leader) I tell them I have the secret to success in life. The secret to success is to stay in love. Staying in love gives you the fire to really ignite other people, to see inside other people, to have a greater desire to get things done than other people. A person who is not in love doesn't really feel the kind of excitement that helps them to get ahead and lead others and to achieve. I don't know any other fire, any other thing in life that is more exhilarating and is more positive a feeling than love is.

Army Major General John H. Stanford (Kouzes & Posner, 1987)

On July 15, 1982, Don Bennett, a Seattle businessman, was the first amputee ever to climb Mount Rainier (reported by Kouzes & Posner, 1987). He climbed 14,410 feet on one leg and two crutches. It took him five days. When asked to state the most important lesson he learned from doing so, without hesitation he said, "You can't do it alone."

What did he mean? There were many ways in which others helped him achieve his goal, including his daughter. During one very difficult trek across an ice field in Don Bennett's hop to the top of Mount Rainer, his daughter stayed by his side for four hours and with each new hop told him, "You can do it, Dad. You're the best dad in the world. You can do it, Dad." There was no way Bennett would quit hopping to the top with his daughter yelling words of love and encouragement in his ear. His daughter's encouragement kept him going, strengthening his commitment to make it to the top. The team and the organization are similar. With members of their cooperative group cheering them on, members amaze themselves and their superiors with what they can achieve. With members of their team cheering them on, members amaze themselves and their colleagues with what they can accomplish.

There is growth and decline. Staying the same is not an option. Growth takes leadership, not management. There is a difference. Some individuals manage, some individuals lead. The difference may be found in the root meanings of *lead* and *manage* (Kouzes & Posner, 1987). The root origin of *lead* is a word meaning "to go," denoting travel from one place to another. Leaders are those who "go first," pioneering unexplored territory and showing others the direction they should take. By comparison, the root origin of *manage* is a word meaning "hand." Managing seems to connote "handling" things by controlling and maintaining the status quo. Managers tend to handle things, leaders tend to get us going somewhere. **The unique role of the leader is to take us on journeys to places we have never been before.**

The metaphor of the journey may be the most appropriate one for discussing the tasks of leaders. Individuals can manage what now exists, the status quo, or take staff members on a journey to increase their expertise and create a new and better organization.

Perhaps more than anything else, leadership is about the creation of a new way of life within organizations. Leadership is inextricably connected with the process of innovation, of bringing new ideas, methods, or solutions into use. Leaders are agents of change. Change requires leadership, a "prime mover" to push for implementation of strategic decisions. The leader highlights the challenges the organization faces and makes them shared challenges for the staff. **Leaders create a "family" within which staff members care deeply about each other and the mutual vision they are trying to actualize.** Managers get other people to do, but leaders get other people to *want* to do.

There are a series of leadership issues that must be faced in order to maximize the productivity of the organization (Kouzes & Posner, 1987; Johnson & Johnson, 1994):

1. How to **challenge the status quo** of the traditional competitive and individualistic models of management.
2. How to **inspire a clear mutual vision** of what the organization should and could be, a clear mission that all members are committed to achieving, and a set of goals that guide members' efforts.
3. How to **empower members through cooperative teamwork.** Doing so enables each individual member to take action to increase his or her expertise and effectiveness, both technically and interpersonally.
4. How to **lead by example** by (a) using cooperative team procedures and (b) taking risks to increase expertise.
5. How to **encourage the heart** of members to persist and keep striving to improve their technical and interpersonal expertise.

Challenging the Status Quo

Organizations (and groups) are sites for an inevitable and external conflict. On one side are the forces of maintenance and continuity (i.e., the status quo), which strive to create and sustain the use of orderly and predictable procedures. Opposing them are the forces of innovation and discontinuity, which seek to alter established practices. Both seek the same goal of team and organizational productivity. Both are needed. The creative tension between the two is what powers considered and thoughtful development and change.

These same two forces operate within the individual member. Group members will experience the conflict between the security of the past and the satisfactions of growth in expertise and accomplishment. The status quo side wants to continue what he or she has done in the past. The enhanced expertise side strives for growth, change, and increased competence. Leaving the status quo and risking one's current success against the potential of being even better in the future requires courage.

In challenging the status quo, leaders highlight that **if members are not working to increase their expertise, they are losing their expertise.** Expertise is a process, not an end product. Any person or organization is constantly changing. If expertise is not growing, then it is declining. The minute a person believes he or she is an expert and stops trying to learn more, then that person is losing his or her expertise. **Leaders must lead members towards enhanced expertise, not manage for bureaucratic control. The clearest and most direct challenge to traditional competitive and individualistic actions is the adoption of cooperative teams within the organization.** The organization needs to be transformed into an interlocking network of cooperative teams in order to increase productivity, promote more supportive and committed relationships, and increase members' psychological adjustment and self-esteem.

Creating a Shared Vision

The second leadership responsibility is to create a joint vision of what the team or organization should and could be, a clear mission that all members are committed to achieving, and a set of goals that guide members' efforts. To do so, a leader must:

1. Have a vision/dream of what the organization could be.
2. Communicate that vision with commitment and enthusiasm.

3. Make it a *shared* vision that staff members adopt as their own.
4. Make it a rational vision based on theory and research and sound implementation procedures.

Leaders enthusiastically and frequently communicate the dream of the team and the organization being places where individuals share, help, encourage, and support each other's efforts to achieve and succeed. Places where *we* dominates *me*. Where working together to get the job done creates caring and committed relationships that propel people forward in their mutual search for excellence.

Leaders inspire a shared vision. It is the common vision that creates a basic sense of "sink or swim together" (i.e., positive interdependence) among members. Leaders breathe life into the hopes and dreams of others and enable them to see the exciting possibilities the future holds by striving for a common purpose. **The vision and its advocacy, furthermore, has to be rational.** The new practices have to be backed up with a knowledge of the relevant research and theory. A person with no followers is *not* a leader, and people will not become followers until they accept a vision as their own. It is the long-term promise of achieving something worthwhile and meaningful that powers an individual's drive toward greater expertise. **You cannot command commitment, you can only inspire it!**

Empowering Members Through Cooperative Teams

The most important of all the five leadership practices is empowering individuals by organizing them into cooperative teams. To be effective a cooperative team must be carefully structured to include positive interdependence, face-to-face promotive interaction, individual accountability, social skills, and group processing (Johnson, Johnson, & Holubec, 1998a, 1998b).

The one-word test to detect whether someone is on the road to becoming a leader is *we*. Leaders do not achieve success by themselves. It is not *my* personal best leaders inspire, it is *our* personal best. The most important thing a leader can do is to organize members so that they work cooperatively with each other, for at least two reasons.

The first is to promote committed and caring relationships among organization members. This is achieved through a "team" approach. Having members work as part of cooperative teams fosters committed and caring relationships. Cooperative efforts result in trust, open communication, and interpersonal support, all crucial ingredients for productivity. When trust is broken by competition, harsh feelings, criticism, negative comments, and disrespect, productivity suffers.

The second is to empower staff members through teamwork. The "real world" involves working with and through many different people to get the job done. By organizing members into cooperative teams, leaders increase members' confidence that if they exert effort, they will be successful. Teams empower their members to act by making them feel strong, capable, and committed. Being part of a team enables members to innovate, experiment, take risks, and grow professionally.

Leading by Example

One does not improve through argument but through examples. . . . Be what you wish to make others become. Make yourself, not your words, a sermon.

Henri Frederic Amiel

To provide leadership, you will need to model (a) using cooperative procedures and (b) taking risks to increase your technical and interpersonal expertise. You model the way by practicing what you are preaching. **You lead by example.** To do so, you must be clear about your belief in cooperative efforts, you must be able to speak coherently about your vision and values, and your actions must be congruent with your words. **You begin leadership by becoming a role model that exemplifies the organizational and leadership values you believe are important.** You show your priorities through living your values.

One thing you can count on for certain. **Every exceptional leader is a learner.** The self-confidence required to lead comes from trying, failing, learning from mistakes, and trying again. We are all involved in a continuous process of increasing our technical and interpersonal expertise. From making your own journey to actualize your vision, you model the way for others. Remember, it is not the cry, but the flight of the wild duck that leads the flock to fly and follow (a Chinese proverb).

Encouraging the Heart of Staff Members

Love 'em and lead 'em.

Major General John H. Stanford,
   Commander, U.S. Army

Leaders are vigilant about the little things that make a big difference. Each spring at Verstec, annual bonuses are given to about 2,000 nonmanagerial personnel (Kouzes & Posner, 1987). In a recent year, the president arrived at the celebration dressed in a satin costume, riding atop an elephant, and accompanied by the Stanford Marching Band. The president frequently says, "If you are going to give someone a check, don't just mail it. Have a celebration."

This example may seem extreme. It usually does not take a marching band and an elephant to make organizational members feel appreciated. **What makes a difference to each individual staff member is to know that his or her successes are perceived, recognized, and celebrated.** Leaders search out "good news" opportunities and orchestrate celebrations. Striving for increased technical and interpersonal expertise is an arduous and long-term enterprise. Members become exhausted, frustrated, and disenchanted.

They often are tempted to give up. **Leaders must inspire members to continue the journey by encouraging the heart** (Kouzes & Posner, 1987). Leaders inspire staff members by giving them the courage and hope to continue the quest. This does not require elephants and marching bands (although they are not a bad idea). What it does require is:

1. The recognition of individual contributions to the common vision.
2. Frequent group celebrations of individual and joint accomplishments.

Members do not start the day with a desire to fail. It is the leader's job to show them that they can succeed. **The primary tools for doing so are individual recognition and group celebration.** A leader becomes a master of celebration. Leaders should give out stickers, T-shirts, buttons, and every other conceivable award when members achieve a milestone. One leader sends out cards that have "I heard something good about you" printed at the top. **Leaders find ways to celebrate accomplishments.** If you do not show your appreciation to your members, they are going to stop caring, and then, in essence, you are going to find yourself out of business.

To give individual recognition and have a group celebration requires a cooperative organizational structure. In competitions, to declare one person a winner is to declare all others losers. Group celebrations do not take place in competitive/individualistic organizations. In such environments, praise may be perceived to be phony or satirical and recognition may be the source of embarrassment and anxiety about future retaliation by colleagues. **Within cooperative enterprises, however, genuine acts of caring draw people together and forward. Love of their work and each other is what inspires many members to commit more and more of their energy to their jobs.** Establishing a cooperative structure and encouraging the development of caring and committed relationships among members may just be the best-kept secret of exemplary leadership.

Exercise 5.7: The Furniture Factory

The purpose of this exercise is to give participants an opportunity to observe task-leadership and maintenance-leadership actions within a decision-making group. The procedure is as follows:

1. The class divides into groups of seven. Two members should volunteer to be observers. The task of the observers is to record the frequency of task and maintenance actions within the group. The observation sheets to be used are on page 216.
2. The task of each group is to read and discuss the problem description that follows and rank the five possible solutions on the basis of how effective they would be in ensuring the least resistance to the proposed changes in work procedures. Each member of the group must be willing to sign the group answer sheet, indicating that he or she agrees with the group's ranking and can explain the rationale for ranking the possible solutions in the order that the group did so.
3. After deciding how the possible solutions are to be ranked, members discuss the nature of leadership within the group. The following questions may be used as a starter:
   a. What leadership actions were present and absent in the group?
   b. What leadership actions did each member engage in?
   c. How do the members feel about their participation in the group?

    d. How might the task effectiveness of the group be improved?

    e. How might the relationships among group members be improved?

4. Each group shares its conclusions with the class.

5. The ranking of possible solutions by experts on organizational change appears on page 581.

PROBLEM DESCRIPTION: FURNITURE FACTORY EXERCISE

Lazy-Days Manufacturing Company is located in a small northern town. This small, family-owned business manufactures school furniture. Because of the opportunities for work available in a larger town located about fifty miles away, Lazy-Days must attract whomever it can and train them to do the job. Most of the four hundred workers are women and young people just out of high school. Lazy-Days also hires some physically and mentally disabled adults as part of a special community program.

    Until now, Lazy-Days has manufactured school furniture, but, because of a tightening of the economy, management has realized a dire need to diversify its manufacturing capabilities. After a study of the market, the decision was made to add showroom display cases as a new product. If well made, this line will bring increased income and security to Lazy-Days Manufacturing.

    Because of the difficulties in getting new workers, particularly trained ones, Lazy-Days would like to divert current personnel to the new jobs. However, the current workers are very set in their ways and are highly resistant to and suspicious of changes at work. The last time changes were needed, workers demanded higher wages, threatened to unionize, and a few key people quit. If the new line is successful, Lazy-Days could raise wages, but this is not possible under current conditions that require using available income to help purchase the new equipment and finance necessary remodeling to accommodate the new equipment.

    Michael Days, president of Lazy-Days, has listed several ways of approaching the workers about the needed changes. He has asked you to decide which alternative to use. As a group, rank these alternatives from 1 to 5 in terms of their effectiveness in bringing about the desired changes with the least resistance from the workers. Number 1 would be the most effective, 2 the next most effective, and so on through 5, the least effective. Remember, your decision can make the difference between the success or failure of Lazy-Days Manufacturing Company.

_____ a. Mr. Days would send a written memo to all employees that would tell them about the needed changes. He would then make the changes and lay off any employees who did not comply with the changes in their jobs.

_____ b. Mr. Days would meet with small groups of employees. He would explain the need for the changes and the reasoning behind the changes. He would then ask everyone to help in designing and implementing the new jobs.

_____ c. Mr. Days would meet with large groups of his employees. He would enthusiastically describe the needed changes and present multicolored charts and filmclips to make his points dramatically and forcefully. He would then implement the changes.

_____ d. Mr. Days would send a written memo to all employees that would explain the need for the changes and ask the employees to go along with the changes for the good of the company.

_____ e. Mr. Days would meet with large groups of his employees. He would explain the need for the changes and the reasoning behind the changes. He would then have the employees select representatives to work with him in designing and implementing the new jobs.

Observation Sheet for Task Actions

Actions	Group Members				
Information and opinion giver					
Information and opinion seeker					
Direction and role definer					
Summarizer					
Energizer					
Comprehension checker					

Observation Sheet for Maintenance Actions

Actions	Group Members				
Encourager of participation					
Communication facilitator					
Tension reliever					
Process observer					
Interpersonal problem solver					
Supporter and praiser					

Observation Sheet for Task and Maintenance Actions

Actions	Group Members				
Information and opinion giver					
Information and opinion seeker					
Direction and role definer					
Summarizer					
Energizer					
Comprehension checker					
Encourager of participation					
Communication facilitator					
Tension reliever					
Process observer					
Interpersonal problem solver					
Supporter and praiser					

Leaping the Abyss of Failure

When you look into the abyss, the abyss is looking into you.

Nietzsche

Leaders give organizational members the courage they need to take the risks necessary to increase technical and interpersonal expertise. Members can choose to play it safe in the short run by traveling on the path of the status quo, thereby facing guaranteed long-term failure through obsolescence, atrophy, and burnout. Adherents to the status quo slowly and gradually descend into the abyss of failure. They are descending even though they may not always realize it. Managers organize the easy walk downward into the abyss of failure along the path of the status quo. Leaders encourage and inspire members to take the difficult leaps toward increase technical and interpersonal competence. They take a leap over the abyss of failure to reach enhanced expertise. Sometimes their leap falls short and they fail. Sometimes they soar high above the abyss to land safely on the other side. Leaders encourage the risks of short-term failure in order to enhance long-term productivity.

WHAT IF YOU DO NOT WANT TO BE A LEADER?

If you follow the following rules carefully, you can be guaranteed never to be a leader:

1. Be absent from group meetings as frequently as possible.
2. When you do attend, contribute nothing.
3. If you do participate, come on strong early in the discussion. Demonstrate your knowledge of everything, including your extensive vocabulary of big words and technical jargon.
4. Indicate that you will do only what you have to and nothing more.
5. Read the paper or knit during meetings.

Exercise 5.8: Tower Building

This exercise is aimed at providing participants with an opportunity to observe leadership behavior in a situation of intergroup competition in which verbal communication is not allowed. Several groups are needed for this exercise, all of which should have at least seven members. The task of each group is to build a tower from supplied materials. A large room is needed so that the groups can work separately (but within sight of one another). The time needed to complete the exercise is approximately one hour. The procedure is as follows:

1. Two judges are selected to determine which tower is (a) the highest, (b) the strongest, (c) the most beautiful, and (d) the cleverest.
2. The class forms groups of at least seven members.
3. Each group selects two of its members to observe leadership in the group. The observers (using the observation sheets on page 216) are to note:
   a. How the group organizes for work.
   b. How decisions are made by the group.
   c. Whether participation and influence is distributed throughout the group, or whether a few members dominate.

d. What task and maintenance actions are needed to improve the functioning of the group.

e. How the group reacts to winning or losing.

4. Each group receives a box of supplies containing construction paper, newsprint, tape, magazines, crayons, pipe cleaners, scissors, and glue.

5. The groups have twenty minutes to build their towers. This is a *nonverbal exercise: No talking among group members or between groups is allowed.*

6. During the twenty minutes the judges meet to decide how they will evaluate the towers on the basis of the four criteria given. At the end of the twenty minutes the judges decide which tower wins and award a box of candy (provided by the person conducting the exercise) to the winning group.

7. The groups meet with their observers and discuss the exercise. All impressions concerning how the group functioned and what leadership patterns were present and absent should be presented and reviewed.

Exercise 5.9: Selecting A City

The purposes of this exercise are for participants to develop through role playing an understanding of the distributed-actions theory of leadership and to observe task and maintenance actions in a decision-making group. Instructions for the coordinator are as follows:

1. Introduce the exercise by stating the objectives. Then explain the following leadership actions (see page 199 for definitions):

   a. Information and opinion giver
   b. Information and opinion seeker
   c. Direction and role definer
   d. Summarizer
   e. Encourager of participation
   f. Communication facilitator
   g. Process observer
   h. Tension reliever

2. Form heterogeneous groups of eight. Two members from each group should volunteer to be observers.

3. Explain the task-behavior and maintenance-behavior observation form to the observers and instruct them to look for:

   a. What leadership actions are present and absent in the group.
   b. How well participation is distributed among group members.
   c. What specific leadership actions each group member provides.

4. Place a large envelope containing role-playing instruction envelopes in the center of each group; give no further instructions or information.

5. After the exercise has been completed, instruct each group to discuss its experience, using the following questions as starters.

   a. What leadership actions was each member supposed to role play, and how were they carried out?
   b. What leadership actions were present and absent in the group decision making, and what were the consequences of the presence or absence of these actions?
   c. What were the feelings and reactions of the group members?
   d. What conclusions about leadership and group functioning can be drawn from this exercise?

6. Have each group share its conclusions with the class.

ENVELOPE INSTRUCTIONS

Instructions written on the large envelope, which contains all other envelopes:

> Enclosed you will find three envelopes containing directions for the phases of this group session. You are to open the first one (labeled Envelope I) at once. Later instructions will tell you when to open the second (Envelope II) and third (Envelope III).

Envelope I contains the following directions:

Directions for Envelope I:

> Time allowed: Fifteen minutes
>
> Special instructions: Each member is to take one of the enclosed envelopes and follow the individual role-playing instructions contained in it.
>
> Task: The group is to select a city.
>
> DO NOT LET ANYONE ELSE SEE *YOUR* INSTRUCTIONS!
>
> (After fifteen minutes, go on to the next envelope.)

Envelope II contains the following directions:

Directions for Envelope II:

> Time allowed: Five minutes
>
> Task: You are to choose a group chairperson.
>
> (After five minutes go on to the next envelope.)

Envelope III contains the following directions:

Directions for Envelope III:

> Time allowed: Ten minutes
>
> Task: You are to evaluate the first phase of this group session.

Special instructions for the second phase: The newly selected chairperson will lead a discussion on the roles and actions of group members in the process of decision making and their feelings and reactions to that process. The discussion should begin with the report of the observers.

> (After ten minutes return the directions to their respective envelopes and prepare for a general discussion of the exercise.)

ROLE-PLAYING INSTRUCTION ENVELOPES FOR PHASE I

Here are the contents of the six individual instruction envelopes to be used in the first phase of the exercise. Each envelope contains an assigned leadership action and a position concerning which city to select. Two of the envelopes also contain special knowledge concerning the selection process.

1. *Leadership Action:* Direction and Role Definer
   Position: Introduce and support Albuquerque. Oppose San Diego.
2. *Leadership Action:* Encourager of Participation
   Position: Introduce and support San Diego. Oppose Albuquerque.
   Special Knowledge: The group is going to select a chairperson later in the exercise. You are to conduct yourself in such a manner that they will select you.
3. *Leadership Action:* Information and Opinion Seeker
   Position: Introduce and support New York City.

4. *Leadership Action:* Summarizer and Process Observer
   Position: Oppose New York City.
5. *Leadership Action:* Communication Facilitator
   Position: When there seems to be a clear polarity in the discussion, suggest a compromise city, such as Minneapolis or Frameswitch, Texas.
6. *Leadership Action:* Tension Reliever
   Position: Support San Diego.
   Special Knowledge: The group is going to select a chairperson later in the exercise. You are to conduct yourself in such a manner that they will select you.
7. (if needed) *Leadership Action:* Any
   Position: Any

Selecting a City Exercise Observation Sheet

	Group Members				
Actions					
Information and opinion giver					
Information and opinion seeker					
Direction and role definer					
Summarizer					
Encourager of participation					
Communication facilitator					
Process observer					
Tension reliever					

Exercise 5.10: *Are Groups Run by Great Persons?*

The purpose of this exercise is to compare two opposing theories of leadership: the great-person theory and the interaction-process-analysis theory. According to the great-person theory, the leader is the best-liked member of the group and is perceived as being the most important member for achieving the group's goals. The interaction-process-analysis theory suggests that task actions and maintenance actions are ordinarily executed by different persons, so that a group will usually have two complementary leaders. The procedure for the exercise is as follows:

1. Each participant locates a group that has worked together for some time and has a stable group structure. The group should be small enough so that every member knows every other member well enough to evaluate them on likability and task ability.
2. Give every member of the group a questionnaire consisting of two items:
   a. Rank the members from best to worst at helping the group complete its tasks.
   b. Rank the members of the group from most to least likable.
3. Construct two sociometric matrices from the group. The task-ability matrix is constructed by:
   a. Listing the names of the group members down the left-hand side of the matrix and also across the top of the matrix.
   b. Listing the ranks given by each group member to all other members on task ability in the rows. Each column then represents the rankings received for one member by all the other members of the group.
   c. Compute the mean rank of each member.

4. Repeat this process for the likability rankings.
5. By graphing the mean ranking of the members on the two dimensions (see Figure 5.7), the answer to which theory holds in that group can be determined. If the two sets of rankings correspond, the graph should resemble a straight line, and the great-person theory of leadership is confirmed. If any pattern other than a straight line results, the theory of two complementary leaders or another theory of leadership is supported.
6. The class divides into groups of five. Share with each other your graphs. Discuss the following questions:
   a. How do the graphs of the different groups compare with one another?
   b. What overall conclusions concerning group leadership can be made from the five graphs?
   c. What have you learned about leadership by analyzing and comparing the leadership patterns of the five groups?

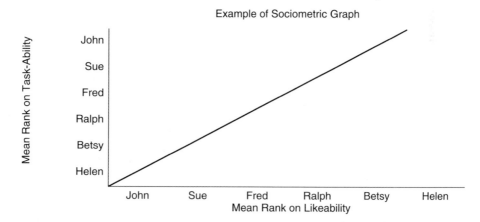

Figure 5.7 Sociometric matrix and graph.

Exercise 5.11: Hollow Square

The Hollow Square Exercise is a problem-solving situation in which you can observe leadership functions. You can see the processes of group planning, the problems of communication between a planning group and an implementing group, and the problems with which an implementing group must cope when carrying out a plan it did not make itself, all of which require effective leadership behavior. The specific objectives for the exercise are to provide a problem-solving task in which you can observe leadership behavior, to increase your awareness of the problems involved in using a formal hierarchy in group problem solving, and to give you practice in observing groups and in giving the group feedback on your observations.

The exercise is carried out in clusters of ten to twelve persons. Each cluster is divided into three subgroups: four persons are planners, four are implementers, and the rest observers. The planners decide how they will instruct the implementers to do a task, the implementers carry through the task as best they can, and the observers watch the process of both groups in the two phases. Here is the specific procedure for the coordinator of the exercise:

1. Tell the participants the objectives of the exercise and divide them into four-person planning teams, four-person implementing teams, and observers. Each team goes to a separate room or different parts of a large room (out of earshot) to await instructions.
2. Hand out the appropriate instruction sheets to each team. Give them adequate time to read them, then review them with each team. The observers should be fully briefed first, the planners next, and the implementers last.
3. The planners are given the general diagram sheet and the pieces of the puzzle and are instructed to begin phase I. Each planner is given four pieces of the puzzle. The exact distribution of the pieces is not crucial, but they should not have any labels marked on them. Phase I lasts forty-five minutes. All information the planners need to know is on their briefing sheet. The answer to how the puzzle fits together is on page 581.
4. At the end of phase I the planning team gives the implementing team its instructions. The planners are then prohibited from giving any further help; they must remain silent and uninvolved as the implementing team works.
5. Implementers are to finish the task, phase II, according to their instructions, taking as much time as necessary.
6. When the task is completed a discussion is held involving all the members of each cluster. This discussion is to include reports from the observers, planners, and implementers, and a comparison of similarities between the exercise and other organizational and group experiences of the members. Questions for the discussion should include:
   a. What leadership functions were present and absent in the planning and implementing teams? What were the consequences of the functions being present or absent?
   b. What leadership functions were needed for each type of activity?
   c. How could the functioning of each team have been improved?
   d. Were the leadership functions distributed among all the team members? Was participation and influence evenly distributed throughout the team?
   e. How was communication between the planning and implementing teams handled? How could it have been improved?
   f. What did it feel like to wait for the planners' instructions, and what did it feel like to watch the implementers carry them out?
7. The major points of the discussion should be summarized with an emphasis placed upon the conclusions about the leadership functions being present, absent, and dis-

tributed within the teams. Other types of learning that typically take place during the exercise are

a. Planners often place limitations on team behavior that do not appear in the instructions, thereby making their task harder. They could, for example, ask the implementing team to observe their planning meeting.

b. There is considerable frustration in planning something that others will carry out without yourself being involved. The commitment to implement a plan is usually built through the planning process, and when the planners cannot put the plan into effect they often experience frustration.

c. Planning is so interesting and absorbing that planners can forget what their implementing team is experiencing. Implementers can become anxious because they do not know what the task will be, though this concern does not usually enter the minds of the planners.

d. Planners often fail to use all the resources at their disposal to solve the problem, such as getting the silent members of the planning team to participate.

e. Planners can spend so much time planning the task that they do not allow enough time to communicate their plans adequately to the implementers, which results in wasting much of their effort.

f. In communicating their plan to the implementing team, the planning team often does not take into account the implementers' anxieties, their needs for being physically comfortable, and so on. Their preoccupation with giving information under pressure blinds them to the needs of the members of the implementing team, which reduces the effectiveness of the communication.

g. Implementers usually develop some feelings of antagonism or hostility toward their planners while they are waiting for their instructions. This antagonism increases if they are given complex instructions in a short amount of time and left confused as they take responsibility for finishing the task.

INSTRUCTION SHEET FOR OBSERVERS

You will be observing a situation in which a planning team decides how to solve a problem and gives instructions to an implementing team. The problem consists of assembling sixteen flat pieces into a square containing an empty square in its middle. The planning team is supplied with a general diagram of the assembled pieces. The planners are *not* allowed to put the puzzle together themselves; they are to instruct the implementing team on how to assemble the pieces in minimum time. You will be silent observers throughout the process. Half of you should observe the planners throughout the entire exercise and half of you should observe the implementers. Observation sheets focusing upon task and maintenance leadership behaviors are provided to help you observe. Make sure you understand the behavioral roles before you begin. Some suggestions for observers are:

1. Each observer should watch the general patterns of leadership behavior.
2. During phase I, consider the following questions:
   a. What kinds of behavior block or help the process?
   b. Are the team members participating equally?
   c. How does the planning team divide its time between planning and instructing?
   d. What group functions are not provided by the group members?
3. During the instructing process, note these behavioral questions:
   a. At the beginning of the instruction, how do the planners orient the implementers to their task?

b. What assumptions made by the planning team are not communicated to the implementing team?

c. How effective are the instructions?

d. Does the implementing team appear to feel free to ask questions of the planners?

e. What leadership functions are present and absent?

4. During the assembling period, seek answers to the following questions:

a. How does the implementing team show that instructions were clearly understood or misunderstood?

b. What nonverbal reactions do planning team members show as they watch their plans being implemented or distorted?

c. What leadership functions are present and absent?

5. You should each have two copies of the observation sheets, one for phase I and one for phase II.

INSTRUCTION SHEET FOR PLANNERS

Each of you will be given a packet containing four pieces of a puzzle. When all the pieces from all four packets are properly assembled, they will form a large square containing an empty place in the middle. A sheet bearing a diagram of the completed puzzle is provided for your team. Your task is to:

1. Plan how the sixteen pieces distributed among you can be assembled to solve the puzzle.

2. Decide on a plan for instructing your implementing team on how to carry out your plan for putting the puzzle together.

3. Call the implementing team and begin instructing them at any time during the next forty minutes.

4. Give them at least five minutes of instructions; the implementing team must begin assembling the puzzle forty-five minutes from now.

Before you begin, read these rules

1. During planning

a. Keep the pieces from your packet in front of you at all times.

b. Do not touch the pieces nor trade any with other persons, either now or during the instruction period.

c. Do not assemble the square; that is the implementers' job.

d. Do not mark any of the pieces.

2. During instruction

a. Give all instructions in words. Do not show the diagram to the implementers; hide it. Do not draw any diagrams yourselves, either on paper or in the air with gestures. You may give your instructions orally or on paper.

b. The implementing team must not move the pieces until the signal is given to start phase II.

c. Do not show any diagram to the implementers.

d. After the signal is given for the assembly to begin, you may not give any further instructions; stand back and observe. You may not touch the pieces or in any way join in the implementers' work.

INSTRUCTION SHEET FOR IMPLEMENTERS

1. Your team will have the responsibility of carrying out a task in accordance with instructions given you by your planning team.

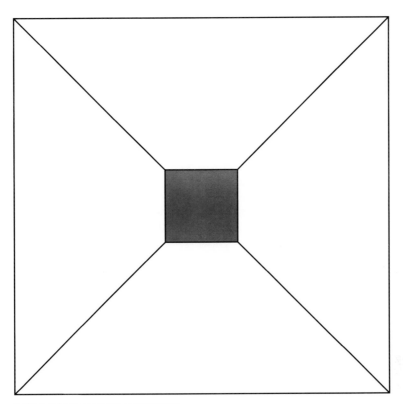

HOLLOW SQUARE PATTERN

2. Your task will begin forty minutes from now.
3. Your planning team may call you in for instruction at any time during the next forty minutes.
4. If the planning team does not call you during the next forty minutes, you must report to it on your own at the end of that time.
5. You may send notes to the planners and they may send notes in reply.
6. Once you have begun the task of assembling the puzzle, your planning team will not be allowed to give you any further instructions. Finish the assigned task as quickly as possible.
7. While you wait for a call from your planning team, do the following:
   a. Individually, write on a piece of paper the concerns you feel while waiting for instructions.
   b. As a group, think of anything you can that might help you follow instructions or keep you from doing so. Write actions that will help you on one sheet of paper and those that will hinder you on another.
   c. Make notes on how the four of you can organize as a team to receive and follow the instructions.
   d. Keep handy the sheets on which you have written these notes. You may find them useful during the discussion that takes place after you have completed the task.

Exercise 5.12: Other Leadership Exercises

1. An exercise for an ongoing group is to place the task and maintenance functions singly on 3 × 5-inch cards, shuffle the cards, and deal each member one or two of them face down. During a meeting of the group, each member then practices the task or maintenance function on the card he or she received. There must be at least two observers. After the meeting the group discusses which functions different members fulfilled and which ones they were trying to fulfill.
2. The class forms groups of six. Each group chooses a leader and then analyzes why it selected that person.
3. Members lie on the floor with their heads toward the center of the group and begin a group fantasy about what the perfect leader for this group would have to be like. When the fantasy is over the group reviews the experience.
4. Working as a group, members paint or draw a picture of the perfect leader for their group. Members then discuss both the process of making the picture and the picture itself.

Exercise 5.13: Your Leadership Behavior

Now that you have completed some or all of the exercises in this chapter and have read some or all of the information presented, it may be helpful for you again to take stock of your leadership behavior. Here is a procedure for doing so.

1. Describe the task and maintenance actions in which you usually engage.
2. Describe the task and maintenance actions you would like to practice and become better at.
3. Ask other members of your group to describe your usual task and maintenance actions and help you decide which ones would be helpful for you to practice.
4. Plan how you can practice being a process observer in order to determine which task and maintenance actions would be most helpful for the group to focus on.
5. Plan how you can encourage other group members to engage in needed task and maintenance actions.

Exercise 5.14: Why I Am a Leader!

Working individually, rank the five theories of leadership from:

a. Most difficult to least difficult to implement.
b. First choice to last choice for your personal plan to improve your leadership abilities.

Form a group of four members. Working cooperatively, rank the five theories, reaching consensus as to (a) the difficulty to implement and (b) the group's choice to improve members' leadership abilities.

Difficulty	Theory	My Personal Plan
____	I plan to be genetically superior to most other people. They will realize I was born to lead and they were born to follow me.	____
____	I plan to do things with such great style that I will be the leader of any group to which I belong.	____
____	I plan to know how to influence people so skillfully that they will gladly follow me.	____
____	I plan to be appointed or elected leader of every group to which I belong.	____
____	I plan to learn the goal and relationship skills required for groups to function effectively.	____

SUMMARY

Small group leadership may be defined in a variety of ways. It has been defined as a set of traits, a personal style, the ability to influence others, a role in an authority hierarchy, or the situational fulfillment of functions necessary for achieving the group's goals and maintaining effective working relationships among members. Organizational leadership involves a process of challenging the status quo, inspiring a mutual vision, empowering members through teams, leading by example, and encouraging the heart to persist.

The third guideline for creating an effective group is to ensure leadership and participation are distributed among all group members. All members are responsible for providing leadership. The equalization of participation and leadership makes certain that all members are involved in the group's work, committed to implementing the group's decisions, and satisfied with their membership. It also (a) assures that the resources of every member are fully utilized and (b) increases the cohesiveness of the group.

ANSWERS

Page 199: 1. c; 2. g; 3. j; 4. b; 5. i; 6. h; 7. f, 8. a; 9. 1; 10. e; 11. k; 12. d.
Page 200: 1. e; 2. k; 3. j; 4. c; 5. h; 6. a; 7. 1; 8. i; 9. b; 10. f; 11. d; 12. g.

6 *Using Power*

Basic Concepts to Be Covered in This Chapter

In this chapter a number of concepts are defined and discussed. The major ones are listed below. Divide into pairs, define each concept (noting the page on which it is defined and discussed), making sure that both you and your partner understand the meaning of each concept. Then join with another pair to make a group of four. Compare the answers of the two pairs. If there is disagreement, look up the concept in the chapter and clarify it until all members agree on and understand the definition.

Concepts

1. Power
2. Dynamic-interdependence approach to power
3. Trait-factor approach to power
4. Credibility
5. Attractiveness
6. Forewarning
7. Innovation
8. Reward power
9. Coercive power
10. Legitimate power
11. Referent power
12. Expert power
13. Informational power
14. Outcome dependence
15. Information dependence
16. Resistance
17. Manipulation
18. Rule of self-direction

Exercise 6.1: Is Power a Personal or Relationship Attribute?

There has been some controversy over whether power is an attribute of a person or an aspect of a relationship between two or more persons. The purpose of this exercise is to structure a critical discussion of the issue. The procedure is as follows:

1. **Assignment of Positions:** The class forms groups of four. Each group is ultimately to write a report summarizing its position:

   Position A: Power is a personal attribute. Some people are naturally born to wield power (and some are not). Because of their innate personality and makeup, they are able to influence others and rise to positions of power.

   Position B: Power is an attribute of a relationship. For power to exist, there must be both an influencer and an influencee. As circumstances and situations change, the relationship changes and power changes.

   The report is to contain the group's overall conclusions and the facts and rationale supporting its position. The supporting facts and rationale may be obtained from this chapter, the entire book, and outside reading.

2. **Preparation Pairs:** Each group divides into pairs. One pair is assigned Position A (power is a personal attribute) and the other pair is assigned position B (power is an attribute of a relationship). Each pair reviews the supporting sections of this chapter, the procedure for the exercise, and the guidelines for constructive controversy (pp. 330). The pair members prepare a persuasive "best case" rationale for their assigned position that includes as many facts and research findings as possible. Ten minutes are allowed for this phase.

3. **Presentations:** One member of each pair changes chairs. A "personal attribute" person should be seated with a "relationship attribute" person. The "personal attribute" person has up to three minutes to present the best case possible for the position, being as forceful and persuasive as possible. The "relationship attribute" person takes notes and asks for clarification of anything that is not fully understood. The "relationship attribute" person then presents.

4. **Open Discussion** (Refute and Rebut): There is an open discussion of whether power is a personal attribute or an aspect of a relationship. Each side presents as many facts and research findings as it can to support its point of view. Members listen critically to the opposing position and ask for supporting facts for any conclusions made by the opponent. Participants should ensure that all the facts supporting both sides are brought out and discussed. The guidelines for constructive controversy should be followed. About ten minutes are allowed for this phase.

5. **Perspective Reversal:** Members of each pair change chairs. The "personal attribute" person presents in three minutes the best case possible for the "relationship attribute" position. He or she should be as forceful and persuasive as he or she can and add new arguments or facts if possible. The "relationship attribute" person then similarly presents the best case possible for the "personal attribute" position.

6. **Synthesis and Integration:** Participants drop all advocacy and come to their best reasoned judgment as to whether power is an attribute of a person or a relationship. The pair members summarize the information and arguments for each position and come to an agreement. Each pair prepares a short presentation on their conclusion to the rest of the class. Because other groups will have other conclusions, each group may need to explain the validity of its position to the class. About ten minutes are allowed for this phase.

7. **Whole Class Discussion:** The coordinator samples the decisions made by the groups of four by having several of them present their position to the class. The class then discusses similarities and differences among the positions, and the coordinator summarizes what the participants have learned about power and influence.

INTRODUCTION

The price of greatness is responsibility.

        Winston Churchill

In Orwell's fable, *Animal Farm,* the livestock of a farm overthrow their human masters and form an egalitarian system. At first, the ideology of the new order is summarized in several simple maxims that included "All animals are equal." As the story unfolds, however, the pigs (who assume the managerial positions on the farm) soon take advantage of their new status and power to bestow all kinds of special treatment on themselves. For instance, they do none of the many arduous chores that are the essence of farm work and they claim the farmhouse (which is the most comfortable spot on the farm). Eventually, the swine legitimize their behaviors by formally changing the farm's ideology. They delete six of the seven maxims, retaining only the equality principle, which they qualify with the addendum: "But some animals are more equal than others." In Orwell's world, the pigs, by assuming superior power and status, come to see themselves as privileged and meriting favorable treatment. What is true for pigs may also be true for humans.

Even though we sometimes do not like to admit it, power is a basic aspect of social life. It can be seized or given up, increased or lost. It can be used for good, evil, or trivial purposes. All relationships—with family, friends, lovers, co-workers—involve power and influence. Yet many persons are unaware of the influence they exert on others, and many people are unaware of how necessary and constructive mutual influence is in building effective groups and collaborative relationships among members. Being skillful in influencing other group members and taking responsibility for such influence are important parts of being a member of a group.

WHAT IS POWER?

The **fourth guideline** for creating an effective group is to ensure that the use of power is distributed among group members and that patterns of influence vary according to the needs of the group. In order to explicate this guideline, it is first necessary to define

What Is Power?

Everyone knows that power exists, but there is disagreement as to what it is. Several definitions follow. Rank these definitions from most clear to least clear. Find a partner. Come to an agreement on a joint ranking.

Power Is:

	The ability to influence others and to resist others' influence.
	The ability to control others' outcomes.
	The control of valuable resources.
	The capacity to affect another person's rewards and costs.
	The capacity to affect another's goal accomplishment.

The Image of Power

When you think of power, what images come to mind? Do you think of a football player (physical strength), a great orator, a semi-truck, or a gun? Write down the images you have when you think of power. Find a partner. Share your images and listen carefully to your partner's images. Then choose the two images most illustrative of the concept of power.

1. _____   4. _____

2. _____   5. _____

3. _____   6. _____

power. The definition of power used is the ability to influence others and to resist others' influence attempts (Dahl, 1957; Johnson, 1970). Power is also commonly defined as the amount of control over the other's outcomes (Fiske, 1993; Fiske & Morling, 1996); this definition is congruent with French and Raven's (1959; Raven, 1993) distinction between power that involves control of others' outcomes (e.g., reward and coercive power) and bases of power that do not (e.g., expert, informational, referent). The latter forms of power are more indirect and involve the willing cooperation and deference of the influencee. In order to understand power, it is also necessary to understand the nature of influence and control. **Influence** is using power to change another person in a desired direction. **Control** is the influencee behaving as the influencer intended. In this chapter, power and influence are used interchangeably.

The direct use of power is examined from two points of view: the dynamic-interdependence perspective and the trait-factor perspective. Several topics are discussed that deal with the use of power to increase the group's effectiveness: personal power and personal goal accomplishment, the bases of power, power and problem solving, interaction between high- and low-power members, and power and conflict. Finally, power may be exerted indirectly as well as directly (see Figure 6.1). Group norms are often implemented to serve as a substitute for direct influence procedures. At times, a "group mind" will influence and even control the actions of group members.

DIRECT		INDIRECT
Interdependence Approach	**Trait-Factor Approach**	**Group Factors**
Nature of relationship: Cooperative versus competitive	Source: Credibility, attractiveness	Group norms
Bases for power	Message characteristics	Group mind
Unequal levels of power	Receiver states	
Use in problem solving		
Use in conflicts		

Figure 6.1 The nature of power.

THE DYNAMIC-INTERDEPENDENCE VIEW OF POWER

Dynamic means in a constant state of change; **interdependence** means that each member's actions affect the outcomes of other members. The **dynamic-interdependence approach of power** posits that who is influencing whom to what degree changes constantly as members strive to achieve the group's goals. Members' power is based on expertise, ability, and access to information, not on authority or personality characteristics. The theory is based on two important principles:

1. Power exists in relationships, not individuals. It takes two persons for power to exist. A person cannot be an influencer if there is no influencee and vice versa. The use of power is inherent in any relationship. Any two persons who interact constantly influence and are influenced by each other.

2. For power to be constructive, the context in which it is used has to be cooperative. In a **competitive context** power is used to gain advantage and to promote one's own success at the expense of the other person. In a **cooperative context** power is used to maximize joint benefits or to promote the achievement of mutual goals. Individuals with cooperative goals (compared with individuals with competitive goals) tend to be more open to influence, more positive towards those who exercise power, and more appreciative of the way power is used (Tjosvold, 1995b).

When group members work together to achieve mutual goals, the use of power is inevitable, essential, dynamic, and distributed. *First,* power is inevitable—it exists in all relationships. By definition, a group is a cooperative enterprise. In order to achieve their mutual goals, group members must influence and be influenced by each other. Mutual influence goes on continuously, as group members act and react and adjust to each other's actions. They take turns talking, modify the expression of their attitudes and beliefs to take into account the reactions of other members, and speed up or slow down their activity to stay coordinated with one another.

Second, the use of power is essential to all aspects of group functioning. Goals cannot be established and communication cannot take place without mutual influence. Leadership cannot exist without using power. Decisions cannot be made without members influencing one another. Controversies and conflicts of interest cannot be managed

Dynamic-Interdependence View of Power

	Characteristics
Dynamic	Focuses on the changing nature and patterns of influence within a group as members strive to achieve mutual goals rather than on who possesses power.
Holistic	Assumes that power is a complex phenomenon that has to be studied as a whole and cannot be meaningfully broken into components.
Phenomenological	Stresses the immediate experience of group members and the ways they influence each other in the present rather than focusing on members' history and genetics.
Deductive	Applies and validates theoretical principles concerning the nature and use of power.
Distributed	Stresses power is distributed among all group members and every group member has some influence over each other and what takes place in the group.
Inevitable	Assumes power exists in all relationships. In small groups mutual influence goes on continuously, as group members act and react and adjust to each other's actions.
Pervasive	Assumes the use of power is essential to all aspects of group functioning—goal setting, communication, leadership, decision making, conflict resolution.

or resolved without the use of power. Every group member should be aware of his or her power, accept it, and take responsibility for its use.

Third, the use of power is dynamic. The patterns of influence among group members change constantly as the group progresses toward its goals, the costs (in energy, emotion, time, and so forth) of working together vary, and alternative relationships and groups become available in which the goals of group members might be better achieved (Cartwright, 1959; Thibaut & Kelly, 1959). If the group members make progress towards achieving their goals and the costs of working together go down so that no other group would be as rewarding, the ability of members to influence each other increases. If, on the other hand, the group is not making progress toward goal accomplishment, if the costs to group members in terms of emotion and energy are high, and if other groups are available that are more effective and less demanding, the ability of group members to influence each other decreases. In the latter case, members may even terminate their membership and join other groups, thereby reducing to zero the capacity of the original group members to influence and be influenced by them.

Fourth, power is distributed among all group members. Every group member has some influence over other members and what takes place in the group. Each member has power over the others and is open to influence by each other member. Group members use their power to ensure (a) the joint goals are achieved and (b) their personal goals (reasons for being a member of the group) are also accomplished.

The dynamic-interdependence approach to power is ideal for describing the exercise of power in groups where individuals are constantly interacting.

PERSONAL POWER AND PERSONAL GOAL ACCOMPLISHMENT

Most groups are formed because the group can accomplish goals that any one individual, working alone, cannot. Members cooperate in achieving these goals. Based on the dynamic-interdependent view of power, each group member (a) has the power to promote or obstruct the goal achievement of other members and (b) is dependent on the assistance of other members to achieve his or her own goals. The process by which group members mobilize their power in order to accomplish their goals consists of five steps (Figure 6.2).

1. **Determining Your Goals:** The first step in using your power within a group is to clarify your personal goals. Goals are desired future states based on wants, needs, and interests. Typically, goals are consciously sought, but some are obtained unconsciously. In order to plan to attain your goals you must be aware of them, accept them as valuable and worthwhile, and be willing to enlist the aid of other group members to accomplish them.

2. **Assessing Your Relevant Resources:** The second step in using your power is to contribute your resources to achieving the group's and your goals. You must be aware of and accept your resources in order to use them effectively. Moreover, it is only when you know your own resources that you understand (a) what other resources you need to achieve your goals, (b) how you can help other group members achieve their goals, and (c) how the resources of all members may be combined to achieve the group's goals.

3. **Determining Your Needed Coalitions:** The third step in using your power is to assess what coalitions you need to secure the information and resources necessary to achieve your goals. Coalitions are formed by (a) identifying the group members who have the information and resources you need, (b) identifying how your information and resources could contribute to their goal accomplishment, and (c) negotiating a mutual support agreement in which each agrees to contribute to the other's success.

4. **Negotiating a Mutual Support Agreement:** The fourth step in using your power is to negotiate an agreement with the appropriate group members to mutually support each other's efforts to his or her goals. In planning how resources will be utilized to help achieve the group's goals, group members often develop formal or informal contracts with one another. The contract usually includes (a) the resources you want from the group members, (b) the resources other

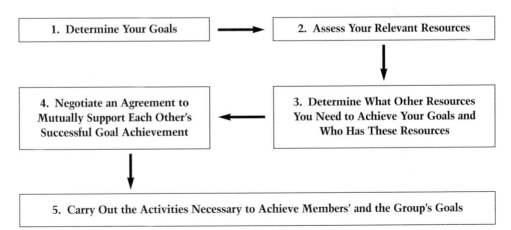

Figure 6.2 Mobilizing power to accomplish goals.

group members want from you, and (c) how members will coordinate their effects so that everyone can accomplish his or her goals. In essence, the contracts are a plan for group members to apply their resources in certain ways towards the achievement of the group's goals.

5. **Implementing the Contracts:** The fifth step in using your power is to carry out the activities necessary to achieve your goals.

Exercise 6.2: *Personal Power and Personal Goal Accomplishment*

The purpose of this exercise is to give you an opportunity to experience the process of increasing your personal power step-by-step.

1. Form heterogeneous groups of four.
2. Read Step 1 **(Determining Your Goals).** Each person should first state all the goals that he or she might work towards in this group. After everyone has had his or her say, each member should state which three goals he or she would like the group to accomplish first. Write these on newsprint, and include your name. Then go on to the next step.
3. Read Step 2 **(Assessing Your Relevant Resources).** Assess your resources by creating a list of your skills, talents, abilities, or personal traits that help you function more productively. The object is to increase your awareness of (a) your strengths so that you may more consciously mobilize them to achieve your goals and (b) other resources you need. The procedure for each group is as follows:
   a. Individually, think of all the things you do well, all the things you are proud of having done, all the things for which you feel a sense of accomplishment. List all your positive accomplishments and your successes.
   b. Share your lists with one another. Then, with the help of the other group members examine your past successes and identify the personal strengths you used to achieve them. Make a list of these strengths.
   c. After you have all made your list of strengths, give one another feedback about additional strengths. Add to each person's list the qualities, skills, and characteristics she has overlooked or undervalued.
   d. Each member should then discuss the question *"What might be keeping me from using all my strengths?"* The group helps members explore the ways in which they can free themselves from constraints on the use of their strengths.
   e. Review the material on self-acceptance and the acceptance of others in Johnson (2000).
4. Read Step 3 **(Determining Your Needed Coalitions).** As a group, look for similarities among your goals. Decide as a group upon the three goals that are most in accord with the personal goals of each member. List them on newsprint. Review the strengths listed in Step 2. Try to determine what resources are needed for the accomplishment of each of the three goals, and who has them. In participating in this exercise you may experience either the frustration of finding little or no compatibility between your own goals and those of the other group members or the rejection of having your resources overlooked, undervalued, or underused. Do not at this point make any formal coalitions with other group members. Limit yourself to determining what coalitions are needed. Then go on to the next step.
5. Read Step 4 **(Negotiating a Mutual Support Agreement).** Negotiate formal contracts with other group members and form open coalitions. In doing so, focus specifically on (a) what you want from the group members, (b) what the other group members want from

you, (c) what you exchange so that all members can accomplish their goals. Write your contracts on newsprint so that all members can see and read them. In essence, these contracts are a plan for group members to apply their resources cooperatively to achieve the group's goals.

6. Read Step 5 **(Implementing the Contracts).** Carry out the actions specified in the contract.

DISCUSSION

After completing the steps above, the groups should discuss their experiences. The following questions may be used to stimulate discussion:

1. What was the outcome of the five steps? To what extent were everyone's goals integrated into the group's goals, and to what extent were everyone's resources committed to the accomplishment of the group's goals?
2. What are the present reactions and feelings of each group member to the five steps?
3. On the basis of the group's experiences, what conclusions can be made about the use of power in a group? Groups should write their answers on newsprint. When all groups have finished their discussion, the conclusions should be shared.

THE TRAIT-FACTOR APPROACH TO POWER

One night long, long ago, a princess lay down to sleep on a bed that contained thirteen mattresses. At the bottom of the pile of mattresses had been placed a tiny pea. The princess tossed and turned all night, unable to sleep. This fairy tale princess was unable to sleep because it is part of the nature of princesses to be disturbed by provocations that those of us with mundane natures do not even notice. The princess illustrates the trait-factor approach to power and influence. She is credited with having innate dispositions that differentiated her from all other females. Who can deny her divine spark?

The **trait-factor approach to power** may be traced to Aristotle, whose rhetoric dealt at some length with the characteristics of an effective influencer and gave detailed advice on the techniques of persuasion. From the trait-factor point of view, influence is a function of the characteristics of (a) the person exerting the influence, (b) the person receiving the influence, and (c) the influence attempt itself. The assumption is that a person's traits explain why the person is as he or she is, how the person became so, and why the person stays the same despite circumstances, fortune, and opportunities. Thus, certain individuals are born with a self-contained capacity to influence others.

Trait-Factor Approach To Power

Characteristics	
Static	Focuses more on continuity than on change.
Atomistic	Assumes complex phenomena can be analyzed into component parts.
Historical	Assumes that causation of present behavior is a function of genetic and experiential factors acting cumulatively over relatively long periods of time.
Inductive	Stresses accounting for empirically observed phenomena more than seeking empirical validation for general theoretical statements.

The major post–World War II application of the trait-factor approach to power was the Yale Attitude Change Program, which was headed by Carl Hovland (Hovland, Lumsdaine, & Sheffield, 1949). Most of the research in this program focused on the area in which the trait-factor view is strongest—the effects of a single attempt to influence people delivered through the mass media. In situations where a politician is giving a speech to an audience, an announcer is delivering a television commercial, or a health official is warning the public about a health danger, the findings from the Yale Program are quite useful. In each of these situations the contact between the communicator and the receiver of the communication is brief and not repeated. Moreover, the communication is one-way; there is no interaction between the two parties. Because single instances of one-way communication are essentially static, a trait-oriented theory is quite helpful in analyzing them.

Hovland's wartime studies of propaganda were organized around the question "Who says what to whom with what effect?" Investigators have usually broken this question down into variables relating to the source (the characteristics of the communicator), the message (the characteristics of the communication), and the receiver (the characteristics of the person receiving the message). The exercise of power may thus be seen as a credible and attractive communicator's delivery of an effectively organized message to a vulnerable or influenceable audience. Trait-factor researchers assume that people are rational in the way they process information and are motivated to attend to a message, learn its contents, and incorporate it into their attitudes.

The Effects of the Source

Credibility.   Aristotle noted that an effective communicator must be a person of good sense, goodwill, and good moral character. Following this notion, most of the research on the personal characteristics of the communicator has focused on the dimension of credibility. **Credibility** is the perceived ability to know valid information and be motivated to communicate this information without bias. More specifically, credibility depends on (Giffin, 1967; Hovland & Weiss, 1952; Johnson, 1973):

1. Objective indicators of *expertise* relevant to the topic under discussion (for example, a Ph.D. or an affiliation with a prestigious organization).
2. *Reliability* as an information source (for example, of communicator's perceived character such as his dependability, predictability, and consistency).
3. The *motives* and *intentions* of the communicator. (Communicators who argue against their own self-interest or who appear not to be attempting to influence a receiver tend to be regarded as more trustworthy than communicators who overtly attempt to influence on the basis of self-interest.)
4. The expression of *warmth* and *friendliness.*
5. The *dynamism* of the communicator. (A confident, forceful, and active communicator tends to be regarded as more credible than a self-conscious, listless communicator.)
6. The *majority opinion* of others concerning the expertness and trustworthiness of the communicator.

Attractiveness.   The attractiveness of the communicator is an important influence on the power to influence an audience. We are likely to change our attitudes to agree with those of the people we like (e.g., Roskow-Ewoldsen & Fazio, 1992). The following factors have been found to be determinants of how attractive one person appears to another:

1. *Cooperativeness and goal facilitation* (Johnson & Johnson, 1989). A person likes others who are cooperating with him and facilitating his goal achievement.
2. *Physical appearance* (Berscheid & Walster, 1974). Other personal attributes being equal, physically attractive persons tend to be liked better than homely persons.
3. *Liking* (Byrne, 1969). If one person knows that she is liked by another, she is apt to reciprocate that liking.
4. *Similarity* (Byrne, 1969). Although the point is controversial, considerable evidence suggests that individuals who perceive themselves to be similar in basic values and other characteristics tend to like each other.
5. *Competence* (Blanchard, Weigel, & Cook, 1975). Persons who are perceived to be competent in important areas tend to be liked.
6. *Warmth* (Johnson, 1971). Warm, friendly persons tend to be liked.
7. *Familiarity and propinquity* (Berscheid & Walster, 1969; Watson & Johnson, 1972). Although the point is equivocal, some findings suggest that a person likes others with whom he or she is familiar. "To know them is to love them."

The Effects of the Message

Without a message there can be no influence exerted on another person. Like Aristotle, the Yale researchers were deeply concerned with the nature of arguments, their logical coherence and emotional appeal, and the language used by the communicator to convey the message. The basic findings from the research on message variables are (Aronson, 1972; McGuire, 1969; Watson & Johnson, 1972):

1. In general, messages that inspire fear tend to be persuasive with receivers who have high self-esteem but not with those who have low self-esteem. High-fear appeals with specific instructions for action tend to be more persuasive than high-fear appeals without specific instructions.
2. With intelligent receivers, messages that acknowledge opposing viewpoints (two-sided messages) are more persuasive than are one-sided messages. With less intelligent receivers, one-sided messages tend to be more effective.
3. When a communicator is credible, the greater the discrepancy between the position advocated and the receiver's initial position, the greater the change. If a communicator is not credible, mildly discrepant positions are most effective.

The Effects of the Receiver

There are a multitude of personality characteristics that affect the acceptance of a persuasive message. The most salient and consistent of these characteristics are:

1. *Self-esteem* (McGuire, 1969; Watson & Johnson, 1972). The experimental evidence indicates that receivers with low self-esteem are more persuadable than receivers with high self-esteem. When long-term self-esteem is measured and correlated with persuasion, this clearly negative relationship is less frequent and less pronounced.

2. *The receiver's present attitudes* (Watson & Johnson, 1972). Receivers may refuse to listen to messages that disagree with their present attitudes, or they may misinterpret what the communicator is stating. Attitudes that are integral to the individual's self-conception appear to be more difficult to change than less integral attitudes (Rokeach, 1968).

3. *Forewarning* (Watson & Johnson, 1972). Forewarning receivers of the communicator's intention of converting them to his or her point of view creates resistance to the message.

4. *Role playing* (Watson & Johnson, 1972). Actively role playing a previously unacceptable position increases its acceptability to the receiver.

5. *Inoculation* (McGuire, 1964). Having receivers practice defending their position and then giving them additional arguments to support it decreases their susceptibility to attempts to influence them.

6. *Distraction* (Baron, Baron, & Miller, 1973). Receivers are generally more susceptible to influence when they are distracted during the communicator's statement of her message.

7. *Intelligence* (McGuire, 1969). Intelligence and influence are negatively related in the middle and upper portions of the IQ distribution and positively related in the lower portion.

Summary

Attempts to exert power over others are enhanced if one is credible and attractive; if one phrases one's messages so that they are two sided, action oriented, and discrepant with members' current beliefs; and if the other group members have low self-esteem, see their attitudes under modification as peripheral to them, have no forewarning of the influence attempt, role play positions that agree with one's own, have not been inoculated, are distracted while one is presenting the message, and are not very intelligent. The trait-factor approach to influence, however, is weak both logically and empirically in situations where two or more individuals are constantly interacting.

THE BASES OF POWER

It was the first of November in the year of 1095 that Pope Urban II delivered a speech in an open field outside of the town of Clermont in France in which he urged the crowd to arm itself and drive the "wicked race" of pagans from the Holy Land. Moved by the pope's words, the crowd began to yell, "It is the will of God!" Thus began the long series of wars for the cross of Christianity known as the Crusades. The first was organized in 1096 by Peter the Hermit. Unarmed men, priests, monks, and even women became captivated by the promise of salvation, the lure of riches, and the promise of adventure. Almost all of them died. Yet the Crusades lasted until 1291, when the Muslims regained full control of the Holy Land. What gave Pope Urban II the power to launch such a 200-year effort?

According to social exchange theory, power is based on the control of valuable resources. If a person has control over a resource you want, that person has power over

Bases of Power

Rank the following bases of power from most to least effective in influencing others.

Rank	Base of Power
	Ability to deliver positive consequences or remove negative consequences in response to their behavior.
	Ability to mete out negative consequences or remove positive consequences in response to the behavior of group members.
	Possession of a position in the group or organization (such as a president) or special role responsibilities (such as X-ray technician).
	Modeling behavioral patterns and personal qualities that others want to imitate out of respect, liking, and wanting to be liked.
	Possession of some special expertise that is useful in accomplishing the goal and that is not available anywhere else.
	Possession of resources or information that is useful in accomplishing the goal and that is not available anywhere else.

you unless, of course, you have an alternative source for the resource. Different types of power can be specified based on what types of resources are under a person's control (French & Raven, 1959; Frost & Stahelski, 1988; Raven & Kruglanski, 1970): reward, coercive, legitimate (based on position in a hierarchy), referent, expert, and informational.

A person has **reward power** over other group members if he or she has the ability to deliver positive consequences or remove negative consequences in response to their behavior. A person's power will be greater the more the group members value the reward, the more they believe that the person can dispense the reward, and the less their chances appear of getting the reward from someone else. The successful use of reward power will generally produce a "moving towards" the person. Group members will comply with the person's requests, seek him or her out, increase their liking for the person, and communicate effectively with him or her. Under certain conditions, however, the reward power can backfire. Too many rewards or the development of suspicion on the part of the group members that they are being bribed or conned into going along can lead to a "moving away" or "moving against" the person.

A person has **coercive power** over other group members if the person can mete out negative consequences or remove positive consequences in response to the behavior of group members. Punishment for a member who fails to get the group to go along with his or her wishes often increases the pressure on group members to engage in the desired behavior. Coercive power frequently causes group members to avoid the person and to like him or her less. Group members may do what the person wants, but they tend to avoid interacting with the person in the future. Only when the use of coercive power brings a conflict out into the open to be resolved can it have many positive effects.

When a person has **legitimate power,** group members believe the person ought to have influence over them because of his or her position in the group or organization (such as an employer) or because of his or her special role responsibilities (such as those of a policewoman). Group members invariably believe it their duty to follow the commands of a person with legitimate power, even when it means restricting themselves to a limited set of behaviors. Legitimate power is often used to reduce conflict—when the person with it plays the role of an arbitrator or mediator or when those with less power simply conform to the person's wishes.

When a person has **referent power,** group members identify with or want to be like the person and therefore do what he or she wants out of respect, liking, and wanting to be liked. Generally, the more the person is liked, the more the group members will identify with him or her.

When a person has **expert power,** group members see the person as having some expertise that will be useful in accomplishing the goal and that is not available anywhere else. They believe the person is not trying to deceive them for selfish purposes. The successful use of expert power results in liking for the person, as group members are convinced of the correctness of the influence attempts. Only if her expertise fosters feelings of inadequacy in the group members will it have negative effects.

When a person has **informational power,** group members believe that the person has resources or information (not available anywhere else) that will be useful in accomplishing the goal. The person's power is based upon the logic of the person's arguments or the superiority of his or her demonstrated knowledge; it has effects similar to those that result from the use of expert power.

Although resources may create the basis of power, power is still expressed through behavior. Sometimes power is exerted in conversation. How we talk to another person often reflects and reinforces the balance of power between us. Gender relations are no exception. There is evidence that men are more likely to dominate discussions of neutral topics and masculine topics, whereas women dominate discussions only on traditionally feminine subjects (Brown, Dovidio, Ellyson, 1990). Men tend to interrupt and touch women more than vice versa (Hall & Veccia, 1990; Major, Schmidlin, & Williams, 1990; West & Zimmerman, 1983), both of which have been interpreted as indicators of men's greater social power.

It should be noted that it is the *perception* of a group member's power base that affects the behavior of other members, not the actual resources. A member can have considerable resources that are unknown or ignored by other group members and therefore have little power over the others. On the other hand, a group member can have few resources but be seen as having many resources and thereby have a great deal of influence over the other group members.

French and Raven's theory of power bases has been one of the most influential in the field. The research, however, has not found a consistent relationship between influence attempts and effectiveness (Falbe & Yukl, 1992; Yukl & Falbe, 1991; Yukl & Tracey, 1992; Tjosvold, 1995b). There have been two approaches to develop more consistent evidence. The first approach is to develop new instruments (Hinkin & Schriesheim, 1989; Rahim, 1989). Despite significant methodological improvements, the studies using these new instruments are only partially consistent with previous findings and with each other. The findings on power bases seem to depend heavily on how they are measured.

The second approach is to improve the theory. The most exciting theorizing on power has been formulated by Dean Tjosvold (1990a, 1993, 1995b). Tjosvold notes that

(a) the same power source can be used to reward or to punish (a reward that is considerably below what is expected tends to be perceived to be a punishment) and (b) the context in which the power source is used affects how it is perceived. Based on social interdependence theory (Deutsch, 1962), he hypothesized that in a competitive (or an individualistic) context, individuals tend to resent and resist influence attempts because they perceive them as being intended to block and obstruct their goal accomplishment. In a cooperative context, individuals tend to be open to influence because they perceive the intent of the influence to promote mutual success.

Tjosvold (1995b) conducted an experiment in which undergraduates in a Canadian university participated in a simulation where power was used (a) to reward or punish and (b) in a cooperative, competitive, or individualistic context. Each participant was told he or she was an employee in a consulting company that specialized in solving problems of other organizations and would be working with another participant who was assigned the role of manager. All participants were given four chances in a lottery for $50. In one condition participants were given a reward of four additional chances for their efforts and in another condition the four chances were taken away. Tjosvold found that the use of **power to reward** (as opposed to punish) induced more openness and open-mindedness, feelings of acceptance and warmth, beliefs that power was used wisely, attraction and positive attitudes towards the manager, and a stronger work relationship. He also found that participants in a **cooperative context** (compared with participants in a competitive or individualistic context) were more open-minded, felt greater warmth and were more confident in the work relationship, believed more strongly that power was used wisely, and perceived the power holder as being more likable, fair, and trustworthy. Previously, Tjosvold (1981, 1989, 1990a) found that even with unequal power, cooperators exchange resources and productively complete tasks whereas unequal power in competition arouses suspicions and refusal to exchange resources; individualistic goals had a similar impact on power dynamics as did competition.

Bases of Power

Match the following bases of power with their definitions. Find a partner and compare answers.

___	1. Reward	a. Group members believe the person has useful knowledge not available elsewhere.
___	2. Coercive	b. Group members believe the person ought to have power because of her position or responsibilities.
___	3. Legitimate	c. A person can deliver positive consequences or remove negative consequences.
___	4. Reference	d. Group members believe the person has a special knowledge or skill and is trustworthy.
___	5. Expert	e. Group members do what the person wants out of respect, liking, and wanting to be liked.
___	6. Informational	f. A person can deliver negative consequences or remove positive consequences.

CONFLICT MODEL OF SOCIAL INFLUENCE

The French social psychologist Serge Moscovici (1980, 1985a) proposed an intergroup conflict model of social influence in which power defines whether a group is a majority or a minority. He assumes that both majorities and minorities are sources and targets of influence attempts. Majorities tend to use their power to force minorities to yield and conform to the majorities' expectations. Minorities tend to convert majorities to the minorities' position. What defines the majority and the minority groups is the amount of power they have. A **power majority** is the group that has the most control over how important resources are distributed (they may be the numerical minority). A **power minority** is a group that has little control over the distribution of important resources (they may be a numerical majority). In the United States and Europe, for example, white males (a numerical minority) have traditionally controlled the distribution of the top posts in government and industry (they have been the power majority), whereas Asians and others are part of the power minorities (Shinagawa, 1997). In Japan, however, "pure Japanese" are the power majority and white Europeans are a power minority.

Exercise 6.3: Unequal Resources

This exercise gives participants a chance to observe how groups (a) use resources that have been unequally distributed and (b) negotiate to obtain the resources they need. It is conducted with four groups, each having two to four members. If there are more persons than needed for the exercise, they may participate without being group members. Should more than one cluster of four groups participate, the coordinator may wish to add the element of competition between as well as within the clusters. The exercise should take less than one hour. The procedure for the coordinator is as follows:

1. Introduce the exercise as an experience with the use of resources needed to accomplish a task that have been distributed unequally among groups. Form the groups. Have at least two observers for each cluster. Groups should be placed far enough away from each other so that their negotiation positions are not compromised by casual observation.
2. Meet briefly with the observers and discuss what they might focus upon. Any aspect of negotiation and problem solving can be observed.
3. Distribute an envelope of materials and a copy of the accompanying task sheet to each group. Explain that each group has different materials, but that each must complete the same tasks. Explain that the groups may negotiate for the use of materials and tools in any way that is agreeable to everyone. Emphasize that the first group to finish all the tasks is the winner. (If clusters are competing, there will be both a group winner and a cluster winner.) Give the signal to begin.
4. When the groups have finished, declare the winner. Then conduct a discussion on using resources, sharing, negotiating, competing, and using power. Ask the observers to participate in the discussion. Then ask each cluster to summarize its conclusions about the use of power that manifested itself during the exercise.

GROUP MATERIALS

Group 1: Scissors, ruler, paper clips, pencils, two 4-inch squares of red paper, and two 4-inch squares of white paper.

Group 2: Scissors, glue, and two sheets each of gold paper, white paper, and blue paper, each 8 × 11 inches.

Group 3: Felt-tipped markers and two sheets each of green paper, white paper, and gold paper, each 8 × 11 inches.

Group 4: Five sheets of paper, 8 × 11 inches—one green, one gold, one blue, one red, and one purple.

UNEQUAL RESOURCES EXERCISE TASK SHEET

Each group is to complete the following tasks:

1. Make a 3 × 3-inch square of white paper.
2. Make a 4 × 2-inch rectangle of gold paper.
3. Make a 3 × 5-inch T-shaped piece of green and white paper.
4. Make a four-link paper chain, each link in a different color.
5. Make a 4 × 4-inch flag in any three colors.

The first group to complete all the tasks is the winner. Groups may negotiate with each other for the use of needed materials and tools on any mutually agreeable basis.

Exercise 6.4: Power Politics

The objective of this exercise is to examine the dynamics of negotiating for power. Group members with different amounts of power negotiate to form coalitions. The exercise takes one hour. The procedure is as follows:

1. Divide the participants into groups of twelve. Each participant needs a pencil and a pad of paper for writing notes.
2. *Task:* In this exercise group members are to select a chairperson for the governing board of a political party. Each group member has a different amount of power. It takes 4,000 votes to elect a chairperson. The chairperson cannot be elected unless members form coalitions and vote as a block.
3. Each group member receives (a) a copy of the instruction sheet and (b) a slip of paper indicating the number of votes the participant controls (the numbers range from 100 to 1,200 votes). Each group member controls a different number of votes (one member controls 100 votes, one member 200 votes, another member 300 votes, and so on with one member controlling 1,200 votes). *Do not show your slip of paper with the number of your votes to other group members.*
4. Two rounds of negotiations will take place before the first vote is taken. Each negotiation round will last five minutes. During negotiations, members write notes to one another. No verbal communication is permitted. Members may write as many notes to as many other members as they wish. Notes should include the names of the sender and the receiver. These notes are not to be read until the end of the five-minute period.
5. Give the signal to begin round one. At the end of five minutes stop all note passing and allow members to read their notes.
6. Give the signal to begin round two. The same rules apply. At the end of five minutes stop all note passing and allow members to read their notes.
7. Ask the group members if they are ready to vote on their chairperson. If seven members want to vote, a vote is taken. All voting takes place by secret ballot. On the ballot, write the number of votes you control and to whom you commit them. If the group is

not ready to vote, or if no one has enough votes to become chairperson, round three begins.

8. Give the signal to begin round three. Group members may negotiate verbally with one another. There are no restrictions on negotiations during this round, which also lasts for five minutes. At the end of round three, call for a vote. The vote is again by secret ballot.

9. If no one has enough votes to become chairperson, give the signal to begin round four. Allow a ten-minute free-negotiation period. Then take a final vote.

10. Discuss the experience, using the following questions as guides:
    a. What deals were made? How was power used in making those deals?
    b. What negotiation strategies were used?
    c. What criteria did members use to decide to whom to commit their votes?
    d. What were the feelings and reactions of the members to the experience?
    e. How did it feel to control a small number of votes? How did it feel to control a large number of votes?
    f. What strategies did members use to create allies and develop power blocs?
    h. What conclusions can you make about the use of power? (Write these on newsprint to share with other groups.)

POWER POLITICS EXERCISE INSTRUCTION SHEET

This is a game of power politics. Your group is to become the governing body of a political party, and you and the other group members must select a general chairperson. A member must receive 4,000 votes to become chairperson. This is a crucial decision for the party. The person you elect chairperson will control who gets how much patronage from the party. The chairperson will have 100 units of patronage to distribute to deserving group members. Group members may negotiate for votes and the distribution of the patronage. One member controls 100 votes, a second controls 200, a third controls 300, and so on, with one member controlling 1,200 votes. The number of votes each member has is on a slip of paper handed out by the coordinator of the exercise. Keep this slip. *Do not show it to any other group member.* You may commit your votes to any member you wish; you may split your votes among several members if you wish.

POWER AND PROBLEM SOLVING

In the two previous exercises the resources of the group were distributed unequally among its members. This will be the case with most of the problems a group faces. Yet because resources are unequally distributed does not mean that there are members who are powerless. Every group member has some power; every group member is able to influence other group members in some way. Some group members, for example, may have a high degree of informational power, whereas others may have legitimate power. *How* a group manages power has an important bearing on group effectiveness.

The effectiveness of any group is improved when (a) power is relatively balanced among its members, and (b) power is based upon competence, expertise, and information. The ability of the group to solve problems increases as all group members come to believe they share equally in influencing the direction of the group effort, and as the group climate becomes relatively free of domination by a few of the most powerful members. When members have equal power they are more cooperative in their interactions, more responsive to the cooperative initiatives of other members, and more committed to implementing the group decision. Studies have found that even within organizations the satisfaction of subordinates increases when they believe they can influence particular aspects of the organization's decision making (Tjosvold, 1995b). Unequal power interferes with the trust and communication necessary for managing group conflicts constructively. Thus, the problem-solving ability of a group is improved when the group has dynamic power patterns that in the long run equalize influence among group members.

A group's decisions are invariably of higher quality when power is based upon competence, expertise, and relevant information—not upon authority or popularity. The problem-solving capacity of many groups is seriously damaged when the member with the most authority is most influential at a time that calls for expertise and accurate information as the bases of power. When power is not distributed equally among group members, or when the use of authority dominates and expertise and informational bases of power are ignored, group effectiveness is undermined. The next exercise deals with the unequal distribution of power and the consequences it can have for both high- and low-power group members.

Exercise 6.5: Power to the Animals

The objective of this exercise is to examine the interaction among groups of different power as they negotiate with one another. The exercise takes two hours. The coordinator should read the accompanying instructions regarding the distribution of marbles and then follow this procedure:

1. Introduce the exercise as one that highlights interaction among groups having unequal power. Divide the class into groups of twelve. Explain that within each group are three mammals, four birds, and five fish; the status of the members in each group is determined by how well they negotiate—for marbles. (Even if there are more than twelve participants in a group, keep the number of mammals under five.) Hand out a copy of the general instructions to every participant.

2. Distribute twelve bags of marbles randomly within each group. Make sure that the members understand their instructions. Give them time to examine what marbles they have, warning them not to let other participants see the marbles. Then begin negotiation session 1, which is to last five minutes.

3. During the negotiation session place on newsprint three headings: "Mammals," "Birds," and "Fish." After five minutes stop the negotiating and have the participants compute their scores. Take the three highest scores and place them, along with the persons' initials, under the heading "Mammals." (Even if there are more than twelve participants in a group, keep the number of mammals under five.) Place the next four scores, together with the persons' initials, under the heading "Birds." Place the remaining five scores, with the persons' initials, under the heading "Fish." Have each person make a name tag indicating what he is and put it on.

4. Begin negotiation session 2. After five minutes end it and ask for scores. Read just the individual scores, placing the three highest in the mammals column, the next four in the birds column, and the next five in the fish column. Members who change columns on the basis of their score will have to exchange their name tags.

5. Conduct negotiation session 3 in the same way.

6. Conduct negotiation session 4 in the same way.
7. Announce that the mammals now have the authority to make the rules for the exercise and that although anyone else can suggest rules, the mammals will decide which ones will be implemented. Inform the mammals that they may make any rules they wish, such as a rule that all marbles must be redistributed so that everyone has equal points, or a rule that all fish and birds must give mammals the marbles they ask for whether they want to or not. Have the mammals record their rules on newsprint.
8. After the new rules are established, conduct negotiation session 5. Then allow five minutes for the mammals to discuss and make any rule changes.
9. Repeat this cycle twice. Then give the birds and the fish copies of the list of strategies for influencing a high-power group. The birds and the fish have ten minutes to discuss the strategies and decide which ones to adopt. Then continue with another negotiation session.
10. After a variety of strategies have been tried by the birds and the fish, or when they refuse to continue, conduct a discussion of the experience. The following questions may be used as guides:
    a. What were your feelings and your reactions to the experience?
    b. Are there any parallels between the system set up by the game and the system in which we live?
    c. Would it have made much difference if the members who were fish had been the mammals?
    d. Were the mammals acting with legitimate authority?
    e. Are there any parallels between the exercise and the relations among racial groups, rich and poor, and adults and students?
    f. What negotiation strategies were used?
    g. What feelings arose from the unequal distribution of power? How did it feel to have high power? How did it feel to have low power?
    h. How did the strategies for changing the high-power group work? What contributed to their effectiveness or ineffectiveness?
    i. What conclusions about the use of power can be made from your experiences in the exercise?

DISTRIBUTION OF MARBLES

1. The total number of marbles needed is seventy-two (six times the number of group members).
2. The number of green marbles needed is five (the number of mammals plus two).
3. The number of yellow marbles needed is ten (the number of birds plus the number of fish plus one).
4. The number of red, white, and blue marbles needed is fifty-seven, nineteen of each.

Give each participant a bag of six marbles. Five bags are each to contain one green marble, one yellow marble, and four marbles randomly selected from the colors red, white, and blue. Three bags are to contain one yellow marble and five marbles randomly selected from the colors red, white, and blue. The remaining four bags are to contain a random assortment of red, white, and blue marbles. These twelve bags are to be distributed at random within each group.

GENERAL INSTRUCTIONS

In this exercise there are three levels of power, based on marbles in each group. Group members have the chance to progress from one level of power to another by obtaining marbles through negotiation. The three members who get the most power will be declared the winners when the exercise ends. You will be given six marbles each. The scoring system for the marbles is given below. Additional points are awarded if a member is able to get several marbles of the same color:

Color	Points	Number of a Kind	Points
Green	50	4	50
Yellow	25	3	30
Red	15	2	20
White	10	1	10
Blue	5		

For example, a person's total score if she had six green marbles would be 300 (6 × 50) plus 50 (for 6 of a kind), or 350 points. The rules for negotiation are as follows:

1. You have five minutes to improve your score.
2. You improve your score by negotiating with other group members.
3. Members must be holding hands to have an agreement.
4. Only one-for-one trades are legal. Two for one or any other combination is illegal.
5. Once a member touches the hand of another member, a marble of unequal value (or color) must be traded. If two members cannot make an agreement, they will have to hold hands for the entire negotiating round.
6. There is no talking unless hands are touching. This rule must be strictly followed.
7. Members with folded arms do not have to negotiate with other members.
8. All marbles must be hidden. This rule must be strictly followed.

STRATEGIES FOR INFLUENCING A HIGH-POWER GROUP

1. Build your own organizations and resources in order to make the low-power group less vulnerable.
2. Form coalitions.
3. Change the attitudes of high-power group members through education or moral persuasion.
4. Use existing legal procedures to bring pressures for change.
5. Search for ways in which to make high-power group members dependent upon the low-power group.
6. Use harassment techniques to increase the high-power group's costs of sticking with the status quo.

UNEQUAL POWER

One of the most common settings for realistic conflict exists between high- and lower-power groups. **Power** is the capacity to affect another person's goal accomplishment. **High power** is the capacity to have considerable influence on another person's goal accomplishment whereas **low power** is the capacity to have little influence on another person's goal accomplishment. When the distribution of power is obviously unequal, both the high- and the low-power members may have troubles, the overall group effectiveness may suffer, the gains members receive from being members decrease, and severe maintenance problems result. In discussions of theory and research pertaining to high and low power, the usual reference is to our society rather than to a small, problem-solving group. Yet the same dynamics between high-power and low-power persons can be found in a group of any size, even one as large as our society. In the previous exercise you yourself experienced, depending on your marbles, what it means to have a great deal of power or very little power. Compare your experience with the following discussions of high- and low-power group members.

High-Power Members

In Greek mythology, the king of Phrygia, Midas, showed unusual kindness to Dionysus' teacher, Silenus. In appreciation, Dionysus offered to grant any wish King Midas requested. Midas asked that all he touched would turn to gold. When even his food became gold, he implored Dionysus for relief and was directed to bathe in the river Pactolus (which has since had golden sands). His touch returned to normal, King Midas had gained the wisdom to know that the exercise of power does not always turn out the way it is intended.

Life generally seems good for high-power persons. Everything goes right, every problem is easily solved, everyone seems to like and appreciate them and everything they do. High-power persons are typically happy with their situation and tend not to see how much the use of power is involved in their relationships. They are convinced that low-power persons really do like them, that everyone communicates honestly with them, that no one hides information from them, and that they are really seen as "nice" persons. When this enjoyable world is threatened by dissatisfaction expressed by low-power persons, however, high-power persons tend not to react benevolently. They are hard to move towards cooperation, conciliation, and compromise, and they will largely ignore the efforts of their low-power groupmates to increase cooperative problem solving. To them, low-power persons somehow never learn to "know their place"; they insist on "rocking the boat" out of ignorance and spite.

There are at least two strategies that high-power group members use to make it more difficult for low-power members to reduce the differences in power between them (Jones & Gerard, 1967). The first is to institute norms or rules in the group that legitimize their power and make wrong any attempt by others to change the status quo. The first action taken by most groups who attain power is to make their holding of it legitimate and to establish regulations and norms that make illegitimate any change in the existing power relationships. For example, in most communities the white power structure has established strong norms as to where minority-group members may live, what occupations they may have, and where they must go to school—as well as procedures for making both whites and nonwhites believe that the status quo is "legitimate" and "right." This strategy may be described as the "power-defines-injustice" strategy, or the "might-is-right" strategy.

The second strategy high-power members employ to solidify their position is to make the risk of attempting to change the status quo so great that the low-power members are deterred from trying to do so. They can invoke this strategy by establishing

severe penalties against those who might attempt to change the status quo and by offering the low-power members a variety of benefits or rewards on the condition that
they refrain from rebelliousness. Of the two, the second seems to be more effective. The
threat of punishment has never worked effectively to deter behavior, but the paternal-
istic leadership that tries to keep everyone happy has been applied successfully in com-
bating labor and racial unrest in many parts of the country. This strategy may be defined
as the "this-hurts-me-more-than-it-will-hurt-you" strategy, or the "if-only-you-would-
behave-neither-of-us-would-go-through-this-suffering" strategy.

Powerful group members have been found to (a) make more attempts to influence
the behavior of the low-power members, (b) devalue the performance of the low-power
members, (c) attribute the efforts of the low-power members to their own use of power
rather than to the low-power members' motivations to do well, (d) view the low-
power members as objects of manipulation, and (e) express a preference for the maintenance of psychological distance from the low-power members (Kipnis, 1972). Kipnis
(1987) found that husbands, wives, and business managers who used controlling tactics of influence to get their way viewed persons they influenced as less worthy than
themselves and moved away from them socially and psychologically. He labeled these
changes the **metamorphic** effects of power. Participants who were randomly assigned
to central positions in a communication network (the more powerful positions) not
only viewed themselves as powerful but also rated themselves as more capable than
the participants who were randomly assigned peripheral positions (Stotle, 1978).
Tjosvold (1978) notes that high-power group members (a) feel more secure than low-
power members, (b) underestimate the low-power members' positive intentions,
(c) devalue low-power persons, (d) are inattentive to the communications of low-
power persons, (e) are unresponsive to cooperative gestures by the low-power members, and (f) attempt to protect their superior power by rejecting demands for change.
High-power group members also seem uninterested in learning about the intentions
and plans of low-power members (Tjosvold & Sagaria, 1978). High-power individuals
tend to make fewer concessions in conflict situations (Lawler & Yoon, 1994), claim a
larger share of available resources (Murnighan & Pillutla, 1995), and are less cooperative and more exploitative of the other's cooperation (Lindskold & Aronoff, 1980).
High-power individuals tend to be more angered by a lower person's harm than when
positions are reversed (Baumeister, Smart, & Boden, 1996). As Aristotle noted, people
think it "right that they should be revered by those inferior to them" (384–322
B.C./1991, p. 143) and they find it particularly vexing to be insulted or harmed by
someone who should actually treat them with deference.

Using power may alter the high-power person (Kipnis, Castell, Gergen, & Mauch,
1976). *First*, the desire for power becomes a need in and of itself, apart from the larger
goals that power is intended to fulfill, such as accomplishing the task. *Second*, the ease
in using power encourages power holders to use power to benefit themselves, at the
expense of those under their power. *Third*, power holders receive unwarranted positive
feedback, even adulation, from others, thereby producing an inflated sense of self-
worth. *Fourth*, power may lead to the devaluation of others, reflected in a tendency to
see the worst in others. *Fifth*, having an inflated view of one's power may also lead
power holders to overstep the bounds of its appropriate use. *Sixth*, a recent meta-analysis
indicates that as a person's power increases, the performance ratings of others become

increasingly negative (effect size = 0.29) and self-evaluations become increasingly positive (effect size = 0.45) (Georgesen & Harris, 1998). High power seems to result in an egocentric or self-serving bias (Harris & Schaubroeck, 1988), resulting in inflating their self-evaluations to maintain their benefits such as employment, promotions, and perks.

The **power-devaluation theory,** proposed by Kipnis and his colleagues (Kipnis, 1972; Kipnis, Castel, Gergen, & Manch, 1976; Kipnis, Schmidt, Prince, & Stitt, 1981; Wilkinson & Kipnis, 1978), posits that as a person's power increases, he or she will make more attempts to influence others. As more influence attempts are made, the person comes to believe that he or she controls other people's behavior and is the causal agent in producing the outcomes. The performances of low-power others are devalued, and the high-power person takes responsibility for any successes associated with the work of others.

High-status positions invoke a sense of privilege (Messe, Kerr, & Sattler, 1992). Occupants of high-status positions come to believe they are entitled to special treatment simply because of the position they hold. Messe and his associates demonstrated that (a) privilege behaviors are a central component of people's role schema for "supervisor"; (b) due to this sense of privilege, supervisors expend less effort than subordinates on shared tasks; and (c) occupants of high-status positions act in a privileged manner by taking more than an equal share of the rewards offered to the group. In an earlier study, Johnson and Allen (1972) found that having high status and high power in an organization results in an enhanced self-perception that leads to altruistic behavior but disdain for the worker. But when individuals had high status but low power in an organization that rewards high power, they engaged in selfish behavior (they deviated from the prescribed norms in order to increase their own rewards) and expressed respect for the worker.

There is an association between power and stereotyping (Fiske, 1993; Fiske & Morling, 1996). The general premise of **power-stereotyping theory** is that persons in positions of power are especially vulnerable to stereotyping subordinates because they pay less attention to them. High-power individuals may lack cognitive capacity to attend to subordinates because power requires attending to more people and more issues at the same time. High-power individuals may ignore subordinates because the high-power person's outcomes do not depend on subordinates. High-power individuals may not attend to subordinates because they have a dominant personality trait and may attempt to control their interactions with others to such an extent that they ignore the actions and motivations of others. Regardless of its cause, decreases in attention make powerful individuals more likely to depend on stereotypes in interacting with subordinates.

Folklore emphasizes two aspects of high power. The first is, "Power corrupts." High power is believed to result in arrogance and corruption. The second is that the greater a person's power, the more insufficient it is likely to seem, simply because the claims upon it increase faster than the power to fulfill them (Halle, 1967). The Ford Foundation, for example, though by far the richest of American foundations, is undoubtedly the most inadequately endowed in terms of the expectations it is called on to meet.

Low-Power Members

Low-power individuals generally find their relationships with high-power people threatening and debilitating. Low-power individuals are apt to feel frustrated and uncertain about their future goal facilitation because they depend heavily on the unpredictable

behavior of the high-power members (Tjosvold, 1978). These feelings of uncertainty and anxiety provoke (a) increased vigilance and attempts to understand and predict the high-power members' behavior; (b) distorted perceptions of the positive intent of the high-power members towards them; (c) attraction to, mixed with fear of, the high-power members; (d) stifling of criticism of the high-power members; (e) unwillingness to clarify one's position to the high-power members; (f) ingratiation, conformity, flattery, and effacing self-presentation so as to induce the high-power members to like and to reward them; and (g) the expectation of exploitation (low-power members tend to believe that, because they have no retaliatory capability, they are vulnerable and helpless and will be exploited). Low-power members have been found to direct much of their communication and attention to high-power members and to keep on good terms with them.

On the other hand, low-power group members have been found to resist attempts by high-power members to control them. Tjosvold (1978) notes that low-power members have been found to defy threats, to counterthreaten, to refuse to comply with an influence attempt even when resistance is costly, to dislike the high-power members, and to perceive the relationship as competitive. Johnson and Allen (1972) found that low-power group members who believed they were equal to their high-power peers felt underrewarded and attempted to obtain increased rewards from the group while emphasizing the incompetence, uncooperativeness, lack of generosity, and unfairness of the high-power members. In addition, they disliked their high-power peers.

Compared to high-power individuals, low-power individuals tend to be more cooperative (e.g., Lindskold & Aronoff, 1980), to make more concessions (e.g., Lawler & Yoon, 1993), and to be more compliant in response to threat while negotiating (e.g., Lawler & Yoon, 1993). Managers tend to yield to their superiors when interpersonal conflicts arise (e.g., Kramer, 1996). Low-power individuals tend to behave less aggressively than those having high power (e.g., Epstein & Taylor, 1967; Ohbuchi & Saito, 1986). It may be adaptive for the weaker person to be submissive (e.g., Gilbert, 1992) and can be seen as "the natural order of things according to which the big ones always peck the little ones" (Heider, 1958, p. 260). Finally, low-power individuals may experience psychological reactance more than high-power individuals. **Reactance** is a motivational state that is aroused whenever persons feel that their freedom has been abridged or threatened (Brehm, 1966). It is the reactions individuals have to a loss of control or freedom of choice. Threats to personal freedom motivate persons to take actions that will help them regain their freedom and control.

Deutsch (1969) assumes that the goal of low-power members is to establish authentic, cooperative, equal-power relationships with the high-power members. He states that the ability of low-power members to offer and engage in authentic cooperation means that they are aware that they are neither helpless nor powerless, even though they are at a disadvantage. Cooperative action requires a recognition that a person has the capacity to "go it alone" if necessary; unless a person has the freedom to choose not to cooperate, there can be no free choice to cooperate. Thus, the low-power members in a group need to build enough cohesiveness and strength to function independently of the high-power members if this is necessary. In addition, the high-power members must be motivated to cooperate with the low-power members. This means that the latter must find goals that are important to the high-power members, especially goals they cannot accomplish without the cooperation of the low-power members.

A variety of strategies for influencing high-power members are available to low-power members (Deutsch, 1969). By building their own organizations and developing their own resources, low-power members not only can make themselves less vulnerable to exploitation but also can add to their power by providing themselves with alternatives that preclude their being dependent solely upon the high-power members. Low-power members can add to their power by allying themselves with third parties. Another strategy is to try to use existing legal procedures to bring pressures for change. Further, low-power members can search for attachments with the high-power members that, if made more obvious, could increase the latter's positive feelings toward or outcome dependence upon the low-power members. Low-power members can try to change the attitudes of those in high power through education or moral persuasion. Finally, the low-power members can use harassment techniques in order to increase the high-power members' costs of staying with the status quo. In planning how to increase their power in relation to the high-power members, low-power members of a group should first clarify their goals, then take stock of their resources, and finally study how to make the high-power members more aware of their dependence on them and of their compatibility (if any) of goals.

Relationships Between High- and Low-Power Groups

The basic rule of authority hierarchies is that each person should obey the directives of those with higher authority. There are times when this rule seems inappropriate. In 1971, for example, Lieutenant William Calley was convicted of premeditated murder of at least twenty-two Vietnamese civilians in March 1968 at what is known as the My Lai massacre. In his defense, Calley declared that he was acting as a good soldier and following orders. One manifestation of authority is a uniform. Even when a stranger is approached on the street and given a directive that has nothing to do with the authority hierarchy ("give that person a dime"), individuals more frequently follow the directive when the person giving it is in a uniform (guard or firefighter) (Bickman, 1974; Bushman, 1984).

Being placed in a high-power or low-power position can change a person's behavior patterns. Zimbardo (1972, 1973) conducted a field study to explore the roles of guards and prisoners in a prison situation. From over one hundred applications to participate in the two-week experiment, Zimbardo carefully selected twenty-four participants on the basis of extensive psychological testing to ensure they were "normal" and representative of intelligent, middle-class, male youth. Participants were randomly assigned to be guards or prisoners. The setting was made realistic with bars on the doors, prison uniforms, clubs for the guards, and strict visiting hours for anyone wanting to meet with the prisoners. The guards were simply instructed to keep order. The surprising outcome of this simulation was that it had to be abandoned after only six days because the treatment of the prisoners by the guards was far more aggressive and dehumanizing than had been expected. The prisoners broke down and became passive acceptors of brutal treatment, and the guards seemed to enjoy thinking up new ways to degrade prisoners. What makes these findings so shocking is the expectation that normal, bright, young, middle-class men would not act in this way.

Revenge

Interaction between high- and low-power individuals often results in the low-power person feeling abused and mistreated. Revenge is arguably the driving force behind a large portion of conflicts. Power asymmetry between parties affects whether revenge will be carried out or suppressed (Heider, 1958; Raven & Kruglanski, 1970). In general, people of low power are less likely to take revenge against a more powerful harm doer (than high-power people are to take revenge against a less powerful harm doer)—if only because they must fear the consequences of the high power's counterrevenge. In the presence of a third party concerned with justice issues, however, upward revenge by low-power participants was greater than downward revenge (high-power participants taking revenge against low-power participants) (Kim, Smith, & Brigham, 1998).

Relationships Among Low-Power Groups

Although there has been considerable examination of relationships between high- and low-power groups, there has been little research on how low-power groups relate to each other. There are two views. Based on the similarity-attraction hypothesis (Byrne, 1971; Brown, 1984) and on the common-enemy position (Sherif, 1966), it is argued that two disadvantaged groups will be attracted to each other. On the other hand, disadvantaged groups may perceive their similar status as a threat to their distinctiveness, which may decrease the integrity of their identity and self-esteem, thus motivating the group to derogate other low-power out-groups to enhance differentiation (Brown, 1984; Turner, 1978).

Rothgerber and Worchel (1997) conducted a set of studies examining the relationship between a disadvantaged, low-power group and (a) an advantaged, high-power group and (b) other disadvantaged, low-power groups. They found that disadvantaged groups relate differently to other disadvantaged groups than they do to an advantaged group. They tend to be more sensitive to the actions of a disadvantaged out-group than to the actions of an advantaged out-group. Good fortune for the disadvantaged out-group excites negative behavior towards that group, whereas good fortune for the advantaged group elicits either little response or more positive behavior towards that group. Thus, it seems that low-power groups respond competitively to each other. When the performance of a low-power group increases over time and it may gain more power, other low-power groups may try to restrain their progress and keep them from bettering themselves. This, of course, helps the high-power group keep its power advantage.

Power and Conflict

Power and conflict are interrelated. Although power is always present in interpersonal and group interaction, conflict occurs only when a group member wants something to happen and does not have the power to make it happen. No conflict exists when (a) a person wants group members to do something and they want to do it (even when the person does not have the power to influence them to do so) and (b) a person wants group members to do something and has the power to influence them to do it. Conflict does exist when a person wants other group members to do something they do not want to do and the person does not have enough power to overcome their unwillingness. Conflict often ends when the use of power is successful but is escalated when influence attempts are unsuccessful; that is, when the desire to influence is not matched by the capacity to influence.

The destructive management of conflict results in fewer and fewer bases of power being effective. Informational power and expertise power are apt to be rejected because each participant sees the other as being untrustworthy and as trying to use expertise for personal gain. Hostility and distrust undermine legitimate power and mutual referent power. Reward power can arouse suspicions of bribery or suggest that one is attempting to increase another's dependence. Only coercive power is left and thus is relied on more and more.

The use of coercive power is destructive for many reasons. It exacerbates the conflict, thereby increasing hostility, resentment, lies, threats, retaliation, revenge, and distrust. Threats often lead to aggression and counterthreats. Coercion and threats can sometimes shorten or control a conflict through behavioral compliance or withdrawal. Coercion decreases the frequency and reliability of communication. The reliance on coercive power results in a separation of high- and low-power groups and a redefinition of behavior by low-power groups. A political uprising is a "crime of violence" from the high-power perspective but a "humanitarian attempt at liberation" from the low-power perspective. The low-power group's revolutionary hero is the high-power group's terrorist. From the high-power perspective, it makes strategic sense to define any act of political rebellion as "aggressive," in order to weaken the opposition. For these and many other reasons, the use of coercive power should be avoided in conflicts.

Exercise 6.6: Power Among Summer Students

The purpose of this exercise is to provide an opportunity for a discussion as to how power is used and how leadership is developed in peer groups. It achieves this purpose by examining the interrelationships among ten college students attending summer school and living together in a small dormitory. The procedure is as follows:

1. Form groups of five members. One member volunteers to be an observer. The task of the observer is to record the nature of leadership and power within the group as members complete the task.
2. Each participating group member (four in all) is given the description of two of the college students (ten in all). The group as a whole is given a copy of the Characteristics Chart. The task of the group is to decide by consensus the answers to the following ques-

tions. Each member must agree with the answers, be able to explain them, and be confident that every other member can explain the reasoning of the group in arriving at the answers.
  a. Who are the members of each subgroup?
  b. What is the base of power for each subgroup member?
  c. Who is the leader of each subgroup?
  d. What characterizes the interactions among members of different subgroups?
3. When the group has come to consensus about the answers to the questions in step 2, members are to write a description of power that includes the answers to the following questions. Group members are to agree by consensus to the answers (i.e., their written description of power and influence).
  a. How do the students exert influence on each other?
  b. What bases of power does each student use?

Characteristics of the Summer Students

Characteristics	Virginia	Renee	Pat	Debbie	Janice
Religion	Catholic	Catholic	Nonsectarian	Methodist	Presbyterian
Attendance	Frequent	Occasional	Never	Frequent	Rare
College major	Math	Education	Business Mgt.	Home Ec.	Accounting
Grade average	B	C	A	B	A
Family income	Medium	Medium	Medium	Low	High

Characteristics	Diane	Gail	Cindy	Cathy	Heidi
Religion	Baptist	Christian	Baptist	Catholic	Baptist
Attendance	Frequent	Occasional	Occasional	Occasional	Frequent
College major	History	Pre-law	Languages	Home Ec.	Music
Grade average	B	A	B	C	C
Family income	Medium	High	Medium	Low	Low

4. When the group has finished step 3, members are to write a description of leadership that includes answers to the following questions. Each group is to agree by consensus to all the points included in its written description of leadership.
  a. What leadership qualities do the students identified as leaders have?
  b. How do the leaders of the subgroups exercise their leadership?
5. The groups should share their descriptions of leadership and power with each other in a discussion involving the entire class.

DESCRIPTION OF THE SUMMER STUDENTS

  Virginia is a social person who often talks to others. She is quite attractive and dresses well. She dates often. When she has problems, she shares them with Renee or Pat. She sometimes borrows clothes from them. At night she is usually in her room or in Cathy's room. She sometimes sneaks out of the dorm at night and always gets back without being caught. She shares the food and beer that she sneaks into the dorm with Renee, Cathy, and sometimes Janice.

Renee is a fairly attractive, rather insecure person. She smokes and drinks. She dates occasionally, often double-dating with Cathy. She borrows clothes from Virginia and Debbie. At night she is usually in Virginia's or Cathy's room and confides in them. At times she sneaks out of the dorm at night and is helped by Virginia to get back in. She shares food and liquor with Cathy and Virginia.

Pat is a clearheaded person with a perceptive mind. She does not drink and is fairly traditional in her ideas. She is quiet and seldom dates; she never double-dates. She lends clothes to Janice, Virginia, Gail, and Heidi, but does not borrow them. She is a good listener and others confide in her, but she does not reciprocate. At night she can be found in her own room, but she is often accompanied by one of the other students.

Debbie is a rather wild person who dates frequently, occasionally double-dating with Janice. She seems mostly interested in boys—her main topic of conversation. She shares clothes with Virginia and Janice, and at night can usually be found in one of their rooms. At times she sneaks out of the dorm at night and is helped to get back in by Virginia. She shares food with Janice, Virginia, and occasionally Cathy. She confides in Janice.

Janice is an outgoing person who is quite attractive and dresses well. She dates often and sometimes double-dates with Debbie. When she has problems she goes to see Pat. She borrows clothes from Pat or Debbie. At night she is usually in her own room. She is a good talker and is successful in debating most of the other students. She is well versed in clothes, dating, and men and has lots of spending money. She shares food from home with Debbie, Virginia, and Gail.

Diane is a neat, well-groomed, modest person with strong moral convictions. She seldom dates and does not smoke or drink. She is very active in church work and attends several times a week. When she has a personal problem, she goes to see Pat or her minister. She lends clothes to Cindy. At night she is usually in her own room. She likes to read and has been known to remind the students about quiet hours, which has caused some resentment from Janice and Renee.

Gail is a wealthy, well-traveled, sophisticated person who seems to relate well to everyone on a casual level. She dates occasionally but never double-dates. She sometimes borrows clothes from Pat, with whom she shares her problems. She is mature and understanding of others but does not seem to form very close friendships. At night she can be found in the room of Pat or Diane. She shares food with Diane, Pat, and sometimes Janice.

Cindy is a very shy person who seldom dates. She doesn't smoke or drink. She occasionally goes to a movie with Diane, sometimes Heidi. At night she can be found in Diane's or Janice's room. She shares food with Diane or Janice. She avoids Renee and Virginia.

Cathy is a rather loud, chunky person. She often swears and is heard telling dirty jokes. She occasionally double-dates with Renee. She likes to smoke and drink. She shares her problems with Virginia and Renee. At night she is in her room or Virginia's room. She shares food with Virginia, Renee, and sometimes Debbie.

Heidi is an overweight person who tries to be friendly with everyone. She goes out of her way to run errands and otherwise tries to please the other students. She does not smoke, drink, or date. She attends movies with Cindy or Diane. She does not dress well, and Pat is the only one who will lend her clothes. At night she is either in her own room or Pat's or Diane's room. She shares her problems with Pat or Diane. She shares food with Diane, Cindy, Gail, and Pat.

Exercise 6.7: Group Power Experiences

1. With your classmates, form groups of five. Place all the change the group members have in a hat. Decide who in the group gets all the money. Discuss the experience.

2. Stand by the walls of the room with your classmates. Each of you picks a spot in the center of the room in which you would like to sit. At a signal from a coordinator, go sit in that spot. Once all of you are settled, discuss your experience with the nearest person.

3. Stand in the circle with your classmates, touching fingertips with the person on either side. Pick a spot in the room to which you would like the group to go. Do not talk. When the signal is given, try to get the group to move to your chosen spot. Discuss what you have learned with a partner.

4. Stand in a circle with your classmates. Each member helps with one hand to hold a sheet of paper. No verbal communication is allowed. At the signal the paper suddenly becomes "power." See what happens and discuss.

5. Pair up with a classmate. Sit in chairs facing each other. You have five minutes to decide, nonverbally, who is going to sit on the floor. At the end of that time one person must be on the floor. See what happens and discuss.

6. Sit in a circle with your classmates. Each of you close your eyes and imagine you live in a small rural village. You have been handed an important message to deliver to someone in a much more powerful neighboring village. You begin to walk to the other village. You pass a girl on a bridge. You pass a man on a bicycle. You pass a family having a picnic. You hear the sound of birds singing, you see trees moving in the breeze, and you smell the grass and the earth. Rounding a bend, you suddenly come upon a wall. It continues in both directions as far as you can see. The village you need to get to is beyond the wall. For a few minutes think of what happens. Then open your eyes and share stories of what happened at the wall. Discuss from the standpoint of power.

7. Sit in a circle with your classmates. Close your eyes and picture the group in which you are a member. In your fantasy, begin a game of follow-the-leader. At first see yourself as the leader and note what happens among the followers. Now shift leaders and see someone else at the head of the line. Keep going until all the members of your group have had a chance to be the leader. Then open your eyes and discuss the following questions: *What kinds of things did different persons lead the group to do? What feelings did you imagine among the followers? How did you picture the group behaving when you were the leader? Who seemed the most "natural" in the role? Who seemed the least "natural' in the role?*

8. Divide into groups of four with your classmates. Make a picture or collage of power, using available resources—magazines, pencils, paints, crayons, newspapers, and so forth. At the end of thirty minutes discuss the picture of each group. If Polaroid cameras are available, go out and take a picture of power instead of making a picture of power. Then come back and discuss.

9. This exercise is for a group that has been working together on a task. Arrange yourselves in a line according to how powerful you see yourselves, from most powerful to least powerful. Before beginning, mark one end of the line as the spot for the most powerful person so that all members will know how to arrange themselves. After the line has stabilized, ask if anyone wants to move to a different location. Discuss self-perceptions and perceptions of others. How does your power as perceived by other members compare with how you see it? Were there disagreements among members about who is the most powerful? Does the group have certain biases about power, such as the richest person being seen as the most powerful?

YOUR POWER BEHAVIOR

You have now participated in a series of exercises on power as well as having read a summary of much of the current theory and research on the use of power. Power has been discussed in several previous chapters. At this point, form a group with two of your classmates. Discuss what you have learned about yourself and your behavior in power situations. What are your feelings when you are being opposed and have to rely upon power to further your goals? How do you feel when others quickly conform to what you wish them to do? How do you react when others force you to comply to their wishes? What basis of power do you usually rely upon? Have you ever been manipulated or conned? If so, what did it feel like? Any question about power and its use should be discussed if it increases your understanding of yourself and the other members of your group. Write down your conclusions about yourself and your use of power.

Exercise 6.8: Developing Land Areas

The purpose of this exercise is to examine the consequences of unequal power among nations of individuals. Group members are representatives of large land areas and strive to advance the standard of living of its residents. Materials needed are copies of the game board for each member (or one large one for each group, with six individual markers); one hundred tokens for each group (coins, small strips of paper, etc.); resource cards—five for each member, thirty for each group; six cards for each group with the land areas written on them; and copies of the rules for each group. Groups need six members each. The procedure for the coordinator is as follows:

1. Introduce the exercise as a game focusing upon the consequences of unequal power among nations or individuals. Each person will represent a land area and will attempt to improve the standard of living of his or her area.
2. Form groups of six. On 3 × 5 inch cards, write the names of the following land areas: Asia, Africa and Mideast, South America, the former Soviet countries, Europe, and North America. Turn the cards face down and mix them. Each member chooses a card to find out which land area he or she will represent.
3. Tokens are distributed to the group members in the following way:
   a. Asia is given 1.
   b. Africa and Mideast are given 2.
   c. South America is given 2.
   d. Russia and the members of the former Soviet Union are given 8.
   e. Europe is given 13.
   f. North America is given 26.
   Tell the group members that these numbers represent the approximate gross national product of their areas divided by the population. Forty-eight additional tokens are put in the middle as a common bank from which members can draw according to game instructions.
4. Five resource cards marked with the land area are given to each member. These represent the natural resources of the area and can either each represent one token or can be used as collateral on loans from other land areas. In order to advance to level 7, however, members must possess all their resource cards.

5. Distribute a game board to each member. Members keep track of their progress by covering each square with a token. They must advance sequentially. (Alternative: Make one large game board per group and have members mark their places with representative markers.) Members begin on the square that represents the number of tokens they were initially given.
6. Go over the rules with the class. Give them a few minutes to study their positions, then have them begin.
7. After the game, discuss the following questions with the large group:
   a. How did it feel to begin the game with the number of tokens you did?
   b. How did the number of your tokens make a difference in the strategies you used?
   c. How difficult was it to develop an alliance or get a loan? Why?
   d. How many people called "Attack"? How successful was it as a strategy?
   e. What did you learn about the dynamics of unequal power from playing this game?

RULES FOR DEVELOPING LAND AREAS EXERCISE

1. The purpose of this game is to advance your land area as many spaces as you can. You do this by gaining tokens; one token will advance you one space. You must keep all previous spaces filled, although you may go backward (by loaning tokens, for example) as well as forward. If you give as collateral a resource card you have used as a token, you must fill that empty space first.
2. You start out with the number of tokens that represent your land area's approximate wealth (according to the 1980 gross national product divided by population size). That number determines where you will start the game (put all your tokens on your game board to begin). In addition, you will each get five resource cards, which represent your area's natural resources. These can be used to add to your position by representing one token or can be used as collateral for loans from other countries. You can use a resource card you hold from another land area as collateral as one token.
3. There will be ten rounds. Appoint a timekeeper. Starting with Asia and rotating clockwise, you will each get three minutes to find a way to increase your tokens. Once you have added tokens, your turn is over. If you are unsuccessful at the end of three minutes, you lose your turn and the round continues. The game ends after ten rounds or if a stalemate develops.
4. You can gain tokens in four ways:
   a. **Progress:** When you fill a line with tokens, you get additional ones from the World Bank according to the number noted at the end of the line. If, in lending out or losing tokens, you fall below a line previously passed, you do not have to repay that token. You may collect (or recollect) tokens when you fill that line again. However, if you use resource cards as tokens, you may take them off a space only if you negotiate a loan and must thereby give the card to the lender.
   b. **Form an Alliance:** If you and another land area negotiate an alliance, you both get two tokens from the World Bank. You may negotiate an alliance only once with a particular land area.
   c. **Call an Attack:** If you call "Attack," each land area that does not hold any of your resource cards or is not in alliance with you must pay you one token. You may call an attack only twice during the game.
   d. **Negotiate a Loan:** Any land area can lend tokens to another land area in exchange for a resource card, which serves as collateral and can later be repurchased. The amount of the loan and the repurchase are negotiable.

Game Board for Developing Land Areas Exercise

Level VII Nirvana	**Self-Sufficiency:** *You can sit back and watch everyone else play, or . . .*						
Level VI Secure	31 Secure food	32 Secure homes	33 Secure work	34 Secure health	35 Secure education	36 Secure energy	Buy back resource cards
Level V Specialized	25 Extra food	26 Luxury homes	27 Comfortable work	28 Specialized medicine	29 Specialized education	30 Solar energy	Receive five tokens
Level IV Mass production	19 Abundant food	20 Large houses	21 Factories	22 Hospitals	23 Higher education	24 Oil energy	Receive four tokens
Level III Mechanized	13 Sufficient food	14 Small houses	15 Mechanized farms	16 Health clinics	17 Basic education	18 Dam energy	Receive three tokens
Level II Basic	7 Subsistance food	8 Basic shelter	9 Rudimentary farming	10 Folk medicine	11 Early education	12 Forest energy	Receive two tokens
Level I Predevelopment	1 Malnutrition	2 Lack of shelter	3 Inefficient farming	4 Disease	5 Folklore	6 Wood gathering	Receive one token

GROUP NORMS: INDIRECT POWER

"What's it to be? Pizza or hamburgers?" Six friends who had just exited a movie theater were trying to decide what to eat. "Pizza!" immediately said five. "Hamburgers!" Keith answered. In rapid fire everyone talked to Keith. "We always get pizza." "Pizza is our group's official food. " "You can have hamburger on your pizza." "We never eat hamburgers; hamburgers are for kids!" "Don't be a killjoy!" "OK," said Keith. "Let's get pizza." This scenario occurs many times a day. The majority of a group decide on a particular course of action that another member prefers not to do. The majority reminds the dissenter of group norms designed to pressure and persuade the member to adopt the group perspective. The incident concludes when the member capitulates and conforms to the group's norms.

Group norms often serve as substitutes for the direct use of power among group members (Kelley & Thibaut, 1978). **Norms** are prescribed modes of conduct and belief that guide the behavior of group members. Group members (whether they have high or low power) tend to gain from having mutually acceptable norms that introduce regularity and control into their relationship without making direct interpersonal application of power necessary. The direct use of power requires the expenditure of considerable energy and resources and has numerous costs. Group norms are often implemented to substitute for direct influence procedures. Indirect influence through group norms avoids the resistance and lack of wholehearted cooperation that may result from the direct application of power. Group norms control the behavior of high-power members as well as low-power members and set limits on the use of power. Group members give up part of their personal power to the norms to protect themselves from the capricious or inconsistent use of power and constantly checking on each other's behavior to make sure everyone is behaving appropriately. Individuals let themselves be influenced by norms in ways that they would never permit themselves to be influenced by others, because norms often take on the characteristics of moral obligations (they have a specific "ought to" and "must" quality). At the very least, conformity to group norms is a requirement for continued membership in the group.

Conforming to Group Norms

As for conforming outwardly, and living your own life inwardly,
I do not think much of that.

Henry David Thoreau

A man stands up and faces the group. "My name is Dale," he says. "I am an alcoholic. I have not had a drink for three years, two months, and six days." The group applauds. This is a meeting of Alcoholics Anonymous. One group norm is to take the "first step" and admit that you are an alcoholic. Another group norm is to stay sober, one day at a time. Dale has just publicly testified that he is conforming to these normative expectations. The group is giving him support and recognition for doing so. This scenario occurs countless times daily in families, businesses, schools, churches, and all other groups. A group cannot exist, cannot survive, cannot function, and cannot be productive unless most members conform to its norms most of the time.

In our society conformity has acquired a generally negative connotation. Many people think of conformity as a blind, unreasoning, spineless, weak, slavish adherence to the demands of the majority of peers or authority figures. Even among social psychologists there is a common conception of conformity as agreement with the majority or for the sake of agreement. Conformity to group norms is frequently viewed as a violation of one's principles in order to obtain group acceptance, or a selling out of one's individuality in order to get ahead. Much of the research on conformity is based on behaviors such as lying about one's perceptions or beliefs. These pejorative connotations of conformity, however, are inaccurate and are based on a misunderstanding of the complexity of the process of conforming to group norms. There are conditions under which conformity to group norms may violate important values and principles of an individual, and other conditions under which conforming will support these values and beliefs.

Conformity is defined as changes in behavior that result from group influences. The changes include **compliance** (behavioral change without internal acceptance) and **private acceptance** (changes in both behavior and attitudes). Conforming to group norms frequently improves the functioning of a group at no expense to the individual's principles or beliefs. Conforming to a classroom norm that one should provide help and assistance to classmates, for example, is beneficial for the group and the students involved.

The classic studies on conformity under group pressures were conducted by Solomon Asch (1956). Asch was born in 1907 in Poland. He arrived in the United States at age thirteen. In 1928 he received a B.S. degree from City College of New York. In 1932 he received a Ph.D. degree from Columbia University. He was an unusually independent person and of him it has often been said that it took the least conformant of social psychologists to defend conformity and to point out that an essential feature of social life is the willingness to trust the observations of others. In his experimental studies on conformity he asked participants to choose which of several lines came closest in length to a line they had just seen (see Figure 6.3). There was an obvious right answer. Yet each participant found him or herself faced with most or all fellow group members (group size ranged from three to fifteen) agreeing on an obviously wrong answer. The participant was thus faced with a conflict: Accepting the evidence of his or her own eyes or going along with the group's perception. Sixty-eight percent of the individual estimates remained independent; 32 percent were deflected part or all of the way to the unanimous judgment of the fellow group members. One fourth of the participants made no concessions to the unanimous majority; one third conformed in half or more of the trials. Whether the majority consisted of three or fifteen members made little difference,

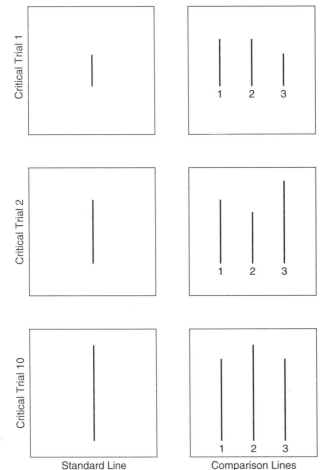

Figure 6.3 The Asch experiments. On twelve of the eighteen trials, the majority of the group members purposely picked the incorrect comparison line. On the first of these critical trials, the standard line was 3 inches long, and Comparison Line 3 was the correct answer. However, the group chose Line 1, which was actually 3¾ inches long. On Critical Trial 2 the correct answer was 1, but the group unanimously answered with 2. Finally, the stimuli used in the tenth critical trial are also shown; the correct answer in this case was 2, but the group suggested 1.

Source: S. Asch, "An Experimental Investigation of Group Influence," in *Symposium on Preventive and Social Psychology*, Walter Reed Army Institute of Research (Washington, D.C.: U.S. Government Printing Office, 1957).

as long as it was unanimous. If one other member agreed with the participant, the tendency to err in the direction of the majority estimate dropped from 32% to 10%. If the participant reported his estimates secretly, furthermore, the promajority errors were fewer. The results of the Asch experiments were somewhat shocking, as they seemed to indicate that many persons would go along with an erroneous group judgment even when they knew it was false. Most social psychologists reacted to the results of Asch's studies as if they agreed with Thoreau.

In discussing conformity to group norms we must differentiate two dimensions: conformity versus anticonformity and independence versus dependence (Allen 1965; Hollander and Willis, 1967). The conformers and anticonformers both react to the group norm and base their behavior on it: The conformers agree with the norm, the anticonformers disagree with the norm, and both behave accordingly. An independent person, on the other hand, does not give undue importance to the group norm in making her judgment.

Not all behaviors are covered by group norms. Not many groups care what foods their members eat or whether they prefer one type of drink to another. Group norms deal primarily with the behavior affecting the accomplishment of the group's task and the ability of the group to maintain itself over time. In general, the more relevant the individual's behavior to the accomplishment of the group's task and the maintenance of the group, the more the pressures toward conformity. Many years ago observers in industrial organizations noted that members of male work groups typically established production standards (norms) that were adhered to by most members (Homans, 1950; Roethlisberger and Dickson, 1939). When a worker deviated too much from the standard, he or she was subjected to ridicule and other sanctions. If the worker produced too much, he or she was referred to as a "speed king" or a "rate-buster"; if he produced too little, the worker was a "chiseler." Schachter (1951), Emerson (1954), and Schachter and his associates (1954) all found in their studies of deviation from group norms that the more relevant the deviation to the purposes of the group, the greater the rejection of the deviant by the other group members. Festinger (1950) and Allen (1965) concluded that there is greater pressure to conform to task-related norms if goal attainment depends on the coordinated behavior of the group members. Raven and Rietsema (1957) found that the clearer the group goal and the path to the goal are to the group members, the stronger are the pressures towards uniformity in task behavior. In general, nonconforming behaviors are accepted if they are perceived by the group's members as potentially improving the group's ability to accomplish its task and maintain itself; they are not accepted if they interfere with group maintenance and task accomplishment.

Implementing Group Norms

There are several ways in which norms can be initiated (Johnson, 1970). One frequent method is for a member to state the norm directly and tell other members to accept it. A member might say, for example, "I think we should express our feelings openly about this topic," and tell other members to do so. Norms can be initiated through modeling, wherein members learn to conform to a group norm by watching others conform. Norms can also be imported from other groups. People usually learn cultural norms of **social responsibility** (you should help someone who is in need of help), **fair play,** (don't kick someone when he's down), and **reciprocity** (if someone does you a favor, you should do her a favor in return) from others, and these norms can be incorporated into one's own group. All in all, however, perhaps the most effective way of starting group norms is through group discussion.

Johnson (1970) has presented a set of general guidelines for the establishment and support of group norms. Group members will accept and internalize group norms when they:

1. Recognize that the norms exist, see the other members accepting and following the norms, and feel some commitment to the norms.
2. See the norms as helping accomplish the goals to which members are committed. It is helpful, therefore, for a group to clarify how conformity to a norm will help goal accomplishment.
3. Feel a sense of ownership for the norms. Ownership is usually established through involvement in establishing the norms.
4. Enforce the norms on each other immediately after a violation. Consistent enforcement enhances both understanding of the norms and commitment to them.
5. See appropriate models and examples of conforming to the norms and have a chance to practice the desired behaviors.
6. Import cultural norms that promote goal accomplishment and group maintenance and growth into the group.
7. Perceive that the norms are flexible so that at any time more appropriate norms can be substituted to increase group effectiveness.

THE GROUP MIND

In 1212 bands of children and young people in Germany and France responded to the Church's call to reconquer Jerusalem. They began the Children's Crusade convinced that only the pure in spirit could succeed in taking the Holy Land from the Muslims. In Germany, a boy named Nicholas led the children from town to town gathering increasing numbers. They walked across the Alps into Italy and then to the sea. The children expected the sea to divide so they could walk to the Holy Land. It did not. Confused, some returned home and merchants sold some into slavery. No one knows if any reached the Holy Land. Why did thousands of children join the Crusade? Why did their parents let them?

There are unexplained ways in which groups have powerful influences on members. Group members sometimes engage in **collective behavior,** where they spontaneously perform atypical actions such as in riots, panics, and mass hysteria (the spontaneous outbreak of atypical thoughts, feelings, or actions in a group, including psychogenic illness, common hallucinations, and bizarre actions [Pennebaker, 1982; Phoon, 1982]). In 1903, for example, there was a panic at Chicago's Iroquois Theater. A small fire broke out backstage and the management tried to calm the audience. When the fire became visible to the crowd, however, the audience stampeded for the exits. Some died by jumping from the fire escapes to the pavement. Many more were killed as fleeing patrons trampled them. Some were burned. Nearly six hundred people were killed. From the Crusades to the French revolution to rock-and-roll concerts, membership in groups and mass hysteria have been associated together.

A number of explanations have been proposed to examine such group influences. The *first* was the group mind proposed by Le Bon. In 1895 Gustave Le Bon published his classic study *The Crowd* to explain why persons in a mob lose their sense of responsibility. Le Bon argued that people in crowds show "impulsiveness, irritability, incapacity to reason," and "exaggeration of sentiments" (p. 40). No matter what the individual qualities of the people in the group, once they fall under the "law of the mental unity of crowds," they *all* act in ways that are impulsive, unreasonable, and extreme.

Le Bon believed that three mechanisms contributed to the formation of crowd behavior. The first is **anonymity** because people feel less responsible for their behavior when they cannot be identified. Crowds create relative anonymity and thus reduce individual responsibility. People then commit acts for which they believe they cannot later be held responsible. The second is **contagion** because emotional states spread from person to person like diseases spread. Le Bon was a physician, and so he viewed the collective mind as a kind of disease that began at one point in the group and then spread throughout the rest of the crowd. Similar to how germs are spread from person to person, emotions and behaviors are transmitted from one person to another, resulting in the tendency for group members to behave in very similar ways. The third is **suggestibility** as crowd members completely accept all suggestions made to them, just as if they were hypnotized.

A *second* possible explanation is convergence theory. According to **convergence theory,** individuals join the group because they possess similar needs and personal characteristics. Crowd action represents the convergence of people with compatible needs, desires, motivations, and emotions. By joining in the group, the individual makes possible the satisfaction of these needs, and the crowd situation serves as a trigger for the spontaneous release of previously controlled behaviors. A specific event brings together people who share similar convictions and predispositions. Members bring a common mood to the crowd (as in a protest demonstration). The crowd eventually acts out this mood. Crowd behavior could be predicted, therefore, by identifying the latent tendencies and beliefs of large numbers of people. Although the predisposing features may be latent or virtually unrecognizable, they are the true causes of the formation of both large and small collectives. Convergence theory seeks to identify the latent tendencies in people that cause them to act alike, the circumstances that bring people with such tendencies together, and the kinds of events that will cause these tendencies to be released (Freud, 1922; Turner & Killian, 1972, p. 19). Sigmund Freud (1922) believed that people join collectives to satisfy repressed unconscious desires that otherwise would never be fulfilled. In the group situation, control over behavior is transferred to the leader or other group members, and each person is thus freed from the bonds of restraint and guilt. As a result, formerly repressed needs come to motivate behavior, and atypical actions become more likely.

A *third* explanation is emergent-norm theory. Ralph Turner and Lewis Killian (1972) argue that crowds are quite heterogeneous and do not have a "mental unity." Rather the members all adhere to norms that are relevant to the given situation. They hypothesized that all crowds share a number of common elements. Crowds form in ambiguous situations in which the participants' behaviors are unplanned. A sense of urgency characterizes the feelings of the crowd members. As the crowd gets larger, norms are communicated throughout the crowd about appropriate moods, imagery, and actions. The dominant mood, imagery, and actions come to be viewed as right, as those to which the crowd members should conform. A group norm thus emerges. Uniformity ultimately results from the interaction among the initially dissimilar members. Individuals become highly susceptible to suggestions consistent with the emergent norm. As a result, the participants may engage in actions they would ordinarily inhibit.

The *fourth* theory is deindividuation theory. **Deindividuation** is a state of relative anonymity, in which group members do not feel singled out or identifiable (Festinger, Pepitone, & Newcomb, 1952). When people cannot be identified, they are more likely to perform antisocial acts. Festinger, Pepitone, and Newcomb (1952) argued that people in groups feel themselves to be "submerged in the group" and lose their personal identity, that is, they experience deindividuation. This feeling creates a "reduction of inner restraints" and, in the extreme, atypical actions.

Philip Zimbardo's **deindividuation theory** attempts to explain the reduction of inner constraints by dividing deindividuation into three interrelated components (inputs, internal changes, outputs):

1. Conditions of deindividuation **(Inputs):** These include (a) anonymity, (b) reduced responsibility, (c) membership in a large group, and (d) arousal.
2. The state of deindividuation **(Internal Changes):** A subjective experience in which the individual group members experience "a lowered threshold of normally restrained behavior" based on (a) low self-awareness and (b) altered experiencing.
3. Deindividuated behaviors **(Outputs):** Extreme, atypical, or polarized actions. Deindividuation can result in a range of positive outcomes, but for the most part it is the antisocial behaviors such as violence, destruction, and hostility that are most often discussed.

The **conditions of deindividuation** begin with anonymity, which exists when others cannot identify or single out a person for evaluation, criticism, judgment, or punishment. Second, personal responsibility is reduced by the demands for compliance by an authority figure, the separation of the consequences from the act itself, and a diffusion of responsibility among group members. Third, the larger the group the greater the deindividuation. Finally, arousal is increased through altered temporal perspective, sensory overload, heightened involvement, and the lack of situational structure.

Individuals, when deindividuated, experience profound changes in emotions, memory, and self-regulation. *Deindividuation is experienced by* (a) a **loss of self-awareness** (minimal self-consciousness, lack of conscious planning, uninhibited speech, and performing uninhibited tasks) and (b) **altered experiencing** (disturbances in concentration and judgment, the feeling that time is moving slowly or rapidly, extreme emotions, a sense of unreality, and perceptual distortions). People who are deindividuated have lost self-awareness and their personal identity in the group situation. **Altered experiencing** involves cognitive and emotional changes, including disturbances in concentration and judgment, the feeling that time is moving slowly or rapidly, extreme emotions, a sense of unreality, perceptual distortions, and intense pleasure.

Finally, **deindividuated behaviors** replace reason and order with impulse and chaos. Zimbardo states (1975, p. 53) the conditions that reduce a person's sense of uniqueness and individuality are the wellsprings of antisocial behaviors, such as aggression, vandalism, stealing, cheating, rudeness, as well as a general loss of concern for others. The deindividuated person is quite reactive to emotions and situational cues that may lead to uninhibited behaviors and is less concerned with norms, personal punishment, or long-term consequences.

Power can be exercised by the group as a whole. Groups do influence members in profound and powerful ways. Power can be exercised by the group as a whole through such processes as the group mind, converging with people who share similar convictions and predispositions, following norms that emerge in the group, or members' becoming deindividualized. Being influenced by the group is not all bad. Although theory and research on group power may be cast in negative ways (e.g., mass hysteria and panic), it should also be noted that groups can encourage members to behave altruistically.

Review of Important Concepts

Match the following concepts with their definitions. Find a partner and compare answers.

____	1. Power	a.	Prescribed modes of conduct and belief that guide the behavior of group members.
____	2. High power	b.	Changes in behavior that result from group influences.
____	3. Low power	c.	Behavioral change without internal acceptance.
____	4. Power majority	d.	Capacity to affect another person's goal accomplishment.
____	5. Power minority	e.	State of relative anonymity, in which group members do not feel singled out or identifiable.
____	6. Norms	f.	Individuals spontaneously perform atypical actions such as in riots, panics, and mass hysteria.
____	7. Conformity	g.	Capacity to have considerable influence on another person's goal accomplishment.
____	8. Compliance	h.	Capacity to have little influence on another person's goal accomplishment.
____	9. Collective behavior	i.	Group that has the most control over how important resources are distributed (they may be the numerical minority).
____	10. Deindividuation	j.	Group that has little control over the distribution of important resources (they may be a numerical majority).

Exercise 6.9: Your Power Behavior

Having completed this chapter, it may be helpful to focus again on your behavior in exercising power. Form a group of three with two persons who know you well and who have participated with you in some of the exercises in this book. Then complete the following tasks, taking at least two hours to do so.

1. Reflect silently on how each member uses power. Give each other feedback about the animal, song, or book that each member reminds the others of on the basis of how he or she deals with power. Each person explains why he or she chose the animal, song, or book that he or she did.
2. Write down your individual strengths in using power constructively and effectively. Share your lists. Members should add to each other's lists.
3. Write down the individual skills you need to develop in order to use power more constructively and effectively. Share your lists. Members should add to each other's lists.
4. Discuss the feelings each member has in using power and why he or she reacts that way. Help each other think of alternative ways of reacting to the use of power.
5. From magazine pictures and any other materials, build a collage about the way in which you exercise power. Share the collage with the other members. Add ideas to each other's collages.

SUMMARY

The dynamic-interdependence approach to influence views power as an attribute of an interpersonal relationship. In a relationship people are dependent on each other for outcomes and information. There is an aversion to being controlled and, therefore, the direct use of power in a relationship has to be done carefully. The base of the use of power may make a difference. Power may be based on the ability to deliver rewards, the ability to deliver punishments, a position of authority, being a referent for others, being an expert, and having needed information. When the distribution of power is unequal, both the high- and low-power person have problems. Although the use of power is ever present in a relationship, it is during conflicts that individuals become most conscious of its use.

The trait-factor approach to influence views power as an attribute of a person. A person exerts power by (a) being credible and attractive; (b) phrasing messages so that they are two sided, action oriented, and discrepant with members' current beliefs; and (c) playing on others' low self-esteem and low intelligence, giving them no forewarning of the influence attempt, distracting them during the influence attempt, convincing them the attitudes under modification are peripheral to them, and having them role play positions counter to their beliefs.

Finally, besides the direct use of power, there are indirect ways to exert influence. The primary way is through group norms. When group members conform to the normative expectations, they are being influenced. Most power is exerted through indirect means such as group norms. The mass hysteria and panic that are sometimes observed in groups may have their origins in the group mind, converging with people who share similar convictions and predispositions, following norms that emerge in the group, or members' becoming deindividualized. Being influenced by the group is not all bad. The group can encourage members to behave altruistically.

You should now have a good understanding of power and how it can help or hinder a group. You have experienced high- and low-power situations and know the dangers of each. In the next chapter you will learn how to make effective decisions in small groups.

Decision Making

Basic Concepts to Be Covered in This Chapter

In this chapter a number of concepts are defined and discussed. The major ones are listed below. Divide into heterogeneous pairs. Each pair is to (a) define each concept, noting the page on which it is defined and discussed and (b) ensure that both members of the pair understand the meaning of each concept. Then combine into groups of four. Compare the answers of the two pairs. If there is disagreement, look up the concept in the chapter and clarify it until all members agree on and understand the definition.

Concepts

1. Decision
2. Effective decision
3. Consensus
4. Majority vote
5. Minority control
6. Averaging opinions
7. Defensive avoidance
8. Groupthink
9. Concurrence-seeking
10. Dissonance reduction
11. Vigilance
12. Critical evaluation

MAKING EFFECTIVE DECISIONS

Imagine yourself driving down the street. A police officer stops you for a minor traffic violation and then notices that your appearance matches the description of a person who has just robbed a nearby bank. He arrests you and, to your horror, no fewer than six eyewitnesses identify you as the bank robber. You cannot provide a good alibi for the time of the robbery (you were driving around by yourself) and no one pays any attention to your protestations of innocence. The ordeal drags on until the day you go on trial and face your accusers. As the trial begins you realize that the only barrier between you and a prison sentence is a small group of your peers. The jury members are strangers to one another, chosen randomly from your community, unschooled in legal principles, and unpracticed in group decision making. They hold your fate, your future, your well-being in their hands.

Trial by a jury of peers to determine guilt and innocence has formed the foundation of judicial systems for hundreds of years. As far back as the eleventh century juries were used both to provide information about the actions of the accused and to weigh the evidence. Gradually, juries evolved into finders of fact that weigh the testimony of each person before deciding if a law has in fact been broken.

A jury is only one of the small groups in our society that have to make vital decisions. Governments, large corporations, military units, and virtually all other social entities entrust their key decisions to groups. As a result, most of the laws, policies, and practices that affect our daily lives (as well as the future course of society) are determined by teams, committees, boards of directors, and similar groups, *not* by single individuals. Many groups exist to make decisions in our society. Thousands of small groups are making most of the vital decisions every day. How good the decisions are depends on how effective the groups are. Groups are continually making decisions, some as important as whether a peer accused of a crime will live or die, others as ordinary as when and where the group will meet, what course of action it will take towards accomplishing goals, and what procedures it will use in discussions.

The purpose of group decision making is to decide upon well-considered, well-understood, realistic action towards goals every member wishes to achieve. A *group decision* implies that some agreement prevails among group members as to which of several courses of action is most desirable for achieving the group's goals. Making a decision is just one step in the more general *problem-solving process* of goal-directed groups—but it is a crucial one. After defining a problem or issue, thinking over alternative courses of action, and weighing the advantages and disadvantages of each, a group will decide which course is the most desirable for them to implement.

Typically, groups try to make their decisions as effectively as possible. There are five major characteristics of an *effective group decision.*

1. The resources of group members are fully utilized.
2. Time is well used.
3. The decision is correct, or of high quality.
4. The decision is implemented fully by all the required group members.
5. The problem-solving ability of the group is enhanced, or at least not lessened.

A decision is effective to the extent that these five criteria are met; if all five are not met, the decision has not been made effectively.

Not everyone agrees that group decision making is a good idea. For decades social scientists have disagreed over whether individuals or groups make better decisions. The first issue examined in this chapter, therefore, is the comparative effectiveness of individual and group decision making. Second, different methods a group can use to arrive at a decision are explained. Third, the factors that facilitate and hinder an effective group decision are detailed. Finally, a process groups may use to ensure effective decision making is discussed. Figure 7.1 contains an overview to delineate further how these issues are broken down in the chapter.

Individual Versus Group Decision Making

Process Gain	Involvement and Commitment
Correct Each Other's Errors	Changed Behavior and Attitudes
Social Facilitation	Type of Task
Risk Taking	Potential Group Productivity

Methods of Decision Making

Decision by Authority Without Group Discussion	Decision by Minority
Decision by Expert	Decision by Majority Vote
Decision by Averaging Individuals' Opinions	Decision by Consensus
Decision by Authority After Group Discussion	Time and Decision Making

Essential Components	*Hindering Factors*	
Positive Interdependence	Lack of Group Maturity	
Face-to-Face Promotive Interaction	Dominant Response	
Individual Accountability	Social Loafing	
Social Skills	Free Riding	
Group Processing	Not Being a Sucker	
	Groupthink	Conflicting Goals
	Egocentrism of	Homogeneity
	Group Members	Inappropriate Size
	Production Blocking	Lack of Skills
	Dissonance Reduction	
	Lack of Incentives for and Barriers to Contributing	

Considered and Thoughtful Decision Making

Identifying and Defining Problem	Deciding on a Solution
Gathering Information About Problem	Second-Chance Meeting
Forming Alternative Solutions	Presenting Recommendation to Organization
Force Field Analysis	Evaluating Success of Implementation
Vigilant Analysis	
Barriers	

Problems with Theorizing on Decision Making

Figure 7.1 Overview of chapter.

Exercise 7.1: Individual Versus Group Decision Making

There has been some controversy over whether individual or group decision making is more effective. The purpose of this exercise is to structure a critical discussion of the issue.

1. *Assignment to groups.* Assign participants to groups of four. Each group is to write a short statement summarizing and explaining its position on whether individual or group decision making is more effective.
2. *Assignment to pairs and positions.* Divide each group into two pairs. Pair One is assigned the position that individuals are superior to groups in making decisions and given Briefing Sheet One. Pair Two is assigned the position that groups are superior to individuals in making decisions and is given Briefing Sheet Two. The procedure and guidelines for constructive controversy may be reviewed (page 330).
3. *Preparation of positions.* The pairs meet separately. They have ten minutes to prepare a forceful and persuasive three-minute presentation of their position. Anything in this chapter or in the field of decision making may be included in the presentation. Both members of the pair have to be ready to give the presentation.
4. *Presentations of positions.* New pairs are formed consisting of one person from Pair One and one person from Pair Two. Each person presents his or her assigned position. The listener takes notes and asks for clarification of anything that is not fully understood. Each person can present for only three minutes.
5. *Attack and defend discussion.* A ten-minute discussion of the issue is conducted. Each person critically analyzes the opposing position and points out its shortcomings. Each person defends his or her position from the attacks of the opponent. The discussion should focus on theory, research, and facts, not on opinions and impressions.
6. *Reverse perspectives.* Each person has two minutes to summarize the opponent's position and best reasoning. The summary should be complete and accurate.
7. *Joint report.* The pair writes one statement summarizing and explaining its conclusions on whether individual or group decision making is more effective. The best reasoning from both sides should be synthesized or integrated into a position they both believe is valid. The statement should include theory, research, and facts.
8. *Conclusions and processing.* The pairs join together into a group of four and compare the two statements, write down three conclusions about what they have learned concerning the relative advantages of individual and group decision making. Finally, each person tells each other group member one thing the person liked about working with him or her.

BRIEFING SHEET ONE: INDIVIDUALS MAKE SUPERIOR DECISIONS

Your position is that individuals make higher-quality decisions than groups. To support your position, use the two quotations below, any material from this chapter that is applicable, and what you know from your outside reading.

> If anything, group membership blunts ethical perception and fetters moral imagination, because we then uncritically and possibly let others think for us (LaBarre, 1972, p.14).

> When a hundred clever heads join a group, one big nincompoop is the result, because every individual is trammeled by the otherness of others. (Jung, quoted in Illing, 1957, p. 80.)

BRIEFING SHEET TWO: GROUPS MAKE SUPERIOR DECISIONS

Your position is that groups make higher-quality decisions than individuals. To support your position, use the quotation on page 277, any material from this chapter that is applicable, and what you know from your outside reading.

Group operations have two kinds of potential advantage over action by a single individual. One is the caliber of thinking, the range of resources, and the critical scrutiny which enter the problem solving. The other is the willingness with which people carry out decisions they have helped to make. . . . Groups may sometimes be more sane, moderate, well-balanced and wise than their average member. . . . A thoughtful group may make its members more rational, more self-critical, and more ready to revise personal prejudices in the light of objective evidence, than these members would be if they were studying alone. (Watson & Johnson, 1972, pp. 130–131.)

INDIVIDUAL VERSUS GROUP DECISION MAKING

Which is more productive, groups or individuals? One of the earliest studies to compare individual and group decision making was conducted by Goodwin Watson (1931). Watson received his Bachelor of Arts degree from the University of Wisconsin and his masters and doctorate from Columbia University. He taught at Columbia University from 1925 to 1962. In 1970 he founded and became director of the Graduate School of the Union for Experimenting Colleges and Universities. A vigorous, dedicated psychologist, Watson fought against all types of discrimination and challenged the value of standardized intelligence tests. In his 1931 study he used three equivalent forms of an intelligence test, each consisting of nine tasks suited to bright adults. Sixty-eight graduate students participated in the study. Each student took the first test alone; students then joined with one another in groups of four or five to solve the second test cooperatively. The third form of the test was taken by each individual alone. The two individual performances were averaged. Groups had no previous practice in working together, and were allowed only ten minutes per task. Eleven of the fifteen groups scored higher than their average member and six of the fifteen groups scored higher than their best individual performer. The typical group attained a level of intellectual performance of about the seventieth percentile of its members working alone.

Marvin Shaw (1932) conducted a study in which individuals and four-person groups attempted to solve a series of intellectual puzzles. One puzzle had three married couples trying to cross a river in a boat that can hold only three passengers. There were constraints that reflected the sex and marital norms of the day: Only the husbands could row and no husband would allow his wife to be in the presence of any of the other husbands unless he was also present. Puzzles such as these are called *eureka tasks*—if the correct solution is proposed, it is clear that it is correct (Lorge, Fox, Davitz, & Brenner, 1958). Only three out of twenty-one individuals were able to solve the "husbands and wives" puzzle in Shaw's study, while three of five groups were able to do so.

As a result of studies such as these, Thorndike (1938) concluded that the superiority of group to individual problem solving and decision making to have been proved. More recent reviews have also concluded that groups generally learn faster, make fewer errors, recall better, make better decisions, and are more productive with a higher-quality product than individuals (Baron, Kerr, & Miller, 1992; Davis, 1969; Johnson & Johnson, 1989; Laughlin, 1980). But why are groups superior to individuals (see Figure 7.2)? *One explanation (based on the results of Goodwin Watson's study) is that in groups there is process gain—the interaction among group members results in ideas, insights, and strategies that no one member had previously thought of.* Similar to Watson, Barnlund (1959) found that after a group discussion, decisions surpassed both the average of the decisions of individual members and the best individual members' answers. Falk and Johnson (1977) and Hall and Williams (1966) found that group discussions led to decisions that none of the participants had thought of before the discussion. Groups discussing problems have been found to derive more crucial insights into how best to solve the problems than do individuals working alone (Johnson, Skon, and Johnson, 1980; Skon, Johnson, and Johnson, 1981). Ames and Murray (1982) even demonstrated that when two young children did not know the basic principles of conservation, working together cooperatively resulted in the children spontaneously generating and sharing conservation judgments and explanations where none existed on the pretests. The conservation insights were sustained through both immediate and delayed posttests and affected responses to items that were not part of the experimental session. While only 6% of the children working alone gave conservation answers and explanations on the first posttest, 42% of the children in the cooperative condition did so. Overall, it may be concluded that process gain often occurs in groups, as the discussion often stimulates ideas that might not occur to the individual working alone. In a musical jam session, for example, each member responds continuously to the stimulation of others in building a creative product.

Another explanation is that in groups incorrect solutions are more likely to be recognized and rejected. Shaw (1932) concluded from her study that a group is better able to recognize and reject incorrect solutions and suggestions than are individuals working alone. Ziller (1957) concluded that in groups, chance errors and blind spots may be corrected (as it is usually easier to see others' mistakes than one's own) and members can remedy each other's mistakes.

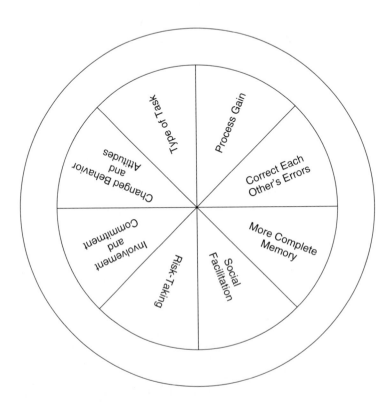

Figure 7.2 Effective group decision making.

A third explanation is that groups have a more accurate memory of facts and events than do individuals. Bekhterev and DeLange (1924) briefly showed a picture to groups and asked members to write down all the details they could remember from the picture. A discussion period followed in which the group tried to reach a consensus about each item. The group decision corrected many of the mistaken recollections of the members. Villasenor (1977) notes that the jurors in the Juan Corona trial remembered far more collectively about the evidence and the testimony than they did individually.

Other reasons why groups may make better decisions than individuals are:

1. Groups facilitate higher motivation to achieve.
2. Groups make riskier decisions than individuals.
3. Involvement in decision making increases members' commitment to implement the decision.
4. Involvement in group decision making facilitates the changes in behavior and attitudes required to implement the decision.

Each of these explanations is discussed below. Finally, the issue of whether decision making groups work up to their potential is examined.

Social Facilitation

Another reason that groups may make better decisions and outperform individuals is that groups provide a cooperative context in which members promote each other's success and give each other help and assistance. When individuals work alone, the presence of other people may be a source of competitive feelings, fear of being obstructed, and evaluation apprehension. For the past one hundred years researchers have studied the impact of the presence of other people on individual performance. In the social facilitation research, the individual or alone condition typically involves the performance of an individual in front of an observant experimenter, whereas the group condition involves people working in the presence of co-actors and an experimenter on similar yet independent tasks. The participants in the groups can see and be seen by one another, which produces an implicitly competitive situation (Geen, 1980).

Social facilitation researchers have shown that working in the presence of others improves performance on a variety of tasks such as fishing-reel winding (Triplett, 1898), dressing in familiar clothes (Markus, 1978), recognition of salient stimuli (Cottrell, Wack, Sekerak, & Rittle, 1968), negotiating simple mazes (Hunt & Hillery, 1973), and copying simple material (Sanders & Baron, 1975). On the other hand, they have found that working in the presence of others impairs performance on other tasks, such as solving difficult anagrams (Green, 1977), dressing in unfamiliar clothes (Markus, 1978), recognition of novel stimuli (Cottrell et al., 1968), negotiating difficult mazes (Hunt & Hillery, 1973), and copying difficult material (Sanders & Baron, 1975). Thus, having others around us appears to facilitate simple tasks and impair performance on complex ones (Bond & Titus, 1983). Social facilitation and impairment effects, furthermore, occur in a wide range of species. There are a number of explanations for these findings.

Most researchers believe that the underlying reason is that feelings of competition increase anxiety, evaluation apprehension, and drive, which increase the likelihood that the dominant or most probable response will occur (Baron, Kerr, & Miller, 1992). If the dominant response includes behaviors that lead to successful performance (as in the case of simple tasks), then people do better when in a drive state. If the dominant response primarily includes behaviors that lead to poor performance (as in the case in difficult tasks), then people do worse when in a drive state.

There are a number of theoretical explanations of how social conditions produce drive-arousal that then facilitates dominant responding. They involve the mere presence of others, learned drives, and distraction. Zajonc (1965) argued that social facilitation and impairment both occur because we are excited and aroused by the mere physical presence of speciesmates. As a result, we try harder. Cottrell (1972) suggests that the presence of speciesmates elevates drive/arousal because, through learning, we have come to associate speciesmates with a variety of rewards and punishments. Social facilitation should occur primarily in competitive or evaluative situations, because such situations have the strongest past associations with rewards and punishments from others. Robert Baron and his associates (1978) proposed that social facilitation occurs because audiences, co-actors, and even bystanders often lead performers into "attentional temptation" in which they are placed in conflict regarding whether to attend to their speciesmates or to the ongoing task. Because the performer wishes to pay attention to more than he or she can manage, the resulting conflict leads to drive-arousal and stress, which in turn produces the social facilitation or impairment effects. Distraction during a simple task will actually improve performance if it triggers attentional conflict (Baron, 1986; Sanders, 1981).

All of the above theories assume that social conditions produce drive-arousal that then facilitates dominant responding. There are three theoretical explanations of social facilitation/impairment that instead focus on self-awareness, self-presentation, and attention. Duval and Wicklund (1972) proposed that social facilitation occurs because (a) audiences or co-actors heighten self-consciousness and (b) self-aware individuals will try harder. Social impairment occurs on difficult tasks because when self-aware people see that they are not succeeding, their motivation drops and they stop trying. Bond (1982) argues that audiences and co-actors affect performance by increasing our concerns about projecting a positive self-image to onlookers. From this self-presentation perspective, social impairment occurs on difficult tasks because initial failures produce embarrassment, which then disrupts performance. Finally, Geen (1976, 1980a) suggests that information overload occurs when a person tries to attend to both the task and the audience. When we are bombarded with attentional demands, our focus of attention actually shrinks. On simple tasks that have become more or less automatic, our performance is facilitated because we have to process only a narrow range of cues. On nonautomatic tasks, however, a narrow attentional focus screens out needed cues.

The social facilitation research over the past ninety years has identified a number of conditions under which the presence of others will disrupt an individual's performance. From this work we can conclude that group decision making will be more effective than individual decision making because in groups the cooperation and social support among group members will moderate arousal and reduce competitiveness, evaluation apprehension, fear of punishment, attentional conflicts, fear of making a negative impression on others, fear of embarrassment, and the narrowing of perceptual focus that creates information overload. In other words, the stronger the positive interdependence and the more social support and assistance given in a group, the greater the social facilitation and the less the social impairment. The security of the group, furthermore, encourages members to take risks in their conclusions and judgments.

Group Polarization

Groups seem to be more secure than individuals in adopting positions that are more liberal or conservative than those originally held by the members (Myers & Lamm, 1976). A group discussion can polarize decisions by causing the group to adopt a position more extreme than the positions individual members held beforehand. When divergent and creative thinking is required and new perspectives are needed, such risk-taking enhances the quality of group decisions.

In 1961 James Stoner (1961), then an MIT graduate student in industrial management, compared risk-taking by individuals and groups for his master's thesis. He wanted to test the commonly held belief that groups were more conservative in their decisions than individuals were. Stoner's procedure, which was followed in dozens of later experiments, posed some decision dilemmas to people by themselves. Each problem described a decision faced by a fictitious person. The subject's task was to advise the person how much risk to take. For example, what advice would you give the person in this item?

Henry is a writer who is said to have considerable creative talent but who so far has been earning a comfortable living by writing cheap westerns. Recently he has come up with an idea for a potentially significant novel. If it could be written and accepted it might have considerable literary impact and give a big boost to his career. On the other hand, if he is not able to work out his idea or if the novel is a flop, he will have expended considerable time and energy without remuneration.

Imagine that you are advising Henry. Please check the *lowest* probability that you would consider acceptable for Henry to attempt to write the novel. Henry should attempt to write the novel if the chances that the novel will be a success are at least:

—— 1 in 10	—— 4 in 10	—— 7 in 10
—— 2 in 10	—— 5 in 10	—— 8 in 10
—— 3 in 10	—— 6 in 10	—— 9 in 10

—— 10 in 10 (Place a check here if you think Henry should attempt the novel only if it is certain that the novel will be a success.)

After marking their advice on a dozen items similar to this one, subjects would be placed in groups of five or so members and discuss each item and reach a unanimous decision on how much risk the person should take. Much to everyone's surprise, the decisions chosen by the group were by and large riskier than those selected before discussion. The finding was immediately dubbed the **risky shift** phenomenon. Over 300 research studies have since been conducted on this issue. Most of these studies used Stoner's method and found that group decisions were indeed riskier. Other research indicates that group discussion intensifies all sorts of attitudes, beliefs, values, judgments, and perceptions (Myers, 1982).

More recently, researchers have realized that although group discussion often produces a shift in individual opinions, such a shift is not necessarily in the direction of greater risk. It could be in the direction of greater cautiousness (a *caution shift*). If the initial opinions of the group tend toward conservatism, then the shift resulting from group discussion will be toward a more extreme conservative opinion (Fraser, 1971; Myers & Bishop, 1970). The term **group polarization,** therefore, has replaced the term *risky shift*. When people discuss issues in groups, there is a tendency to polarize decisions by deciding on a more extreme course of action than would be suggested by the average of their individual judgments, but the direction of this shift depends on what was initially the dominant point of view. Groups seem to be more secure than individuals in adopting positions that are more liberal or conservative than those originally held by the members (Myers & Lamm, 1976). See Figures 7.3 and 7.4.

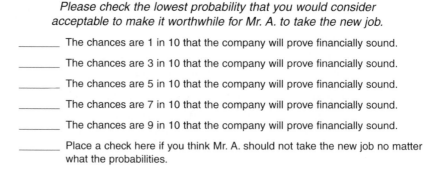

Mr. A., an electrical engineer who is married and has one child, has been working for a large electronics corporation since graduating from college five years ago. He is assured of a lifetime job with a modest, though adequate, salary and liberal pension benefits upon retirement. On the other hand, it is very unlikely that his salary will increase much before he retires. While attending a convention, Mr. A. is offered a job with a small, newly founded company that has a highly uncertain future. The new job would pay more to start and would offer the possibility of a share in the ownership if the company survived the competition of the larger firms.

Imagine that you are advising Mr. A. Listed below are several probabilities or odds of the new company proving financially sound.

Please check the lowest probability that you would consider acceptable to make it worthwhile for Mr. A. to take the new job.

_____ The chances are 1 in 10 that the company will prove financially sound.

_____ The chances are 3 in 10 that the company will prove financially sound.

_____ The chances are 5 in 10 that the company will prove financially sound.

_____ The chances are 7 in 10 that the company will prove financially sound.

_____ The chances are 9 in 10 that the company will prove financially sound.

_____ Place a check here if you think Mr. A. should not take the new job no matter what the probabilities.

Figure 7.3   A choice-dilemma questionnaire item.
Source: M. Wallach, N. Kogan, and D. Bem, "Group Influence on Individual Risk Taking," *Journal of Abnormal and Social Psychology,* 65 (1962), 75–86.

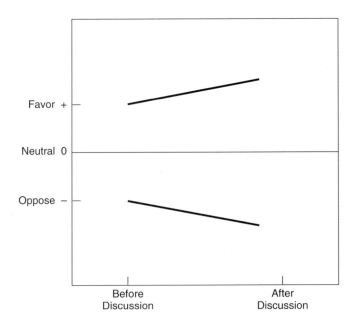

Favor +

Neutral 0

Oppose –

Before
Discussion

After
Discussion

Figure 7.4 The group polarization hypothesis predicts that an attitude shared by group members will usually be strengthened by discussion. For example, if people initially tend to favor risk on a life dilemma question (such as that concerning Henry), they tend to favor it even more after discussion. If initially they tend to oppose risk (as in the case of Roger's decision about selling his life insurance), they tend to oppose it even more after discussion.

At least three explanations have been given for the group polarization effect.

1. *Normative influences.* Groups may polarize because members want to create a favorable impression on others and, therefore, (a) compare their opinions to those of other group members and (b) modify their opinions to be a strong advocate of the group's position. Such normative influence is more likely when the topic concerns values, tastes, and preferences as opposed to factual issues (Laughlin & Early, 1982) or when the situation or topic is ambiguous (Boster & Hale, 1989).

2. *Informational influences:* Groups may polarize because members learn new information that causes them to modify their opinions (Kaplan & Miller, 1987) and members are confronted with persuasive arguments that are (a) compelling (logical and well thought out) and (b) new to some of the group members (Burnstein & Vinokur, 1977; Isenberg, 1986). Recent research on *information sampling theory* indicates that group members have a strong tendency to discuss primarily the information that they share in common and to fail to mention important information that is known only to single individuals (e.g., Stasser & Titus, 1987). Group members seem reluctant to introduce unique ideas unless they detect some social support for doing so.

3. *Social identification:* Groups may polarize because individuals want to identify with the group and be considered members (Isenberg, 1986; Kaplan & Miller, 1987).

The group polarization effect is limited and even reversed when groups make decisions that have real, binding, costly consequences for all group members (Baron, Roper, & Baron, 1974).

Involvement In Decision Making

There are at least two reasons for involving all group members in the group's decision making. *The first reason is to increase the quality of the decision by fully utilizing the resources of all members.* In general, high involvement in decision making increases the use of the members' resources, which in turn increases the quality of the decision. The more group members who participate in making a decision, the more resources available and, consequently, the higher quality the decision. The members responsible for implementing the decision may be especially knowledgeable about what the decision should be and, therefore, especially should be involved in making the decision.

The second reason is to increase members' commitment to implement the decision. Involvement in decision making also tends to increase members' allegiance to the group. One of the most famous research studies of the 1940s dealt with involving workers in decisions about how their work should be conducted. An associate of Kurt Lewin and the personnel manager of a clothing factory teamed up to do a study on overcoming the resistance of workers to changes in their work activities (French & Coch, 1948). The workers in question resisted management's changes in work activities by quitting their jobs, lowering their level of production, and expressing verbal hostility towards the plant and co-workers. French and Coch decided to try out three methods of instituting changes in job duties. One group of workers was simply told about the planned changes in their jobs and what was expected of them; they did not participate in the decision making. The second group appointed representatives from among themselves to meet with management to consider problems involved in changing work methods. All members of the third group met with management, participated actively in discussions, shared many suggestions, and helped plan the most efficient methods for mastering the new jobs. The differences in outcome were dramatic. Average production in the nonparticipating group dropped 20% immediately and did not regain the prechange level, and 9% of the group quit. Morale fell sharply, as evidenced by marked hostility toward the supervisor, by slowdowns, by complaints to the union, and by other instances of aggressive behavior. The group that participated through representatives required two weeks to recover its prechange output. Their attitude was cooperative, and none of the members quit their jobs. The consequences in the total-participation group were even more positive. Members of this group regained the prechange output after only two days, and then climbed steadily until they reached a level of about 14% above the earlier average. No one quit, all members of the group worked well with their supervisors, and there were no signs of aggression. Zander and Armstrong (1972), furthermore, found that when work groups in a slipper factory were asked to set their own daily production goals, they tended to aim for goals even higher than the standard set by the manager.

Perhaps the only times decisions should be made by one or a few persons are (a) when the decisions are about matters that do not need committed action by most members of the group, (b) when the decisions are so simple that coordination among group members and understanding of what to do are easy, and (c) when the decisions have to be made quickly.

Changing Behavioral Patterns And Attitudes

It is easier to change individuals formed into a group than to change any of them separately.

Kurt Lewin (1951, p. 228)

Participating in a decision-making discussion within a group can have an impact on a person's subsequent behavior and attitudes. The classic experiments demonstrating this were conducted by Kurt Lewin and his associates. During World War II there was considerable concern in the U.S. government about the reactions of the public to food rationing and the need to promote the use of foods not ordinarily eaten by U.S. citizens. Lewin was persuaded to come to Washington and help. He and his associates conducted a series of experiments to determine what procedures were most effective in changing behavioral patterns and attitudes. More specifically, the studies focused on determining what procedures were most effective in persuading citizens to eat foods they considered undesirable, and to recommend these to the government. In the first study Lewin (1943) attempted to encourage housewives to use less popular meat products, such as kidneys and sweetbreads. The subjects were six groups of Red Cross volunteers ranging from thirteen to seventeen members each. Half of the groups were given an interesting lecture arguing for greater use of these meat products, and the other half were led through a group discussion that developed the same arguments as those presented in the lecture. At the end of the group discussion, the group leader asked for a show of hands by those willing to try one of the undesirable meat products. A follow-up survey revealed that only 3% of those in the lecture groups had served one of these meats, whereas 32% of those in the group-decision groups had served them.

A second study was conducted with six groups of housewives, ranging from six to nine members (Radke and Klishurich, 1947). The attempt in this study was to increase the consumption of milk. The groups were temporary and the same person served as both lecturer and group decision leader. Again, an interesting lecture was given to half of the groups and the other half participated in a group discussion about the use of milk. A follow-up was made after two weeks and again after four weeks. In both cases the increase in the use of milk was greater among those in the group decision situation.

A third study was conducted in which an attempt was made to increase the consumption of orange juice and cod-liver oil by babies (Radke and Klishurich, 1947). In this study farm mothers with their first baby either examined interesting materials on the use of orange juice and cod-liver oil or participated in group discussions covering the same material. Again, the group decision procedure was more effective in getting the mothers to actually use more orange juice and cod-liver oil.

A number of studies have confirmed the findings of Lewin and his associates (Kostick, 1957; Levine and Butler, 1952) and highlighted two causes of the success of group discussion: public commitment to peers to eat the foods and the degree of perceived consensus in the group (Bennett, 1955; Pelz, 1958; Pennington, Haravey, and Bass, 1958). In a related study, Preston and Heintz (1949) compared the impact of participatory and supervisory leadership roles on students' attitudes. The participatory leader was told to be sure that each member of his or her group was considered, to encourage all members to take part in the discussion, to discourage chance methods of decision making, and to complete the group's assigned work in the allotted time. The supervisory leader was instructed not to participate in the discussion and to limit his or her responsibility to seeing that the work was done in the allotted time. The results showed that participatory leadership was more effective than supervisory leadership in changing students' attitudes. Participatory group members also were more satisfied with their group's decision than members of the supervisory groups, found the task more interesting and meaningful, and rated their group discussions as more friendly and enjoyable.

Overall, the results of these and other studies indicate that if you wish to change people's behaviors and attitudes, you should involve them in group discussions that lead to (a) public commitment to the new behaviors and attitudes and (b) the perception that all members of the group support the new behaviors and attitudes. A participatory leadership pattern may also facilitate changes in behaviors and attitudes.

Type of Task

Whether groups or individuals are more productive may depend on the type of task. If the task is one that allows group members to pool their efforts (such as pulling on a rope in a tug-of-war), groups should do better than individuals (with comparable abilities). But if the task requires extremely precise coordination of action (such as splitting a diamond, driving a car), a well-trained individual will outperform a group. Steiner (1966, 1972) proposed that tasks can be (a) divisible or unitary and (b) maximizing (amount and speed of work) or optimizing (quality of work). On divisible, maximizing, and optimizing tasks, groups tend to do better than individuals. On unitary tasks, comparisons between groups and individuals are more complex. Steiner stated that there are four types of unitary tasks: **disjunctive** (group score is that of best individual member), **conjunctive** (group score is that of worst individual member), **additive** (group score is the sum of group member contributions) and **discretionary** (group score is any combination of individual efforts the group wants to put together). Baron, Kerr, and Miller (1992) present an interesting illustration of this task taxonomy. Imagine three track groups each containing four runners competing in the 400-meter run. The finishing times of group A are 46 seconds, 47 seconds, 47 seconds, and 49 seconds. For group B the finishing times are 44 seconds, 45 seconds, 49 seconds, and 53 seconds. For group C the finishing times are 45 seconds, 45 seconds, 46 seconds, and 51 seconds. Which group wins? It depends on how group performance is defined. If the winning group is the group of the first runner to cross the finish line (disjunctive task demands), then group B wins. If every member of the group must cross the finish line before the group has finished the race (conjunctive task demands), then group A is the winner. If the group score is the simple sum of the times of its four runners (additive task demands), then Group C wins. Although groups outperform individuals on most tasks, there are tasks that are better done by individuals.

Potential Group Productivity

A number of psychologists believe that there is one way in which groups are typically inferior to individuals—the productivity per person. If, for example, instead of simply comparing groups and individuals on the time needed for a solution (which tends to favor groups in most studies), the number of *person-minutes* required were compared (i.e, solution time × size of the group), then individuals solve the problem in fewer person-minutes than groups.

Steiner (1966, 1972) proposed that the most important question is not whether groups are more productive than individuals, but rather if groups are as productive as they should be. He defined a group's *potential productivity* as the group's maximum possible level of productivity at a task and suggested that it depends on two factors—member resources and task demands. He proposed that groups rarely achieve up to their potential because of *process loss* due to *coordination losses* that occur when group members do not organize their efforts optimally and *motivation losses* that occur when members are not optimally motivated. In other words:

Actual Productivity = Potential Productivity – Process Loss

There are problems with Steiner's model. *First,* it implies that there exists a single, unique potential productivity baseline that constitutes an upper boundary on group performance. This is true for certain very simple tasks, but on more complex tasks there is more than one way to define a group's potential productivity. *Second,* Steiner assumes that individuals cannot be any more motivated in groups than they are when working individually, but people may have higher motivation levels in some group settings (Hackman & Morris, 1975). It is possible that groups exhibit motivational gains as well as motivational losses (the social facilitation research is an example). *Finally,* Steiner seems to assume that individuals are always performing up to their potential. Individuals rarely achieve up to their potential. An individual's potential also depends on the person's resources and the demands of the task. Individuals also can suffer process loss due to lack of motivation.

For many reasons groups generally make better decisions than do individuals, even if the groups do not always work up to their potential. There are, however, a variety of methods of making decisions, and they are not equally effective under all conditions. Certain factors enhance the effectiveness of group decision making, and other factors inhibit groups from making good decisions. The methods of decision making and the factors that enhance and inhibit group decision-making effectiveness are discussed in the following sections.

Exercise 7.2: The Bean Jar (I)

The purpose of this exercise is to compare the reactions of group members to the seven methods of decision making discussed in the next section of this chapter. A large jar full of a known quantity of beans is required for the exercise. The procedure for the coordinator is as follows:

1. Set a large jar of beans in front of the participants. You need to know exactly how many beans are in the jar. Inform the participants that they will be asked to estimate how many beans the jar contains.
2. Divide the participants into heterogeneous groups of six. Seven groups are ideal for this exercise. Appoint one member of the group to be the recorder. After the group has made its decision and all group members have completed the postdecision questionnaire (at

the end of this exercise), the recorder collects the results and computes a group average for each question by totaling the individual scores for each question and dividing the sum by the number of members in the group.

3. State that each group has to estimate the number of beans the jars contains. Assign one method of decision making to each group. The instructions of each method are as follows:

a. The member with the most authority makes the decision. One member is appointed leader by the coordinator. This person should exercise control by such means as telling the group how to sit while waiting for the decision to be made and how to use their time while she is deciding. The leader then estimates how many beans are in the jar and announces her decision to the group. All members of the group then complete the postdecision questionnaire.

b. The member with the most expertise makes the decision. The coordinator appoints the member with the most training in mathematics to be the leader. The expert then considers how many beans are in the jar, makes a decision, and announces it to the group. All group members then complete the postdecision questionnaire.

c. The opinions of the individual members are averaged. Each member of the group backs away from the group so that he cannot see the answers of other group members and they cannot see his answer. Each member independently estimates the number of beans in the jar without interacting with the other group members. The recorder then asks each member for his estimate, adds the estimates, and divides the sum by the number of members. The resulting number is announced as the group's decision. All group members then complete the postdecision questionnaire.

d. The member with the most authority makes the decision following a group discussion. One member is appointed leader by the coordinator, and she calls the meeting to order. She asks the group to discuss how many beans are in the jar. When she thinks she knows how many beans are in the jar, she announces her decision to the group. This is not consensus or majority vote—the leader has full responsibility and makes the decision she thinks is best. All members of the group then complete the postdecision questionnaire.

e. A minority of group members makes the decision. The coordinator appoints an executive committee of two members. The committee meets away from the group to decide how many beans are in the jar. They announce their decision to the group. All group members then complete the postdecision questionnaire.

f. Majority vote. Each group member estimates the number of beans in the jar, and the group then votes on which estimate is to be its decision. When the majority of members agree on an estimate, the group decision is made. All group members then complete the postdecision questionnaire.

g. Consensus. All members of the group participate in a discussion as to how many beans are in the jar. Discuss the issue until all members of the group can live with and support the group's estimate. Follow the basic guidelines for consensual decision making given on page 296. When an estimate is agreed on, all members of the group complete the postdecision questionnaire.

4. Collect the results from the postdecision questionnaires and enter them in the summary table on page 289. Instruct each group to make four conclusions as to what is to be learned from these results. Have each group share its conclusions with the class. Then conduct a class discussion on how the conclusions agree or disagree with the material presented in this chapter. Point out the following relationships:

a. The extent to which a member feels understood and influential in the group is related to how well his or her resources are utilized.

b. The extent to which a member is committed to the decision and responsible for its implementation is related to his or her commitment to implement the decision.

c. The extent to which a member is satisfied with his or her participation and the positiveness of the atmosphere of the group is related to the future problem-solving ability of the group.

5. Note how accurate each group's estimate was. Usually, the more group members directly involved in the decision making, the more effective the decision.

POSTDECISION QUESTIONNAIRE

On a sheet of paper record your answers to the following questions. Then hand the paper to the recorder in your group.

1. How understood and listened to did you feel in your group?
   Not at all   1 : 2 : 3 : 4 : 5 : 6 : 7 : 8 : 9   Completely
2. How much influence do you feel you had in your group's decision making?
   None   1 : 2 : 3 : 4 : 5 : 6 : 7 : 8 : 9   A great deal
3. How committed do you feel to the decision your group made?
   Very uncommitted   1 : 2 : 3 : 4 : 5 : 6 : 7 : 8 : 9   Very committed
4. How much responsibility do you feel for making the decision work?
   None   1 : 2 : 3 : 4 : 5 : 6 : 7 : 8 : 9   A great deal
5. How satisfied do you feel with the amount and quality of your participation in your group's decision making?
   Very dissatisfied   1 : 2 : 3 : 4 : 5 : 6 : 7 : 8 : 9   Very satisfied
6. Write one adjective that describes the atmosphere in your group during the decision making.

Results of Postdecision Questionnaire

Method of Decision Making	Understanding	Influence	Commitment	Responsibility	Satisfaction	Atmosphere
Decision by authority without discussion						
Expert member						
Average member						
Decision by authority after discussion						
Minority rule						
Majority rule						
Consensus						

METHODS OF DECISION MAKING

Think about the groups to which you belong. How do they make decisions? Do different groups use different methods? Does your family use the same procedure for making decisions that you and your friends do? Among the alternatives that follow, which decision-making method would you prefer for the groups to which you belong? Table 7.1 summarizes the advantages and disadvantages of these decision-making methods.

1. Rely on the person in charge of the group. The designated leader has the responsibility; he or she should also have the power to make the decisions.
2. Postpone making a decision and wait it out. Time takes care of everything; with a little luck a decision will never have to be made if the group waits long enough.
3. Let the expert make the decision. Give the person with the most expertise in the group the authority to make whatever decision he or she thinks best.
4. Find out what each member thinks, and then choose the most popular alternative. With this method the group does not even have to meet; members are polled individually.
5. Flip a coin, roll the dice, or pick a number out of a hat.
6. Rely on the person in charge of the group to make the decision, but only after the group has thoroughly discussed the issue with that person.
7. Put the decision in the hands of a knowledgeable and qualified committee that will look at the issues, decide what the group should do, and tell the group members its decision.
8. Take a vote and let the majority rule. The issues should be presented to the group, discussed, and then a vote held, with the majority deciding.
9. Ask the group next door what it is going to do and then do just the opposite.
10. Obtain a basic agreement among everyone in the group as to what the decision should be. The issues should be thoroughly discussed, each member participating, until all agree on what the group should do.

There are many ways in which a group can make a decision. We shall take up seven of the major ones. Each decision-making method has its uses and is appropriate under certain circumstances. Each also has its particular consequences for the group's future operation. An effective group understands each method of decision making well enough to choose the method that is best for the

1. Type of decision to be made.
2. Amount of time and resources available.
3. History of the group.
4. Nature of the task being worked on.
5. Kind of climate the group wishes to establish.
6. Type of setting in which the group is working.

Method 1: Decision by Authority Without Group Discussion

In this method the designated leader makes all the decisions without consulting the group members in any way. This method is quite common in organizations. It is an efficient method in the sense that it can take a short time to execute, but it is not very effective. Even if the designated leader is a good listener who sorts out the correct

Table 7.1 **Advantages and Disadvantages of Decision-Making Methods**

Method of Decision Making	Disadvantages	Advantages
1. Decision by authority without discussion	One person is not a good resource for every decision; advantages of group interaction are lost; no commitment to implementing the decision is developed among other group members; resentment and disagreement may result in sabotage and deterioration of group effectiveness; resources of other members are not used.	Applies more to administrative needs; useful for simple, routine decisions; should be used when very little time is available to make the decision, when group members expect the designated leader to make the decision, and when group members lack the skills and information to make the decision any other way.
2. Expert member	It is difficult to determine who the expert is; no commitment to implement the decision is built; advantages of group interaction are lost; resentment and disagreement may result in sabotage and deterioration of group effectiveness; resources of other members are not used.	Useful when the expertise of one person is so far superior to that of all other group members that little is to be gained by discussion; should be used when the need for membership action in implementing the decision is slight.
3. Average of members' opinions	There is not enough interaction among group members for them to gain from each other's resources and from the benefits of group discussion; no commitment to implement the decision is built; unresolved conflict and controversy may damage group effectiveness in the future.	Useful when it is difficult to get group members together to talk, when the decision is so urgent that there is no time for group discussion, when member commitment is not necessary for implementing the decision, and when group members lack the skills and information to make the decision any other way; applicable to simple, routine decisions.
4. Decision by authority after discussion	Does not develop commitment to implement the decision; does not resolve the controversies and conflicts among group members; tends to create situations in which group members either compete to impress the designated leader or tell the leader what they think he or she wants to hear.	Uses the resources of the group members more than previous methods; gains some of the benefits of group discussion.

(continued)

Table 7.1 **Advantages and Disadvantages of Decision-Making Methods** *(Continued)*

Method of Decision Making	Disadvantages	Advantages
5. Majority control	Usually leaves an alienated minority, which damages future group effectiveness; relevant resources of many group members may be lost; full commitment to implement the decision is absent; full benefit of group interaction is not obtained.	Can be used when sufficient time is lacking for decision by consensus or when the decision is not so important that consensus needs to be used and when complete member commitment is not necessary for implementing the decision; closes discussion on issues that are not highly important for the group.
6. Minority control	Does not utilize the resources of many group members; does not establish widespread commitment to implement the decision; unresolved conflict and controversy may damage future group effectiveness; not much benefit from group interaction.	Can be used when everyone cannot meet to make a decision, when the group is under such time pressure that it must delegate responsibility to a committee, when only a few members have any relevant resources, and when broad member commitment is not needed to implement the decision; useful for simple, routine decisions.
7. Consensus	Takes a great deal of time and psychological energy and a high level of member skill; time pressure must be minimal, and there must be no emergency in progress.	Produces an innovative, creative, and high-quality decision; elicits commitment by all members to implement the decision; uses the resources of all members; the future decision-making ability of the group is enhanced; useful in making serious, important, and complex decisions to which all members are to be committed.

information upon which to make his or her decision, it is still the group that has to act on the decision, and under this method the involvement of the other group members is very small. Furthermore, when the designated leader makes the decision, not all members of the group may understand what it is; they may not, therefore, be able to implement it. If they disagree with it, they may not want to implement it. Under this method, how well the decision is implemented is particularly crucial.

Method 2: Decision by Expert

Group decisions can be made by letting the most expert member in the group decide what the group should do. The procedure for this method is to select the expert, let him or her consider the issues, and then have that person tell the group what the decision is. The group does not discuss the issue, but rather lets the expert decide on his or her own.

There is one major problem with this method: how to tell which member has the most expertise. On most complex issues, individuals disagree as to what the best approach is, and this makes it difficult for them to identify the expert among them. Personal popularity and the amount of power a person has over the group members often interfere with the selection of the most expert member. The classic illustration of this point is the story of the general with a college education and several captains with Ph.D.s in engineering discussing how a bridge should be built. Needless to say, it is the general who designs the bridge, simply because he has the most power. Individuals with a great deal of power are notorious for overestimating their expertise while underestimating the expertise of others. Unless there is a clear and effective way to determine who the expert is, this method does not work very well. Moreover, it too fails to win the involvement of other group members, which is necessary for implementing the decision.

Method 3: Decision by Averaging Individuals' Opinions

This method consists of separately asking each group member his or her opinion and then averaging the results. When the chair of a group, for example, calls each member on the telephone, asks what the member's opinion is, and then takes the most popular opinion as the group's decision, the chair is using the averaging method. This procedure is like majority voting, except that the group's decision may be determined by less than 50% of the members (the most common opinion is not necessarily the opinion of more than half of the members) and no direct discussion is held among members as to what decision the group should make.

Because individual errors and extreme opinions tend to cancel themselves out under this method, it is usually a better procedure to follow than the designated leader method (without a group discussion). At least members are consulted in this method. The disadvantage of the method is that the opinions of the least knowledgeable members may annul the opinions of the most knowledgeable members. Letting the most expert member make the decision is always better than using a group average to decide. Although group members are consulted before the decision is made, they are still little involved in the decision making itself. Consequently, their commitment to the decision is not very strong. If implementation of a decision made by this method requires the efforts of all group members, the effectiveness of the decision will probably be slight.

There are group decision-making methods that were created to average group opinions while eliminating or controlling members' interactions with one another. The *Delphi technique* was developed by Dalkey, Helmer, and their colleagues at the Rand Corporation (Dalkey, 1969, 1975). Its original purpose was to improve judgmental forecasting (e.g., economic forecasts and cost of fringe benefits) by providing practical procedures for eliciting expert opinions. First, members are asked to provide individual estimates for the focal quality and their opinions are collected and summarized in a way that assures the anonymity of each member. Then a summary of the members' opinions is circulated among the members. The members are then provided an opportunity to revise their earlier forecasts. This procedure is repeated several times until individual opinions stabilize; that is, members change no more. The median or mean of the set of individual estimates is taken as the final group forecast. Dalkey claimed that the procedure avoided the "biasing effects of dominant individuals, or irrelevant communications, and of group pressure toward conformity" (1969, p. 408).

A *nominal group technique* meeting begins with individual assessment of the focal problem; individuals first generate ideas concerning the issue without any discussion. Each participant then presents personal ideas in a face-to-face group meeting, and these ideas are recorded. After all the ideas are recorded, group discussion begins, and is primarily focused on clarifying the stated ideas. Finally, each member evaluates the priorities of these ideas by ranking them, and these rankings are combined mathematically to yield a group judgment (Delbecq, Van de Ven, & Gustafson, 1975).

Both of these methods are based on the assumption that groups are so poorly structured and members so unskilled that interaction among members is better avoided.

Method 4: Decision by Authority After Group Discussion

Many groups have an authority structure that clearly indicates that the designated leader will make the decisions. Groups that function within organizations, such as businesses and government agencies, usually employ this method of decision making. The group does originate ideas and hold discussions, but it is the designated leader who makes the final decision. Under this method the designated leader calls a meeting of the group, presents the issues, listens to the discussion until he is sure of what he thinks the decision should be, and then announces his decision to the group.

Listening to a group discussion will usually improve the accuracy of a decision made by the group's leader. The greater the designated leader's skill as a listener, the greater will be the benefits of the group discussion. But although members can become involved in the discussion, they have no part in the decision making, which does not help the decision's effectiveness. As a result, the group members may tend to either compete to impress the leader or tell the leader what they think he wants to hear.

Method 5: Decision by Minority

A minority—two or more members who constitute less than 50% of the group—can make the group's decisions in several ways, some legitimate and some illegitimate. One legitimate method is for the minority to act as an executive committee composed of only a few members, making all but the most important decisions for the group. Another is for the minority to act as a temporary committee that considers special problems and decides what action the group should take. The illegitimate methods involve railroading. For instance, two or more members may come to a quick agreement on a course of action, challenge the rest of the group with a sudden "Does anyone object?" and, if no one replies fast enough, proceed with a "Let's go ahead, then." Or a minority may forcibly recommend a course of action—implying that anyone who disagrees is in for a fight—and then move ahead before other members can consider the issue carefully. We shall focus on the legitimate methods of minority decision making; group members should be able to tell when they are being railroaded.

The minority members who make the decision may be committed to it, but the majority may not only be uncommitted, they may even want to prevent the decision from being implemented. When a few members railroad a decision, furthermore, they seem to assume that persons who are silent agree. But often a majority of group members need more time to organize their thoughts against a proposal, or sometimes members keep silent because they are afraid they are the only ones who disagree. When a group has a large number of decisions to be made and not enough time to deal with them all, decision-making committees can be efficient. This method may also be effective if a large number of decisions do not need member involvement in order to be implemented. In general, however, decision by minority is not a good method of decision making.

Method 6: Decision by Majority Vote

Majority vote is the method of group decision making most commonly used in the United States. Its procedure is to discuss an issue only as long as it takes at least 51% of the members to decide on a course of action. This method is so common in our society—indeed, it is almost a ritual—that it is often taken for granted as the natural way for any group to make decisions. It is certainly one of the methods that is used most often. On the surface, majority voting resembles our election system, but critical differences exist between elections and the use of majority vote in most groups. In our political system minority rights are carefully protected through the Bill of Rights and the Constitution, and political minorities always have the right to compete on equal terms in the next election in order to become a majority. In most groups, however, minority opinions are not always safeguarded. Thus, majority voting often splits a group into winners and losers, encourages either/or thinking (when there may be other ways of looking at a problem), and fosters blind arguments rather than rational discussion. A majority that has often been outvoted is not contributing its resources towards influencing the decision. This circumstance not only reduces the quality of the decision but often creates coalitions of individuals who resent losing the vote and who try to regroup, pick up support, and overturn the decision. When a task needs the support of everyone in the group, when the lack of support or sabotage by one or more members could seriously damage the undertaking, a decision by vote can be dangerous. Where commitment by everyone is not essential, of course, a majority vote can serve very well. If majority voting is to be used, however, the group must be sure that it has created a climate in which members feel they have had their day in court and will feel obliged to support the majority decision.

Method 7: Decision by Consensus

Consensus is the most effective method of group decision making, but it also takes the most time. Perfect consensus means that everyone agrees what the decision should be. Unanimity, however, is often impossible to achieve. There are degrees of consensus, all of which bring about a higher-quality decision than majority vote or other methods of decision making. **Consensus** is more commonly defined as a collective opinion arrived at by a group of individuals working together under conditions that permit communications to be sufficiently open—and the group climate to be sufficiently supportive—for everyone in the group to feel that he or she has had a fair chance to influence the decision. When a decision is made by consensus, all members understand the decision and are prepared to support it. That means that all members can rephrase the decision to show that they understand it, that all members have had a chance to tell the group how they feel about the decision, and that those members who continue to disagree or have doubts will nevertheless say publicly that they are willing to give the decision a try for a period of time.

To achieve consensus, members must have enough time to state their views and, in particular, their opposition to other members' views. By the time the decision is made they should be feeling that others really do understand them. Group members, therefore, must listen carefully and communicate effectively. Decisions made by consensus are sometimes referred to as synergistic decisions, because the group members working together arrive at a decision of higher quality than the decision they would obtain if each one worked separately. In reaching consensus, group members need to see differences of opinion as a way of (a) gathering additional information, (b) clarifying issues, and (c) forcing the group to seek better alternatives.

The basic guidelines for consensual decision making are as follows:

1. *Avoid arguing blindly for your own opinions.* Present your position as clearly and logically as possible, but listen to other members' reactions and consider them carefully before you press your point.
2. *Avoid changing your mind only to reach agreement and avoid conflict.* Support only solutions with which you are at least somewhat able to agree. Yield only to positions that have objective and logically sound foundations.
3. *Avoid conflict-reducing procedures* such as majority voting, tossing a coin, averaging, and bargaining.
4. *Seek out differences of opinion.* They are natural and expected. Try to involve everyone in the decision because they present a wide range of information and opinions, thereby creating a better chance for the group to hit upon more adequate solutions.
5. *Do not assume that someone must win and someone must lose* when discussion reaches a stalemate. Instead, look for the next most acceptable alternative for all members.
6. *Discuss underlying assumptions,* listen carefully to one another, and encourage the participation of all members.

Consensus is the best method for producing an innovative, creative, and high-quality decision that (a) all members will be committed to implementing, (b) uses the resources of all group members, and (c) increases the future decision-making effectiveness of the group. But it is often difficult to reach (Kerr, Atkin, Stasser, Meek, Holt, & Davis, 1976). Consensus is characterized by more conflict among members, more shifts of opinion, a longer time to reach a conclusion, and more confidence by members in the correctness of their decision (Nemeth, 1977). To reach consensus group leaders should encourage all members to participate, encourage differences of opinions to be expressed, and express acceptance of different positions and perspectives (Torrance, 1957). Group leaders should also encourage minority opinions and conflict among members (Maier & Solem, 1952).

Relation Between Time and Decision Making

Every method of decision making takes a different amount of time to carry out. Obviously, methods that involve group discussion take more time than methods that do not. Usually, the more persons involved in the decision making the longer it will take to reach a decision. Figure 7.5 summaries the relationship among the number of persons involved, the type of method used, the quality of the decision, and the time needed to

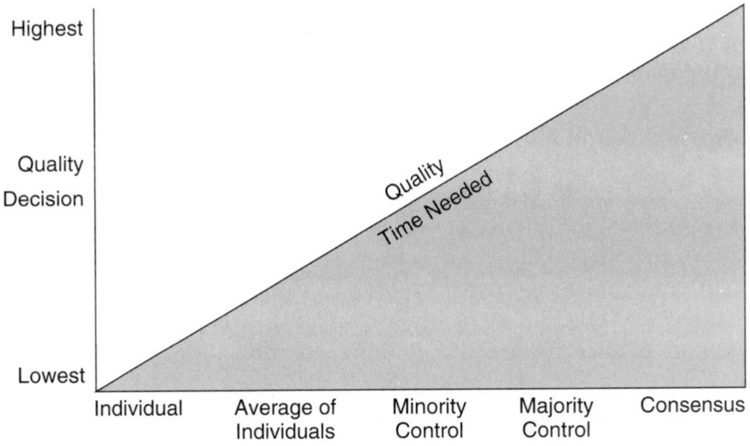

Figure 7.5 Quality of decision and time needed, as a function of number of decision-makers.

arrive at a decision. If the time needed for both making and implementing a decision is considered, however, the time factor becomes less clear. Often the extra time taken to make a consensual decision will greatly reduce the time needed to implement it. Thus, many group authorities insist that if the whole process of decision making and implementation is considered, consensus is the least time-consuming method.

Generally, you are better off making important decisions in groups than you are having one person make the decision. This does not mean, however, that there is something magical about having a group make a decision. Some groups have a difficult time making decisions. Groups can make bad decisions as well as good ones. To help assure that their group will arrive at effective decisions, members must not only take advantage of the factors that facilitate effective decision making but also pay attention to the factors that may block effective decision making.

FACTORS ENHANCING GROUP DECISION MAKING

Whether a group decision is good or bad depends on how the group is structured. When you want to maximize the likelihood that the group will make a good decision, you need to structure five essential elements into group life: positive interdependence, face-to-face promotive interaction, individual accountability, social skills, and group processing (see Chapter 1). Whenever you want the group to make a good decision or to work productively, make sure the five elements are present.

FACTORS HINDERING GROUP DECISION MAKING

Although groups tend to make higher-quality decisions than individuals working alone, there is nothing magical about groups. There are conditions under which groups function inefficiently and ineffectively. As we saw in a previous section, six of the fifteen groups in the Watson (1931) study excelled the decision of their best member. There are a number of possible reasons why more of the groups did not do so. The potential barriers of group decision-making effectiveness are briefly discussed below.

Lack of Group Maturity

In the study conducted by Goodwin Watson (1931) and in most of the other studies conducted on group decision making, college students are assigned groups in which they know none of the other members and in which they stay together for only one hour or so. Such temporary ad hoc groups do not have time to develop enough maturity to function with full effectiveness. Group members need time and experience working together to develop into an effective decision-making group.

Uncritically Giving One's Dominant Response

Poor decisions are often made because group members quickly decide on a solution based on their dominant response and, therefore, do not think of the proper alternatives or do a poor job of evaluating and choosing among the alternatives being considered (Maier & Thurber, 1969). Both Berlyne (1965) and Maier (1970) have theorized that responses are hierarchically arranged and when confronted with a problem individuals may place low probabilities on the correct solution. Dominant responses may be based on (a) physical states such as hunger that affect which stimuli a person attends to (Levine, Chein, & Murphy, 1942; McClelland & Atkinson, 1948), (b) psychological states such as attitudes and beliefs that affect what one perceives (Allport & Postman, 1945; Iverson & Schwab, 1967); (c) general cultural perspectives that lead to distortions in information perceived (Bartlett, 1932); (d) mental sets that cause the same words to have different meanings for different persons (Foley & MacMillan, 1943); (e) expectations that bias how ambiguous events are interpreted (Bruner & Minturn, 1955) and create a sensitivity to perceiving some stimuli and not others (Neisser, 1954); (f) fixation on the first reasonable solution thought of (Simon, 1976); (g) laziness that results in available information not being cognitively processed and alternative ways of understanding such information not being fully considered (Langer, Blank, & Chanowitz, 1978; Taylor, 1980); and (h) adoption of solutions that have been previously useful (Luchins, 1942).

Social Loafing: Hiding In the Crowd

In certain groups (such as sports groups and combat units) there are factors (such as contagious excitement, strong norms favoring maximal effort, and intense feelings of commitment, loyalty, and obligation) that cause group members to demonstrate levels of motivation and effort far beyond what would be expected from an individual acting alone. During a college basketball game in 1989, for example, Jay Burson, a player on the Ohio State University group, continued to play in a game after he had suffered a broken neck. There are many other examples where people like Jay Burson double their efforts or place themselves in great jeopardy because of their devotion and loyalty to other group members. Most of the research, however, has focused on how being a group member can lower motivation.

A French professor of agricultural engineering named Max Ringelmann wanted to assess the relative efficiency of humans, oxen, and machinery in pulling and pushing loads. In the course of his investigations, he studied additive tasks by having individuals and groups of 2, 3, and 8 males pull on a rope attached to a pressure gauge (reported in Moede, 1927). Two people, of course, pulled harder than one person. Three people pulled harder than two people. Individuals, on the average, exerted 63 kg of pressure, dyads about 118 kg, triads about 160 kg, and groups of eight about 248 kg of pressure. The intriguing aspect of these findings was that each person added did not increase the performance by 63 kg. Triads, for example, performed at only 2.5 times as much as the performance of one individual. The inverse relationship between the number of people in a group and the quality and/or magnitude of individual performance on additive tasks was dubbed the *Ringelmann effect.* Similar results have been observed for groups working on intellectual puzzles (Taylor & Faust, 1952), creativity tasks (Gibb, 1951), and perceptual judgments and complex reasoning (Ziller, 1957).

Ingham, Levinger, Graves, and Peckham (1974) replicated Ringelmann's study to determine if the loss of effort was due to (a) group process problems such as difficulty in coordinating the efforts of group members (on pulling a rope, for example, everyone has to position themselves to get a good hold on the rope and then they have to pull and pause at the same time) or (b) some group members loafing. They demonstrated that as groups got larger members pulled less hard at least partially because they were less motivated. A similar replication conducted a few years later used a new task—cheering as loud as possible (Latane, Williams, & Harkins, 1979). Latane called the decline in motivation social loafing. **Social loafing** is a reduction of individual effort when working with others on an additive group task. **Additive tasks** require the summing together of individual group members' inputs to maximize the group product. *Social loafing* has been demonstrated on a variety of additive tasks such as rope pulling, shouting, clapping, evaluation of poems and editorials, cheering, cycling, pumping air or water, producing ideas, typing, and detecting signals. It has also been demonstrated in many different cultures, including India (Weiner, Pandy, & Latane, 1981), Japan, (Williams & Williams, 1984), and Taiwan (Gabrenya, Wang, & Latane, 1983).

Several situational and social factors appear to have an important impact on the magnitude of the effect. For instance, social loafing has been shown to occur especially when group members lack identifiable contributions (Williams, Harkins, & Latane, 1981); when there is an increased likelihood of redundant efforts (Harkins & Petty, 1982); when there is a lack of cohesiveness among group members (Williams, 1981); when there is lessened responsibility for the final outcome (Petty, Harkins, Williams, & Latane, 1977); when the task is boring, as opposed to challenging, appealing, or involving (Brickner, Harkins, & Ostrom, 1986); when there is no spirit of commitment to the group (Hackman & Walton, 1986); and when group members believe that others are loafing (Zaccaro, 1984). In some four dozen studies we see that, when individuals are working on additive tasks believe that they are lost in a crowd and, therefore, are not accountable and cannot evaluate their own efforts, responsibility is diffused across all group members (see Figure 7.6).

Social loafing seems most likely to occur when there is no strong incentive to perform the task for individuals or for groups. That is, it may be eliminated if group cohesion is sufficiently high (Williams, 1981), the group sets performance goals (Brickner, 1987), and the task is sufficiently involving (Brickner, Harkins, & Ostrom, 1986), attractive (Zaccaro, 1984), or intrinsically interesting (Petty, Cacioppo, & Kasmer, 1985).

When the contribution of each group member is identifiable (Williams Harkins, & Latane, 1981; Kerr & Bruun, 1981) and when the contribution is going to be evaluated by groupmates and oneself (Harkins, 1987; Harkins & Jackson, 1985; Harkins & Szymanski, 1987; Szymanski & Harkins, 1987), no social loafing tends to occur. An opportunity for group members to evaluate the group's (but not individual members') performance can likewise motivate group members to work (Harkins & Szymanski, 1989).

Social loafing, therefore, seems to be restricted to a fairly narrow range of situations, where the task has to be additive and where evaluation of member or group performance by anyone is unlikely. In essence, social loafing is related to social facilitation through

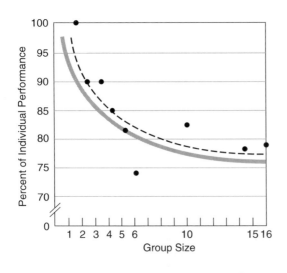

Figure 7.6 This chart represents a summary of 49 studies involving more than 4,000 participants that disclosed that effort decreases (loafing increases) as the size of the group increases. Each dot represents the aggregate data from one of these studies.
Source: J. Jackson and K. Williams, *A Review and Theoretical Analysis of Social Loafing* (unpublished manuscript, Fordham University).

evaluation apprehension. When people believe that their individual performance is being closely monitored by others, their concern about being evaluated goes up and their performance on simple additive tasks may increase. But when they believe that their efforts are lost in a crowd, their evaluation concerns decrease and social loafing may occur.

Free Riding: Getting Something for Nothing

When one works alone, success or failure is entirely one's own responsibility. When one works in a group, however, the responsibility for the group's success or failure is often shared among group members. In an emergency, for example, the responsibility for helping appears to be diffused among bystanders, such that the larger the group, the less likely it is that any particular individual will provide help (Darley & Latane, 1968; Latane & Nida, 1981). Helping in an emergency is a *disjunctive task*—if one person does it, everyone receives the benefit. Similarly, if you are sharing an apartment with several other people, if one person cleans the apartment no one else has to do so at that time. On disjunctive tasks, there is the possibility of a **free ride** (Olson, 1965); that is, to benefit from the task efforts of other group members while doing no work oneself. Under certain conditions, group members are sensitive to the dispensability of their efforts (Kerr, 1983; Kerr & Bruun, 1983). When group members perceive their contributions to be dispensable, such that group success or failure depends very little on whether or not they exert effort, and when that effort is costly, they are less likely to exert themselves on the group's behalf. The opportunity to free ride—to get something for nothing—is not the same as the opportunity to socially loaf—to hide in the crowd.

Motivation Losses Due to Perceived Inequity: Not Being a Sucker

What would you do if you were sharing an apartment and found that you were the only person who cleaned it; that is, everyone else was enjoying the benefits of your cleaning but was making no attempt to help keep the apartment clean? Kerr (1983) labeled the tendency to reduce your efforts when other group members were engaging in free riding the **sucker effect**. He demonstrated that people were willing to reduce their efforts (and thereby their rewards) rather than play the sucker and be exploited by a free-riding partner. This does not mean that everyone has to contribute the same amount to the group's efforts. People generally do not feel like a sucker when another group member is trying hard to contribute but is unable to do so (Kerr, 1983; Tjosvold, Johnson, & Johnson, 1981).

Groupthink and Defensive Avoidance

Decision makers are often reluctant to take action; are beset by conflict, doubts, and worry; and struggle with incongruous longings, antipathies, and loyalties. They sometimes seek relief in **defensive avoidance**—procrastinating, rationalizing, or denying responsibility for their own choices. When group decision making is dominated by defensive avoidance, poor decisions are often made. Social psychologist Irving Janis (1971, 1982) analyzed the decision-making procedures that led to several major fiascoes, such as:

1. *Pearl Harbor.* In the weeks preceding the 1941 Pearl Harbor attack, military commanders in Hawaii were fed a steady stream of information about Japan's

preparations for attack—somewhere. Then military intelligence lost radio contact with Japanese aircraft carriers, which had begun moving full-steam straight for Hawaii. Air reconnaissance could have spotted the carriers, or at least provided a few minutes of warning of the impending attack. But the commanders decided against such precautions.

2. *Bay of Pigs Invasion.* "How could we have been so stupid?" asked President John Kennedy after the 1961 invasion of Cuba by 1,400 CIA-trained Cuban exiles. Nearly all the invaders were soon killed or captured, the United States was humiliated, and Cuba allied itself even closer to the USSR.

3. *Vietnam War.* From 1964 to 1967 President Lyndon Johnson and his "Tuesday lunch group" of policy advisers escalated the Vietnam War on the assumption that the escalations (U.S. aerial bombardment, defoliation, and search-and-destroy missions) were likely to bring North Vietnam to the negotiating table. The escalation decisions were made despite warnings from government intelligence experts as well as from leaders of nearly all U.S. allies. The resulting disaster cost 56,500 American lives and more than 1 million Vietnamese lives, drove Lyndon Johnson from office, and created huge budget deficits that helped fuel inflation in the 1970s.

Janis (1972, 1982) coined the word *groupthink* to describe the decision-making process in these fiascoes. **Groupthink** is the collective striving for unanimity that overrides group members' motivation to realistically appraise alternative courses of action and thereby leads to (a) a deterioration of mental efficiency, reality testing, and moral judgment, and (b) the ignoring of external information inconsistent with the favored alternative course of action. Groupthink leads to **concurrence-seeking**—group members inhibiting discussion in order to avoid any disagreement or arguments, emphasizing agreement, and avoiding realistic appraisal of alternative ideas and courses of action. Quick compromises and censorship of disagreement are characteristic of groups dominated by concurrence-seeking. *Groupthink* is promoted when the group is highly cohesive, when it is insulated from outside criticism, when the leader is directive and dynamic, and when the group does not search for and critically evaluate alternatives (see Figure 7.7). Group members rely on shared illusions and rationalizations to bolster whatever option is preferred by the leader. In seeking concurrence and avoiding disagreement, members become trapped in the dynamics of groupthink.

1. *Self-censorship.* Each member minimizes any doubts about the apparent group consensus.

2. *Illusion of unanimity.* Each member assumes that everyone (except oneself) is in agreement. There is a state of pluralistic ignorance where members falsely assume that the silence of other members implies consent and agreement.

3. *Direct pressure on dissenters.* Anyone expressing doubts is pressured to conform.

4. *Mind guards.* Certain group members try to prevent dissenters from raising objections.

5. *Illusion of invulnerability.* Members develop an illusion of invulnerability, characterized by unwarranted optimism and excessive risk-taking. They often believe that the group is above attack and reproach.

6. *Rationalization.* Group members invent justifications for whatever action is about to be undertaken, thus preventing misgivings and appropriate reconsideration.

7. *Illusion of morality.* Members ignore the ethical consequences of the favored alternative and assume that the group's actions are morally justified.

8. *Stereotyping.* Group members dismiss competitors, rivals, and potential critics as too weak or stupid to react effectively or as too evil to warrant genuine attempts at negotiation. These aspects of groupthink lead to a number of defects in the decision-making process including an incomplete survey of alternatives and objectives, failure to examine risks of the preferred choice, poor information search, selective bias in processing information, failing to reappraise alternatives, and making no contingency plans.

Aldag and Fuller (1993) conducted an extensive review of literature and concluded that most support for groupthink has come from retrospective case studies that have focused on decision fiascoes rather than comparing the decision-making processes associated with good versus bad decisions. Overall, the research does not

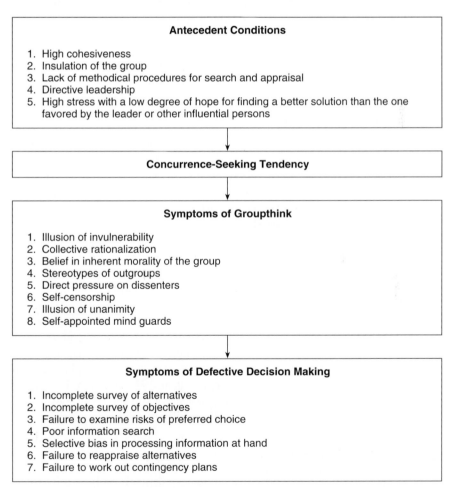

Antecedent Conditions

1. High cohesiveness
2. Insulation of the group
3. Lack of methodical procedures for search and appraisal
4. Directive leadership
5. High stress with a low degree of hope for finding a better solution than the one favored by the leader or other influential persons

Concurrence-Seeking Tendency

Symptoms of Groupthink

1. Illusion of invulnerability
2. Collective rationalization
3. Belief in inherent morality of the group
4. Stereotypes of outgroups
5. Direct pressure on dissenters
6. Self-censorship
7. Illusion of unanimity
8. Self-appointed mind guards

Symptoms of Defective Decision Making

1. Incomplete survey of alternatives
2. Incomplete survey of objectives
3. Failure to examine risks of preferred choice
4. Poor information search
5. Selective bias in processing information at hand
6. Failure to reappraise alternatives
7. Failure to work out contingency plans

Figure 7.7 A model of groupthink.

provide convincing support for the validity of the groupthink phenomenon or for the suggestion that groupthink characteristics lead to negative outcomes. Controlled experimental research on the groupthink process has been sparse. There is research in the laboratory that high cohesion has generally not produced the poor discussion quality Janis' theory predicts (e.g., Flowers, 1977; Leana, 1985), but directive leadership results in low-quality group problem solving (e.g., Flowers, 1977). The historical examples that Janis presents have to be viewed with caution because we cannot be certain that contradictory examples have not been overlooked (Longley & Pruitt, 1980). Tetlock (1979), however, did a quantitative content analysis of public statements made by key decision makers and found that for policy decisions Janis had categorized as exemplifying groupthink, decision-makers' perceptions of the issue were much more simplistic than was true for decisions that Janis categorized as nongroupthink. Herek, Janis, and Huth (1987) report a negative correlation between the number of groupthink symptoms and the quality of the decision—the greater the groupthink, the more negative was the outcome of the decision. McCauley (1989) did an historical analysis and found that two key groupthink decisions discussed by Janis were characterized by compliance processes that overrode decision-makers' serious reservations regarding the group's decision. McCauley's analysis also suggests that directive leadership (stating the leader's views early), homogeneity among group members, and insulation of the group from outside influence are particularly crucial factors in the groupthink process.

Conflicting Goals of Group Members

Members bring to a group a variety of motives. Some may wish, consciously or unconsciously, to sabotage the group effort. Others have self-oriented needs that may interfere with attention to making an effective decision. Members may be competing with one another in ways that reduce their effectiveness in working together. Even when members are genuinely work oriented and anxious to achieve results, they may have different ideas about how to proceed.

Egocentrism of Group Members

A critical aspect of effective decision making is the ability to view the issues being discussed from a variety of points of view. When members egocentrically present their opinions and coldly evaluate the extent to which the information and conclusions of other members agree with their own, a competition over whose ideas are going to dominate develops. A number of studies indicate that an egocentric approach to decision making results in lower quality decisions than an approach emphasizing understanding of other members' perspectives (Falk & Johnson, 1977; Johnson, 1977, 2000). The more members are embedded in their own perspective and the more they refuse to consider the perspectives of others, the lower the quality of the group's decisions will be.

Lack of Sufficient Heterogeneity

Whether a group will be optimally productive depends on how fully the necessary information, skills, and viewpoints are represented. The more homogeneous the participants, the less each member adds to the resources present in the others. In general, homogeneous groups make less effective decisions than heterogeneous groups (Johnson, 1980a). The more heterogeneous the group, the more frequent conflict among group members (Bass, 1960; Hoffman, 1959), the less willing members are to accept incorrect responses from each other (Goldman, Dietz, & McGlynn, 1968), and the greater the group productivity (Goldman et al., 1968; Hoffman & Maier, 1961).

Interference or Production Blocking

Because only one person can talk (and be heard by all the others) at any one time, participants in a discussion often have to wait to make their point. Sometimes the delay is so long that the whole course of the discussion has changed before the would-be speaker gets a chance to be heard. He or she may then drop the idea entirely, which deprives the group, or may bring the idea belatedly, which causes the others to backtrack from the issues they have moved on to. There are times when the participation of one member may interfere with the participation of other members and lower the decision-making effectiveness of the group. When groups are given the task to generate as many ideas as possible, they usually produce fewer (sometimes less than 50% as many) ideas as nominal groups (Diehl & Stroebe, 1987; Lamm & Trommsdorff, 1973). One of the reasons for this process loss is production blocking—only one group member can talk at any one time.

Inappropriate Group Size

Some decisions require that a large number of persons participate; other decisions need only one or two individuals. An inappropriate group size may interfere with effective group decision making. There are a number of ways that group size can interfere with group effectiveness. *First, the greater the discrepancy between functional group size and actual group size, the more ineffective the group will be.* Stephan and Mishler (1952) found that the proportion of active speakers in discussion groups declined with group size. As groups get larger, therefore, only a few of its members are actively trying to solve the problem. The functional size could be much smaller than the actual group size. Bray, Kerr, and Atkin (1978), for example, found that in most instances groups were solving problems about as fast as the fastest solver when group size was two. In ten-person groups there is clearly considerable process loss occurring. In groups of more than eight or nine members, a few participants are likely to dominate and others are likely to remain passive (Watson & Johnson, 1972).

Second, the less group members see their efforts as essential for group success, the less effective the group will be. Generally, as the group gets larger and larger, members are less likely to see their own personal contribution to the group as being important to the group's chances of success (Kerr, 1989; Olson, 1965). Social loafing, therefore, increases as the size of the group increases. The smaller the size of the group, furthermore, the greater the individual accountability (Messick & Brewer, 1983). Morgan, Coates, and Rebbin (1970) found that team performance actually improved when one team member was missing from five-person teams, perhaps because members believed that their contributions were more necessary. As group size increases, individual team members tend to communicate less frequently, which may reduce the amount of information utilized in arriving at a decision (Gerard, Wilhelmy, & Conolley, 1968; Indik, 1965). Finally, as group size increases so does the likelihood individuals may alter their statements to conform to the perceived beliefs of the overall team (Gerard, Wilhelmy, & Conolley, 1968; Rosenberg, 1961).

Third, generally the greater the complexity of group structure and the more time it takes to organize joint efforts, the less effective the group will be. There is a certain amount of time needed to organize a group that is unnecessary for individuals (Bales & Strodtbeck, 1951). The larger the group the more time is needed to organize it and coordinate efforts among members.

Fourth, the less the effort of each member, the less effective the group will be. In Ringelmann's (1913) experiment mentioned earlier, in which subjects were supposed to pull on a rope as hard as they could, he found that as group size increased, the average pull per member decreased.

Fifth, the less members identify with the group, the less effective the group will be. Kramer and Brewer (1986) have shown that a strong sense of belonging or social identity leads to cooperative behavior. They suggest that the more you feel part of the group, the less strongly you distinguish between your personal welfare and the group's welfare. Small groups are easier to identify with than are large groups.

Sixth, the less members follow the group's norms, the less effective the group will be. Enforcement of group norms requires (a) the ability to monitor members' behavior so that norm violations will be detected and (b) that the social sanctions the group uses to punish norm violation will be salient. Reducing group size makes it easier to monitor members' behavior, and it increases members' attachment to the group, thereby making rejection from the group more salient (Fox, 1985).

Decision-making groups should be large enough that the needed resources are present, but small enough so that every member's resources are fully utilized, participation is high, acceptance and support by all members is possible, and coordination is easy (Johnson, 1980a). Overall, the larger the group, the harder it is to make it effective, though there are ways to do it. Perhaps the most important way of increasing the effectiveness of large groups is to strengthen the positive interdependence among group members. The larger the group, the stronger the positive interdependence among members has to be. Seta, Paulus, and Schkade (1976) found that for a complex task, larger groups performed worse than smaller groups when given competitive instructions, and better when given cooperative instructions. They also found that cooperative groups performed better when they are in close proximity and competitors performed better when they were not in close proximity.

Premature Closure and Dissonance Reduction

Making a decision prematurely and then reducing any dissonance felt by group members can contribute to ineffective decision making. According to the dissonance theory developed by Leon Festinger (1957), anytime one is forced to choose between two attractive options, postdecision dissonance is present. **Cognitive dissonance** exists when a person possesses two cognitions that contradict each other. Dissonance exists, for example, if a group member knows the group selected one alternative as the most desirable option when other attractive alternatives also exist. A state of dissonance is assumed to motivate group members to reduce or eliminate it. One way to reduce the dissonance is to increase the perceived desirability of the decision made and decrease the perceived desirability of the alternatives that were not adopted. The more difficult or important the decision, the more likely group members are to find reasons that support the choice that was made and to minimize the attractive qualities of the foregone choice. This spreads apart the alternatives so that the one chosen is viewed as more attractive (in comparison with the other alternatives) after the decision than before it. If the group needs to reconsider the decision or reopen the decision making, dissonance reduction may interfere with its doing so.

Members Not Having Relevant Skills

If group members do not have the needed skills to complete the task and work together effectively, the decisions they make will not be effective. There are two types of relevant skills—those required to complete the task (taskwork skills) and those required to work as part of a group (groupwork skills). Groups with incapable members may often underperform a skilled individual. A skilled lumberjack, for example, could undoubtedly cut, trim, split, and load more timber on his own than any given group of college professors. It is not enough for a group member to know the correct answer to the problem. The member must share the solution with the rest of the group and persuade them to accept it. Factors that may interfere with doing so include the member's status in the group (Torrance, 1954), the confidence the member has in his or her solution, and the amount of his or her participation in the discussion (Thomas & Fink, 1961). In other words, when the most capable members of a problem-solving group are not confident, have low status, or are not talkative, the group is likely to underutilize its resources. If taskwork and groupwork skills are low, the quality of the group's decision making will suffer.

Lack of Individual Incentives for and Barriers to Contributing

Shepperd (1993) concluded after a meta-analysis of the literature that when there is a lack of incentives for contributing, members make little effort to achieve group goals. Correspondingly, there may be barriers that undermine the value of contributing or provide a motive to withhold contributions. When contributing to the group takes time and energy that would better be spent elsewhere or when a person believes his contributions are being exploited by others, there is an incentive for not contributing to a group effort.

Summary

Although groups tend to make higher-quality decisions than individuals working alone, there is nothing magical about groups. In order for high-quality decision making to take place within a group, the group needs to work together long enough to mature and to develop effective patterns of interaction among members. Any tendency towards uncritically giving the dominant response to the situation or social loafing needs to be avoided. Conflicting goals of individual members need to be resolved. All members need to participate and have the necessary social skills to present their information and ensure that it is incorporated into the group's deliberations. Egocentric refusal to consider any ideas but one's own needs to be avoided by group members. Avoidance and suppression of conflict and disagreement must also be avoided. A group needs sufficient heterogeneity among its members to ensure that different viewpoints and resources will be contributed to the discussion. Participation of members needs to be managed so that all members contribute without interfering with one another's thinking process. Group size needs to be appropriate to the problem, the problem has to be important to group members, and there needs to be sufficient time to deal with the problem. Power within the group needs to be managed constructively, and members' motivation needs to be sustained. Quick decisions and premature closures need to be avoided.

Exercise 7.3: *Winter Survival*

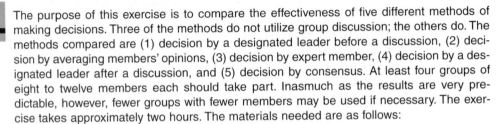

The purpose of this exercise is to compare the effectiveness of five different methods of making decisions. Three of the methods do not utilize group discussion; the others do. The methods compared are (1) decision by a designated leader before a discussion, (2) decision by averaging members' opinions, (3) decision by expert member, (4) decision by a designated leader after a discussion, and (5) decision by consensus. At least four groups of eight to twelve members each should take part. Inasmuch as the results are very predictable, however, fewer groups with fewer members may be used if necessary. The exercise takes approximately two hours. The materials needed are as follows:

> Instructions for observers.
> A description of the situation and a decision form.
> A group summary sheet.
> Instructions for groups that decide by consensus.
> Instructions for groups whose leader decides.
> A summary table.

The coordinator for the exercise should use the following procedure:

1. State that the purpose of the exercise is to compare several different methods of decision making. Set the stage by pointing out that group decision making is one of the most significant aspects of group functioning, that most consequential decisions are made by groups rather than individuals, that though many decisions are routine others are extremely crucial, and that participants in this exercise are now in a situation where the decisions they make as a group may determine whether or not they survive.

2. Divide the participants into groups of approximately eight members—six participants and two observers. Give each group a number or name for purposes of identification, ask the observers to meet at a central place to be briefed, and then distribute the description and decision forms to the participants. Review the situation with the participants, again emphasizing that their survival depends upon the quality of their decision. In half the groups designate one person as the leader; in the other groups make no mention of leadership. Then instruct the participants to complete the decision form quietly and by themselves so that the results indicate their own decisions. They have fifteen minutes to complete the decision form and make a duplicate copy of their ranking. The designated group leaders should write "leader" on their duplicate copy, and all participants must write their group designation on their duplicate copy. At the end of the fifteen minutes, collect the duplicate copies.

3. While the participants are completing their decision forms, brief the observers. Give each a copy of the instructions for observers and copies of the description and decision form (to orient them to the group task). Review the instructions to make sure the observers understand their task.

4. Distribute one copy of the group summary sheet and the appropriate instruction sheet to each participant. (The groups with a leader receive one instruction sheet and the groups without a leader the other instruction sheet.) Observers should also receive a copy of the instructions for their group. The groups should be placed far enough apart so that they cannot hear each other's discussions or be aware that they have different in-structions. The groups have forty-five minutes to decide upon a group ranking of the items on the decision form. They are to make a copy of their group ranking with their group designation clearly written on the top.

5. While the groups are working on their rankings, score the individual decision forms in the following way:

    a. Score the net difference between the participant's answer and the correct answer. For example, if the participant's answer were 9 and the correct answer is 12, the net difference is 3. Disregard all plus or minus signs; find only the net difference for each item. (The correct ranking appears in the Appendix.)

    b. Total these scores; the result is the participant's score. The lower the score the more accurate the ranking.

    c. To arrive at an average member's score, total all members' scores for each group and divide by the number of members.

    d. Put the scores in order from best to worst for each group. This ranking will be used to compare how many members, if any, had more accurate scores than the group's score.

    e. In the summary table that follows the instruction sheets for the groups, enter the av-erage member's score for each group and the score of the most accurate group mem-ber. Then, for the groups with a designated leader, enter the score of that person.

6. At the end of forty minutes, give a five-minute warning. After forty-five minutes instruct the groups to complete their ranking in the next thirty seconds and, with the group num-ber or name clearly marked on the paper, to turn in their group ranking. Quickly score the groups' rankings and enter them in the appropriate place in the summary table. Re-cruit one or two observers to help if you need them.

7. In a session with all the participants, give the correct ranking and the rationale for each item. The correct ranking and the rationale appear on pages 582–584 in the Appen-dix. Then explain how the rankings are scored so that each person can determine his or her score.

INSTRUCTION TO OBSERVERS

This exercise looks at the process by which groups make decisions. Crucial issues are how well the group uses the resources of its members, how much commitment to implement the decision is mustered, how the future decision-making ability of the group is affected, and how members feel about and react to what is taking place. As an observer, you may wish to focus on the following issues:

1. Who does and does not participate in the discussion? Who participates the most?

2. Who influences the decision and who does not? How is influence determined (expertise, sex, loudness of voice)?

3. Who is involved and who is uninvolved?

4. What are the dominant feelings of the group members? How would you describe the group atmosphere during the meeting?

5. What leadership behaviors are present and absent in the group? You may wish to use the task-behavior and maintenance-behavior observation sheets on page 216.
6. What are the basic causes for the members' resources being used or not being used?

WINTER SURVIVAL EXERCISE: THE SITUATION

You have just crash-landed in the woods of northern Minnesota and southern Manitoba. It is 11:32 A.M. in mid-January. The light plane in which you were traveling crashed on a lake. The pilot and copilot were killed. Shortly after the crash the plane sank completely into the lake with the pilot's and copilot's bodies inside. None of you is seriously injured and you are all dry.

The crash came suddenly, before the pilot had time to radio for help or inform anyone of your position. Because your pilot was trying to avoid a storm, you know the plane was considerably off course. The pilot announced shortly before the crash that you were twenty miles northwest of a small town that is the nearest known habitation.

You are in a wilderness area made up of thick woods broken by many lakes and streams. The snow depth varies from above the ankles in windswept areas to knee-deep where it has drifted. The last weather report indicated that the temperature would reach minus 25 degrees Fahrenheit in the daytime and minus 40 at night. There is plenty of dead wood and twigs in the immediate area. You are dressed in winter clothing appropriate for city wear—suits, pantsuits, street shoes, and overcoats.

While escaping from the plane, the several members of your group salvaged twelve items. Your task is to rank these items according to their importance to your survival, starting with 1 for the most important item and ending with 12 for the least important one.

You may assume that the number of passengers is the same as the number of persons in your group and that the group has agreed to stick together.

WINTER SURVIVAL DECISION FORM

Rank the following items according to their importance to your survival, starting with 1 for the most important and proceeding to 12 for the least important.

_____ ball of steel wool   _____ sectional air map made of plastic
_____ newspapers (one per person) _____ 20 × 20-ft piece of heavy-duty canvas
_____ compass   _____ extra shirt and pants for each survivor
_____ hand ax   _____ can of shortening
_____ cigarette lighter (without fluid) _____ quart of 100-proof whiskey
_____ loaded .45-caliber pistol   _____ family-size chocolate bar (one per person)

INSTRUCTIONS FOR GROUPS WITHOUT A LEADER

This is an exercise in group decision making. Your group is to employ the method of group consensus in reaching its decision. This means that the ranking for each of the twelve survival items *must* be agreed upon by each group member before it becomes a part of the group decision. Consensus is difficult to reach. Therefore, not every ranking will meet with everyone's complete approval. Try, as a group, to make each ranking one with which all group members can at least partially agree. Here are some guidelines to use in reaching consensus:

1. Avoid arguing *blindly* for your own opinions. Present your position as clearly and logically as possible, but listen to other members' reactions and consider them carefully before you press your point.

2. Avoid changing your mind just to reach agreement and avoid conflict. Support only solutions with which you are able to agree to at least some degree. Yield only to positions that have objective and logically sound foundations.
3. Avoid conflict-reducing procedures such as majority voting, tossing a coin, averaging, and bargaining.
4. Seek out differences of opinion. They are natural and expected. Try to involve everyone in the decision process. Disagreements can improve the group's decision because a wide range of information and opinions improves the chances of the group to hit upon more adequate solutions.
5. Do not assume that someone must win and someone must lose when discussion reaches a stalemate. Instead, look for the next most acceptable alternative for all members.
6. Discuss underlying assumptions, listen carefully to one another, and encourage the participation of *all* members—the especially important factors in reaching decisions by consensus.

Winter Survival: Group Summary Sheet

Item	Members						Summary
	1	2	3	4	5	6	
Ball of steel wool							
Newspapers							
Compass							
Hand ax							
Cigarette lighter							
.45-caliber pistol							
Sectional air map							
Canvas							
Shirt and pants							
Shortening							
Whiskey							
Chocolate bars							

Summary Table: Accuracy of Decisions

Group	Before Group Discussion			After Group Discussion		Gain or loss over designated leader's score	Gain or loss over average member's score	Gain or loss over accurate member's score	Number of members superior to group score
	Designated leader's score	Average member's score	Most accurate member's score	Leader-group score	Consensus-group score				
1									
2									
3									
4									

INSTRUCTIONS FOR GROUPS WITH A LEADER

This is an exercise in how a leader makes decisions after participating in a group discussion. Your group is to discuss what the ranking of the survival items should be, but the final decision rests with the designated leader of your group. At the end of forty-five minutes your group's leader will hand in what he or she considers to be the best ranking of the items. The role of the group members is to provide as much help as the leader wants in trying to determine how the items should be ranked.

Exercise 7.4: They'll Never Take Us Alive (see page 584 for correct ranking)

This exercise uses the same procedure as the Winter Survival Exercise.

THEY'LL NEVER TAKE US ALIVE RANKING SHEET

In a recent survey, *Dun's Review* lists the most perilous products or activities in the United States, based on annual death statistics. Below are listed fifteen of these death-causing hazards. Your task is to rank them in order of dangerousness according to the number of deaths caused each year. Place 1 by the most dangerous, 2 by the next most dangerous, and so forth:

_____ swimming   _____ pesticides
_____ railroads   _____ handguns
_____ police work   _____ bicycles
_____ home appliances   _____ firefighting
_____ alcohol   _____ mountain climbing
_____ nuclear power   _____ vaccinations
_____ smoking   _____ surgery
_____ motor vehicles

APPROACHES TO DECISION MAKING

Neither life nor liberty nor sacred honor are safe while the legislature is in session.

Revere's Canon

This country has come to feel the same when Congress is in session as when a baby gets hold of a hammer.

Will Rogers

Involving all group members in the decision making ensures that a considered and thoughtful decision is made that everyone is committed to implementing. Making a considered and thoughtful decision is much harder than it sounds. Many times decisions are made by trying to:

1. *Stay with the status quo.* The decision makers complacently decide to continue whatever they have been doing, clinging to tradition, ignoring information about its in-

effectiveness and the risks of losses. This is often a nonrational resistance to change, such as clinging to tradition, inertia and habit, overdependence on authority, illusions of powerlessness, or insecurity about the consequences of the change for oneself.

2. *Change as little as possible.* The decision makers adopt a new course of action that requires as little effort to implement as possible. Lindbloom (1959) notes that decision-makers engage in *disjointed incrementalism* where decisions differ incrementally from existing policies and, therefore, only small changes ever result.

3. *Delay and avoid making the decision.* The decision-makers believe that they are "damned if they change and damned if they don't." Because they believe there are serious risks no matter what they do, they defensively avoid the decision. *Defensive avoidance* is characterized by (a) procrastination (turning attention away from the conflict to other less distressing matters), (b) shifting of responsibility or buck-passing to someone else (enabling them to evade the dilemma and providing them with a handy scapegoat should the decision prove to have undesirable outcomes), or (c) psychological escape by means of inventing fanciful rationalizations in support of one of the choice alternatives (selectively attending to only the good aspects of that alternative and ignoring or distorting negative information about it so that decision makers feel invulnerable to threat and danger) (Mann & Janis, 1983). This latter procedure is often known as groupthink.

4. *Choose the first likely solution without considering all alternatives.* The decision-makers feel pressure to make the decision immediately. Fear and anxiety about the consequences of the decision may result in vacillation, panic, and impulsively seizing a hastily contrived solution without understanding its full implications. The new course of action that requires minimal change, is most salient, or is most strongly advocated is uncritically adopted action without much thought. Hoffman (1961) notes that decisions are adopted when they reach a minimum level of support necessary for acceptance. There is a reduced time perspective, reduced memory span, simplistic and repetitive thinking, and cognitive rigidity, all of which lead to a higher value on immediate goals, premature closure, restricted search for alternatives, and less rigorous evaluation of alternatives and their consequences (Mann & Janis, 1983).

5. *Encourage considered and thoughtful decision making in which all major alternatives are given a fair and thorough hearing.* Group members search for relevant information, assimilate it in a relatively unbiased way, and carefully evaluate the major alternatives before making a choice. Considered and thoughtful decision-making can be best achieved from the small-group / large-group decision-making procedure using advocacy subgroups. This procedure is discussed in depth in Chapter 8.

The first four methods are so easy but so inadequate compared to considered and thoughtful decision making.

CONSIDERED AND THOUGHTFUL DECISION MAKING

Decision making occurs within the context of problem solving. In order to consider the steps to making considered and thoughtful decisions, the whole problem-solving procedure has to be discussed (Johnson & Johnson, 1989).

Identifying and Defining the Problem or Issue

The first step of a decision-making group is to identify and define the problem. A **problem** is a discrepancy or difference between an actual state of affairs and a desired state of affairs. Problem solving requires both an idea about where the group should be and valid information about where it is now. The more clear and accurate the definition of the problem, the easier it is to do the other steps in the problem-solving processes. The group's vision, mission, and goals are relevant to defining the problem. There are three steps in defining the problem:

1. Reaching agreement on what the desired state of affairs is (that is, the group's purposes, goals, and objectives).
2. Obtaining valid, reliable, directly verifiable, descriptive (not inferential or evaluative), and correct information about the existing state of affairs.
3. Discussing thoroughly the difference between the desired and actual state of affairs, because it is from the awareness of this discrepancy that the commitment and motivation to solve the problem is built.

Because problem-solving groups often progress too quickly towards a solution to the problem without first getting a clear, consensual definition of the problem itself, members of the group should see to it that everyone understands what the problem is before trying to assess its magnitude.

Defining a workable problem is often the hardest stage of the problem-solving process. Suggestions for procedures are as follows:

1. List a series of statements about the problem. Describe it as concretely as possible by mentioning people, places, and resources. There should be as many different statements of the problem as the members are willing to give. Write them on a blackboard where everyone can see them. Avoid arguing about whether the problem is perfectly stated.
2. Restate each problem statement so that it includes a description of both the desired and actual state of affairs. Take out alternative definitions that are beyond the resources of the group to solve. Choose the definition that the group members agree is most correct. *The problem should be important, solvable, and urgent.*
3. Write out a detailed description of what group life will be like when the problem is solved. The more detailed and specific the scenario is, the better.

There are a number of potential barriers to identifying and defining problems. The first is *prematurely defining the problem.* The direction a group first takes in defining the problem may keep it from finding a successful solution (Maier, 1930); therefore, the group should be careful not to agree prematurely on the definition of its problem. The second is a *lack of clarity in stating the problem.* Much of the initial effort of groups in solving a problem is directed towards orienting members to what the problem is. This phase is extremely important, and it deserves sufficient time and effort to identify the problem, to define it, and, through this process, to get the members involved in and committed to solving it. Often, groups are doomed to failure when they inadequately define the nature of their problem. Third, a *critical, evaluative, competitive climate* prevents creative and workable solutions from being discovered. A supportive, trusting, cooperative atmosphere is necessary for solving problems successfully. If group members are afraid that other members are evaluating their ideas, effective problem solving is destroyed. Fourth, if group members have *inadequate motivation to solve the problem* a compelling solution will not be found. Any problem-solving group must have the motivation to solve its problems. If the group members are not motivated, they must be persuaded to see the importance of the problem and the necessity for seeking a solution. Members who leave the work to others clearly lack motivation.

Gathering Information About the Existence of the Problem

The second step in the problem-solving process is diagnosing the existence, magnitude, and nature of the problem. Valid information must be gathered. Then the information must be thoroughly discussed and analyzed to ensure that all task force members understand it. Actual frequency of occurrence of the problem, the magnitude of the forces helping the group to move towards the desired state of affairs, and the forces hindering this movement need to be documented. Determining what forces are acting upon the problem situation is called **force field analysis** (Lewin, 1944; Myrdal, 1944). In force field analysis the problem is seen as a balance between forces working in opposite directions—some helping the movement towards the desired state of affairs and others restraining such movement. The balance that results between the helping and restraining forces is the actual state of affairs—a **quasistationary equilibrium** that can be altered through changes in the forces (Figure 7.8).

The ideal state of affairs towards which the group is working is on the right side and is represented by a plus sign. The worst state of affairs, on the left side of the figure, is represented by a minus sign. The vertical line in the middle signifies the current state of affairs—a middle ground. On any problem numerous forces are at work, some restraining change and others helping change. There are two basic steps for a group to follow in doing a force field analysis:

1. Make up lists of forces by first brainstorming all the helping forces and then all the restraining forces. The list should include all possible forces, whether psychological, interpersonal, organizational, or societal. If a force seems to be a complex of variables, each variable should be listed separately. Critical judgment should be avoided; it is essential that every member's ideas are publicly requested and aired.

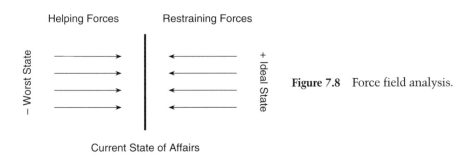

Figure 7.8 Force field analysis.

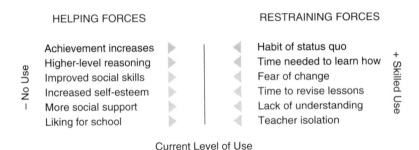

Figure 7.9 Implementing cooperative learning.

2. Rank the forces according to their importance in affecting the present situation. Agree on the most important helping and restraining forces, which may total from three to six each. Rate the important forces according to how easily they can be resolved, and avoid spending time discussing those that the group cannot influence with their current resources.

An example is as follows. The implementation of cooperative learning within a school may be seen as a balance between forces helping teachers implement cooperative learning and restraining teachers from using cooperative learning. The use of cooperative learning is promoted by the teachers' awareness that it will increase student achievement, higher-level reasoning, social skills, self-esteem, and social support. The use of cooperative learning is restrained by teachers habitually using other instructional procedures, not being willing to commit the time to learn how to use cooperative learning, inherent fear of change, lack of willingness to revise their standard lessons, and incomplete understanding of what cooperative learning is (Figure 7.9).

There are two major *barriers* to gathering valid information about the nature and magnitude of the problem. The first is *not getting the needed information.* When information is minimal, the definition of the problem will be inadequate, fewer alternative strategies for the solution will be generated, and potential consequences of those alternatives will not be properly explored. The result is relatively low-grade solutions. Great emphasis must be placed on fact finding in order to solve a problem effectively. The second barrier is *poor communication within the group.* Poor communication among group members has the same effect as the lack of information, with the added problem that it makes the implementation of any action that requires coordination among group members difficult. Effective communication among all group members is necessary for effective problem solving.

Without defining the problem correctly and specifically, it cannot be adequately understood. And without an accurate and precise understanding of the forces involved, the alternative strategies for the solution of the problem cannot be formulated.

Formulating and Considering Alternative Solutions

The overall purpose of a decision-making group is to make a free and informed choice of a solution to the problem based on having and understanding the relevant information. To achieve that purpose a cooperative structure must be established, the problem must be accurately identified and defined, and valid information about the existence, magnitude, and nature of the problem must be gathered and organized so it is easily understood. Once the nature and magnitude of the problem is accurately understood, alternative ways to solve it may be identified.

The third step in problem solving is identifying and analyzing alternative ways to solve the problem. Groups often make poor decisions because they (a) do not think of the proper alternative solutions and/or (b) do a poor job of evaluating and choosing among the alternatives considered. *Systematically evaluating each alternative and analyzing the advantages and disadvantages of each alternative before making a final decision are the most important factors in effective decision making.* The more explicit the systematic evaluation, the less likely that an alternative will be overlooked or rationalized away. If decision-makers do know what the alternatives are and have correctly diagnosed each alternative's inherent advantages and disadvantages, they will not choose a certain course of action unless its advantages are expected to exceed its disadvantages.

Identifying and analyzing alternative ways to solve the problem requires creative, divergent, and inventive reasoning. Such higher-level thinking and analysis comes primarily from intellectual disagreement and challenge, (i.e., controversy). Controversy is discussed in Chapter 8. By definition, all decisions involve controversy as decision making is a choice among alternative courses of action. Controversy is structured within problem-solving groups through the use of advocacy subgroups. In order to participate competently in the controversy process, group members must be able to prepare a position, advocate it, defend it from criticism, critically evaluate the alternative positions, be able to view the problem from all perspectives, and be able to synthesize and integrate the best parts of all solutions.

Force-Field Analysis. Force field analysis is a particularly useful way of specifying alternative strategies for solving a problem. It is based on the assumption that changes in the present situation will occur only as the helpful and restraining forces are changed so that the level where they are balancing is altered. *There are two basic methods for changing the equilibrium point between the two sets of forces:* increasing the strength or number of the helping forces and decreasing the strength or number of the restraining forces. Of the two, the preferable strategy is to reduce the strength or eliminate the restraining forces. Increasing the pressure for change in the present situation by strengthening the helping forces also increases natural resistance to change, reducing the strategy's effectiveness. Restraining forces may be reduced or eliminated without creating resistance. *Reducing the restraining forces, therefore, is usually the more effective of the two strategies.* The fewer the forces acting upon the present situation, furthermore, the lower the tension level of the people in the situation.

The two methods are not mutually exclusive. Often you will wish to reduce restraining forces and increase helping forces at the same time. When this can be done, it is very effective. One way of intervening simultaneously with both types of forces is to modify a restraining force so that it becomes a helping force. One of the most successful strategies for changing the direction of a restraining force is to involve the group members who are resisting the desired changes in diagnosing the problem situation and in planning the solutions (Watson & Johnson, 1972). *People enjoy and affirm the changes they make themselves, and they resist changes imposed upon them by others.*

Involvement of resisters in the diagnosing and planning of change often means a more difficult planning process, but it virtually guarantees that they are committed to the proposed changes. It also helps clear up any misunderstandings and differences of opinion before the strategies are implemented, and it uses the resources of the opposition.

Force field analysis is useful for two reasons. First, it avoids the error of a single-factor analysis of a problem; using it will keep attention on the problem situation until a number of relevant factors are identified. *Second,* by helping to identify a number of problem-related factors, it gives group members several points at which they may intervene in their attempt to produce a change. Because any change is the result of a number of factors, an effective change strategy involves plural actions that are directed toward several of those factors. When an approach is made through modifying several factors at the same time, the possibility is increased that the improvement will be permanent.

In specifying alternative strategies for change, group members should think of as many ways as possible in which the forces holding the group from moving towards the desired state might be reduced. They should obtain ideas from everyone in the group. If group members do not have many ideas, outside consultants can always be invited to lend assistance. Bringing in an expert who knows a lot about the substance of the problem is often extremely helpful at this point. Group members should try to take each restraining force in turn and think up ways to reduce its strength or to eliminate it altogether. Divergent thinking should be encouraged.

Vigilant Analysis.   Janis and Mann (1977) recommend a procedure they believe eliminates the possibility of defensive avoidance and ensures that vigilant consideration of each alternative solution takes place. The group systematically evaluates each alternative solution on the basis of four factors.

1. The tangible gains and losses for the group members.
2. The tangible gains and losses for significant others such as other members of the organization.
3. Member self-approval or self-disapproval (Will we feel proud or ashamed if we choose this alternative?).
4. The approval or disapproval of the school by significant others (Will important people we are connected with think we made the right decision?).

The group ensures that these four factors are used to analyze each alternative in the following way:

1. A balance sheet is completed for each course of action considered. A balance sheet consists of listing the tangible gains from adopting the alternative on one side and the tangible losses on the other.
2. Each gain or loss is rated in terms of its importance on a ten-point scale from "1" (no importance) to "10" (extremely important).
3. After a balance sheet is completed for each alternative course of action, the balance sheets are compared and the alternatives are ranked from "most desirable" to "least desirable."

Using a balance sheet to ensure systematic evaluation has been found to be related to level of satisfaction with a decision, commitment to a decision, and security about the correctness of a decision (Janis & Mann, 1977).

Other procedures for ensuring that high-quality decisions are made by preventing groupthink and by structuring systematic evaluation include the following (Janis and Mann, 1977; Mann and Janis, 1983):

1. *Impartial leadership.* The leader abstains from communicating his or her position at the outset so that members cannot adopt it uncritically. By not stating preferences and expectations at the outset and by not advocating specific proposals, the leader allows members to develop an atmosphere of open inquiry and to explore impartially a wide range of policy alternatives.

2. *Critical evaluator role for every member.* Group members are encouraged to express doubts and objections freely. The leader assigns each member the role of critical evaluator, giving high priority to the airing of objections and doubts and accepting criticism of judgments in order to discourage group members from soft-pedaling their disagreements.

3. *Devil's advocate.* One or more group members are assigned the role of challenging the testimony of all those who support the majority opinion. Members are chosen to represent unpopular positions in the group.

5. *Outside experts.* Outside experts are invited to group meetings and asked to challenge the views of group members.

Barriers. There are a number of barriers to formulating and considering alternative solutions to the problem. The first is a *failure to identify the proper alternative courses of action.* If a course of action is not identified, it cannot be considered and evaluated. The second is *premature elimination of courses of action without proper analysis and evaluation, or uninformed and premature choice.* Groups often make poor decisions, not because they did not think of the proper alternatives, but because they did a poor job of evaluating and choosing among the alternatives they considered (Maier & Thurber, 1969). For most people, ideas are fragile creations, easily blighted by a chill, or even indifferent reception. As groups proceed in their problem-solving activities, they must avoid all tendencies to squelch each idea as it comes along; instead, they should create an atmosphere that supports the presentation and the pooling of a wide assortment of ideas. All alternative solutions should receive a fair hearing. Only then can the group avoid becoming fixated on the first reasonable solution suggested and critically evaluate the worth of all alternatives. The third is *pressures for conformity.* Pressures for conformity and compliance slow down the development of different and diverse ideas. Divergent thinking as well as convergent thinking are necessary for sound problem solving. The fourth is a *lack of inquiry and problem-solving skills.* Some groups may need special training in how to use inquiry and problem-solving methods to advantage. Training may be accomplished through an expert member of the group, or the group may wish to call in an outside consultant. The fifth is a *lack of procedures to aid analysis and synthesis.* The forces creating the problem must be understood and systematically analyzed in order for new alternatives to be created.

Deciding on a Solution

Once all the possible solutions have been identified and formulated in specific terms, the group needs to select the solution it will implement. Making a decision involves considering possible alternatives and choosing one. The purpose of group decision making is to decide on well-considered, well-understood, realistic action towards goals every member wishes to achieve. Whenever possible, decisions by task forces should be made by consensus. Consensus is not easy to achieve as it is characterized by more conflict among members, more shifts of opinion, a longer time to reach a conclusion, and more confidence by members in the correctness of their decision. It is, however, worth the time and trouble.

Second-Chance Meeting.   Even when decisions are made by consensus, there are times when members fixate on an alternative without thinking through all its consequences. One procedure for ensuring that a decision is not made too hastily is *second-chance meeting.* Alfred Sloan, when he was Chairman of General Motors, once called an executive meeting to consider a major decision. He concluded the meeting by saying,

> Gentlemen, I take it we are all in complete agreement on the decision here. . . . Then I propose we postpone further discussion until our next meeting to give ourselves time to develop disagreement and perhaps gain some understanding of what the decision is all about (quoted in Drucker, 1974, p. 472).

After a preliminary consensus on the best alternative, a *second-chance meeting* can be held in which all members are encouraged to express any remaining doubts and criticisms. Second-chance meetings help prevent premature consensus and concurrence seeking.

There have been societies that assumed that under the influence of alcohol there would be fewer inhibitions against expressing residual doubts about a preliminary decision made when everyone was sober. According to Herodotus, the ancient Persians would make important decisions twice—first sober and then drunk. According to Tacitus, the Germans in Roman times also followed this practice. In Japan, where an emphasis is placed on harmony and politeness, a decision is frequently reconsidered after work in a bar. *Saki talk* takes place after each person has had a couple of cups of saki and, therefore, is no longer required to be polite. How group members really feel about the decision is then revealed.

Presenting the Recommendation to the Organization

It is not enough to make a decision. All persons who must implement the decision need to be convinced that it is the best thing to do. Thus, the solution recommended has to be clearly communicated to the organization as a whole and the relevant others must have an opportunity to modify the decision if they are to be committed to implementing it. If the people who must implement the decision are not involved in making it, they will have little or no commitment to help implement the decision. People tend to affirm, support, and implement decisions they have helped make whereas they tend to resist implementating decisions imposed on them. The key to this step is to ensure that everyone participates, everyone is involved in making the decision, and, therefore, everyone is committed to implementing the decision once it is made. The *barrier* to effective decision making at this point is inadequate involvement of the individuals who have to implement the decision.

Evaluating Extent and Success of Implementation

The responsibilities of the group members do not end when the group makes a decision. The decision has to be implemented. *Decision implementation* is a process of taking the necessary actions that result in the execution of the decision. *Decision implementation requires internal commitment by relevant group members to the decisions made.* No decision is worthwhile unless it is implemented. Once the group decides, the next step is to go out and do what members have decided to do.

To evaluate the success of the solution the group has decided to implement, members must determine (a) whether the solution was successfully implemented and (b) what the effects were. The first activity is sometimes called *process evaluation* because it deals with the process of implementing a strategy. The second is called *outcome evaluation* because it involves assessing or judging the consequences of implementing the strategy. Planners should establish criteria for or ways in which to judge the effectiveness of their actions in implementing the strategy, and review their progress as each action step occurs. The major criterion for assessing the outcome of an implemented strategy is whether the actual state of affairs is closer to the desired state of affairs than it was before the strategy was carried out. The group documents the extent to which implementation takes place, notes barriers to implementation, and evaluates the success of the decision.

If the group finds that its solution has been successfully implemented, but has failed to substantially change the current situation into the ideal state of affairs, a new solution must be chosen and implemented until the group finds one that is effective. The solution of one set of problems, however, often brings other problems into the open, and in trying out various strategies the group may find that it has not been working for the solution of the most critical problem in the situation. The final result of the evaluation stage, therefore, should be to show the group what problems have been solved and to what extent, what problems still need to be solved, and what new problems have come up. Evaluation should result in a new definition of a problem, a rediagnosis of the situation, and beginning of a new problem-solving sequence.

PROBLEMS WITH THEORIZING ON DECISION MAKING

There are at least two major problems with the theorizing and research on decision making in small groups. The *first* is that much of the research has focused on whether the decisions made by groups are of high or low quality. In the real world many decisions cannot be objectively evaluated in terms of success or failure because their long-term effects cannot be fully measured. To evaluate long-term success or failure, one would need to take into account the negative consequences of the decision made, the positive consequences that would have resulted if each of the other alternatives were adopted as the decision, the positive consequences of the decision, and the negative consequences that would have resulted if each of the other alternatives had been adopted. Obviously, it is difficult if not impossible to quantify these factors.

The *second* problem is that much of the theorizing and research on decision making has assumed that decision-makers are completely informed (that they know all the possible courses of action and the potential outcomes of each), infinitely sensitive (they see each alternative in all its complexity), and always rational (they always maximize the outcomes of their action). Real-life decision-makers, however, are not always completely informed (they do not or cannot know all courses of action and their potential outcomes), do not understand fully the intricacies of various alternatives, and are rarely completely rational. Real-life decision-makers often seem beset by conflicts, doubts, and worries: They struggle with conflicting loyalties, antipathies, and longings and engage in procrastination, rationalization, and denial of responsibility for their decisions. Instead of determining the solution that maximizes their outcomes, many decision-makers look only for the alternative that meets a minimal set of requirements (this is called satisficing) and make quick decisions (Hoffman, 1961; Simon, 1976). Ineffective groups seem to operate under a variety of decision-making rules, such as "Tell a qualified expert about the problem and do whatever he or she says—that will be good enough" and "Do what we did last time if it worked, and the opposite if it didn't work." Real-life decision-makers also realize how expensive it is in time, effort, and money to collect and dissect the huge amounts of information a group needs in order to use an ideal form of decision making.

Researchers can alleviate these two problems by studying the process of decision making rather than focusing on quality, and by specifying procedures that encourage real-life decision-makers to become more systematic and rational in their decision making.

Exercise 7.5: A Problem Diagnosis Program

This program is designed to help you in diagnosing a problem that involves people working together in a group. In this program eleven separate steps are presented, each of which contains a complete and separate idea, question, or instruction. Be sure that you understand and complete each step before going on to the next one.

1. Identify the problem you wish to work on. Describe the problem as you now see it.

   _____

   _____

   _____

2. Most problem statements can be rephrased so that they describe two things:
   a. The situation as it is now.
   b. The situation as you would like it to be (the ideal).
   Restate your problem situation in these terms. _____

   _____

   _____

   _____

3. Most problem situations can be understood in terms of the forces that push towards and against change—in other words, helping forces and restraining forces. It is useful to analyze a problem by making lists of the helping and restraining forces affecting a situation. Think about these now, and list them. Be sure to list as many as you can, not worrying at this point about how important each one is. Use additional paper if you need to.

Helping	*Restraining*

4. Review the two lists. Underline those forces that seem to be the most important right now, and that you think you might be able to influence constructively. Depending on the problem, there may be one specific force that stands out, or there may be two or three helping forces and two or three restraining forces that are particularly important.
5. Now, for each restraining force you have underlined, list some possible courses of action that you might be able to plan and carry out to reduce the effect of the force or to eliminate it completely. Brainstorm. List as many action steps as possible, without worrying about how effective or practical they would be. You will later have a chance to decide which are the most appropriate.

   Restraining force A. Possible action steps to reduce this force:

   _____

   _____

Restraining force B. Possible action steps to reduce this force:

_____

_____

Restraining force C. Possible action steps to reduce this force:

_____

_____

6. Now do the same with each helping force you underlined. List all the action steps that come to mind that would increase the effect of each helping force.

Helping force A. Possible action steps to increase this force:

_____

_____

Helping force B. Possible action steps to increase this force:

_____

_____

Helping force C. Possible action steps to increase this force:

_____

_____

7. You have now listed action steps to change the key forces affecting your problem situation. Review these possible action steps and underline those that seem promising.

8. List the steps you have underlined. Then for each action step list the materials, people, and other resources available to you for carrying out the action.

Action Steps	*Resources Available*

9. Review the list of action steps and resources and think about how each might fit into a comprehensive action plan. Take out those items that do not seem to fit into the overall plan, add any new steps and resources that will round out the plan, and think about a possible sequence of action.

_____

_____

_____

_____

10. Plan a way of evaluating the effectiveness of your action program as it is implemented. Think about this now, and list the evaluation procedures you will use.

_____

_____

_____

_____

11. You now have a plan of action to deal with the problem situation. The next step is for you to implement it.

Exercise 7.6: *The Bean Jar (II)*

The purpose of this exercise is to show that the involvement of more persons in the decision-making process affects the accuracy of the decision. The exercise can be done in an hour, and it requires only a large jar full of a known quantity of beans. The procedure for the coordinator is as follows:

1. Explain that the exercise focuses on the accuracy of the decisions made by different combinations of individuals. Then set a large jar of beans in front of the participants. You need to know exactly how many beans are in the jar. Tell the participants they will be asked to estimate how many beans the jar contains.
2. Have each person estimate the number of beans, working alone. Record the estimates.
3. Have each participant pick a partner. Have the two-person teams work out a system for estimating how many beans are in the jar, and record their estimates.
4. Have each pair pick another twosome and the four-person teams estimate the number of beans. Record their estimates.
5. Have each quartet pick another foursome and the eight-member groups estimate the number of beans. Record their estimates.
6. Have each octet pick another group and the sixteen-member groups estimate the number of beans. Record their estimates.
7. Ask for the final estimates and then tell the participants the number of beans in the jar. Have the class form groups of eight and discuss their experience, how they felt during the decision making, and the way in which they operated in the groups. Finally, ask the groups of eight to build a set of conclusions about the effect that an increasing number of members has on the accuracy of the decision and why the number of members influenced decision accuracy in the way it did. Have each group share its conclusions with the rest of the participants, and then have a class discussion of the conclusions.

Exercise 7.7: *Your Decision-Making Behavior*

Before this chapter ends it might be useful for you to consider your decision-making behavior. How do you usually behave in a decision-making group? How would you like to behave? Here is a closing exercise for you to do in a group with two of your classmates:

1. Throw all your loose change into the center of the group. Decide (using consensus) how to use the money. Then look at the group decision in terms of the behaviors of each member. How did each of you behave? What task and maintenance functions did you yourself fulfill? How did you feel about your participation? How did your usual behavior reveal itself in the group decision making?
2. Review as a group the task and maintenance functions listed in Chapter 5. Discuss what other functions could be added. Examples are
   a. *Clarification or elaboration.* Interpret or reflect on ideas or suggestions; clear up confusion; bring up alternatives and new issues before the group; give examples.
   b. *Summarization.* Pull together related ideas; restate suggestions after the group has discussed them.
   c. *Consensus testing.* Check with the group to see how much agreement has been reached; test to see if the group is nearing a decision.
   d. *Communication of feeling.* Express your feelings about the issues the group is discussing and the way in which it is functioning.

e. *Verification of feeling.* Ask other members how they are feeling; check to see if your perception of their feelings is correct.

Pick the task and maintenance functions you usually engage in; pick those you would like to perform better. Give one another feedback about each member's behavior.

3. Have you received any feedback on your behavior that has increased your awareness of how you behave? How would you now describe your behavior in decision-making situations?

4. Decide as a group when to end this exercise.

HOW I BEHAVE QUESTIONNAIRE

The purpose of this questionnaire is to help you look at how you behave in a group that is making a decision. Different persons act in different ways when they are members of groups that are making decisions. Moreover, the same person may act differently at different times, depending on the group, the decision to be made, and the circumstances. But, in general, how do you act when a group in which you are a member is making a decision? In each of the following three statements, choose the best description of the way in which you behave when a group to which you belong is making a decision. Be as objective and honest as you can; the results are for your use only.

1. When my group is making a decision, I
   _____ Passively defer to others.
   _____ Work for a decision that satisfies everyone without worrying about how good it is.
   _____ Look entirely at the merits of the alternatives without thinking about how the members of the group feel or how satisfied they are.
   _____ Look for alternatives that work, though I might not personally think they are the best.
   _____ Work for a strong, creative decision having a common basis of understanding among group members.

2. When my group is facing a decision, I
   _____ Show little interest in the decision or the other group members.
   _____ Think mostly about how the members of the group are getting along, without worrying about what the decision will be.
   _____ Push for a really good decision and view the other members only as contributors of resources that will help make a better decision.
   _____ Work for good relations among the members and a good solution, though I am willing to sacrifice a little of each to get the job done.
   _____ Avoid compromise and try to get everyone to agree to and be satisfied with a decision that is based upon looking at the situation in a realistic way.

3. When my group is making a decision, I
   _____ Wait for the group to tell me what to do and accept what they recommend for me.
   _____ Help others participate by giving them moral support and by testing to see if members can agree.
   _____ Give information, evaluate how well the group is working towards completing the task, set ground rules for behavior, and see that everyone stays at the task.
   _____ Summarize periodically what has been discussed, call for things to be made clearer, and encourage members to compromise.
   _____ Help the group think of alternatives, discuss how practical the alternatives are, and work out ways in which the group can come to an agreement.

You can plot this self-assessment on the task–maintenance grid in Figure 5.1 (page 198). Each of the preceding statements can be completed in five possible ways. The first alternative for each statement is a (6,6) response; it shows that this person has little or no interest in either maintaining the group or helping it accomplish its task of making a decision. The second alternative is a (6,30) response, showing that this member emphasizes group maintenance while ignoring the task. The third alternative is a (30,6) response; here the person focuses on getting the task done but ignores group maintenance. The fourth alternative is an (18,18) response, indicating a member who compromises on both task and maintenance in order to reach a decision. The fifth alternative for each question is a (30,30) response; this person tries to achieve a creative, consensual decision, and emphasizes both the task and maintenance functions of the group.

Look at your three responses. Locate each on the task–maintenance grid. Then discuss the results in groups of three, comparing your responses here with those you gave on the leadership surveys in the previous chapter, and with the way you would like to act in groups.

SUMMARY

Typically, groups make more effective decisions than do individuals because groups create the possibility for social facilitation, risk taking, member commitment to the group, appropriate behavioral and attitudinal patterns being adopted, and the likelihood that the task is better done in a group. Once a group is given the responsibility for making the decision, there are seven methods to choose from, including letting the member with the highest authority decide to averaging individual opinions to group consensus. In using the decision-making methods, there are components that must be carefully structured (positive interdependence, promotive interaction, individual accountability, social skills, and group processing) and there are factors that hinder the group's decision-making efforts. The hindering factors include the lack of group maturity, taking the dominant response, social loafing, free riding, fear of being a sucker, groupthink, conflicting goals, members' egocentrism, homogeneity, production blocking, inappropriate size, dissonance reduction, and the lack of necessary taskwork and teamwork skills. In order to structure the essential components and avoid the hindering factors, the group has to engage in considered and thoughtful decision making. The steps for doing so are to identify and define the problem, gather the information needed to diagnose it, formulate alternative solutions, decide on the solution to implement, present the group's recommendations to the larger organization (if appropriate), and evaluate the success of the implementation to determine if the problem is now solved.

An essential aspect of decision making is deciding among alternative solutions. To do so effectively, conflict among members' preferences, analyses, conclusions, and theories must be encouraged and resolved constructively. The next chapter focuses on structuring decision-making controversies and ensuring that it leads to creative problem solving.

8 *Controversy and Creativity*

Basic Concepts to Be Covered in This Chapter

In this chapter a number of concepts are defined and discussed. The major ones are listed below. The procedure for learning these concepts is as follows:

1. Divide into heterogeneous pairs.
2. The task for each pair is to:
   (a) Define each concept, noting the page on which it is defined and discussed.
   (b) Ensure that both members of the pair understand the meaning of each concept.
3. Combine into groups of four. Compare the answers of the two pairs. If there is disagreement, the members look up the concept in the chapter and clarify it until they all agree on the definition and understand it.

Concepts

1. Controversy
2. Conceptual conflict
3. Cognitive perspective
4. Perspective-taking
5. Concurrence-seeking
6. Debate
7. Epistemic curiosity
8. Creativity
9. Dogmatism
10. Open-mindedness
11. Differentiation of positions
12. Integration of positions
13. Brainstorming

Exercise 8.1: Controversy

Task: In the book, *Peter Pan,* a case is made for staying young forever in Never-Never Land. Is this a good idea? Would you like to live in Never-Never Land and never grow up? Write a report on the issue *Was Peter Pan right or wrong? Should you grow up or stay a child?* The report should present a position and the reasons why the position is valid.

Cooperative: Write one report for the group, in which everyone has to agree, and everyone has to be able to explain the choice made and the reasons why the choice is a good one.

PROCEDURE

1. *Research and prepare your position.* Your group of four has been divided into two pairs. One pair has been assigned the pro position and the other pair has been assigned the con position. With your partner, plan how to present to the other pair the best case possible for your assigned position in order to make sure it receives a fair and complete hearing. Research your position and get as much information to support it as possible. Make sure both you and your partner are ready to present.
2. *Present and advocate your position.* Forcefully and persuasively present the best case for your position to the opposing pair. Be as convincing as possible. Take notes and clarify anything you do not understand when the opposing pair presents.
3. *Open discussion.* Argue forcefully and persuasively for your position, presenting as many supporting facts as you can. Critically evaluate the opposing pair's arguments, challenge their information and reasoning, and defend your position from their attacks. Keep in mind that you need to know both sides to write a good report.
4. *Reverse perspectives.* Reverse perspectives and present the best case for the opposing position. The opposing pair will do the same. Strive to see the issue from both perspectives simultaneously.
5. *Synthesis.* Drop all advocacy. Synthesize and integrate the best evidence and reasoning from both sides into a joint position that all members can agree to. Then (a) finalize the group report, (b) present your conclusions to the class, (c) individually take the test covering both sides of the issue, and (d) process how well you worked together as a group and how you could be even more effective next time.

CONTROVERSY RULES

1. I am critical of ideas, not people. I challenge and refute the ideas of the opposing pair, but I do not indicate that I personally reject them.
2. I remember that we are all in this together, sink or swim. I focus on coming to the best decision possible, not on *winning.*
3. I encourage everyone to participate and to master all the relevant information.
4. I listen to everyone's ideas, even if I don't agree.
5. I restate what someone has said if it is not clear.
6. I first bring out *all* ideas and facts supporting both sides, and then I try to put them together in a way that makes sense.
7. I try to understand both sides of the issue.
8. I change my mind when the evidence clearly indicates that I should do so.

Exercise 8.2: *Your Behavior in Controversies (I)*

The purposes of this exercise are to (a) make you more aware of your typical actions when involved in a controversy and (b) make your group more aware of the pattern of members' actions when they are involved in a controversy. The procedure is as follows:

1. Working by yourself, complete the following questionnaire.
2. Using the scoring table, determine (a) your scores and (b) the average of all group members' scores.
3. Engage in a group discussion of (a) the strategies used most frequently during a controversy and (b) how controversies may be managed more constructively.

UNDERSTANDING MY CONTROVERSY BEHAVIOR

Each of the following questions describes an action taken during a controversy. For each question write a 5 if you always behave that way, 4 if you frequently behave that way, 3 if you occasionally behave that way, 2 if you seldom behave that way, and 1 if you never behave that way.

_____ 1. When I disagree with other group members, I insist that they change their opinions to match mine.

_____ 2. If someone disagrees with my ideas and opinions, I feel hurt and rejected.

_____ 3. I often infer that persons who disagree with me are incompetent and ignorant.

_____ 4. When others disagree with me, I try to view the issue from all points of view.

_____ 5. I try to avoid individuals who argue with me.

_____ 6. When others disagree with me, I view it as an interesting opportunity to learn and to improve the quality of my ideas and reasoning.

_____ 7. When I get involved in an argument with others, I become more and more certain that I am correct, and argue more and more strongly for my own point of view.

_____ 8. When others disagree with my ideas, I get hostile and angry at them.

_____ 9. When I disagree with others, I am careful to communicate respect for them as persons while I criticize their ideas.

_____ 10. I am careful always to paraphrase thinking and feelings of others when they present ideas and opinions that are different from mine.

_____ 11. When others disagree with me, I generally keep my ideas and opinions to myself.

_____ 12. When others disagree with me, I encourage them to express their ideas and opinions fully, and seek to clarify the differences between their position and perspective and mine.

_____ 13. I view my disagreements with others as opportunities to see who wins and who loses.

_____ 14. I often insult those who criticize my ideas and opinions.

_____ 15. When another person and I disagree, I carefully communicate, "I appreciate you, I am interested in your ideas, but I disagree with your current position."

_____ 16. When others disagree with me, I keep thinking of my ideas and opinions so that I do not forget them or get confused.

_____ 17. I am careful not to share my ideas and opinions when I think others may disagree with them.

_____ 18. When I disagree with others, I listen carefully to their ideas and opinions and change my mind when doing so is warranted by their information and reasoning.

_____ 19. When others and I disagree, I try to overpower them with my facts and reasoning.

_____ 20. I tend to dislike those who disagree with my ideas and opinions.

_____ 21. When I am disagreeing with and criticizing others' ideas and opinions, I let them know that I like them as individuals.

_____ 22. I try to view the situation and issue from my opponent's shoes when involved in a disagreement about ideas and opinions.

_____ 23. I refuse to get into an argument with anyone.

_____ 24. When others disagree with me, I try to clarify the differences among our ideas and opinions, clarify the points of agreement, and seek a creative integration of all our ideas and information.

_____ 25. When others and I disagree, I have to convince them that I am right and they are wrong.

_____ 26. When others disagree with my ideas and opinions, it means that they are angry with me and dislike me.

_____ 27. While I am disagreeing with others I let them know that I appreciate their ability to present a challenging and thought-provoking position.

_____ 28. When I am involved in an argument, I restate and summarize the opposing positions.

_____ 29. When others disagree with me, I stay very quiet and try to avoid them in the future.

_____ 30. When I am involved in an argument, I never forget that we are trying to make the best decision possible by combining the best of all our facts and reasoning.

SCORING

Write your answer for each question in the space provided and total your answers for each controversy-managing strategy. The higher the total score for each controversy strategy, the more frequently you tend to use that strategy; the lower the total score for each controversy strategy, the less frequently you tend to use it. Add the scores of all group members for each strategy and divide by the number of members in the group. This will give your group average for each strategy.

Win–Lose	Rejection	Confirmation
_____ 1.	_____ 2.	_____ 3.*
_____ 7.	_____ 8.	_____ 9.
_____ 13.	_____ 14.	_____ 15.
_____ 19.	_____ 20.	_____ 21.
_____ 25.	_____ 26.	_____ 27.
_____ TOTAL	_____ TOTAL	_____ TOTAL
_____ GROUP AVERAGE	_____ GROUP AVERAGE	_____ GROUP AVERAGE

Perspective-Taking	Avoidance	Problem Solving
_____ 4.	_____ 5.	_____ 6.
_____ 10.	_____ 11.	_____ 12.
_____ 16.*	_____ 17.	_____ 18.
_____ 22.	_____ 23.	_____ 24.
_____ 28.	_____ 29.	_____ 30.
_____ TOTAL	_____ TOTAL	_____ TOTAL
_____ GROUP AVERAGE	_____ GROUP AVERAGE	_____ GROUP AVERAGE

*Reverse the scoring on this question by substituting 1 for 5, 2 for 4, and so on.

CONTROVERSY QUESTIONNAIRE: INTERPRETATION

Write your scores in the spaces provided below. If your score is above 15, it means that you are likely to engage in this strategy. If your score is less than 15, it means that you are not likely to engage in this strategy. Add the scores of all group members for each strategy and divide by the number of members in the group. This will give you your group average for each strategy.

Constructive Strategy	Your Score	Group Average	Destructive Strategy	Your Score	Group Average
Problem solving	____	____	Win–Lose	____	____
Confirmation	____	____	Rejection	____	____
Perspective-taking	____	____	Avoidance	____	____

Procedure

1. Compare your scores for the constructive and destructive strategies.
2. Compare your scores with your actual behavior (as reported by observer) in the controversy exercise.
3. Discuss the strategies that are difficult for you to engage in.
4. On the basis of the group average scores and the actual behavior of the group members in the controversy exercise, characterize the group's tendencies towards constructive and destructive controversy.

CONTROVERSY AND DECISION MAKING

Since the general or prevailing opinion on any subject is rarely or never the whole truth, it is only by the collision of adverse opinion that the remainder of the truth has any chance of being supplied.

John Stuart Mill

A large pharmaceutical company faced the decision of whether to buy or build a chemical plant (*Wall Street Journal,* October 22, 1975). To maximize the likelihood that the best decision was made, the president established two advocacy teams to ensure that both the buy and the build alternatives received a fair and complete hearing. An advocacy team is a subgroup that prepares and presents a particular policy alternative to the decision-making group. The buy team was instructed to prepare and present the best case for purchasing a chemical plant, and the build team was told to prepare and present the best case for constructing a new chemical plant near the company's national headquarters. The buy team identified over 100 existing plants that would meet the company's needs, narrowed the field down to 20, further narrowed the field down to 3, and then selected one plant as the ideal plant to buy. The build team contacted dozens of engineering firms and, after four months of consideration, selected a design for the ideal plant to build. Nine months after they were established, the two teams, armed with all the details about cost, (a) presented their best case and (b) challenged each other's information, reasoning, and conclusions. From the spirited discussion, it became apparent that the two options would cost about the same amount of money. The

company, therefore, chose the build option because it allowed the plant to be conveniently located near company headquarters. This procedure represents the structured use of controversy to ensure high-quality decision making.

In almost every meeting room within every organization, people are disagreeing with each other. Whether the organization is a business, an industry, a government agency, a hospital, a school, a law firm, or a family, disagreements occur as decisions are made and problems are solved. Involved participation in such situations means that different ideas, opinions, beliefs, and information will surface and clash. The result is **controversy**—the conflict that arises when one person's ideas, information, conclusions, theories, and opinions are incompatible with those of another person, and the two seek to reach an agreement. Controversies are resolved by engaging in what Aristotle called **deliberate discourse** (i.e., the discussion of the advantages and disadvantages of proposed actions) aimed at synthesizing novel solutions (i.e., *creative problem solving*). When a group has to make an important decision, the group identifies a number of alternative courses of action and ensures that each alternative the group considers gets a fair and complete hearing by going through the following steps (Johnson, 1970; Johnson, Johnson, & Johnson, 1976; Johnson & Johnson, 1979, 1989, 1995a):

1. *Research and prepare a position.* Each alternative course of action is assigned to a two-person advocacy team. The advocacy teams are given the time to research their assigned alternative course of action and find all the supporting evidence available. They organize what is known into a coherent and reasoned position. They plan how to present their case so that all members of the group understand thoroughly the advocacy pair's position, give it a fair and complete hearing, and are convinced of its soundness.

2. *Present and advocate their position.* Each advocacy pair presents its position forcefully, sincerely, and persuasively. Other group members listen carefully and critically, but with an open mind.

3. *Engage in an open discussion.* Each advocacy pair (a) continues to advocate its position, (b) attempts to refute opposing positions, and (c) rebuts attacks on its position. Each alternative course of action is thus given a trial by fire.

4. *Reverse perspectives:* Advocacy pairs reverse perspectives and present each other's positions. In arguing for the opposing position, group members summa-

rize it in a forceful, sincere, and persuasive way. They add any new information that the opposing pairs did not think to present. They strive to see the issue from all perspectives simultaneously.

5. *Reach a decision through consensus as to which course of action to implement.* Group members drop all advocacy and integrate what they know into a reasoned decision to which all members agree. This requires reconceptualizing the issue by synthesizing and integrating the best information and reasoning from all sides. The group's decision then reflects their best reasoned judgment.

Structured controversies are most commonly contrasted with concurrence-seeking, debate, and individualistic decision making. **Debate** exists when two or more individuals argue positions that are incompatible with one another and a judge declares a winner on the basis of who presented his or her position the best. An example of debate is when each member of a group is assigned a position as to whether more or fewer regulations are needed to control hazardous wastes and an authority declares as the winner the person who makes the best presentation of his or her position to the group.

Concurrence-seeking occurs when members of a group inhibit discussion to avoid any disagreement or arguments, emphasize agreement, and avoid realistic appraisal of alternative ideas and courses of action. An example of concurrence-seeking is when a group is to decide whether more or fewer regulations are needed to manage hazardous waste, with the stipulation that group members are not to argue but rather to compromise quickly whenever opposing opinions are expressed. Most group decision-making situations are dominated by concurrence-seeking (Walton, 1987). Concurrence-seeking is close to the *groupthink* concept of Janis (1982), in which members of a decision-making group set aside their doubts and misgivings about whatever policy is favored by the emerging consensus so as to be able to concur with the other members. The underlying motivation of groupthink is the strong desire to preserve the harmonious atmosphere of the group on which each member has become dependent for coping with the stresses of external crises and for maintaining self-esteem.

Individualistic decision making occurs when isolated individuals independently decide on a course of action without any interaction or consultation with each other; each decision-maker comes to his or her decision without interacting with others or discussing the information upon which the decision is being made. The processes generated by controversy, debate, concurrence-seeking, and individual decision making are summarized in Table 8.1.

A key to the effectiveness of conflict procedures for promoting learning is the mixture of cooperative and competitive elements within the procedure (see Table 8.2). The greater the cooperative elements and the fewer the competitive elements, the more constructive the conflict (Deutsch, 1973). Cooperative elements alone, however, do not ensure maximal productivity. There has to be both cooperation and conflict. Thus, controversy is characterized by both positive goals and resource interdependence as well as by conflict. Debate has positive resource interdependence, negative goal interdependence, and conflict. Within concurrence-seeking there is only positive goal interdependence, and within individualistic learning situations there is neither interdependence nor intellectual conflict.

Table 8.1   **Controversy, Debate, Concurrence-Seeking, and Individualistic Processes**

Controversy	Debate	Concurrence-Seeking	Individualistic
Categorizing and organizing information to derive conclusions	Categorizing and organizing information to derive conclusions	Categorizing and organizing information to derive conclusions	Categorizing and organizing information to derive conclusions
Presenting, advocating, elaborating position and rationale	Presenting, advocating, elaborating position and rationale	Active presentation of position	No oral statement of positions
Being challenged by opposing views	Being challenged by opposing views	Quick compromise to one view	Presence of only one view
Conceptual conflict and uncertainty about correctness of own views	Conceptual conflict and uncertainty about correctness of own views	High certainty about the correctness of own views	High certainty about the correctness of own views
Epistemic curiosity and perspective-taking	Epistemic curiosity	No epistemic curiosity	No epistemic curiosity
Reconceptualization, synthesis, integration	Closed-minded adherence to own point of view	Closed-minded adherence to own point of view	Closed-minded adherence to own point of view
High productivity, positive relationships, psychological health and social competencies	Moderate productivity, relationships, psychological health	Low productivity, relationships, psychological health	Low productivity, relationships, psychological health

Controversies are common within decision-making situations. In the mining industry, for example, engineers are accustomed to addressing issues such as land use, air and water pollution, and health and safety. The complexity of the design of production processes, the balancing of environmental and manufacturing interests, and numerous other factors often create controversy. Most groups waste the benefits of such disputes, but every effective decision-making situation thrives on what controversy has to offer. Decisions are by their very nature controversial, as alternative solutions are suggested and considered before agreement is reached. When a decision is made, the controversy ends and participants commit themselves to a common course of action.

Table 8.2   **Nature of Decision-Making Procedures**

	Controversy	Debate	Concurrence-Seeking	Individualistic
Positive goal interdependence	Yes	No	Yes	No
Resource interdependence	Yes	Yes	No	No
Negative goal interdependence	No	Yes	No	No
Conflict	Yes	Yes	No	No

THE AVOIDANCE OF CONTROVERSY

Within most organizations there is considerable conflict that is managed in costly and time-consuming ways. Thomas and Schmidt (1976) found that between 20 and 25% of managers' time is spend directly dealing with conflicts. Accountemps, a division of Robert Half International Inc., found in a recent survey that managers of America's leading corporations spend over four working weeks a year dealing with the problems caused by employees who just don't get along with each other. Janz and Tjosvold (1985) determined in an interview study the cost of interpersonal conflicts in employee time, materials, and project days. Included in their broad definition of conflict was refusing to communicate directly, ignoring advice and suggestions, being disinterested in learning from others, viewing problems from only one's own point view, involving only others that support one's point of view, embarrassing and blaming others, and seeing design flaws but not bringing them up because of wanting others to look bad. They estimated that the cost in employee time and materials for ineffectively managing interpersonal conflicts was about $15,000 (Canadian dollars) per employee per year, and over $40,000 per employee per year if project days were taken into account. Conflicts, therefore, are pervasive within most organizations and frequently mismanaged. There is a need to train managers and other organizational personnel in the procedures and skills needed to manage conflicts constructively.

If a group is to make effective decisions and solve problems competently, controversies should not only be encouraged and sought out, but deliberately structured. Yet too few organizational members seek to stimulate or structure controversy. There are at least three reasons why. The first reason is that too few people understand controversy to be able to accept and utilize it effectively. There is insufficient knowledge and understanding of the procedures involved in controversy and the advantages and potentially constructive outcomes that can result from disagreements. A second reason is that many people seem to lack the interpersonal skills and competencies needed to stimulate controversy and ensure that it is managed constructively. Although most managerial training programs, for example, spend years providing technical training, the interpersonal skills needed to manage decision-making and problem-solving situations are not systematically and extensively taught.

Thirdly, the discussion of conflicting ideas may not be a standard and common practice within decision-making and problem-solving situations because of the fear and anxiety most people seem to feel in conflict situations. A general feeling in our society is that conflicts are bad and should be avoided; consequently, many people believe that an effective group is one in which there are no conflicts among members. Many discussions of conflict see it only as causing divorce, separation, psychological distress, social disorder, violence, divisiveness, and even war. The disintegration of many groups and organizations have been blamed on conflict. Within most groups, members either try to shun conflict or crush it. Neither strategy works. Avoidance or force only raises the level of the conflict and becomes part of the problem rather than being the solution.

A healthy group does not suffer from a lack of conflict. Rather, the absence of conflict may signal apathy, disinterest, noninvolvement, and alienation—not maturity. In a healthy group, conflicts among members are inevitable. Thus, the issue is not whether conflicts can be prevented, but rather how they are managed, for conflicts can have both highly constructive and highly destructive effects on group and organizational functioning.

Being able to initiate conflicts and capitalize on their constructive outcomes are essential group and managerial skills. Nowhere is that more true than in decision-making situations.

There are a number of hypotheses as to why conflict is so avoided and suppressed in decision-making situations (Johnson, 1970; Johnson, Johnson & Johnson, 1976; Johnson & Johnson, 1979, 1989, 1995c). *The first hypothesis is that fear blocks group members from engaging in controversies.* Because destructively managed conflicts create divisiveness and hostility, when conflicts occur group members may have some anxiety as to whether constructive or destructive outcomes will result. Palmer (1991, 1992), for example, believes that fear of conflict blocks constructive behavior and recommends that group members have the courage to promote intellectual conflict despite their apprehensions about doing so.

The second hypothesis is that ignorance of how to engage in controversy blocks group members from doing so. Until recently there has not been a clear set of procedures that group members can use in a wide variety of decision-making and problem-solving situations. The development of structured controversy gives group members a clear procedure they can use to structure decisional conflicts in ways that increase the quality of their decision making.

The third hypothesis is that lack of training programs to teach group members how to use decisional conflict effectively blocks group members from engaging in them. Most group members have not been trained in how to create intellectual conflicts and how to use the conflicts to increase the quality of their decision making and problem solving. Such training programs exist only in a few organizations. As a consequence, most group members do not know how to take advantage of the decisional conflicts when they occur.

The fourth hypothesis is that our culture is so anticonflict that group members do not see the promotion of decisional conflicts as a possibility. The view that conflict is a potentially positive and powerful force on decision making and problem solving may be culturally unacceptable. A general feeling in our society is that conflicts are bad and should be avoided. The possibility of conflict being constructive is not viewed within the realm of possibility. Many people, consequently, believe that a well-run group is one in which there are no conflicts among members.

The fifth hypothesis is that group norms may block group members from engaging in intellectual conflicts. Current norms in most groups promote getting along and not challenging each other's reasoning. In such a climate, the norms of what is acceptable behavior may not include creating decisional conflict among members.

The sixth hypothesis is that inertia, the power of the status quo, may be so great that group members just do not try anything new. Group members may choose to play it safe by not disagreeing or challenging groupmates because it is their personal tradition and the tradition of the group.

These six barriers are formidable obstacles to overcome if group members are to utilize the power of conflict during decision making and problem solving.

Experts and Group Decision Making

When two men in business always agree, one of them is unnecessary.

William Wrigley, Jr.

Organizations are filled with individuals who have expertise in their limited areas and must interact and make joint decisions with each other. Important decisions are typically made by small groups of individuals with diverse expertise. To maximize the quality of the decision, expertise must be exchanged. Most important group decisions involve more than one expert and, as Tversky and Kahneman (1981) note, most decision-makers are normally unaware of alternative perspectives and frames of reference and of their potential effects on the relative attractiveness of options. Thus, two different experts, with different information and perspectives, can make directly opposing decisions without recognizing the limitations of their frames of reference. Each expert does not see the whole world; they see only the part they specialize in. Because they are capable of all sorts of rationalizations about their areas of expertise—mainly in the direction of enhancing its importance—any decision made by a single expert is suspect. Lord, Ross, and Lepper (1979) found that individuals who hold strong beliefs about an issue are apt to examine relevant evidence in a biased manner, by accepting confirming evidence at face value and subjecting disconfirming evidence to highly critical evaluation.

When experts with different information and perspectives come together to make a joint decision, conflict and disagreement result. Their points of departure need to be explicitly highlighted so that they will be able to sort out their differences and arrive at a mutually acceptable synthesis. Most decisions have to be made under the condition of uncertainty (the probability of desired outcomes resulting from the alternative course of action are unknown). Individuals with a wide variety of expertise and frames of reference are brought together to make such decisions. Conflict among their ideas, information, opinions, preferences, theories, conclusions, and perspectives is inevitable. Having the skills to manage the controversies constructively and knowing the procedures for exchanging information and perspectives among individuals with differing expertise are essential for organizational effectiveness and growth.

Expertise is not only developed but it must be maintained. If experts are not gaining new information and knowledge, not refining their theories and conceptual frameworks, and not challenging their conclusions, they may soon lose their expertise. With the rapid growth of knowledge in almost all fields, individuals can quickly lose their expertise if they do not stay current and push beyond their present levels of understanding. To do so they must generate an epistemic curiosity about their field of knowledge, promote their internal conceptual conflict by seeking out different perspectives and theories that contradict their own, adopt new and broader perspectives, and incorporate new information into their conceptual frameworks. Controversy is an essential factor in obtaining and maintaining expertise.

Exercise 8.3: Stranded in the Desert

There is nothing as beautiful as a desert night. And there are few places more dangerous to be stranded than the desert during the night or day. In such a situation, effective decision making is a matter of life or death, and because the emotional content of the arguments over what a stranded group should do will be high, skills in managing controversies constructively are essential. The purpose of this exercise is to examine the dynamics of controversy and its effects on the decision making of a group caught in a survival dilemma. The materials needed for the exercise are a description of the situation, a group decision form, a postdecision questionnaire, a summary table, a constructive controversy checklist, and a controversy observation form. Approximately 60 minutes are needed for the exercise. The procedure for the coordinator is as follows.

1. Introduce the exercise by stating its objective and reviewing the overall procedure and tasks.
2. Divide the class into five groups. Give each group member a Stranded in the Desert Situation Sheet and a copy of the appropriate role-playing instructions. The role-playing instructions for each group are as follows:
   a. *Group 1.* Your position is that the group members have to walk to the nearest ranch if they are to survive. Plan carefully the best procedure for doing so. Select the five or six possessions of the group that are most important for implementing your plan and rank them from 1 (most important) to 5 or 6 (the least important).
   b. *Group 2.* Your position is that the group members have to signal search planes and vehicles if they are to survive. Plan carefully the best procedure for doing so. Select the five or six possessions of the group that are most important for implementing your plan and rank them from 1 (most important) to 5 or 6 (the least important).
   c. *Group 3.* Your position is that the group members have to protect themselves from the heat of the day and the cold of the night if they are to survive. Plan carefully the best procedure for doing so. Select the five or six possessions of the group that are most important for implementing your plan and rank them from 1 (most important) to 5 or 6 (the least important).
   d. *Group 4.* Your position is that the group members must stay by the wreck and keep physical movement to a minimum if they are to survive. Plan carefully the best procedure for doing so. Select the five or six possessions of the group that are most important for implementing your plan and rank them from 1 (most important) to 5 or 6 (the least important).
   e. *Group 5.* Your responsibility is to be observers. The observer's role is to record the nature of each member's participation in the group, using the accompanying observation form. Each observer needs two copies of this form. Make sure all members understand the role of the observer and how to use the observation form.
3. Within each group have participants divide into preparation pairs (one triad if there are an odd number of participants in the group). The preparation pairs are responsible for:
   a. Planning a rationale for their assigned position.
   b. Selecting the five or six possessions of the group that are most important for implementing their plan and ranking them from 1 (most important) to 5 or 6 (the least important).
   c. Planning a persuasive presentation of their position and its rationale.
4. Introduce the situation. Have the groups read the description of the situation and their role assignment sheets. Tell them to construct as good a rationale for their position as possible and plan a persuasive presentation of it. Give them fifteen minutes to do so.
5. Form new groups of five by taking one participant from each of the previous groups and placing them together in a new group. Each member of the group should be representing a different position (with the exception of the observer).
6. Have the new groups read the situation description and then rank the twelve possessions of the group from 1 (the most important possession for the survival of the group members) to 12 (the least important possession). All members must agree on the ranking and be able to explain the rationale for why it is ranked where it is. Give the groups twenty minutes to decide on their ranking.
7. Have participants complete the postdecision questionnaire and give their responses to the group observer. Have the observers determine the group mean for each question

while you share the correct/experts' ranking (see page 584 in the Appendix). Have each group score their ranking.

8. Record the results from each group in the Summary Table.
9. Instruct each group to discuss its experience and derive at least four conclusions, using:
   a. The decision and questionnaire results.
   b. The information collected by the observers.
   c. The impressions of the group members.
   d. The constructive controversy checklist.
10. Have each group share its conclusion with the entire class.

STRANDED IN THE DESERT SITUATION

You are one of the members of a geology club that is on a field trip to study unusual formations in the New Mexico desert. It is the last week in July. You have been driving over old trails, far from any road, in order to see out-of-the-way formations. At about 10:30 A.M. the specially equipped minibus in which your club is riding overturns, rolls into a twenty-foot ravine, and burns. The driver and professional adviser to the club are killed. The rest of you are relatively uninjured.

You know that the nearest ranch is approximately forty-five miles east of where you are. There is no closer habitation. When your club does not report to its motel that evening you will be missed. Several persons know generally where you are, but because of the nature of your outing they will not be able to pinpoint your whereabouts.

The area around you is rather rugged and very dry. There is a shallow water hole nearby, but the water is contaminated by worms, animal feces and urine, and several dead mice. You heard from a weather report before you left that the temperature would reach 108 degrees, making the surface temperature 128 degrees. You are all dressed in lightweight summer clothing and you all have hats and sunglasses.

While escaping from the minibus each member of your group salvaged a couple of items; there are twelve in all. Your group's task is to rank these items according to their importance to your survival, starting with 1 for the most important and proceeding to 12 for the least important.

You may assume that the number of club members is the same as the number of persons in your group and that the group has agreed to stick together.

STRANDED IN THE DESERT DECISION FORM

Rank the following items according to their importance to your survival, starting with 1 for the most important and proceeding to 12 for the least important.

_____ magnetic compass

_____ 20 × 20-ft piece of heavy-duty, light blue canvas

_____ book, *Plants of the Desert*

_____ rearview mirror

_____ large knife

_____ flashlight (four-battery size)

_____ one jacket per person

_____ one transparent, plastic ground cloth (6 × 4 ft) per person

_____ .38-caliber loaded pistol

_____ one 2-quart plastic canteen per person, full of water

_____ accurate map of the area

_____ large box of kitchen matches

STRANDED IN THE DESERT: POSTDECISION QUESTIONNAIRE

1. To what extent did other members of the group listen to and understand your ideas?
   Not at all   1 : 2 : 3 : 4 : 5 : 6 : 7 : 8 : 9   Completely
2. How much influence do you feel you had on the group's decision?
   None at all   1 : 2 : 3 : 4 : 5 : 6 : 7 : 8 : 9   A great deal
3. To what extent do you feel committed to and responsible for the group's decision?
   Not at all   1 : 2 : 3 : 4 : 5 : 6 : 7 : 8 : 9   Completely
4. To what extent are you satisfied with your group's performance?
   Very dissatisfied   1 : 2 : 3 : 4 : 5 : 6 : 7 : 8 : 9   Very satisfied
5. How much did you learn about the issue under discussion?
   Nothing at all   1 : 2 : 3 : 4 : 5 : 6 : 7 : 8 : 9   A great deal
6. Write two adjectives describing the way you now feel. _____

Summary Table: Response to Postdecision Questionnaire

Group	Group Score	Understanding	Influence	Commitment	Satisfaction	Learning	Feelings
1							
2							
3							
4							

Determine the group means from the questionnaire responses and record them in the appropriate column, except for the first and the last columns. In the Feelings column put representative adjectives from the questionnaire.

CONSTRUCTIVE CONTROVERSY CHECKLIST

_____ 1. There was no winner or loser, only a successful, creative, and productive solution. The cooperativeness of group members should outweigh by far their competitiveness.
_____ 2. Disagreements among members' positions were initiated.
_____ 3. Every member's contributions were listened to, respected, and taken seriously.
_____ 4. Effective communication skills were listened to, respected, and taken seriously.
_____ 5. Issues and problems were viewed from all available perspectives.
_____ 6. Group members criticized ideas and positions, not individuals. Members disagreed with each other while confirming each other's competence.
_____ 7. Group members viewed disagreement as an interesting situation from which something could be learned, not as personal rejection or a sign that they were being perceived as incompetent or ignorant.
_____ 8. There was appropriate pacing of differentiation and integration of member's positions. Differentiation took place first, followed by integration.
_____ 9. Emotions were allowed and members were encouraged to express them
_____ 10. The rules of rational argument were followed. Members presented organized information to support their positions, reasoned logically, and changed their minds when others presented persuasive and convincing arguments and proof.
_____ 11. The arguments of all members were given equal consideration, regardless of how much formal power a member had.

CONTROVERSY OBSERVATION FORM

Behaviors	Participants					Total
Contributes ideas and opinions						
Asks others for their ideas and opinions						
Emphasizes mutual goals						
Emphasizes win–lose competition						
Asks others for proof, facts, and rationale						
Paraphrases, summarizes						
Criticizes and disagrees with others' ideas						
Criticizes other members as persons						
Differentiates positions						
Integrates positions						
Total						

Insert the name of a group member above each of the columns. Then record the frequency with which each member engages in each behavior. After the group meeting is over, total columns and rows.

Exercise 8.4: Who Should Get the Penicillin?

The purpose of this exercise is to examine the dynamics of controversy within the context of a social studies lesson. The materials needed for the exercise are a description of the situation, a briefing sheet for the medical point of view, a briefing sheet for the military point of view, a postdecision questionnaire, a summary table, a constructive controversy checklist, and a controversy observation form. (The last four items are the same as in the previous exercise, and are also used in the following three exercises.) Approximately ninety minutes are needed for the exercise. The procedure for the coordinator is as follows:

1. Introduce the exercise by stating its objective and reviewing the overall procedure.
2. Form groups of five members. One member from each group should volunteer to be an observer. The observer's role is to record the nature of each member's participation in the group, using the controversy observation form.

3. Divide the remaining four members of each group into two pairs. Give one pair a copy of the medical viewpoint and the other pair a copy of the military viewpoint.

4. Introduce the situation. Instruct the pairs to build as good a rationale for their assigned position as they can in fifteen or twenty minutes, using the information on the briefing sheet as a guide.

5. Instruct the pairs to meet together as a group of four. The group is to come to a decision that all four members can agree to. The decision should reflect the best reasoning of the entire group. The group discussion should follow these steps:

   a. Each pair presents its position as forcefully and persuasively as it can while the opposing pair takes notes and clarifies anything the two members do not fully understand.

   b. Have an open discussion in which members of each pair (1) argue forcefully and persuasively for their position, presenting as many facts as they can to support it, and (2) listen critically to members of the opposing pair, asking them for the facts that support their point of view. This is a complex issue and members need to know both sides in order to come to a thoughtful decision.

6. Instruct the pairs to reverse their perspectives by switching sides and arguing for the opposite point of view as forcefully and persuasively as possible. Members should see if they can think of any new facts that the opposing pair did not present in support of its position, and should elaborate on that position.

7. Instruct the groups to come to a joint decision by

   a. Summarizing the best arguments for both points of view.

   b. Detailing the facts they know about World War II and the African campaign.

   c. Achieving consensus among the members.

   d. Organizing the rationale supporting the decision that they will present to the rest of the class. They should be ready to defend the validity of their decision to groups who may have come to the opposite decision.

8. Instruct participants to complete the postdecision questionnaire. Then have the observers determine the group mean for each question.

9. Summarize the decision of each group in front of the entire class. Then summarize the results of the postdecision questionnaire, using the summary table.

10. Instruct each group to discuss their experience, using

    a. The decision and questionnaire results.

    b. The information collected by the observers.

    c. The impressions of the group members.

    d. The constructive controversy checklist.

    The following questions may help the groups discuss how they managed the controversy:

    a. How did the group manage disagreements among its members? (Use the checklist for constructive controversy as a guide.)

    b. From its experience, what conclusions can the group make about the constructive handling of controversies?

    c. Did the opinions of the group members change as a result of the group's discussion? Did members gain insight into the other point of view through the perspective reversal procedure? Did members learn anything new about World War II?

    d. What did members learn about themselves and other group members? How did each member react to the controversy?

11. Have each group share its conclusions about the constructive management of controversy with the rest of the class.

WHO SHOULD GET THE PENICILLIN EXERCISE SITUATION

In 1943 penicillin, which is used for the prevention of infection, was in short supply among the U.S. armed forces in North Africa. Decisions had to be made whether to use this meager supply for the thousands of hospitalized victims of venereal disease or for the thousands of victims of battle wounds at the front. If you were a member of a team of medical and military personnel, for whom would you use the penicillin?

_____ victims of venereal disease

_____ victims of battle wounds

Share your position and rationale with your group. Stick to your guns unless logically persuaded otherwise. At the same time, help your group achieve consensus on this issue.

BRIEFING SHEET: THE MEDICAL VIEWPOINT— WHO SHOULD GET THE PENICILLIN EXERCISE

Your position is to give the penicillin to the battle-wounded. Whether or not you agree with this position, argue for it as strongly and as honestly as you can, using arguments that make sense and are rational. Be creative and invent new supporting arguments. Seek out information; ask members of other groups who may know the answers to your questions. Remember to learn the rationale for both your position and the military position. Challenge the military position; think of loopholes in its logic; demand facts and information that back up its arguments.

1. Our responsibility is to treat the wounded and save as many lives as possible. Without the penicillin many of the wounded will die needlessly. Minor wounds will get infected and become major, life-threatening wounds.
2. Our strategies must be based on the premise that human life is sacred. If one person dies needlessly, we have failed in our responsibility. The soldiers who have sacrificed so much to help us win the war must be treated with all the care, concern, and resources we can muster. Our soldiers must be able to fight harder than the German soldiers.
3. Troop morale is vital. Nothing raises troop morale as much as the men's knowledge that if they are wounded they will receive top-notch medical treatment.
4. Morale at home is vital. People must make sacrifices to produce the goods and materials we need to win the war. Nothing raises morale at home more than knowing that sons and brothers are receiving the most effective medical care that is humanly possible. It would be devastating for word to reach the United States that we were needlessly letting soldiers die for lack of medical care.
5. Even though we are at war, we must not lose our humanity. It will do no good to defeat Germany if we become Nazis in the process.
6. At this point the war is going badly in North Africa. Rommel and the German army are cutting through our lines like butter. We are on the verge of being pushed out of Africa, in which case we will lose the war. Rommel must be stopped.
7. Fresh troops and supplies are unavailable. The German submarines control the Atlantic, and we cannot get troop ships or supply ships into African ports. We have to make do with what we have.
8. Penicillin is a wonder drug that will save countless lives if it is used to treat the wounded.

**BRIEFING SHEET: THE MILITARY VIEWPOINT—
WHO SHOULD GET THE PENICILLIN EXERCISE**

Your position is to give the penicillin to the VD patients. Whether or not you agree with this position, argue for it as strongly and as honestly as you can, using arguments that make sense and are rational. Be creative and invent new supporting arguments. Seek out information that supports your position. If you do not have needed information, ask members of other groups who may. Remember to learn the rationale for both your position and the medical position. Challenge the medical position; think of loopholes in its logic; demand facts and information that back up its arguments.

1. Our responsibility is to win the war for our country at all costs. If we lose Africa, we will lose Europe to Hitler, and eventually we will be fighting in the United States.
2. Our strategies to win must be based on the premise of the greatest good for the greatest number. We may have to sacrifice soldiers in order to win the war, save our democracy, and free Europe.
3. Troop morale is vital. Our soldiers must be able to fight harder than the German soldiers. Nothing raises troop morale like seeing fresh troops arrive at the front.
4. Morale at home is vital. People must make sacrifices to produce the goods and materials we need to fight the war. Nothing raises morale at home like hearing of battles won and progress being made in winning the war. Victories give our people at home more dedication.
5. At this point, the war is going badly in North Africa. Rommel and the German army are cutting through our lines like butter. We are on the verge of being pushed out of Africa, in which case we will lose the war. Rommel must be stopped at all costs!
6. Penicillin is a wonder drug that will send VD into remission, and within twenty-four hours the VD patients will be free from pain and able to function effectively on the battlefield.

Exercise 8.5: *Fallout Shelter*

The purpose of this exercise is to provide a decision-making situation in which controversy will occur. The procedure for the exercise is as follows:

1. Form groups of six. One member should volunteer to be an observer. The observer should use the controversy observation form on page 343.
2. Each group member individually completes the fallout shelter ranking task.
3. The group decides by consensus on the best ranking possible on the fallout shelter items. There should be one ranking for the group; every member should agree with the ranking and be able to explain the rationale behind the ranking of each item.
4. Members complete the postdecision questionnaire. Compute the group means for each question and place them in the summary table.
5. Score the accuracy of the group's ranking by comparing it with the experts' ranking on pages 586–587 in the Appendix. Find the absolute difference between the group's ranking and the experts' ranking for each item and add them together. The lower the score the more accurate the group's ranking.
6. Using the observer's information, the postdecision questionnaire results, the members' impressions, and the accuracy score for the ranking, discuss the way in which controversy was managed in the group. The constructive controversy checklist and the discussion questions given on page 342 may be helpful. The group should write down its conclusions about the constructive management of controversy.
7. Groups should share their conclusions with the entire class.

FALLOUT SHELTER EXERCISE: RANKING TASK

The possibility of a nuclear war has been announced and the alert signal has been sounded. You and the members of your group have access to a small basement fallout shelter. When the attack warning signal is announced, you must immediately go to the shelter. In the meantime, you must decide what to take with you to help you survive during and after the attack. You are outside the immediate blast areas. The greatest danger facing you is from radioactive fallout. In order to help in your decision making, rank the following items in order of their importance to your survival in the shelter (answers on pages 586–587 of Appendix).

_____ one large and one small garbage can with lids

_____ broom

_____ containers of water

_____ blankets

_____ canned heat stove

_____ matches and candles

_____ canned and dried foods

_____ liquid chlorine bleach

_____ vaporizing liquid fire extinguisher

_____ flashlight and batteries

_____ battery-powered radio

_____ soap and towels

_____ first-aid kit with iodine and medicines

_____ cooking and eating utensils

_____ Geiger counter

OUTCOMES OF CONTROVERSY

*Have you learned lessons only of those who admired you, and were
tender with you, and stood aside for you?*
*Have you not learned great lessons from those who brace themselves
against you, and disputed the passage with you?*

Walt Whitman

When controversy is suppressed and concurrence-seeking is emphasized, several defects in making decisions will appear. When NASA, for example, decided to launch the space shuttle *Challenger,* engineers at the Morton Thiokol Company (which makes the shuttle's rocket boosters) and at Rockwell International (which manufactures the orbiter) had opposed the launch because of dangers posed by the subfreezing temperatures. The Thiokol engineers feared that the cold would make the rubber seals at the joints between the rocket's four main segments too brittle to contain the rocket's superhot gases. Several months before the doomed mission, the company's top expert had warned in a memo that it was a "jump ball" as to whether the seal would hold, and that if it failed "the result would be a catastrophe of the highest order" (Magnuson, 1986). In a group discussion the night before the launch, the engineers argued for a delay with their uncertain managers and the NASA officials who wanted to launch on schedule. Because the engineers could not prove there was danger, they were silenced (illusion of invulnerability). Conformity pressures were aimed at the engineers, such as when one of the NASA officials complained, "My God, Thiokol, when do you want me to launch, next April?" The NASA managers made a coalition with the Thiokol managers to shut the engineers out of the decision making (illusion of unanimity). Finally, to mindguard, the top NASA executive who made the final decision to launch was never told about the engineers' concerns, nor about the reservations of the Rockwell officials. Protected from the disagreeable information, he confidently gave the go-ahead to launch the *Challenger* on its tragic flight.

How could such faulty decision making take place? The answer is, because of the lack of controversy. NASA officials never gave the alternative of delaying the launch a fair and complete hearing. Disagreement was stifled rather than utilized. Often in group discussions if a margin of support for one alternative develops, then better ideas have little chance of being accepted. In mob lynchings, for example, misgivings, if not immediately expressed, were drowned out. Drawing on biased information is evident in some group polarization experiments; often the arguments that surfaced in group discussion tended to be more one sided than those volunteered by individuals privately. Group discussions can exacerbate tendencies toward overconfidence, thereby heightening an illusion of judgmental accuracy (Dunning & Ross, 1988), and minority opinions can be suppressed. When initially only one member of a six-member group knew the correct answer, in almost 75% of the cases the single member failed to convince the others because they were not given a fair and complete hearing (Laughlin, 1980; Laughlin & Adamopoulos, 1980). Group decision making often goes wrong because alternatives are not considered carefully, minority opinions are silenced, and disagreement among members' conclusions is suppressed.

Without controversy, group decisions may always be less than optimal. Over the past twenty years there have been more than twenty-three experimental studies on controversy. The nature and results of those studies are summarized in Johnson and Johnson (1989, 1995c). These studies form a solid body of evidence that controversy promotes high productivity and quality of decision making, creativity, task involvement, positive interpersonal relationships, and psychological health.

Productivity and Quality of Decision Making

Compared with concurrence-seeking, debate, and individualistic efforts, controversy typically produces higher group productivity, individual achievement, and quality of decision making (Johnson & Johnson, 1979, 1989, 1995c). In a meta-analysis of the available research, Johnson and Johnson (1989) found that controversy produced greater productivity and higher achievement than did concurrence seeking (effect size = 0.42), debate (effect size = 0.77), or individualistic efforts (effect size = 0.65) (see Table 8.3). Controversy also tends to result in greater ability to transfer learning to new situations and more frequent use of higher-level reasoning strategies. Finally, group members tend to exert more physical and psychological energy in working on the decision when controversy occurs.

Table 8.3 **Mean Effect Sizes of Controversy on Productivity**

Condition	Mean	*sd*	*n*
Controversy/Concurrence-seeking	0.42	0.57	49
Controversy/Debate	0.77	0.41	20
Controversy/Individualistic	0.65	0.32	20
Debate/Individualistic	0.36	1.03	3

Compared with concurrence-seeking, debate, and individualistic efforts, controversy tends to result in higher-quality decisions and solutions to complex problems for which different viewpoints can plausibly be developed. Even a minority in a group can have influence over group decision making when they are consistent in their advocacy of their views (Wood, Lundgren, Quelletter, Busceme, & Blackstone, 1994). An interesting real-world example is a study conducted by Dean Tjosvold (1990b) within airline flight crews. Most air accidents result from pilot error resulting from the failure of crew members to use their information expeditiously to cope with safety hazards. Tjosvold interviewed twenty-seven pilots, first officers, and second officers, and eight flight attendants on how specific incidents that threatened the safety of the airplane were managed. Sixty incidents were provided. Respondents were asked to describe in detail a recent, significant incident in which they managed an air safety problem effectively and one they managed ineffectively. Hierarchical regression analyses indicated that the open discussion of conflicting views and ideas within a cooperative context were powerful antecedents to using safe procedures expeditiously.

An interesting question concerning controversy and problem solving is what happens when erroneous information is presented by participants. Simply, can the advocacy of two conflicting but wrong solutions to a problem create a correct one? The value of the controversy process lies not so much in the correctness of an opposing position, but rather in the attention and thought processes it induces. More cognitive processing may take place when individuals are exposed to more than one point of view, even if the point of view is incorrect. A number of studies with both adults and children have found significant gains in performance when erroneous information is presented by one or both sides in a controversy. Ames and Murray (1982) compared the impact of controversy, modeling, and nonsocial presentation of information on the performance of nonconserving, cognitively immature children on conservation tasks. The cognitive immature children were presented with erroneous information that conflicted with their initial position. Ames and Murray found modest but significant gains in conservation performance. Three children with scores of 0 out of 18 scored between 16 and 18 out of 18 on the posttest, and 11 children with initial scores of 0 scored between 5 and 15. They conclude that conflict *qua* conflict is not only cognitively motivating, but that the resolution of the conflict is likely to be in the direction of correct performance. In this limited way, two wrongs came to make a right.

Creativity

By blending the breath of the sun and the shade, true harmony comes into the world.

Tao Te Ching

Disagreements and arguments among individuals with diverse information and ideas are all important aspects of gaining creative insight. Compared with concurrence-seeking, debate, and individualistic efforts, group members participating in a controversy tend to generate more potential solutions, have more creative insights into the problem, view the problem from different perspectives, and reformulate the problem in ways that allow new orientations to emerge (Glidewell, 1953; Hoffman, Harburg, and Maier, 1962a; Johnson & Johnson, 1989, 1995c; Maier and Hoffman, 1964;

C. Rogers, 1970). Controversy increases the number of ideas, quality of ideas, creation of original ideas, the use of a wider range of ideas, originality, the use of more varied strategies, and the number of creative, imaginative, novel solutions (Bahn, 1964; Bolen and Torrance, 1976; Dunnette, Campbell, and Jaastad, 1963; Triandis, Bass, Ewen, and Mieksele, 1963). Studies further demonstrated that controversy encouraged group members to dig into a problem, raise issues, and settle them in ways that showed the benefits of a wide range of ideas being used, as well as resulting in a high degree of emotional involvement in and commitment to solving the problems the group was working on.

Task Involvement

Task involvement refers to the quality and quantity of the physical and psychological energy that individuals invest in their efforts to achieve. Task involvement is reflected in the attitudes participants have towards the task and towards the controversy experience. Individuals who engaged in controversies tended to like the task and procedure better and generally had more positive attitudes towards the experience than did individuals who engaged in concurrence-seeking discussions, individualistic efforts, or debate. Compared with concurrence-seeking, debate, and individualistic efforts, controversy tends to result in greater task involvement reflected in greater emotional commitment to solving the problem, more feelings of stimulation, and greater enjoyment of the process (see Johnson & Johnson, 1989, 1995c). As Samuel Johnson once stated, "I dogmatize and am contradicted, and in this conflict of opinions and sentiments I find delight." Controversy not only creates high involvement in and commitment to solving a problem, it tends to be fun, enjoyable, and exciting.

Interpersonal Attraction Among Participants

It is often assumed that the presence of conflict within a group will lead to difficulties in establishing good interpersonal relationships and will promote negative attitudes towards groupmates. It is also assumed that arguing leads to rejection, divisiveness, and hostility among members. Within controversy and debate there are elements of disagreement, argumentation, and rebuttal that could result in individuals disliking each other and could create difficulties in establishing good relationships. The research indicates otherwise (Johnson & Johnson, 1979, 1989, 1995c). Controversy has been found to promote greater liking and social support among group members than does debate, concurrence-seeking, and individualistic efforts. Spirited disagreement and intellectual challenge can bind people into deeper and more meaningful relationships.

Psychological Health and Social Competence

There are a number of components of psychological health that are strengthened by participating in academic controversies (see Johnson & Johnson, 1989, 1995c). Compared with concurrence-seeking, debate, and individualistic efforts, controversy tends to result in higher task-oriented self-esteem and greater perspective-taking accuracy. Being able to manage disagreements and conflicts constructively enables individuals to cope with the stresses involved in interacting with a variety of other people.

PROCESS OF CONTROVERSY

Difference of opinion leads to inquiry, and inquiry to truth.

> Thomas Jefferson

The process by which controversy sparks high-quality decision making, increased productivity, better relationships, increased psychological health, and other positive outcomes for the group is outlined in Figure 8.1. During a constructive controversy, decision-makers proceed to do the following (Johnson & Johnson, 1989, 1995c):

1. When individuals are presented with a problem or decision, they have an initial conclusion based on categorizing and organizing incomplete information, their limited experiences, and their specific perspective.
2. When individuals present their conclusion and its rationale to others, they engage in cognitive rehearsal, deepen their understanding of their position, and discover higher-level reasoning strategies.
3. Individuals are confronted by other people with different conclusions based on other people's information, experiences, and perspectives.
4. Individuals become uncertain as to the correctness of their views. A state of conceptual conflict or disequilibrium is aroused.
5. Uncertainty, conceptual conflict, and disequilibrium motivate an active search for more information, new experiences, and a more adequate cognitive perspective and reasoning process in hopes of resolving the uncertainty. Berlyne (1965) calls this active search *epistemic curiosity*. Divergent attention and thought are stimulated.
6. By adapting their cognitive perspective and reasoning through understanding and accommodating the perspective and reasoning of others, a new, reconceptualized, and reorganized conclusion is derived. Novel solutions and decisions are detected that are, on balance, qualitatively better.

A discussion of each of these premises follows. These premises are illustrated in Figure 8.2.

Step 1: Organizing Information and Deriving Conclusions

In order to make high-quality decisions, individuals have to think of the proper alternatives, do a good job of evaluating them, and choosing the most promising one. When individuals are presented with a problem or decision, they have an initial conclusion based on categorizing and organizing incomplete information, their limited experiences, and their specific perspective. Individuals organize their current knowledge and experiences, within the framework of their perspective, into a conceptual framework from which they can derive a conclusion (through the use of inductive and deductive logic). The conceptual frameworks formed, however, often lead to inaccurate conclusions

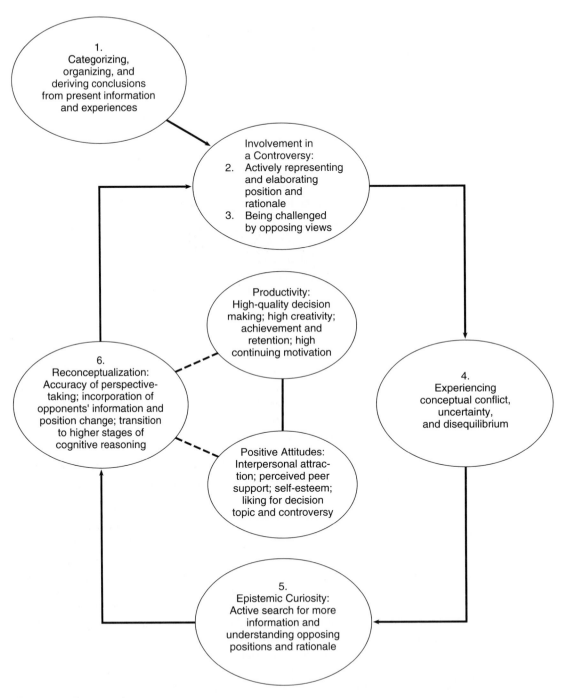

Figure 8.1 Process of controversy.

Source: D. W. Johnson and R. Johnson, *Creative Conflict* (Edina, MN: Interaction Book Company, 1987).

Figure 8.2   Illustration of controversy.

because of the limitations of perspective, one's expectations and mental set at the time, a tendency to give one's dominant response to the situation, or fixation on the first seemingly satisfactory solution generated.

Step 2: Presenting and Advocating Positions

Edward R. Murrow, the journalist, said, "To be persuasive we must be believable; to be believable we must be credible; to be credible, we must be truthful." Most students get few opportunities to present and advocate a position. Within a controversy students present and advocate positions to others who, in turn, are advocating opposing positions. *Advocacy* may be defined as the presenting of a position and providing reasons why others should adopt it. Decisions and conclusions are then reached through a process of argument and counterargument aimed at persuading others to adopt, modify, or drop positions. Advocating a position and defending it against refutation require engaging in considerable cognitive rehearsal and elaboration, increased understanding of the position, and the discovery of higher-level reasoning processes. Disagreements within a group have been found to provide a greater amount of information and variety of facts as well as changes in the salience of known information.

Step 3: Being Challenged by Opposing Views

*Has anything escaped me?" I asked with some self-importance. I trust there
is nothing of consequence that I have overlooked?*

I'm afraid, my dear Watson, that most of your conclusions were erroneous.
When I said that you stimulated me I meant, to be frank, that in noting
your fallacies I was occasionally guided towards the truth.

Sir Arthur Conan Doyle, *The Hound of the Baskervilles*

In controversy, individuals' conclusions are challenged by the advocates of opposing positions. Members critically analyze each other's positions in attempts to discern weaknesses and strengths. They attempt to refute opposing positions while rebutting the attacks on their position. At the same time, they are aware that they need to learn the information being presented and understand the perspective of the other group members.

The direct evidence indicates that individuals engaged in controversy are motivated to know the others' positions and to develop understanding and appreciation of them (see Johnson & Johnson, 1989, 1995c). Furthermore, hearing opposing views being advocated stimulates new cognitive analysis and frees individuals to create alternative and original conclusions. When contrary information is not clearly relevant to completing the task at hand, it may be ignored, discounted, or perceived in biased ways in favor of supporting evidence. When individuals realize, however, that they are accountable for knowing the contrary information some time in the near future, they will tend to learn it. Even being confronted with an erroneous point of view can result in more divergent thinking and the generation of novel and more cognitively advanced solutions.

Step 4: Conceptual Conflict and Uncertainty

Hearing other alternatives being advocated, having one's position criticized and refuted, and being challenged by information that is incompatible with and does not fit with one's conclusions, leads to conceptual conflict and uncertainty. Conceptual conflict exists when incompatible ideas exist simultaneously in a person's mind or when information being received does not seem to fit with what one already knows. The greater the disagreement among group members, the more frequently disagreement occurs, the greater the number of people disagreeing with a person's position, the more competitive the context of the controversy, and the more affronted the person feels, the greater the conceptual conflict and uncertainty the person experiences (see Johnson & Johnson, 1989, 1995c).

Step 5: Epistemic Curiosity and Perspective-Taking

Macbeth said, "Stay, you imperfect speakers, tell me more." When faced with intellectual opposition within a cooperative context, students will ask each other for more information. Conceptual conflict motivates an active search for more information (called *epistemic curiosity*) in hopes of resolving the uncertainty. Indices of epistemic curiosity include individuals' actively (a) searching for more information, (b) seeking to understand opposing positions and rationales, and (c) attempting to view the situation from opposing perspectives.

Step 6: Reconceptualization, Synthesis, Integration

André Gide said, "One completely overcomes only what one assimilates." Nothing could be more true of controversy. When overt controversy is structured within a problem-solving, decision-making, or learning group by identifying alternatives and assigning members to advocate the best case for each alternative, the purpose is not to choose the best alternative. The purpose is to create a synthesis of the best reasoning and conclusions from all the various alternatives. **Synthesizing** occurs when individuals integrate a number of different ideas and facts into a single position. It is the intellectual bringing together of ideas and facts and engaging in inductive reasoning by restating a large amount of information into a conclusion or summary. Synthesizing is a creative process involving seeing new patterns within a body of evidence, viewing the issue from a variety of perspectives, and generating a number of optional ways of integrating the evidence. This requires **probabilistic** (i.e., knowledge is available only in degrees of certainty) rather than **dualistic** (i.e., there is only right and wrong and authority should not be questioned) or **relativistic thinking** (i.e., authorities are seen as sometimes right but that right and wrong depend on your perspective). The dual purposes of synthesis are to arrive at the best possible decision or solution and to find a position that all group members can agree on and commit themselves to. There is evidence that controversy leads to accuracy of perspective-taking, incorporation of others' information and reasoning into their own position, attitude and position change, and transition to higher stages of cognitive reasoning, all of which contribute to the quality of individuals' reconceptualization, synthesis, and integration.

CONDITIONS DETERMINING THE CONSTRUCTIVENESS OF CONTROVERSY

He that wrestles with us strengthens our nerves, and sharpens our skill.
Our antagonist is our helper.

       Edmund Burke, *Reflections on the French Revolution*

Although controversies can operate in a beneficial way, they will not do so under all conditions. As with all types of conflicts, the potential for either constructive or destructive outcomes is present in a controversy. Whether there are positive or negative consequences depends on the conditions under which controversy occurs and the way in which it is managed. These key elements include the context within which the controversy takes place, the heterogeneity of participants, the distribution of information among group members, the level of group members' social skills, and group members' ability to engage in rational argument (Johnson & Johnson, 1979, 1989, 1995c).

Cooperative Goal Structure

Deutsch (1973) emphasizes that the context in which conflicts occur has important effects on whether the conflict turns out to be constructive or destructive. There are two possible contexts for controversy: cooperative and competitive. A cooperative context facilitates constructive controversy, whereas a competitive context promotes destructive controversy in several ways (Johnson & Johnson, 1987; Johnson & Johnson, 1989):

1. In order for controversy to be constructive, information must be accurately communicated. Communication of information is far more complete, accurate, encouraged, and utilized in a cooperative context than in a competitive context.
2. Constructive controversy requires a supportive climate in which group members feel safe enough to challenge each other's ideas. Cooperation provides a far more supportive climate than competition.
3. In order for controversy to be constructive, it must be valued. Cooperative experiences promote stronger beliefs that controversy is valid and valuable.
4. Constructive controversy requires dealing both with feelings and with ideas and information. There is evidence that cooperativeness is positively related and competitiveness is negatively related to ability to understand what others are feeling and why they are feeling that way.
5. How controversies are defined has a great impact on how constructively they are managed. Within a cooperative context, controversies are defined as problems to be solved, whereas in a competitive situation controversies tend to be defined as win-lose situations.
6. Constructive controversy requires a recognition of both similarities and differences between positions. Group members participating in a controversy within a cooperative context identify more of the similarities between their positions than do members participating in a controversy within a competitive context.

In a series of studies, Dean Tjosvold and his associates studied the impact of cooperative and competitive contexts (Tjosvold, 1995a). They found that controversy within a competitive context promoted closed-minded disinterest and rejection of the opponent's ideas and information. Competitors tend to refuse to incorporate any of the opponents' viewpoints into their own position. The increased understanding that resulted from controversy tended to be ignored for a defensive adherence to the competitors' own positions. When competitors are unsure of the correctness of their position, they selected to be exposed to disconfirming information when it could easily be refuted, presumably because such refutation could affirm their own beliefs. Avoidance of controversy results in little interest in or actual knowledge of opposing ideas and information and the making of a decision that reflects one's own views only. Within a cooperative context, controversy induces feelings of comfort, pleasure, and helpfulness in discussing opposing positions, an open-minded listening to the opposing positions, motivation to hear more about the opponent's arguments, more accurate understanding of the opponent's position, and the reaching of more integrated positions where both one's own and one's opponent's conclusions and reasoning are synthesized into a final position.

Skilled Disagreement

Controversy requires a complex set of procedures and skills. For controversies to be managed constructively, people need collaborative and conflict-management skills (Johnson, 1991, 2000; Johnson & Johnson, 1989, 1995c). One of the most important skills is to be able to disagree with each other's ideas while confirming each other's personal competence. Disagreeing with others, and at the same time imputing that others are incompetent, tends to increase their commitment to their own ideas and their rejection of the other person's information and reasoning. Disagreeing with others while simultaneously confirming their personal competence, however, results in being better liked and in opponents being less critical of others' ideas, more interested in learning more about others' ideas, and more willing to incorporate others' information and reasoning into their own analysis of the problem.

Another important set of skills for exchanging information and opinions within a controversy is perspective-taking. More information, both personal and impersonal, is disclosed when one is interacting with a person who is engaging in perspective-taking behaviors, such as paraphrasing, which communicates a desire to understand accurately. Perspective-taking ability increases one's capacity to phrase messages so that they are easily understood by others and to comprehend accurately the messages of others. Engaging in perspective-taking in controversies results in increased understanding and retention of the opponent's information and perspective (Johnson, 1971). Perspective-taking facilitates the achievement of creative, high-quality problem solving (Falk and Johnson, 1977; Johnson, 1977). Finally, perspective-taking promotes more positive perceptions of the information-exchange process, of fellow group members, and of the group's work. To obtain a creative synthesis of all positions in a controversy, group members must obtain a clear understanding of all sides of the issue and an accurate assessment of the validity and relative merits of each position. In order to do this fully, they must accurately perceive the frame of reference from which the other person is viewing and analyzing the situation and problem.

A third set of skills involves the cycle of differentiation of positions and their integration. Group members should ensure that there are several cycles of differentiation (bringing out differences in positions) and integration (combining several positions into one new, creative position). Differentiation must precede integration. Differentiation involves seeking out and clarifying differences among members' ideas, information, conclusions, theories, and opinions. It involves highlighting the differences among members' reasoning and seeking to understand fully what the different positions and perspectives are. All different points of view must be presented and explored thoroughly before new, creative solutions are sought. Integration involves combining the information, reasoning, theories, and conclusions of the various group members so that all members are satisfied. After it has differentiated positions, the group needs to seek a new, creative position that synthesizes the thinking of all the members. The group should never try to integrate members' positions before adequate differentiation has taken place. The potential for integration is never greater than the adequacy of the differentiation already achieved. Most controversies go through a series of differentiations and integrations before reaching a final decision.

Rational Argument

During a controversy, group members have to follow the canons of rational argumentation. Within a controversy group members present their position and its rationale while asking other members for proof that their analyses and conclusions are valid. Rational argumentation includes generating ideas, collecting and organizing relevant information, using inductive and deductive logic, and making tentative conclusions based on current understanding. Rational argumentation requires that participants keep an open mind, changing their conclusions and positions when others are persuasive and convincing in their presentation of rationale, proof, and logical reasoning. The abilities to gather, organize, and present information, to challenge and disagree, and to engage in reason logically are essential for the constructive management of controversies.

STRUCTURING ACADEMIC CONTROVERSIES

In conducting a controversy within a group there are a series of steps to follow.

1. *Propose several courses of action that will solve the problem under consideration.* When the group is making a decision, identify a number of alternative courses of action for the group to follow.

2. *Form advocacy teams.* To ensure that each course of action receives a fair and complete hearing, assign two group members to be an advocacy team to present the best case possible for the assigned position. **Positive interdependence** is structured by highlighting the cooperative goal of making the best decision possible (goal interdependence) and noting that a high-quality decision cannot be made without considering the information that is being organized by the other advocacy teams (resource interdependence). **Individual accountability** is structured by ensuring each member participates in preparing and presenting the assigned position. Any information discovered that supports the other alternatives is given to the appropriate advocacy pair.

3. *Engage in the controversy procedure.*

a. Each advocacy team researches its position and prepares a persuasive presentation to convince other group members of its validity. The assigned alternative course of action is thoroughly researched through consultants, relevant articles and books, and experts. Persuasive arguments are organized into a presentation.

b. Each advocacy team presents without interruption the best case possible for its assigned alternative course of action to the entire group. Other advocacy teams listen carefully, taking notes, and striving to learn the information provided.

c. There is an open discussion characterized by advocacy, refutation, and rebuttal. The advocacy teams give opposing positions a trial by fire, seeking to refute them by challenging the validity of their information and logic. They defend their own position while attempting to persuade other group members of its validity. For higher-level reasoning and critical thinking to occur, it is necessary to probe and push each other's conclusions. Members ask for data to support each other's statements, clarify rationales, and show why their position is the most rational one. Group members refute the claims being made by the opposing teams, and rebut the attacks on their own position. They take careful notes on and thoroughly learn the opposing positions.

Members follow the specific rules for constructive controversy. Sometimes a time-out period is needed so that pairs can caucus and prepare new arguments. Members should encourage spirited arguing and playing devil's advocate. Members are instructed to: "Argue forcefully and persuasively for your position, presenting as many facts as you can to support your point of view. Listen critically to the opposing pair's position, asking them for the facts that support their viewpoint, and then present counterarguments. Remember this is a complex issue, and you need to know all sides to make a good decision."

   d. Advocacy teams reverse perspectives and positions by presenting one of the opposing positions as sincerely and forcefully as team members can. Members may be told, "Working as a pair, present an opposing pair's position as if you were they. Be as sincere and forceful as you can. Add any new facts you know. Elaborate their position by relating it to other information you have previously learned."

   e. All members drop their advocacy and reach a decision by consensus. They may wish to summarize their decision in a group report that details the course of action they have adopted and its supporting rationale. Often the chosen alternative represents a new perspective or synthesis that is more rational than the two assigned. All group members sign the report, indicating that they agree with the decision and will do their share of the work in implementing it. Members may be instructed to: "Summarize and synthesize the best arguments for *all* points of view. Reach a decision by consensus. Change your mind only when the facts and the rationale clearly indicate that you should do so. Write a report with the supporting evidence and rationale for your synthesis that your group has agreed on. When you are certain the report is as good as you can make it, sign it."

   f. Group members process how well the group functioned and how their performance may be improved during the next controversy.

    4. *Implement decision.* Once the decision is made, all members commit themselves to implement it regardless of whether they initially favored the alternative adopted.

GUIDELINES FOR CONSTRUCTIVE CONTROVERSY

There are no cookbook rules for making controversies productive, but the following guidelines can help group members argue more constructively and transform disagreement among themselves into a positive experience.

    1. *Emphasize your common ground of making the best possible decision.* Statements such as "We are all in this together" and "Let's make the best possible decision" should dominate the group, not "I am right and you are wrong." The context within which the controversy takes place should be cooperative, not competitive. The issue is not to establish who has the best answer but to make the best group decision possible by exploring different perspectives and integrating different information.

2. *Look for opportunities to engage in controversy.* Highlight contrasting viewpoints, point out disagreements, and promote challenging tasks. Include diverse people in the group. People who differ in background, expertise, opinions, outlook, and organizational position are likely to disagree.

3. *Prepare the best case possible for your position.* Develop your thesis statement and research the best rationale possible to support it. It is up to you to ensure that your position is seen in its best light. Consult relevant articles, books, and experts to compile information and experiences to support your position. List relevant facts, information, and theories.

4. *Advocate your position forcefully but with an open mind.* Speak up. Make sure everyone listens. It is up to you to ensure that your position gets a fair and complete hearing.

5. *Encourage others to advocate their positions forcefully.* Express a warm, intense interest in all contributions. Every member should share his or her position and ideas in order to get comments and reactions from other members that will help improve the quality of group work. Value, respect, and take seriously everyone's contributions. Help all members, regardless of their status, to speak out confidently.

6. *Understand, then challenge opposing ideas and positions.* Ask questions. Ask for the supporting facts, information, and theories in order to understand the opposing positions more thoroughly. Understanding the statements of another group member is not enough; the frame of reference from which the member is speaking must also be clearly understood. View the issue under discussion from a variety of perspectives. Then, point out fallacies in information and logic. Try to refute their thesis statements and claims. Group members should be critical of ideas, not of persons. Arguments should concern ideas, not personality traits. Group members should be highly critical

of each other's ideas at the same time affirming each other's competence and communicating respect and appreciation for the member as a person. Any inference of incompetence or weakness and any hint of rejecting another member should be avoided. Criticize opposing ideas while confirming the competence of the other group members. Combine personal regard with intellectual challenge. Say, "We are friends," "I am interested in what you have to say." Then say, "I do not agree with you on that point," "I have come to a different conclusion," "I appreciate you, I am interested in your ideas, but I disagree with your current position." Do not say, "You are stupid and ignorant and I do not like you!" Insults or imputations that challenge another member's integrity, intelligence, and motives are to be avoided.

7. *Do not take personally other members' disagreements and rejection of your ideas.* That other members disagree with your ideas and conclusions should be taken as an interesting situation from which something can be learned, not as a personal attack. Do not confuse rejection of your ideas and opinions with personal rejection. Separate the validity of your thinking from your competence and worth as a person.

8. *Ensure that there are several cycles of differentiation and integration.* Differentiation involves bringing out differences in positions and integration involves combining several positions into one new, creative position. Differentiation must come before integration is attempted.

9. *Put yourself in the other member's shoes.* Controversy is an opportunity to improve the quality of your own reasoning by seeing the issue from a variety of perspectives. Ensure that you understand the perspectives underlying positions as well as their content.

10. *Follow the canons of rational argument.* Generate ideas, collect and organize relevant information, use deductive and inductive logical procedures, and make tentative conclusions. Avoid premature evaluations.

11. *Synthesize the best ideas from all viewpoints and perspectives.* The end result is a synthesis that is better than any single position advocated. Think creatively until it is discovered.

BEING A CITIZEN IN A DEMOCRACY

The word *democracy* comes from the Greek word *demokratia,* which is a combination of *demos* (people) and *kratos* (rule). Thomas Jefferson believed that rule by the people required free and open discussion in which knowledge is the basis of influence within society, not the social rank within which a person was born. American democracy was thus founded on the premise that truth will result from free and open discussion in which opposing points of view are advocated and vigorously argued. Before a decision is made, every citizen is given the opportunity to advocate for his or her ideas. A vote is then taken and the majority rules. The minority is then expected to willingly go along with the majority because they know (a) they received a fair and complete hearing and (b) they will have another chance in two or four years. To be a citizen in our democracy individuals need to master the process of advocating one's views, challenging opposing positions, making a decision, and committing oneself to implement the decision made (regardless of whether one initially favored the alternative adopted).

SUMMARY

Decision making typically involves considering possible alternatives and choosing one. By definition, all decision-making situations involve some conflict as to which of several alternatives should be chosen. Within decision-making groups, that conflict takes the form of controversy. Controversy exists when one individual's ideas, information, conclusions, theories, and opinions are incompatible with those of another, and the two seek to reach an agreement. Such intellectual conflict among individuals may be avoided and suppressed or it may be structured and encouraged. Simply by emphasizing concurrence-seeking, intellectual conflict among group members may be avoided. If it does occur, it may be suppressed by stating that it is against the rules.

Most intellectual conflicts are avoided and suppressed. Yet there is evidence that controversy can be a powerful tool. Conflicts among ideas, conclusions, theories, information, perspectives, opinions, and preferences are inevitable. Such conflicts are (a) an inherent aspect of decision making, problem solving, reasoned judgment, and critical thinking; and (b) inevitable. If individuals get intellectually and emotionally involved in cooperative efforts, controversies will occur no matter what participants do. They are critical events that may bring (a) increased learning, creative insight, high-quality problem solving and decision making; (b) closer and more positive relationships; and (c) greater social competence and psychological health. Or they may bring closed minds and poorly conceived decisions, lasting resentment and smoldering hostility, and psychological scars, rigidly ineffectual behavior, and a refusal to change or learn.

Controversy begins when your group, faced with a decision that has to be made, assigns the major alternatives to advocacy subgroups and has each subgroup (a) develop its alternative in depth and (b) plan how to present the best case possible for its alternative to the rest of the group. First, group members prepare a position to present to the rest of the group based on their current information, experiences, and perspective. Second, they then present and advocate your position to the rest of the group who, in turn, are advocating opposing positions. High-quality decisions and conclusions are reached through a process of argument and counterargument aimed at persuading others to adopt, modify, or drop positions. Third, group members are confronted by other group members with different positions based on their information, experiences, and perspectives. Members attempt to refute opposing positions while rebutting the attacks on their position. Fourth, faced with these opposing positions, criticisms of your position, and information that is incompatible with and does not fit with their conclusions, they become uncertain as to the correctness of your views. A state of conceptual conflict or disequilibrium is aroused. Group members experience conceptual conflict and uncertainty when faced with (a) opposing positions with their rationales and (b) challenges to the validity of their own position and its rationale. Being challenged by conclusions and information that are incompatible with and do not fit with their reasoning and conclusions results in conceptual conflict, uncertainty, and disequilibrium. Fifth, members' uncertainty, conceptual conflict, and disequilibrium motivates an active search for more information, new experiences, and a more adequate cognitive perspective and reasoning in hopes of resolving the uncertainty. Epistemic curiosity, divergent attention and thought are stimulated. Members search for more information and experiences to support your position, seek to understand the opposition's, and attempt to view the problem from opposing perspectives. This results in a reorganization and reconceptualization of their conclusions.

Finally, members adapt their cognitive perspective and reasoning through understanding and accommodating the perspective and reasoning of others and derive a new, reconceptualized, and reorganized conclusion. Novel solutions and decisions that, on balance, are qualitatively better are detected. The purpose of controversy is not to choose the best of the alternatives. The purpose of controversy is to create a synthesis of the best reasoning and conclusions from all the various alternatives. To do so, members have to keep conclusions tentative, accurately understand opposing perspectives, incorporate new information into their conceptual frameworks, and be willing to change their attitudes and position. This process is repeated until the differences in conclusions among group members have been resolved, a decision is reached, and the controversy has ended.

Controversies tend to be constructive when the situational context is cooperative, there is some heterogeneity among group members, information and expertise is distributed within the group, members have the necessary conflict skills, and the canons of rational argumentation are followed. An essential aspect of controversy is the creativity that is derived from the collision of adverse opinion.

Exercise 8.6: The Johnson School

Form groups of six. Give one set of cards to each group. Each member should take one of the cards. The cards should contain the following statements, one on each card.

1. The strongest coach coached wrestling second.
   Track was a sport coached at the Johnson School.
   Dale offered to recruit cheerleaders for the school.

2. Members of your group have all the information needed to find the answer to the following question. (Only one answer is correct.) *In what sequence did the Johnsons coach the sports taught at their school?* Some of the information your group has is not relevant and will not help your group solve the problem.

3. Frank coached wrestling third.
   The strongest coach had been coaching longer than the other coaches.
   Edye's favorite sport was eating.

4. The strongest coach coached first the sport that David liked the best.
   All coaches coached all the sports.
   Keith preferred telling others what to do rather than doing it himself.

5. Helen had been coaching longer than any of the other coaches.
   David coached basketball third.
   Each coach coached the sport they liked best second.

6. Roger preferred to coach golf more than the other sports.
   All coaches preferred or liked one sport above the others.
   All coaches coached at the same time.

   Give the following instructions: You have all the information you need to define a problem and solve it. You have twenty to forty minutes. One rule you must follow: Although you may tell your group what is on your card, you may not pass it around for others to read. All communication in the group is to be verbal. I repeat, you may not let others read what is on your card; you may only tell them what it says.

Exercise 8.7: Avoiding Controversies

People often find ingenious methods to keep from having to deal directly with controversies. How do you behave when you want to avoid a dispute? How do the other members of your group behave?

The following exercise is designed to produce feedback about how other group members see your behavior when you want to avoid a controversy. Its objective is for participants to examine their own behavior in controversies and disagreements. Understanding avoidance behavior, or how people avoid responding, can be as helpful as increasing their awareness of constructive behaviors. The procedure for the coordinator is as follows:

1. Introduce the exercise as a chance for each group member to get feedback from other group members on his or her behavior.
2. Tell each group member to place a sheet of newsprint on the wall with his or her name clearly written at the top.
3. Have group members walk around the room writing down their impressions on the newsprint of how each of the others behaves when he or she wants to avoid a controversy. You may wish to use the checklist below to start ideas.
4. All members should classify themselves according to the checklist below and then read the remarks other group members have written on their sheet.
5. Divide the participants into groups of three and have them discuss the content of the remarks written on their sheets, their own perceptions of their behavior, and the feelings generated by the exercise. Note that although the defenses against directly facing controversy are not helpful to the group and will promote destructive outcomes, they are at times very helpful and of constructive value to the individual. Participants should ask themselves whether there are ways to protect themselves without being harmful to the group.

DEFENSES AGAINST CONTROVERSY

1. *Ostrich:* Deny the controversy exists; refuse to see the potential or actual disagreement.
2. *Turtle:* Withdraw from the issue and the persons disagreeing with you.
3. *Lemming:* Give in and accept the other person's point of view or ideas.
4. *Weasel:* Rationalize by stating that the issue is not important, that you really don't hold an opposing opinion, that the issue is one on which you have no expertise, and so on.
5. *Gorilla:* Overpower the other members by forcing them to accept your ideas and point of view.
6. *Owl:* Intellectualize about the issue and ideas so that all feelings and emotions are hidden.
7. *Sheep:* Formulate, support, and conform to group norms forbidding the expression of opposition and disagreement in the group.

Exercise 8.8: Beliefs about Creativity

The purpose of this exercise is to provoke a discussion concerning the nature of creativity. The procedure is as follows:

1. Working by yourself, answer the following questions about creativity.
   a. Creativity and intelligence are (1) unrelated, (2) highly related to each other in the sense that creativity promotes cognitive development.

b. Creativity is a (1) stable trait that some persons are born with and others lack, (2) process of problem solving characterized by an interaction between group members and the challenges of their environment.

c. Creativity: (1) is at the same level across situations—a creative person is creative in every situation—(2) varies a great deal from situation to situation, depending on the problem-solving process being used.

d. Creativity is something that (1) cannot be taught because it is an inborn trait, (2) can be taught because it is a problem-solving process.

e. The role of the school is to (1) discover or identify creative students and place them in accelerated programs so that their creativity is utilized, (2) develop creative competencies in all students by providing the needed challenges and teaching them the problem-solving skills necessary for a creative response.

2. Form heterogeneous groups of six and arrive at a group consensus for each question.
3. Compare your group's answers with those of the other groups in the class.

CREATIVITY

One of the most compelling outcomes of decisional and intellectual conflict is creative problem solving. Creative thinking and reasoning, while vitally important to effective groups, is hard to find in the real world and little understood even in the laboratory. Creativity is a process of bringing something new into existence, consisting of a sequence of overlapping phases (Johnson, 1979). *First, group members must recognize that a problem exists and it is challenging enough to motivate them to solve it.* For the possibility of creativity to exist, group members need to be aroused to a level of motivation sufficient to sustain problem-solving efforts despite frustrations and dead ends (Deutsch, 1969). This level of motivation, however, cannot be so intense that it overwhelms members or keeps them too close to the problem. The motivation to persist is increased by both controversy and a group tradition supporting the view that with time and effort constructive solutions can be discovered or invented for seemingly insoluble problems.

Second, group members must gather the necessary knowledge and resources within the group and plan an intense, long-term effort to solve the problem. The more members are immersed in and focused on the problem and the relevant information and circumstances, the greater the likelihood they will achieve a creative insight.

Third, a cooperative context must be highlighted in order for the necessary level of social support to be achieved within the group. Members must not feel threatened or under too much pressure (Deutsch, 1969; Rokeach, 1960; Stein, 1968). Feeling threatened prompts defensiveness and reduces both tolerance of ambiguity and receptiveness to the new and the unfamiliar. Too much tension leads to stereotyping of thought processes. Feeling threatened and under pressure prevents group members from becoming sufficiently detached from their original viewpoint to be able to see the problem from new perspectives.

Fourth, group members need to seek out different perspectives and different ways of viewing the problem. They then can reformulate it in a way that lets new orientations to a solution emerge. Creative insight usually depends on (a) the availability of diverse information and viewpoints and (b) group members disagreeing and challenging

each other's reasoning and perspectives. The more varied the members of a group, the more likely the group will arrive at a creative solution. Both male and female, lower-class and middle-class, white and minority, high-achieving and low-achieving persons should be placed in the same cooperative problem-solving groups to maximize the possibility of creative solutions being found. The members with diverging ideas and perspectives must disagree and challenge each other's reasoning and perspectives. Once diverse ideas and perspectives are available, the exchange of ideas has to be encouraged so that they can be put together into new and varied patterns. Each group member needs the freedom, support, and self-confidence to express him- or herself without being afraid of censure. The resulting conflict among group members will tend to spark new ideas and approaches, broaden the range of available solutions, and produce moments of insight or inspiration by one or more group members. Creative insight is often accompanied by intense emotional experiences of illumination and excitement and leads to the formulation of a tentative solution.

Fifth, group members need to experience an incubation period during which they feel frustration, tension, and discomfort due to their failure to produce an adequate solution to the problem and temporarily withdraw from the issue. In order for group members to derive creative answers to problems they are working on, they must be allowed time to reflect. Instant answers should not be demanded. Creative thinking "is commonly typified by periods of intense application and periods of inactivity" (Treffinger, Speedie, and Brunner, 1974, p. 21). After all sides of a controversy have been presented, group members should be allowed to think about solutions for a day or so before trying to put things together in new and varied patterns.

Sixth, group members formulate a new and unique solution to the problem, elaborate on it and work out the details of implementing it, and test it against reality. If the implementation is successful, group members than give the validated solution to relevant audiences.

DEVELOPING AND FOSTERING CREATIVITY

How do you increase group members' creative thinking? There are no easy answers to this question. From the process perspective, here is a set of procedures that can be used to promote creativity.

1. Reaffirm the cooperative goal of making the best decision possible.

2. Promote controversy among ideas, opinions, information, theories, and perspectives of group members. Members should promote different points of view, critically analyze each other's information and reasoning, serve as a devil's advocate to challenge other member's positions and creative diversity of opinion, and recombine already known facts into new combinations and relationships. Members should be enthusiastic about originality in thinking and problem solving, and become immersed in the perspectives and approaches to approaching and solving the problem.

3. Set aside time for members to reflect on the diverse ideas and perspectives generated by the controversy process. Encourage persistence in solving the problem, no matter how difficult it is. Creative insights come out of struggle, not quick reflection. Creative individuals such as Einstein and Picasso experienced great difficulties before achieving insight.

4. Meet to make final decisions, but do not rush to judgment. Creative insights cannot be hurried.

David and Houtman (1968) are the authors of a book intended to teach creativity. They suggest four methods of generating novel ideas that can be taught: part changing, using a checkerboard figure, using a checklist, and finding something similar. The *part-changing method* involves group members in identifying the parts or attributes of something that might be changed. The following is an example:

> Four qualities of a chair are color, shape, size, and hardness. Invent a new kind of chair by listing fifteen different colors, ten different shapes, five sizes, and five grades of hardness. Try to think of different ideas, and do not worry about whether or not they are any good. Think of different ways to change each part of the chair. Use your imagination.

The *checkerboard method* involves making a checkerboard figure with spaces for entering words or phrases on the vertical and horizontal axes. Different sets of properties or attributes are listed on the axes. Then group members examine the interaction or combination of each pair of things or attributes. For example:

> Your group is to invent a new sport. Place materials and equipment along the top horizontal axis and place the things the players do (such as running, batting, kicking, hanging from their knees) down the side or vertical axis. Then examine the combination of each item on each axis with all the other items on the other axis.

The *checklist method* involves developing and using checklists to make sure that something is not left out or forgotten. David and Houtman suggest a checklist that includes these procedures:

1. Change color.
2. Change size.
3. Change shape.
4. Use new or different material.
5. Add or subtract something.
6. Rearrange things.
7. Identify a new design.

A group can apply this checklist to any object or problem.

The *"find something similar" method* involves encouraging group members to come up with new ideas by thinking of other persons, animals, or social units in the world that perform the same acts the group wants to perform. Here is an example:

Imagine your city has a parking problem. Find ideas for solving this problem by thinking of how bees, squirrels, ants, shoe stores, clothing stores, and so on store things.

Another technique designed to enhance the creativity of group members is *synectics,* developed by William J. Gordon (1961). Gordon stresses the importance of psychological states in achieving creativity and the use of metaphor in achieving the proper psychological state. He suggests using three interrelated techniques for making the strange appear familiar and the familiar strange:

1. *Personal analogy* in which persons imagine how it feels to be part of the phenomenon they are studying. Asking them how they would feel if they were an incomplete sentence or if they were Paul Revere's horse are examples.
2. *Direct analogy,* in which group members are asked to think about a parallel situation in order to gain insight into what they are studying. Asking them to describe how a book is like a lightbulb or how a beaver chewing on a log resembles a typewriter are examples.
3. *Compressed conflict,* in which group members are forced to perceive an object or concept from two frames of reference. Asking them to give examples of repulsive attraction or cooperative competition are illustrations.

Exercise 8.9: Creativity

This problem requires creativity on the part of the group that is attempting to solve it. The class should divide into groups of three. Each group's assignment is to connect all nine dots with only four straight and connected lines. (Answer is on page 587 in the Appendix.)

●   ●   ●

●   ●   ●

●   ●   ●

Exercise 8.10: Joe Doodlebug

This problem also requires group creativity to solve. It is taken from Rokeach (1960). The procedure for the coordinator is as follows:

1. Have the class divide into groups of three.
2. Hand out copies of the problem sheet and state that it contains all the ncessary information. The problem is *why* Joe *has* to take *four* jumps to reach the food, which is only three feet away. The groups have thirty minutes to come up with an answer. Explain that you will give hints after fifteen, twenty, and twenty-five minutes if the groups have not solved the problem.
3. After fifteen minutes give the first hint, after twenty minutes the second, and after twenty-five minutes the third (see page 587 in the Appendix).
4. At the end of thirty minutes stop the groups and give them the answer (it appears on page 587 in the Appendix). After clarifying the answer, conduct a discussion of moving outside one's belief system to solve a problem. Then ask the group to discuss how they worked together, listened to each other, handled controversies, and so on.

THE PROBLEM

Joe Doodlebug has been jumping all over the place getting some exercise when his master places a pile of food three feet directly west of him. Joe notices that the pile of food is a little larger than he. As soon as Joe sees all this food he stops dead in his tracks facing north. After all his exercise Joe is hungry and he wants to get the food as quickly as possible. Joe examines the situation and then says, "I'll have to jump four times to get the food." Why does Joe have to take four jumps to get to the food?

Joe Doodlebug, a strange sort of imaginary bug, can and cannot do the following things: (1) He can jump only in four different directions: north, south, east, and west (he cannot jump diagonally, such as southwest); (2) once he starts in any direction he *must* jump four times in that direction before he can change direction; (3) he can only jump, not crawl, fly, or walk; (4) he cannot jump less than one inch per jump or more than ten feet per jump; (5) Joe cannot turn around.

OPEN VERSUS CLOSED BELIEF SYSTEMS

A key element of creative problem solving is the open-mindedness to view the problem from diverse perspectives. When a group member is willing to attend to, comprehend, and gain insight into information, ideas, perspectives, assumptions, beliefs, conclusions, and opinions discrepant from his or her own, the member is *open-minded.* When the member resists such opportunities, the member is *closed-minded* and dogmatic. Group members must be open-minded about different beliefs, opinions, information, ideas, perspectives, and assumptions. The extent to which a member can receive, evaluate, and act on relevant information on its own merits (as opposed to viewing it only from his or her own perspective) defines the extent to which the student is open-minded (as opposed to being closed-minded) (Rokeach, 1960). Without seeing the problem from several perspectives, members will not be able to analyze it and synthesize various ideas to produce creative solutions. Controversy is an essential ingredient in discovering new perspectives on the problem being solved.

How do you tell if a group is open- or closed-minded? *Closed-minded groups are characterized by* (a) emphasis on the differences between what they believe and what they do not believe; (b) denial of information that is contrary to what they believe; (c) the existence of contradictory beliefs that go unquestioned; (d) the discarding as irrelevant of similarities between what they believe and what they reject; and (e) the avoidance of exploring differences in beliefs and distortion of information that does not fit their beliefs. *Open-minded groups are characterized by* (a) the seeking out of opposing and differing beliefs; (b) the discovery of new beliefs; (c) the remembering of information that disagrees with currently held beliefs; and (d) the organization of new beliefs that lead to the solution of the problem. Open-mindedness is an important requirement for creative problem solving.

Rokeach (1954, 1960) has developed the concept of dogmatism to categorize persons in terms of the openness or closedness of their belief system. He defines *dogmatism* as "(a) a relatively closed cognitive organization of beliefs and disbeliefs about reality, (b) organized around a central set of beliefs about absolute authority which, in turn, (c) provides a framework for patterns of intolerance toward others." This research indicates that *closed-minded persons,* compared with open-minded individuals (Ehrlich & Lee, 1969; Vacchiano, Strauss, & Hochman, 1968):

1. Are less able to learn new beliefs and to change old beliefs.
2. Are less able to organize new beliefs and integrate them into their existing cognitive systems during problem solving, and thus take longer to solve problems involving new beliefs.
3. Are less accepting of belief-discrepant information.
4. Are more resistant to changing their beliefs.
5. More frequently reject information that is potentially threatening to their perceptual and attitudinal organization.
6. Have less recall of information that is inconsistent with their beliefs.
7. Evaluate information that is consistent with their beliefs more positively.
8. Have more difficulty in discriminating between the information received and its source, so that the status of an authority is confused with the validity of what the authority is stating; in other words, dogmatic persons tend to accept what authorities say as the truth and discount what low-status individuals say as invalid.
9. Resolve fewer issues in conflict situations, are more resistant to compromise, and are more likely to view compromise as defeat.

The creative solution of problems requires open-mindedness. In being open-minded, group members must be willing to give up their current beliefs about the situation and adopt new ones. The new beliefs help them synthesize an unforeseen but effective solution. The replacement of old beliefs with new beliefs is called the *analytic phase* of the problem-solving process. Once new beliefs have superseded the old ones, group members must organize their new beliefs in a way that leads them to the solution of the problem. This organizational step is called the *synthesizing phase* of the problem-solving process.

In solving the Joe Doodlebug problem, for example, group members must first overcome three beliefs, one by one, and replace them with three new beliefs. The *first* belief to be replaced is the facing belief. In everyday life we have to face the food we are to eat. But Joe does not have to face the food in order to eat it, he can land on top of it. The *second* is the direction belief. In everyday life we can change direction at will. But Joe is not able to do this because he must forever face north. The only way Joe can change direction is by jumping sideways and backward. The *third* belief that must be replaced is the movement belief. When we wish to change direction in everyday life, there is nothing to stop us from doing so immediately. But Joe's freedom of movement is restricted by the fact that once he moves in a particular direction (north, south, east, or west) he has to continue four times in that direction before he can change it. Many group members assume that Joe is at the end rather than possibly in the middle of a jumping sequence.

The replacement of old beliefs that limit a group's thinking with new beliefs that enable whole new orientations and perspectives depends on the old beliefs being challenged and disconfirmed. It is conflict that sparks the cognitive changes that enable creative insight. If group members are to engage in creative problem solving, they must be open-minded and be challenged with opposing positions, which results in seeing the issue from a variety of perspectives, which leads to developing a creative synthesis that solves the problem. Controversy, replacement of old beliefs with new ones, and the synthesis of new beliefs are all essential.

BRAINSTORMING

Problem solving depends on developing divergent views that conflict with each other. Often groups suffer by members not producing a wide variety of diverse ideas that can be contrasted with each other. Before group members can converge on a creative course of action, they must develop a wide variety of possibilities to be explored. Brainstorming was invented to (a) encourage divergent thinking, (b) produce many different ideas in a short period of time, and (c) ensure the full participation of all group members. **Brainstorming** is a procedure in which group members are asked to produce as many, and as uninhibited, ideas as they possibly can and to withhold criticism in order to optimize creativity. All criticism is withheld in order to reduce evaluation apprehension. The engaging of free association of ideas is supposed to open new avenues of thought. Brainstorming tends to increase member participation and involvement, generate lots of ideas in a relatively short period of time, and reduce the need to look for the "right" idea in order to impress authority figures in the group. During brainstorming, the ground rules are:

1. All criticism or evaluation of ideas is ruled out. Ideas are simply placed before the group.
2. Wild ideas are expected in the spontaneity that evolves when the group suspends judgment. Practical considerations are not important at this point. The session is to be freewheeling.
3. The quantity of ideas counts, not their quality. All ideas should be expressed, and none should be screened out by any individual. A great number of ideas will increase the likelihood of the group discovering good ones.
4. Build on the ideas of other group members when possible. Pool your creativity. Everyone should be free to build onto ideas and to make interesting combinations from the various suggestions.

5. Focus on a single problem or issue. Don't skip around to various problems or try to brainstorm a complex, multiple problem.
6. Promote a congenial, relaxed, cooperative atmosphere.
7. Make sure that all members, no matter how shy and reluctant to contribute, get their ideas heard.
8. Record all ideas.

After the period of brainstorming, all the ideas are categorized, and the group critically evaluates them for possible use or application. Priorities are selected and the best ideas are applied.

The rationale for using brainstorming is the belief that many ideas are never born or are quickly stifled due to domineering members, stereotypes of each other's expertise and intelligence, interpersonal conflicts, habitual patterns of uninvolvement and silence, fear of ridicule or evaluation. It is like a vice president in charge of a group of managers saying, "Those opposed will signify by clearing out their desks, putting on their hats, and saying 'I resign.' "

There is only one problem with brainstorming. Most research suggests that it is less effective than allowing the same number of people to generate ideas on their own, independent from any group experience (Diehl & Stroebe, 1987; Mullen, Johnson, & Salas, 1991). The primary reason for the lack of effectiveness of brainstorming is in part due to production blocking. *Production blocking* reflects the common group norm that only one person is to speak at a given time. This prevents members from blurting out their ideas the moment they think of them and thereby the ideas may be forgotten or censored. Groups (compared to isolated individuals), therefore, are at a definite disadvantage for generating lots of ideas in a short period of time. Yet the use of brainstorming remains widespread. The reasons may include that (a) people enjoy working in groups and are therefore more motivated to produce ideas in a group setting (Stroebe, Diehl, & Abukoumkin, 1992), and (b) the dynamics of group brainstorming create better analysis, adoption, and implementation in later stages of group problem solving.

The thinking of all of us is highly influenced by the thinking of those with whom we talk and otherwise interact. It is almost always possible to be part of a group process that encourages, supports, and rewards our potential for creativity. The ideas of others spark our own. The theory of one group member may help build a much more creative theory by touching off all sorts of new ideas among the rest of the members. Untold amounts of creative problem solving may occur when diversity and controversy are sought and used.

Exercise 8.11: Brainstorming

The objective of this exercise is to come up with a large number of ideas or solutions to a problem by temporarily suspending criticism and evaluation—in other words, to experience the process of brainstorming. The procedure is as follows:

1. The ground rules for brainstorming are reviewed by the group.
2. The group is presented with a problem: One of the authors of this book has been cast ashore nude on a desert island with nothing but a glass peace symbol on a leather thong.

3. The group has fifteen minutes to generate ideas as to what can be done with this object.
4. The group has another fifteen minutes to critically select their best ideas.
5. The group discusses how well it applied the rules of brainstorming and what its results were. Was creativity enhanced? Did it help the group to discover interesting ways of using the object?

After initial exposure to brainstorming, a group should pick a specific problem it is working on and apply brainstorming to it to see if new, creative perspectives can be gained. If, however, a second practice session is desired, the following story can be used:

> A small wholesaler in the hinterland of New Mexico called his buyer in Santa Fe and asked him to obtain a large order of pipe cleaners from Mexico. The buyer agreed. He also agreed to advance the wholesaler the money to finance the deal. A month later, just as the shipment of pipe cleaners was arriving, the buyer received a disastrous phone call from the wholesaler: His warehouse and outlet store had burned down and there simply was no more business. The buyer was suddenly faced with the prospect of trying to sell 20,000 pipe cleaners.

In one minute group members should generate as many ideas as possible (with a recorder counting the number of different ideas) for selling pipe cleaners. (A relatively spontaneous group will create approximately twenty-five ideas in a little more than a minute. If the group creates fifteen ideas or less, it should be given more training in brainstorming.)

In brainstorming a group problem, it is important that the problem be well defined and specific. It must also be a problem that the group has the power to do something about. If possible, the group members should be notified in advance about the issue to be explored so that they will have given some thought to it.

Exercise 8.12: *Creativity Warm-up*

Have you ever felt in a rut? Have you ever felt embarrassed about sharing new or wild ideas? Have you ever ignored your thinking because you felt it was too far out? Do you ever enjoy letting your imagination and thoughts run wild? Have you ever been so critical of your own thoughts that you could not get started?

Here are six short, fun exercises to loosen up group thinking and warm up group creativity:

1. The group sits in a circle (group size should be limited to eight members or so). The person nearest the window says the first thing that comes to his mind. The statement should be short, not over a sentence or two. Without pause the person to his left says what comes to her mind. Her statement must be relevant to something the first person said. The relevance may be of any kind—an association, a contrast, an alternative, a continuation, and so on. The process continues at high speed until at least three rounds have been completed. Members critique the process by discussing the feelings they had during the exercise.
2. The group sits in a circle and identifies a problem or issue. The person nearest the door states his solution. Each subsequent group member (to his left) states his or hers, using as many ideas of previous speakers as one can. The process is continued until a plan generally acceptable to all the group members is arrived at. When a member cannot add anything new, he or she passes. Finally, members' reactions to and feelings about the experience are discussed.
3. The group sits in a circle and a group problem or issue is identified. The first person states her solution to the problem. The next person immediately states what her opposition

to the first person's solution is. The third person immediately states his or her opposition to the second person's opposition. The process is continued until everyone in the group has spoken at least three times. The emphasis is upon generating creative ideas in arguments. Members' reactions to and feelings about the experience are discussed.

4. The group lies on the floor, members' heads toward the center of the room. The first person begins with a fantasy about what the group could be like. After no more than two or three minutes, the fantasy is passed on to the next group member, who continues it, adding his own associations and fantasies. The process continues until everyone has spoken at least three times. Members' reactions to and feelings about the exercise are examined.

5. The group has before it a number of assorted materials, such as clay, water paints, Tinker Toys, magazines, newspapers, and so on. It then creates something out of the materials—a mural, a collage, a design. If more than one group participates, they end the exercise by discussing one another's creations.

6. The group acts out a walk through the woods. Each member takes the leadership role for a while and directs the walk, indicating what he or she is experiencing and seeing. What the members learn about one another, the group, and walking through the woods should be discussed.

Exercise 8.13: Your Behavior in Controversies (II)

How do you behave in controversies? Has your behavior changed as a result of your experiences connected with this chapter? How would you now describe your behavior?

1. When a difficult decision is to be made
   _____ I seek out people who agree with me and see the situation the same way I do.
   _____ I seek out people who disagree with me and see the situation much differently than I do.
2. When I disagree with other members of my group, I
   _____ Become more and more certain I am right and try to overpower any opposition so that I win by having the final decision reflect what I want to do.
   _____ Present my point of view but listen carefully to everyone else's ideas and change my mind when I am logically persuaded to do so.
3. When other members of the group disagree with my ideas, I
   _____ Feel hurt and rejected.
   _____ Believe they may have important information and insights that my help me better understand the situation.
4. When other group members disagree with me, I
   _____ Try to stand in their shoes and see the situation from their point of view.
   _____ Am puzzled that they cannot see the situation as accurately and completely as I do.
5. When other members of my group disagree with me, I
   _____ State my position and my feelings so that everything is out in the open.
   _____ Keep quiet and sit the discussion out.
6. When I get involved in an argument, I
   _____ Incorporate other members' ideas into my thinking, try to see the situation from all perspectives, and search for a creative synthesis that is better than my original position.

_____ Become more and more certain that I am correct and argue more and more strongly for my point of view.

7. Disagreement and arguments among group members are

_____ Constructive because they clear the air and enhance involvement and commitment of group members while improving the creativity and quality of decision making.

_____ Destructive because they lead to dislike, rejection, and defeat.

Compare your answers with the answers you gave to the questionnaire at the beginning of the chapter. Have you changed? How would you now describe your behavior in controversy situations? Write a description of your controversy behavior and share it with two persons who know you well and who have participated in some of the controversy exercises with you. Ask them to add to and modify your self-description.

FINAL NOTE

This chapter focused on the use of the controversy procedure to increase the creativeness and quality of a group decision making. The next chapter will focus on the constructive resolution of conflicts of interest.

9 Managing Conflict of Interests

Basic Concepts to Be Covered in This Chapter

In this chapter a number of concepts are defined and discussed. The major ones are listed below. Divide into heterogeneous pairs. Each pair is to (a) define each concept, noting the page on which it is defined and discussed and (b) ensure that both members of the pair understand the meaning of each concept. Then combine into groups of four. Compare the answers of the two pairs. If there is disagreement, look up the concept in the chapter and clarify it until all members agree on and understand the definition.

Concepts

1. Conflict of interests
2. Conflict positive group
3. Withdrawal
4. Forcing
5. Smoothing
6. Compromise
7. Negotiation
8. Distributive, win–lose negotiations
9. Integrative, problem-solving negotiations
10. Dilemma of trust
11. Dilemma of openness and honesty
12. Norm of reciprocity
13. Goal dilemma
14. Steps of integrative negotiating
15. Psychological reactance
16. Fundamental attribution error
17. Attribution theory
18. Frustration-aggression process
19. Superordinate goal
20. Self-fulfilling prophecy
21. Stereotype
22. Mediation

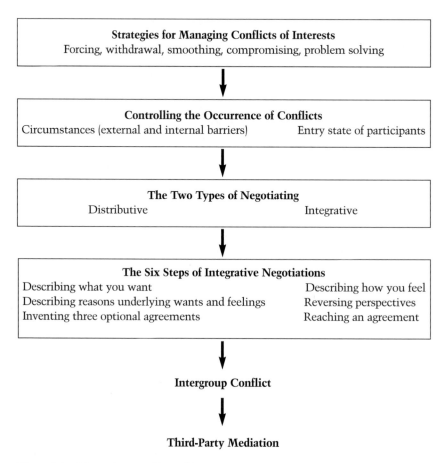

Figure 9.1   Managing conflicts of interests.

CONFLICT POSITIVE GROUP

Groups can be either conflict negative or conflict positive (Tjosvold, 1991b) (see Table 9.1). In a **conflict negative group** conflicts are suppressed and avoided and, when they occur, are managed in destructive ways. In a **conflict positive group** conflicts are encouraged and managed constructively to maximize their potential in enhancing the quality of decision making and problem solving and group life in general. Group members create, encourage, and support the possibility of conflict.

In order to create a conflict positive group, you must understand:

1. The nature of conflicts of interests.
2. The five strategies most commonly used to manage conflicts of interests.
3. The nature of distributive and integrative negotiations.
4. The steps for using integrative negotiations.
5. The nature of intergroup conflict.
6. How to apply constructive procedures to intergroup conflict.

Table 9.1 **Conflict Negative and Conflict Positive Groups**

Conflict Negative Group	Conflict Positive Group
Sees conflict as unitary.	Recognizes different types of conflicts.
Sees conflict as the problem.	Sees conflict as part of the solution.
Avoids, suppresses, contains conflicts.	Seeks out and encourages conflicts.
Believes conflict is inherently destructive.	Believes conflict is potentially constructive.
Sees no value to conflict.	Sees many values to conflict.
Conflicts create anxiety and defensiveness.	Conflicts create excitement, interest, focus.
Individuals go for a "win."	Individuals try to "solve the problem."

NATURE OF CONFLICTS OF INTERESTS

Imagine you are part of a group that has just been given five thousand dollars to spend in any way it wishes over the next two weeks. Your group has six members: Jane, Mary, Joe, John, Edythe, and yourself. Jane and Mary want to donate the money to the women's liberation movement. Edythe, John, and Joe want to give a series of parties for all their friends. You want the group to use the money for a college scholarship for your younger brother. Your group is in conflict, and it is more than just a matter of opposing opinions. There is a scarce resource (money) that the group must decide to allocate among the competing needs of the members. Because different members have vested interests in spending the money in different ways, your group has a conflict of interests.

According to the *World Book Dictionary*, a **conflict** is a fight, struggle, battle, disagreement, dispute, or quarrel. A conflict can be as small as a disagreement or as large as a war. Probably the most influential definition is that of Deutsch (1973), who states that a conflict exists whenever incompatible activities occur. An activity that is incompatible with another activity is one that prevents, blocks, or interferes with the occurrence or effectiveness of the second activity. Incompatible activities may originate in one person, between two or more people, or between two or more groups. The word *conflict* is derived from the Latin *conflictus,* meaning a "striking together with force." There are times when group members' needs and preferences "strike together" and produce disruptive effects.

We are all unique individuals with our separate needs and goals and conflicts of interests result. To understand conflicts of interests, you must first understand what wants, needs, goals, and interests are (Johnson & Johnson, 1995a) (see Table 9.2). There

Table 9.2 **Understanding Conflicts of Interests**

Concept	Definition
Want	Desire for something.
Need	Universal necessity for survival.
Goal	Desired ideal state of future affairs.
Interests	Potential benefits to be gained by achieving goals.
Conflict of interests	Actions taken by person A to achieve goals that prevent, block, or interfere with actions taken by person B to achieve goals.
Negotiation	Process by which persons who have shared and opposed interests and want to come to an agreement try to work out a settlement.

are many things each of us want. A **want** is a desire for something. Each person basically has a unique set of wants. A **need** is a necessity for survival. Needs are more universal. Every person needs to survive and reproduce (water, food, shelter, sex), belong (loving, sharing, cooperating), have power, have freedom, and have fun (Glasser, 1984). On the basis of our wants and needs we set goals. A **goal** is an ideal state of affairs that we value and are working to achieve. Our goals are related through social interdependence. When we have mutual goals we are in a cooperative relationship; when our goals are opposed we are in a competitive relationship. Our **interests** are the potential benefits to be gained by achieving our goals.

A **conflict of interests** exists when the actions of one person attempting to maximize his or her needs and benefits prevent, block, interfere with, injure, or in some way make less effective the actions of another person attempting to maximize his or her needs and benefits (Deutsch, 1973). Conflict among interests can be based on: (a) differences in needs, values, and goals; (b) scarcities of certain resources, such as power, influence, money, time, space, popularity, and position; or (c) rivalry. **Both because they occur naturally and because they are deliberately created, conflicts of interests are common.** The management of conflicts of interests is an important aspect of maintaining the cooperation among group members that is needed for group effectiveness.

CONFLICTS CAN BE DESTRUCTIVE OR CONSTRUCTIVE

When conflicts are managed constructively they have many desirable outcomes (Deutsch, 1973; Johnson, 1970; Johnson & Johnson, 1995a, 1995c). The Chinese character for crisis represents a combination of the symbol for danger and the symbol for opportunity. Inherent in any conflict is the potential for destructive or constructive outcomes. On the **destructive** side, conflicts can create anger, hostility, lasting animosity, and even violence. Conflicts can result in pain and sadness. Conflicts can end in lawsuits, divorce, and war. Destructively managed conflicts are highly costly to a group, destroying the group's effectiveness, ripping apart relationships, sabotaging work, delaying and decreasing teaching and learning efforts, and devastating individuals' commitment to the group's goals, sense of security, and personal feelings (Janz & Tjosvold, 1985). Poorly managed conflicts result in group members spending time brooding and fighting rather than teaching and learning.

Conflicts, however, carry the potential for many important **positive outcomes.** Conflicts can focus attention on problems that have to be solved and energize and motivate you to solve them. Conflicts can clarify how you need to change. Patterns of behavior that are dysfunctional are highlighted and clarified by conflicts. Conflicts can clarify what you care about and are committed to. You fight over only those wants and goals you value. You fight much more frequently and intensely with people you value and care about. The more committed you are to your goals, and the more committed you are to the other person, the more frequent and intense the conflicts. Conflicts can clarify who you are and what your values are. It is through conflicts that your identity is developed. Conflicts can help you understand who the other person is and what his or her values are. It is through conflicts that the identity of your friends and acquaintances is clarified. Conflicts (a) keep the relationship clear of irritations and resentments and (b) strengthen relationships by increasing your confidence that the two of you can resolve your disagreements. A good conflict may do a lot to resolve the small tensions of interacting with others and increase your confidence that the relationship can survive stress and adversity. A conflict a day keeps depression away! Conflicts can release anger, anxiety, insecurity, and sadness that, if kept inside, make us mentally sick. Conflicts can be fun. Being in a conflict reduces boredom, gives you new goals, motivates you to take action, and stimulates interests. Life would be incredibly boring if there were no conflict. Finally, when conflicts of interests are managed properly, they can help ensure that all group members are committed to implementing the group's decisions and that the group's problem-solving ability does not deteriorate during the decision-making process.

It is not the presence of conflicts, but the way in which they are managed, that determines whether they are destructive or constructive. **Conflicts are constructive to the extent that they:**

1. Result in an agreement that allows all participants to achieve their goals. The agreement maximizes joint outcomes, benefits everyone, and is in all participants' best interests.
2. Strengthen the relationship among participants by increasing their liking, respect, and trust for each other.
3. Increase participants' ability to resolve future conflicts with each other constructively.

Exercise 9.1: Your Conflict Strategies

Different persons learn different ways of managing conflicts. The strategies you use to manage conflicts may be quite different from those used by your friends and acquaintances. This exercise gives you an opportunity to increase your awareness of what conflict strategies you use and how they compare with the strategies used by others. The procedure is as follows:

1. With your classmates, form groups of six. Make sure you know the other members of the group. Do not join a group of strangers.
2. Working by yourself, complete the following questionnaire.
3. Working by yourself, read the accompanying discussion of conflict strategies. Then make five slips of paper. Write the names of the other five members of your group on the slips of paper, one name to a slip.
4. On each slip of paper write the conflict strategy that best fits the actions of the person named.
5. After all group members are finished, pass out your slips of paper to the persons whose names are on them. In turn, you should end up with five slips of paper, each containing a description of your conflict style as seen by another group member. Likewise, each member of your group should end up with five slips of paper describing his or her conflict strategy.
6. Score your questionnaire, using the table that follows the discussion of conflict strategies. Rank the five conflict strategies from the one you use the most to the one you use the least. This will give you an indication of how you see your own conflict strategy. The second most frequently used strategy is your backup strategy, the one you use if your first one fails.
7. After drawing names to see who goes first, one member describes the results of his or her questionnaire. This is the member's view of his or her own conflict strategies. The

member then reads each of the five slips of paper on which are written the views of the group members about his or her conflict strategy. Next he or she asks group members to give specific examples of how they have seen him or her act in conflicts. The group members should use the rules for constructive feedback. The person to the left of the first member repeats this procedure, and so on around the group.

8. Each group discusses the strengths and weaknesses of each of the conflict strategies

HOW YOU ACT IN CONFLICTS

The proverbs listed below can be thought of as descriptions of some of the different strategies for resolving conflicts. Proverbs state traditional wisdom, and these proverbs reflect traditional wisdom for resolving conflicts. Read each of the proverbs carefully. Using the following scale, indicate how typical each proverb is of your actions in a conflict.

5 = very typical of the way I act in a conflict
4 = frequently typical of the way I act in a conflict
3 = sometimes typical of the way I act in a conflict
2 = seldom typical of the way I act in a conflict
1 = never typical of the way I act in a conflict

_____ 1. It is easier to refrain than to retreat from a quarrel.
_____ 2. If you cannot make a person think as you do, make him or her do as you think.
_____ 3. Soft words win hard hearts.
_____ 4. You scratch my back, I'll scratch yours.
_____ 5. Come now and let us reason together.
_____ 6. When two quarrel, the person who keeps silent first is the most praiseworthy.
_____ 7. Might overcomes right.
_____ 8. Smooth words make smooth ways.
_____ 9. Better half a loaf than no bread at all.
_____ 10. Truth lies in knowledge, not in majority opinion.
_____ 11. He who fights and runs away lives to fight another day.
_____ 12. He hath conquered well that hath made his enemies flee.
_____ 13. Kill your enemies with kindness.
_____ 14. A fair exchange brings no quarrel.
_____ 15. No person has the final answer but every person has a piece to contribute.
_____ 16. Stay away from people who disagree with you.
_____ 17. Fields are won by those who believe in winning.
_____ 18. Kind words are worth much and cost little.
_____ 19. Tit for tat is fair play.
_____ 20. Only the person who is willing to give up his or her monopoly on truth can ever profit from the truths that others hold.
_____ 21. Avoid quarrelsome people as they will only make your life miserable.
_____ 22. A person who will not flee will make others flee.
_____ 23. Soft words ensure harmony.
_____ 24. One gift for another makes good friends.
_____ 25. Bring your conflicts into the open and face them directly; only then will the best solution be discovered.
_____ 26. The best way of handling conflicts is to avoid them.
_____ 27. Put your foot down where you mean to stand.
_____ 28. Gentleness will triumph over anger.
_____ 29. Getting part of what you want is better than not getting anything at all.

_____ 30. Frankness, honesty, and trust will move mountains.
_____ 31. There is nothing so important you have to fight for it.
_____ 32. There are two kinds of people in the world, the winners and the losers.
_____ 33. When one hits you with a stone, hit him or her with a piece of cotton.
_____ 34. When both give in halfway, a fair settlement is achieved.
_____ 35. By digging and digging, the truth is discovered.

Scoring

Withdrawing	*Forcing*	*Smoothing*	*Compromising*	*Problem Solving*
_____ 1.	_____ 2.	_____ 3.	_____ 4.	_____ 5.
_____ 6.	_____ 7.	_____ 8.	_____ 9.	_____ 10.
_____ 11.	_____ 12.	_____ 13.	_____ 14.	_____ 15.
_____ 16.	_____ 17.	_____ 18.	_____ 19.	_____ 20.
_____ 21.	_____ 22.	_____ 23.	_____ 24.	_____ 25.
_____ 26.	_____ 27.	_____ 28.	_____ 29.	_____ 30.
_____ 31.	_____ 32.	_____ 33.	_____ 34.	_____ 35.
_____ Total	_____ Total	_____ Total	_____ Total	_____ Total

The higher the total score for each conflict strategy, the more frequently you tend to use that strategy. The lower the total score for each conflict strategy, the less frequently you tend to use that strategy.

CONFLICT STRATEGIES: WHAT ARE YOU LIKE?

Dealing with a conflict of interests is like going swimming in a cold lake. Some people like to test the water, stick their foot in, and enter slowly. Such people want to get used to the cold gradually. Other people like to take a running start and leap in. They want to get the cold shock over quickly. Similarly, different people use different strategies for managing conflicts. Usually, we learn these strategies in childhood so that later they seem to function automatically on a "preconscious" level. We just do whatever seems to come naturally. But we do have a personal strategy and, because it was learned, we can always change it by learning new and more effective ways of managing conflicts.

When we become engaged in a conflict, we have to take two major, dual concerns into account (Johnson & Johnson, 1995a):

1. **Reaching an agreement that satisfies our needs and meets our goals.** We are in conflict because we have a goal or interests that conflicts with another person's goal or interests. Our goal may be placed on a continuum between being of little importance to being highly important.
2. **Maintaining an appropriate relationship with the other person.** Some relationships are temporary whereas some are permanent. Our relationship with the other person may be placed on a continuum between being of little importance to being highly important.

The dual concern model of conflict resolution has its origins in Blake and Mouton's (1964) managerial grid and has been articulated by several theorists (Cosier & Ruble, 1981; Filley, 1975; Johnson, 1991; Pruitt & Rubin, 1986; Rahim, 1983; Thomas, 1976). Other labels are sometimes given to the two concerns, such as "concern for self" and "concern for other."

In a conflict of interests, how you behave depends on how important your goals are to you and how important you perceive the relationship to be. Given these two concerns, there are five basic strategies (see Figure 9.2) that may be used to manage conflicts:

1. **The Owl (Problem-Solving Negotiations):** Owls highly value their own goals and relationships. When both the goal and the relationship are highly important to you, you initiate problem-solving negotiations to resolve the conflict. Solutions are sought that ensure both you and the other person fully achieve your goals and resolve any tensions and negative feelings between the two of you. This strategy requires risky moves, such as revealing your underlying interests while expecting the other to do the same.

2. **The Teddy Bear (Smoothing):** To teddy bears the relationship is of great importance whereas their own goals are of little importance. When the goal is of no importance to you but the relationship is of high importance, you give up your goals in order to maintain the relationship at the highest quality possible. When you think the other person's interests are much stronger or important than yours, you smooth and give the other person his or her way.

3. **The Shark (Forcing or Win–Lose Negotiations):** Sharks try to overpower opponents by forcing them to give in. When the goal is very important but the relationship is not, you seek to achieve your goal by forcing or persuading the other to yield. You compete for a win. Tactics used to force the other to yield include making threats, imposing penalties that will be withdrawn if the other concedes, and taking preemptive actions designed to resolve the conflict without the other's consent (such as taking a book home that the other insists is his). Tactics to persuade the other to yield include presenting persuasive arguments, imposing a deadline, committing oneself to an "unalterable" position, or making demands that far exceed what is actually acceptable.

4. **The Fox (Compromising):** Foxes are moderately concerned with their own goals and their relationships with others. When both the goal and the relationship are moderately important to you, and it appears that both you and the other person cannot get what you want, you may need to give up part of your goals and sacrifice part of the relationship in order to reach an agreement. Compromising may be meeting in the middle so each gets half or flipping a coin to let chance decide who will get his or her way. Compromising is often used when disputants wish to engage in problem-solving negotiations but do not have the time to do so.

5. **The Turtle (Withdrawing):** Turtles withdraw into their shells to avoid conflicts. When the goal is not important and you do not need to keep a relationship with the other person, you may wish to give up both your goals and the relationship and avoid the issue and the other person. Avoiding a hostile stranger, for example, may be the best thing to do. Sometimes you may wish to withdraw from a conflict until you and the other person have calmed down and are in control of your feelings.

In using these strategies there are five important points to consider. **First, to be competent in managing conflicts, you must be able to engage competently in each strategy.** You need to practice all five strategies until they are thoroughly mastered. You do not want to be an overspecialized dinosaur who can deal with conflict in only one way. Each strategy is appropriate under a certain set of conditions and, based on the dual concerns of one's goals and the relationship with the other person, you choose the conflict strategy appropriate to the situation.

Second, some of the strategies require the participation of the other disputant and some may be enacted alone. You can give up your goals by using withdrawing and smoothing no matter what the other disputant does. When you try to achieve your goals by using forcing, compromising, and problem solving, the other disputant has to participate in the process.

Third, the strategies tend to be somewhat incompatible in the sense that choosing one of them makes choosing the others less likely. Though sometimes used in combination (temporarily withdrawing before initiating problem-solving negotiations), withdrawing implies lack of commitment to one's goals, whereas negotiating implies high commitment to one's goals. Forcing implies low commitment to the relationship whereas smoothing implies high commitment to the relationship. Essentially, the five strategies are independent from each other and when you engage in one the likelihood of your being able to switch effectively to another is not high.

Fourth, certain strategies may deteriorate into other strategies. When you try to withdraw, and the other disputant pursues you and will not allow you to withdraw, you may respond with forcing. When you try to initiate problem-solving negotiations and the other disputant responds with forcing, you may reciprocate by engaging in win–lose tactics. When time is short, problem-solving negotiations may deteriorate into compromising.

Fifth, whether problem-solving or win–lose negotiations are initiated depends on your perception of the future of the relationship. When conflicts arise, the potential short-term gains must be weighed against potential long-term losses. When you perceive the relationship as being unimportant, you may go for the "win" by attempting to force the other person to capitulate or give in. The relationship may be perceived as unimportant because (a) there will be only one or a few interactions or (b) you are so angry at the other person that only the present matters. When you perceive the relationship as being important, then you will try to solve the problem in a way that achieves the other person's goals as well as your own. The relationship is perceived to be important because it is ongoing and long-term or there are strong positive emotions (such as liking and respect) that bond you to the other person.

The shadow of the future looms largest when interactions among individuals are durable and frequent. Durability ensures that individuals will not easily forget how they have treated, and been treated by, each other in the future. **Frequency** promotes stability by making the consequences of today's actions more salient for tomorrow's dealings. When individuals realize they will work with each other frequently and for a long period of time, they see that the long-term benefits of cooperation outweigh the short-term benefits of taking advantage of the other person. In ongoing relationships, the future outweighs the present so that the quality of the relationship is more important than the outcome of any particular negotiation. In schools, all relationships are long-term and, therefore, the shadow of the future is ever present.

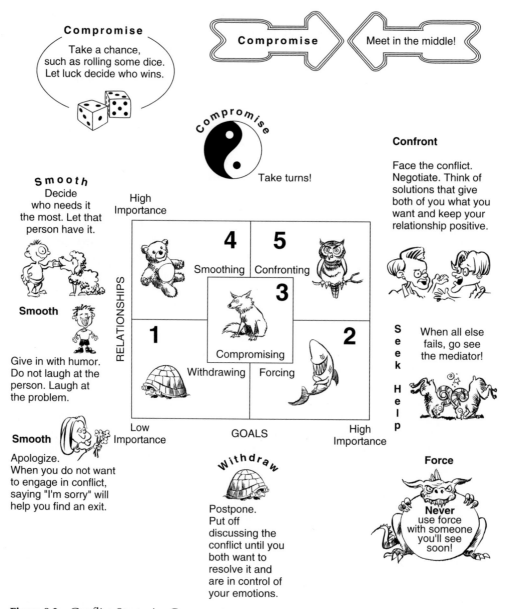

Compromise
Take a chance, such as rolling some dice. Let luck decide who wins.

Compromise Meet in the middle!

Compromise Take turns!

Confront

Face the conflict. Negotiate. Think of solutions that give both of you what you want and keep your relationship positive.

Smooth
Decide who needs it the most. Let that person have it.

Smooth
Give in with humor. Do not laugh at the person. Laugh at the problem.

Smooth
Apologize. When you do not want to engage in conflict, saying "I'm sorry" will help you find an exit.

High Importance

RELATIONSHIPS

4 Smoothing

5 Confronting

3 Compromising

1 Withdrawing

2 Forcing

Low Importance

GOALS

High Importance

Seek Help
When all else fails, go see the mediator!

Withdraw
Postpone. Put off discussing the conflict until you both want to resolve it and are in control of your emotions.

Force
Never use force with someone you'll see soon!

Figure 9.2 Conflict Strategies Game
Reprinted by permission: Johnson, D. W., & Johnson, R. (1995a). *Teaching Students to be Peacemakers.* (3rd Ed.) Edina, MN: Interactive Book Company.

Field studies have found problem solving to be strongly associated with constructive resolution of conflicts and high organizational performance whereas forcing the other person to accept one's position was strongly associated with ineffective conflict management (Burke, 1969, 1970; Lawrence & Lorsch, 1967). Experimental studies have found that high concern about both one's own and the other's outcomes produced high joint outcomes;

high concern about one's own outcomes but low concern about the other's outcomes tended to result in attempts to dominate and persuade; low concern about one's own outcomes but high concern about the other's outcomes resulted in low joint benefit (Ben-Yoav & Pruitt, 1984a, 1984b; Carnevale & Keenan, 1990; Pruitt & Syna, 1983).

CONTROLLING THE OCCURRENCE OF CONFLICTS

Not everything that is faced can be changed but
Nothing can be changed until it is faced.

James Baldwin

When a conflict of interests arises it is usually advisable to face and resolve it. There are times, however, when you may wish to postpone the occurrence of a conflict. You can control the occurrence of a conflict when you understand (a) the circumstances that brought about the conflict and (b) the entry state of the participants. The **circumstances** that surround the conflict include both the barriers to the beginning of negotiations and the events that trigger expressions (Walton, 1987). **Internal barriers** include negative attitudes, values, fears, anxieties, and habitual patterns of avoiding conflict. **External barriers** may include task requirements, group norms for avoiding conflict, pressure to maintain a congenial public image, and faulty perceptions of one's vulnerability and others' strength. Physical separation is a frequently used barrier to the expression of conflicts of interests. Placing members in different locations, avoiding being in the same room with certain other members, and removing a member from the group, can all suppress a conflict of interests. A **triggering event** may be as simple as two group members being physically near each other or as complex as two members being in competition. Negative remarks, sarcasm, and criticism on sensitive points are common triggering events, as is the feeling of being deprived, neglected, or ignored. Some events may trigger a destructive cycle of conflict and others may trigger problem solving; group members will want to maximize the latter type of triggering event.

The diagnosis of a conflict involves discovering (a) the barriers to negotiation and (b) what triggers open expression of the conflict. From such knowledge group members can choose the time and place for negotiations. If an appropriate time is not immediately available, the barriers to expressing the conflict can be increased and the triggering events can be decreased in order to avoid the conflict temporarily. To **avoid** the conflict, you remove the triggering events and build up the barriers to negotiations. To **resolve** the conflict, you increase the frequency of the triggering events and decrease the barriers to negotiations.

The second factor in controlling the occurrence of a conflict is the entry state of the disputants. The **entry state** of a group member is that person's ability to deal constructively with the conflict. Members' level of self-awareness, their ability to control their behavior, their skills in communicating and in other ways being interpersonally effective (see Johnson, 2000), their ability to withstand stress, and their ability to incorporate their strengths in constructive conflict behavior are all important aspects of their entry state. Your opponent may be too anxious, defensive, or psychologically unstable to negotiate effectively, or his or her motivation to change may be very low. Group support and consultation can raise the entry state of each participant.

Not every conflict of interest is negotiable. It is a mistake to assume that you can always openly negotiate the resolution of a conflict. There are times when conflicts are better avoided. Usually, however, through careful attention to the entry state of participants and the circumstances that trigger or prevent a conflict, a time optimal for constructive resolution can be chosen.

THE NATURE OF NEGOTIATIONS

Negotiation is woven into the daily fabric of our lives. Many individuals, however, do not know how to negotiate and those who do often negotiate very poorly. Negotiating with skill and grace is not easy. It must be learned. **Negotiation** is a process by which persons who have shared and opposed interests and want to come to an agreement try to work out a settlement (Johnson & Johnson, 1995a). Negotiations are aimed at achieving an agreement that specifies what each group member gives to and receives from each other. Negotiation may involve **distributive issues,** where one member benefits only if the opponent agrees to make a concession, or **integrative issues,** where the two members are working together to seek a solution that will benefit everyone. You spend a great deal of time negotiating, even when you (a) do not think of yourself as doing so and (b) are not fully aware that negotiations are taking place. You can tell you are negotiating by using the following checklist:

_____ Is there another person involved and are you dependent on each other for information (about what is a reasonable agreement) and an agreement (you get what you want only if the other person agrees and vice versa)?
_____ Are both cooperative elements (we both wish to reach an agreement) and competitive elements (we both wish the agreement to be as favorable to ourselves as possible) present in the situation?
_____ Are both primary and secondary gains a concern?
_____ Are there contractual norms on how negotiation should be conducted?
_____ Is there a beginning, a middle, and an end?
_____ Do you wish to propose an agreement that is favorable to yourself but not so one-sided that it drives the other away from negotiations?

There are several important points to be made about negotiations. The *first* is that there are three types of interdependence inherent in any negotiations: participation interdependence, outcome interdependence, and information interdependence. **Participation interdependence** is that it takes at least two to negotiate, whether it is two group members, two groups, two organizations, or two nations. You cannot negotiate by yourself. It takes the consent and participation of others. **Outcome interdependence** exists as an agreement that can be reached only with the cooperation of the other disputant. Both members must commit themselves to an agreement and, therefore, each is dependent upon the other for the outcome. All negotiating is aimed at achieving certain outcomes for oneself, but those outcomes are possible only if the other negotiator agrees to them. **Information dependence** exists because negotiators are dependent upon each other for information about a possible agreement. Such information can be secured in one of two ways: Negotiators can openly and honestly share their preferences, needs, and expectations, or they can deduce what the other wants from his or her behavior during the negotiations. This is a complicated issue because negotiators often do not know what their own expectations should be until they learn what the other negotiator's expectations are. To the point that negotiators know both what the other wants and what is the least the other will accept, they will be able to develop an effective negotiating position. Information dependence sets up two dilemmas: the dilemma of trust and the dilemma of honesty and openness. The **dilemma of trust** involves a choice about whether to believe the other negotiator. To believe the other negotiator is to risk potential exploitation. Disbelieving the other negotiator reduces the possibility of any agreement being reached. The **dilemma of honesty and openness** involves the risk of either being exploited for disclosing too much too quickly or seriously damaging the negotiating relationship by refusing to disclose information and thereby seeming deceitful or distrusting. Both of these dilemmas are the result of information dependence.

Second, within any negotiations there are both cooperative and competitive elements. The mixed-motive situation is created by the desire to reach an agreement and the desire to make that agreement as favorable to oneself as possible (see Figure 9.3). The two motives can seriously interfere with each other. The balance between the cooperative and competitive elements determine how negotiations are conducted.

Third, both primary and secondary gains must be attended to in negotiations. The **primary gain** is determined by the nature of the agreement: The more favorable the agreement is to a member's short-term goals, the greater the primary gain for her. The **secondary gain** is determined by factors influencing the effectiveness of the working relationship between the disputants, the impact of an angry and revengeful person on the quality of one's life, the future effectiveness of the group, and relatively unimportant benefits to oneself. The more effective the group, the more the member's long-term goals will be met, and therefore the greater the long-term gain for her. Consequently, in negotiating a resolution to a conflict a group member has to be concerned not only with what is more desirable for him or her in the short term but also with what is most desirable for improving the effectiveness of the group, relationships with group members, and other possible future outcomes.

Fourth, during negotiations **contractual norms** are developed that spell out the groundrules for conducting the negotiations and managing the difficulties involved in reaching an agreement. Two common norms are the **norm of reciprocity** (a negotiator should return the same benefit or harm given him or her by the other negotiator) and the **norm of equity** (the benefits received or the costs assessed by the negotiators should be equal).   .

Fifth, negotiations have important time dimensions. There is a beginning, a middle, and an end. The strategies and tactics used to initiate negotiations, exchange proposals and information, and precipitate an agreement can be quite different and sometimes contradictory.

Sixth, in negotiations disputants face a **goal dilemma:** how to reach an agreement favorable to oneself but not so one-sided that the other negotiator will refuse to agree. In resolving the goal dilemma, negotiators must decide on a "reasonable" proposal, one that not only will get the most for oneself but also will have a good chance of being acceptable to the other. Inasmuch as there is rarely any obvious "correct" agreement, each must decide during the negotiations what is a reasonable outcome for oneself and for the other negotiator.

Figure 9.3 Integrative negotiations.

Negotiating skills are one of your keys to success in life. There is no overstating the importance of being able to negotiate well. A recent survey conducted for Accountemps (a large accounting, bookkeeping, and data processing temporary personnel service that is a division of Robert Half International Inc.) of vice presidents and personnel directors of 100 of the nation's 1,000 largest corporations found that the people who manage America's leading corporations spend over 4 working weeks a year dealing with the problems caused by employees who cannot resolve their conflicts with each other. In answer to the question "What percent of management time is spent dealing with conflicts among employees?" respondents revealed that executives spend an average of 9.2% of their time or, based on a 40-hour week, 4.6 weeks a year attempting to deal with employee conflicts and the difficulties and disruptions they cause. In addition to taking up valuable management time, employee conflicts can seriously reduce any company's productivity and its ability to compete effectively in the marketplace. Knowing how to negotiate constructive resolutions to conflicts of interests is an essential skill for any career.

Exercise 9.2: *Making a Profit*

The purpose of this exercise is to give participants an opportunity to negotiate a profit–loss situation so that they may examine the dynamics of bargaining. The exercise can be conducted in less than an hour. The procedure for the coordinator is as follows:

1. Introduce the exercise as an opportunity to study the dynamics of negotiation between two persons with different interests. The negotiation is between a buyer and a seller in a wholesale market. Explain that the exercise has three parts: (a) preparing for negotiations, (b) negotiating, and (c) discussing what happened in negotiations.
2. Divide the class into heterogeneous groups of four. Divide each group into two pairs. Assign one pair the role of buyers and the other pair the role of sellers. Give each pair the appropriate profit schedule (see page 588 in the Appendix). *Their first task is to prepare for negotiations.* Both pair members need to (a) understand the profit schedule so that they know which agreements are most and least profitable for them and (b) are ready to negotiate an agreement that is beneficial to them. On the profit schedule are three commodities (oil, gas, coal). The nine prices for each commodity are represented by the letters A to I. Next to each price is the profit the person would make. The following questions may clarify whether pair members understand the profit schedule:
   a. What is your most important commodity? _____
   b. What is your least important commodity? _____
   c. For price B for coal, what would your profit be? _____
   d. For price D for gas, what would your profit be? _____
   Make sure participants understand that all communication during negotiations will be verbal only—they cannot show their profit schedules to the opposing negotiator.
3. One member of each pair switches chairs so that a buyer is facing a seller. *The second task is to negotiate one agreement that includes a price for each of the three commodities* (oil, gas, coal), such as AAA, III, or BDC. Each person is expected to make and respond to proposed agreements. They can say anything they want to each other, but they may not show each other their profit schedule. When an agreement is reached, write it down and sign it. Each negotiator then writes down (without asking each other) (a) which commodity was most important to the opponent and (b) which commodity was least important to the opponent.

4. The two pairs combine into a group of four and complete *The third task* by discussing the following questions:
   a. What were the agreements reached by the members of the group? Each person writes down: (1) the buyer's total profit, (2) the seller's total profit, and (3) the joint profit (the buyer's and seller's profits added together).
   b. How did negotiators communicate information about their profit schedule, and how did they learn about the profit schedule of their opponent? Were their perceptions of which commodities were most and least important to their opponent correct? Was information exchange direct (did buyer and seller accurately tell each other their profit schedules)? Or was it indirect (did they deduce each other's profit schedule by comparing each other's responses to different package offers)?
   c. Did negotiators try to win (maximize own profit at other's expense) or solve the problem (maximize joint profit)?
   d. Did the negotiators make package deals or did they negotiate the commodities one at a time?
   e. What conclusions can the group make about negotiations on the basis of their experience and discussion?
5. Have each group share its conclusions with the rest of the class.

Exercise 9.3: Group-Member Excellence

The objective of this exercise is to examine the dynamics of negotiation among members of the same group. The exercise can be conducted in less than one hour. The procedure for the coordinator is as follows:

1. Randomly divide the class into groups of seven: six participants and one observer. You need at least two groups.
2. For each group, make up six bags of marbles (one for each participating member) consisting of varied colors (see the following table).

Distribution of Marbles to the Six Negotiators

Member	Red	Blue	Green	White
1	4	3	2	1
2	1	4	3	2
3	2	1	4	3
4	3	2	1	4
5	3	3	2	2
6	2	2	3	3

3. From each group, collect one dollar from each member (excluding the observer). The money will be awarded to group members who negotiate successfully and achieve the assigned goal.
4. Distribute the instructions:
   a. One copy of the general instruction sheet to all group members (six negotiators and one observer).
   b. One copy of the observers' instructions to each observer.
   c. Without letting the groups know that they are getting different instructions, give half of the groups a copy of the "win-lose negotiation instructions" and the other half a copy of the "problem-solving negotiation instructions."

5. Meet with the observers to make sure they understand their responsibilities.
6. Distribute a bag of marbles to each group member. Each member has ten marbles. The number of each color varies from member to member.
7. **Negotiations Task:** "*The goal of negotiations is to collect fifteen marbles of the same color.* In addition, for each marble over fifteen you will receive a 10% bonus. Thus, if you turn in eighteen green marbles, you will receive the regular award for fifteen marbles plus thirty percent more. You may only negotiate with members of your group." Answer any questions members have about the exercise. Announce that participants have ten minutes to achieve the goal. Give the signal to begin.
8. **Self-Monitoring Task:** After ten minutes announce, "Time is up! Stop negotiating. Write down *two adjectives* that describe your feelings during the negotiations."
9. Determine how many negotiators succeeded in collecting fifteen marbles of the same color. Determine bonuses for collecting more than fifteen. Divide the money accordingly. If no group member collected fifteen marbles, the money goes into a class fund to purchase food for the next class session.
10. **Small Group Processing:**
    a. In each group the observer reports his or her observations. Members are to discuss and summarize the experience:
       (1) What negotiation strategies were used?
       (2) How did members react to each other's strategies?
       (3) How successful was each strategy?
       (4) How often did coalitions form in which two or more members pooled their marbles and negotiated with other members as a bloc?
       (5) What side agreements were made about the money?
       (6) Did any member collect two colors of marbles in order to be flexible until the last few minutes? What other interesting strategies were used?
    b. Record the adjectives written down by each member.
    c. Summarize (1) members' negotiation strategies, their success, and the reactions of groupmates; (2) members' adjectives; and (3) conclusions group members draw from the experience. Plan how to make a five-minute presentation of your summary to the class as a whole.
11. **Whole Class Processing:**
    a. Have each group (1) share its instructions for negotiation (problem solving or win–lose) and (2) present a five-minute summary of members' experiences and conclusions. Record the results on the following table.

Group	Problem-Solving Instructions		Win–Lose Instructions	
	# Successful	**Adjectives**	**# Successful**	**Adjectives**
1				
2				
3				
4				
5				
6				
Total				

Conclusions: _____

_____

    b. Ask participants to reflect on the information from all the groups and share their conclusions about the effectiveness of the problem-solving and win-lose strategies. Summarize the major points of the discussion.

12. Have participants read the subsequent sections on negotiation and compare their conclusions about the exercise with the material in those sections.

GENERAL INSTRUCTIONS

Systems for evaluating the performance of group members have many shortcomings. Different members behave in different ways to accomplish their objectives. These variations make most comparisons difficult and unfair. To overcome this problem, we have developed a simulation. All members will participate (except for the observer). From your behavior in this exercise we will be able to tell if you are a poor, average, good, or excellent group member. The exercise provides an impartial and equal measure of your performance.

    You are being issued a bag containing ten marbles of four different colors: red, green, blue, and white. Each negotiator has ten marbles but different negotiators have different numbers of each color (you may have two white marbles but another member may have four). *Your goal is to collect fifteen marbles of the same color. You will receive a 10% bonus for each marble over the fifteen that you collect.* Thus, if you collect eighteen green marbles, you will receive the regular award for fifteen marbles *plus* 30% more. The money collected will be divided among the group members who succeed in obtaining fifteen or more marbles.

    You have ten minutes to negotiate with other members of your group (you may not negotiate with members of the other group).

OBSERVERS' INSTRUCTIONS

As an observer your task is to obtain as much information about the interaction among group members as possible. Concentrate on:

1. What strategies of negotiation group members are using.
2. How group members are reacting to each other's strategies.
3. How successful the strategies are.

Observations of any other aspect of group behavior will also be helpful. Write down your observations. Make as many observations as possible.

INSTRUCTIONS FOR WIN–LOSE NEGOTIATION

In this exercise your group is to adopt a win–lose negotiation strategy in which each member will try to obtain more marbles of the same color than anyone else. Obviously, some of the members of your group are going to win and some are going to lose. You want to be a winner. Be a tough negotiator. Make extreme opening offers and compromise slowly. Hide as much information from other group members as you can. Trust no one. Say whatever will be helpful in negotiating with the other members. During the negotiations try to achieve the best outcome for yourself, and use your power and skill in any way that helps you do so. Remember, if you keep the other group members from winning, you will increase your own chances of winning.

INSTRUCTIONS FOR PROBLEM-SOLVING NEGOTIATION

In this exercise your group is to adopt a problem-solving negotiation strategy in which members try to find a creative solution to the problem that benefits as many members as possible. In negotiating with other group members, communicate openly and honestly about what you want and try to identify as many ways as possible to maximize joint gain. Search for a rational agreement that ensures both your own and other group members' success. Avoid all threats and deceptions, which might destroy trust among group members. The problem is to figure out how as many group members as possible can achieve the goal.

TWO TYPES OF NEGOTIATING

Storms are a natural and unavoidable aspect of Earth's weather system. Storms range in intensity from rainstorms to hurricanes. Some are accompanied by gentle rain, others by thunder and lightning. Similarly, interpersonal storms are a natural and unavoidable aspect of life within groups that vary in intensity from mild to severe. To resolve them you may wish to negotiate. When you use negotiations to resolve a conflict of interests, you have a choice. You can go for a "win" by acting like a shark and using forcing or distributive procedures, or you can go for solving the problem in a mutually beneficial way by acting like an owl and using integrative or problem-solving procedures. Both are appropriate under certain circumstances (see Table 9.3).

Distributive Negotiations: Win–Lose Negotiations

People . . . are trying to either shun conflict or crush it. Neither strategy is working. Avoidance and force only raise the level of conflict . . . They have become parts of the problem rather than the solution.

DeCecco and Richards, 1974

When the negotiation is with a person whose continued goodwill and cooperation is not necessary (such as a car salesperson), then you negotiate to win (this means the other person loses). In **distributive negotiations** the goal is to maximize your outcomes while minimizing the other person's outcomes. You try to reach an agreement more favorable to you than to the other person. You go for the win when your wants, needs, and goals are important and you have a temporary, ad hoc relationship with the other person. In some cultures, where bargaining is a way of life, this type of negotiating is both recreation and an art form.

In distributive negotiations a sequence of behavior occurs in which one party presents a proposal, the other evaluates it and presents a counterproposal, the first party replies with a modified proposal, and so on until a settlement is reached (Chertkoff & Esser, 1976; Johnson, 1974; Johnson & Johnson, 1995a; Rubin, Pruitt, & Kim, 1994; Walton & McKersie, 1965). The negotiators use this sequence of behaviors to obtain information that helps resolve the dilemma of goals. On the basis of the other party's opening offer, the proposals one receives, and the counterproposals one offers, a negotiator can obtain an idea as to what sort of settlement the person will agree to. A common win–lose negotiating pattern is for both negotiators to set a relatively high but tentative goal at first; they can then change it on the basis of the other person's reactions and counterproposals. This sequence of behaviors, which allows one negotiator to assess the second negotiator's points of potential settlement, can also be used to influence the second negotiator's assessment of the first's points of potential settlement. Through their opening offers and their counterproposals, negotiators can influence the other's expectations

Table 9.3   **The Two Types of Negotiating Strategies**

Distributive (Win–Lose)	Integrative (Problem Solving)
Presenting an opening offer very favorable to oneself and refusing to modify that position.	Describing what you want.
Gathering information about what the other considers a "reasonable" agreement from the other's opening offer and proposals.	Describing how you feel.
Continually pointing out the validity of one's own position and the incorrectness of the other person's.	Describing reasons underlying wants and feelings.
Using a combination of threats and promises to convince the other person that he or she has to accept one's offer.	Reversing perspectives.
Committing oneself to a position in such a way that if an agreement is to be reached, the other person has to agree to one's terms.	Inventing at least three optional agreements that maximize joint outcomes.
Agreeing if one's benefits are greater than the other's or if no better outcome is available elsewhere.	Choose one alternative and agree.

of what they consider a "reasonable" agreement. Ideally, a win–lose negotiator would like to obtain the maximal information about the other's preferences while disclosing the minimal, or misleading, information about her own preferences. Helpful hints for engaging in distributive negotiations, therefore, are:

1. Identify triggering events and barriers to negotiations. Trigger the conflict at a moment when it is most advantageous to you and least advantageous to your opponent.
2. **Make an extreme opening offer** (if you are willing to pay $1,500, offer $500) to (a) establish a negotiating range skewed in your favor, (b) influence the other's expectations about one's anticipated minimal terms (do not let the other person know how much you are willing to pay), (c) change the other's beliefs about his or her minimum terms, and (d) create an impression of "toughness." Perceptions of toughness have considerable influence on determining how far a negotiator thinks he can push an opposing negotiator (that is, what terms the opponent will finally agree to).
3. **Compromise slowly** (try to get the other person to compromise first). A slow rate of compromise is aimed at creating an image of toughness and influencing the opponent's expectations as to (a) what a reasonable outcome is for him or her and (b) what one's expectations of a reasonable outcome are. As the opponent **reconnoiters the negotiating range** for possible points of agreement, he or she seeks information to reduce the uncertainty as to what the agreement might be. Every action a negotiator makes affects the opponent's conclusions about what to propose next.
4. **Use threats, promises, sticking doggedly to a committed position, and arguments** to (a) coerce and entice the opponent to accept one's proposal, (b) convince the other person what he or she wants is unreasonable and unattainable, and (c) change the other's evaluation of how many concessions are required to reach

an agreement. A **threat** states that if the other negotiator performs an undesired act, you will harm him or her. A **promise** states that if the other negotiator performs a desired act, you will provide benefits. A **preemptive action** is designed to resolve the conflict without the other's consent (such as taking up residence on a disputed piece of land). A **persuasive argument** is pointing out the validity of your position and the incorrectness of the other's. **Committing oneself to an "unalterable" position** is making it clear that it is the other negotiator who has the last chance of avoiding "no agreement." Plugging up your ears until the other negotiator says yes is an example.

5. **Be ready to walk away with no agreement.** Every negotiator is faced with a continual threefold choice of (a) accepting the available terms for agreement, (b) trying to improve the available terms through further negotiation, and (c) discontinuing negotiations without agreement and with no intention of resuming them. If you cannot walk away with no agreement, you must accept what the opponent is willing to give.

For a goal-oriented group a win–lose strategy of negotiation has some fundamental shortcomings. Although it will often result in more favorable primary gains for some group members, the damage it can cause to future cooperation among group members significantly reduces its secondary gains. Because a win–lose strategy emphasizes power inequalities, it undermines trust, inhibits dialogue and communication, and diminishes the likelihood that the conflict will be resolved constructively. Attempts to create cooperative relations between negotiators are more effective if their power is equal (Deutsch, 1973). Walton (1987) notes that **when power is unequally distributed the low-power person will automatically distrust the high-power person because he or she knows that those with power have a tendency to use it for their own interests.** Usually, the greater the difference in power, the more negative the attitudes towards the high-power person and the less likely the low-power person is to present his or her views in a clear and forceful way. The high-power person, on the other hand, tends to underestimate the low-power person's positive intent and will react with hostility whenever the low-power person tries to reduce his or her power. Even when an agreement is reached, losers have little motivation to carry out the actions agreed upon, resent the winner, and often try to sabotage the agreement. The winner finds it hard to enforce the agreement. Damage to interpersonal relationships results as winners and losers are often hostile towards each other.

In going for the win you assume that the relationship is unimportant and has no future. This is often a mistake. There are very few times in your life when you negotiate with someone you will never interact with again. If you go for a win and then have to face the same person the next day, sooner or later the other person gets revenge! In most situations, therefore, you want to try to resolve the conflict by maximizing joint outcomes. A famous example is the dispute between Egypt and Israel. When Egypt and Israel sat down to negotiate at Camp David in October 1978, it appeared that they had before them an intractable conflict. Egypt demanded the immediate return of the entire Sinai Peninsula; Israel, which had occupied the Sinai since the 1967 Middle East war, refused to return an inch of this land. Efforts to reach agreement, including the proposal of a compromise in which each nation would retain half of the Sinai, proved completely unacceptable to both sides. As long as the dispute was defined in terms of what percentage of the land each side would control, no agreement could be reached. Once both realized that what Israel really cared about was the security that the land offered, whereas Egypt was primarily interested in sovereignty over it, the stalemate was broken. The two countries were then able to reach an integrative solution: Israel would return the Sinai to Egypt in exchange for assurances of a demilitarized zone and Israeli air bases in the Sinai.

Integrative Negotiations: Negotiating to Solve the Problem

By blending the breath of the sun and the shade, true harmony comes into the world.

Tao Te Ching

Imagine that you and another person are rowing a boat across the ocean and you cannot row the boat by yourself. Although the two of you may have conflicts about how to row, how far to row, what direction to row, and so forth, you seek food and water for the other person as well as for yourself. Otherwise, you may perish. Your conflicts become mutual problems that must be solved to both persons' satisfaction. In **integrative negotiations,** the goal is to maximize joint benefits. Maintaining a high-quality relationship with other group members is usually more important than getting your way on any one issue. In a family, for example, ensuring the survival of the family is almost always more important than "winning" on any one issue. In integrative negotiations, therefore, there is a hardheaded, side-by-side search for a fair agreement that is advantageous to both sides.

In ongoing relationships, conflicts are often resolved by a procedure known as the **one-step negotiation.** Each person (a) assesses the strength of his or her interests, (b) assesses the strength of the other person's interests, and (c) agrees that whoever has the greatest need gets his or her way. Marital satisfaction, for example, has been found to be higher when couples allocated decision-making power such that each person exercised more power on decisions that mattered to that individual (Beach & Tesser, 1993). The one-step negotiation procedure works only if it is reciprocal. Each should get his or her way half of the time. Ongoing relationships are guided by a **norm of mutual responsiveness** (you help them reach their goals and they help you reach your goals). One-way relationships never last long.

When disputants have to achieve their goals and, therefore, the one-step procedure is not appropriate, they engage in integrative negotiations. There are six basic steps in negotiating a workable solution to a problem that maximizes joint outcomes:

1. Each person explains what he or she wants in a descriptive, nonevaluative way.
2. Each person explains how he or she feels in a descriptive, nonevaluative way.
3. Each person explains his or her reasons for wanting what he or she wants and feeling the way he or she does.
4. Each person reverses perspectives by summarizing what the other person(s) wants and feels and the reasons underlying those wants and feelings.
5. The participants invent at least three good optional agreements that would maximize joint outcomes.
6. The participants choose the agreement that seems the wisest and agree to abide by its conditions.

Exercise 9.4: *Negotiating Resolutions to Conflicts of Interest*

The purpose of this exercise is to stimulate a discussion on how to negotiate constructive resolutions to conflicts of interests. The procedure is as follows:

1. Form groups of four. Divide each group into two pairs. Assign one pair the role of Chris and the other pair the role of Pat or the instructor. Brief descriptions of several conflicts of interests appear below. Taking one at a time, the pair prepares to role play its assigned character by reading the description of the situation and writing out the answers to the following questions:
   a. What do you want?
   b. How do you feel?
   c. What are your reasons for wanting what you want and feeling like you do?
2. One person from each pair changes chairs. A Chris and a Pat should now be seated together. They role play negotiating an agreement that resolves the conflict. The role play will be more interesting if you overdramatize somewhat.
3. Combine both pairs into a group of four. Each group is to share the agreements negotiated, discuss what made the conflict difficult to resolve, come to a consensus about how it could be managed most constructively, and write out the ideal agreement to be negotiated. Each group shares its solution with the rest of the class.

CONFLICT DESCRIPTIONS

1. Chris enters a large lecture class and takes an aisle chair. Before the class begins Chris places his/her books and then leaves to get a drink of water. Upon returning, Chris finds his/her books sitting in the aisle and Pat in the chair. What do you do? Role play the exchange.
2. Chris tells Pat (a friend) in confidence about someone Chris would like to date. The next day several people comment on it. Chris gets Pat alone to talk about it. What do you do? Role play the exchange.
3. Chris has been sick for several weeks. The science instructor refuses to extend the deadline for Chris' final project. Because Chris cannot finish the project in time, this means that Chris will receive a low grade in the class. Chris believes the instructor is being very unfair. Chris decides to try talking to the instructor again. Role play the exchange.
4. Chris borrows Pat's history book. The next day, when Chris returns the book, it is muddy and the cover is torn. Pat believes that when you borrow something, you are responsible for taking care of it. Pat spends twenty minutes cleaning the book and taping the cover back together. Chris laughs and calls Pat a "neatness freak." What do you do? Role play the exchange.

HAMLET AND HIS FATHER'S GHOST

Using the same instructions as given above, role play the negotiations between Hamlet and his father's ghost.

Situation

The scene is the battlements of the castle of the king of Denmark. It is midnight, the witching hour. The ghost of Hamlet's father appears and beckons Hamlet to follow the ghost for a private talk. They have a conflict that must be resolved. Find a partner. Flip a coin to see who will be Hamlet and who will be his father. Then resolve the conflict using the problem-solving negotiation procedure.

Ghost

I am your father's spirit. Listen to me. If you ever loved me you must avenge my foul, strange, and most unnatural murder. I was not bitten by a poisonous snake. The serpent that bit me now wears my crown. He is an incestuous beast. He seduced your mother, a seemingly virtuous queen. Then, when I was asleep in the garden, he poured poison into my ear. My own brother, your uncle, killed me to gain both my crown and my wife. This is horrible! Horrible! You must kill him! You are my son and it is your duty to avenge my death. I cannot rest in my grave until my murder is avenged. You must fulfill your obligation and put me to rest. Denmark will not prosper with such a man on the throne. The king must be committed to the welfare of Denmark, not himself. Besides, if he has a son you will lose your birthright.

Hamlet

I did not know you were murdered. I thought you died of a snake bite. This is a complete surprise to me. The fact that my uncle murdered you is even more of a surprise. I have a relationship with this man. I certainly want justice, but let's not be hasty. Asking me to kill him is a serious request. First, I may be too young and inexperienced to do it right. You would do better to ask one of your generals to do it. Second, killing my uncle could seriously damage my future career options and quality of life. Don't be so bloodthirsty. Think of my future! Third, this is not the time for me to kill someone. I am a carefree youth! I am in love. I'm still in school. I have years of learning and maturing left before I will be ready to kill someone. Fourth, I would never rest in my grave, and I might even go to hell, if I killed my uncle. Finally, killing my uncle is a complex task. I have to catch him alone doing something wicked so his soul will go to hell. What use is it if I kill him when he is doing something virtuous and he goes to heaven? This is not one of the usual "walk into the room and stab him" killings. This one is very complex and difficult. I'm not sure I want to do that much work!

THE INTEGRATIVE NEGOTIATING PROCEDURE

Step 1: Describe What You Want (Your Interests)

If a man does not know to which port he is sailing, no wind is favorable.

Seneca

In describing what you want, you assert your wants and listen carefully to the other person's wants. Describing your wants and goals includes describing (not evaluating) the other person's actions and defining the conflict (a) as a mutual problem and (b) in as small and specific a way as possible.

Describing What You Want.   Negotiating begins when you describe what you want. **Everyone has a perfect right to their wants, needs, and goals** (Alberti & Emmons, 1978). Two of the major mistakes in defining a conflict is to be **aggressive** by trying to hurt the other person or to be **nonassertive** by saying nothing, giving up your interests, and keeping your wants to yourself. You can **assert** your wants, needs, and goals directly to another person in an honest and appropriate way that respects both yourself and the other person. On the other hand, **everyone has a perfect right to refuse to meet your wants and needs or facilitate your goal accomplishment if they see it as destructive to their own interests to do so.** No one has to act against his or her best self-interests just to

Table 9.4 **Respect for Self and Others**

My Respect for Me	My Respect for You
I Have a Perfect Right To:	**You Have a Perfect Right To:**
My needs and wants	Your wants and needs
Tell you what I want	Tell me what you want
Tell you how I feel	Tell me how you feel
Refuse to give you what you want	Refuse to give me what I want

We Have a Perfect Right to Negotiate with Each Other

please someone else. After asserting your needs and goals, therefore, do not expect the other person to do exactly as you wish. **Do not confuse letting others know what you want with demanding that they act as you think they should.** Providing others with information about your interests is different from trying to force others to act in the ways you wish them to.

Communicating what you want involves taking ownership of your interests by making personal statements that describe your wants and goals (see Table 9.4). To clearly communicate your wants and goals to the other person (Johnson, 1996; Johnson & Johnson, 1995a):

1. **Make personal statements** that refer to *I, me, my,* or *mine.*
2. **Be specific about your wants, needs, and goals** and establish their legitimacy.
3. **Acknowledge the other person's goals as part of the problem.** Describe how the other person's actions are blocking what you want. In doing so, separate the behavior from the person. More specifically, a **behavior description** includes:
   a. A **personal statement** that refers to *I, me, my,* or *mine.*
   b. A **behavioral description statement** that includes the specific behaviors you have observed and does *not* include any judgment or evaluation or any inferences about the person's motives, personality, or attitudes.
4. **Focus on the long-term cooperative relationship.** During most conflicts of interests you will be discussing the current problems in your relationship. Negotiations within a long-term cooperative relationship include discussing how the relationship can be changed so the two of you can work together better. During such conversations, you will need to make relationship statements. A **relationship statement** describes some aspect of the way the two of you are interacting with each other. A good relationship statement indicates clear ownership (refers to *I, me, my, or mine*) and describes how you see the relationship. "I think we need to talk about our disagreement yesterday" is a good relationship statement.

Furthermore, how you present your proposed agreement has implications for both your commitment to your current position and the response to it by other group members. To persuade others you may overemphasize the factors that favor your position, and this overattention to positive arguments results in selective retention of position-consistent information. In addition, arguing for your position tends to result in increased commitment to it (Hovland, Janis, & Kelley, 1953) and a belief that you are committed through self-perception (Bem, 1972). If you are too demanding in your presentation, however, your attempts to persuade may boomerang. Jack Brehm (1976; Brehm & Brehm, 1981) demonstrated that persuasive attempts that are viewed as coercive or biased often backfire by causing others to reject what you are saying and increase their commitment to their original positions. This intensification is called **psychological reactance**—the need to reestablish your freedom whenever it is threatened. In one of the Bem studies, for example, two teammates had to choose between two alternatives marked 1-A or 1-B. When the partner stated, "I prefer 1-A," 73% chose 1-A but when the partner stated, "I think we should both do 1-A," only 40% chose 1-A (Brehm & Sensenig, 1966). Similarly, 83% of the members of a group refused to go along with a member who stated, "I think it's pretty obvious all of us are going to work on task A" (Worchel & Brehm, 1971).

Listening to the Other Person's Wants. Your success as a negotiator depends largely on showing the other person how his or her needs and goals may be met through accepting your proposals. In order to make a persuasive case for your position, you have to understand clearly what the other person's interests (and feelings) are. This requires careful listening and being able to see the situation from the other person's perspective. There is no set of skills more important for negotiating than being a good listener (see Johnson, 1991, 2000). **To listen to another person you must (a) face the person, (b) stay quiet (until your turn), (c) think about what the person is saying, and (d) show you understand.** The keystone to good listening is paraphrasing. **Paraphrasing** is restating, in your own words, what the person says, feels, and means. This improves communication in several ways. *First*, it helps you avoid judging and evaluating. When you are restating, you are not passing judgment. *Second*, restating gives the sender direct feedback as to how well you understand the messages. If you do not fully understand, the sender can add messages until you do. If you are interpreting the message differently from the way he intended it, the sender can clarify. Being able to clarify and elaborate are important for making sure communication is taking place. *Third*, paraphrasing communicates to the sender that you want to understand what he is saying. It shows that you care about him enough to listen carefully, that you are interested, that you take what he is saying seriously, and that you want to understand. *Finally*, paraphrasing helps you get into the sender's shoes. It helps you see the message from the sender's perspective. By restating the message as accurately and fairly as possible, you begin to see things from the sender's point of view.

Paraphrasing is often a simple restatement of what has been said. At first, it may feel dumb to restate what another person has said. It may feel awkward and unnatural until you get used to doing it. But the speaker will be grateful for a chance to clarify or add to his original statement, and he will feel grateful for being understood. Paraphrasing becomes harder when it includes feelings as well as ideas. It is not limited to only the words the sender uses. Nonverbal cues are also important.

Often in a conflict it is helpful to follow the **paraphrasing rule** (Johnson, 1971): Before you can reply to a statement, restate what the sender says, feels, and means correctly and to the sender's satisfaction. When you use paraphrasing, there is a rhythm to your statements. The rhythm is "You said . . . ; I say. . . ." First you say what the sender said (You said). Then you reply (I say). Paraphrasing is often essential in defining a conflict so that a constructive resolution may be negotiated.

Describing the Other Person's Actions.   Imagine you and a close friend are in a conflict. Your friend believes you have behaved in a very destructive way. You believe your behavior was caused by extenuating circumstances, the actions of other people, and a desire to do the right thing. You conclude that your friend should understand and forgive you. Your friend, however, insists that your behavior was caused by your negative personal characteristics such as poor judgment, irresponsibility, selfishness, a lack of concern, a tendency to show off, and incompetence. You are deeply hurt and counterattack, accusing your friend of being a person of low moral character who is irresponsible and selfish, has poor judgment, and lacks any concern for you. Both you and your friend consider the other's attributions to be unfair and unreasonable and, therefore, the conflict is escalated. Harold Kelley and his associates (Kelley, 1979; Orvis, Kelley, & Butler, 1976) found just such a cycle in a study of 700 conflicts in 41 marriages.

Conflicts are created and escalated when individuals engage in destructive acts. The harm destructive acts do cannot be easily repaired, no matter how considerate and thoughtful a person is later. Destructive acts are exceptionally detrimental to relationships, whereas constructive acts do not yield commensurately positive consequences (e.g., Billings, 1979; Gottman, 1993; Jacobson & Margolin, 1979; Markman, 1981; Rusbult & Van Lange, 1996). In conflicts, there are two general classes of destructive acts:

1. Directly hurting the other person.
2. Inferring that the other person's actions are the result of dispositional (personality, beliefs, attitudes, and values) factors.

Avoiding directly hurtful actions is always a good idea. More difficult to control, however, are the inferences you make about other people's behavior. Especially in conflicts, there is a tendency to attribute the causes of the opponent's behavior to his or her inner psychological state (Blake & Mouton, 1962; Chesler & Franklin, 1968; Sherif & Sherif, 1969) while at the same time attributing the causes of your own behavior to situational (environmental) factors. This is known as the **fundamental attribution error** (Ross, 1977; Ross & Nisbett, 1991). Inferences about the causes of behaviors and events are known as attributions. **Attribution theory** posits that people continually formulate intuitive causal hypotheses so that they can understand and predict events that transpire in the group (Heider, 1958). Attributions are especially important in conflict, because attributions influence perceptions of groupmates' motives and intentions (Steiner, 1959) and mediate reactions to groupmates' behaviors (Horai, 1977; Messe, Stollak, Larson, & Michaels, 1979). If attributions are accurate, they help group members understand each other better. If attributions are inaccurate, conflicts become destructive. Like everyone else, opponents want to appear strong and capable to others, and if they believe you are trying to label them as sick, weak, incompetent, or ineffective they will refuse to negotiate flexibly (Brown, 1968; Pruitt & Johnson, 1970; Tjosvold, 1974, 1977).

During conflicts, attributing the causes of the opponent's behavior often follows a two-step process. First, there is an automatic (without conscious awareness) attribution of the causes of the opponent's behavior to dispositional (not situational) causes (Gilbert & Malone, 1995). Second, there is a reflective, thoughtful analysis during which the dispositional inferences are qualified with relevant situational information about the context of behavior and the initial dispositional inferences are corrected (Gilbert, McNulty, Giuliano, & Benson, 1992; Reeder, 1993). Whether or not the second step occurs may depend on how constructively the conflict is being managed.

Defining a conflict is like lacing your shoes. If you start out wrong, the whole thing gets messed up. Separate the person from the problem. Negotiate over issues, not personalities. Avoid personalized attacks. Describe the other's actions toward you!

Defining the Conflict as a Mutual Problem

A house divided against itself cannot stand.

Abraham Lincoln

Two drivers, coming from different directions, are roaring down a one-lane road. Soon they will crash head-on. If the two drivers define the situation as a competition to see who will "chicken out," they will probably crash and both will die. If the two drivers define the situation as a problem to be solved, they will tend to see a solution in which they alternate giving each other the right-of-way. Even simple and small conflicts become major and difficult to resolve when they are defined in a competitive, "win–lose" way. Even major and difficult conflicts become resolvable when they are defined as problems to be solved.

A conflict defined as a problem to be solved is much easier to resolve constructively than a conflict defined as a win–lose situation (Blake & Mouton, 1962; Deutsch & Lewicki, 1970). The total benefits for all sides in negotiations are higher than when problem-solving strategies are used (Lewis & Pruitt, 1971). One of the most constructive things you can do in a conflict is to define the conflict as a mutual problem to be solved. Doing so will tend to increase communication, trust, liking for each other, and cooperation. No one tends to lose when you and the other person sit down to solve a mutual problem!

To define a conflict jointly, group members have to use a common language about conflicts. The group language may include such terms as *win–lose, problem solve, confront, beltline,* and *gunnysack* (i.e., to store up grievances for a long time and then unload them all on an offending group member). A common language about conflicts facilitates the identification of constructive and destructive strategies of negotiation. Groups may develop their own vocabulary for describing conflict behaviors and procedures.

Defining the Conflict as Being Small and Specific.

Fred wants to join a baseball game on the playground. "You can't play," Ralph shouts. "We already have our teams!" "You are no longer my friend!" Fred shouts back. "You're selfish and mean! I'll never help you with your homework again!" In defining a conflict there is an unfortunate tendency to be global and general. Fred is defining the conflict as being one of friendship and gratitude. This creates difficulty in resolving the conflict. He could just as easily have defined the conflict as being one of arriving late or finding a way to make the teams even.

In defining a conflict, the smaller and more specific it is defined, the easier it is to resolve. The smaller and more precise the definition of a conflict, the easier it will be to resolve (Deutsch, Canavan, & Rubin, 1971). Think small. The more global, general, and vague the definition of the conflict, the harder the conflict is to resolve. Defining a conflict as "She always lies," makes it more difficult to resolve than defining it as "Her statement was not true." When it comes to resolving conflicts, small is easy, large is hard!

Step 2: Describe Your Feelings

Many of us in business, especially if we are very sure of our ideas, have hot tempers. My father knew he had to keep the damage from his own temper to a minimum.

Thomas Watson, Jr., Chairman Emeritus, IBM

The second step of negotiating to solve a problem is to describe how you feel. Expressing and controlling your feelings is one of the most difficult aspects of resolving conflicts. It is also one of the most important, for several reasons (Johnson, 1996; Johnson & Johnson, 1995a). *First,* many conflicts cannot be resolved unless feelings are openly recognized and expressed. If individuals hide or suppress their anger, for example, they may make an agreement but they keep their resentment and hostility towards the other person. Their ability to work effectively with the other person is damaged as is their ability to resolve future conflicts constructively. The conflict will tend to reoccur regardless of what the agreement is. *Second,* it is through experiencing and sharing feelings that close relationships are built and maintained. Feelings provide the cement holding relationships together as well as the means for deepening relationships and making them more effective and personal. *Third,* feelings that are not accepted and recognized can (a) create bias in your judgments, (b) create insecurities that make it more difficult to deal with the conflict in constructive ways, and (c) reduce your control over your behavior. For many reasons it is often best to communicate your feelings directly when conflicts are building.

Fourth, the only way other people can know how you are feeling and reacting is for you to tell them (see Johnson, 1996 and Johnson & Johnson, 1995a for specifics). In order to communicate your feelings you must be aware of them, accept them, and be skillful in expressing them constructively.

Step 3: Exchange Reasons for Positions

To be persuasive we must be believable; to be believable we must be credible; to be credible, we must be truthful.

Edward R. Murrow, Journalist

Once both you and the other person have expressed what you want and how you feel, listened carefully to each other, and jointly defined the conflict as a small and specific mutual problem, you must exchange the reasons for your positions. To do so, negotiators have to:

1. Express cooperative intentions.
2. Present your reasons and listen to the other person's reasons.
3. Focus on wants and interests, not positions.
4. Clarify the differences between your and the other's interests before trying to integrate them into an agreement.
5. Empower the other person.

Expressing Cooperative Intentions: Enlarging the Shadow of the Future.

One of the most constructive things you can do in resolving a conflict is to highlight the long-term cooperative relationships. This is done in three ways. The *first* is to stress the dealing with the conflict in a problem-solving way. You want to say such things as, "This situation means that we will have to work together," "Let's cooperate in reaching an agreement," "Let's try to reach an agreement that is good for both of us." The *second* is to state that you are committed to maximizing the joint outcomes. Successful negotiation requires finding out what the other person really wants and needs and showing him or her a way to get it while you get what you want. The *third* is to enlarge the shadow of the future by stating that you are committed to the continuation and success of the joint cooperative efforts. In doing so, you must wish to point out (a) the long-term mutual goals and (b) the ways the two of you will be interdependent for the foreseeable future.

The clear and unambiguous expression of cooperative intentions in negotiations results in higher-quality agreements being reached in a shorter amount of time (i.e., better agreements faster). The other person becomes less defensive, more willing to change his or her position, less concerned about who is right and who is wrong, and more understanding of your views and ideas (Johnson, 1971, 1974; Johnson, McCarty, & Allen, 1976). The other person tends to see you as an understanding and trustworthy person whom he or she can confide in.

The expression of competitive intentions, such as threats and punishments, tend to escalate the conflict (Deutsch & Krauss, 1960, 1962). Imagine you own a trucking company that carries merchandise over the roads pictured in Figure 9.4.

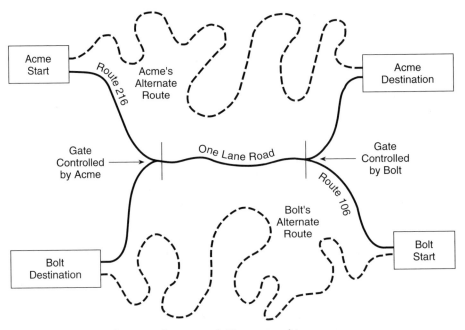

Figure 9.4   The road map in the Deutsch-Krauss trucking game.
Source: M. Deutsch, *The Resolution of Conflict: Constructive and Destructive Processes* (New Haven, CT: Yale UP, 1973). Reprinted by permission.

Each time your truck reaches its destination, you earn sixty cents minus the operating cost of one cent for each second it takes. A part of the road is one-way. If you encounter a truck going the opposite way, one of you will have to reverse to let the other through. If the other person refuses to back up, you can close a gate at the other end and then he or she will have to back up and take the alternative route. You can then open the gate for yourself and proceed rapidly to your destination. Describe how you would behave.

Morton Deutsch and Robert Krauss (1960, 1962) used this imaginary situation to determine how the use of threats affects hostility, counterthreats, and unwillingness to compromise. In the unilateral-threat condition, only one participant had a gate. In the bilateral-threat condition, both sides had gates. In the control condition no gates were present. When no gate was present, the participants learned to alternate in their use of the one-way road and both made a profit of about $1.00. When one participant had a gate, participants lost an average of $2.03 per person, although the participant with the gate lost less than the participant without the gate. When both participants had a gate, participants lost an average of $4.38 per person. Thus, the use of threats was counterproductive, intensifying the destructive aspects of the conflict. In considering the use of threats, you may be advised to remember the advice of Niccolo Machiavelli, an adviser to sixteenth-century Florentine princes:

> I hold it be a proof of great prudence for men to abstain from threats and insulting words toward anyone, for neither . . . diminishes the strength of the enemy; but the one makes him more cautious and the other increases his hatred of you and makes him more persevering in his efforts to injure you.

Presenting Your Reasons, Listening to the Other Person's Reasons.   To say what you want and how you feel is not enough. You must also give your reasons for wanting what you want and feeling as you do. It is not enough to say, "I want to use the computer now and I'm angry at you for not letting me have it." You must also say, "I have an important homework assignment due today and this is my only chance to get it done." Your reasons are aimed at (a) informing the other person and (b) persuading him or her to agree with you.

Many times you will have to ask the other person why he or she has taken a certain position. You may ask a friend to study with you. She may reply "no." Until you understand the reasons for the "no" you will not be able to think creatively of ways for both of you to get what you want. The statement in doing so is, "May I ask why?" If the answer is vague, you add, "Could you be more specific?" or "What do you mean when you say . . . ?" "I'm not sure I understand." Your tone of voice is as important as the words when you ask these questions. If you sound sarcastic your attempt to understand the other person will backfire.

In listening carefully to the needs and wants of the other person, you must **stay flexible, changing your position and feelings when persuaded to do so.** Negotiating is a rational process. You are seeking a way to reach your goals and the other person is doing the same. How successful you are in reaching an agreement depends on how creatively you can think of alternatives that are good for both. This requires flexibility and a willingness to change your mind when you are persuaded that it is rational to do so.

Once both of you have explained your reasons, either of you may agree or disagree to help the other person to reach his or her goals. The decision to help the other person reach his or her goals or keep negotiating is based on two factors:

1. How important your goal is to you.
2. How important the other person's goal is to him or her (based on the reasons he or she presents).

You must listen carefully to the reasons given and decide whether they are valid or not. If you decide that the other person's goals are far more important to him or her than yours are to you, then you may wish to agree at this point. Giving up your goals to help the other person reach his or her goals only works if he or she does the same for you about 50% of the time. This is known as the **one-step negotiation procedure.**

If the other person's reasons are not valid, you need to point that out so he or she may see the inadequacies of his or her proposals. If neither you nor the other person is convinced to give up your own goals in order to fulfill the goals of the other person, then the two of you must reaffirm your cooperative relationship and explore each other's reasons at a deeper level.

Focusing on Wants and Interests, not Positions. Susan is usually a compliant student in Mr. Johnson's English class. Today, however, she comes up to Mr. Johnson's desk and states, "I won't do this homework assignment. I don't care what you do to me, I'm not going to do it!" Mr. Johnson, having read this book, immediately recognizes that Susan is presenting a position, and he does not yet know what her needs and wants are. He says, "May I ask why?" In order to negotiate successfully and reach an agreement that satisfies both people, you have to approach the other person on the basis of his or her wants and goals.

The classic example of the need to separate interests from positions is that of two sisters, each of whom wanted the only orange available. One sister wanted the peel of the orange to make a cake; the other wanted the inner pulp to make orange juice. Their positions ("I want the orange!") were opposed, but their interests were not. Often, when conflicting parties reveal their underlying interests, it is possible to find a solution that suits them both.

The heart of negotiations is meeting the goals of the other person while ensuring your goals are being met. The success of negotiations depends in finding out what the other person really wants and showing him or her a way to get it while you get what you want. For a wise decision, therefore, reconcile wants and goals, not positions. For every want or goal, there usually exist several possible positions that could satisfy it. A common mistake is to assume that because the other person's position is opposed to yours, his or her goals must also be opposed. Behind opposed positions lie shared and compatible goals, as well as conflicting ones. To identify the other person's wants and goals, ask "Why?" or "Why not?" and think about his or her choice, and realize that the other person has many different wants and goals.

Focusing on needs and goals rather than positions eliminates many of the traps that cause conflicts to become destructive. One such trap is the aggression that arises from being frustrated by the opponent's refusal to agree with your position. The link between frustration and aggression is one of the oldest social psychological explanations of hostility and physical violence. The **frustration-aggression process** may be summarized in the following way (Berkowitz, 1978). Individuals who are unable to attain the goals they desire because of personal limitations or external influences sometimes experience frustration. This frustration produces a readiness to respond in an aggressive manner, which may boil over into hostility and violence if situational cues that serve as "releasers" are present. Negotiators can become frustrated and, at any sign of belligerence or hostility by others, release verbal and, in some cases, physical violence. What often prevents high levels of frustration is the continual clarification of needs and goals and the search from new positions that let all members reach their goals.

Differentiating Before Integrating. Conflicts cannot be resolved unless you understand what you are disagreeing about. If you do not know what you are disagreeing about, you cannot find a way to reach an agreement. You must understand the differences between your wants and needs and those of the other person. Only then will you be able to think of ways to satisfy both yourself and the other person so that the conflict can be resolved constructively. Your ability to come up with satisfactory solutions depends on your understanding of how the other person's thoughts, feelings, and needs are different from yours. The more you differentiate between your interests and those of the other person, the better you will be able to integrate them into a mutually satisfying agreement. In discussing a conflict you try to find the answers to these questions: (a) What are the differences between my wants and needs and yours? (b) Where are our needs and goals the same? (c) What actions of the other person do I find unacceptable? and (d) What actions of mine does the other person find unacceptable?

Empowering the Other Person. During negotiations it is important that you do not let the other person feel powerless. Shared power and wise agreements go hand in hand. **There are two ways to empower the other person.** The *first* is by being open to negotiations and flexible about the option you like the best. If he or she can negotiate with you, then he or she has power and options. Willingness to negotiate is based on being open to the possibility that there may be a better option available than you now realize. Staying tentative and flexible means that you do not become overcommitted to any one position until an agreement is reached. The *second* is to provide power through choice among options. Generate a variety of possible solutions before deciding what to do. If Susan says to Mr. Johnson, "You have to agree to let me not do my homework!" he will feel powerless. If Susan said, "Let's think of three possible agreements, and then choose the one that seems the best!" both she and Mr. Johnson feel powerful.

The psychological costs of being helpless to resolve grievances include frustration, anxiety, and friction. When a person is powerless, either he or she becomes hostile and tries to tear down the system or becomes apathetic and throws in the towel. You do not want the other person to do either one. We all need to believe that we have been granted a fair hearing and that we should have the power and the right to gain justice when we have been wronged. If it becomes evident that we cannot gain justice, frustration, anger, depression, and anxiety may result (Deutsch, 1985).

Staying Flexible. **Stay flexible, changing your position and feelings when persuaded to do so.** Negotiating is a rational process. You are seeking a way to satisfy your needs and reach your goals and the other person is doing the same. How successful you are in reaching an agreement that is good for you depends on how creatively you can think of alternatives that also are good for the other person. This requires flexibility and a willingness to change your mind when you are persuaded that it is rational to do so. It is very easy and quite common to become entrapped in your commitment to a position and close your mind to alternatives. Allan Teger (1980), for example, studied the entrapment process through conducting "dollar auctions." A dollar is auctioned off to the highest bidder with the rule that although the highest bidder gets to keep the dollar, the second highest bidder must pay the amount he or she bid. Thus, if a person bid eighty cents for the dollar and someone else bid ninety cents, the person is entrapped in bidding higher to avoid losing the eighty cents. Negotiators need to be vigilant against being entrapped by their commitment to old proposals and positions.

Coordinating Motivation to Negotiate in Good Faith.   There are often differences in motivation to resolve a conflict. You may want to resolve a conflict but other group members could care less. Your groupmate may be very concerned about resolving a conflict with you, but you may want to avoid the whole thing. Usually, a conflict cannot be resolved until both persons are motivated to resolve it at the same time. **The motivation to resolve a conflict is based on the costs and gains of continuing the conflict for each person.** The costs of continuing a conflict may be the loss of a friendship, the loss of enjoyment from work, the loss of job productivity, the loss of a friend, or the loss of respect from the other person. The gains for continuing the conflict may be satisfaction in expressing your anger or resentment and the protection of the status quo. By protecting the status quo, you avoid the possibility that things will get worse when the conflict is resolved. Answering the following questions may help you clarify your motivation and the motivation of the other person to resolve the conflict:

1. What do I gain from continuing the conflict?
2. What does the other person gain from continuing the conflict?
3. What do I lose from continuing the conflict?
4. What does the other person lose from continuing the conflict?

A person's motivation to resolve a conflict can be changed. By increasing the costs of continuing the conflict or by increasing the gains for resolving it, the other person's motivation to resolve it can be increased. Through changing the costs and gains, you can change both your and the other person's motivation to resolve the conflict.

When the outcomes of negotiations are presented as gains, more concessions are made than when the outcomes are presented as losses. Negotiators who think in terms of losses or costs are more likely to take the risk of losing all by holding out in an attempt to force further concessions from the opponent. A negotiator should try to present information in a way that leads the opposition to see what they have to gain from a settlement.

It is within the exchange of proposals and feelings that the dilemmas of trust and openness arise. The better negotiators understand each other's interests, the better the agreement that can ultimately be achieved. A negotiator faces the dilemmas of whether or not to (a) trust opponents to tell the truth about their interests and (b) tell the truth about his or her own interests to the opposing negotiators. Deutsch (1958, 1960, 1973) used the **Prisoner's Dilemma Game** (PDG) to study the issue of trust within conflict situations. The PDG derives its name from a hypothetical situation studied by mathe-

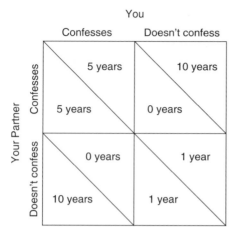

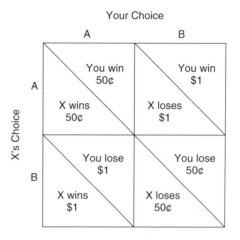

Figure 9.5 The Prisoner's Dilemma Game.

matical game theorists (Luce & Raiffa, 1957). Imagine that you and your partner have just robbed a bank, hidden the money, and are arrested by police who are sure you are guilty but have no proof. The police's only hope of convicting you is for you to confess. The officers take you and your partner into separate rooms to question you (see Figure 9.5). You are both presented with two alternatives: Confess to the crime or remain silent. If neither of you confesses, you both will be tried on a minor charge that carries the light sentence of one year in prison. If you both confess, then each will spend five years in prison. If your partner confesses and you do not, your partner will go free but you will get ten years in prison. Conversely, if you confess and your partner does not, you will go free and your partner will go to prison for ten years. The dilemma for you and your partner is whether to trust the other to remain silent and not exploit your silence if you remain silent. If both you and your partner trust the other to keep silent, both of you will benefit.

To conduct research on trust, Deutsch used the prisoner's dilemma situation in a game format in which pairs of participants were paid according to the combination of their choices (see Figure 9.5). If both choose A, both receive fifty cents. If both choose B, both lose fifty cents. If one chooses A and the other chooses B, the person choosing B wins one dollar and the person choosing A loses one dollar. Although the PDG has been overused in research on conflict, it was a remarkable methodological breakthrough when Deutsch initiated its use. One of its most important uses was by Robert Axelrod (1984) in his studies of the evolution of cooperation (see Chapter 4). What the results of research using the PDG demonstrate is that the pursuit of self-interests by each group member leads to a poor outcome for all. In the long run, only cooperative behavior based on trust ensures the well-being of all group members.

Potential Problems. There are two problems in analyzing underlying interests. *First,* sometimes a person does not understand the interests underlying his or her position and preferences and, therefore, cannot describe them to others. *Second,* disputants may not wish to reveal their interests out of fear that the other will use this information to personal advantage. Revealing one's wants, goals, and interests always carries the risk of having one's vulnerability exploited. A person's interests are often organized into hierarchical trees, with the initial interests discussed being the tip of the iceberg. With more and more discussion, deeper and deeper interests may be revealed.

Step 4: Understand the Other's Perspective

The test of a first-rate intelligence is the ability to hold two opposed ideas in the mind at the same time, and still retain the ability to function.

F. Scott Fitzgerald

To reach a wise agreement, you must have a clear understanding of all sides of the issue, an accurate assessment of their validity and relative merits, and the ability to think creatively to come up with potential solutions that maximize joint outcomes and fulfill the interests of all disputants. To do all this, you must be able to (a) see the conflict from both your own and the other person's perspective and (b) keep both perspectives in mind at the same time. A **perspective** is a way of viewing the world (as well as specific situations) and one's relation to it. **Social perspective-taking** is the ability to understand how a situation appears to another person and how that person is reacting cognitively and emotionally to the situation. The opposite of perspective-taking is **egocentrism** or being unaware that other perspectives exist and that one's own view of the conflict is incomplete and limited. There are two types of social perspective-taking (Batson, Early, & Salvarani, 1997). The first is understanding how another person feels; it creates empathy and evokes altruistic motivation. The second is understanding how you would feel if you were the other person; it creates a combination of empathy for the other person and personal distress, and evokes egoistic motivation. In engaging in perspective-taking, it is important to place oneself in the other's shoes and understand the situation from the other's perspective, not imagine how one would feel if one were the other person.

Engaging in social perspective-taking may be difficult given the following aspects of perspectives. **First, each person has a unique perspective that is different from the perspectives of others.** Your perspective is developed as a result of the ways in which you respond to your experiences as an infant, child, youth, and adult. Other people have developed their perspectives on the basis of their responses to their life experiences. This means that different people have different perspectives. No two people will see an issue in exactly the same way. Each person will interpret identical events differently.

Second, a person's perspective selects and organizes what the person attends to and experiences. All experiences are interpreted and understood within the perspective in which they are viewed. People tend to see only what their perspective allows them to see. A rich person and a poor person may see a homeless person differently because they have two quite different perspectives. To make the situation worse, people tend to see only what they want to see. Out of a mass of detailed information, people tend to pick out and focus on those facts that confirm their prior perceptions and to disregard or misinterpret those that call their perceptions into question. Each side in a negotiation tends to see only the merits of its case, and only the faults of the other side. It is not enough to understand logically how the other person views the problem. If you want to influence the other person, you also need to understand empathetically the power of his or her point of view and to feel the emotional force with which he or she believes in it.

You may see on the table a glass half full of water. The other person may see a dirty, half-empty glass about to cause a ring on the mahogany finish. Change a person's perspective and you change what the person attends to and the way the person interprets the events in his or her life. Understand the other's perspective, and you change your ability to find integrative solutions to the conflict.

Third, each person can have different perspectives at different times. If you have been lifting hundred-pound bags of cement and someone tosses you a forty-pound bag, it will seem very light. But if you have been lifting twenty-pound bags, the forty-pound bag will seem very heavy. When you are hungry, you notice all the food in a room. When you are not hungry, the food does not attract your attention. As your job role, experiences, assumptions, physiological states, and values change, your perspective will change.

Fourth, the same message can mean two entirely different things from two different perspectives. A teasing comment may be perceived as a sign of friendliness by a co-worker or as a sign of hostile insubordination by your boss. Different perspectives may result in the message being given different meanings.

Fifth, misunderstandings often occur because we assume that everyone sees things from the same perspective as we do. If we like Italian food, we assume that all our friends like Italian food. If we are interested in sports, we assume that everyone is interested in sports. If we get angry when someone laughs at our behavior, we assume that everyone will get angry when they are laughed at. If we think a teacher is stupid, we are surprised when a peer thinks the teacher is brilliant.

Accurate perspective-taking is one of the most difficult aspects of conflict resolution. It is also one of the most important, for a number of reasons (see Johnson & Johnson [1989] for a complete review of the research).

First, perspective-taking improves communication and reduces misunderstandings and distortions by influencing how messages are phrased and received. Negotiators often misunderstand and distort the positions of the others involved in the conflict due to poor communication. The better you understand the other person's perspective, the more able you are to phrase messages so the other person can easily understand them. If a person does not know what snow is, for example, you do not refer to "corn snow" or "fresh powder." In addition, understanding the other person's perspective helps you accurately understand his or her messages and retain them over time. For example, if the other person says, "That's just great!" the meaning reverses if you know the person is frustrated. You must be able to stand in the sender's shoes to understand accurately the meaning of the messages that person is sending you. The better negotiators are at perspective-taking, the more information, both personal and impersonal, they disclose.

Second, perspective-taking facilitates the development of creative and high-quality solutions to the joint problem. Creative problem solving is enhanced by the understanding of a variety of ways to view the conflict. Understanding a wide variety of perspectives on an issue, seeing the merits of other positions and the shortcomings of your position, incorporating information from other positions into one's own, and feeling the emotional force with which others hold their positions all help spark the creativity needed to find integrative solutions to the joint problem.

Third, engaging in perspective-taking tends to improve the relationship with the other person. You are more liked and respected when the other person realizes that you are seeing his or her perspective accurately and using it to create potential agreements that benefit both sides equally. You also will tend to have a more positive view of the negotiations.

Fourth, taking the other person's perspective transforms a disputant's motivation from immediate, self-interests to long-term concerns about joint outcome and the well-being of the relationship. Being locked in one's own perspective results in acting on the basis of immediate self-interest (Dehue, McClintock, & Liebrand, 1993; Yovetich & Rusbult, 1994). Adopting the partner's perspective activates broader concerns including joint outcomes and the well-being of the partner and relationship (Davis, Conklin, Smith, & Luce, 1996; Johnson, 1971). Adopting the other person's perspective results in more positive and less negative emotion and cognition, such as situationally based, less blameful construals of the partner's seemingly destructive acts (Johnson, 1971; Jones & Nesbett, 1972; Regan & Totten, 1975; Storms, 1973). Adopting the perspective of the other person (a) increases positive emotional reactions (caring, affectionate), attributional interpretations (relationship enhancing), and behavior preferences (constructive and active behaviors), and (b) reduces negative emotions (annoyed, bitter), attributions (blaming the partner), and behavioral preferences (destructive and passive behaviors) (Arriaga & Rusbult, 1998).

You ensure that you accurately see the situation from the other person's perspective by (a) asking for clarification or correction to make sure your understanding is accurate (this is called **perception checking**), (b) stating your understanding of the other's wants and needs (i.e., **paraphrasing**), and (c) presenting the other's position from his or her perspective.

The most effective way to gain insight into the other person's perspective is to role play that you are the other person and present the other person's position and reasoning as if you were he or she. Then have the other person do the same. The more involved the two of you get in arguing for the other's position, the more you will understand how the conflict appears from the other person's viewpoint. Such role playing is invaluable in finding solutions that are mutually acceptable. A systematic series of studies on the impact of perspective reversal on the resolution of conflicts has been conducted (Johnson, 1971d). The results indicated that skillful role reversal increases cooperative behavior between negotiators, clarifies misunderstanding of the other's position, increases understanding of the other's position, and aids one's ability to perceive the issue from the other's frame of reference. He also found the role reversal skillfully used can result not only in a reevaluation of the issue and a change of attitude towards it, but also in the role reverser being perceived as a person who tries to understand the other's position, as an understanding person in general, as a person willing to compromise, and as a cooperative and trustworthy person. Temporarily arguing your opponent's position does result in insight into your opponent's perspective and changes your attitudes about the issues being negotiated.

There is nothing more important to resolving conflicts constructively than understanding how the conflict appears from the other person's perspective. Once you can view the conflict from both your own perspective and the other person's perspective, you can find mutually beneficial solutions. You can also communicate to the other person that you really understand his or her thoughts, feelings, and needs. It is usually much easier to resolve a conflict when the other person feels understood. The more skilled you are in seeing things from other people's shoes, the more skilled you will be in resolving conflicts constructively.

Rules to Follow in Taking the Other's Perspective

1. Do not deduce the other person's intentions from your fears. People often tend to assume that whatever they fear, the other side intends to do.

2. Do not blame the other person for your problem. Blaming is an easy habit to fall into. Even if blaming is justified, it is counterproductive. It will make the other person defensive and closed-minded.

3. Discuss each other's perceptions.

4. Look for opportunities to act inconsistently with the other person's negative perceptions.

5. Give the other person a stake in the outcome by making sure he or she participates in the process. Agreement becomes much easier if both people feel ownership of the ideas.

6. Make your proposals consistent with the other person's goals and values and, thereby, help him or her "save face."

Step 5: Invent Options for Mutual Gain

One completely overcomes only what one assimilates.

Andre Gide

The fifth step of negotiating is to identify several possible agreements. One will rarely do. People have a tendency to agree to the first reasonable solution that is proposed. But doing so shuts off consideration of even more advantageous agreements. Thus, make sure you generate at least three good alternative agreements before deciding on which one to adopt. To invent a number of potential agreements, you must avoid a number of obstacles and you must think creatively.

Avoiding Obstacles.   Inventing options does not come naturally. Not inventing options is the normal state of affairs, even within the easiest negotiations. In most negotiations four major obstacles inhibit the inventing of a number of options:

1. **Judging prematurely.** Nothing is so harmful to inventing options as a critical attitude waiting to pounce on the drawbacks of any new idea. Premature criticism is the first impediment to creative thinking.

2. **Searching for the single answer.** Premature closure and fixation on the first proposal formulated as the single best answer is a sure short circuit of wise decision making.

3. **Assuming a fixed pie.** This inhibits creative thinking. Do not assume that the less for you, the more for me. Rarely, if ever, is this assumption true. Expanding the pie is a key to flexible problem solving. Imagine you want to see one movie and your date wants to see another movie. You also know your date likes to eat at a certain restaurant. By enlarging the pie to include which restaurant you go to for dinner before going to a movie, an integrative agreement is possible (one picks the restaurant, one picks the movie).

4. **Being concerned only with your own immediate needs and goals.** In a relationship, to meet your needs you also have to meet the other person's needs. Short-sighted self-concern leads to partisan positions, partisan arguments, and one-sided solutions.

5. **Defensively sticking with the status quo to avoid the fear of the unknown inherent in change.** Changing creates anxiety about potential new and unknown problems and guilt over ineffective or inappropriate behavior in the past. Many times people try to justify their past actions by refusing to change.

Inventing Creative Options.   Follett (1940) gives an example of a conflict between two people reading in a library room. One wants to open the window for ventilation, the other to keep it closed in order not to catch cold. To resolve their conflict they search for creative options. They finally agree to open a window in the next room, thereby letting in fresh air while avoiding a draft. Finding potential agreements that will maximize joint outcomes often takes creative problem solving. To invent creative options, you need to:

1. **Think of as many options as possible.** The more the options, the greater the room for negotiations. Find ways to expand the number of options on the table rather than looking for a single answer. One of the keys to wise decision making is selecting from a great number and variety of options.

2. **Separate the act of inventing options from the act of judging them.** Invent first, judge later.

3. **Gather as much information as possible about the problem.** The more you know about the problem, the easier it is to find solutions.

4. **See the problem from different perspectives and reformulate it in a way that lets new orientations to a solution emerge.** Such a reformulation often produces a moment of insight by one or both participants. The insight is often accompanied by intense emotional experiences of illumination and excitement and leads to the reformulation of the problem so that solutions emerge.

5. **Search for mutual gains.** There always exists the possibility of joint gain. Look for solutions that will leave the other person satisfied as well. Try to maximize joint outcomes.

6. **Invent ways of making decisions easily.** Give the other person choices that are as painless as possible. If you want a horse to jump a fence, do not raise the fence! Propose "yesable" agreements.

7. **Test each proposed agreement against reality.** What are its strengths and weaknesses? What does each person gain and lose? How does it maximize joint outcomes?

The types of agreements that help maximize joint outcomes include:

1. **Expand the pie** by finding ways to increase the resources available. Many conflicts arise from a perceived resource shortage. In such circumstances, integrative agreements can be devised by increasing the available resources.

2. **Package deals** in which parties include several related issues in one agreement. A package deal involving homework, in-class behavior, and helping another student may be easier to reach than trying to negotiate each separately.

3. **Trade-offs** in which two different things of comparable value are exchanged. A student may agree to do his homework if the teacher agrees never to call on him in class.
4. **Tie-ins** in which an issue considered extraneous by the other person is introduced and you offer to accept a certain settlement provided this extraneous issue will also be settled to one's satisfaction.
5. **Carve-outs** in which an issue is carved out of a larger context, leaving the related issues unsettled. This is the opposite of a tie-in.
6. **Logrolling** in which each party concedes on his or her low-priority issues that are high priority to the other person.
7. **Cost cutting** in which one person gets what he or she wants and the other's cost of conceding on those issues is reduced or eliminated.
8. **Bridging the initial positions** by creating a new option that satisfies both parties' interests that is different from what each originally thought he or she wanted. Rubin, Pruitt, and Kim (1994), for example, discuss a married couple in conflict over whether to vacation at the seashore or in the mountains. After some discussion, they identified their interests as swimming and fishing. They then agreed to visit a lake region that was neither at the seashore or in the mountains, but offered excellent swimming and fishing.

After inventing a number of options, you and the other person will have to agree on which one to try out first. Some realistic assessment of the alternatives then takes place. In trying to decide which alternative to try first it may help to remember Aesop's fable about the mice in trouble. The mice were saying, "It's terrible! Just terrible! We really must do something about it! But what?" The mice were talking about the cat. One by one they were falling into her claws. She would steal up softly, then spring suddenly, and there would be one mouse less. At last the mice held a meeting to decide what to do. After some discussion a young mouse jumped up. "I know what we should do! Tie a bell around the cat's neck! Then we would hear her coming and we could run away fast!" The mice clapped their little paws for joy. What a good idea! Why hadn't they thought of it before? What a very clever little fellow this young mouse was! But now a very old mouse, who hadn't opened his mouth during the whole meeting, got up to speak. "Friends, I agree that the plan of the young mouse is very clever indeed. But I should like to ask one question. Which of us is going to tie the bell around the cat's neck?" The moral is that there is no use adopting an option that cannot be implemented by one or both persons.

Once a variety of optional agreements are invented that maximizes mutual gain and fulfills the interests of all parties, one of the options is selected to be the initial agreement.

Step 6: Reach a Wise Agreement

*I never let the sun set on a disagreement with anybody who means
a lot to me.*

Thomas Watson Sr., Founder, IBM

Given that we are all separate individuals with our own unique wants and needs, whenever we interact with others, we will have some interests that are congruent and other interests that are in conflict. It takes wisdom to manage the combination of shared and opposed interests and reach an agreement. **Wise agreements** are those that are fair to all participants, are based on principles, strengthen participants' abilities to work together cooperatively, and improve participants' ability to resolve future conflicts constructively. In other words, wise agreements are those that meet the following criteria.

The first requirement for a wise agreement is that the agreement must meet the legitimate needs of all participants and be viewed as fair by everyone involved. In deciding on which option to adopt, keep in mind the importance of shared good feelings, preserving mutual interests, and preserving your shared history. Focus on the long-term relationship to ensure that the agreement is durable. Point out that your long-term survival and happiness should not be jeopardized by any agreement reached. To meet your and the other person's legitimate interests the agreement should clearly specify the responsibilities and rights of everyone involved in implementing the agreement. This includes:

1. **The ways each person will act differently in the future.** These responsibilities should be stated in a *specific* (tells who does what when, where, and how), *realistic* (each can do what he or she is agreeing to do), and *shared* (everyone agrees to do something different) way.

2. **How the agreement will be reviewed and renegotiated if it turns out to be unworkable.** This includes (a) the ways in which cooperation will be restored if one person slips and acts inappropriately and (b) the times participants will meet to discuss whether the agreement is working and what further steps can be taken to improve cooperation with each other. You cannot be sure the agreement will work until you try it out. After you have tested it for a while, it is a good idea to set aside some time to talk over how things are going. You may find that you need to make some changes or even rethink the whole problem. The idea is to keep on top of the problem so that the two of you may creatively solve it.

The second requirement for a wise agreement is that it is based on principles that can be justified on some objective criteria (Fisher & Ury, 1981). The objective criteria may be:

1. Everyone has an equal chance of benefiting (such as flipping a coin; one cuts, the other chooses; or letting a third-party arbitrator decide).

2. Fairness (taking turns, sharing, equal use). One way to assess fairness is to list the gains and losses for each person if the agreement is adopted and then see if they balance.

3. Scientific merit (based on theory, tested out, evidence indicates it will work).

4. Community values (those who are most in need are being taken care of first).

Evaluate each of the proposed options on the basis of one of these objective criteria. Think through which standards are most appropriate to evaluate the options and make a decision based on principle. The more you do so, the more likely you are to produce a final agreement that is wise and fair.

Using objective criteria to evaluate a possible agreement may result in clarifying what is "fair" and "just" from both sides of the issue. Remember King Solomon. One of the first problems the new King Solomon was presented with involved two women who both claimed the same baby. They wanted him to decide whose it was. Sitting on his throne, Solomon listened carefully. The two women lived together in the same house. Their babies had been born only three days apart. Then one of the babies died. The first woman said, "This woman's child died in the night. She then arose and took my son from beside me and placed the dead child next to me. When I woke to feed my baby, I found her dead child in my arms." "No!" the other woman cried frantically. "The living child is my son!" Solomon calmly said, "Bring me a sword and bring me the baby. Divide the living child in two and give half to the one and half to the other." Everyone was shocked. "No! Please don't!" screamed the real mother. "She can have the child. Don't kill it!" "No," the other woman said, "let the child be neither mine nor yours, but divide it." "Aha!" said Solomon. "Now I know to whom the child belongs." Then pointing to the woman who had asked that the baby's life be spared, he said, "Give her the living child. She is its mother."

The third requirement for a wise agreement is that the agreement and the process of reaching the agreement strengthen participants' ability to work together cooperatively in the future (the trust, respect, and liking among participants should be increased). All participants in the conflict must remain moral persons who are caring and just. They should see each other as being entitled to caring and justice. When conflicts are resolved constructively, **commitment to the long-term survival of the relationship** is increased. The more committed individuals are to their relationship, the more they inhibit negative emotions (annoyance, bitterness), negative attributions (it is all the other person's fault), and negative behaviors (passiveness, destructive acts) (Arriaga & Rusbult, 1998). Commitment appears to involve the *inhibition* of destructive processes rather than the *activation* of constructive processes. Individuals inhibit destructive patterns of thinking (e.g., do not think bad things about us [Rusbult et al., 1996]), drive away thoughts of tempting alternative relationships (Johnson & Rusbult, 1989), and think in collective terms (e.g., *we, us, our* rather than *I, me, mine* [Agnew et al., 1998]).

The fourth requirement for a wise agreement is that the agreement and the process of reaching the agreement strengthen participants' ability to resolve future conflicts constructively. Conflicts of interests will reoccur frequently and each time one is faced and resolved, the procedures and skills used should be strengthened and validated.

It is important that both you and the other person understand which actions trigger anger and resentment in the other. Criticism, put-downs, sarcasm, belittling, and other actions often trigger a conflict. If the two of you understand what not to do as well as what to do, the conflict will be resolved much more easily.

One way to understand how constructive agreements may be reached is to look at a few examples.

1. Roger was a coin collector; his wife, Ann, loved to raise and show championship rabbits. Their income did not leave enough money for both to practice their hobbies, and splitting the cash they did have would not have left enough for either. Solution: Put all the first year's money into the rabbits, and then after they were grown use the income from their litters and show prizes to pay for Roger's coins.
2. Edythe and Buddy shared an office but had different work habits. Edythe liked to do her work in silence whereas Buddy liked to socialize in the office and have the radio on. Solution: On Mondays and Wednesdays Buddy would help keep silence in the office, and on Tuesdays and Thursdays Edythe would work in a conference room that was free. On Fridays the two worked together on joint projects.

3. Keith loved to spend his evenings talking to people all over the world on his ham radio set. His wife, Simone, felt cheated out of the few hours of each day they could spend together. Keith did not want to give up his radio time and Simone was not willing to forego the time they had together. Solution: Four nights each week Keith stayed up late and talked to his ham radio friends after spending the evening with Simone. On the following mornings Simone drove Keith to work instead of having him go with a carpool, which allowed him to sleep later.

TRY, TRY AGAIN

Difference of opinion leads to inquiry, and inquiry to truth.

Thomas Jefferson

When you fail at negotiating an integrative agreement that is wise, the next step is to start over. To be successful at negotiating in a problem-solving way, you must remember to try, try again. No matter how far apart the two sides seem, no matter how opposed your interests seem to be, keep talking. With persistent discussion a viable and wise decision will eventually become clear.

Exercise 9.5: Negotiating Within an Organization

This exercise consists of two situations in which members of the same organization or group have to negotiate a resolution to a conflict of interests. In each situation the basic procedure for the coordinator is the same. The exercise takes less than one hour to complete.

1. Introduce the exercise as one in which the dynamics of negotiation among members of a group become apparent. Divide the class into groups of three (two participants and one observer) for case studies 1 and 2. You need at least two groups. Distribute the accompanying background sheets and role-playing sheets to the participants and observers. Give each observer one copy of the observers' instructions used in the previous exercise. Without letting the groups know that they are getting different instructions, give half of them copies of the accompanying bargaining instructions and the other half copies of the role-reversal instructions.
2. Meet with the observers to make sure they understand what they are expected to do.
3. Give them the signal to begin. Groups have up to twenty-five minutes to negotiate an agreement. If they finish before their time is up, note how long it took them to negotiate an agreement and what type of negotiation instructions they had.
4. At the end of twenty-five minutes announce that the time is up and the negotiations must end. Ask each participant to write on a sheet of paper two adjectives describing his feelings during the negotiations and hand it to you. Record how many groups negotiated an agreement and which type of instructions (bargaining or role reversal) they had.
5. Ask each group to discuss its experience with its observer. The main topics of the discussion should be the negotiation strategies used, how members reacted to one another's strategies, and how successful the different strategies were. Then, on a sheet of newsprint, have each group summarize its strategies, how successful they were, how members reacted to them, and any conclusions members can make about their effectiveness.

6. In a general session have each group share its instructions for negotiation, the strategies its members used, and its conclusions about their effectiveness. You can then reveal how participants with bargaining instructions reacted to the negotiations compared with participants with role-reversal instructions, how many groups with each type of instructions completed the negotiations successfully, and how long it took these groups to do so. Summarize the main points of the discussion.

7. Have the participants read the subsequent sections on negotiation and compare their conclusions with the material in those sections.

NEGOTIATION EXERCISE: CASE STUDY 1

Background

Jim and Chris (a female) both work for a research firm but in different divisions. Chris has been assigned project leader of a study, and Jim has been assigned from the other division to work on it. This does not necessarily imply that Chris is Jim's boss. This arrangement has been in effect for about a year and is relatively unsatisfactory to Chris, who would like to have Jim taken off the project. Meetings of the project team are often dominated by arguments between Chris and Jim. As a result Chris has often held meetings without notifying Jim. Jim and Chris are meeting to see if the conflict between them can be resolved.

Chris

Jim is a know-it-all who is always trying to tell you how to run your project. You do not agree with his approach. Jim comes into meetings, slumps down in a chair, and demands that everyone pay attention to him, even if he is late and they have already started. What he wants to study is not the subject of the research. You cannot stand Jim's voice. He has an extremely grating voice that he uses with imperious overtones. He is generally obnoxious. Jim doesn't give others a chance to talk and always interrupts if they do get a chance.

Jim does not care about the project. If he finds something else to do that he likes better, he simply ignores his responsibilities for completing work on the project. The group had to miss one deadline because he chose to do something else, and in the report before, you had to rewrite one whole section because what he turned in was not adequate. He was busy working on something for the director of the organization just to make a name for himself. Meanwhile, he sacrificed your reputation by causing your project to be late and your group to produce inferior work.

Jim

You do not agree with Chris' approach to the project. Working with her is difficult, because her main emphasis is on something that is not relevant to the real problems. She is ignoring the immediate problems that need to be solved and focusing on future issues that are not yet relevant. You believe you cannot tell her this, because Chris thinks she is better than anyone else around here and only the research she is doing is any good. She is a prima donna who thinks all the other work in the organization is "trash" except for hers. Consequently, you do not really feel involved in the project, especially because Chris accepts what everyone else on the project is doing, but she chooses your area to criticize. Occasionally you have worked on other projects. The director, for example, had you working on something more important for the organization for a while. But Chris is not willing to agree that anyone except herself can do anything well.

NEGOTIATION EXERCISE: CASE STUDY 2

Background

Juanita and Richard both work for a research organization. Originally the director of the organization was the leader of a project. Richard was interviewed for a position on that project and hired by the director. Juanita also interviewed Richard and strongly opposed his being hired for the project. Juanita thought Richard wasn't competent to do the job. Five or six months after work on the project began, the director decided she wanted to be relieved and proposed that Richard and Juanita conduct it jointly. Juanita agreed only reluctantly—with the stipulation that it be made clear she was not working for Richard. The director consented. They were to have a shared directorship. Within a month Juanita was angry because Richard was acting towards others as though he were the director of the entire project and she were working for him. Juanita and Richard are meeting to see if the conflict between them can be resolved.

Juanita

Right after the joint-leadership arrangement was reached with the director, Richard called a meeting of the project team without even consulting you about the time or content. He just told you when it was being held and said you should be there. At the meeting Richard reviewed everyone's paper line by line—including yours, thus treating you as just another team member working for him. He sends out letters and signs himself as project director, which obviously implies to others that you are working for him. You are hurt, angry, and determined to reestablish your position as joint director of the project.

Richard

You think Juanita is all hung up with feelings of power and titles. Just because you are project director, or sign yourself that way, doesn't mean that she is working for you. You do not see anything to get excited about. What difference does it make? She is too sensitive about everything. You call a meeting and right away she thinks you are trying to run everything. Juanita has other things to do—other projects to run—so she does not pay too much attention to this one. She mostly lets things slide. But when you take the initiative to set up a meeting, she starts jumping up and down about how you are trying to make her work for you.

NEGOTIATION EXERCISE: WIN–LOSE NEGOTIATING INSTRUCTIONS

Win–lose negotiation exists when each person attempts to reach an agreement as more favorable to oneself than to the other person. Strategies used to be successful include:

1. Presenting an opening offer very favorable to oneself and refusing to modify that position.
2. Gathering information about what the other considers a "reasonable" agreement from the other's opening offer and proposals.
3. Continually pointing out the validity of one's own position and the incorrectness of the other person's.
4. Using a combination of threats and promises to convince the other person that he or she has to accept one's offer.
5. Committing oneself to a position in such a way that if an agreement is to be reached, the other person has to agree to one's terms.

NEGOTIATION EXERCISE: ROLE-REVERSAL INSTRUCTIONS

Role reversal is defined as a negotiating action in which one person accurately and completely paraphrases, in a warm and involved way, the feelings and position of another. It is the expression of a sincere interest in understanding the other person's position and feelings. The basic rule for role reversal is this: Each person speaks up for himself only after he has first restated the ideas and feelings of the other person accurately and to the other's satisfaction. In other words, before one person presents his point of view it is necessary for him to achieve the other person's perspective or frame of reference and to understand her position and feelings so well that he can paraphrase them accurately and completely. General guidelines for role reversal are as follows:

1. Restate the other person's expressed ideas and feelings in one's own words rather than parroting the words of the other person.
2. Preface your reflected remarks with "You think . . . ," "Your position is . . . ," "You feel . . . ," "It seems to you that . . . ," and so on.
3. Avoid any indication of approval or disapproval in paraphrasing the other person's statements. It is important to refrain from interpreting, blaming, persuading, or advising.
4. Make your nonverbal messages congruent with your verbal paraphrasing. Look attentive, be interested in and open to the other's ideas and feelings, and appear to be concentrating on what the other person is trying to communicate.

In this exercise you are to engage in role reversal during the entire negotiating session and use it to arrive at the solution to the problems you and the other person(s) are facing.

NEGOTIATING IN GOOD FAITH

You can bring your credibility down in a second. It takes a million acts to build it up, but one act can bring it down. . . . People are suspicious because for several thousand years that suspicion was warranted . . . we try very hard not to do things that will create distrust.

Howard K. Sperlich, President, Chrysler Corporation

Everyone has a negotiating reputation. The promises of some people are to be believed. Other people rarely keep their commitments. You want to build a reputation of being someone who is honest, truthful, trustworthy, and, therefore, fulfills your promises. You want your word to be good. When your word has not been good in the past, there are at least three strategies you can use to increase your credibility:

1. **Pay your debts.** Whatever you have agreed to do in the past and not yet done, do it. Once you have fulfilled past promises, your current promise will be more credible.
2. **Use collateral.** The collateral should be something of value, something the other person does not expect you to give up. While being significant enough to be meaningful, the collateral should not be something so outrageous that it is not believable. Promising to give someone $1,000 if you break your word is not believable.
3. **Have a cosigner who guarantees your word.** Find someone who trusts you that the other person trusts, and have him or her guarantee that you will keep your word.

REFUSAL SKILLS: THIS ISSUE IS NOT NEGOTIABLE

Not all issues are negotiable. Group members must be able to:

1. Know when an issue is and is not negotiable.
2. Be able to say "no" or "I refuse to negotiate this issue."

There are times when group members should not negotiate. Group members must always have the option of saying "no" to negotiations. There are clear reasons for doing so, such as the issue being illegal, inappropriate, it will hurt other people, or they do not think they can keep their word. There are also unclear reasons, such as intuition, being unsure, not seeing the right option, and having changed their mind (see Table 9.5). You will save considerable time and trouble by not persuading others to make agreements they do not wish to make and not letting others persuade you to agree to something you do not wish to do.

Table 9.5 **Reasons for Saying "No"**

Clear	Unclear
Illegal.	My intuition tells me "no."
Inappropriate.	I am not sure.
It will hurt other people.	The right option is not there.
I will not be able to keep my word.	I have changed my mind.

Exercise 9.6: Breaking Balloons

This exercise seeks to demonstrate a nonverbal conflict—which is a complete change from the previous highly verbal activities. The procedure is as follows:

> Each participant is to blow up a balloon and tie it to his or her ankle with a string. Then when the coordinator gives the signal, the participants are to try to break one another's balloons by stepping on them. The person whose balloon is broken is "out" and must sit and watch from the sidelines; the last person to have an unbroken balloon is the winner. The participants can then discuss their feelings of aggression, defense, defeat, and victory. Strategies for protecting one's balloon while attacking others should be noted. A variation on the exercise is to have teams with different-colored balloons competing against each other.

Exercise 9.7: Intergroup Conflict

This exercise studies the dynamics of intergroup conflict and negotiation among groups with conflicting positions. It takes two hours. The procedure for the coordinator is as follows:

1. Introduce the exercise as an experience in intergroup conflict and negotiation. Divide the participants into four groups of no fewer than six members each and distribute a copy of one of the accompanying instruction sheets to each group. Emphasize that the exercise will determine which group is best.
2. Have each group meet separately to select a negotiator and to develop its proposals on the issue. They have half an hour to do this. At the end of this period give them the ac-

companying reaction form and ask them to answer only questions 1, 2, and 5 and to write the name of their group at the top.

3. Have the negotiators meet in the center of the room, each with her group sitting behind her. Give each group representative five minutes to present her group's proposals. After each representative has completed her presentation, have all participants complete the reaction form, answering all questions.

4. Tell the groups to reconvene separately and brief their negotiator on the best way to proceed in a second presentation of their position. The groups have fifteen minutes to confer. At the end of this period they again answer questions 1, 2, and 5 on the reaction form.

5. Have the negotiators again meet in the center of the room with their groups seated behind them. They have up to half an hour to reach an agreement. Group members can communicate with their negotiator through written notes. At the end of fifteen minutes stop the negotiations and have everyone again complete the questionnaire. Negotiations then resume, and at the end of the thirty-minute period everyone answers the reaction form for the last time.

6. Conduct a general session in which the results of the questionnaire are presented and discussed. Ask group members how they feel about the experience and then focus upon the experience of the negotiators.

7. Have the groups meet separately to discuss how well they worked together and what the experience was like for them. Develop a list of conclusions about intergroup conflict and place it on newsprint.

8. Again conduct a general session, this time to discuss the conclusions reached by each group.

INSTRUCTIONS TO COORDINATOR FOR USE OF THE REACTION FORMS

1. Pick one person in each group—as many assistants as you need—to hand out and collect the reaction forms and to compute the group mean for each question each time the forms are used.

2. Copy the four accompanying charts on a chalkboard or large sheets of newsprint. After each use of the reaction forms, calculate the group means and place them on the charts, using a different color for each group. The response to question 5 should be listed for use in the discussion sessions. Do not let the participants see the results until the general session in which the results are discussed.

3. In discussing the results of each question, look for certain trends. The response to question 1 should be somewhat high in the beginning, increase after comparison with other group's proposals, and drop off if agreement is reached. If no agreement is reached it should not drop off. For question 2, look for the "hero–traitor" dynamic: Satisfaction goes up if the negotiator convinces other groups that her proposals are best, and goes down if she compromises the group's position. It is often helpful to look at the notes passed to the negotiator to see how the group is reacting. The responses to question 3 should be the reverse of the responses to question 1 (if satisfaction with one's own group's proposal is high, satisfaction with the other groups' proposals is low, and vice versa). This usually amounts to devaluing the other group's proposals and a loss of objectivity in evaluation. Question 4 usually demonstrates overconfidence in one's own group's proposal, though this sense of superiority gradually slips from an initial high as negotiations progress.

INTERGROUP CONFLICT EXERCISE: TEACHERS' GROUP

You are residents of Engleston, a medium-sized but quickly growing suburban community that is within commuting distance of a large city. Engleston has recently been torn by a number of civil rights demonstrations centering on the issue of school integration. Two of the public schools in Engleston contain approximately 90% of the underprivileged, culturally different white and black children in the community. Moreover, the high school drop-out rate (60%) has shown the inadequacy of the educational program for these youngsters. Acts of vandalism and other forms of juvenile delinquency have been pronounced and costly to the town, and most of those responsible are among the drop-outs. Four opposing groups in the community, yours among them, have suggested various solutions to some of these problems. The school board has asked the four groups to get together and settle on a single set of four to six proposals, which it will then implement. As a member of the teachers' group, you are essentially opposed to breaking up the schools in any way. You are interested in creating better schools and are generally in favor of expanding the educational program.

Your group is to submit four to six recommendations for dealing with the problems at a meeting at which your representative and one from each of the other three groups will be present. You and your groupmates may prepare a simple chart of the *main* points you wish to emphasize. Try to make your recommendations original and creative, because it will be to your advantage if the other groups accept your proposals. After the representatives have presented their group's proposals, they will negotiate a *composite proposal* of four to six points to be presented to the school board.

PARENTS' GROUP

You are residents of Engleston, a medium-sized but quickly growing suburban community that is within commuting distance of a large city. Engleston has recently been torn by a number of civil rights demonstrations centering on the issue of school integration. Two of the public schools in Engleston contain approximately 90% of the underprivileged, culturally different white and black children in the community. Moreover, the high school drop-out rate (60%) has increasingly shown the inadequacy of the educational program for these youngsters. Acts of vandalism and other forms of juvenile delinquency have become pronounced and costly to the town, and most of those responsible are among the drop-outs. Four opposing groups in the community, yours among them, have suggested various solutions to some of these problems. The school board has asked the four groups to get together and settle on a single set of four to six proposals, which it will then implement. You are a member of the parents' group. Because the tax rate is already one of the highest in the state, you favor solutions that will *not* increase your taxes. You feel that teachers and administrators have been lax, and that what is needed is more efficient and immediate use of the present resources. You are absolutely against any busing of students and want all students to attend the school closest to their home.

Your group is to submit four to six recommendations for dealing with the problems at a meeting at which your representative and one from each of the other three groups will be present. You and your groupmates may prepare a simple chart of the *main* points you wish to emphasize. Try to make your recommendations original and creative, because it will be to your advantage if the other groups accept your proposals. After the representatives have presented their group's proposals, they will negotiate a *composite proposal* of four to six points to be presented to the school board.

CIVIL RIGHTS GROUP

You are residents of Engleston, a medium-sized but quickly growing suburban community that is within commuting distance of a large city. Engleston has recently been torn by a number of civil rights demonstrations centering on the issue of school integration. Two of the public schools in Engleston contain approximately 90% of the underprivileged, culturally differ-ent white and black children in the community. Moreover, the high school drop-out rate (60%) has increasingly shown the inadequacy of the educational program for these youngsters. Acts of vandalism and other forms of juvenile delinquency have become pronounced and costly to the town, and most of those responsible are among the drop-outs. Four opposing groups in the community, yours among them, have suggested various solutions to some of these problems. The school board has asked the four groups to get together and settle on a single set of four to six proposals, which it will then implement. As a member of the civil rights group, you are totally committed to immediate integration. You believe the schools have to be integrated through immediate busing of students. You feel that reforms generally take place too slowly, and you are extremely dissatisfied with the present situation.

Your group is to submit four to six recommendations for dealing with the problems at a meeting at which your representative and one from each of the other three groups will be present. You and your groupmates may prepare a simple chart of the *main* points you wish to emphasize. Try to make your recommendations original and creative, because it will be to your advantage if the other groups accept your proposals. After the representatives have presented their group's proposals, they will negotiate a *composite proposal* of four to six points to be presented to the school board.

SCHOOL ADMINISTRATORS' GROUP

You are residents of Engleston, a medium-sized but quickly growing suburban community that is within commuting distance of a large city. Engleston has recently been torn by a num-ber of civil rights demonstrations centering on the issue of school integration. Two of the public schools in Engleston contain approximately 90% of the underprivileged, culturally deprived white and black children in the community. Moreover, the high school drop-out rate (60%) has increasingly shown the inadequacy of the educational program for these young-sters. Acts of vandalism and other forms of juvenile delinquency have become pronounced and costly to the town, and most of those responsible are among the drop-outs. Four op-posing groups in the community, yours among them, have suggested various solutions to some of these problems. The school board has asked the four groups to get together and settle on a single set of four to six proposals, which it will then implement. As a member of the school administrators' group, you are generally satisfied with the way things are and be-lieve that anything but gradual and carefully planned change would lead to chaos. More-over, you believe that the complaining has been done chiefly by extremist groups at work in the community. In your opinion all school policy decisions should be made by your group—and parents, teachers, and community groups should not butt in.

Your group is to submit four to six recommendations for dealing with the problems at a meeting at which your representative and one from each of the other three groups will be present. You and your groupmates may prepare a simple chart of the *main* points you wish to present. Try to make your recommendations original and creative, because it will be to your advantage if the other groups accept your proposals. After the representatives have presented their groups' proposals, they will negotiate a *composite proposal* of four to six points to be presented to the school board.

REACTION FORM

Group _____

1. How satisfied are you with your own group's proposals?
   Very dissatisfied 1 : 2 : 3 : 4 : 5 : 6 : 7 : 8 : 9 Very satisfied

2. How satisfied are you with the negotiator your group has selected?
   Very dissatisfied 1 : 2 : 3 : 4 : 5 : 6 : 7 : 8 : 9 Very satisfied
3. How satisfied are you with the proposals of the other groups?
   Very dissatisfied 1 : 2 : 3 : 4 : 5 : 6 : 7 : 8 : 9 Very satisfied
4. How do you think the final composite proposal will compare with your group's proposals?
   Very inferior 1 : 2 : 3 : 4 : 5 : 6 : 7 : 8 : 9 Very superior
5. Write one adjective describing the way you now feel about what is taking place. _____

CHART A: SATISFACTION WITH OWN GROUP'S PROPOSALS

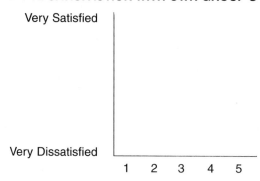

CHART B: SATISFACTION WITH NEGOTIATOR

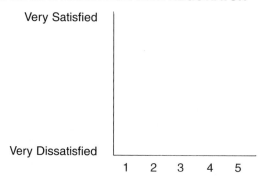

CHART C: SATISFACTION WITH OTHER GROUPS' PROPOSALS

CHART D: SATISFACTION WITH COMPOSITE PROPOSAL

Very Satisfied

Very Dissatisfied

1 2 3 4 5

Other Intergroup Conflict Exercises

Other intergroup conflict exercises can easily be created around the general procedure given on pages 424–425. The task can be to state the five most important principles of leadership, the qualities of an effective supervisor, the five most important things for a teacher to know, and so on. The dynamics of intergroup conflict are so predictable that if participants are divided into groups and told to compete, develop their position, and represent that position in negotiations, the dynamics are bound to occur.

INTERGROUP CONFLICT

About 1260 B.C. one of the great intergroup conflicts in history occurred between the powerful Greek king of Sparta (Menelaus) and his allies and Paris from the city of Troy. During the ten-year war Troy was destroyed and Greece lost some of its greatest warriors and kings. It took another ten years for one of the Greek heroes (Odysseus) to get home. The conflict was over Helen (the most beautiful woman in the world at the time). It began at the wedding of Peleus, a mortal king, and Thetis, an immortal sea nymph. During the ceremony the goddess Eris (goddess of strife and discord) appeared. Angered that she was not invited to the wedding, Eris left a golden apple that she proclaimed would go to the most beautiful goddess. This understandably created a conflict. Hera (supreme goddess of heaven), Athena (goddess of wisdom), and Aphrodite (goddess of love) were all convinced that they were the most beautiful goddess. They began to argue and the argument raged until Zeus stepped in and ordered Paris, the son of Priam the king of Troy, to decide. Each of the three goddesses offered Paris a bribe. Hera promised to make him ruler of the entire world if he named her the most beautiful, Athena offered him glory in war, and Aphrodite offered him the most beautiful woman in the world, Helen. Paris chose Aphrodite's offer and named her the most beautiful of the goddesses.

Paris then set sail for Greece to claim his prize. The problem was that Helen was already married to the powerful Greek king of Sparta, Menelaus. Because of Helen's beauty, when Menelaus was courting her, virtually every unmarried Greek male wanted her for his wife. Helen's father, realizing that no matter whom he chose to wed his daughter the others would feel slighted and would very likely seek revenge, consulted the advice of Odysseus (who was famed for his cleverness) and made each of Helen's suitors swear an oath (a) that he would defend the marriage no matter who won her hand and (b) if she were ever carried off they would aid in getting her back.

When Paris arrived at the palace of Menelaus he was given food, shelter, and gifts according to the rules of hospitality. When Menelaus left, however, Paris and Helen, who was irresistibly attracted to him thanks to Aphrodite, eloped to Troy. When Menelaus returned to find his wife taken he invoked the oath that the other suitors had taken, and began preparations for a huge invasion force to win back Helen. The Trojan War was the result. Not all intergroup conflicts are as famous as that of the Trojan War. Such deadly intergroup quarrels can also start over trivial reasons. Battles resulting in the death of street gang members, for example, have started from a perceived insult or the intrusion of a member of one gang into an area controlled by another gang.

The tendency to see the world in an "us-versus-them" framework is well documented. If you selected ten people at random and randomly divided them into two groups of five, they would quickly come to value their own group and discriminate in favor of it. There is an **in-group–out-group bias,** in which we hold less favorable views about groups to which we do not belong, while holding more favorable opinions about groups to which we do belong (Wilder, 1986, 1990; Perdue et al., 1990). Individuals tend to reward members of their own group at the expense of members of other groups, and they do so in ways that magnify the differences in reward between the two groups. Tajfel and Turner (1979, p. 38) demonstrated that a systematic in-group bias in groups where "the mere awareness of the presence of an out-group is sufficient to provoke intergroup competition or discriminatory responses on the part of the in-group." Such social categorization often leads to the **out-group homogeneity bias,** which is the belief that there is less variability among the members of the out-groups than within one's own in-group (Linville, Fisher, & Salovey, 1989).

If such dynamics are found in groups that are minimally differentiated from each other and where members are anonymous, it is hardly surprising that the bias against out-groups would be even stronger when the out-groups have very obvious and salient differences from in-groups. Three of the dynamics of the in-group–out-group and out-group homogeneity biases are intergroup competition, bias favoring the in-group over the out-groups, and the depersonalization of members of the out-groups. The two theories that discuss the issues most directly are social identity and social categorization theories.

Social identity theory (formulated by Henri Tajfel [1982] and John Turner [1987]) is based on the hypothesis that individuals seek a positively valued distinctiveness for their own groups compared to other groups to achieve a positive social identity (see Figure 9.6). **Social identity** is the individual's knowledge that he or she belongs to certain social groups that have emotional value significant to the individual (Tajfel, 1982). According to social identity theory, people strive to enhance their self-esteem, which has two components: a personal identity and various social identities derived from the groups to which they belong (Tajfel & Turner, 1986; Tajfel, 1974; Turner et al., 1992). Thus, people may boost their self-esteem by viewing their in-groups more favorably than out-groups. In other words, our quest for a positive social identity leads us to in-

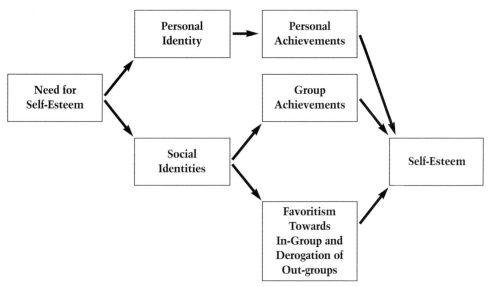

Figure 9.6   Social Identity Theory.

flate the positive aspects of the group to which we belong and belittle groups to which we do not belong (Tajfel & Turner, 1986; Tujfel, 1974; Turner et al., 1992). When a group is successful, members' self-esteem can rise and conversely when members' self-esteem is threatened, they feel a heightened need for in-group favoritism (attraction to own group and disparagement of out-groups) which in turn enhances their self-esteem (Crocker & Luhranen, 1990).

The differentiation between in-groups and out-groups is based on **social categoriza-tion.** Social categories function as cognitive "labor-saving devices" by helping you place other people into meaningful categories. While you may use a wide range of categories for classifying people (for example, male, friend, stranger, Christian, neighbor, political, athlete), two very basic social categorizations are (a) member of my group and (b) member of another group (Hamilton, 1979). **Social categorization theory** is based on the hypothesis that personal and social identity are self-categorizations (Turner & Oakes, 1989) that in and of themselves are sufficient to create discriminatory intergroup behavior. Social identity is based on differentiating among groups (I am American, male, and Protestant as opposed to Canadian, female, and Catholic) and is assumed to be a more inclusive, superordinate level of abstraction than personal identity in the categorization of the self.

A premise of social identity and social categorization theories is that the process of making categorical distinctions to understand the social world involves minimizing perceived differences within categories and accentuating intercategory differences (Tajfel, 1969). This results in three principles:

1. The **intergroup accentuation principle**—there is assimilation within category boundaries and contrast between categories, such that all members of the in-group are perceived to be more similar to the self than to members of the out-group.

2. The **ingroup favoritism principle**—positive affect (trust, liking) is selectively generalized to fellow in-group members but not to out-group members.
3. The **social competition principle**—intergroup social comparison is based on perceived negative interdependence (competition) between in-group and out-group.

There is some evidence that the desire to see oneself as fair-minded can mitigate against discriminating against out-group members (Singh, Choo, & Poh, 1998).

The second premise of social identity and social categorization theories is that because individual persons are themselves members of some social categories and not others, social categorization carries with it implicit in-group–out-group (we–they) distinctions resulting in (a) intergroup competition, (b) mutual distrust between in-group and out-groups, and (c) in-group members receiving preferred treatment (Turner, 1985). Even when social categorizations are imposed on people (given the acceptance and internalization of the categories), members of the in-group are liked more and treated better than members of the out-group. In addition, there is a tendency to depersonalize members of the out-group ("they" are all alike).

It should be remembered that people do not categorize themselves in the same way in every situation. When in Indiana, a person may say, "I'm from Muncie," when in California, a person may say, "I'm from Indiana," and in Singapore, a person may say, "I'm from the United States." As situations change, so do the ways people categorize themselves and others.

Thus, categorization results in competition among groups, social identity, the depersonalization of members of the out-groups, and a bias towards the in-group and against the out-group. Social identity and social categorization theories explain how this happens. In order to overcome these effects, a process of decategorization and then recategorization must take place.

Decategorization: Personalizing Interaction

A primary consequence of categorization is the depersonalization of members of out-groups. Individual members of an out-group tend to be treated as undifferentiated representatives, not as unique individuals. In order to reduce in-group bias and the depersonalization of out-group members, contact among members of the different groups is required. These intergroup interactions should be structured so as to reduce the salience of category distinctions and to promote opportunities to get to know out-group members as individuals (Miller, Brewer, & Edwards, 1985). Contact will be most effective when interactions are highly personalized rather than category based (Brewer & Miller, 1984). Attending to personal characteristics of out-group members tends to disconfirm category stereotypes and decreases the perception of out-groups as homogeneous units.

Recategorization: Building a Common In-group Identity

Johnson and Johnson (1992a) and Gaertner and his associates (1993) posited that in-group bias and the depersonalization of out-group members can be reduced by structuring the contact among members of different groups so attention is focused on a superordinate category identification that encompasses both in-group and out-group in a single social group representation. Although there may be white Americans, black

Americans, Asian Americans, and Hispanic Americans, for example, highlighting the superordinate identity of "American" can unite all citizens into a single social category and identification. Thus, attention to category differences is minimized by creating a new inclusive group identity. This is facilitated by assigning majority and minority members the same role (Bettencourt et al., in press; Bettencourt & Dorr, 1998). The more that individuals perceive the superordinate identity as a single entity, rather than as an aggregate of separate groups, evaluation of former out-group members becomes more positive.

It should be noted that decategorization and recategorization are not mutually exclusive. Cooperation and superordinate goals promote formation of common identity. Equal-status, personalized interactions promote decategorization and individuation.

Sherif's Studies of Intergroup Conflict

A number of social scientists have worked to develop an intergroup theory. They include Muzafer Sherif, Robert Blake, and Jane Mouton. Intergroup conflicts also include clashes among cultures and clarifying resulting misunderstandings.

Perhaps the most interesting and best-known studies of intergroup conflict were performed under the direction of Muzafer Sherif (1966). Sherif was born in 1906 in Izmir, Turkey. After attending Izmir International College, he studied at the University of Istanbul, receiving a master's degree in 1928. Awarded a fellowship in national competition for study abroad, he went to Harvard University in 1929, received another master's degree in 1932, and then traveled to Germany where he attended Kohler's lectures and the University of Berlin. He then taught in Turkey, returned to Harvard to conduct research, and subsequently studied at Columbia University (1934–1936), where he received a Ph.D. degree in 1935. His dissertation was published as a book, *The Psychology of Group Norms* (discussed in Chapter 1). He studied in Paris and taught in Turkey until January 1945, when he returned to the United States. After teaching at both Princeton and Yale, he became director of the Institute of Group Relations at the University of Oklahoma, a position he held from 1949 to 1966. In 1966 he moved to Pennsylvania State University. It was during the years he spent at Oklahoma that he encountered his famous research on superordinate goals.

To study intergroup conflict and its resolution, Sherif, his students, and his colleagues ran a summer camp for twelve-year-old boys in the early 1950s. All the boys were strangers to one another prior to attending the camp, so there were no established relationships among them. The camp setting, isolated from outside influences, afforded the experimenters a unique opportunity to manipulate the conditions and circumstances of interaction among the camp members. The investigators were interested in studying intergroup relations, and especially the effectiveness of various techniques for reducing hostility between groups. To create intergroup conflict, the experimenters divided up the campers into groups and instilled in each group an esprit de corps by such procedures as assigning names like Bull Dogs and Red Devils to the groups and structuring their daily activities so that interdependent, coordinated activity among the group members was necessary for achieving desired goals (the food, for example, needed to be cooked over a campfire and distributed among the group members).

Following the successful development in the camp of two in-groups characterized by mutual good feeling between their members, the experimenters attempted to induce conflict between the two groups by requiring them to participate in competitive activities in which the winning group was rewarded and the losing group was not. For a time the two groups displayed good sportsmanship, but in the course of the competitive activities they became increasingly hostile towards each other. Eventually the two groups were having garbage fights—throwing mashed potatoes, leftovers, bottle caps, and the like—in the dining hall.

Sherif (1966) and his associates next tested several different methods of reducing the conflict between the groups. To find out the effects of social contact between groups on intergroup conflict, Sherif devised several pleasant situations in which members of the rival groups could engage in such contact. These situations included eating together in the same dining room, watching a movie together, and shooting firecrackers in the same area. These contact situations had no effect in reducing intergroup conflict. If anything, they were utilized by members of both groups as opportunities for further name-calling and other forms of conflict. Sherif concluded that contact between groups in pleasant situations does not in itself decrease existing intergroup tension.

The next strategy researched by Sherif (1966) and his associates was the establishment of a common enemy. Sherif did demonstrate that it is possible to reduce the hostility between two groups by presenting them with a common enemy against whom they are banded together. He arranged a softball game in which the two groups in conflict were combined to play against a group of boys from a nearby town. The common enemy did bring the two groups of campers together and reduced some of the hostility between them. This approach, however, has little promise for conflict resolution, as it fails to resolve the conflict but only transfers it from two small groups to one larger group. Bringing some groups together against another means larger and more devastating conflicts in the long run.

Sherif (1966) hypothesized that contact between the rival groups would resolve the conflict only when the groups came together to work cooperatively towards goals that were more important to the groups than the continuation of their conflict. Because cooperation towards common goals had been effective in forming the two in-groups, Sherif reasoned, it would be effective in reducing the conflict between the groups. Sherif therefore arranged a series of superordinate-goal situations for the two antagonistic groups of campers to engage in. He defined **superordinate goals** as goals that cannot be easily ignored by members of two antagonistic groups, but whose attainment is beyond the resources and efforts of either group alone; the two groups, therefore, must join in a cooperative effort in order to attain the goals. One such goal was to repair the water-supply system, which the experimenters had earlier sabotaged. Another was to obtain money to rent a movie that both groups wanted to see. Still another was to push a truck to get it started after it had suddenly broken down on its way to a camp-out with food. After the campers had participated in a series of such activities, their attitude towards members of the out-group changed; several friendships among members of different groups were formed, members of the rival group were no longer disliked, and the friction between the groups disappeared.

The characteristics of the superordinate goals introduced by Sherif and his associates in their studies were as follows:

1. They were introduced by a more powerful third party (the experimenters).
2. They were perceived by campers to be natural events in no way identified with the third party.

3. They were not perceived by the two groups of campers as being aimed at resolving the conflict.
4. They transcended the conflict situation and restructured the competitive relationship between the groups into a cooperative one.

In most conflict situations such superordinate goals are not feasible alternatives. A third party, for example, rarely had the power to initiate goals with the above characteristics. Nor could a participant in a conflict easily initiate such a goal in an attempt to resolve the conflict.

Although Sherif's studies provide clear documentation that cooperative groups will produce interpersonal attraction even when the individuals start out as enemies, the cooperative goals that were introduced were presented to the campers as "acts of God." Johnson and Lewicki (1969) conducted a study on intergroup conflict in which two types of superordinate cooperative goals were introduced, one appearing to be an "act of God" and the other introduced by one of the groups engaged in the conflict. The "act of God" cooperative goal did in fact resolve the intergroup conflict whereas the opposing group refused to accept the superordinate cooperative goal proposed by one of the parties involved. The opposing group tended to view the superordinate cooperative goal as part of a competitive strategy aimed at furthering the initiating group's vested interests. Thus, to be effective in promoting interpersonal attraction among "enemies," cooperative goals may have to be presented by a third party or appear to be natural tragedies or opportunities independent of the parties involved in the conflict.

Sherif's notion of resolving conflicts through the use of superordinate goals is an elaboration of the principle that groups that cooperate with one another towards the accomplishment of common goals will have harmonious and friendly relations. Deutsch's (1949a, 1962) theory of cooperation and competition states such a principle, and a number of research studies support the principle's validity (Johnson and Johnson, 1987). Deutsch's theory predicts that even when there is intense hostility between two groups, cooperative action to accomplish goals that are of vital importance to both will result in mutual liking and continued cooperation.

Blake and Mouton Studies of Intergroup Conflict

The more the intergroup conflict is defined as a win–lose situation, the more predictable are the effects of the conflict on the relationships of members within the group, on relationships between the groups, on negotiations between the groups, on the group that wins, and on the group that loses (Blake & Mouton, 1962, 1983). A group in the throes of an intergroup conflict experiences a strong upward shift in cohesion as members join together to defend their group against defeat. The group becomes more closely knit and gleans greater loyalty from its members; members close ranks and "table," or put aside, some of their conflicts with one another. There is a sharpening and banding together of the in-group power structure as militant leaders take control and group members become more willing to accept autocratic leadership. Maintenance needs become secondary to task needs, and the group becomes more tightly structured and organized. Satisfaction among the members runs high, along with their sense of identification with the group and with its position on the issues in the conflict. At the same time the opposing group and its positions are belittled and devalued. Conformity is demanded; "a solid front" must be presented.

Between the groups, an attitude of hostility develops. Each sees the other as the enemy. Inaccurate and uncomplimentary stereotypes form. Distortions in perception (see Johnson, 2000) increase. Each group sees only the best parts of itself and the worst parts of the other group. Interaction and communication decrease between members of the conflicting groups. Doubt is cast upon the validity of the position of the other group; its position is seen as distinctly inferior to that of one's own group. Group members tend to listen only to what supports their own position and stereotypes. They misperceive and fail to listen carefully to the other group's position. All of these dynamics only intensify the conflict and deepen distrust.

In win–lose negotiations, there are distortions of judgment about the merits of the conflicting positions, with one's own position recognized as *good* and the other group's position assessed as *bad*. Negotiators are relatively blind to points of agreement between their own and the other side's proposals, and they tend to emphasize the differences. The orientation of the negotiators for the two sides is to win for their group, not to reach an agreement that satisfies everyone. This stance inevitably results in the **hero–traitor dynamic**—the negotiator who *wins* is seen as a *hero* and the one who *loses* as a *traitor*. When a neutral third party decides who is right and who is wrong, the winner considers the third party to be impartial and objective; the loser views the third party as biased and thoughtless. Each side sees itself as objective and rational and the other side as unjust and irrational—thereby excluding from the negotiations any elements of genuine objectivity. With the only loyalty being to one's own group's position, the common result of win–lose negotiations is a deadlock. The win–lose strategy can result, of course, in the representative being caught in a conflict between his own beliefs and perceptions and the mandate given him by his group.

The group that wins becomes even more cohesive. It also tends to release tension, lose its fighting spirit, and become self-satisfied, casual, even playful. The leadership that was responsible for the victory is consolidated. Although there is a high concern for maintenance, there is little tendency to work. Members believe that winning has confirmed their positive stereotype of their group and the negative stereotype of the other group, and that as a result there is little need to reevaluate perceptions or reexamine group operations to learn how to improve them.

The group that loses frequently splinters, seeks the reasons for its defeat, and then reorganizes. Members bring to the surface unresolved conflicts among themselves in an effort to find the reasons for the defeat. Tension increases and the group begins to work even harder. Maintenance concerns abate as task concerns rise in a group effort to recover from defeat. The group often seeks someone to blame for the defeat—the leader, the judges, those who made the rules of the conflict situation, the least conforming members, and so on—and replaces the leadership responsible for the loss. If future victories seem impossible, members may become completely demoralized and assume a defeatist, apathetic attitude towards the group. The losing group tends to learn a great deal about itself because its positive stereotype of itself and its negative stereotype of the other group have been upset by the loss; it has therefore had to reevaluate its perceptions. Consequently, the losing group is likely to reorganize and become more cohesive and effective once it has accepted the loss realistically.

Blake and Mouton (1983) emphasize that those who use this procedure must avoid three basic traps that lead to increased, rather than decreased, conflict. The first to avoid is the **win–lose dynamic**—seeing every action of the other group as a move to dominate,

Important Concepts

Demonstrate your understanding of the following concepts by matching the definitions with the appropriate concept. Find a partner. Compare answers.

	Concept	Definition
_____	1. Psychodynamic fallacy	a. Seeing every action of members of other groups as a move to dominate, create an advantage, or win.
_____	2. Win–lose dynamic	b. The capacity to affect another person's goal accomplishment.
_____	3. Hero–traitor dynamic	c. Feelings of discontent aroused by the belief that one fares poorly compared to others.
_____	4. Superordinate goals	d. Seeing the motivation for the behavior of members of other groups in terms of personality factors rather than the dynamics of intergroup conflict.
_____	5. Power	e. When a person is frustrated but cannot attack the source because of fear or simple unavailability, the person attacks an innocent third party because the party is available and has less power.
_____	6. Relative deprivation	f. Goals that cannot be easily ignored by members of two antagonistic groups, but whose attainment is beyond the resources and efforts of either group alone.
_____	7. Displaced aggression	g. Antagonism between groups arises from real conflicts of interests and the frustrations these conflicts produce.
_____	8. Authoritarian personality	h. Your expectations cause you to behave in a way that provokes behavior from others that confirms your expectations.
_____	9. Realistic group conflict	i. Prejudice arises when one group frustrates the other group's goal achievement and the frustrated group reacts with aggression.
_____	10. Self-fulfilling prophecy	j. Conflict over basic values occurring among individuals from different cultures.
_____	11. Culture clash	k. The negotiator who *wins* is seen as a *hero* and the one who *loses* as a *traitor*.
_____	12. Frustration-aggression theory	l. Person characterized by exaggerated submission to authority, rigid conformity to conventional norms, self-righteous hostility, and harsh punitiveness towards anyone considered different.

create an advantage, or win. The participants must learn to recognize win–lose attitudes and behaviors and be able to set norms that stress their avoidance. The second trap to avoid is the **psychodynamic fallacy**—seeing the motivation for the behavior of members of another group in terms of personality factors rather than the dynamics of intergroup conflict. It is much easier to blame the conflict on sick, vicious, power-hungry persons than to view the other group's behavior as a predictable result of intense intergroup conflict. The final trap to avoid is the use of a **self-fulfilling prophecy.** For example, one group assumes that the other is belligerent and proceeds to engage in hostile behavior in an attempt to defend itself by mounting a good offense—thereby provoking belligerence on the part of the other group, which confirms the original assumption.

More recent evidence indicates that when third parties decide how to resolve intergroup and cross-cultural conflict (i.e., arbitration), the decision will be evaluated more strongly through judgments about the treatment of disputants (relational concerns) in conflicts within groups and more strongly in terms of the decision's favorability (instrumental concerns) in disputes across groups (Tyler, Lind, Ohbuchi, Sugawara, Huo, 1998).

Exercise 9.8: Intergroup Confrontation (I)

This procedure was developed by Blake and Mouton (1962). It has been used successfully in intergroup conflicts in a variety of organizations for every type of intergroup conflict you can imagine. Its purpose is to change the win–lose orientation to a problem-solving orientation. This exercise takes at least two hours to conduct (Blake and Mouton usually took about twenty hours to use the procedure in actual union–management conflicts).

1. Introduce the exercise as an experience in resolving conflicts between two or more groups. The objective is to change a win–lose to a problem-solving orientation. Discuss the previous success Blake and Mouton have had with the procedure in difficult union–management conflicts. Use the accompanying descriptions of a union–management conflict to set up a role play that participants can use in the exercise.
2. Each group meets separately and develops on newsprint (a) how it sees itself as a group and (b) how it sees the other group. Allow the groups at least thirty minutes to complete this task.
3. The two groups come together and share their descriptions. They compare how each side sees itself with how the other group sees it. Often each group sees the other as unreasonable, unethical, and unwilling to cooperate while seeing itself as extraordinarily reasonable, ethical, and cooperative. The differences in the perception of how each group sees the other group are then clarified.
4. The two groups meet separately for twenty minutes to diagnose their present relationship. They should answer such questions as: "What problems exist?" "Why aren't the problems being constructively solved?" "What does the other group contribute to the conflict?" "What does one's own group contribute to the conflict?" The groups should place this material on newsprint to share with the other group.
5. The groups meet together to share their diagnoses. They summarize the key issues causing the conflicts and the main sources of friction. The two groups should keep the integrative, problem-solving negotiation procedure in mind as they plan the next steps in resolving their conflict.
6. The two groups assess their reactions to the exercise and summarize what they have learned about resolving intergroup conflict. Conclusions about preventing intergroup conflict should also be presented and discussed.

UNION–MANAGEMENT CONFLICT

The union in a midsize manufacturing company has asked the management for across-the-board increases in pay and fringe benefits. The management has refused to meet these "excessive demands" and has made an offer that the union leadership considers unacceptable. Still without a contract agreement at midnight of the day before the old contract expires, the union has voted to go on strike and remain on strike until a satisfactory agreement is reached. Divide into union and management groups and carry out the above procedure.

Contact Theory

Resolving intergroup conflict is based on the assumption that contact between members of different groups will result in positive relationships and a reduction of stereotyping and prejudice. One of the most studied intergroup conflicts is that between white and minority individuals. Historically, social scientists believed that sheer ignorance about African Americans and their lives contributed to erroneous and oversimplified racial stereotypes (Myrdal, 1944). Contact was seen as the solution. A wide variety of studies conducted in the 1930s, 1940s, and 1950s indicated that such contact was not a straightforward matter. It seemed to be the nature of the contact between members of different ethnic groups, not the frequency, that promoted favorable intergroup attitudes. Researchers studied the effects of actual contact between blacks and whites, utilizing visiting black lecturers in classrooms (Young, 1932), meetings with black professionals (Smith, 1943), school integration (Horowitz, 1936), joint recreational activities in integrated summer camps (Yarrow, Campbel, & Yarrow, 1958; Williams, 1948), voyages of white merchant seamen serving with black seamen (Brophy, 1945), and contact within combat infantry platoons (Mannheimer & Williams, 1949; Star, Williams, & Stouffer, 1965). Many of the earliest research studies used questionnaires in which respondents were asked to note their attitudes towards members of an ethnic group and then to describe the nature and frequency of their contact with members of that group (Allport & Kramer, 1946; Harlan, 1942; MacKenzie, 1948; Rosenblith, 1949). Somewhat later studies were based on postwar occupational and educational desegregation (Gray & Thompson, 1953; Gundlach, 1950; Harding & Hogerge, 1952; Minard, 1952; Reed, 1947; Rose, 1948; Williams & Ryan, 1954) and desegregated residential settings (Deutsch & Collins, 1951; Irish, 1952; Jahoda & West, 1951; Kramer, 1951; Wilner, Walkey, & Cook, 1952, 1955; Winder, 1952). These latter studies indicated that the greater the degree of cooperation growing out of involuntary residential proximity between white and black residents, the more likely the development of friendly ethnic relationships.

Years later, we realize that the issue is not so simple. Sometimes intergroup contact is associated with less prejudice. As these early studies indicated, according to national surveys, having more black friends or more contact with gay men and lesbians is associated with less prejudice (Herek & Capitanio, 1996; Jackman & Crane, 1986). Contact, however, is also correlated with more prejudice. Whites who have had the most contact with illegal immigrants (Espenshade & Calhoun, 1993) and whites living in areas of the South with the largest concentration of African Americans have the most prejudiced political attitudes (Giles & Buckner, 1993; Key, 1949). Thus, contact can either increase or decrease prejudice and discrimination.

Based on these early studies, in 1947 Goodwin Watson published a review of the previous research and writings on intergroup relations. He concluded that contact between members of different ethnic groups was likely to be more effective in changing behavior and attitudes than were such alternative experiences as exposure to correct information or persuasive communication, given that the contact met a number of conditions. The conditions included:

1. Cooperative action to achieve mutual goals (the diverse individuals had to engage in cooperative activities together).
2. Personal interactions among individuals from the different groups.
3. Social norms and authorities favoring equalitarian cross-ethnic contact.
4. Equal-status contact.

In the same year, Williams (1947) published a similar list of conditions for constructive cross-ethnic contact, as did Kenneth Clark in 1953, and in 1954 Gordon Allport published his famous book, *The Nature of Prejudice,* in which he identified a similar list of conditions. Stuart Cook followed with a review in 1957.

Between the years of 1950 and 1970 there were approximately forty studies on cross-ethnic interaction (Amir, 1969; Cook, 1969; Stephan, 1978). The reviewers of this research concluded that the evidence was inconclusive as to whether cross-ethnic contact resulted in more favorable cross-ethnic attitudes and relationships. Under favorable conditions contact seemed to reduce prejudice and under unfavorable conditions contact seemed to increase prejudice. The major determinant of whether cross-ethnic contact produced positive attitudes and relationships was cooperative interaction among the individuals involved.

The most recent formulations of contact theory specify that the following conditions must exist for contact to result in a reduction of prejudice, stereotyping, and racism:

1. **Cooperative action to achieve mutual goals.** What largely determines whether interaction results in positive or negative relationships is the context within which the interaction takes place. Rather than requiring members of different groups to compete to see who is best or work individualistically on their own, they must work together to achieve mutual goals. This is the best supported of the conditions. Two meta-analyses indicated that cooperative experiences promote more positive relationships among heterogeneous individuals (Johnson & Johnson, 1989; Johnson, Johnson, & Maruyama, 1983). When people cooperate, they tend to like each other more, trust each other more, be more candid with each other, and be more willing to listen to and be influenced by each other than are people competing or working individualistically (Johnson & Johnson, 1989). In addition, there is considerable evidence that cooperative experiences, compared with competitive and individualistic ones, promote more positive, committed, and caring relationships regardless of differences in ethnic, cultural, language, social class, gender, ability, or other differences (Johnson & Johnson, 1989).

2. **Personal interactions among individuals from the different groups.** In-group members tend to assume that out-group members are all alike. Through intimate, one-on-one interaction, those categories should break down and out-group members should be perceived in more individualized terms (Brewer & Miller, 1984; Marcus-Newhall et al., 1993; Urban & Miller, in press; Wilder, 1986). In schools, individual contact among individuals from different groups is unusual and uncommon. Students associate with members of their own group. Tracking (ability grouping) ensures that white and minority students are separated. Desegregation does not ensure integration. Teachers must create the conditions and opportunities for personal interactions among diverse students in order for positive relationships to develop and stereotyping and prejudice to decrease. Such interactions also increase students' sophistication (see following section).

3. **Support from social norms and authorities.** The social norms, defined in part by relevant authorities, should favor intergroup contact. Norms have a powerful impact on individuals' behavior. Greenberg and Pyszczynski (1986) demonstrated that participants expressed more prejudice after they overheard a confederate utter a racial slur. Blanchard and his associates (1991) demonstrated that college students being interviewed about a racial incident on campus conveyed more racist sentiment after they heard a fellow student do the same. Wilder and Shapiro (1991) demonstrated participants were more likely to rate an out-group member as "typical" when they were with fellow in-group members than when they were alone.

4. **The two groups should be of equal status in the contact situation.** Desegregation situations that provided equal-status contact, as in the army and public housing projects, have been successful (Pettigrew, 1969). When the public schools were desegregated, however, white children were coming from more affluent families, were better prepared, and were academically more advanced than their black peers (Cohen, 1984).

In addition to these four conditions, recent research has focused on additional conditions that may be required for contact between diverse individuals and groups to have constructive rather than destructive effects. **The first is the salience of social categories.** When category distinctions are highly salient in an intergroup contact situation, group members are more apt to respond in ways that are category-based (Brewer & Miller, 1984; Hong & Harrod, 1988; Oakes, 1987; Tajfel, 1978; Wilder & Shapiro, 1989a, 1989b) and are more biased in their intergroup attitudes (Haunschild, Moreland, & Murrell, 1994; Hong & Harrod, 1988). Three ways to reduce the salience of social categories are:

1. Make shared categories salient. In-group bias is higher when people differ on two real social categories (such as ethnicity and gender) than when they differ on one category but share another (Brewer, Ho, Lee, & Miller, 1987; Commins & Lockwood, 1978; Islam & Hewstone, 1993; Urban & Miller, in press). Similar results have been found in laboratory studies on nominal group categories (Deschamps, 1977; Deschamps & Doise, 1978; Vanbeselaere, 1987, 1991).

2. Have equal representation of majority and minority members in cooperative groups (Rogers, Hennigan, Bosman, & Miller, 1984; Worchel, Andreoli, & Folger, 1977). Members of numerical minorities are more aware of their social category than are members of numerical majorities (McGuire, McGuire, Child, & Fujioka, 1978; McGuire, McGuire, & Winton, 1979; Mullen, 1983), express more in-group bias than do numerical majorities (Brewer, Manzi, & Shaw, 1993; Gerard & Hoyt, 1974; Mullen, Brown, & Smith, 1992; Sachdev & Bourhis, 1984, 1991), and are less accepting of members of other groups (Miller & Davidson-Podgorny, 1987). Groups for whom category salience is high are more biased in their intergroup attitudes (Haunschild, Moreland, & Murrell, 1994; Hong & Harrod, 1988).

3. Create a common identity among majority and minority members (Johnson & Johnson, 1999b). When majority and minority members are assigned the same role, for example, they perceive themselves as sharing a common identity (Bettencourt et al., in press; Bettencourt & Dorr, 1998).

The second potential addition to contact theory is the role of intergroup friendship. In a survey of 3,806 respondents in seven 1988 national probability samples of France, Great Britain, the Netherlands, and West Germany, Pettigrew (1997) found that intergroup friendship is a strong and consistent predictor of reduced prejudice and pro-immigrant policy preferences. The reduction of prejudice among those with diverse friends generalized to more positive feelings about a wide variety of out-groups. There seems to be a benevolent spiral in which intergroup friendship reduces prejudice and, in turn, reduced prejudice increases the likelihood of further intergroup friendships. Similar effects were not found when the individual had an out-group co-worker or neighbor (but not a friend). Herek and Capitanio (1996) found that multiple out-group friends have a strong negative relationship with prejudice. Wright, Aron, McLaughlin-Volpe, and Ropp (1997) found that knowledge that an in-group member had a close relationship with an out-group member results in more positive intergroup attitudes.

Since its original formulation fifty years ago, extensive research has been inspired by contact theory. The research has generally confirmed the theory across a variety of societies, situations, and groups. These include German children in school with Turkish children (Wagner, Hewstone, & Machleit, 1989), the elderly (Caspi, 1984), and the mentally ill (Desforges et al., 1991). The theory has been confirmed by laboratory (e.g., Cook, 1978; Johnson & Johnson, 1989), survey (e.g., Sigelman & Welch, 1993), field (e.g., Meer & Freedman, 1966; Johnson & Johnson, 1989), and archival (e.g., Fine, 1979) research.

There are problems with contact theory. The *first* is that the proliferation of required conditions renders the theory meaningless. As a result of all the diverse research, many social scientists have suggested revisions to contact theory. Some of the revisions have been situational (such as intimacy [Amir, 1976] or salience of social categories [Brewer & Miller, 1984]) and some individual (such as low authoritarianism [Weigel & Howes, 1985]). The danger to contact theory is that too many factors will render it meaningless. Contact theory may become a "grocery list" of necessary conditions rather than a coherent model of attitude and behavior change. The proliferation of conditions may result from social scientists confusing facilitating with essential conditions. Some of the conditions suggested for optimal contact may be catalytic (not essential for harmonious relationships but related to underlying mediating processes). Pettigrew (1997) suggested four broad, encompassing processes: (a) learning about the out-group, (b) empathizing with the out-group, (c) identifying with the out-group, and (d) reappraising the in-group. Some of the conditions proposed as requirements for constructive contact may actually be facilitators of one or more of these processes.

The *second* problem is the need to specify more precisely the mediation of contact effects. Social judgment theory, which is discussed at length in the next chapter, is an attempt to be more specific about the mediators of contact and positive relationships.

The *third* problem is that while contact theory is about interaction among members of diverse groups, it focuses on interpersonal interaction. It needs to refocus on the contact of group with group (Hewstone & Brown, 1986), rather than on contact of individuals from two groups. There is evidence that the perceived collective other is a qualitatively different kind of actor than a perceived individual other. Groups evoke stronger reactions than an individual engaging in the same behavior and actions by groups and individuals elicit differing preferences for redress (Abelson, Dasgupta, Park, & Banaji, 1998). When observers perceive individuals as part of a cohesive group (as opposed to an aggregate of unrelated individuals), the observers express stereotypic judgments about the individuals and infer that their behavior was shaped by the presence of others (Oakes & Turner, 1986; Oakes, Turner, & Haslam, 1991; Wilder, 1977, 1978b). A racial slur by an individual, for example, provokes a different reaction than a racial slur delivered by a group. Considerably more research is needed on intergroup (as opposed to interpersonal) contact.

Awakening "the Sense of Injustice"

Discrimination against out-groups may be decreased by reducing stereotyping and prejudice. Discrimination may be viewed as a form of injustice (Deutsch, 1985). Removing discrimination, therefore, requires awakening **a sense of injustice** in majority members about their treatment of minority and low-power group members. Deutsch posits that no change in discriminatory practices is possible until a sense of injustice is awakened. To awake the majority's sense of injustice follow the steps given below.

Awakening a sense of injustice depends on prejudice being more than a uniform set of attitudes and values. Rather than having uniformly negative or positive attitudes towards out-groups, many individuals have conflicting tendencies (Gaertner & Dovidio, 1986; Katz & Hass, 1988; Katz, Wachenhut, & Hass, 1986; McConahay, 1986; Monteith, 1996b). A number of studies, for example, found that approximately 78% of the sampled populations indicated that they should respond with less prejudice than is apparent in their actual responses (Devine, Monteith, Zuwerink, & Elliot, 1991; Monteith, 1996a, 1996b; Monteith, Devine, & Zuwerink, 1993; Zuwerink, Monteith, Devine, & Cook, 1996). This finding held for both high- and low-prejudiced individuals.

Given that many people are highly prejudiced but feel conflicted about it, awakening their sense of injustice will tip the scales in favor of respect and appreciation. Monteith and Walters (1998) found that many high-prejudiced white individuals feel morally obligated to (a) be less prejudiced and (b) have relatively low-prejudiced personal standards for responding to blacks. These obligations appear to originate from an egalitarian self-image that defines egalitarianism in terms of equality of opportunity. Their belief in the right of every American to have an equal opportunity is more powerful than their prejudices.

How to Awaken a Sense of Injustice

Step 1 Remove the majority's ignorance of the injustices experienced by minorities. Often the majority "insulates" itself from the victims by avoiding contact (living in all-white suburbs) or structuring the contact in ways that prevent the possibility of becoming aware of the discrimination (such as "employee of the month" celebrations). This **insulated ignorance** protects majority-group members from being aware of the consequences of their behavior (Hornstein & Johnson, 1966).

Step 2 Delegitimize the officially sanctioned ideologies and myths that "justify" the injustices (i.e., "The cream rises to the top"). Majority-group members are largely content and tend to have a vested interest in preserving the status quo (which ensures their superior roles and privileges). Awaking a sense of injustice requires majority-group members becoming aware of their ideologies, questioning the ideologies, and deciding the ideologies are no longer legitimate.

(continued)

How to Awaken a Sense of Injustice *(continued)*

Step 3 Expose the majority to new ideologies, models, and reference groups that support action to undo the disadvantages of the minorities. Majority-group members must interact with minority-group members, come to understand their perspective and experience, and form a new reference group that includes both majority and minority individuals. The new reference group must support change. The action steps must be clear.

Step 4 Stimulate the hope of the majority that they can effectively reduce injustice. Once victimization has become deeply embedded in social institutions, individual action to overcome it is frequently seen to be futile and costly. There must be hope of success in order for majority-group members to take action.

Step 5 Increase majority's belief they will benefit from reducing injustice. This involves (a) reducing the fear of the majority that their new actions will have costly, harmful consequences for them and (b) enhancing the majority's prospect of material and psychic gains from a positive change in their relationships with the minority. Both the majority and the minorities must be seen as being better off as a result of decreasing discrimination.

Step 6 Increase the majority's belief that continuation of the old relationship will no longer produce the material benefits and gains the majority has experienced in the past. Thus, continuing the status quo may have costly, harmful consequences for the majority.

Exercise 9.9: Intergroup Confrontation (II)

The following is a conflict resolution procedure for establishing cooperative goals among conflicting groups so that all members are committed to achieving their joint goals (Beckhard, 1969). The objective is provide a framework for resolving conflicts through highlighting common goals. Beckhard conducts the exercise as a one-day activity, but it can be shortened to a couple of hours when used strictly for learning.

1. Introduce the exercise as an experience in setting cooperative goals among groups in conflict with each other. Emphasize that the exercise is an opportunity for participants to learn how to resolve intergroup conflict. They should be open and honest in the expression of their ideas and feelings. The union–management situation used in the previous exercise can be applied here for role-playing purposes.
2. Divide the participants into groups of four or five and have them meet separately. The task of these conflicting groups is to think of ways in which life would be better for their members and their relationships with other groups. Ask each group to make a list of the ideas and place them on newsprint. This phase takes between thirty and forty-five minutes.
3. You and the participants categorize the ideas listed.
4. Have the groups complete the following tasks:
   a. Go through the entire list and select three or four items that most affect you and your group. Rephrase the items into goals, determine what actions your group will take to achieve them, and establish a timetable for doing so. Prepare to report your decisions in a general session.

    b. Go through the list again and select those items you think all groups should give high-
       est priority but that your group cannot achieve alone.
5. In a general session have the groups share the results of their meetings. Combine the
   lists. The groups should then outline plans of action for implementing their decisions and
   determine the necessary follow-up procedures. During the discussion they should emphasize intergroup cooperation.
6. Ask the groups to assess their reactions to the exercise and summarize what they have
   learned about resolving intergroup conflicts. Conclusions about preventing intergroup
   conflict should also be presented and discussed.

THIRD-PARTY MEDIATION

William Ury often tells a tale of an old gentleman who in his will requests that his estate be divided among his three sons in the following manner: One half to his eldest son,
one third to his middle son, and one ninth to his youngest son. When the loving father
died his estate consisted of seventeen camels. The three sons attempted to divide up the
estate according to their father's wishes but quickly found that they could not do so
without cutting some of the camels into pieces. They argued and argued without agreeing on how to divide the camels. Eventually, a village elder rode up on his own dusty
camel and inquired about their problem. The three brothers explained the situation. The
elder then offered to make his own camel available if that might help. It did. With eighteen camels, the brothers could solve the problem. The oldest soon took nine camels
(one-half of eighteen), the middle son choose six more (one-third of eighteen), and the
youngest son extracted two camels (one-ninth of eighteen). Nine plus six plus two
equals seventeen. Almost before the three brothers knew what had happened, the wise
man climbed back onto his own camel and rode off into the setting desert sun.

    This story illustrates what a clever and creative mediator can do. A **mediator** is a
neutral person who helps two or more people resolve their conflict by assisting them
through the steps of problem-solving negotiations so that an agreement is reached that
both believe is fair, just, and workable. A mediator does *not* tell disputants what to do,
decide who is right and who is wrong, or talk about what he or she would do in such a
situation. The mediator is simply a facilitator with no formal power over either disputant. **Mediation** exists, therefore, when a neutral and impartial third party assists two
or more people in negotiating a constructive resolution to their conflict. The participants in the conflict who seek mediation are called **disputants.** Mediation is an extension of the negotiation process and is a collection of strategies to promote more efficient
and effective negotiations. When mediation has been successful:

1. The conflict will be resolved so that all disputants have benefited.
2. The relationship between the disputants will be as good as or even better than ever.
3. Individuals' negotiating skills and self-confidence in using them will be increased.
    An important purpose of the mediator is to teach negotiation procedures and skills
    so that the individuals can manage their conflicts on their own in the future.

    When two individuals or groups cannot resolve their conflict constructively, they
often seek the help of a mediator. Mediation is an extension of the negotiation process
and is a collection of strategies to promote more efficient and effective negotiations.
The main difference between negotiating and mediation is that a third party, the

mediator, ensures that both parties engage in each step of the problem-solving negotiating process. Mediation is unlikely to be effective when the relationship between the two parties is poor and when resources are scarce. Under such conditions, the likelihood of finding a mutually acceptable compromise is not very high. Conversely, mediation is most likely to be successful when both parties are highly motivated to use the mediation process. In general, disputants are likely to be satisfied with the mediation process, as most studies show satisfaction rates of 75% or higher (Kressel & Pruitt, 1985). Mediation facilitates conflict resolution in the following ways (Raven & Rubin, 1976, p. 462):

1. Reducing emotional upset by giving parties an opportunity to vent their feelings.
2. Presenting alternative solutions by recasting the issues in different or more acceptable terms.
3. Providing opportunities for "graceful retreat" or face saving in the eyes of one's adversary, one's constituency, the public, or oneself.
4. Facilitating constructive communication among parties.
5. Controlling contact between the parties, including such aspects as the neutrality of the meeting site, the formality of the setting, the time constraints, and the number and kinds of people at the meeting.

To be successful, mediators need to possess certain characteristics and adopt particular strategies. Mediators need to be perceived as being trustworthy and able (Rubin, Pruitt, & Kim, 1994). Mediators need to convey an impression of legitimacy, social position, and expertise in order to gain the confidence of both parties and to win acceptance for the proposed solution (Kolb, 1985). Mediators tailor tactics to particular situations. Mediators may lower hostility by being very directive and using humor but being nondirective with inexperienced parties who lack expertise in negotiating (Carnevale & Pegnetter, 1985). When mediation fails, an arbitrator may be brought in. **Arbitration** is a binding settlement of a conflict determined by a disinterested third party.

Mediator Guidelines

A good mediator is impartial, neutral, nonjudgmental, patient, understanding, imaginative, knowledgeable, analytical, respectful, and trustworthy. A mediator acts and talks in ways that show he or she has these qualities. Some guidelines for doing so are as follows:

1. Listen, don't talk. A mediator cannot listen and talk at the same time. When you do talk, use words and phrases that are impartial and nonjudgmental.
2. Find out the facts. Find out what happened and what must be done to resolve the conflict. Ask each disputant, "What has to happen in order for this conflict to be resolved to your satisfaction?"
3. Analyze what you hear to see if agreement is possible. You must do more than listen. You must think about what is being said so that you can help disputants separate their interests from their positions and think of creative solutions to their problem.
4. Be firm in enforcing the rules. You will not help anyone if you permit disputants to interrupt, insult, or shout at each other. The rules ensure that the procedures are fair.

5. Be patient. Some things take time to resolve.
6. Respect each disputant. They will not participate effectively unless they believe that you respect them.

Exercise 9.10: Your Conflict Behavior

Having completed this chapter, it may be helpful to focus again on your behavior in conflict situations. Form a group of three with two persons who know you well and who have participated with you in some of the exercises in this book. Then complete the following tasks, taking at least two hours to do so.

1. Reflect silently on how each member deals with conflict. Give one another feedback about the animal, song, or book that each member reminds the others of on the basis of how he or she deals with conflict. Each person explains why he or she chose the animal, song, or book that he or she did.
2. Write down your individual strengths in managing conflicts constructively. Share your lists. Members can add to each other's lists.
3. Write down the individual skills you need to develop in order to manage conflict more constructively. Share your lists. Members should add to each other's lists.
4. Discuss the feelings each member has in conflict situations and why he or she reacts that way. Help each other think of alternative ways of reacting to conflict situations.
5. From magazine pictures and any other materials, build a collage about the way in which you behave in conflict situations. Share the collage with the other members. Add ideas to each other's collages.

SUMMARY

Guideline 7 is for group members to face their conflicts of interests (conflicts promoted by incompatible needs or goals, scarce resources, and by competitiveness) and engage in problem-solving (integrative) negotiations to resolve them. There are five basic strategies to manage conflicts of interests: withdrawal, forcing (distributive, win–lose negotiations), smoothing, compromise, and problem solving (integrative negotiations). The more effective the group, the more frequently conflicts of interests will be valued for their potential constructive outcomes and resolved through problem-solving negotiations. Where problem-solving negotiations fail, another group member needs to mediate. Even in intergroup conflicts, problem-solving negotiations need to be used. When they are resolved constructively, conflicts are an important and indispensable aspect of increasing group effectiveness.

Now that you are acquainted with the dynamics involved in resolving conflicts of interests and have practiced resolving them, you are ready to encounter power. You will do so in the next chapter.

10

Valuing Diversity

Basic Concepts to Be Covered in This Chapter

In this chapter a number of concepts are defined and discussed. The major ones are listed below. Divide into pairs, define each concept (noting the page on which it is defined and discussed), making sure that both you and your partner understand the meaning of each concept. Then join with another pair to make a group of four. Compare the answers of the two pairs. If there is disagreement, look up the concept in the chapter and clarify it until all members agree on and understand the definition.

Concepts

1. Demographic diversity
2. Personal diversity
3. Ability and skill diversity
4. Stereotype
5. Illusionary correlation
6. Prejudice
7. Ethnocentrism
8. Discrimination

9. Blaming the victim
10. Personal identity
11. Superordinate group identity
12. False consensus bias
13. Causal attribution
14. Self-serving bias
15. Culture clash
16. Sophistication

Exercise 10.1: Diversity: Beneficial or Harmful?

Task: Your tasks are to (a) write a group report on the issue *"Is diversity beneficial or harmful?"* and (b) individually pass a test on the information from both sides of the issue. Your report should provide details of the advantages and disadvantages of diversity. A controversy about the value of diversity is raging. Imagine that you are a committee of the top officials who are trying to decide whether or not diversity should be encouraged or discouraged. To ensure that both sides get a complete and fair hearing, you have divided the committee into two groups to present the best case possible for each side of the issue. Your thesis will be either of the following two choices:

_____ Diversity is a resource that has many beneficial influences.

_____ Diversity is a problem that has many harmful influences.

Cooperative: Write one report for the group of four. All members have to agree. Everyone has to be able to explain the choice made and the reasons why the choice is a good one. To help you write the best report possible, your group of four has been divided into two pairs. One pair has been assigned the position that diversity is beneficial and the other pair has been assigned the position that diversity is harmful.

PROCEDURE

1. **Research and Prepare Your Position:** Your group of four has been divided into two pairs. Each pair is to (a) research your assigned position, (b) organize it into a persuasive argument (thesis, rationale, conclusion), and (c) plan how to present the best case for your position to the other pair.
2. **Present and Advocate Your Position:** Make sure your assigned position receives a fair and complete hearing. Forcefully and persuasively present the best case for your position to the opposing pair. Be as convincing as possible. Take notes and clarify anything you do not understand when the opposing pair presents.
3. **Open Discussion (Advocate, Refute, Rebut):** Argue forcefully and persuasively for your position. Critically evaluate and challenge the opposing pair's information and reasoning. Defend your position from attack.
4. **Reverse Perspectives:** Reverse perspectives and present the best case for the opposing position. The opposing pair will present your position. Strive to see the issue from both perspectives simultaneously.
5. **Synthesis:** Drop all advocacy. Synthesize and integrate the best information and reasoning from both sides into a joint position that all group members can agree to. Then (a) finalize the group report, (b) plan how to present your conclusions to the class, (c) ensure that all group members are prepared to take the test, and (d) process how well you worked together as a group and how you could be even more effective next time.

CONTROVERSY RULES

1. I am critical of ideas, not people. I challenge and refute the ideas of the opposing pair, but I do not indicate that I personally reject the other persons.
2. I remember that we are all in this together, sink or swim. I focus on coming to the best decision possible, not on winning.
3. I encourage everyone to participate and to master all the relevant information.
4. I listen to everyone's ideas, even if I don't agree.
5. I restate what someone has said if it is not clear.

6. I first bring out all ideas and facts supporting both sides, and then I try to put them together in a way that makes sense.
7. I try to understand both sides of the issue.
8. I change my mind when the evidence clearly indicates that I should do so.

DIVERSITY IS BENEFICIAL

You represent the prodiversity perspective. Your position is *Diversity is a resource that has many beneficial influences.* Arguments that support your position follow. Summarize the evidence given. Research your position and find as much additional information to support it as possible. Arrange your information into a compelling, convincing, and persuasive argument that your position is valid and correct. Plan how to present your assigned position best to ensure it receives a fair and complete hearing. Make at least one visual to help you present a persuasive case for your position.

1. **Diversity decreases stereotyping and prejudice.** It is only through direct contact and interaction with diverse individuals that stereotypes can be disconfirmed, personal relationships can be built, and prejudice can be reduced.
2. **Diversity increases the positiveness of relationships.** There is evidence that we like people we work with to achieve mutual goals. The positive relationships can lead to acceptance, respect, appreciation, and a commitment to equality.
3. **Diversity renews the vitality of society** by providing a source of energy and creativity. Music, dance, art, literature, and other aspects of culture are enriched and advance by the mixture of different cultural traditions and ways of perceiving the world.
4. **Diversity increases achievement and productivity.** Diverse groups have a wider range of resources available for completing the task and, therefore, tend to have higher achievement and be more productive than homogeneous groups are.
5. **Diversity increases creative problem solving.** Diverse groups tend to be more creative in their problem solving than homogeneous groups. The conflicts and disagreements that arise from the different perspectives and conclusions generate more creativity than is available in homogeneous groups.
6. **Diversity fosters growth in cognitive and moral reasoning.** Cognitive and moral growth depend on at least two different perspectives being applied to the same issue. Without such diversity, cognitive and moral growth cannot take place.
7. **Diversity fosters perspective-taking** and a broader, more sophisticated view of the world and what happens within it. Without exposure to other perspectives, perspective-taking ability cannot develop. The more able a person is to take a wide variety of perspectives, the more sophisticated the person is. Being sophisticated means that one can see the world, events, and issues from a variety of perspectives. It is through diversity that sophistication is created.
8. **Diversity builds a commitment to American democracy.** It is not possible to value a fully American democracy in a homogeneous environment. The values advocated in the Constitution and the Declaration of Independence can best be understood through the protection of minority rights and the ability of minorities to influence the decisions of the majority.

DIVERSITY IS HARMFUL

You represent the antidiversity perspective. Your position is *Diversity is a problem that has many harmful influences.* Arguments that support your position follow. Summarize the evidence given. Research your position and find as much additional information to support it as possible. Arrange your information into a compelling, convincing, and persuasive argument that your position is valid and correct. Plan how to present your assigned position best to ensure it receives a fair and complete hearing. Make at least one visual to help you present a persuasive case for your position.

1. **Diversity increases stereotyping and prejudice.** Before actual contact takes place, only vague impressions of members of other groups may exist. With actual contact with diverse individuals, stereotypes can be confirmed and prejudice can be strengthened.
2. **Diversity creates interaction strain** (feeling discomfort and uncertainty as to how to behave). Interaction strain inhibits interaction, creates ambivalence, and fosters atypical behavior such as overfriendliness followed by withdrawal and avoidance.
3. **Diversity increases the negativity of relationships.** There is evidence that we like people we see as similar to ourselves and we dislike people who seem different. The dislike can lead to rejection, scapegoating, bullying, hostility, and even racism.
4. **Diversity lowers productivity.** Diversity creates difficulties in communication, coordination, and decision making. These difficulties result in more time being spent in trying to communicate and less time being spent on completing the task. Productivity suffers.
5. **Diversity makes life more complex and difficult.** It is so easy to relate to similar people. You never have to stop and think about what to say or do. The more diverse the group, the more you have to monitor your statements and behavior to ensure that you do not inadvertently insult or hurt someone's feelings.
6. **Diversity requires more effort to relate to others.** Even talking to a person from another culture takes more concentration and effort. Accents can be distracting. Phrases can be unusual. Communicating effectively with diverse individuals takes more effort than with individuals just like yourself.
7. **Diversity can be threatening,** which creates defensiveness, egocentrism, and closed-minded rejection of new information. The more defensive a person, the more closed-minded and the less receptive to new information the person becomes.
8. **Diversity creates internal dissonance and anxiety** by challenging the standard ways of thinking and doing things. Strange, new ways of perceiving the world and completing tasks can create dissonance about one's traditional behavior and anxiety results. People are calmer and happier when they are with homogeneous peers.

INTRODUCTION

In the story *Beauty and the Beast,* Beauty, to save her father's life, agrees to live in an enchanted castle with the Beast. Although initially very fearful of the Beast, and horrified by his appearance, she is able to look beyond his monstrous appearance into his heart. Considering his kind and generous nature, her perception of his appearance changes. She no longer is repelled by the way he looks but instead is drawn to his loving nature. The better she gets to know him, the less monstrous he seems. Finally, finding him dying of a broken heart, she reveals her love for him, which transforms the beast into a handsome prince. Beauty and the Beast not only live happily ever after, but all those who stumbled into their domain in despair are changed, finding on their departure that their hearts are now filled with goodness and beauty.

This is an often repeated story. Many times we are repelled by those we do not know. Yet after they have become our friends, we do not understand how once they seemed monstrous to us. Nowhere is Beauty and the Beast more apparent than in small groups. For it is in small groups that diversity among individuals is most often faced and eventually valued.

Pluralism and diversity among individuals creates an opportunity, but like all opportunities, there are potentially positive or negative outcomes (Johnson & Johnson, 1989). In other words:

1. **Diversity among group members can result in beneficial consequences,** such as increased achievement and productivity, creative problem solving, growth in cognitive and moral reasoning, increased perspective-taking ability, improved relationships, and general sophistication in interacting and working with peers from a variety of cultural and ethnic backgrounds.
2. **Diversity among group members can result in harmful consequences,** such as lower achievement and productivity, closed-minded rejection of new information, increased egocentrism, and negative relationships characterized by hostility, rejection, divisiveness, scapegoating, bullying, stereotyping, prejudice, and racism.

Whether diversity leads to positive or negative outcomes largely depends on your (Johnson & Johnson, 1989, 1995a, 1995c, 1999b):

1. Recognizing that diversity exists and is a valuable resource.
2. Building a coherent personal identity that includes (a) your own cultural/ethnic heritage and (b) a view of yourself as an individual who respects and values differences among individuals.
3. Understanding the internal cognitive barriers (such as stereotyping and prejudice) to building relationships with diverse peers and working to reduce the barriers.
4. Understanding the dynamics of intergroup conflict (see Chapter 9).
5. Understanding the social judgment process and knowing how to create the process of acceptance while avoiding the process of rejection (see Chapter 3).
6. Creating a cooperative context in which positive relationships among diverse individuals will be built (see Chapter 3). This requires structuring cooperation (as opposed to a competitive or individualistic effort). It is within a cooperative context that diverse individuals develop personal (as opposed to impersonal) relationships.
7. Managing conflicts in constructive ways. This includes:
   a. Intellectual conflicts that are part of decision-making and learning situations (controversy) (see Chapter 8).
   b. Conflicts of interests that are resolved by problem-solving negotiations and mediation (see Chapter 9).
8. Learning and internalizing pluralistic, democratic values.

DIVERSITY

Diversity in America

Most countries are becoming more pluralistic. Historically, the United States always has been pluralistic. Our common culture has been formed by the interaction of subsidiary

Waves of Immigration

Origin	1820–1860	1901–1921	1970–1986
Northern, Western Europe	95%	41%	6%
Southern, Eastern Europe		44	9
Latin America			37
Asia		4	41
North America	3	6	3
Other	2	1	4

Sources: Population Reference Bureau, Bureau of the Census, Immigration and Naturalization Service.

cultures and has been influenced over time by a wide variety of willing (and sometimes unwilling) European, African, and Asian immigrants as well as American Indians. American music, art, literature, language, food, and customs all show the effects of the integration of diverse cultures into one nation.

The diversity of the United States is still increasing. In the 1980s alone, over 7.8 million people from over 150 different countries and speaking dozens of different languages immigrated to the United States. The Carnegie Foundation (1995) notes that from 1980 to 1990 the number of immigrant children increased by 24%, the number of children with limited proficiency in English increased 20% thereby linguistically isolating those children of households where no one over 14 speaks English very well. In 1970, 20% of students were from minority groups whereas in 1992 it had increased to 40%. The percentage of students with disabilities, from families in poverty, and suffering from abuse is increasing. There is every reason to expect the diversity of individuals' cultural and experiential backgrounds, knowledge, abilities, and skills to continue to increase in the future.

Sources of Diversity

The major sources of diversity are (a) demographic characteristics, (b) personality characteristics, and (c) abilities and skills. **Demographic diversity** includes culture, ethnicity, language, handicapping conditions, age, gender, social class, religion, and regional differences. North America, for example, is becoming more multicultural and multilingual.

In addition to demographic diversity, individuals can have different **personal characteristics.** Groups can be composed of introverts as well as extroverts and of people who approach problems randomly as well as sequentially. Group members also can have different values, attitudes, opinions, lifestyles, styles of interaction, and commitments. Attitudes, values, and beliefs vary systematically with demographic variables. Age cohorts have had different attitudes towards economic conditions and war, males and females have had different attitudes towards interpersonal relationships, and education has been related to attitudes towards innovation and reductions in prejudice.

Finally, individuals differ in the **abilities and skills** they bring to the group. Experts from a variety of fields, for example, may be brought together to solve a problem or con-

duct a project. Representatives from design, manufacturing, distribution, and sales may form a team to bring a new product to market. Accountants and creative artists may work together to revitalize a neighborhood. It is difficult if not impossible to find a productive group whose members do not have a wide variety of abilities and skills.

IMPORTANCE OF MANAGING DIVERSITY

The more voices we allow to speak about one thing, the more eyes, different eyes we can use to observe one thing, the more complete will our concept of this thing, our objectivity, be.

Nietzsche

Utilizing diversity is one of the major challenges facing modern societies. Dealing with diversity is increasingly important for several reasons.

First, we increasingly live in one world. The problems that face each person, each community, each country cannot be solved without global cooperation and joint action. Changes in the world economy, transportation, and communication are resulting in increased levels of interdependence among individuals, groups, organizations, communities, and societies. The more interdependent the world becomes, the more diverse the membership of any one group will likely be. In a global village, highly diverse individuals are interdependent and, therefore, have to interact and work together.

Second, diversity in most settings is inevitable and, therefore, individuals need the skills to interact effectively with people from a wide variety of backgrounds. For 200,000 years humans lived in small hunting and gathering groups, interacting only infrequently with other nearby small groups. It is only with the recent development of worldwide interdependence and communication and transportation systems that diverse individuals have begun to interact, work with, and live next to each other. In North America, Europe, and throughout the world individuals increasingly interact with people who come from different cultures and ethnic backgrounds, speak different languages, and have grown in markedly different conditions. In addition, interaction between genders and generations is quite different from what it used to be. Such diversity is relatively new. Diversity among acquaintances, classmates, co-workers, neighbors, and friends is increasingly inevitable.

Third, economically there has been a globalization of business reflected in the increase in multinational companies, coproduction agreements, and offshore operations. More and more companies must translate their local and national perspectives into a worldview. Companies that are staffed by individuals skilled in building relationships with diverse individuals will have an advantage in the global market. A telephone survey of 408 opinion leaders about human resource issues in business (e.g., executives, consultants, faculty), for example, asked respondents to think ahead about the strategic issues that business will face, and found that managing a more diverse workforce was the one issue that was repeatedly mentioned (Sirota, Alpher, & Pfau, 1989).

With increasing interdependence, diversity cannot be avoided or bypassed. Any group may consist of members who are diverse on (a) a wide number of personal characteristics and (b) the abilities and skills they contribute to the group's efforts. The diversity of the group membership may enhance or hinder the performance of the group. Diversity among individuals creates an opportunity, but like all opportunities, there is the potential for either positive or negative outcomes. **Tomorrow's effective groups (including large groups such as organizations and nations) will be those that have learned to be productive with a diverse membership.** This chapter, therefore, focuses on the ways groups can take full advantage of the positive consequences of diversity and can minimize the potential negative consequences. This chapter is divided into four sections. First, the sources of diversity and the increasing interdependence are discussed. Second, the evidence is reviewed that indicates diversity in group composition increases productivity on a variety of tasks. Third, the difficulties with diversity that have to be faced, such as prejudice, blaming the victim, and culture clash, are discussed. Finally, the practical procedures that groups can use to ensure that diversity is a resource and not a hindrance are presented.

THE VALUE OF DIVERSITY

The research that documents the value of diversity has primarily focused on performance on a variety of tasks. There is also some research examining the impact of diversity on cohesion and conflict, which are determinants of absenteeism, turnover, and satisfaction. Outcomes often are nearly as important as group performance in organizational settings.

Group Composition and Performance on Tasks

How does heterogeneity of group membership affect group performance? Researchers have studied the degree of homogeneity–heterogeneity among members' (a) demographic attributes, (b) personal attributes (including personality, attitudes, values), and (c) abilities and skills (both technical and social). Three types of tasks have been studied: (a) performance on clearly defined production tasks, (b) performance on cognitive or intellective tasks, and (c) creative idea generation and decision making related to ambiguous judgmental tasks (McGrath, 1984; Jackson, 1992; Johnson & Johnson, 1989). The combination of sources of diversity and types of task is presented in Table 10.1 (Jackson, 1992).

Production tasks have objective standards for performance evaluation and require the proficient use of perceptual and motor skills (McGrath, 1984). A comprehensive review of research on group composition and performance tasks, covering studies conducted primarily between 1940 and 1968, was conducted by Haythorn (1968). Shaw (1981), McGrath (1984), and Driskell, Hogan, and Salas (1987) have conducted subsequent reviews. From these reviews it may be seen that relatively few studies, with mixed results, have assessed the impact of personal attribute composition on performance tasks. Two studies found performance to be higher in groups whose members were homogeneous in personal attributes (Clement & Schiereck, 1973; Fenelon & Megaree, 1971). Terborg, Castore, and DeNinno (1976), however, found attitude heterogeneity–homogeneity to be unrelated to performance in a longitudinal study of student groups working on land-surveying tasks.

Groups composed of members with heterogeneous technical abilities may do better on production tasks than groups composed of members with homogeneous technical abilities (Jackson, 1992). Pelz (1956) found that more productive scientists and engineers tended to create informal communication networks with dissimilar peers.

Table 10.1 **Group Composition and Types of Tasks**

Types of Diversity Investigated	**Types of Tasks**
Demographic attributes	Performance on clearly defined production tasks
Personal attributes (personality, attitudes, values)	Performance on cognitive or intellective tasks
Abilities and skills (technical, social)	Creative idea generation and decision making on ambiguous judgmental tasks

The productivity among scientists and engineers was positively correlated with the extent to which they were in frequent contact with colleagues whose training and expertise were dissimilar to their own. Such networks resemble loosely structured heterogeneous groups. Voiers (1956) found that heterogeneous abilities facilitated performance of B-29 bomber crews when the crews could take advantage of the ability heterogeneity by assigning members to those tasks to which they were best suited. Athletic teams with more diverse skills (good offensive and defensive units) have been found to outperform teams with less diverse skills (Jones, 1974).

Intellective tasks are problem-solving tasks with correct answers (McGrath, 1984). Wood (1987) reviewed the research on the impact of sex differences on group performance. He found twelve studies in which objective performance results (accuracy and speed) could be compared for same- versus mixed-sex groups. He found weak support for the conclusion that mixed-sex groups tend to outperform same-sex groups of either males or females. Similar findings have been reported with more complex learning tasks (Johnson, Johnson, Scott, & Ramolae, 1985; Peterson, Johnson, & Johnson, 1991). Laughlin and colleagues (see Laughlin, 1980) have demonstrated that typically in problem-solving groups "truth supported wins." When heterogeneity increases the probability of the group containing some members who are capable of determining the correct answer to the problems being solved, mixed-attribute groups should outperform homogeneous groups. For "Eureka" tasks, the group needs only one member with the ability to discover the correct answer. Other studies demonstrated that groups made up of individuals with different ability levels (high, medium, low) outperformed individuals on intellective tasks (Johnson & Johnson, 1989).

Decision-making tasks involve reaching consensus about the best solution to a problem when the "correct" answer is not known (McGrath, 1984). Research reviews indicate that heterogeneous groups are more likely than homogeneous groups to be creative and to reach high-quality decisions (Fiedler, Meuwese, & Conk, 1961; Filley, House, & Kerr, 1976; Frick, 1973; Hoffman, 1979; Johnson, 1977; Johnson & Johnson, 1989; McGrath, 1984; Shaw, 1981; Torrance, 1961; Webb, 1977). The conclusion holds for a variety of personal attributes, including personality (Hoffman & Maier, 1961), leadership abilities (Ghiselli & Lodahl, 1958), types of training (Pelz, 1956), and attitudes (Hoffman, Harburg, & Maier, 1962b; Triandis, Hall, & Ewen, 1965; Willems & Clark, 1971). Ziller, Behringer, and Goodchilds (1962) created heterogeneity in groups by changing the people who made up the group (open groups) versus groups with stable membership (closed groups). They asked the groups to write cartoon captions. Captions written by the heterogeneous (open) groups were judged to have greater fluency and originality. Pelz and Andrews (1966) also found that groups with fluid membership are likely to be more creative, even when the groups are initially interdisciplinary. They concluded that when scientists of interdisciplinary teams worked closely together on a daily basis, within three years they were found to have become homogeneous in their perspectives and approach to solving problems. Whereas diverse perspectives are potentially advantageous, heterogeneous groups may not always function at an optimal level. Hill (1982) reviewed several studies that found on creative and decision-making tasks, the performance of interacting groups was less than their potential (as estimated by statistical pooling). Hall and Williams (1966), however, found just the opposite. Furthermore, in a field study of 119 top management teams in the banking industry in 6 midwestern states, Bantel and Jackson (1989) found that the more heterogeneous (in terms of job expertise) the decision-making teams, the more frequently the bank adopted new, innovative practices.

Ability composition of groups affects their performance on creative and decision-making tasks. Laughlin and Bitz (1975) used a word-association task to compare the performance of groups composed of members with dissimilar ability levels with the performance of individuals whose ability was equivalent to that of highest ability group member. They found that the groups outperformed the high-ability individuals. Their findings suggest that high-ability members can benefit from interaction with others who have less ability, perhaps because (a) the high-ability individuals take on the role of teacher, which leads them to sharpen their own thinking, or (b) the questions and inputs of more naive members encourage the more expert members to unbundle the assumptions and rules they automatically use when dealing with issues and problems in which they are experts (Simon, 1979). This unbundling increases the likelihood that unwarranted assumptions are reexamined and decision rules are reexamined for exceptions. Overall, the evidence indicates that when working on complex, nonroutine problems (a situation that requires some degree of creativity), groups are more effective when composed of individuals with diverse types of skills, knowledge, abilities, and perspectives.

The results of the research on group composition and task performance are summarized in Table 10.2. There is little or no research on the impact of heterogeneity of demographic attributes on performance of production, intellective, and decision-making tasks. Heterogeneity of membership, both in personal characteristics and abilities and skills, tends to facilitate performance on creative and decision-making tasks. Heterogeneity of abilities and skills seems to be beneficial for performance tasks. There are too few studies on intellective tasks to make a conclusion. Homogeneity of personal characteristics and abilities does not seem to facilitate performance on any of the types of tasks.

Table 10.2 **Impact of Group Composition on Outcomes**

Types of Outcomes	**Personal Attributes**	**Abilities and Skills**
Production tasks	The few studies found mixed results, so no clear effect of group composition on performance is proved.	The few studies found that heterogeneity of types and levels of ability increases productivity.
Intellective tasks	Overall, not enough studies to draw a conclusion. Mixed-sex groups may outperform same-sex groups.	Almost no directly relevant research.
Decision-making tasks	Heterogeneous groups outperform homogeneous groups.	Heterogeneity of ability levels is beneficial.
Cohesion	Heterogeneous groups are somewhat less cohesive and have higher turnover rates.	Almost no direct research.
Conflict	More conflicts tend to occur in heterogeneous groups.	Almost no direct research.

Other Outcomes

Absenteeism, turnover, and satisfaction often are nearly as important as group performance to groups and organizations (Nadler, Hackman, & Lawler, 1979; Schmidt, 1974). These outcomes are determined largely by cohesion and conflict. Haythorn (1968) reviewed the evidence and concluded that the effects of **personality heterogeneity–homogeneity** on cohesion depended on a number of factors, including personality characteristics, task characteristics, and extent of interpersonal contact. Bantel and Jackson (1989), in their field study of decision-making teams at 119 banks in 6 states, found no relationship between team heterogeneity and cohesiveness. Jackson, Brett, Sessa, Cooper, Julin, and Peyronnin (1991), in a follow-up study, found that (a) the demographically homogeneous teams had lower turnover and (b) were more likely to fill vacancies with employees from inside the firm, both of which may indicate higher cohesion. **Turnover** tends to be higher in work groups composed of members who are more diverse with respect to their **ages and years of organizational tenure** (e.g., Jackson et al., 1991; McCain, O'Reilly, & Pfeffer, 1983; O'Reilly, Caldwell, & Barnett, 1989; Wagner, Pfeffer, & O'Reilly, 1984) and who are heterogeneous in terms of **college alma mater, curriculum studied,** and **industry experiences** (Jackson, et al., 1991). **Attitude similarity** has been found to be mildly related to group cohesion. There is evidence that people are attracted to others with similar attitudes (Byrne, 1971; Heider, 1958; Newcomb, 1961) and that group members tend to become more similar in their attitudes as they interact over time (Newcomb, 1956). Terborg, Castore, and DeNinno (1976), however, conducted one of the few studies in which attitudes were assessed directly and then used to assemble groups. In their longitudinal investigation of student groups, cohesiveness was assessed at six points in time. At each assessment, cohesiveness was greater in the groups composed of attitudinally similar members, although the magnitude of the effect of attitude similarity on cohesiveness did not approach statistical significance until the last three assessments.

Finally, the heterogeneity among group members promotes increased argumentation and **conflict** (Nijhof & Kommers, 1982). Such conflicts can be beneficial for completing complex problem-solving tasks (Cosier, 1981; Janis, 1972; Johnson & Johnson, 1979, 1989, 1992a; Schweiger, Sandberg, & Rechner, 1989; Schwenk, 1983).

Disadvantages of Homogeneity of Membership

There are a number of disadvantages to members being homogeneous. First, homogeneous groups may lack the controversy and clash of perspectives so essential to high-quality decision making and creative thinking. Too many members who think alike and see the world the same make for a very dull and mediocre group. Second, homogeneous groups tend to be risk-avoidant (Bantel & Jackson, 1989) and may, therefore, miss opportunities to increase their productivity. Third, homogeneous groups more frequently engage in groupthink (Janis, 1972). Fourth, homogeneous groups tend to function best in static situations. They have trouble adapting to changing conditions.

Bringing diverse individuals together does not automatically result in positive outcomes (Johnson & Johnson, 1989). Proximity is a necessary condition for the positive potential of diversity to be realized, but it is not sufficient in and of itself. What proximity does create is visibility and initial contact. The initial contact is often dominated by **interaction strain** (individuals feeling discomfort and uncertainty as to how to behave). Interaction strain inhibits interaction, creates ambivalence, and fosters atypical behavior such as overfriendliness followed by withdrawal and avoidance. Under competitive and individualistic conditions, furthermore, pluralism and diversity may cause problems. Diversity can result in lower achievement due to increased difficulties in communication and coordination. It can create threat, defensiveness, increased egocentrism, and closed-minded rejection of new information. Direct interaction among diverse individuals in competitive situations can create negative relationships characterized by hostility, rejection, divisiveness, scapegoating, bullying, stereotyping, and prejudice.

Conclusions

There are a number of problems with the group composition research. **First, in considering member heterogeneity, it is difficult to determine what attributes are important.** The research has focused on personal attributes (such as personality, attitudes, gender, ethnicity) and skills and abilities. These two categories have been focused on because they can be measured and group members can be selected based on them. It is not clear that they are the variables that affect team performance.

Second, no one attribute is likely to make much difference in the complexity of real work. Thus, multiattribute research may be more important. Instead of studying the impact of gender, ethnicity, age, or cognitive style, studies that track composition along all of these dimensions simultaneously are needed.

Third, organizations employ people to perform a wide variety of both simple and complex tasks that involve perceptual and motor performance, intellective performance, creativity, and judgmental decision making. Groups may be working on a variety of tasks simultaneously, and the tasks that they are doing today may not be the tasks they are working on tomorrow. What tasks a team may have to do at any given time are unpredictable. Over time, the tasks that a group faces are unpredictable and, therefore, the safest thing to do is to maximize the heterogeneity in the group.

Fourth, it is difficult to determine what is and is not diversity. What outsiders may define as heterogeneity may not be perceived as being heterogeneous by insiders. Turner (1987), in his discussion of self-categorization theory, argues that many group phenomena (including cohesiveness and cooperation) are influenced by the self-categorizations of group members. Specifically, psychological in-groups form when people perceive themselves to be relatively similar to each other on some dimension(s) and relatively different from comparison others, who are viewed as the out-group. Thus, in order to judge whether a group is heterogeneous or homogeneous with respect to an attribute, it is important to consider how the attribute is distributed among nonteam members.

Fifth, very little is known about precisely how group composition and tasks interact to affect performance. Thus, recommendations cannot be made about the procedures and strategies group members should use to utilize their diversity to improve their productivity. If not enough is known to make recommendations about specific, limited, artificial situations, then in the complexity of the real world, recommendations about using heterogeneous groups are impossible.

Finally, group members are simultaneously both heterogeneous and homogeneous. Each person has hundreds of characteristics and abilities. Members that are homogeneous on one or two attributes are heterogeneous with respect to other attributes. Conversely, group members that are heterogeneous with respect to several attributes still share common attributes. It is probably impossible to create a homogeneous group. **Clearly, it is unrealistic to cope with the diversity of people by attempting to completely control the composition of groups.** Instead, ways need to be found to manage groups to ensure that the positive consequences of heterogeneity are maximized and potential negative consequences of heterogeneity are minimized.

Because diversity is inevitable and increasing, the choice to avoid diversity does not exist for most people. In school, on the job, and in the community, you will be interacting with people different from you in many ways whether you wish to or not. The promise of diversity far outweighs the problems as long as the individuals involved understand how to capitalize on the benefits while avoiding the pitfalls. The greater the understanding of human relations, for example, the more constructive will be the results of diversity.

BARRIERS TO INTERACTING WITH DIVERSE PEERS

Diversity among members is an important resource to be utilized to improve the group's productivity. Doing so may not be easy. There are a number of barriers to interacting effectively with diverse peers (see Johnson, 2000; Johnson & Johnson, 1999). They include stereotyping, prejudice, the tendency to blame the victim, and cultural clashes.

Stereotypes

When we see a red-breasted bird, we say to ourselves "robin." When we see a crazily swaying automobile, we think, "drunken driver." . . . A person with dark brown skin will activate whatever concept of Negro is dominant in our mind.

Allport (1954, p. 20)

Stereotypes are everywhere and everyone has them. Stereotypes are a product of the way the mind stores, organizes, and recalls information. The use of stereotypes cannot be avoided. They are used to describe differences among groups and to predict how others will behave. They reduce complexity, help us make quick decisions, fill in the gaps in what we know, help us make sense out of who we are and what has happened to us, and help us create and recognize the patterns needed to draw conclusions. Unfortunately, stereotypes can also support unfairness and injustice.

The term *stereotype* was first used in the eighteenth century to describe a printing process designed to duplicate pages of type. In the nineteenth century the term *stereotypy* was used by psychiatrists to describe a behavior of persistent repetitiveness and unchanging mode of expression. Modern use of the term *stereotype* was originated by Lippmann (1922) in his book, *Public Opinion.* He argues that "there is neither time nor opportunity for intimate acquaintance. Instead we notice a trait which marks a well known type, and fill in the rest of the picture by means of the stereotypes we carry about in our heads" (p. 59). The world is simply too complicated to attend to every detail and, therefore, the perceiver relies on stereotypes to simplify social perception. Katz and Braly (1933) conducted the first classic empirical study of stereotypes and linked them to attitudes and prejudice.

A **stereotype** is a belief that associates a whole group of people with certain traits. Stereotypes are (a) cognitive; (b) reflect a set of related beliefs rather than an isolated bit of information; (c) describe the attributes, personalities, and characters so groups can be compared and differentiated; and (d) are shared by individuals and groups holding them (Ashmore & Del Boca, 1979). Stereotypes function as simplifiers and organizers of social information. They reduce the complexity of the social environment and make it more manageable. Examples of stereotypes are the following. Women have been stereotyped as being more emotional than men. Men have been stereotyped as being more competitive than women. Tall, dark, and handsome men have been stereotyped as being mysterious. Stereotypes are often influenced by past events. Stereotypes of the Japanese in the 1940s, for example, were heavily influenced by the surprise attack on Pearl Harbor in World War II.

You form stereotypes by (a) categorizing (you sort single objects into groups rather than thinking of each as unique) and (b) differentiating between the in-group (the groups with which you identify) and out-groups. You commonly assume that the members of out-groups are quite similar while realizing that the members of the in-group are quite diverse (**out-group homogeneity effect**). The failure to notice differences among out-group members may result from lack of personal contact with a representative sample of the out-group. A white person, for example, may see all Hispanics as being alike, but someone with a wide variety of Hispanic friends may see little similarity among Puerto Ricans, Cubans, Mexicans, and Argentineans.

An efficient cognitive system does more than simply make things easy for people at all costs. Rather, it distributes limited resources in ways that maximize the informational value gained for the effort expended. There are several reasons why stereotyping is efficient. *First,* the social categorization that precedes stereotyping reduces the amount of information that must be attended to. When you group social stimuli together and treat them as functionally equivalent, you reduce the need to form individualized impressions of each category member (Allport, 1954; Brewer, 1988; Fiske & Neuberg, 1990; Hamilton & Sherman, 1994; Lippmann, 1922). *Second,* stereotypes expand your base of knowledge by allowing you to infer a person's attributes without having to attend carefully to the person's behavior (Brewer, 1988; Fiske & Neuberg, 1990; Hamilton & Sherman, 1994; Medin, 1988; Sherman, 1996). Through the relatively simple act of social categorization, stereotypes allow you to gain a large amount of "functionally accurate" information (Swann, 1984), thus resulting in a beneficial ratio of information gained to effort expended. Stereotypes are particularly useful when processing capacity is constrained, processing resources are scarce, and when accurate social perception is difficult to achieve. Stereotypes facilitate the encoding of both stereotype-consistent and stereotype-inconsistent information when processing capacity is low (Sherman, Lee, Bessenoff, & Frost, 1998). The energy saved by encoding stereotype-consistent information is then used to understand stereotype-inconsistent information. Stereotypes may be automatically activated when people experience a threat to their self-image (Spencer, Fein, Wolfe, Fong, & Dunn, 1998).

People who hold strong stereotypes are prone to the **fundamental attribution error.** They attribute negative behavior on the part of a minority-group member to dispositional characteristics and positive behavior by a minority-group member to situational factors, whereas one's own negative behavior is attributed to situational causes and one's own positive behavior is viewed as dispositional. When a minority-group member acts in an undesirable way, the attribution is "That's the way those people are" or "Those people are born like that." If the minority-group member is seen engaging in desirable behavior, the person holding the stereotype can view the minority person as an exception to the rule or view the minority person's behavior as due to luck, the situational context, or extraordinary motivation and effort.

Stereotypes are perpetuated and protected in four ways. *First,* stereotypes influence what we perceive and remember about the actions of out-group members. The social categories we use to process information about the world controls what we tend to perceive and not perceive. Our prejudice makes us notice the negative traits we ascribe to the groups we are prejudiced against. Furthermore, when individuals expect members of an out-group to behave in a certain way, they tend to recall more accurately instances that confirm rather than disconfirm their expectations. Hence, if an out-group is perceived to be of low intelligence, individuals (a) would tend to remember instances in which an out-group member was confused in class or failed a test but (b) would tend to forget instances in which an out-group member achieved a 4.0 grade point average or became class valedictorian (Rothbart, Evans, & Fulero, 1979).

There is an association between power and stereotyping (Fiske, 1993; Fiske & Morling, 1996). The general premise of this work is that persons in positions of power are especially vulnerable to stereotyping subordinates because they pay less attention to them. High-power individuals may lack cognitive capacity to attend to subordinates because power requires attending to more people and more issues at the same time. High-power individuals may ignore subordinates because the high-power persons' outcomes do not depend on subordinates. High-power individuals may not attend to subordinates because they have a dominant personality trait and may attempt to control their interactions with others to such an extent that they ignore the actions and motivations of others. Regardless of its cause, decreases in attention make powerful individuals more likely to depend on stereotypes in interacting with subordinates.

Second, stereotypes create an oversimplified picture of out-group members. The act of categorization itself leads people to assume similarity among the members of a category. Even when the distinctions between groups are arbitrary, people tend to minimize the differences they see among members of the same group and to accentuate the differences between members of two different groups. When processing information about their in-group and out-groups, people develop relatively simplistic and nonspecific pictures of out-groups. The larger the out-group, the more likely oversimplifications will occur. Individuals, furthermore, do more than simply note the differences between their in-group and the out-groups. They attempt to emphasize the differences, and take actions that will discriminate in favor of their own group.

Third, individuals tend to overestimate the similarity of behavior among out-group members. Because out-groups are perceived to be very homogeneous, the actions of one member can be generalized to all.

Why Do Stereotypes Endure?

Given below are several reasons why stereotypes persist. Rank them from most important (1) to least important (7). Write down your rationale for your ranking. Find a partner and share your ranking and rationale, listen to his or her ranking and rationale, and cooperatively create a new, improved ranking and rationale. Then find another pair and repeat the procedure in a group of four.

Rank	Reason
	The tendency for people to overestimate the association between variables that are only slightly correlated or not correlated at all (i.e., **illusionary correlation).** Many people, for example, perceive that being poor and being lazy are associated. Any poor person who is not hard at work the moment you notice him or her may be perceived to be lazy. Low-power groups can acquire negative traits easily and once acquired, the stereotype is hard to lose.
	Your prejudice makes you notice the negative traits you ascribe to the groups you are prejudiced against, and you more readily believe information that confirms your stereotypes than evidence that challenges them. People tend to process information in ways that verify existing beliefs. This is known as the **confirmation bias** (the tendency to seek, interpret, and create information that verifies existing beliefs).
	You tend to have a **false consensus bias** by believing that most other people share your stereotypes (see poor people as being lazy). You tend to see your own behavior and judgments as quite common and appropriate, and to view alternative responses as uncommon and often inappropriate.
	Your stereotypes tend to be **self-fulfilling.** Stereotypes can subtly influence intergroup interactions in such a way that the stereotype is behaviorally confirmed. You can behave in ways that elicit the actions you expect from out-group members, thus confirming your stereotype.
	You dismiss individuals who do not match your stereotype as exceptions to the rule or representatives of a subcategory.
	Your stereotypes often operate at an implicit level without your conscious awareness.
	You often develop a rationale and explanation to justify your stereotypes and prejudices.

Fourth, stereotypes can lead to scapegoating. A **scapegoat** is a guiltless but defenseless group that is attacked to provide an outlet for pent-up anger and frustration caused by another group. The term comes from a biblical guilt-transference ritual:

> And Aaron shall lay both his hands upon the head of the live goat, and confess over him all the iniquities of the children of Israel, and all their transgressions in all their sins, putting them upon the head of the goat, and shall send him away by the hand of a fit man into the wilderness (Leviticus 16:21).

In most instances, if group 1 interfered with group 2, group 2 would respond by retaliating against group 1. If, however, group 1 is extremely powerful, too distant, or too difficult to locate, group 2 may respond by turning its aggression on to group 3. Group 3, although in no way responsible for the difficulties group 2 experienced, would nonetheless be blamed and thereby become the target of group 2's aggressive actions. Stereotypes of certain out-groups can create a continual scapegoat that is blamed for all problems and difficulties no matter what their origins.

Stereotypes can be changed. The more personal information you have about someone, the less you stereotype. The more time and energy you have to consider the person's characteristics and behavior, the less you stereotype. The more motivated you are to form an accurate impression of someone, the less you stereotype. The more you perceive the person to be typical of the stereotyped group, the more your interaction will change your stereotypes. What these factors indicate is that in order for stereotypes to change, members of different groups need to interact for prolonged periods of time under conditions where they get to know each other personally and see each other as being typical members of his or her group.

Stereotypes not only affect the ones who hold them, stereotypes also affect the ones targeted. When a widely known negative stereotype (e.g., poor intellectual ability) exists about a group, it creates for its members a burden of suspicion that acts as a threat. This threat arises whenever individuals' behavior could be interpreted in terms of a stereotype, that is, whenever group members run the risk of confirming the stereotype. Steele and Aronson (1995) in studying **stereotype threat** found that negative stereotypes about blacks' intellectual ability create a "situational pressure" that distracts black students and depresses their academic performance. They argue that the possibility of being judged by a stereotype can cause so much anxiety that intellectual performance is disrupted. Steele and Aronson suggest that stereotype threat is the reason for the underachievement of black students. Seventy percent of black college students drop out of college (as opposed to about 35% of white students), and the drop-out rate is the highest among black students ranked in the top third by SAT scores. In addition, black students with the highest SAT scores fail more frequently than black students with lower scores and at a rate more than three times that of whites with similar scores. When placed in achievement situations, the negative stereotypes are activated and black students become more self-conscious and work less efficiently. Similar findings were reported on a study of lower-class individuals (Croizet & Claire, 1998). Stereotype threat is eliminated in programs such as the University of Michigan's Twenty-First Century Program where black and white students are randomly recruited, live together, study together cooperatively, and have personal discussions on social issues.

Prejudice

To know one's self is wisdom, but to know one's neighbor is genius.

Minna Antrim

To be prejudiced means to prejudge. **Prejudice** can be defined as an unjustified negative attitude towards a person based solely on that individual's membership in a group other than one's own. Prejudices are judgments made about others that establish a superiority/inferiority belief system. If one person dislikes another simply because that other person is a member of a different ethnic group, sex, or religion, we are dealing with prejudice.

One common form of prejudice is ethnocentrism. **Ethnocentrism** is the tendency to regard one's own ethnic group, nation, religion, culture, or gender as better or more "correct" than others. The word is derived from *ethnic*, meaning a group united by similar customs, characteristics, race, or other common factors; and *center*. When ethnocentrism is present, the standards and values of our culture are used as a yardstick to measure the worth of other ethnic groups. Ethnocentrism is often perpetuated by **cultural conditioning.** As children we are raised to fit into a particular culture. We are conditioned to respond to various situations as we see others in our culture react.

Stereotypes lead to prejudices. **Racism** is prejudice directed at people because of their ethnic membership. **Sexism** is prejudice directed at a person because of his or her gender. **Ageism** is prejudice against the elderly. There are many other types of "isms."

The concept of race assumes biological differences that are most evident in physical appearances. The evidence indicates that there is only one human race (with many variations). Although race has dubious value as a scientific classification system, it has had real consequences for the life experiences and life opportunities of African Americans. Race is a socially constructed concept that is the defining characteristic for African American group membership. Race has social meaning suggesting one's status within the social system. It introduces power differences as people of different races interact with one another. Racism and prejudice deal with the forming of unfounded and often inaccurate opinions about a group, leading to biased behavior against members of that group. Racism gives permission to individuals to treat racial groups differently because it mistakenly assumes that (a) humans may be divided into clearly defined racial groups and (b) these groups vary in capabilities and aptitudes.

Modern Racism

Traditionally, in the United States racism and sexism were expressed through such statements as "Blacks are not as smart as whites" and "Women are too emotional to be good managers." Traditional racism and sexism directly and explicitly contain negative evaluations of minorities and females and use the "natural world order" as a justification ("Nature intended it to be this way").

Beginning with the civil rights movement in the 1960s, however, there has been increasing public pressure to see each person as an individual, not as a member of an ethnic group. This has influenced the way whites talk about minorities. Modern racism is a more subtle form of prejudice in which people appear, on the surface, not to be prejudiced, but actually do hold racist attitudes (Dovidio & Gaertner, 1991). Modern racism and sexism camouflage prejudices within more sophisticated principles of meritocracy and justice through such statements as "Blacks and women have gone too far—they are pushing for jobs they do not deserve" (Swim, Aikin, Hall, & Hunter, 1995).

Modern racism and sexism use indirect and implicit negative evaluations of minorities and females and use "protecting cherished social values such as meritocracy from attack by minorities" as a justification. The concept of modern racism posits that if we scratch the apparently nonracist surface of many people, we will find bigotry lurking beneath. Modern racism arises because people can see themselves as being fair, humanitarian, and egalitarian while at the same time holding a somewhat negative view of members of groups other than their own.

Having prejudiced thoughts, however, does not necessarily make you a racist (Devine et al., 1991). Even those who completely reject prejudice may sometimes experience unintentional prejudiced-like thoughts and feelings due to prior learning. In this case, racism is like a lingering bad habit that surfaces despite people's best efforts to avoid it. As with all bad habits, with enough commitment and support, racism can be licked.

Discrimination.   When prejudice is put into action, it is discrimination. **Discrimination** is an action taken to harm a group or any of its members. It is a negative, often aggressive action aimed at the target of prejudice. Discrimination is aimed at denying members of the targeted groups treatment and opportunities equal to those afforded to the dominant group. When discrimination is based on race or sex, it is referred to as racism or sexism. To reduce your prejudices and use of stereotypes, these steps may be helpful (Johnson, 2000):

1. Admit that you have prejudices (everyone does, you are no exception) and commit yourself to reducing them.
2. Identify the stereotypes that reflect your prejudices and modify them.
3. Identify the actions that reflect your prejudices and modify them.
4. Seek feedback from diverse friends and colleagues about how well you are communicating respect for and valuing of diversity.

Blaming the Victim

It is commonly believed that the world is a just place where people generally get what they deserve. If you win the lottery, it must be because you are a nice person who deserves some good luck. If you are robbed, it must be because you were careless and wanted to be punished for past misdeeds. Any person who is mugged in a dark alley while carrying a great deal of cash may be seen as "asking to be robbed." Most people tend to believe that they deserve what happens to them. Most people also believe that others get what they deserve in the world. It is all too easy to forget that victims do not have the benefit of hindsight to guide their actions.

But what happens when situations appear to be unjust? One method is to blame the victim by convincing ourselves that no injustice has occurred. When someone is a victim of prejudice, stereotyping, and discrimination, all too often he or she is seen as "doing *something* wrong." **Blaming the victim** occurs when we attribute the cause of discrimination or misfortune to the personal characteristics and actions of the victim. The situation is examined for potential causes that will enable us to maintain our belief in a just world. If the victim can be blamed for causing the discrimination, then we can believe that the future is predictable and controllable because we will get what we deserve.

Attribution Theory.   Blaming the victim occurs as we try to attribute a cause to events. We constantly interpret the meaning of our behavior and events that occur in our lives. Many times we want to figure out *why* we acted in a particular way or why a certain outcome occurred. If we get angry when someone infers we are stupid, but we

Errors in Making Decisions about Diverse Others

Making a decision requires gathering information on each major alternative action and inferring from the information which alternative will maximize gain and minimize costs.

Errors in Making Inferences

Relying on small samples	Small samples are highly unreliable.
Relying on biased samples	People often ignore clear information about how typical and representative a sample is.
Underutilization of base-rate information	People tend to pay more attention to a single concrete instance than to valid base-rate information, perhaps because the single concrete instance is vivid and salient and thus more compelling.

Errors from Cognitive Heuristics

Availability heuristic	Estimating the frequency of some event by the ease with which you can bring instances to mind. People tend to overestimate the frequency of events that are easy to remember.
Representativeness heuristic	Seeing how well the information matches some imagined average or typical person in the category; the closer the person is to the prototype, the more likely we are to judge the person to be in the category.

Weighing Information

Positive frame	People avoid risks and opt for "sure thing."
Negative frame	People take risks to avoid "costs."
Postdecision rationalization	Alternative chosen becomes more attractive and alternatives not chosen become less desirable.

could care less when someone calls us "clumsy," we want to know why we are so sensitive about our intelligence. When we are standing on a street corner after a rainstorm and a car splashes us with water, we want to know whether it was caused by our carelessness, the driver's meanness, or just bad luck. This process of explaining or inferring the causes of events has been termed **causal attribution.** An attribution is an inference drawn about the causes of a behavior or event. Any behavior or event can have a variety of possible causes. We observe the behavior or event and then infer the cause. When our boss criticizes our work, for example, we can attribute his or her behavior to a grouchy mood, being under too much pressure, disliking us, or the sloppiness of our work. Early in childhood we begin observing our own behavior and draw conclusions about ourselves. We seem to have a fundamental need to understand both our own behavior and the behavior of others. In trying to understand why a behavior or event occurred, we generally choose to attribute causes to either of the following:

1. Internal, personal factors (such as effort and ability).
2. External, situational factors (such as luck, task difficulty, or the behavior/ personality of other people).

Dimensions of Attributions

	Stable	Unstable
Internal	Ability	Effort
External	Task difficulty	Luck

For example, if you do well on a test, you can attribute it to your hard work and great intelligence (an internal attribution) or to the fact that the test was incredibly easy (an external attribution). When a friend drops out of school, you can attribute it to a lack of motivation (an internal attribution) or a lack of money (an external attribution).

People make causal attributions to explain their successes and failures. Frequently such attributions are **self-serving,** designed to permit us to take credit for positive outcomes and to avoid blame for negative ones. We have a systematic tendency to claim our successes are due to our ability and efforts whereas our failures are due to bad luck, obstructive people, or task difficulty. We also have a systematic tendency to claim responsibility for the success of group efforts ("It was all my idea in the first place and I did most of the work") and avoid responsibility for group failures ("If the other members had tried harder, this would not have happened").

Attribution theory recommends that students be trained to make **self-serving attributions.** Students should attribute their academic success to ability and effort and avoid attributing successes to luck or other people. Students should attribute academic failures to bad luck or lack of effort and avoid attributing failures to personal factors such as lack of ability.

Attribution theorists assume that how people explain their successes and failures determines how hard they work on subsequent tasks. If minority students, for example, attribute academic failure to lack of ability, it can eventually lead to **learned helplessness** (the feeling that no amount of effort can lead to success) (Seligman, 1975). Learned helplessness is associated with shame and self-doubt. Students with a long history of attributing failure to lack of ability simply make no effort to learn. Teachers should ensure that students (especially minority students) think through why they succeeded or failed, and guide them towards the conclusion that their failure is caused by either (a) a lack of effort or (b) using the wrong strategy. What emotions teachers express towards students seem to affect the attributions students make about the causes of their success or failure (Graham, 1991). Teacher sympathy for failure tends to be interpreted as indicating low ability whereas teacher anger towards failure seems to be interpreted as indicating low effort.

Success Orientation

	Stable	Unstable
Success	Ability	Effort
Failure	Task difficulty	Luck

Culture Clash

Another common barrier to interacting effectively with diverse groupmates is cultural clashes. **Culture clash** is conflict over basic values that occurs among individuals from different cultures. The most common form is when members of minority groups question the values of the majority. Common reactions by majority-group members when their values are being questioned are feeling:

1. **Threatened:** Their responses include avoidance, denial, and defensiveness.
2. **Confused:** Their responses include seeking more information in an attempt to redefine the problem.

Guidelines for Action

1. Recognize that diversity among members is ever present and unavoidable.
2. Recognize that the more interdependent the world becomes, the more important it is to be able to work effectively with diverse groupmates.
3. Maximize heterogeneity among members in both personal characteristics and abilities in order to maximize the group's productivity and success.
4. With heterogeneous membership comes increased conflict. Structure constructive procedures for managing conflicts among group members.
5. Face and resolve the barriers to the utilization of diversity (stereotyping, prejudice, blaming the victim, cultural clashes).
6. Ensure that diversity is utilized as a resource by strengthening the positive interdependence within the group in order to create the context in which diversity is a resource, not a hindrance.
7. Ensure diversity is utilized as a strength by uniting the personal identities of members of diverse groups. Create a superordinate identity based on a pluralistic set of values. Encourage individuals to develop:
   a. An appreciation for their gender, religious, ethnic, and cultural backgrounds.
   b. An appreciation for the gender, religious, ethnic, and cultural backgrounds of other group members.
   c. A strong superordinate identity of "group member" that transcends the differences among members.
   d. A pluralistic set of values concerning equality, freedom, the rights of individual members, and the responsibilities of group membership.
8. Ensure that diversity is utilized as a strength by fostering personal relationships among members that allow for candid discussions that increase members' sophistication about their differences.
9. Ensure that diversity is utilized as a strength by clarifying miscommunications among diverse group members.

3. **Enhanced:** Their responses include heightened anticipation, awareness, and positive actions that lead to solving the problem. Many cultural clashes develop from threatening, to confusing, to enhancing. Once they are enhancing, they are no longer a barrier.

As prejudice, stereotyping, and discrimination are reduced, the tendency to blame the victim is avoided, and cultural clashes become enhancing, the stage is set for recognizing and valuing diversity.

MAKING DIVERSITY AMONG MEMBERS A STRENGTH

Diversity among members is a potential source of creativity and productivity. For group members to capitalize on their differences, they must:

1. Ensure that high levels of positive interdependence exist among group members.
2. Create a superordinate group identity that (a) unites the diverse personal identities of group members and (b) is based on a pluralistic set of values.
3. Gain sophistication about the differences among members through personal relationships that allow for candid discussions.
4. Clarify miscommunications among group members from different cultures, ethnic and historical backgrounds, social classes, genders, age cohorts, and so forth.

Structuring and Strengthening Positive Interdependence

In order to build a superordinant group identity that unites all members and build personal relationships that allow for candid conversations that result in increased sophistication, positive interdependence must be structured into group life and periodically strengthened to remind members that they are engaged in a joint enterprise. **Positive interdependence** exists when group members perceive that they can reach their goals if and only if the other members also do so (Deutsch, 1962; Johnson & Johnson, 1989). Group members must believe that they "sink or swim together" in striving to achieve important mutual goals. Positive interdependence may be structured through mutual goals, joint rewards, shared resources, complementary roles, divisions of labor, and a mutual identity.

Strength through diversity does not automatically occur with proximity. Bringing diverse individuals into the same room does not ensure that constructive results will occur. The discords of diversity are not automatically transformed into a symphony when people are brought face-to-face. Prejudice, stereotyping, and discrimination often increase with proximity. What largely determines whether interaction results in positive or negative relationships is the context within which the interaction takes place. Rather than requiring group members to compete to see who is best or work individualistically on their own, group members must work together to achieve mutual goals. When people cooperate, they tend to like each other more, trust each other more, are more candid with each other, and are more willing to listen to and be influenced by each other (Johnson & Johnson, 1989). When people compete or work individualistically, then liking, trust, influence, and candor tend to decrease. There is considerable evidence that cooperative experiences, compared with competitive and individualistic ones, promote more positive, committed, and caring relationships regardless of differences in ethnic, cultural, language, social class, gender, ability, or other differences (Johnson & Johnson, 1989). The impact of positive interdependence will be enhanced when members have equal status and social norms and authorities promote positive relationships and friendship formation (Watson, 1947; Williams, 1947; Allport, 1954).

Creating a Superordinate Group Identity

Diverse individuals from different gender, religious, social class, ethnic, and cultural backgrounds come together in small group settings. The results will be positive if group members get to know each other, appreciate and value the vitality of diversity, learn how to use their diversity for creative problem solving and enhanced productivity, and internalize a common superordinate identity that binds them all together. In order for group members to actualize the positive potential of their diversity, they must recognize that diversity exists and then learn to value and respect fundamental differences among people. The goal of managing diversity is not to assimilate all members so that everyone is alike. The goal is for members to work together to achieve mutual goals while recognizing their diversity among members and valuing and respecting fundamental differences. Creating an *unum* from *pluribus* is done in four steps.

First, group members develop an appreciation for their historic, cultural, ethnic, and religious background as well as their other important personal characteristics. Members should value and recognize the culture, history, and homeland of their ancestors. A **personal identity** is a consistent set of attitudes that defines "who you are" (see Johnson [2000] for a full discussion on developing a personal identity). An identity helps a person cope with stress, it provides stability and consistency to the person's life, and it directs what information is attended to, how it is organized, and how it is remembered. A personal identity consists of multiple subidentities that are organized into a coherent, stable, and integrated whole. The subidentities include a **gender identity** (fundamental sense of maleness or femaleness), a **cultural identity** (sense of origins and membership in a culture), an **ethnic identity** (sense of belonging to one particular ethnic group), a **religious identity** (sense of belonging to one particular religious group), and so forth. Each of these subidentities should be recognized and valued, and they need to be organized into a coherent, stable, and integrated overall sense of self. Respect for one's subidentities may be the basis for self-respect.

Second, group members develop an appreciation for the historic, cultural, ethnic, and religious backgrounds (and other important personal characteristics) of others. A critical aspect of developing a historical, cultural, and ethnic identity is whether ethnocentricity is inherent in one's definition of oneself. A personal identity that includes one's heritage must be developed in a way that does not lead to rejection of the heritage of other members. There are many examples where being a member of one group requires the rejection of other groups. There are also many examples where being a member of one group requires the valuing and respect for other groups. Other heritages may be seen as collaborators rather than competitors. The degree to which a person's identity leads to respect for and valuing of others' diversity depends on developing a superordinate identity that subsumes both one's own heritage and the heritage of all other group members. Members need to learn how to express respect for diverse backgrounds and value them as a resource that increases the quality of life and adds to the viability of the group.

Third, encourage members to develop a strong superordinate identity of "group member" that transcends the differences among members. Being the member of a work group is creedal rather than racial or ancestral. The work group unites as one widely diverse people. In essence, the work group has its own culture that supersedes the individual cultures of members. Members need to learn how to highlight the group's superordinate identity and use it to resolve conflicts based on members' differences.

Fourth, group members adopt a pluralistic set of values concerning democracy, freedom, liberty, equality, justice, the rights of individuals, and the responsibilities of citizenship. All members have a say in how the group operates. All members are free to speak their minds and give their opinions. All members are considered to be of equal value. Every member has the right and responsibility to contribute his or her resources

Being an American

Being an American is creedal rather than racial or ancestral. It is our beliefs that "all humans are created equal and endowed by their creator with certain inalienable rights" (i.e., our commitment to the Constitution, Bill of Rights, and Declaration of Independence of the United States) that provide our superordinate identity as Americans. To be an American is to adopt a pluralistic set of values concerning democracy, freedom, liberty, equality, justice, the rights of individuals, and the responsibilities of citizenship (Johnson & Johnson, 1994). It is these values that form the American creed. The common commitment to equality, justice, and liberty for all unites us as one people, even though we are the descendants of many cultures, races, religions, and ethnic groups. Each cultural group is part of the whole, and members of each new immigrant group, while modifying and enriching our national identity, learn they are first and foremost Americans. America is one of the few successful examples of a pluralistic society where different groups clashed but ultimately learned to live together through achieving a sense of common nationhood. In our diversity, there has always been a broad recognition that we are one people. Whatever our origins, we are all Americans. It is from the four steps given above that the United States creates an *unum* from *pluribus*.

1. I respect, appreciate, and value my religious, ethnic, and cultural background.

2. I respect, appreciate, and value the religious, ethnic, and cultural backgrounds of others.

3. I have a strong superordinate identity as an "American." Being an American is creedal. I believe in the American creed.

4. I have pluralistic values. I value democracy, freedom, liberty, equality, justice, the rights of individuals, and the responsibilities of citizenship.

and efforts towards achieving the group's goals. Each member has a right to expect the group to be considerate of his or her needs and wants. All members must at times put the good of the group above their own needs and desires. It is these values that form the group or organizational culture. In the group, members must respect basic human rights, listen to dissenters instead of rejecting them, have freedom of speech, and have open discussion of differences. It is these values that bind group members together. Most groups are or will become a multicultural unit knitted together by a common set of values.

Gaining Sophistication Through Intergroup Relationships

Some people are **sophisticated** about how to act appropriately within many different cultures and perspectives. They are courteous, well-mannered, and refined within many different settings and cultures. Other people are quite **provincial,** knowing only how to act appropriately with their narrow perspective. To become sophisticated a person must be able to see the situation from the cultural perspective of the other people involved. Much of the information about different cultural and ethnic heritages and perspectives cannot be attained through reading books and listening to lectures. Only through knowing, working with, and personally interacting with members of diverse groups can individuals really learn to value diversity, utilize diversity for creative problem solving, and work effectively with diverse peers. Understanding the perspective of others from different ethnic and cultural backgrounds requires more than information. It requires the personal sharing of viewpoints and mutual discussion of situations.

To gain the sophistication and skills required to build relationships with diverse peers, you need to develop friends from a wide variety of cultural, ethnic, social class, and historical backgrounds. There are many aspects of relating to individuals different from you that can be learned only from friends being candid about misunderstandings you are inadvertently creating. To gain the necessary sophistication and skills to relate to, work with, and become friends with diverse peers, you need:

1. **Actual Interaction:** Seek opportunities to interact with a wide variety of peers. You do so because you value diversity, recognize the importance of relating effectively to diverse peers, and recognize the importance of increasing your knowledge of multicultural issues.
2. **Trust:** Build trust by being open about yourself and your commitment to cross-cultural relationships and being trustworthy when others share their opinions and reactions with you. Being trustworthy includes expressing respect for diverse backgrounds and valuing them as a resource that increases the quality of your life and adds to the viability of your society.
3. **Candor:** Persuade your peers to be candid by openly discussing their personal opinions, feelings, and reactions with you. There are many events that seem neutral to you that are offensive and hurtful to individuals from backgrounds different from yours. In order to understand what is and is not disrespectful and hurtful, your peers must be candid about their reactions and explain them to you.

If you are not sophisticated and skilled in building relationships with diverse peers, you are in danger of unconsciously colluding with current patterns of discrimination. **Collusion** is conscious and unconscious reinforcement of stereotypic attitudes, behaviors, and prevailing norms. People collude with discriminatory practices and prejudiced actions through ignorance, silence, denial, and active support. Perhaps the only way not to collude with existing discriminatory practices is to build the friendships with diverse peers that allow you to understand when discrimination and prejudice occur.

Clarifying Miscommunications

Imagine that you and several friends went to hear a speaker. Although the content was good, and the delivery entertaining, two of your friends walked out in protest. When you asked them why, they called your attention to the facts that the speaker continually used "you guys" even though half the audience were women, used only sports and military examples, quoted only males, and joked about senility and old age. Your friends were insulted.

Communication is actually one of the most complex aspects of managing relationships with diverse peers. To communicate effectively with people from a different cultural, ethnic, social class, and historical background, you must increase your:

1. **Language Sensitivity:** Knowledge of words and expressions that are appropriate and inappropriate in communicating with diverse groups. The use of language can play a powerful role in reinforcing stereotypes and garbling communication. To avoid this, individuals need to heighten their sensitivity and avoid using terms and expressions that ignore or devalue others.

2. **Awareness of Stylistic Elements of Communication:** Knowledge of the key elements of communication style and how diverse cultures use these elements to communicate. Without awareness of nuances in language and differences in style, the potential for garbled communication is enormous when interacting with diverse peers.

Your ability to communicate with credibility to diverse peers is closely linked to your use of language. You must be sophisticated enough to anticipate how your messages will be interpreted by the listener. If you are unaware of nuances and innuendoes contained in your message, then you will be more likely to miscommunicate. The words you choose often tell other people more about your values, attitudes, and socialization than you intend to reveal. Receivers will react to the subtleties conveyed and interpret the implied messages behind our words. The first step in establishing relationships with diverse peers, therefore, is to understand how language reinforces stereotypes and to adjust our usage accordingly.

You can never predict with certainty how every person will react to what you say. You can, however, minimize the possibility of miscommunicating by following some basic guidelines:

1. Use all the communication skills discussed in this book and in Johnson (2000).
2. Negotiate for meaning whenever you think the other persons you are talking with misinterpreted what you said.
3. Use words that are inclusive rather than exclusive such as *women, men, participants.*
4. Avoid adjectives that spotlight specific groups and imply the individual is an exception, such as *black doctor, woman pilot, older teacher, blind lawyer.*
5. Use quotes, references, metaphors, and analogies that reflect diversity and are from diverse sources, for example, from Asian and African sources as well as from European and American sources.
6. Avoid terms that define, demean, or devalue others, such as *cripple, girl, boy, agitator.*
7. Be aware of the genealogy of words viewed as inappropriate by others. It is the connotations the receiver places on the words that is important, not your connotations. These connotations change over time so continual clarification is needed. There are "loaded" words that seem neutral to you but highly judgmental to people of diverse backgrounds. The word lady, for example, was a compliment even a few years ago, but today it fails to take into account women's independence and equal status in society and, therefore, is offensive to many women. Words such as *girls,* and *gals* are just as offensive.

SUMMARY

In a global village highly diverse individuals interact daily, studying, working, and playing together in small groups. Rapidly growing global interdependence and the increasing emphasis on teamwork results in groups with quite diverse membership. Diversity among members is no longer the exception, or optional, it is the everyday rule. Global interdependence and diversity among team members go hand-in-hand. With the one, comes the other. Diversity among your acquaintances, classmates, co-workers, neighbors, and friends is increasingly inevitable. You will be expected to interact effectively with people from a wide variety of characteristics and backgrounds. Doing so has many advantages. Heterogeneity of group composition tends to increase group productivity on a variety of tasks, increase the difficulty for developing cohesive relationships among members, and increases the potential conflict among members. Diversity among members is advantageous, but it is not easy to manage.

Accepting others begins with accepting yourself (see Johnson, 2000 for a thorough discussion of self-acceptance). But even for individuals who are quite accepting of themselves and others, there are barriers to building positive relationships with diverse peers. The most notable barriers are prejudice, blaming the victim, and cul-

Important Concepts

Demonstrate your understanding of the following concepts by matching the definitions with the appropriate concept. Find a partner. Compare answers.

	Concept		Definition
	1. Prejudice	a.	Belief that associates a whole group of people with certain traits.
	2. Ethnocentrism	b.	An action taken to harm a group or any of its members.
	3. Stereotype	c.	Unjustified negative attitude towards a person based solely on that individual's membership in a group other than one's own.
	4. Illusionary correlation	d.	Attribute the cause of discrimination or misfortune to the personal characteristics and actions of the victim.
	5. Discrimination	e.	Conflict over basic values that occurs among individuals from different cultures.
	6. Blaming the victim	f.	Conscious or unconscious reinforcement of stereotypic attitudes, behaviors, and prevailing norms.
	7. Collusion	g.	Tendency for people to overestimate the association between variables that are only slightly correlated or not correlated at all.
	8. Scapegoat	h.	Prejudice directed at people because of their ethnic membership.
	9. Racism	i.	Believing that most other people share their stereotypes.
	10. Modern racism	j.	Guiltless but defenseless group that is attacked to provide an outlet for pent-up anger and frustration caused by another group.
	11. False consensus bias	k.	Subtle forms of prejudice in which people appear, on the surface, not to harbor prejudice, but actually do hold prejudiced attitudes.
	12. Stereotype threat	l.	Tendency to regard own ethnic group, nation, religion, culture, or gender as being more correct than others.
	13. Culture clash	m.	Whenever group members run the risk of confirming the stereotype.

ture clash. Minimizing these barriers makes it easier to recognize that diversity exists and fundamental differences among people are to be both respected and valued. For group members to capitalize on their differences, they must ensure high levels of positive interdependence exist among group members (highlight important mutual goals that require cooperative action and develop a common ground on which everyone is co-oriented); create a superordinate group identity that (a) unites the diverse personal identities of group members and (b) is based on a pluralistic set of values, gains sophistication about the differences among members through personal relationships that have sufficient trust to allow for candid discussions, and clarifies miscommunications that arise when group members from different cultures, ethnic and historical backgrounds, social classes, genders, age cohorts, and so forth, work together.

Exercise 10.2: Stereotyping

Once you realize that everyone is socialized to be prejudiced and to stereotype others, you need to clarify just what stereotypes you hold. This exercise is aimed at clarifying (a) what stereotypes you have been taught about other groups, (b) what stereotypes they have been taught about you, and (c) how the process of stereotyping works.

1. Post each word from the following list on sheets of paper around the room:

Male	Female
Teenager	Over age 70
Asian American	African American
Native American	Hispanic American
Blind	Deaf
Lower income	Middle income
Roman Catholic	Protestant
Southern	Midwestern

2. Each participant is to circulate around the room, read the various categories, and write one stereotype he or she has heard under each heading. Participants are told not to repeat anything that is already written down. They are not to make anything up. They are to write down *all* the stereotypes they have heard about each of the groups listed.
3. After everyone is done writing, participants are to read all the stereotypes under each category.
4. Participants discuss:
   a. Their personal reactions.
   b. How accurate the stereotypes of their identities are.
   c. What they have learned about stereotyping others.

Exercise 10.3: Interacting on the Basis of Stereotypes

Stereotypes are rigid judgments made about other groups that ignore individual differences. The purpose of this exercise is to demonstrate how stereotypes are associated with primary and secondary dimensions of diversity.

1. Divide participants into groups of five. The group is to role play a discussion of employees of a large corporation of the ways in which the percentage of people of color and women in higher-level executive positions may be increased from 10% to 50%.
2. Give each member of the group a headband to wear with a particular identity written on it for other group members to see. **Group members are not to look at their own headbands.** The five identities are:

    Single Mother of Two Young Children, Unemployed
    Employee with Physical Disability
    Woman, Age 72
    White Male, Company President
    Black Female, Union Official

3. Stop the discussion after ten minutes or so. Then have the groups discuss:
    a. What each person thinks the label on his or her headband was.
    b. Their personal reactions.
    c. The participation pattern of each member—who dominated, who withdrew, who was interrupted, who was influential.
    d. What they have learned about stereotyping others.

Exercise 10.4: Greetings and Goodbyes

The purpose of this exercise is to increase awareness of how different cultural patterns of greetings and goodbyes can create communication problems. The procedure is as follows.

1. Divide the class into groups of four. Divide each group into two pairs, Americans and Lakians (from a fictitious country named Lake). If possible give each pair something such as colored ribbons or armbands that visually distinguish them from one another.
2. Ask all American pairs to go to one end of the room and the Lakian pairs to go to the other. They receive separate briefings.
3. The participants are to role play that they are business associates who are to engage in an informal discussion of general economic conditions in their countries.
    a. The **American pairs** are instructed to greet their Lakian business associates in the traditional North American fashion. They are to shake hands, say "good to see you again," talk about the economic conditions of North America for a while, and then say goodbye by shaking hands and waving.
    b. The **Lakian pairs** are instructed to greet their American business associates in the traditional Lakian fashion. They are to give the Americans a warm embrace and then to take and hold their hands for at least thirty seconds. They are to talk about the economic condition of Lake for a while. Then they are to say goodbye by giving the Americans a warm embrace, holding both their hands for at least thirty seconds, and telling them how great it was to talk to them.
4. The group of four meets. If they finish the conversation before other groups in the room do, each pair should find another pair from the other country and repeat the experience.
5. The group of four discusses the experience:
    a. What were the cultural differences?
    b. What communication barriers did the cultural differences create?

   c. How did the participants feel during the interchange between the Americans and Lakians?

   d. What are three conclusions about cross-cultural communication that can be made from the experience?

The English and their North American counterparts are sometimes seen as being impoverished when it comes to kinesic communication, using words to denote what gesture or tone would express in other cultures. In North America, for example, people are often quite reserved when greeting others. Body contact is avoided. Yet in some Arab countries men kiss each other on the street when they meet. Nigerian men often walk hand in hand. Italian men embrace warmly and remain touching when engaged in conversation. In some African countries handshakes may be extended for long periods of time, and a hand on the knee among males is not an offense. All of these differences create potential communication problems when members of the different cultures meet.

Exercise 10.5: Time

The purpose of this exercise is to focus attention on the differences in time and timing in different cultures. The procedure is as follows.

1. Divide the class into groups of four. Divide each group into two pairs, Americans and Pinians (from a fictitious country named Pine). If possible give each pair something such as colored ribbons or armbands that visually distinguish them from one another.
2. Ask all American pairs to go to one end of the room and the Pinian pairs to go to the other. They receive separate briefings.
3. The participants are to role play that they have an appointment with a photographer at 12:00 to have their picture taken.
   a. The **American pairs** are instructed that the appointment is at 12:00 sharp because the photographer has another appointment at 12:30 in another part of town. The photographer asked them not to be late.
   b. The **Pinian pairs** are instructed that to them time is not important. Today or tomorrow, it does not matter. Twelve o'clock or one o'clock, what difference does it make? Take it easy, have a cup of coffee, why rush?
4. The group of four meets. It is 11:55 in the morning and it takes five minutes to get to the photographer's studio.
5. The group of four discusses the experience:
   a. What were the cultural differences?
   b. What communication barriers did the cultural differences create?
   c. How did the participants feel during the interchange between the Americans and Pinians?
   d. What are three conclusions about cross-cultural communication that can be made from the experience?

Individuals living in industrialized societies are often seen as being "slaves of time." Individuals living in nonindustrialized societies are sometimes seen as being inconsiderate and unreliable. What happens when the two cultures meet?

Exercise 10.6: Cross-Cultural Communication

The purpose of this exercise is to increase awareness of how cultural differences can create barriers to communication among group members. The procedure is as follows.

1. Form groups of six and divide each group into three pairs.
2. Each pair is assigned a particular cultural identity based on being a citizen of the country of Winkin, Blinkin, or Nod. Their **task** is to plan how they will act during the exercise based on the information about their country given on their briefing sheet. The pair is to work together cooperatively to ensure that both members understand how to act appropriately as a citizen of their country. They have ten minutes to prepare.
3. Two triads are formed (one member from each country). Each triad is assigned the task of identifying the ten most important principles of cross-cultural communication. They have fifteen minutes to do so.
4. The group of six discusses the following questions:
   a. Compare the two lists. How are they different? How are they the same?
   b. How did members react to their assigned roles? Were there any difficulties in enacting them?
   c. What were the communication barriers among the citizens of the three countries? Why did they occur?
   d. How could the communication barriers be avoided or overcome?
   e. What conclusions can be made from the exercise?
   f. What applications does the exercise have for everyday life?

Confidential: To Be Seen by Winkin Citizens Only

Behavioral Characteristics of the Country of Winkin

1. **Orientation Towards Touch:** Touch as much as possible, stand and sit close to people, and give a long handshake (about fifteen to thirty seconds) when you greet a person.

2. **Orientation Towards Eye Contact:** Look other people in the eyes when you talk to them.

3. **Orientation Towards Disclosure:** You are interested only in yourself and you love to share yourself with other people. Talk only about yourself and what interests you. Do not listen to other people—they are boring. You do not want to understand other people better; you want them to understand you. Whenever they start talking you interrupt them and refocus the conversation on yourself.

4. **Orientation Towards Conflict:** You like to argue for the sake of arguing so that people will pay attention to you.

5. **Orientation Towards Helping Others:** You avoid helping people under any circumstances.

Confidential: To Be Seen by Blinkin Citizens Only

Behavioral Characteristics of the Country of Blinkin

1. **Orientation Towards Touch:** Do not touch other people. Stand and sit far away from other people. Greet other people by nodding your head—do not shake hands.

2. **Orientation Towards Eye Contact:** Do not look other people in the eyes when you talk to them. If you happen to look a person in the eyes, look for only a split second.

3. **Orientation Towards Disclosure:** You are genuinely interested in other people. You are inquisitive. You get to know other people by asking them questions about what they are interested in. You listen carefully and let other people finish what they are saying before you speak. You never interrupt. You never talk about yourself.

4. **Orientation Towards Conflict:** You are very uncomfortable with conflict and want to avoid it at all costs. You never argue about a point with which you disagree. Instead you change the subject and try to find something else to talk about.

5. **Orientation Towards Helping Others:** You try to help other people (especially in solving a problem) as much as possible.

Confidential: To Be Seen by Nod Citizens Only

Behavioral Characteristics of the Country of Nod

1. **Orientation Towards Touch:** Touch people only occasionally when you are talking. Stand and sit about an arm's length from a person. Give a short handshake when you are greeting a person.

2. **Orientation Towards Eye Contact:** Look other people in the eyes for only about three seconds at a time when you talk to them.

3. **Orientation Towards Disclosure:** You want to exchange ideas and thoughts. You share your interests and opinions and you want other people to share their interests and opinions with you. You want to talk *with* other people instead of *to* them.

4. **Orientation Towards Conflict:** You seek reasoned judgments. You ignore who is right and who is wrong. You focus on the quality of ideas, seeking a synthesis or integration of different points of view. You listen carefully, add what you want to say, and make an informed judgment based on all positions and perspectives.

5. **Orientation Towards Helping Others:** You help other people only when it benefits you, that is, when it is rational to do so.

Exercise 10.7: Merging Different Cultures

The purpose of this exercise is to merge individuals from two different cultures into one group. The procedure for the exercise is as follows:

1. The materials you need to assemble for the exercise are:
   a. Using poster board, construct ten sets of Figure 10.1 for each participant in Atlantis and one set of Figure 10.2 for every participant taking part in the exercise.
   b. One envelope per participant.
   c. One die for each group in Atlantis.
2. Divide the class into citizens of Atlantis and Mu. Assign participants to the society of Mu for every participant assigned to Atlantis. The citizens of Atlantis meet at one end of the room and the citizens of Mu meet at the other end of the room.
3. At the Atlantis end of the room, assign participants to groups of four and seat each group around a table.
   a. Place enough pieces for ten complete T's per member in the center of each group (pieces for forty T's).
   b. Tell the participants:

   > You are a worker in Atlantis who earns his or her living by constructing T's. A T is formed using four triangles and three squares. Life is hard in Atlantis so everyone looks out for "Number One." You build your T's by taking pieces from the center of the table. You will take turns in acquiring the shapes. When it is your turn you acquire shapes by either (a) taking two pieces from the pile or (b) rolling the die (if you roll an even number [2, 4, 6] you can select that number of pieces, but if you roll an odd number [1, 3, 5] you lose that number of pieces from those you have accumulated thus far, including those composing complete T's). The member with the greatest number of T's will be declared the wealthiest and will survive. The poorest will perish. You can begin.

4. At the Mu end of the room, a second instructor divides the citizens of Mu into groups of four members and seats each group around a table. Their task is to earn their livelihood by constructing T's. Each citizen of Mu is to form a T using the five pieces as shown in Figure 10.2. The instructor takes the pieces to make up the four T's for each group and randomly divides the pieces into four envelopes (five pieces in each), making sure that no one envelope contains the correct five pieces for completing a T. One envelope is given to each group member. The instructor tells the participants:

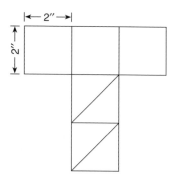

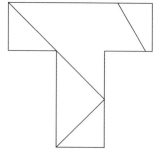

Figure 10.1   Figure 10.2

You are a worker in Mu who earns his or her living by constructing T's. Life is hard in Mu, so everyone looks out for everyone else. There are enough pieces between the members of your group to form one complete T for each member, but no one member has the right combination of pieces to complete his or her T. Mu, however, is a heterogeneous society that does not have a common language. The members of your group, therefore, will not speak to each other. **No verbal communication is allowed.**

Group members must share pieces in order to be successful. You may offer pieces to another group member and accept pieces offered to you by another group member. You cannot offer pieces to more than one person at the same time. You may not ask for a particular piece by pointing, talking, nudging, grimacing, or any other method. When you give a piece to another member, simply hand it to the person without demonstrating how the piece fits into his or her T. You have five minutes to complete this task. You may open your envelopes.

After five minutes the instructor collects each group's pieces and again places the pieces randomly into the envelopes.

5. The Mu groups repeat the task, except that this time they may use any form of communication they wish. All other rules remain in effect. They have five minutes to complete the task.

6. Bring the Atlantis citizens to join the Mu society. Evenly distribute the citizens of Atlantis among the Mu groups. Add to each group's T's one additional T for each new member. Take the combined pieces and randomly distribute them into envelopes, one for each member of the integrated groups. Tell the participants:

The citizens of Atlantis are immigrants to Mu. They are to have a part in the work of Mu, and the sooner they learn to earn a livelihood, the better off Mu will be. Members of Atlantis, however, do not speak Mu's language and the meaning of nonverbal gestures in the two societies is quite different. *There will, therefore, be no talking and no nonverbal signaling such as pointing or gesturing.* Your task is to build T's. The T's are formed differently from those made in Atlantis. You can begin work.

Stop the groups when all groups have built their T's or after ten minutes, whichever one comes first.

7. Have the groups discuss:
    a. How did the members of each society feel about working in integrated units?
    b. How did the two societies differ?
    c. Why was your group successful or unsuccessful in integrating the two societies?
    d. What conclusions can be drawn about work groups consisting of members from more than one society?

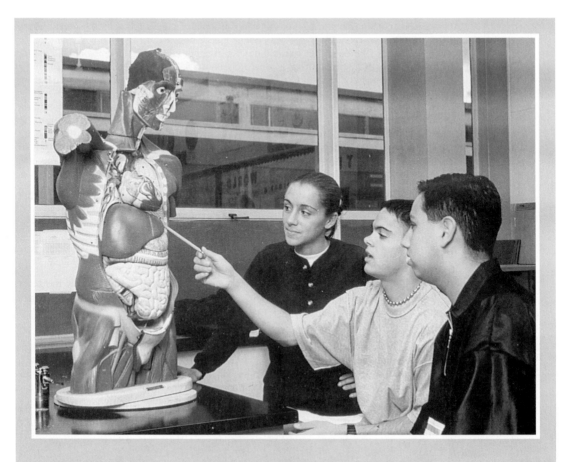

11

Learning and Discussion Groups

Basic Concepts to Be Covered in This Chapter

In this chapter a number of concepts are defined and discussed. The major ones are listed below. Divide into pairs, define each concept (noting the page on which it is defined and discussed), making sure that both you and your partner understand the meaning of each concept. Then join with another pair to make a group of four. Compare the answers of the two pairs. If there is disagreement, look up the concept in the chapter and clarify it until all members agree on and understand the definition.

Concepts

1. Cooperative learning
2. Competitive learning
3. Individualistic learning
4. Formal cooperative learning
5. Informal cooperative learning
6. Cooperative base groups
7. Individual accountability
8. Cooperative school
9. Promotive interaction
10. Group processing

NATURE OF COOPERATIVE LEARNING

Two are better than one, because they have a good reward for toil. For if they
fall, one will lift up his fellow; but woe to him who is alone when he falls and
has not another to lift him up . . . And though a man might prevail against one
who is alone, two will withstand him. A threefold cord is not quickly broken.

Ecclesiastics 4:9–12

Groups have existed for as long as there have been humans (and even before). Groups
have been the subject of countless books. Every human society has used groups to accomplish its goals and celebrated when the groups were successful. It was groups that
built the pyramids, constructed the Temple of Artemis at Ephesus, created the Colos-
sus of Rhodes, and the hanging gardens of Babylon. It is obvious that groups outperform
individuals, especially when performance requires multiple skills, judgments, and experiences. Many educators, however, overlook opportunities to use groups to enhance
student learning and increase their own success.

History of Cooperative Learning

Cooperative learning is an old idea. The **Talmud** clearly states that in order to learn you
must have a learning partner. In the first century, **Quintillion** argued that students could
benefit from teaching one another. The Roman philosopher **Seneca** advocated cooperative learning through such statements as *qui docet discet* (when you teach, you learn
twice). **Johann Amos Comenius** (1592–1679) believed that students would benefit from
both teaching and being taught by other students. In the late 1700s **Joseph Lancaster** and
Andrew Bell made extensive use of cooperative learning groups in England, and the idea
was brought to America when a Lancastrian school was opened in New York City in
1806. Within the **Common School Movement** in the United States in the early 1800s,
there was a strong emphasis on cooperative learning. In the last three decades of the
nineteenth century, **Colonel Francis Parker** brought to his advocacy of cooperative
learning enthusiasm, idealism, practicality, and an intense devotion to freedom, democracy, and individuality in the public schools. His fame and success rested on his power
to create a classroom atmosphere that was truly cooperative and democratic. Parker's
advocacy of cooperation among students dominated American education through the
turn of the century. Following Parker, **John Dewey** promoted the use of cooperative
learning groups as part of his famous project method in instruction. In the late 1930s,
however, interpersonal competition began to be emphasized in schools and in the late
1960s, individualistic learning began to be used extensively. In the 1980s, schools once
again began to use cooperative learning.

Capitalizing on the Power of Groups

The opportunity to capitalize on the power of groups in schools begins with understanding the answers to the following questions (see Table 11.1):

1. What is cooperative learning?
2. Why use cooperative learning?
3. What are the expected outcomes resulting from cooperative efforts?
4. How do you structure formal cooperative learning?

Table 11.1 **Circles of Learning**

Social Interdependence		
Cooperative	Competitive	Individualistic

Research: Why Use Cooperative Learning		
Effort to achieve	Positive relationships	Psychological health

Five Basic Elements				
Positive interdependence	Individual accountability	Promotive interaction	Social skills	Group processing

Cooperative Learning		
Formal Cooperative Learning	**Informal Cooperative Learning**	**Coop Base Groups**
Make preinstructional decisions.	Conduct introductory focused discussion.	Structure opening class meeting to check homework, ensure members understand academic material, complete routine tasks such as attendance.
Explain task and cooperative structure.	Conduct intermittent pair discussions every ten or fifteen minutes.	Structure ending class meeting to ensure members understand academic material, homework assignment.
Monitor learning groups and intervene to improve taskwork and teamwork.	Conduct closure focused discussion.	Members help and assist eachother learn in-between classes.
Assess student learning and process group effectiveness.		Conduct semester or year-long school or class service projects.

Cooperative School		
Teaching teams	Site-based decision making	Faculty meetings

Constructive Conflict			
Students		**Faculty**	
Academic controversy	Negotiating, mediating	Decision-making controversy	Negotiating, mediating

Civic Values				
Work for mutual benefit, common good	Equality of all members	Trusting, caring relationships	View situations from all perspectives	Unconditional worth of self, diverse others

5. How do you structure informal cooperative learning?
6. How do you structure cooperative base groups?
7. How do you use the three types of cooperative learning in an integrated way?
8. What are the basic elements of cooperative learning that make it work?
9. How do you structure cooperation among faculty and staff to ensure that cooperative efforts are institutionalized throughout school life?

What Is Cooperative Learning?

To understand the nature of cooperative learning, it is necessary to place it within the broader context of social interdependence. **Social interdependence** exists when each individual's outcomes are affected by the actions of others (Deutsch, 1949a; Johnson &

What Is It?

Given below are twelve statements. Form a pair and agree on whether each statement reflects a cooperative, competitive, or individualistic situation. Place each statement in the appropriate column in the table given.

STATEMENTS

1. Strive for everyone's success.
2. Strive to be better than others.
3. Strive for own success only.
4. What benefits self does not affect others.
5. Joint success is celebrated.
6. What benefits self benefits others.
7. Only own success is celebrated.
8. Motivated to help and assist others.
9. What benefits self deprives/hurts others.
10. Motivated only to maximize own productivity.
11. Own success and other's failure is celebrated.
12. Motivated to ensure that no one else does better than oneself.

Cooperative	*Competitive*	*Individualistic*

Johnson, 1989). Social interdependence may be positive or negative. **Positive interdependence** (cooperation) exists when individuals work together to achieve mutual goals, and **negative interdependence** (competition) exists when individuals work against each other to achieve a goal that only one or a few may attain. **Social independence,** where the outcomes of each person are unaffected by others' actions, is characterized by individualistic actions.

Cooperation is working together to accomplish shared goals. Within cooperative situations, individuals seek outcomes that are beneficial to themselves and beneficial to all other group members. **Cooperative learning** is the instructional use of small groups so that students work together to maximize their own and each other's learning. It may be contrasted with **competitive** (students work against each other to achieve an academic goal such as a grade of A that only one or a few students can attain) and **individualistic** (students work by themselves to accomplish learning goals unrelated to those of the other students) learning. In cooperative and individualistic learning, you evaluate student efforts on a criteria-referenced basis whereas in competitive learning you grade students on a norm-referenced basis. Although there are limitations on when and where you may use competitive and individualistic learning appropriately, you may structure any learning task in any subject area with any curriculum cooperatively.

Within cooperative learning groups students discuss the material to be learned with each other, help and assist each other to understand it, and encourage each other to work hard. There are three types of cooperative learning groups (see Table 11.2). Cooperative learning groups may be used to teach specific content (**formal cooperative learning groups**), to ensure active cognitive processing of information during a lecture or demonstration (**informal cooperative learning groups**), and to provide long-term support and assistance for academic progress (**cooperative base groups**) (Johnson, Johnson, & Holubec, 1998a, 1998b; Johnson, Johnson, & Smith, 1998). Any assignment in any curriculum for any age student can be done cooperatively. Each of these types of cooperative learning groups will be discussed in this chapter.

FORMAL COOPERATIVE LEARNING: BEING "A GUIDE ON THE SIDE"

At age fifty-five, after his defeat by Woodrow Wilson for president of the United States, Teddy Roosevelt took a journey to South America. The Brazilian government suggested he lead an expedition to explore a vast, unmapped river deep in the jungle. Known as the River of Doubt, it was believed to be a tributary to the Amazon. Roosevelt accepted instantly. "We will go down the unknown river," he declared, and the Brazilian government organized an expedition for the trip. "I had to go," he said later, "it was my last chance to be a boy." Roosevelt, with his son Kermit and a party of eighteen, headed into the jungle. "On February 27, 1914, shortly after midday, we started down the River of Doubt into the unknown," Roosevelt wrote. The journey was an ordeal. Hostile Indians harassed them. Five canoes were shattered and had to be rebuilt. Their food ran short and valuable equipment was lost. One man drowned when his canoe capsized. Another went berserk and killed a member of the expedition and then disappeared into the wilderness. Roosevelt, ill with fever, badly injured his leg when he tried to keep two capsized canoes from being smashed against rocks. Unable to walk, he had to be carried. Lying in a tent with an infected leg and a temperature of 105, he requested to be

Table 11.2 **Types of Cooperative Learning**

Formal Cooperative Learning	Informal Cooperative Learning	Cooperative Base Groups
Completes assignment, lesson, unit, project to maximize own and groupmates' learning.	Discusses assigned questions for few minutes to focus attention, organize knowledge, set expectations, create mood, ensure cognitive processing and rehearsal, summarize, precue next session, provide closure.	Permanent, lasts for one semester, one year, or several years to ensure all members make academic progress and develop cognitively and socially in healthy ways.
Teacher Procedure	**Teacher Procedure**	**Teacher Procedure**
Make preinstructional decisions.	Conduct introductory focused discussion.	Structure opening class meeting to check homework, ensure members understand academic material, complete routine tasks such as attendance, and prepare members for the day.
Explain task and cooperative structure.	Conduct intermittent pair discussions every ten or fifteen minutes.	Structure ending class meeting to ensure all members understand academic material, know what homework to do, and are making progress on long-term assignments.
Monitor learning groups and intervene to improve taskwork and teamwork.	Conduct closure focused discussion.	Members help and assist each other learn in-between classes.
Assess learning and process group effectiveness.		Conduct semester or year-long school or class service projects.

left behind. Ignoring such pleas, Kermit brought his father to safety with the help of the other members of the expedition. Teddy Roosevelt barely survived, but he and his companions accomplished their mission. The party mapped the 1,000 mile River of Doubt and collected priceless specimens for the Museum of Natural History. The river was renamed in his honor, *Rio Theodore.*

An expedition such as Roosevelt's consists of four phases:

1. You make a series of prejourney decisions about the number of people needed, the materials and equipment required, and the route to be taken.
2. You brief all participants on the goals and objectives of the journey, emphasize that members' survival depends on the joint efforts of all, and the behaviors you expect of members of the expedition.

3. You make the journey, carefully mapping the area traveled and collecting the targeted specimens.
4. You report your findings to interested parties, reflect on what went right and wrong with fellow members, and write your memoirs.

Conducting a cooperative lesson is done in the same way. You, the teacher, make a number of preinstructional decisions, explain to students the instructional task and the cooperative nature of the lesson, conduct the lesson, and evaluate and process the results. More specifically, you (Johnson, Johnson, & Holubec, 1994, 1998a):

1. **Make Preinstructional Decisions:** In every lesson you (a) formulate objectives, (b) decide on the size of groups, (c) choose a method for assigning students to groups, (d) decide which roles to assign group members, (e) arrange the room, and (f) arrange the materials students need to complete the assignment.
2. **Explain the Task and Cooperative Structure:** In every lesson you (a) explain the academic assignment to students, (b) explain the criteria for success, (c) structure positive interdependence, (d) explain the individual accountability, and (e) explain the behaviors you expect to see during the lesson.
3. **Monitor and Intervene:** While you (a) conduct the lesson, you (b) monitor each learning group and (c) intervene when needed to improve taskwork and teamwork, and (d) bring closure to the lesson.
4. **Evaluate and Process:** You (a) assess and evaluate the quality and quantity of student achievement, (b) ensure students carefully process the effectiveness of their learning groups, (c) have students make a plan for improvement, and (d) have students celebrate the hard work of group members.

In each class session teachers must make the choice of being "a sage on the stage" or "a guide on the side." In doing so they might remember that **the challenge in teaching is not covering the material *for* the students, it's uncovering the material *with* the students.**

PREINSTRUCTIONAL DECISIONS

Specifying the Instructional Objectives

The Roman philosopher Seneca once said, "When you do not know to which port you are sailing, no wind is favorable." The same may be said for teaching. To plan for a lesson you must know what the lesson is aimed at accomplishing. You need to specify **academic objectives** (based on a conceptual or task analysis) and **social-skills objectives** that detail what interpersonal and small group skills you wish to emphasize during the lesson (Johnson, Johnson, & Holubec, 1994, 1998a). You choose social skills by:

1. Monitoring the learning groups and diagnosing the specific skills needed to solve the problems students are having in working with each other.
2. Asking students to identify social skills that would improve their teamwork.
3. Keeping a list of social skills you teach to every class. The next one on the list becomes the skill emphasized in today's lesson.
4. Analyzing what social skills are required to complete the assignment.

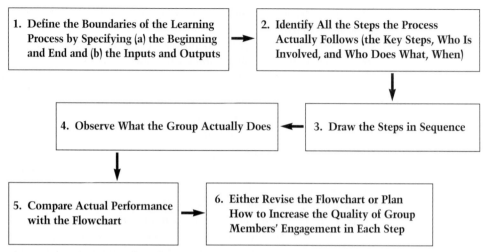

Figure 11.1 Creating a flowchart.

The most sophisticated way to determine the social skills students need to complete a lesson is through creating a flowchart. A **flowchart** is a simple yet powerful visual tool to display all the steps in a process. Creating a flowchart involves six steps (Figure 11.1).

Deciding on the Size of the Group

There is a folk saying about snowflakes. Each snowflake is so fragile and small. But when they stick together, it is amazing what they can do. The same is true for people. When we work together, there is no limit to human ingenuity and potential. For students to work together, they must be assigned to groups. To assign students to groups, you must decide (a) how large a group should be, (b) how students should be assigned to a group, (c) how long the groups will exist, and (d) what combination of groups will be used in the lesson.

> **Group Size Depends on "Team"**
>
> **T** = Time Limits
> **E** = Students' Experience in Working in Groups
> **A** = Students' Age
> **M** = Materials and Equipment Available

Although cooperative learning groups typically range in size from two to four, the basic rule of thumb is: *The smaller the better.* There is, however, no ideal size for a cooperative learning group. A common mistake is to have students work in groups of four, five, and six members before the students have the skills to do so competently. In selecting the size of a cooperative learning group, remember this advice:

1. **With the addition of each group member, the resources to help the group succeed increase.** As the size of the learning group increases, so does (a) the range of abilities, expertise, skills; (b) the number of minds available for acquiring and processing information; and (c) the diversity of viewpoints.

2. **The shorter the period of time available, the smaller the learning group should be.** If there is only a brief period of time available for the lesson, then smaller groups such as pairs will be more effective because they take less time to get organized, they operate faster, and there is more "air time" per member.
3. **The smaller the group, the more difficult it is for students to hide and not contribute their share of the work.** Small groups increase the visibility of students' efforts and thereby make them more accountable.
4. **The larger the group, the more skillful group members must be.** In a pair, students have to manage two interactions. In a group of three, there are six interactions to manage. In a group of four, there are twelve interactions to manage. As the size of the group increases, the interpersonal and small group skills required to manage the interactions among group members become far more complex and sophisticated.
5. **The larger the group, the less the interaction among members.** What results is less group cohesion, fewer friendships, and less personal support.
6. **The materials available or the specific nature of the task may dictate a group size.** When you have ten computers and thirty students, you may wish to assign students to groups of three. When the task is to practice tennis, group size of two seems natural.
7. **The smaller the group, the easier it is to identify any difficulties students have in working together.** Problems in leadership, unresolved conflicts among group members, issues over power and control, tendencies such as sitting back and waiting for others to do the work, and other problems students have in working together are more visible and apparent when groups are small. Groups need to be small enough to ensure all students are actively involved and participating equally.

Assigning Students to Groups

Sic parvis magna (Great things have small beginnings).

Sir Francis Drake's Motto

There is no ideal group membership. What determines a group's productivity is not who its members are, but rather how well the members work together. There may be times when you may use cooperative learning groups that are homogeneous in ability to teach specific skills or to achieve certain instructional objectives. Generally, however, there are advantages to heterogeneous groups in which students come from diverse backgrounds and have different abilities, experiences, and interests:

1. Students are exposed to a variety of ideas, multiple perspectives, and different problem-solving methods.
2. Students generate more cognitive disequilibrium, which stimulates learning, creativity, and cognitive and social development.
3. Students engage in more elaborative thinking, give and receive more explanations, and engage in more frequent perspective-taking in discussing material, all of which increase the depth of understanding, the quality of reasoning, and the accuracy of long-term retention.

To make groups heterogeneous, you assign students to groups using a random or stratified random procedure. **The easiest and most effective way to assign students to a group is randomly.** You divide the number of students in your class by the size of the group desired. If you wish to have groups of three and you have thirty students in your class, you divide thirty by three. You have students number off by the result (e.g., ten). Students with the same number find each other (all 1's get together, all 2's get together, and so forth). A related procedure is **stratified random assignment.** This is the same as random assignment except that you choose one (or two) characteristics of students (such as reading level, learning style, task orientation, or personal interest) and make sure that one or more students in each group have that characteristic. A modified stratified random procedure is to assign students to groups by **preferences.** Have students write their favorite sport to participate in on a slip of paper. Then have them find groupmates who like to participate in the same sport. Variations include favorite food, celebrity, skill, car, president, animal, vegetable, fairy tale character, and so forth.

Teacher-selected groups can be either homogeneous or heterogeneous. When students select their own groups they usually form homogeneous ones.

For additional methods for assigning students to groups as well as a variety of team-building and warm-up activities, see R. Johnson, Johnson, Scott, and Ramolae (1985).

LITERATURE CHARACTERS	GEOGRAPHICAL AREAS
Give students cards with the names of characters in the literature they recently have read. Ask them to group with characters from the same story, play, or poem. Examples are Romeo and Juliet; Captain Hook, Peter Pan, and Wendy; and Hansel, Gretel, Witch, and Stepmother.	List a number of countries or states and have students group themselves according to most preferred to visit. Variations include grouping according to least preferred to visit, similar in terms of climate, similar in geological features, having the same exports, and so forth.
MATH METHOD	STATES AND CAPITALS
There are endless variations to the math method of assigning students to groups. The basic structure is to give each student a math problem and ask them to (a) solve his or her problem, (b) find the classmates whose problems have the same answer, and (c) form a group. This may vary from simple addition in the first grade to complex equations in high school classes. Thus, to form a group of three, you may distribute the following three equations throughout the class $(3 + 3 = \underline{\quad})$, $(4 + 2 = \underline{\quad})$, $(5 + 1 = \underline{\quad})$.	To assign students to groups of two or four, divide the number of students in the class by two $(30 \div 2 = 15)$. Pick a geographic area of the United States and write out on cards the names of fifteen states. Then on another set of cards write out the names of their capital cities. Shuffle the cards and pass them out to students. Then have the students find the classmate who has the matching state or capital. To form groups of four, have two adjacent states and their capitals combine.

Length of Group Life. A common concern is, "How long should cooperative learning groups stay together?" The type of cooperative learning group you use determines one answer to this question. Base groups last for at least one and ideally for several years. Informal cooperative learning groups last for only a few minutes or at most one class period. For formal cooperative learning groups there is no formula or simple answer to this question. Groups usually stay together to complete a task, unit, or chapter. During a course every student should work with every other classmate.

Using Combinations of Cooperative Learning Groups. In many lessons you will want to use a combination of formal and informal cooperative learning groups as well as base groups. You will use more than one size group in any one lesson. You will need ways to assign students to new groups quickly. You will need procedures for making transitions among groups, moving students from pairs to fours to pairs to threes and so forth.

Assigning Roles to Ensure Interdependence

In planning the lesson, you think through what are the actions that need to occur to maximize student learning. **Roles** prescribe what other group members expect from a student (and therefore what the student is obligated to do) and what that person has a right to expect from other group members who have complementary roles. There is a progression for using roles to structure cooperative efforts:

1. Do not assign roles until students get used to working together.
2. Assign only very simple roles to students such as forming roles or the roles of reader, recorder, and encourager of participation. Rotate the roles so that each group member plays each one several times.
3. Add to the rotation a new role that is slightly more sophisticated, such as a checker for understanding. You assign the functioning roles at this point.
4. Over time add formulating and fermenting roles that do not occur naturally in the group, such as an elaborator. Students typically do not relate what they are learning to what they already know until you specifically train them to do so.

The social skills represented by the roles should be taught like a spiral curriculum with a more complex version of the skill taught every year.

Solving and Preventing Problems in Working Together. At times there are students who refuse to participate in a cooperative group or who do not understand how to help the group succeed. You can solve and prevent such problems when you give each group member a specific role to play in the group. Assigning appropriate roles may be used to:

1. Reduce problems such as one or more members' making no contribution to the group or one member dominating the group.
2. Ensure that vital group skills are enacted in the group and that group members learn targeted skills.
3. Create interdependence among group members. You structure **role interdependence** by assigning each member complementary and interconnected roles.

Arranging the Room

The design and arrangement of classroom space and furniture communicates what is appropriate behavior and what learning activities will take place. Desks in a row communicate a different message and expectation than desks grouped in small circles. Spatial design also defines the circulation patterns in the classroom. **Circulation** is the flow of movement into, out of, and within the classroom. It is movement through space. You determine what students see, when they see it, and with whom students interact by the way you design your classroom.

No single classroom arrangement will meet the requirements of all lessons. Reference points and well-defined boundaries of work spaces are needed to move students from rows to triads to pairs to fours to rows. Color, form, and lighting (a) focus students' visual attention on points of emphasis in the classroom (the learning group, you, instructional materials) and (b) define the territorial boundaries of work spaces. You define boundaries by:

1. **Using labels and signs** that designate areas.
2. **Using colors** to attract visual attention and define group and individual spaces as well as different storage areas and resource centers.

Importance of Classroom Design

Form a pair. Rank order the following outcomes of classroom design from most important (1) to least important (9).

	Students' academic achievement. The way in which interior space is designed influences the amount of time students spend on task and other variables affecting achievement.
	Students' visual and auditory focus. The way in which interior space is designed creates overall visual order, focuses visual attention, and controls acoustics.
	Students' participation in learning groups and activities. Classroom design influences the patterns of student (and teacher) participation in instructional activities, the emergence of leadership in learning groups, and the patterns of communication among students and between students and teachers.
	Opportunities for social contact and friendships among students.
	Learning climate. The design of interior space affects students and teachers' feelings (such as comfort, enjoyment, well-being, anger, depression) and general morale. Good spatial definition helps students feel secure by delineating structured learning areas.
	Classroom management. Spatial definition prevents discipline problems by defining how and where students work, how to interact with others, and how to move through the classroom.
	Students' ease of access to each other, teachers, learning materials.
	Students' ability to make quick transitions from one grouping to another.
	Teacher's movement from group to group to monitor student interaction carefully during the lesson.

3. **Taping lines** on the floor or wall to define the different work areas.
4. **Using mobiles and forms** (such as arrows) taped on the wall or hanging from the ceiling to direct attention. You can designate work areas by hanging mobiles from the ceiling.
5. **Using lighting** to define specific work areas. Directed light (illuminating part of the room while leaving other areas dim) intensifies and directs students' attention. Brightly lit areas can draw people towards the areas and suggest activity. More dimly lit areas surrounding the lighted ones become area boundaries. As the activity in the classroom changes, the lighting could also change.
6. **Moving furniture** to define work and resource areas. Even tall plants, when placed in pots with wheels, can be moved to provide spatial boundaries.
7. **Displaying group work** to designate work spaces. If a cooperative group is to remain together for a period of several days or weeks, members may wish to build a poster or collage that designates their work area.

You can use many of these same procedures to control acoustically levels of noise in the classroom.

Planning the Instructional Materials

The types of tasks students are required to complete determine what materials are needed for the lesson. You, the teacher, decide how materials are to be arranged and distributed among group members to maximize their participation and achievement. Usually, you will wish to distribute materials to communicate that the assignment is to be a joint (not an individual) effort. You create:

1. **Materials interdependence** by giving each group only one copy of the materials. The students will then have to work together in order to be successful. This is especially effective the first few times the group meets. After students are accustomed to working cooperatively, teachers can give a copy of the materials to each student.
2. **Information interdependence** by arranging materials like a jigsaw puzzle so that each student has part of the materials needed to complete the assignment. Each group member can receive different books or resource materials to be synthesized. Such procedures require that every member participate in order for the group to be successful.
3. **Interdependence from outside enemies** by structuring materials into an intergroup tournament format and having groups compete to see who has learned the most. Such a procedure was introduced by DeVries and Edwards (1973). In the Teams-Games-Tournament format, students are divided into heterogeneous cooperative learning teams to prepare members for a tournament in which they compete with the other teams. During the intergroup competition the students individually compete against members of about the same ability level from other teams. The team whose members do the best in the competition is pronounced the winner by the teacher.

STRUCTURING THE TASK AND COOPERATIVE STRUCTURE

Explaining the Academic Task

At this point you have planned your lesson by making the preinstructional decisions and preparations. The next step is to face your class and inform them of (a) what to do to complete the assignment and (b) how to do it (Johnson, Johnson, & Holubec, 1994, 1998a). The steps are explained on the flowchart in Figure 11.1.

Explaining Criteria for Success

While explaining to students the academic task they are to complete, you need to communicate the level of performance you expect of students. Cooperative learning requires criterion-based evaluation. **Criterion-referenced** or **categorical judgments** are made by adopting a fixed set of standards and judging the achievement of each student against these standards. A common version of criterion-referenced grading involves assigning letter grades on the basis of the percentage of test items answered correctly. Or you might say, "The group is

Grade	*Percent Correct*
A	95–100
B	85–94
C	75–84
D	65–74
F	Less than 64

not finished until every member has demonstrated mastery." Sometimes improvement (doing better this week than one did last week) may be set as the criterion of excellence. To promote intergroup cooperation, you may also set criteria for the whole class to reach. "If we as a class can score over 520 words correct on our vocabulary test, each student will receive 2 bonus points."

Structuring Positive Interdependence

Positive goal interdependence exists when a mutual or joint goal is established so that individuals perceive they can attain their goals if and only if their groupmates attain their goals (see Johnson & Johnson, 1992a, 1992b). Members know that they cannot succeed unless all other members of their group succeed. Positive interdependence is the heart of cooperative learning. Without positive interdependence, cooperation does not exist. Students must believe that they are in a "sink or swim together" learning situation.

First, you structure positive goal interdependence. Every cooperative lesson begins with positive goal interdependence. To ensure that students think "**We, not me,**" you (the teacher) say to students,

> You have three responsibilities. You are responsible for learning the assigned material. You are responsible for making sure that all other members of your group learn the assigned material. And you are responsible for making sure that all other class members successfully learn the assigned material.

Second, you supplement positive goal interdependence with other types of positive interdependence (such as reward, role, resource, or identity). Positive reward interdependence, for example, may be structured through providing group rewards—"If all members of your group score above 90% on the test, each of you will receive 5 bonus points." Usually, the more ways positive interdependence is structured in a lesson, the better.

Structuring Individual Accountability

In cooperative groups, everyone has to do his or her fair share of the work. **An underlying purpose of cooperative learning is to make each group member a stronger individual in his or her own right.** You hold all group members accountable to learn the assigned material and help other group members learn by:

1. Assessing the performance of each individual member.
2. Giving the results back to the individual and the group to compare to preset criteria. The feedback enables members to (a) recognize and celebrate efforts to learn and contributions to groupmates' learning, (b) provide immediate remediation and any needed assistance or encouragement, and (c) reassign responsibilities to avoid any redundant efforts by members.

Individual accountability results in group members knowing they cannot "hitchhike" on the work of others, loaf, or get a free ride. **Ways of ensuring individual accountability** include keeping group size small, giving an individual test to each student, giving random individual oral examinations, observing and recording the frequency with which each member contributes to the group's work, having students teach what they know to someone else, and having students use what they have learned on different problems.

Structuring Intergroup Cooperation

You can extend the positive outcomes resulting from cooperative learning throughout a whole class by structuring intergroup cooperation. You establish class goals as well as group and individual goals. When a group finishes its work, you encourage members to find other groups that (a) are not finished and help them understand how to complete the assignment successfully or (b) are finished and compare answers and strategies.

Specifying Desired Behaviors

When you use cooperative learning you must teach students the small group and interpersonal skills they need to work effectively with each other. In cooperative learning groups, students must learn both academic subject matter (taskwork) and the interpersonal and small group skills required to work as part of a group (teamwork). Cooperative learning is inherently more complex than competitive or individualistic learning because students have to engage simultaneously in taskwork and teamwork. If students do not learn the teamwork skills, then they cannot complete the taskwork. The greater the members' teamwork skills, the higher will be the quality and quantity of their learning. You define the needed teamwork skills operationally by specifying the behaviors that are appropriate and desirable within learning groups.

Three rules-of-thumb in specifying desired behaviors are as follows. **Be specific.** Operationally define each social skill through the use of a "T-Chart." **Start small.** Do not overload your students with more social skills than they can learn at one time. One or two behaviors to emphasize for a few lessons is enough. **Emphasize overlearning.** Having students practice skills once or twice is not enough. Keep emphasizing a skill until the students have integrated it into their behavioral repertoires and do it automatically and habitually.

MONITORING AND INTERVENING

The only thing that endures over time is the law of the farm: I must prepare the ground, put in the seed, cultivate it, water it, then gradually nurture growth and development to full maturity . . . there is no quick fix.

Stephen Covey

Once the students begin working in cooperative learning groups, the teacher's role is to monitor students' interaction and intervene to help students learn and interact more skillfully (Johnson, Johnson, & Holubec, 1994, 1998a).

Monitoring Students' Behavior

Your job begins in earnest when the cooperative learning groups start working. Resist that urge to get a cup of coffee or to grade papers. You observe the interaction among group members to assess students' (a) academic progress and (b) appropriate use of interpersonal and small group skills.

Observations can be formal (with an observation schedule on which frequencies are tallied) or anecdotal (informal descriptions of students' statements and actions). Based on your observations, you can then intervene to improve students' academic learning and/or interpersonal and small group skills. Remember, **students respect what we inspect.** To **monitor** means to check continuously. **Monitoring has four stages:**

1. **Preparing for observing** the learning groups by deciding who will be the observers, what observation forms to use, and training the observers.
2. **Observing** to assess the quality of cooperative efforts in the learning groups.
3. **Intervening when it is necessary** to improve a group's taskwork or teamwork.
4. **Having students assess the quality of their own individual participation** in the learning groups to encourage self-monitoring, having groups assess the level of their effectiveness, and having both individuals and groups set growth goals.

In monitoring cooperative learning groups, there are a number of guidelines for teachers to follow.

1. Plan a route through the classroom and the length of time spent observing each group so that all groups are observed during a lesson.
2. Use a formal observation sheet to count the number of times they observe appropriate behaviors being used by students. The more concrete the data, the more useful the data are to you (the teacher) and to students.

3. Initially, do not try to count too many different behaviors. At first you may wish simply to keep track of who talks. Your observations should focus on positive behaviors.

4. Supplement and extend the frequency data with notes on specific student actions. Especially useful are descriptions of skillful interchanges that can be shared with students later and with parents in conferences or telephone conversations.

5. Train and utilize student observers. Student observers can obtain more complete data on each group's functioning and may learn important lessons about appropriate and inappropriate behavior.

6. Allocate sufficient time at the end of each group session for discussion of the data gathered by the observers.

Providing Task Assistance

Cooperative learning groups provide teachers with a "window" into students' minds. Through working cooperatively students make hidden thinking processes overt and subject to observation and commentary. From carefully listening to students explain to each other what they are learning, teachers can determine what students do and do not understand. Consequently, you may wish to intervene to clarify instructions, review im-

portant procedures and strategies for completing the assignment, answer questions, and teach both task skills as necessary. In discussing the concepts and information to be learned, you should make specific statements, such as "Yes, that is one way to find the main idea of a paragraph," not "Yes, that is right." The more specific statement reinforces the desired learning and promotes positive transfer by helping the students associate a term with their learning. Metacognitive thought may be encouraged by asking students (a) "What are you doing?" (b) "Why are you doing it?" and (c) "How will it help you?"

Intervening to Teach Social Skills

Cooperative learning groups provide teachers with a picture of students' social skills. The social skills required for productive group work are discussed in detail, along with activities that may be used in teaching them, in Johnson (1991, 2000) and Johnson and Johnson (2000). While monitoring the learning groups, you may intervene to suggest more effective procedures for working together or reinforce particularly effective and skillful behaviors. Choosing when to intervene is part of the art of teaching. In intervening, ask group members to follow the steps of Figure 11.2.

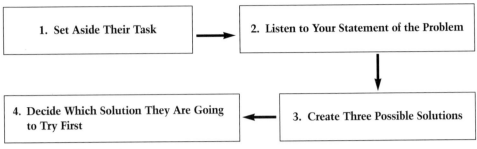

Figure 11.2 When to intervene.

Providing Closure to the Lesson

You provide closure to a lesson by having students summarize the major points in the lesson, recall ideas, and identify final questions for the teacher. Students should be able to summarize what they have learned and to understand how they will use it in the future.

EVALUATING LEARNING AND PROCESSING INTERACTION

Assessing the Quality and Quantity of Learning

The quality and quantity of student learning should be regularly assessed and occasionally evaluated using a criterion-referenced system. This is covered in depth in *Meaningful and Manageable Assessment Through Cooperative Learning* (Johnson & Johnson, 1996b). Cooperative learning, furthermore, provides an arena in which **performance-based assessment** (requiring students to demonstrate what they can do with what they know by performing a procedure or skill), **authentic assessment** (requiring students to demonstrate the desired procedure or skill in a real-life context), and **total quality learning** (continuous improvement of the process of students helping teammates learn) can take place. A wide variety of assessment formats may be used and students may be directly involved in assessing each other's level of learning and then providing immediate remediation to ensure all group members' learning is maximized.

Processing How Well the Group Functioned

When students have completed the assignment, or at the end of each class session, students describe what member actions were helpful (and unhelpful) in completing the group's work and make decisions about what behaviors to continue or change. Group processing occurs at two levels—in each learning group and in the class as a whole. There are four parts to processing:

1. **Feedback:** You ensure that each student and each group and the class receives (and gives) feedback on the effectiveness of taskwork and teamwork. Feedback given to students should be descriptive and specific, not evaluative and general (see Johnson, 2000).

Assessment Procedures

Form a pair. Rank order each of the following columns from most important to you (1) to least important to you.

What Is Assessed	Procedures	Ways Cooperative Learning Helps
_____ Academic learning	_____ Goal setting	_____ Additional sources of labor
_____ Reasoning strategies	_____ Testing	_____ More modalities in assessment
_____ Skills, competencies	_____ Compositions	_____ More diverse outcomes
_____ Attitudes	_____ Presentations	_____ More sources of information
_____ Work habits	_____ Projects	_____ Reduction of bias
	_____ Portfolios	_____ Development of rubrics
	_____ Logs, journals	_____ Implement improvement plan

2. **Reflection:** You ensure that students analyze and reflect on the feedback they receive. You avoid questions that can be answered "yes" or "no." Instead of saying, "Did everyone help each other learn?" you should ask, "How frequently did each member (a) explain how to solve a problem and (b) correct or clarify other members' explanations?"
3. **Improvement Goals:** You help individuals and groups set goals for improving the quality of their work.
4. **Celebration:** You encourage the celebration of members' hard work and the group's success.

Summary

Any assignment in any subject area may be structured cooperatively. In using formal cooperative learning, the teacher makes a number of preinstructional decisions, explains to students the task and the cooperative goal structure, monitors the groups as they work, intervenes when it is necessary, and then evaluates and helps groups process. In addition to formal cooperative learning, teachers use informal cooperative learning and cooperative base groups.

INFORMAL COOPERATIVE LEARNING GROUPS

There are times when instructors need to lecture, show a movie or videotape, give a demonstration, or have a guest speaker. In such cases, informal cooperative learning may be used to ensure that students are active (not passive) cognitively (Johnson, Johnson, & Holubec, 1994, 1998b). **Informal cooperative learning** (see Figure 11.3)

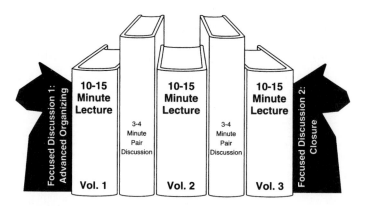

Figure 11.3 Informal Cooperative Learning.

consists of having students work together to achieve a joint learning goal in temporary, ad-hoc groups that last from a few minutes to one class period. Their *purposes* are to focus student attention on the material to be learned, set a mood conducive to learning, help organize in advance the material to be covered in a class session, ensure that students cognitively process the material being taught, and provide closure to an instructional session. Informal cooperative learning groups also ensure that misconceptions, incorrect understanding, and gaps in understanding are identified and corrected, and learning experiences are personalized. They may be used at any time, but are especially useful during a lecture or direct teaching.

During lecturing and direct teaching the instructional challenge for the instructor is to ensure that students do the intellectual work of organizing material, explaining it,

Purposes of Informal Cooperative Learning

Form a pair. Rank order the following purposes of informal cooperative learning from most important (1) to least important (7).

	Focuses student attention on the material to be learned.
	Sets a mood conducive to learning.
	Helps cognitively organize in advance the material to be covered in a class session.
	Ensures that students cognitively process the material being taught.
	Provides closure to an instructional session.
	Allows for identifying and correcting misconceptions, incorrect understanding, and gaps in comprehension.
	Personalizes learning experiences.

summarizing it, and integrating it into existing conceptual networks. This may be achieved by having students do the advance organizing, cognitively process what they are learning, and provide closure to the lesson. Breaking up lectures with short cooperative processing times will give you slightly less lecture time, but will help counter what is proclaimed as the main problem of lectures: "The information passes from the notes of the professor to the notes of the student without passing through the mind of either one."

USING INFORMAL COOPERATIVE LEARNING

The following procedure will help you plan a lecture that keeps students more actively engaged intellectually (Johnson & Johnson, 1999a; Johnson, Johnson, & Holubec, 1998b). It entails having **focused discussions** before and after the lecture (i.e., bookends) and interspersing **pair discussions** throughout the lecture. Two important aspects of using informal cooperative learning groups are to (a) make the task and the instructions explicit and precise and (b) require the groups to produce a specific product (such as a written answer). The procedure is as follows.

1. **Introductory Focused Discussion:** Assign students to pairs. The person nearest them will do. You may wish to require different seating arrangements each class period so that students will meet and interact with a number of other students in the class. Then give the pairs the cooperative assignment of completing the initial (advance organizer) task. Give them only four or five minutes to do so. The discussion task is aimed at promoting **advance organizing** of what the students know about the topic to be presented and **establishing expectations** about what the lecture will cover.

2. **Intermittent Focused Discussions:**
   a. **Lecture Segment 1:** Deliver the first segment of the lecture. This segment should last from ten to fifteen minutes. This is about the length of time a motivated adult can concentrate on a lecture. For unmotivated adolescents, the time may be shorter.
   b. **Pair Discussion 1:** Give the students a discussion task focused on the material you have just presented that may be completed within three or four minutes. Its purpose is to ensure that students are actively thinking about the material being presented. The discussion task may be to (a) give an answer to a question posed by the instructor; (b) give a reaction to the theory, concepts, or information being presented; or (c) relate material to past learning so that it gets integrated into existing conceptual frameworks (i.e., elaborate the material being presented). Discussion pairs respond to the task in the following way:
      (1) Each student formulates his or her answer.
      (2) Students share their answer with their partner.
      (3) Students listen carefully to partner's answer.
      (4) Pairs create a new answer that is superior to each member's initial formulation through the process of association, building on each other's thoughts, and synthesizing.

Randomly choose two or three students to give thirty-second summaries of their discussions. **It is important that students are randomly called on to share their answers after each discussion task. Such individual accountability** ensures that the pairs take the tasks seriously and check each other to ensure that both are prepared to answer.

c. **Lecture Segment 2:** Deliver the second segment of the lecture.

d. **Pair Discussion 2:** Give a discussion task focused on the second part of the lecture.

e. Repeat this sequence of lecture segment and pair discussion until the lecture is completed.

3. **Closure Focused Discussion:** Give students an ending discussion task lasting four to five minutes to summarize what students have learned from the lecture. The discussion should result in students integrating what they have just learned into existing conceptual frameworks. The task may also point students towards what the homework will cover or what will be presented in the next class session. This provides closure to the lecture.

Informal cooperative learning ensures students are actively involved in understanding what they are learning. It also provides time for instructors to gather their wits, reorganize notes, take a deep breath, and move around the class listening to what students are saying. Listening to student discussions can give instructors direction and insight into how well students understand the concepts and material being taught (who, unfortunately, may not have graduate degrees in the topic you are presenting).

In the following sections more specific procedures for the initial focused discussion, the intermittent pair discussions, and the closure focused discussion will be given.

NATURE OF BASE GROUPS

Committed relationships do not develop in a few hours or even a few days. They develop from spending long hours working together in which group members depend upon and support each other. In schools, therefore, it is important that some of the relationships built through cooperative learning groups are long-term. School has to be more than a series of temporary encounters that last for only a few minutes, a class period, an instructional unit, or a semester. Students could be assigned to permanent cooperative base groups (Johnson & Johnson, 1999; Johnson, Johnson, & Holubec, 1998b).

Cooperative base groups are long-term, heterogeneous cooperative learning groups with stable membership. Members' primary responsibilities are to (a) provide each other with support, encouragement, and assistance in completing assignments; (b) hold each other accountable for striving to learn; and (c) ensure all members are making good academic progress. Typically, cooperative base groups (a) are heterogeneous in membership (especially in terms of achievement motivation and task orientation), (b) meet regularly (for example, daily or biweekly), and (c) last for the duration of the class (a semester or year) or preferably until the students are graduated.

Types of Base Groups

There are two ways base groups may be used. The *first* is to have a base group in each course. Class base groups stay together only for the duration of the course. The *second*

Base Groups

Types	Functions	Nature
Class (meet at the beginning and ending of each session or week)	Provide academic support to members	Heterogeneous in membership
School (meet at the beginning and ending of each day or week)	Provide personal support to members	Meet regularly (daily, biweekly)
	Manage class routines and administrative requirements	Last for duration of class, year, or until graduation
	Personalize class and school experience	Ensure all members are making good academic progress

is to organize all students within the school into base groups and have the groups function as an essential component of school life. School base groups stay together for at least a year and preferably for four years or until all members are graduated. The **agendas** of both types of base groups can include:

1. **Academic Support Tasks:** Base group members encourage each other to master course content and complete all assignments. Members check to see what assignments each member has and what help they need to complete them. The group discusses assignments; answers any questions about assignments; provides information about what a member missed; and plans, reviews, and edits papers. Members can prepare each other to take tests and go over the questions missed afterwards. Members can share their areas of expertise (such as art or computers) with each other. Above all, members monitor each other's academic progress and make sure all members are achieving.

2. **Personal Support Tasks:** Base group members listen sympathetically when a member has problems with parents or friends, have general discussions about life, give each other advice about relationships, and help each other solve nonacademic problems. Base groups provide interpersonal relationships that personalize the course.

3. **Routine Tasks:** The base group provides a structure for managing course procedures such as attendance and homework.

4. **Assessment and Evaluation Tasks:** The base group provides a structure for assessing and evaluating student academic learning. Many of the more complex and important assessment procedures can best be used in the context of cooperative learning groups.

Forming Base Groups

Group size: Four (or three)
Assigning students: Random assignment to ensure heterogeneity
Arranging room: Permanent place for each group to meet
Preparing materials: Standard forms students use each meeting; group file folders
Assigning roles: Runner, explainer, accuracy checker, encourager

Class Base Groups

The larger the class and the more complex the subject matter, the more important it is to have class base groups. The base groups meet at the beginning and ending of each class session or (if the class session is fifty minutes or less), at the beginning of the first class session each week, and at the end of the last class session each week. The members of base groups should exchange phone numbers and information about schedules as they may wish to meet outside of class. All members are expected to contribute actively to the group's work, strive to maintain effective working relationships with other members, complete all assignments and assist groupmates in completing their assignments, and indicate agreement with base group's work by signing the weekly contract. At the **beginning of each session** students meet in base groups to:

1. Greet each other and check to see that none of their group is under undue stress. Members ask: "How are you today?" and "Are we all prepared for class?"
2. Complete the next task for the membership grid. This helps members get to know each other better. The task is to answer such questions as: "What is the best thing that has happened to you this week?" "What is your favorite television show?" "Who is your favorite music group?"
3. Pick up their file folders with an attendance sheet, feedback form, and their assignments from the previous class session (with instructor's comments). The group members record their own attendance by writing the date and their initials in the **Attendance** section of the folder. They pass out the assignments from the previous class session and discuss any comments the instructor has made.
4. Check to see if members have completed their homework or need help in doing so. Members ask: "Did you do your homework?" "Is there anything you did not understand?" If extensive help is needed, an appointment is made.
5. In addition to the homework, members review what each member has read and done since the last class session. Each member may be prepared to (a) give a succinct summary of what he or she has read, thought about, and done; (b) share resources they have found; and (c) share copies of assignments they have completed.
6. Students collect each member's work, record it in their **Base Group Progress Report Sheet,** and place the assignments in their file folder. The file folder is returned to the instructor's desk. Periodically, the base groups may be given a checklist of academic skills and assess which ones each member needs to practice.

Base Group Agendas

Opening Tasks	*Closing Tasks*
Greeting and Welcome	Review and clarify assignments
Relationship- and group-building task	Discuss what was learned
Check homework	Discuss applications of learnings
Review progress: ongoing assignments	Celebrate members' hard work

Generally, class base groups are available to support individual group members. If a group member arrives late, or must leave early on an occasion, the group can provide information about what that student missed. Group members may assist one another in writing required papers and completing other assignments. They can discuss assigned work, plan papers, review each other's progress, and edit each other's work. Questions regarding the course assignments and class sessions may be addressed in base groups.

The class session closes with students meeting in base groups. **Closing tasks** may be:

1. Ensure all members understand the assignments. Find out what help each member needs to complete the assigned work.
2. Summarize at least three things members learned in today's class session.
3. Summarize how members will use/apply what they have learned.
4. Celebrate the hard work and learning of group members.

School Base Groups

At the beginning of their freshman year (or any academic year), students should be assigned to base groups. Base groups should stay together for at least a year and ideally, for four years (or until members are graduated). Class schedules should be arranged so that members of base groups are assigned to as many of the same classes as possible. In essence, the computer is programmed to assign base groups to classes (whenever possible) rather than individuals.

When base groups meet twice each week (perhaps first thing on Monday and last thing on Friday), they meet to discuss the academic progress of each member, provide help and assistance to each other, and hold each member accountable for completing assignments and progressing satisfactorily through the academic program. The **meeting on Monday morning** refocuses the students on school, provides any emotional support required after the weekend, reestablishes personal contact among base group members, and helps students set their academic goals for the week (what is still to be done on assignments that are due, and so forth). Members should carefully review each other's assignments and ensure that members have the necessary help and assistance. In addition, they should hold each other accountable for succeeding academically. The **meeting on Friday afternoon** helps students review the week, set academic goals for the weekend (what homework has to be done before Monday), and share weekend plans and hopes.

INTEGRATED USE OF ALL THREE GOAL STRUCTURES

The third step in increasing your expertise in using cooperative learning is to use all three goal structures within an integrated way. While the dominant goal structure within any classroom should be cooperation (which ideally would be used about 60% to 70% of the time), competitive and individualistic efforts are useful supplements. Competition may be used as a fun change-of-pace during an instructional unit that is predominantly structured cooperatively and individualistic learning is often productive when the information learned is subsequently used in a cooperative activity. The integrated use of cooperative, competitive, and individualistic learning is described in Johnson and Johnson (1999) and in Johnson, Johnson, and Holubec (1998b).

Types of Cooperative Learning

Form a pair. In the spaces below, write out the definition of each type of cooperative learning in your own words.

Formal	*Informal*	*Base Groups*

Example of Integrated Use of Cooperative Learning

An example of the integrated use of the cooperative learning procedures is as follows. Students arrive at class and meet in their **base groups** to welcome each other, complete a self-disclosure task (such as "What is each member's favorite television show?"), check each student's homework to make sure all members understand the academic material and are prepared for the class session, and tell each other to have a great day.

The teacher then begins a lesson on the limitations of being human. To help students cognitively organize in advance what they know about the advantages and disadvantages of being human, the teacher uses **informal cooperative learning.** The teacher asks students to form a triad and ponder, "What are five things you cannot do with your human limitations that a Billion-Dollar Being might be designed to do?" Students have four minutes to do so. In the next ten minutes, the teacher explains that although the human body is a marvelous system, we (like other organisms) have very specific limitations. We cannot see bacteria in a drop of water or the rings of Saturn unaided. We cannot hear as well as a deer or fly like an eagle. Humans have never been satisfied in being so limited and, therefore, we have invented microscopes, telescopes, and our own wings. The teacher then instructs students to turn to the person next to them and answer the questions "What are three limitations of humans?" "What have we invented to overcome them?" "What other human limitations might we be able to overcome?"

Formal cooperative learning is now used in the lesson (for the Billion-Dollar Being lesson, see *Topics in Applied Science*, Jefferson County Schools, Golden, Colorado). The teacher has the thirty-two students count off from 1 to 8 to form groups of four randomly. Group members sit so they can face each other and face the teacher. Each member is assigned a role: researcher/runner, summarizer/timekeeper, collector/recorder, and technical adviser (role interdependence). Every group gets one large 2 × 3-foot piece of paper, a marking pen, a rough draft sheet for designing the Being, an assignment sheet explaining the task and cooperative goal structure, and four student self-evaluation checklists (resource interdependence). The **task** is to design a Billion-Dollar Being that overcomes the human limitations thought of by the class and the group. The group

Integrated Use of All Types of Cooperative Learning for Fifty-Minute Session

Step	Activity	Time (in minutes)
1	Welcome and opening base group meeting	10
2	Choice 1: Direct teaching, informal cooperative learning	35
3	Choice 2: Work in formal cooperative learning groups	35
4	Choice 3: Direct teaching, formal coop learning groups	35
5	Choice 4: Academic controversy	35
6	Closing base group meeting	5

Weekly Schedule for Fifty-Minute Class Sessions

Session 1		Session 2		Session 3	
Time	Activity	Time	Activity	Time	Activity
15	Base group meeting	5	Base group meeting	5	Base group meeting
30	Lecture with informal CL	35	Formal CL groups work on assignment or controversy	15	Formal CL groups work on assignment
5	Base group meeting	5	Base group meeting	10	Lecture with informal CL
				15	Base group meeting

Integrated Use of All Types of Cooperative Learning For Ninety-Minute Session

Step	Activity	Time
1	Opening base group meeting	10
2	Direct teaching with informal cooperative learning	25
3	Work on assignment in formal cooperative learning	40
4	Direct teaching with informal cooperative learning	10
5	Closing base group meeting	5

members are to draw a diagram of the Being on the scratch paper and, when they have something they like, transfer it to the larger paper. The teacher establishes **positive goal interdependence** by asking for one drawing from the group that all group members contribute to and can explain. The **criterion for success** is to complete the diagram in the thirty-minute time limit. The teacher ensures **individual accountability** by observing each group to ensure that members are fulfilling their roles and that any one member can explain any part of the Being at any time. The teacher informs students that the **expected social skills** to be used by all students are encouraging each other's participation, contributing ideas, and summarizing. She defines the skill of encouraging participation and has each student practice it twice before the lesson begins. While students work in their groups, the teacher **monitors** by systematically observing each group and intervening to provide academic assistance and help in using the interpersonal and small group skills required to work together effectively. At the end of the lesson the groups hand in their diagrams of the Billion-Dollar Being to be assessed and **evaluated.** Group members then **process** how well they worked together by identifying actions each member engaged in that helped the group succeed and one thing that could be added to improve their group next time.

The teacher uses **informal cooperative learning** to provide closure to the lesson by asking students to meet in new triads and write out six conclusions about the limitations of human beings and what we have done to overcome them.

At the end of the class session the **cooperative base groups** meet to review what students believe is the most important thing they have learned during the day, what homework has been assigned, what help each member needs to complete the homework, and to tell each other to have a fun afternoon and evening.

THE COOPERATIVE SCHOOL

W. Edwards Deming, Joseph Juran, and other founders of the quality movement have stated that over 85% of the behavior of members of an organization is directly attributable to the organization's structure, not the nature of the individuals involved. Your classroom is no exception. If competitive or individualistic learning dominates your classroom, your students will behave accordingly, regardless of whether you have temporarily put them in cooperative groups. If cooperative learning dominates your classroom, your students will behave accordingly and a true learning community will result.

The issue of cooperation among students is part of a larger issue of the organizational structure of schools (Johnson & Johnson, 1994). For decades schools have functioned as "mass production" organizations that divided work into component parts (first grade, second grade; English, social studies, science) to be performed by teachers who are isolated from their colleagues and work alone, in their own room, with their own set of students, and with their own set of curriculum materials. Students can be assigned to any teacher because students are considered to be interchangeable parts in the education machine. By using cooperative learning the majority of the time you are changing the basic organizational structure of your classroom to a team-based, high-performance one. In other words, cooperation is more than an instructional procedure. It is a basic shift in organizational structure that will affect all aspects of classroom life.

In a **cooperative school,** students work primarily in cooperative learning groups, teachers and building staff work in cooperative teams, and district administrators work in cooperative teams (Johnson & Johnson, 1994). The organizational structure of the classroom, school, and district are then congruent. Each level of cooperative teams supports and enhances the other levels.

A cooperative school structure begins in the classroom with the use of cooperative learning the majority of the time (Johnson & Johnson, 1994). Work teams are the heart of the team-based organizational structure and cooperative learning groups are the primary work team. Cooperative learning is used to increase student achievement, create more positive relationships among students, and generally improve students' psychological well-being. Having teachers advocate cooperation to their students, furthermore, changes their own attitudes towards working collaboratively with colleagues.

The second level in creating a cooperative school is to form collegial teaching teams, task forces, and ad-hoc decision-making groups within the school (Johnson & Johnson, 1994). Teacher teams are just as effective as student teams. The use of cooperation to structure faculty and staff work involves (a) collegial teaching teams, (b) school-based decision making, and (c) faculty meetings. Just as the heart of the classroom is cooperative learning, the heart of the school is the collegial teaching team. **Collegial teaching teams** are small cooperative groups (two to five teachers) whose purpose is to increase teachers' instructional expertise and success (Johnson & Johnson, 1994).

A school-based decision-making procedure is implemented through the use of two types of cooperative teams (Johnson & Johnson, 1994). A **task force** considers a school problem and proposes a solution to the faculty as a whole. The faculty is then divided into **ad-hoc decision-making groups** and considers whether to accept or modify the proposal. The decisions made by the ad-hoc groups are summarized, and the entire faculty then decides on the action to be taken to solve the problem.

The third level in creating a cooperative school is to implement administrative cooperative teams within the district (Johnson & Johnson, 1994). Administrators are organized into collegial teams to increase their administrative expertise as well as task forces and ad-hoc decision-making groups.

Willi Unsoeld, a mountain climber and philosopher, gave this advice "as the secret to survival" to all those who set off to climb a mountain: "Take care of each other, share your energies with the group, no one must feel alone, cut off, for that is when you do not make it." The same may be said for everyone entering a school.

SUMMARY

In this chapter we have seen that there are three types of social interdependence: competitive, individualistic, and cooperative, Of the three, cooperation tends to promote the highest achievement, most positive relationships, and greatest psychological health. In order to harness the power of cooperation, however, it is necessary to know what makes it work and apply those elements with discipline and diligence. Like Sandy Koufax, natural talent is not enough to make a great teacher. Being well trained in how to use cooperative learning and unusually well disciplined in structuring the five basic elements in every lesson are also necessary. The five essential components are positive interdependence, individual accountability, promotive interaction, social skills, and group processing. From structuring these five elements into lessons, teachers can create formal cooperative learning lessons, informal cooperative learning lessons, and cooperative base groups. Repetitive lessons and procedures may be turned into cooperative scripts. The use of cooperative learning takes place within an organizational context. If the organizational context emphasizes mass production of educated students, it works against the use of cooperative learning. If the organizational context is a team-based, high-performance structure, then it encourages and supports the use of cooperative learning. In a high-performance school, the five basic elements of cooperation are used to structure teaching teams, faculty meetings, and site-based decision making. Finally, the long-term success of cooperative efforts depends on members having frequent conflicts that are managed constructively.

12

Leading Growth And Counseling Groups

INTRODUCTION

In the past twenty years there has been an explosion in people's participation in growth groups. It is estimated that over five million Americans have at one time or another participated in some type of group activity aimed at personal growth or change. Several million more are members of self-help groups, and tens of thousands have participated in counseling and psychotherapy groups. Special group experiences have been designed to help improve marriages, to bridge the gap between parents and children, to strengthen the communion and unity that have characterized religious organizations in the past, to help people handle conflict more constructively, and to increase people's ability to mediate, "center," and communicate through touch. Training in human relations has become mandatory for potential teachers, and intercultural experiences between minorities and whites are frequently offered as a means of improving teaching and cross-cultural relations. There are sensitivity groups, encounter groups, confrontation groups, personal-growth groups, strength groups, consciousness-raising groups, and such a variety of other groups that no one can keep up with current labels. All such groups are generally referred to as *growth groups* in this book. With such a demand for small-group experiences, and with such an expansion in the types of group experiences available, it is difficult to conceive of a book on groups that does not cover growth groups.

To be an effective growth-group leader a person needs to: (a) understand the unique powers of group experiences, (b) understand the events within groups that promote participant change and growth, (c) understand the goals of growth groups, and (d) perform competently a certain set of skills needed to lead a growth group. Each of these aspects of facilitating personal growth in a group context will be discussed in this chapter. We shall also discuss how one becomes a group facilitator and how the feelings, intuition, and conceptual frameworks of growth-group leaders are related.

THE SOCIAL-SKILLS BASIS OF PERSONAL GROWTH

Jane is a college sophomore who lives in a dorm. She is seeking to participate in a growth group because of her shyness. After a year and a half of college she has made only one friend and finds it hard to talk even to her roommate. Jane is very anxious about approaching others, and she lacks the small group and interpersonal skills she needs in order to interact effectively with others. A social-skills training approach would focus on teaching Jane how to initiate a conversation, how to show interest in another person, and how to build and maintain a relationship. The existence of Jane's anxiety is not ignored, but instead of focusing only on reducing the anxiety a growth-group leader assumes that the anxiety will decrease as Jane acquires more effective skills in relating to others.

Most participants enter growth groups hoping to develop or refine certain skills in relating to others. It is their interpersonal interactions that have led them to depression, anger, anxiety, guilt, capriciousness, and other conflictive feelings. If they could resolve their conflicts with others, influence others in the ways they wish, or manage their feelings constructively, they would do so. Through either a lack of small group and interpersonal skills or an inability to utilize the social skills they have, participants seek the help of a growth group.

It is our interpersonal relationships that provide the warmth, caring, support, and collaboration that give life its excitement and potential for joy and personal fulfillment. It is also in these relationships that both the origin of and the solution to participants' problems can usually be found. Psychological health can be defined as the ability of a person to build and maintain cooperative relationships with family, neighbors, friends, and fellow employees (Johnson, 1979, 1980b). The quality of one's relationships depends largely on one's interpersonal competence. Interpersonal and small group skills form the basic nexus between the individual and others, and if participants are to cope with the stresses, strains, and conflicts involved in building and maintaining productive and ful-filling relationships, they must have a modicum of these skills. The underlying purpose of most growth groups, therefore, is to help participants achieve some kind of behav-ioral and cognitive change that increases their competence in managing their interper-sonal relationships so that they can lead more productive, self-enhancing, and fulfilling lives. The advantages of and procedures for increasing one's interpersonal and small group skills in a growth group form the body of this chapter.

THE UNIQUE POWER OF GROUP EXPERIENCES

Some persons seek isolation and privacy while they try to think through their problems and decide how they are going to improve their relationships. Others seek out a friend or a counselor and discuss their problems and plans in a dyad. Groups, however, have sev-eral unique advantages over solitary contemplation and dyadic discussion for those who want to grow, develop, and change. These unique capacities of groups are as follows.

1. Groups provide a more heterogeneous social setting in which interpersonal skills may be learned, mastered, and integrated into one's behavioral repertoire. Whereas in a dyad only one relationship has to be maintained, in a group several relationships have to be maintained and increased concern about rejection and exclusion for inappropriate behavior may result. In a dyad there is acceptance by only one person; in a group there may be acceptance by many persons. Different persons provoke different feelings and reactions, and in a group more feelings and reactions are generated. In a dyad there is one person to compare oneself with; in a group there are several. The greater number of relationships available in the group provide a richness and potential for learning not pos-sible in a dyad or a solitary situation.

2. Groups generate a sense of community, belonging, support, acceptance, and as-sistance that eases the pain associated with therapeutic exploration and encourages risk-taking in achieving growth goals (Lieberman, Lakin, and Whitaker, 1968). Groups offer a member acceptance by a number of persons, no matter what the member's history or behavior outside of the group. They provide the supportive climate that permits mem-bers to take risks and to reveal themselves. They provide the public esteem and accep-tance that form the basis for increased self-esteem and self-acceptance. Members' confidence in their ability to grow and change may increase as they feel their group-mates become committed to assist and support them in doing so.

3. Groups influence the behavioral and attitudinal patterns of members. A group is able to influence its members in a variety of ways beyond what one other person in a dyad can do. Social pressure to engage in more constructive behavior is greater in a

group setting, the social approval of a number of persons is a more powerful reward than the social approval of one person, the authenticating affirmation of one's peers is more powerful than that of one person, and the threat of expulsion by a whole group is more powerful punishment than the threat of expulsion by one person. Within a group there are group norms that members will be influenced to conform to, and in a growth group the norms will encourage growth and the mastery of more constructive ways of behaving and thinking. Within a group there are a number of persons to identify with and imitate, whereas in a dyad there is only one.

4. Groups may induce and then reduce powerful feelings (Lieberman, Lakin, & Whitaker, 1968). Growth groups provide an environment in which participants may experience previously terrifying feelings with a new sense of acceptance. By finding that the previously feared feelings are not overwhelming or that the feared consequences do not occur, the participant has a corrective emotional experience. The wider variety of persons and the more diverse interpersonal events that take place within a group enable the group to induce more powerful emotions. Yet the support and acceptance within the group make it likely that the emotions will not be completely overwhelming or terrorizing. The experiencing and discussing of the emotions in a supportive and caring environment usually reduce them and decrease their influence on the participant's future behavior and thinking.

5. Groups require the use of a wide variety of interpersonal skills and competencies. While contemplating problems by oneself, there are no interpersonal skills being used. Discussing problems with one person requires some interpersonal skills, but discussing problems and trying out new behaviors in a group requires a far broader range of interpersonal skills and competencies. Listening to others discuss their problems and helping them experiment with more constructive ways of behaving and thinking requires skills and competencies that may never be apparent in a dyadic relationship.

6. Groups provide opportunities for participants to understand and help their peers. In helping other group members to understand their destructive behavioral and attitudinal patterns and facilitating their experimentation with more constructive ways of behaving and thinking, participants build self-esteem, self-insight, and increased interpersonal competence. Helping others is also an important opportunity for altruistic behavior that may be absent from their daily lives. By working to understand others in the group and by caring for the personal struggles that other members are going through, participants gain in a variety of ways.

7. Groups provide a variety of perspectives that stimulate insight into and understanding of one's problems and behavior. By providing labels for the participant's thoughts, feelings, and experiences and by helping the participant reflect on his interactions with them, the other group members help him understand his actions. A group adds to any insight achieved by a member through its consensual validation of the insight.

8. Groups provide sources of comparison for participants (Lieberman, Lakin, & Whitaker, 1968). Members of growth groups often compare their attitudes towards their parents, spouses, children, and friends; their feelings about events within the group; the things that make them sad, happy, guilty, and angry; the ways each member typically deals with and expresses anger and affection; and so on. Such comparisons occur naturally within a group and facilitate possible new ways of feeling, perceiving, and behaving.

9. Groups provide a variety of sources of feedback (Lieberman, Lakin, & Whitaker, 1968). Within a group a person is provided the opportunity to engage in behavior or express observations and feelings, note the consequences of doing so, and hear from other members about his or her impact on them. In a group setting, participants can test their behavior and seek feedback from a variety of persons.

10. Groups provide a remedial environment for the solution of problems. It is within relationships that problems develop and people learn maladaptive patterns of thinking and behaving. A growth group enables participants to work on their problems immediately within a remedial environment. Besides understanding their problems, participants may take immediate corrective steps in their relationships with other members.

11. Groups provide the constructive peer relationships needed for healthy social and cognitive development (Johnson, 1980b). Peer relationships are an absolute necessity for healthy development, and group settings provide access to constructive relationships that may be absent in participants' lives.

EVENTS THAT PROMOTE PARTICIPANT CHANGE

Within growth groups there is a series of events that promote participant change (Lieberman, Yalom, & Miles, 1980). Some of these events directly promote change; others reduce blocks to change. The events are as follows.

1. Change is promoted by the emotional expression of positive and negative feelings toward other group members and about important life events. Participants may express feelings towards other group members. They may also express feelings that they had previously blocked and thereby unburden themselves of an emotional restraint. If participants do not feel free to express positive and negative feelings such as caring and anger in the group, their ability to learn from each other and from their experiences in the group is markedly reduced. Unless participants are free to express both negative and positive feelings towards each other openly and directly, the road to change will be blocked.

2. Change is promoted by the experiencing of intense positive and negative emotions, whether or not they are expressed. Events within the group may unleash feelings certain participants have been previously unable or unwilling to experience. As we have seen, participants may find that such feelings are not overwhelming or that the feared consequences do not occur. Thus, a corrective emotional experience may result even when the feelings are not overtly expressed. Participants may learn a new acceptance of feelings they were previously afraid of.

3. Change is promoted by the observation of other group members having significant emotional experiences. Participants often have beneficial experiences by observing other members having corrective emotional experiences. Other members' emotional experiences may clarify issues for a participant, who may then make use of the experiences in his or her own problematic areas.

4. Change is promoted by the inculcation of hope and a decrease in demoralization. To be demoralized is to be disheartened, bewildered, confused, disordered, and deprived of courage. The demoralized participant feels isolated, hopeless, and helpless. Group situations can generate events that inspire hope in participants, feelings that one can change, and beliefs that one can influence the causes of one's problems. Seeing other members in the group who have successfully grappled with problems or who have changed as a result of their participation in the group is one such event.

5. Change is promoted by the decrease in participants' egocentrism and the increase in their perspective-taking abilities. Through exchanges of ideas about problems and solutions within a context where participants feel understood and accepted, participants will be more aware of and open to other perspectives. Group leaders may also structure perspective reversal situations in which participants switch positions and argue each other's point of view or take the perspective of a significant person outside of the group, such as a mother, boss, or spouse.

6. Change is promoted by self-disclosure, the realization that others have similar feelings, and insight into one's problems. In growth groups self-disclosure consists of the explicit communication of information (a) that a participant believes other group members would be unlikely to acquire unless she told it to them, and (b) that she considers so highly private that she would exercise great caution regarding whom she told it to. Self-disclosure to a group of peers is quite different from self-disclosure to one other person. It feels less dramatic and is a less anxiety-laden action to reveal private information to a single person than to a group. The significance of self-disclosure is not what is disclosed, but rather the response of other members to what one has said. The therapeutic and growth value of self-disclosure lies in the sense of well-being, the trust and confidence in other human beings, and the acceptance by other members that one obtains after disclosing anxiety-producing information to the group and receiving a caring and supportive response from the other members. Self-disclosure can be cathartic when participants discover that no one is shocked by their deeply hidden secrets that have always made them feel ashamed, guilty, depressed, or angry. When several members of a group engage in self-disclosure on similar problems, they feel considerable relief when they discover that they are not the only ones who have reacted the way they have and who experience the feelings they do. There are times when discovering the similarities in their experiences, reactions, actions, and feelings reassures participants that they are normal. Finally, the disclosure of anxiety-producing information to a group facilitates the achievement of insight into one's problems and the dynamics of the situations being discussed.

In summary, self-disclosure helps provide participants with insight into their problems as they organize and think through their experiences in order to share them with others. It creates a sense of relief when participants discover that their problems are not unique and that they are not inherently evil for feeling and behaving as they do. It releases and frees one from anxiety-producing feelings when no one is shocked or horrified by them. Finally, self-disclosure that results in understanding and acceptance by others promotes a sense of personal well-being and trust in others.

7. Change is promoted by experimentation with new behavior and by feedback received from others. The availability of immediate information about how one is perceived by peers is unique to the group situation. There seems to be a basic human need to know how one stands with one's peers and how one is perceived by others. The feedback participants receive from other group members is an important ingredient in increasing their self-awareness and self-esteem. The nature and the value of constructive feedback is discussed at length in Johnson (2000) and Johnson (1991). Along with feedback, growth groups offer participants the opportunity to experiment with new patterns of behavior under low-risk conditions. Having experimented with new behavior patterns in the group, the participants will feel able to engage in the new behaviors in the outside world. Participants must feel that the group setting is safe enough for them to try out new ways of behaving, and they must identify problem areas and new ways of behaving in order to experiment with new behaviors. Feedback is a vital part of experimentation, for the participants need to find out how other members perceive the effectiveness of the new behavioral patterns they are trying out.

8. Change is promoted by other group members modeling constructive behavior and attitude patterns the participants wish to master. One of the best ways to learn new patterns of behaving and thinking is seeing them demonstrated by others. An important element of change, and of the maintaining of changes, is the internalization of how other participants and the group leader would have handled problem situations. Observing others use specific competencies to solve problems and relate more effectively to others can lead to considerable reflection and the discovery of alternative ways to achieve a goal.

9. Change is promoted by cognitive insight into one's problems, behavior patterns, and attitude patterns. Both increased understanding of oneself and the conscious implementation of interpersonal skills depend on cognitive learning. In their classic study of growth groups, Lieberman, Yalom, and Miles (1973) found that it was self-disclosure involving some sort of cognitive mastery or understanding—not self-disclosure in and of itself—that was related to positive change. Many types of growth groups emphasize the learning of specific cognitive skills and frameworks as part of positive change.

ESTABLISHING THE GOALS OF A GROWTH GROUP

When participants join a growth group both they and the group's leader have a set of goals for the group. The participants may wish to improve the state of their feelings or find a more meaningful career. The leader may wish to improve the participants' general interpersonal functioning or even teach growth dynamics. Assuming that the goals of the participants and those of the group leader do not completely overlap, the two must negotiate a set of goals that they can mutually commit themselves to achieving. When participants and the leader have different goals, the goals may initially be cooperative (working to achieve the participants' goals facilitates the accomplishment of the leader's goals, and vice versa) or competitive (working to achieve the participants' goals interferes with the accomplishment of the leader's goals, and vice versa). For the growth group to be successful, the leader and the participants need to negotiate a set of cooperatively structured goals.

Some of the common goals that leaders of growth groups may have are: (a) to facilitate participants' acquisition of self-enhancing patterns of attitudes and behaviors,

(b) to facilitate participants' psychological health, (c) to increase participants' skills and competencies for creating humanizing relationships, (d) to increase participants' interpersonal effectiveness, and (e) to promote participants' self-actualization. Let's look briefly at each of these goals.

Self-Enhancement

Many participants may have developed patterns of behaviors and attitudes that decrease their ability to build and maintain effective relationships with others. These patterns create and sustain negative and self-destructive consequences and ultimately lead to a more painful and troubled life. If a person has no opportunity to change, her self-defeating patterns of attitudes and behaviors will affect all aspects of her life. One of the goals of leaders of growth groups, then, is to help participants identify their self-defeating and self-destructive attitudinal and behavioral patterns and change them to *self-enhancing patterns.*

Psychological Health

It is within interpersonal relationships that psychological illness or health is developed. *Psychological health* can be defined as the ability to be aware of and manage effectively one's cooperative interactions with others (Johnson, 1980b). In order to build and maintain the relationships so necessary for psychological health, individuals need to develop the following (Johnson, 1979):

1. A generalized interpersonal trust in the affection and support of others.
2. The perspective-taking abilities needed for an understanding of how a situation appears to another person and how that person is reacting cognitively and affectively.

3. A meaningful direction and purpose in life, a sense of "where I am going" that is valued by others and similar to the goals of the significant persons in one's life.
4. An awareness of meaningful cooperative interdependence with others.
5. An integrated and coherent sense of personal identity.

Humanizing Relationships

Humanizing relationships reflect the qualities of kindness, mercy, consideration, tenderness, love, concern, compassion, responsiveness, and friendship. One goal of most group leaders is to create humanizing relationships within the group and help participants build the competencies they need to form such relationships outside the group.

Interpersonal Effectiveness

Interpersonal and group skills are based on a person's interpersonal effectiveness. *Interpersonal effectiveness* may be defined as the extent to which the consequences of a person's behavior match his intentions (Johnson, 2000). When two participants interact, for example, they have no choice but to make some impression on each other. When they make the impression they want, their interpersonal effectiveness is high; when they make an impression they do not want, their interpersonal effectiveness is low. All the group skills discussed in this book and the interpersonal skills discussed in Johnson (2000) are relevant to interpersonal effectiveness.

Self-Actualization

Self-actualization may be defined as the psychological need for growth, development, and utilization of potential (Maslow, 1954). A self-actualizing participant will be moving towards the full use of her talents, capacities, and potentialities. Self-actualization involves both self-development and self-utilization: One develops potentialities and then uses them in order to actualize oneself.

LEADING A GROWTH GROUP

Groups are uniquely suited to helping persons grow and change in constructive ways. As we have seen, a number of events may take place in a growth group that facilitate participant growth and help achieve the group's goals. But if these events are in fact to take place, the group leader needs several sets of complex skills:

1. Establishing the conditions for modifying participants' patterns of behavior and attitudes.
2. Being a resource expert on how to learn and change within a group.
3. Teaching needed interpersonal and small group skills.
4. Modeling the constructive use of small group and interpersonal skills.
5. Ensuring that members are provided with constructive confrontations and feedback.
6. Helping define and diagnose the problems of participants.

7. Making sure that members are provided with opportunities for self-disclosure and experimentation with new attitude and behavior patterns.
8. Promoting corrective or reparative emotional experiences within the group.
9. Engineering a problem-solving process with which participants can address their concerns.
10. Negotiating changes in participants' patterns of attitude and behaviors.
11. Engineering an effective group.
12. Establishing and enforcing a contract with participants.
13. Carrying out the executive functions of the group.

Each of these sets of skills is discussed in turn.

Establishing Conditions for Participant Change

This set of skills consists of establishing the conditions for change, helping participants change, and then stablizing the new and more appropriate patterns of behavior and attitudes. Establishing the conditions for change is discussed in detail in Johnson (1980b). These conditions are as follows:

1. A sufficient level of trust among group members to ensure that participants feel free to self-disclose, experiment with new patterns of thinking and behaving, and give and receive feedback. This includes a warm and supportive climate in which participants feel free to take risks.
2. A reduction of participants' egocentrism and the encouragement of their viewing problems and behavior patterns from a variety of perspectives.
3. A reduction of participants' demoralization and an increase in their sense of control and influence over themselves and their lives.
4. The promotion of positive identification by the participant with other members who have the skills and competencies she needs in order to solve the problems she is experiencing.

Being a Resource Expert

An effective group leader must have the skills to act as a resource expert, an educator using inquiry and experiential methods, and a diagnoser of personal, interpersonal, and group dynamics. Any growth-group facilitator should be skilled in the use of inquiry and experiential methods of learning, a subject discussed in Chapters 1 and 2. Almost all types of growth groups emphasize inquiry into the experiences of the group members. This inquiry is usually based upon diagnoses of the personal, interpersonal, and group dynamics being experienced. To make such diagnoses, the facilitator applies a conceptual framework based upon theory and research to the behavior of the group members. To apply such a framework, the facilitator must have expertise in one of the behavioral sciences, such as psychology or sociology. The presentation of conceptual frameworks enables members not only to gain insight into their behavior and their internal reactions to what occurs within the group, but to understand more fully the interpersonal and group dynamics they are involved in. Thus, a facilitator must have a solid knowledge of one of the behavioral sciences, an expertise in inquiry and experiential-learning methods, and the ability to use his knowledge and expertise to help the members understand what they are experiencing. Lieberman, Yalom, and Miles (1973) found that the most effective leaders had a great ability to present conceptualizations that gave meaning to the experiences the members were undergoing. This one ability was the most important variable in promoting member learning that they found in their study. Such conceptualizations are especially useful to members after the group experience has ended, when they are able to use them to understand more fully their day-to-day interpersonal and group situations. The conceptualizations presented in this book and in Johnson (2000) are examples of the types of conceptual frameworks a facilitator must be able to communicate to members.

Teaching Group and Interpersonal Skills

One of the major keys to decreasing self-defeating behavior and increasing self-enhancing behavior is improving participants' group and interpersonal skills. It is often because participants lack social skills or are unable to utilize effectively the group and interpersonal skills they do have that they seek out a growth group to participate in. Improving participants' competency in and utilization of social skills can best be done in a group setting. In order to begin skill teaching, growth-group leaders need to ask themselves questions such as these:

1. What are the group and interpersonal skills every person needs in order to function effectively in our society and lead a fulfilling and self-enhancing life? These skills are detailed in this book and in Johnson (1991, 2000).
2. What interpersonal and group skills are participants failing to utilize effectively?
3. What interpersonal and group skills do participants lack?
4. Will the learning and utilization of the apparently needed group and interpersonal skills reduce participants' self-defeating and self-destructive behavior and thinking and increase their ability to create for themselves a more productive, self-enhancing, and fulfilling life?

In some growth groups interpersonal and group skills are taught directly through exercises like the ones contained in this book. In other growth groups the skill building is conducted through reflection on member's interactions and relationships. Leading growth groups requires the capacity to facilitate the social-skill learning of the participants. Because such skill learning is discussed in depth in Chapters 1 and 2, it will not be discussed here.

Modeling the Constructive Use of Social Skills

A fourth set of skills required of a facilitator consists of modeling the behaviors she hopes members will learn from their group experience. Social-learning theory (Bandura, 1969) emphasizes the importance of modeling desired behaviors and then reinforcing group members (for example, giving recognition and approval for imitating the facilitator); this procedure is probably the most effective way to teach new skills. The behaviors a facilitator may model are discussed in this book and in Johnson (2000). Such behaviors would include, for example, sending and receiving communications, self-disclosure, giving and receiving feedback, experimenting with alternative behaviors, and expressing acceptance and support for others. A willingness to model desired skills means that the facilitator will take an active part in interacting with other group members. Some research indicates that activeness on the part of the facilitator is to be preferred to passiveness (which, when it pertains to members, is associated with anxiety, dissatisfaction, silence, poor attendance, discontinuance, and lack of learning), except when the activeness turns into domination (Bierman, 1969). Peters (1966), in addition, found that members who imitate the facilitator learn more from growth groups than those who do not. Thus, the facilitator may want to be the ideal member in the group in order to promote members' skill development. Finally, it should be noted that simply being an authentic person does not necessarily enable the facilitator systematically to present effective skills to be imitated by group members; a facilitator must be interpersonally effective in order to model desired skills.

Providing Constructive Confrontations and Feedback

The facilitator must be able to make sure that members are provided with constructive feedback and confrontations. Helpful feedback is the sharing, upon request, of a description of how a person sees another person's behavior and its consequences, and a description of how the person is reacting to the other person's behavior. A confrontation is a deliberate attempt to help another person examine the consequences of some aspect of his or her behavior; it is an invitation to engage in self-examination. A confrontation originates from a desire to involve oneself more deeply with the person one is confronting, and it is intended to help the person behave in more fruitful or less destructive ways. The specific skills of feedback and confrontation are presented in Johnson (2000). The point to keep in mind when facilitating feedback and confrontations is the difference among the behavior being observed, the conceptual framework the observer is using, and the inferences and interpretations made about the person engaging in the behavior. A facilitator should never let group members confuse these three elements of giving feedback and confronting other members. The actual behavior being observed will be the same to all group members (assuming that the observations are valid), but the conceptual frameworks used to understand the behavior and to make interpretations and inferences about it can be widely disparate. Selling other group members on one interpretation of what is taking place is a much different activity from arriving at a consensus of what behavior is taking place.

Defining and Diagnosing Participants' Problems

Creating meaning for participants by labeling feelings and events that they undergo and attributing meaning to experiences occurring within the group is a fundamental activity of leaders of growth groups. The increased understanding of participants resulting from such leader behavior reduces their fear and anxiety concerning emotional and interpersonal experiences and provides them with cognitive tools that they can use in becoming more effective persons. In helping participants understand their feelings and experiences, the leader must be careful about the way in which he or she attributes the causes of their problems and must pay attention to the resulting sense of personal control experienced by participants.

A participant's problems may be attributed to something within the participant (internal causation) or something outside of the participant (external causation). Causes may also be viewed as stable (incapable of change) or unstable (capable of change). Depending on the problem and the situation, a leader may wish to help the participant view a problem as having stable, external causes or unstable, internal causes. When a person is deeply depressed about a perceived failure, for example, the leader may wish to help that person focus on the external, unstable causes of the failure. But when he or she succeeds, the leader may wish to emphasize the internal, stable causes of the success in order to improve the person's self-esteem.

Participants' problems should usually be defined in ways that increase their sense of personal control in solving them. Most individuals seem to seek a sense of control over their lives. A belief that one is in control of one's life makes the world more predictable, and one tends to react more positively to the events that take place around oneself and the experiences one has. One of the reasons for severe depressions following major illnesses such as heart attacks is assumed to be the feeling that one has lost control over one's life (Glass, 1977). A belief in one's control over events affects performance on tasks (Glass and Singer, 1973); judgments of the pleasantness of our surroundings and mood (Rodin, Solomon, & Metcalf, 1978); the positiveness of our reactions (Glass, 1977); how active, sociable, and vigorous we are (Langer and Rodin, 1976); and our general health and length of life (Rodin & Langer, 1977). The facilitator of a growth group will usually want to define and diagnose participants' problems in ways that maximize their sense of control over their lives.

Group leaders should also define participants' problems in ways that maximize their sense of freedom in solving them. Brehm (1966) has proposed the concept of psychological reactance to explain some of the reactions individuals have to a loss of control or freedom of choice. **Reactance** is a motivational state that is aroused whenever persons feel that their freedom has been abridged or threatened. Threats to personal freedom motivate persons to take actions that will help them regain their freedom and control. This motivation to regain freedom can be used to change self-defeating to self-enhancing patterns of attitudes and behavior. Being placed in a dependent position, on the other hand, can lead to a significant drop in later performance when one is asked to behave independently on one's own.

Confusion over their feelings and actions increases participants' anxiety and fear concerning their problems. A necessary skill of a growth-group leader, then, is to help participants apply insights and meaningful interpretations to their actions and feelings that will increase their sense of personal control and freedom.

Ensuring Opportunities for Self-Disclosure and Experimentation

Many of the important experiences in growth groups come directly from participants' self-disclosures and experimentation with new patterns of thinking and behaving. An important function of the group leader, therefore, is to ensure that opportunities to do so are present in the group.

Promoting Reparative Emotional Experiences

The facilitator needs to be able to promote corrective or reparative emotional experiences in the group. Highly personalized and relevant learning often arouses emotions—anxiety while the learning is taking place and happiness and satisfaction when it is achieved. To give and receive feedback, to confront and be confronted, to experiment with new behaviors, to bring out personal concerns to be problem-solved—all promote considerable emotional reaction. High levels of warmth, anger, frustration, and anxiety are found in most growth-group experiences. A facilitator may stimulate emotional reaction by confronting group members, by supporting attempts to experiment with alternative behaviors, by promoting feedback and problem solving, by disclosing highly personal material about herself, and by expressing warmth and support for the members of the group. The most effective leaders in the Lieberman, Yalom, and Miles (1973) study engaged in a moderate amount of emotionally stimulating behavior. Though emotional experiences do not mean that learning will take place, genuine learning is often accompanied by emotionality. The facilitator needs to be certain that the members not only experience deep emotion but also are helped to look at the experience objectively, in such a way as to give it meaning for the future. She should emphasize reflection as well as experience and guide members in applying their present experiences. In managing the emotionality of the group, the facilitator must also moderately stimulate learning that arouses emotions and provide conceptualizations that will promote learning from emotional experiences.

Engineering a Problem-Solving Process

Facilitators need to be able to engineer a problem-solving process with which participants can address their concerns. In such a problem-solving process it may be important to bring in information about the person's past behavior and feelings as well as his or her behavior and feelings in the group (Lieberman, Yalom, & Miles, 1973).

Negotiating Changes in Participants' Patterns of Attitudes and Behaviors

Another set of skills for leaders of growth groups consists of helping participants clarify their current attitude and behavior patterns, determining how those patterns are affecting the participants' feelings and interactions with others, strengthening constructive patterns of attitudes and behaviors, and changing destructive patterns that lead to self-defeating cycles of behavior and cause such feelings as guilt, depression, anxiety, fear, anger, and resentment. Encouraging participants to actively take the perspectives of others with whom they are involved, communicating warmth and understanding, highlighting conflict between desired consequences and actual behavior and thinking, and initiating problem-solving discussions are all ways in which a group leader may facilitate participants' mastery of more self-enhancing patterns of attitudes and behaviors. For a more thorough discussion of these methods, see Johnson (1980b) and Johnson and Matross (1977).

Engineering an Effective Group

The facilitator should be able to engineer an effective group. All the skills discussed in this book are useful here. Only in a growth group that is effective can the learning of members take place. The cohesion of the group; group norms that favor moderate emotional intensity, confrontation, and supportive peer control; the distribution of participation and leadership; the quality of communication; the management of conflict—these and all the other aspects of group effectiveness are extremely important for productive growth groups. A facilitator must be able to promote effective group behavior among the members.

Establishing and Maintaining a Contract

It is sometimes useful for a facilitator to have a clear contract with participants concerning their responsibilities as group members. The contract might provide, for example, that members are (a) to be completely open to the group about both past and current behavior, (b) to take responsibility for themselves once they enter the group and not blame others or circumstances for their predicaments, and (c) to get involved with the other group members and cooperate in increasing their learning. When an explicit contract is made the facilitator becomes the keeper of the contract and should see to it that it is enforced.

Carrying Out Executive Functions

Finally, a facilitator may have a variety of executive functions to carry out. Organizing the group, arranging for facilities in which it is to meet, providing it with needed materials, and conducting an evaluation of its success—all of which require a range of administrative and evaluative skills—may be the responsibilities of the facilitator.

BECOMING A FACILITATOR

In the past two decades more and more persons have wanted to become qualified to conduct growth groups. One does not have to be a qualified growth-group facilitator to conduct inquiry- and experiential-learning activities. This book has organized material on group skills so that many different types of educational ventures can use it in the absence of a highly qualified staff. Yet being skilled in conducting inquiry- and experiential-learning activities does not mean that a person is qualified to conduct growth groups.

A person interested in being a facilitator should ask four basic questions. The first question is "Do I have an adequate training in a behavioral science?" A facilitator should have a background in an applied behavioral science (such as social psychology) that places a heavy emphasis upon interpersonal relations and group dynamics. Ideally, one should have a basic knowledge of personality theory, psychopathology, group processes, and interpersonal dynamics. The person should also be connected with some organization, institution of higher education, or other agency that confirms his professional status. A serious commitment to growth groups should be part, but not all, of this person's professional activity. He or she should clearly know his or her intentions and goals as a facilitator, and he or she should understand all the ramifications of the client–facilitator relationship. A familiarity with the research on growth groups is also necessary.

The second question is "How much experience have I had as a participant and a facilitator in growth groups?" Lakin (1972) recommends that before a person can legitimately function as a facilitator, he or she should have had a three-year training sequence something like this:

1. Participate as a member in at least two growth groups.
2. Observe group meetings of at least five growth groups and meet after the sessions with their facilitator to discuss the interactions of members and other relevant processes.

3. Co-lead five groups with experienced facilitators.
4. Lead five groups as sole facilitator, but be observed and discuss with the observer functioning in the facilitator role.
5. Undergo either psychotherapy or some equivalent sustained experiential self-study.
6. Be evaluated by well-qualified local facilitators who not only focus upon your general fitness of character and your preparation, but review with care evaluations others have made of you and their recommendations.
7. Keep up to date by periodically becoming involved in local seminars, supervision by more experienced professionals, and discussions of the ethics of the facilitator's role and function.

The third question is "What is my personal level of sensitivity, self-awareness, self-understanding, and self-actualization?" No matter how much training a person has as a facilitator, if he or she is not self-aware and self-understanding, the person will not be able to resist indulging his or her own personal needs for such things as power and positive responses from participants. The personal qualities of sensitivity to and respect and liking for others are crucial for facilitators. Finally, Maslow (1962) states that a need-deficient person tends to see others in terms of the ways in which they can be of use; the self-actualized person, who is freer and more disinterested, is able to stand off and see others as they are—unique persons with their own problems who can be helped in various ways by various means.

The final question is "Am I certified by a professional organization?" There are many professional organizations that to some extent certify members as being competent as growth-group facilitators. Also, many states license or certify practicing psychologists. A serious facilitator will take the time and trouble to become certified by a professional organization or licensed by his or her state.

FEELINGS, INTUITION, AND CONCEPTUAL FRAMEWORKS

One major requisite of an effective facilitator is the ability to assess accurately his or her feelings, intuition, and conceptual frameworks. To a capable, well-trained, and experienced facilitator the three become integrated. Among poorly trained and inexperienced facilitators, feelings and intuition may be given a "mystical" sense of rightness and followed blindly as a form of emotional anarchy. Though this issue is closely related to the discussion of creativity in Chapter 8, it is important enough to be reviewed briefly at this point.

A person's feelings are great sources of information about what is happening within the group and what sorts of problems are occurring in the relationships among members. But feelings are not infallible. They are susceptible to bias, distortion, and misunderstanding, especially in situations where the person is threatened, defensive, anxious, or tense. Moreover, all people have their blind spots, and in certain situations, or under certain conditions, their feelings can be a reflection of their own fears and anxieties rather than of what is actually taking place in the group. It is important, therefore, for a facilitator to calibrate herself on the validity and reliability of her feelings in different situations, in response to different types of events, and under different conditions. When a person becomes highly emotional, she should be cautious about relying on the accuracy of her feelings, because it is then that they are most susceptible to distortion and bias. Understanding oneself and the potential causes of various feelings is important in learning when to take action on the basis of one's intuitions and feelings.

Awareness of one's feelings and knowledge of the areas in which one can trust one's feelings lead to the issue of intuition as a base for judging what is taking place in the group and how and when to intervene in certain situations. Hunches often prompt a facilitator to intervene without his being able to explain the basis of the intervention's appropriateness. Intuition is a preconscious process: The person does not know quite how the conclusions or impulses were determined. Intuitive thinking characteristically does not advance in careful, well-defined steps: The person has an emotional and cognitive reaction to the total situation and arrives at an answer. He rarely can provide an adequate account of how the answer evolved, and he may be unaware of just what aspects of the problem situation he is responding to. Intuition results from an immersion in the group process and among the members and from a strong identification with and empathy for what is occurring in the group. The greater the familiarity a person has with the issues that concern the group, the greater the likelihood of his intuitions being correct. A wide understanding of and acquaintance and empathy with both human nature and the nature of the group members will enhance one's intuition about the participants more than factual knowledge will. Experience in calibrating one's intuitive abilities is needed because one will find that one's intuition, like one's emotions, is sound on certain types of issues but misleading on others.

The overuse of intuition in leading growth groups has several shortcomings. Facilitators who through lack of training or self-discipline do not have conceptual frameworks from the behavioral sciences or the skills to use such frameworks in gathering information about what is taking place in the group and among its members are ignoring these shortcomings. *First,* hunches often confuse observation with inference; a facilitator begins defending her intuitive inferences as if they were observations and facts. One cannot, for example, prove that a member is projecting his feelings into others. *Second,* facilitators may overrate the validity of their personal observations, believing them more accurate than the witnesses usually are. Research on rumors and testimony, for example, indicates that quite often eyewitnesses' perceptions, memory, and inferences are completely inaccurate even though the witnesses are convinced that they know exactly what happened. *Third,* the history of medicine and clinical psychology gives overwhelming evidence of the folly of treatments based upon intuition. For several centuries, for example, it was intuitively obvious not only that the insane were possessed by demons but also that all diseases were in the blood and a sick person, therefore, could be cured by bleeding. What was intuitively obvious yesterday is often laughed at today. *Fourth,* the research on self-fulfilling prophecies indicates that people quite often engage in behavior that makes an originally false conclusion or perception become valid. Thus, a facilitator whose intuition is wrong may misunderstand a situation but set in action certain dynamics that create the very situation she is trying to correct and thus confirm her original false intuition. A *fifth* shortcoming is that a person's intuitions give her no adequate basis for knowing whether they are accurate. The major fallacy in intuitive thought is not that it may be inaccurate (though we know that many hunches turn out to be mistaken); a person's intuitions may be quite accurate. It is

rather that no basis exists for knowing if it is right or wrong. A facilitator who takes action on the basis of her intuition takes action before she can verify whether or not the action is appropriate. *Finally*, it must be recognized that intuition represents an internal logic based upon one's culture and frame of reference. Intuitive judgments about another culture or another frame of reference can be very misleading.

The need to use feelings and intuitions as a basis for action within the group, even though the dangers of doing so are recognized, reflects the necessity of conceptual frameworks and data-gathering skills that can be used to verify hunches. Facilitators must have the ability to clarify their intuitions to the degree that they are able to formulate hypotheses that can be verified or disproved. It is through conceptualizing what is happening within the group and among its members that the facilitator usually derives effective interventions. It is through the facilitator's communication of his conceptualizations, furthermore, that much of the learning of members takes place. Although facilitators vary in how much they rely on behavioral science conceptualizations and how much they rely on their feelings and intuitions, all have some conceptualization of what is taking place. One always has a set of assumptions from which to operate; the only question is how well formulated and explicit the conceptual framework is, and how systematically it is used to verify one's hunches.

A conceptual framework is nothing more than a way of looking at pieces of behavior in order to make some kind of sense out of them. Individual behaviors, when examined one by one, often have little or no value to the observer. When the pieces are conceptually connected, however, they become understandable and useful. The facilitator uses a conceptual framework to see the connections among and meaning of the individual behaviors of group members. All conceptualizations involve understanding relationships, grasping inherent meaning, or comprehending a structure. The value of conceptualization is that it provides an instrument for decision making. A facilitator is able to use her theoretical system to bring her interventions under rational control. She plans her actions in accordance with a system of related hypotheses rather than on the basis of an intuited procedure. The knowledge now available in the behavioral sciences provides facilitators with the means of organizing their perceptions, making observations systematically in order to promote member learning, checking out their hunches, and communicating their expertise to the members. There is no way to overemphasize the importance to facilitators of explicit conceptual schemes that they can use systematically in helping members learn from their experiences.

As with intuition, however, if facilitators use only their conceptualizations, their effectiveness may suffer. Their behavior in a group may become uncreative and overly structured. They may be pretending that the group is at a level of sophistication and knowledge that it is not, and they will be repressing their capacity for the kind of creativity that provides insights and alternative solutions to the problems the group faces. Though conceptual frameworks do help organize observations and do aid understanding and communication, they do not always help facilitators to draw upon the creativity they need in order to arrive at insights into members' behavior and put fire and zest into their own growth and actualization.

An effective facilitator should be aware of and accept his feelings. He should use them to spark his intuition about what is taking place in the group and among its members. He should also have expertise in using conceptual frameworks to verify hunches, to observe member behavior systematically, and to communicate with members in ways that facilitate their learning. Intuition and theory are both necessary and useful in generating effective interventions within a growth group. Neither should be slighted; neither should be overvalued when employed separately.

GROWTH GROUPS AND PARTICIPANT ANXIETY

During the past twenty years there have been allegations that growth groups create levels of anxiety that are potentially damaging psychologically (Gottschalk, 1966). These allegations have not been supported by evidence. To determine how anxious college students are before and after participating in a growth group, Johnson, Kavanagh, and Lubin (1973), in two separate studies, compared the anxiety level of participants in a growth group with their anxiety level before and after taking a final examination in a course in group dynamics. They found that participant anxiety at the beginning of the growth group was less than that experienced before a final examination, and that participant anxiety after the growth group was over was considerably less than that experienced after a final examination. Participating in a growth group, then, seems less stressful than does taking course examinations.

13 Team Development, Team Training

Basic Concepts to Be Covered in This Chapter

In this chapter a number of concepts are defined and discussed. The major ones are listed below. The procedure for learning these concepts is as follows.

1. Divide into pairs, define each concept (noting the page on which it is defined and discussed), making sure that both you and your partner understand the meaning of each concept.
2. Then join with another pair to make a group of four. Compare the answers of the two pairs. If there is disagreement, the members look up the concept in the chapter and clarify it until all members agree on and understand the definition.

Concepts

1. Team
2. Mass-production organizational structure
3. High-performance organizational structure
4. Organizational development
5. Team building
6. Team training
7. Pareto chart
8. Total quality management

INTRODUCTION

The Killer Bees is a boys' high school basketball team from Bridgehampton, New York (a small, middle-class town on Long Island). Bridgehampton High School's total enrollment has declined since 1985 from 67 to 41, with fewer than 20 males attending the school. There have never been more than 7 players on the team. Yet, since 1980 the Killer Bees have amassed a record of 164 wins and 32 losses, qualified for the state championship playoffs six times, won the state championship twice, and finished in the final four two other times. None of their players was ever really a standout. Not one of the Killer Bees went on to the pros, and the team was never tall. Although every Killer Bee graduated and most went on to college, few had the talent to play ball in college. To win against bigger, supposedly more talented opponents, the Killer Bees had to be the ultimate in versatility, flexibility, and speed. Their game was team basketball.

How did the Killer Bees become so successful with so few players and so little talent? There were a number of factors. The first is that they had a richness and depth of purpose that eludes most teams. Their mission was more than winning basketball games. They were committed to (a) bringing honor and recognition to their community, (b) protecting and enhancing their legacy, and (c) one another. Second, the community really backed the team. Fathers, brothers, and cousins had played on earlier teams, and mothers, sisters, and aunts cheered the team on relentlessly. Third, being a member of the Killer Bees was its own reward. No college scholarships awaited the players. The pros were not interested. No high-paying jobs were waiting. All the reward came from membership in a unique, inspiring, high-performance team. What resulted was team members adopting an incredible work ethic and focus on skill development (starting in preschool, they practiced 365 days a year), and a focus on playing as part of a team, not as an individual.

Teams such as the Killer Bees have been defined as a small group of people so committed to something larger than themselves that they will not be denied (Katzenbach & Smith, 1993). It is the potential for such performances that make teams the key to successful organizations.

Teams typically exist within an organizational context. In organizations, there are a number of different types of teams used. To improve organizational performance, the performance of each team must improve. There are three major ways of doing so: (1) carefully forming, structuring, and nurturing teams; (2) using teams to train organizational members; and (3) implementing team-building programs. To ensure that teams continuously improve the quality of their work, team members must know how to assess their performance and must implement total quality management.

WHAT IS A TEAM?

Productivity through people.

Singapore Management Philosophy

To use teams, and be a team member, you need to know what is and is not a team. Placing people in the same room and calling them a team does not make them one. Aggregates are not groups. To use teams effectively, you first have to know what is and is not a group (see Chapter 1). To be a team, you first have to be a group. In many cases the concepts *small group* and *team* are used interchangeably in the group dynamics literature, even within the same research study. But not all groups are teams. Teams are just one type of small group. You must know what groups are teams and what groups are not teams. A team is *not* just a number of people working together. Committees, task forces, departments, and councils are groups, but they are not necessarily teams. Groups do not become teams simply because that is what someone calls them. No matter how often it is called one, the entire membership of any large and complex organization is *never* a team.

A **team** is a set of interpersonal interactions structured to achieve established goals. More specifically, a team consists of two or more individuals who (a) are aware of their positive interdependence as they strive to achieve mutual goals, (b) interact while they do so, (c) are aware of who is and is not a member of the team, (d) have specific roles or functions to perform, and (e) have a limited life span of membership. Teams can be placed along a continuum according to the amount of collaboration (integration and role differentiation) required (Dyer, 1987). At one end of the continuum are teams such as golf teams, that are composed of a set of individual performers whose individual efforts are combined into a team score. At the other end are teams such as football teams, where division of effort is meshed into a single coordinated result and where the whole is more than and different from the sum of its individual parts.

In a recent field study conducted on actual ongoing work teams, Katzenbach and Smith (1993) distinguished between teams and other forms of working groups in organizations (see Table 13.1). They interviewed hundreds of people in more than fifty different teams in thirty different companies to discover what differentiates various levels

Table 13.1 **Working Groups Versus Teams**

Working Groups	Teams
A strong, clearly focused leader is appointed.	Shared leadership responsibilities exist among members.
The general organizational mission is the group's purpose.	A specific, well-defined purpose that is unique to the team.
Individual work provides the only products.	Team and individual work develop products.
Effectiveness is measured indirectly by group's influence on others (e.g., financial performance of business, student scores on standardized examination).	Effectiveness is measured directly by assessing team work products.
Individual accountability only is evident.	Both team and individual accountability are evident.
Individual accomplishments are recognized and rewarded.	Team celebration. Individual efforts that contribute to the team's success are also recognized and celebrated.
Meetings are efficiently run and last for short periods of time.	Meetings with open-ended discussion and include active problem solving.
In meetings members discuss, decide, and delegate.	In meetings members discuss, decide, and do real work together.

of team performance, where and how teams work best, and how to enhance the effectiveness of teams. In a *working group* interdependence is low and accountability focuses on individual members, not the group as a whole. The product of a working group is the sum of all the work produced by its members. Members do not take responsibility for results other than their own. Members do not engage in tasks that require the combined work of two or more members. In meetings, members share information and make decisions that help each person do his or her job better, but the focus is always on individual performance.

A **team,** on the other hand, is more than the sum of its parts (Katzenbach & Smith, 1993). A team's performance includes team work products that require the joint efforts of two or more members as well as individual work products. Teams not only meet to share information and perspectives and make decisions, they produce discrete work products through members' joint efforts and contributions. The focus is primarily on team accountability. Team members hold themselves and each other accountable for doing high-quality work. Katzenbach and Smith (1993) emphasize that for a real team to exist, there must be a compelling team purpose that is distinctive and specific to the small group and that requires its members to roll up their sleeves and accomplish something beyond individual end products.

TYPES OF TEAMS

Teams may be classified in an infinite number of ways. Three of the most common are discussed here. One way to classify teams is by the setting in which they are used. Teams are primarily found within work, sports, and learning situations. A *work team* is a set of interpersonal interactions structured to (a) maximize members' proficiency and success in doing their jobs and (b) coordinate and integrate each member's efforts with those of the other team members. A *sports team* is a set of interpersonal interactions structured to (a) maximize members' athletic performance and (b) coordinate and integrate each member's efforts with those of the other team members. A *learning team* is a set of interpersonal interactions among peers of equal status structured to (a) maximize each member's acquisition of knowledge and skills and (b) coordinate and integrate each member's efforts with those of the other team members.

A second way to classify teams is by how they may be used in an organization. Three of the most common uses are as follows:

1. *Problem-solving teams* are teams consisting of five to twelve volunteers, hourly and salaried, drawn from different areas of a department. Problem-solving teams meet one to two hours a week to discuss ways of improving quality, efficiency, and work environment. They are off-line discussion groups that have no power to reorganize work or enlarge the role of workers in the production process. Problem-solving teams have been found to reduce costs and improve product quality, but to have little effect on how work is organized or how managers behave. Consequently, they have tended to fade away. They were first implemented on a small scale in the 1920s and 1930s and, based on Japanese Quality Circles, adopted more widely in the late 1970s.

2. *Special-purpose teams* are teams whose duties include such things as designing and introducing work reforms and new technology, meeting with suppliers and customers, and linking separate functions. In organizations that have unions, special-purpose teams have been used to facilitate collaboration between labor and management on operational decisions at all levels. Special-purpose teams involve work in decisions at ever higher levels, creating an atmosphere for quality and productivity improvements. The teams create a foundation for self-managing work teams. Special-purpose teams were implemented in the 1980s as the next step after problem-solving teams. They are still spreading, especially in companies with unions.

3. *Self-managing teams* are teams of five to fifteen employees who produce an entire product or provide an entire service. Team members learn all tasks and rotate from job to job. The teams take over managerial duties, including work and vacation scheduling, the ordering of supplies and materials, and the hiring of new members. Self-managing teams can increase productivity 30% or more and substantially raise quality. They fundamentally change the way work is organized, giving employees control over their jobs, wiping out tiers of managers, and tearing down bureaucratic barriers between departments. A flatter organization results. Self-managing teams were used by a few companies in the 1960s and 1970s and rapidly spread in the mid- to late 1980s. They appear to be the wave of the future.

Another view classifies teams in three ways (Katzenbach & Smith, 1993): teams that recommend things, teams that make or do things, and teams that run things.

1. *Teams that recommend things* include task forces, project groups, and audit, quality, or safety groups asked to study and solve particular problems (Katzenbach & Smith, 1993). Teams that recommend things almost always have predetermined completion dates. Their two most critical issues tend to be (a) getting off to a fast and constructive start and (b) giving their recommendations to the people who have to implement them in an effective way. Not inducing commitment in the implementers is almost always the problem that stymies teams that recommend things. Involving the implementers in the process early and often is an effective strategy. Such involvement may take many forms, including participating in interviews, helping with analyses, contributing and critiquing ideas, and conducting experiments and trials. At a minimum,

anyone responsible for implementation should receive a briefing on the task force's purpose, approach, and objectives at the beginning of the effort. They should also receive regular reviews of the team's progress.

2. *Teams that make or do things* need to have a relentless focus on performance (Katzenbach & Smith, 1993). In deciding where team performance might have the greatest impact, top management should concentrate on the organization's critical delivery points; that is, places in the organization where the cost and value of the company's products and services are most directly determined.

3. *Teams that run things* tend to be rare, especially in large, complex organizations. Despite the fact that many leaders refer to the group reporting to them as a team, few groups of executives really are. Teams at the top are the most difficult to create, but at the same time they are the most powerful when they work well. Often teams at the top are not needed—working groups are adequate for the performance challenge at hand and present fewer risks. At this level, trust is low and destructive conflict tends to be high. Work groups may be less risky and easier to manage. In addition, teams that run things often find it difficult to formulate a purpose that is distinctive and specific to the team, as opposed to the total organizational mission. The organizational mission and the purpose of the team at the top should not be confused. When there are real teams at the top, they tend to be small and informal, mostly having two or three members.

Electronically Linked Teams

Sometimes teams are formed that cannot meet face-to-face. Through the use of modern electronics (such as e-mail, bulletin boards, and computer conferences), teams can be created that are made up of individuals who are widely separated geographically. In an electronically networked team, members can be anywhere in the world. Meetings require only that members are at their terminals. Communication between meetings can be asynchronous and extremely fast in comparison with telephone conversations and interoffice mail. Participation is more equalized and less affected by prestige and status (McGuire, Kiesler, & Siegel, 1987; Siegel, Dubrovsky, Kiesler, & McGuire, 1986). Electronic communication, however, relies almost entirely on plain text for conveying messages, text that is often ephemeral, appearing on and disappearing from a screen without any necessary tangible artifacts. It becomes easy for a sender to be out of touch with his or her audience. It is easy for the sender to be less constrained by conventional norms and rules for behavior in composing messages. Communicators can feel a greater sense of anonymity, detect less individuality in others, feel less empathy, feel less guilt, be less concerned over how they compare with others, and be less influenced by social conventions (Kiesler, Siegel, & McGuire, 1984; Short, Williams, & Christie, 1976). Such influences can lead to both more honesty and more "flaming" (name calling and epithets).

Although electronic communication has many positive features, face-to-face communication has a richness that electronic communication may never match. Meherabian (1971) believed that 93% of peoples' intent was conveyed by tone of voice and facial expression. Harold Geneen, the former head of ITT, believed that his response to requests was different face-to-face than through teletype. "In New York, I might read a request and say no. But in Europe, I could see that an answer to the same question might be yes . . . it became our policy to deal with problems on the spot, face-to-face" (cited in Trevino, Lengel, & Draft, 1987). For this and other reasons (such as lack of effective groupware), teams may be most effective when they use face-to-face rather than electronic interaction. Teams at one site, furthermore, may be electronically linked with other teams in other sites.

The organizational context has profound influences on the success of the team and the actions of team members.

ORGANIZATIONAL CONTEXT

Most teams exist within an organizational context. W. Edwards Deming, J. Juran, and others have stated that over 85% of the behavior of members of an organization is directly attributable to the organization's structure, not the nature of the individuals involved (Walton, 1985). The organizational context in which teams work shapes the behavior of team members by presenting opportunities and constraints. One organizational context, for example, may offer members the opportunity to be included on a number of teams, whereas another organizational context may constrain members from interacting with anyone else. There are basically two organizational contexts—a mass-production organizational structure or a team-based, high-performance organizational structure (Johnson & Johnson, 1989). The *mass-production organizational structure* is designed to drive down the unit costs of long runs of standardized products. In a mass-production organization, an authority hierarchy is rigidly imposed and work is divided into small component parts performed by individuals who work separately from and in competition with other members. The *team-based, high-performance organizational structure* is designed to promote teams that focus on continuous improvement in quality. Organizations may be easily conceptualized as a hierarchy of work teams or "families" that are tied together by linking individuals who are leaders in one team but peer-group members at the next highest organizational level (see Figure 13.1). These individuals are known as *linking pins* (Likert, 1961). Unlike many other organizational theories, Likert's model emphasizes group concepts such as group goals, leadership, and group responsibility rather than individual concepts such as personal motivation and responsibility. Small groups of motivated individuals are the secret to organizational productivity.

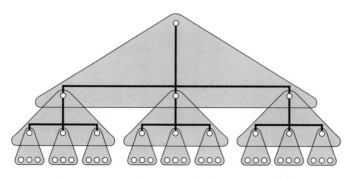

Figure 13.1 The linking-pin model of organizational structure.

Two important aspects of the organizational context are the degree of interdependence structured among members and social support. The greater the interdependence among organization members, the more positive the relations among divisions, departments, teams, and individuals in an organization (Brett & Rognes, 1986). The greater the social support in an organization, the higher performing the teams (Baldwin & Ford, 1988; Sundstrom, Perkins, George, Futrell, & Hoffman, 1990).

Although there is general agreement that organizational contexts greatly influence the behaviors of individuals and groups, there are few research studies that articulate how contextual influences operate. One study that attempted to do so focused on the collision of a Pan Am 747 and a KLM 747 on the ground at Tenerife airport that killed 583 people (Weick, 1990). Weick's analysis of the Tenerife air disaster emphasized contextual factors for cockpit and air-traffic-control crews that interrupted their routines and created such stress that the crews (a) fell back on their most familiar and well-rehearsed response routines and (b) acted as individuals rather than as a team. The high level of stress caused diminished cognitive information-processing capabilities, leading to the "omission of important cues for task performance and an increase in cognitive inefficiency" (Weick, 1990, p. 578). As a result, the flight and air-traffic-control crews made the wrong responses, leading to the deadly crash. Weick suggests that a major contributor to the wrong response patterns was that under a high level of stress crew members acted as individuals, ignoring the need to coordinate their actions with fellow team members.

Organizational Development

Our people's hard work is our most important resource.
> Japanese Management Philosophy

Organizational contexts are not static, they develop and change. Sometimes the changes are planned. **Organizational development** is the use of diagnosis and intervention procedures to promote effective interpersonal, group, and intergroup behavior within the organization. **Organization effectiveness** is the extent to which the organization achieves its goals with the use of minimal resources. In doing so the organization has to achieve its goals, maintain effective cooperation among members, and adapt to the external environment. Organizational effectiveness depends on members (a) having the *interpersonal and small group skills* and *personal attitudes* (i.e., commitment to the team and the organization, caring about colleagues, and caring about reliability and quality of one's work) and *technical competencies* needed to be effective contributors to the organization and (b) committing high levels of *psychological energy* to their work. The commitment of psychological energy and the use of teamwork and taskwork competencies may be encouraged by both the organizational structure and the organizational culture.

Typically referred to as simply OD, organizational development utilizes the **action research** methodology pioneered by Kurt Lewin to improve the effectiveness of organizations. First, the vision and goals of the organization are clarified and their cooperative nature emphasized. Second, the action research methodology is implemented through the following steps:

1. *Diagnosis.* Diagnosis involves three steps:

   a. *Building a normative theory* of how the team or organization should be functioning. Normative theories focus on such factors as cooperation, communication, leadership, decision making, and conflict resolution. Each chapter of this book presents such theories. Without knowledge of what effective leadership looks like, for example, a diagnosis of how effective the leadership of a group or organization is cannot take place.

b. *Measuring current team or organizational functioning* by collecting data through interviews, observations, and questionnaires and by diagnostic group sessions.

c. *Analyzing and organizing the data* so that discrepancies between observed and ideal performance and the causes for the discrepancies can be identified.

2. *Feedback.* The data are reported to those organizational members from whom the data were obtained to highlight the discrepancies between ideal and actual functioning (i.e., problems) of various teams, work groups, departments, and the organization as a whole.

3. *Discussion and planning.* The problems identified by the data are analyzed and the implications for improving the effectiveness of the relevant work groups and departments within the organization are discussed. A plan for improving organizational effectiveness is developed.

4. *Action.* The plan is implemented. Structural supports for the new behaviors and procedures are generated by changing role definitions and group norms. Interventions can be made on the person (skill training or attitude change), group (modifying group structure and procedures), or intergroup (intergroup problem solving) levels.

5. *Rediagnosis.* New data are collected to determine if the plan (a) was implemented and (b) solved the problem. If not, the cycle is repeated.

This process should become continuous and ongoing within most teams and organizations.

Exercise 13.1: Team Structure

Task: Below are three ways of organizing a team. Describe the way team members would interact within each structure and predict the resulting productivity, morale, social support, and professional self-esteem.

Cooperative: One answer from the three of you, everyone must agree, and everyone must be able to explain.

Individual Accountability: One member of your group will be chosen randomly to explain the group's answers.

Expected Behaviors: Everyone participates.

Criterion for Success: Thoughtful answers that have a clear supporting rationale spelled out in detail.

SITUATION 1: MERIT PAY FOR THE BEST TEAM MEMBER

Your organization has decided to implement a competitive merit-pay system for employees. One hundred merit points are given to each team within the organization. You, the manager, are told to rank the team members from best to worst in job performance and divide the bonus points among the team members accordingly. A team member could receive all one hundred points or no points, depending on how his or her job performance is rated for that year. The more merit points given to one team member, the fewer available for the other team members.

To implement this system, criteria on which the team members are to be evaluated have to be determined. On the basis of the selected criteria, team members are ranked from most successful to least successful. The most outstanding member of the team receives fifty merit points, the first runner-up receives thirty points, and the second runner-up receives twenty merit points. The rest of the team members receive no merit points.

SITUATION 2: MERIT PAY FOR OUTSTANDING INDIVIDUAL EFFORTS

Your organization has decided to implement an individualistic merit-pay program for employees. You, the manager, are told to determine how many merit points each of your team members should receive. You decide to reward team members on the basis of how successful they have been this year. All team members who have demonstrated success will receive a merit bonus.

To implement this system, you set criteria for excellent, good, average, poor, and terrible performance. You evaluate the success of each team member. All excellent members are given twenty merit points, good members are given ten merit points, average members are given five merit points, poor members are given one merit point, and terrible members are given no merit points.

SITUATION 3: MERIT PAY FOR OUTSTANDING GROUP EFFORTS

Your organization decides to implement a cooperative merit-pay program for employees. You, the manager, are told to determine how many merit points each of your team members should receive on the basis of how successful their team has been.

To implement the program, you organize all subordinates into teams. You then set criteria for excellent, good, average, poor, and terrible team performance. You evaluate the success of each team. Each member of the excellent teams is given twenty merit points, members of good teams are given ten merit points, members of average teams are given five merit points, members of poor teams are given one merit point, and members of terrible teams are given no merit points.

Exercise 13.2: The Cooperative Team Scenario

A responsibility of team leaders and members is to provide a vision of what the team will be like when the desired changes have been implemented. This vision must be clear and precise.

1. Working individualistically by yourself, write:
   a. Your personal vision of what you hope the team will be.
   b. Your perception of the team's mission.
   c. The immediate goals your team is working to achieve.
   d. The unique talents, skills, competencies, and perspectives you bring to the team's work.

2. Form a triad. Working cooperatively, share your views of the team's mission and goals and come to a consensus as to what the mission and goals of the team should be.
3. In your triad:
   a. Write a detailed, behaviorally oriented scenario that describes what you would expect to see, hear, and feel if most team members acted cooperatively most of the time. Include how interaction and relationships among team members would be affected. This description should be a personalized, realistic, and attainable description of what you are committed to achieving.
   b. It may be helpful to describe the team's *mission,* specify the *environmental demands* on your team, describe the current *response* to these demands, and then describe how cooperative efforts by team members will *contribute* to achieving the team's mission and responding to the current and future demands on your team.
   c. This is a *cooperative* effort. Form a group of three and write one description from the three of you. Everyone must contribute to the description, agree with it, and be able to explain it. Each will need his or her own copy of the scenario. Each will be *individually accountable* to present the group's scenario to another person. Plan how to do so effectively.

Exercise 13.3: Degree of Interdependence Exercise

Task: Decide which team analogy best describes your team and why.
Cooperative: Form groups of three. Agree on one answer and rationale. Everyone must agree, and everyone must be able to explain the group's answer and reasoning.
Individual Accountability: One member of your triad will be selected randomly to present the group's answer and rationale.
Criterion for Success: A reasoned answer backed up by examples and information.
Expected Behaviors: Everyone participates and contributes ideas, analyses, and examples.

TEAMS

1. **Golf Team:** Members all function independently of each other, working to promote as high an individual score as possible, so that when individual scores are combined into team scores, their team wins.
2. **Baseball Team:** Members are relatively independent of one another and, although all members are required to be on the field together, they virtually never interact together all at the same time.
3. **Football Team:** Members are divided into three subteams—offense, defense, and special teams. When the subteam is on the field, every player is involved in every play, but each has a set of specialized skills required by his or her individual position. The teamwork required is centered in the subteam, not the total team.
4. **Basketball Team:** All members play on the team as a whole. Every player is involved in all aspects of the game, offense and defense, and all must pass, run, guard, and shoot. When a substitute comes in, all must play with the new person. True teamwork is like a basketball team where division of effort is meshed into a single coordinated result—where the whole is more than, and different from, the sum of the individual parts.

Exercise 13.4: Roman Army

THE REORGANIZATION OF THE ROMAN ARMY

As a popular and successful general, Caius Marius had been elected consul of the Roman republic five times. In 102 B.C., at the height of his popularity, he reorganized the Roman army—a reform that had been needed for about 50 years. The structural reorganization was relatively simple. The Roman legion consisted of about 6,000 men. Marius divided them into 60 centuries (100 men), each under a centurion. He grouped each century into 10 cohorts, and he had the heads of the cohorts report directly to the general of the legion. This division made the army more efficient, but the real organization was based on changes in society.

Before the reorganization, the army was based on the draft, and under the Roman constitution the draft applied only to citizens who owned a certain amount of property. But over time, the rich landowners, merchants, and others who were eligible no longer had either the aptitude or the taste for military service. The draft was kept, but Marius allowed the poor and unemployed to volunteer. Soon the reluctant farmers and merchants disappeared from the army. The volunteers were those who saw service under a successful general as a prospect for adventure or escape from poverty.

Then, the army began to supply equipment for the soldiers instead of having each individual furnish his own. This meant fewer distinctions based on wealth and ensured that both equipment and training were more standardized.

The bulk of the volunteers were farm laborers or small farmers so heavily in debt that they were in danger of losing their farms. In addition to the prospect of prizes from a successful campaign, a general in search of recruits could promise that, if the army were disbanded, the soldiers would be given an allotment of land. Thus the new Roman army gave more prominence to generals with established reputations whose names would bring in recruits.

The common soldier began to shift allegiance from the republic or the senate to the general. The senate might back down or delay on promises, but the soldiers could count on their generals to fight political battles for them. This made it almost impossible for one general to take an army from another or to remove another general from command.

Thus the army fell more and more under the control of the generals. In turn, the generals became servants of their own armies. They could not retire from public life if their own army were disbanded, because they had to fulfill the promises by which they had obtained volunteers.

Although the Roman soldier respected the constitution, the armies would not hesitate to support their generals against the government if the generals had good reason for attacking it. In 51 B.C., approximately fifty years later, Julius Caesar and Pompeius Magnus (Pompey) began a political struggle. In 50 B.C. Pompey violated the constitution, and Caesar's soldiers enthusiastically followed him. Caesar crossed the Rubicon and invaded Italy, and the civil war began. It ended in 44 B.C. with Caesar being voted a perpetual dictator. This was the beginning of the downfall of the Roman republic.*

*Source: Edgar F. Huse, *The Modern Manager* (St. Paul, MN: West Publishing, 1979), 58–59, as adapted from G. Ferrero, *The Greatness and Decline of Rome* (London: Heinemann, 1909), and F. Marsh, *A History of the Roman World* (New York: Barnes & Noble, 1963).

QUESTIONS

1. Draw an organization chart based on the reorganized Roman army described in this case.
2. What social changes were particularly instrumental in changing the Roman army? How did socioeconomic conditions play a role in these changes?
3. Given hindsight, could the army have been reorganized differently and, perhaps, more effectively?
4. What does this case say about interactions between organizations and their environments?

BUILDING PRODUCTIVE TEAMS

The Plains Indian people, known to whites as the Cheyenne, Crow, and Sioux, are truly the Painted Arrow, the Little Black Eagle, and the Brother People. They follow the *Medicine Wheel Way* (Storm, 1972). Each of the stones within the Medicine Wheel represents one of the many things of the Universe. All things are organized within the Medicine Wheel and all things are equal within it. All things within the Medicine Wheel know of their harmony with every other thing, except for humans. Finding harmony involves recognizing the uniqueness of each person and his or her unity within the Medicine Wheel.

The Medicine Wheel Way states that each person is unique in all ways but one. There is only one thing that all people possess equally, and that is loneliness. No two people on the face of this earth are alike in any one thing except for their loneliness. The only way we can overcome our loneliness is through touching others. The Medicine Wheel Way begins with touching others. Touching others means to be to each other a gift, as is the buffalo. Touching others means nourishing each other, that we all may grow. Through touching others we find our place within the universe and are in harmony with all other things within the universe. We touch others by joining a team and seeing the unity of all members. We are all separate and unique individuals. We are all part of a larger harmony working with each other.

The Plains Indians are not the only ones who believe in unique individuals seeking harmony within a team. Personal productivity in most cases cannot take place without team productivity. A person cannot stand alone. He or she needs a team. Each person needs to be:

1. A unique and valued individual success in his or her own right.
2. Part of a successful (and great) team effort.

The combination of unique individuals who combine into a team fuels productivity. Team productivity depends on ensuring that a clear cooperative structure underlies team efforts and teaching team members the group skills (discussed in this book) they need to be contributing members. In other words, this whole book is about building productive teams. Clear cooperative goals, effective communication, good leadership, effective decision making, constructive conflict management, and positive use of power are all essential (refer back to Figure 1.4 on p. 38).

It takes a team to get extraordinary things done. The productivity of teams is not a simple function of team members' technical competencies and task abilities. Productivity is not guaranteed simply from team members being interested in attaining the team's goals. It takes more than just placing several people in the same room and telling them to work together to create a team effort. Successful team performance requires careful structuring of cooperation among team members.

Using a sales team as an example, there are three ways that relationships among team members may be structured. First, members of the sales team can *compete* with each other to see who is best. Members of the sales team could be ranked from highest to lowest in terms of sales for the month and be given bonuses accordingly. The person who sells the most, for example, would receive a bonus of $500, the second-best salesperson $300, and the third-best salesperson $100. The rest receive no bonus. When a sales staff competes, they will work against each other to be the best. Because helping a competitor hurts one's own chances of winning, the salespersons will be tempted to hide potential customers from colleagues. If a salesperson has more promising leads than he or she can personally follow up on in the near future, for example, the motivation will be towards hiding that information from colleagues in order to lower their sales and thereby increase one's own chances of being the top salesperson. The more one person sells, the less likely it is that others will receive a bonus.

Second, members of the sales team can work *individualistically* to achieve up to a preset criteria. When a sales staff works individualistically, each salesperson will be striving to meet a personal sales quota. A salesperson will receive $500 for selling over $5,000 of products, $300 for selling over $3,000 of products, and $100 for $1,000 of products. Everyone can succeed or everyone can fail, and the efforts of the salespeople are independent. The number of sales one person makes has no positive or negative influence on the success of others.

Third, team members can work *cooperatively* to maximize the productivity of the team. Team members each receive a $500 bonus if the total sales of all members reach $50,000, a $300 bonus if their total sales reach $30,000, and a $100 bonus if the team's total sales reach $10,000. When a sales team works cooperatively, members combine their efforts to maximize the sales of all members. Success depends not only on how many sales one member makes but also on the sales of all other team members. The more successful one's teammates, the more successful one is. If a salesperson has more promising leads than he or she can personally follow up on in the near future, for example, he or she will be motivated to share that information with colleagues in order to increase their sales and thereby increase the overall performance of the team.

Teams structured cooperatively will be more productive than teams structured competitively or individualistically. As was discussed in Chapter 3, the more cooperative the team, the greater the productivity, the more committed team members are to each other, and the greater members' social competencies. The positive results derived from cooperative efforts, however, do not happen automatically. The careful structuring of five essential components (positive interdependence, face-to-face interaction, individual accountability, interpersonal and small group skills, and group processing) is required (Johnson & Johnson, 1989).

If high-quality products and services are to be created, organizations are well advised to use teams. Teams are the basic unit of performance for most organizations. In order to understand the essential role of teams in modern organizations, six issues must be discussed. The *first* is the evidence concerning the effectiveness of teams. The *second* is forming, structuring, and nurturing teams so that they are effective. The *third* is the importance of using teams to train team members in the skills and procedures they need to do their job (taskwork skills) and the skills and procedures they need to coordinate their efforts with other team members (teamwork skills). The *fourth* is the possibility of providing team-building experiences to the team to increase its effectiveness. *Fifth*, the ways in which teams may measure their effectiveness are outlined. *Finally*, the point of carefully structuring teams, training team members, and building team effectiveness is to deliver high-quality products and services to customers.

RESEARCH ON TEAM EFFECTIVENESS

There are hundreds of studies on team effectiveness. Several meta-analyses have been conducted recently to summarize what we know from all this research. Johnson and Johnson (1992b) conducted a meta-analysis on the effectiveness of teams (compared to individuals working competitively or individualistically) for adults (individuals 18 years and older). The studies were divided into those using individual productivity as the measure of success and those using team productivity as the measure of success. Over 120 studies were found that compared team versus individual work on individual productivity. Overall, working in teams resulted in higher individual productivity than did working competitively or individualistically (effect sizes of 0.54 and 0.51, respectively). These results held true for verbal, mathematical, and procedural tasks. Over 57 studies were found that compared team and individual work on team productivity. Overall, working in teams resulted in higher team productivity than did having team members work competitively or individualistically (effect sizes of 0.63 and 0.94, respectively). These results also held true for verbal, mathematical, and procedural tasks. Working in teams was also found to promote more positive relationships and social support among members as well as greater psychological health, self-esteem, and social competencies.

Freeberg and Rock (1987) conducted a meta-analysis on 117 studies of team performance. To be included, the study had to measure team performance as a single entity (rather than the individual performances of team members). An overall mean effect size of 0.42 (sd = 0.43, range = −0.48 – 0.99) was found. Almost all the studies were conducted in a laboratory, used college students as subjects, used very small groups (two to four members), and 50% of the studies were unpublished. More important influences on team productivity were prior experience doing the task, practice, how complex the task was, the way the task was structured, task load, amount of interaction among team members, degree of coordination among team members, and amount of cooperation among team members. Cooperation was especially a major influence on team productivity, both in its direct effects and through mediating processes (such as coordination and cohesion). Team variables were found to be more powerful influences on team productivity than were individual characteristics of members, such as their ability to do the task.

Zhining Qin (Qin, Johnson, & Johnson, 1995) identified sixty-three studies conducted between 1929 and 1989 examining the relative success of cooperative and competitive efforts on individual problem solving. She found that members of cooperative teams outperformed individuals who worked competitively on linguistic, non-linguistic, well-defined, and ill-defined problems.

The productivity of teams, however, is not a simple function of team members' technical competencies and task abilities. To be productive, teams (like all groups) must ensure that members perceive strong positive interdependence, interact in ways that promote each other's success and well-being, be individually accountable, employ their small team skills, and process how effectively the team has been working.

Because teams are effective, teams must be formed, structured, and nurtured. Nurturing teams includes training and retraining members as well as engaging in team-building procedures to ensure that their effectiveness keeps improving.

FORMING, STRUCTURING, AND NURTURING TEAMS

The strength of the wolf is in the pack.

   Rudyard Kipling

Teams and performance go hand in hand. Motorola relied heavily on teams to produce the world's lightest, smallest, and highest-quality cellular phones with only a few hundred parts versus over a thousand for the competition. Ford relied heavily on teams to produce its Taurus model. General Motors relied heavily on teams to produce its Saturn model. At 3M teams are critical to meeting the company's goal of producing half of each year's revenues from product innovations created in the prior five years. General Electric has made self-managing teams a centerpiece of its new organizational approach. Modern tasks often impose greater mental and physical demands than one person can perform in isolation or that working groups can put together from the piecemeal efforts of semi-isolated members. It takes a team effort to be successful in completing demanding and dynamic tasks. *There is, however, a basic discipline that makes teams work.* The role of top management includes the ability to recognize a team's unique potential to deliver results, deploy teams when they are the best tool for the job, and foster the basic discipline that teams need to be effective. There are at least three issues to consider in *forming teams.*

   1. *Keep the size of teams small.* The larger the size of the group, (a) the smaller the percentage of individuals contributing to its efforts and (b) the more anonymous members feel, which often leads to less task involvement and sense of responsibility for the team's success. Virtually all effective teams found by Katzenbach and Smith (1993) ranged between two and twenty-five people. The majority of the effective teams had fewer than ten members. Small size is a pragmatic guide (but not an absolute necessity) for success. Large numbers of people have trouble interacting constructively as a group. Doing real work together is even more difficult. Ten people are far more likely than are fifty to work through their differences and develop a common set of goals that are specific enough for members to hold themselves jointly accountable for the results. Large groups confront more complex constraints on intensely sharing viewpoints needed to build a team. They face difficult logistical issues, such as finding the physical space and time to meet.

2. *Select team members on the basis of their (a) expertise and skills and (b) potential for developing new expertise and skills, not on the basis of their position or personality.* No team succeeds without all the expertise and skills needed to meet its purpose and performance goals. As obvious as this sounds, it is a common failing in potential teams. Usually, teams are heterogeneous, with members who have expertise in different areas. Skill requirements fall into two categories: taskwork skills and teamwork skills. Selecting members with the right mix of skills is not easy. Most teams figure out the skills they will need after they are formed. When team members are chosen for their current skills, the right mix may not be present because it is difficult to know in advance what skills the team will require to achieve its mission. Members' potential for improving existing skills and developing new ones, therefore, should also be considered.

3. *Bring together the resources the team will need to function, such as space, materials, information, time lines, support personnel, and so forth.* Careful planning and preparation are needed to form a team.

Once a team has been formed, it must be *structured* and *nurtured.* Procedures for doing so include the following.

1. *Present the team with its mission, structure positive interdependence among team members, and engage in the process of redefining the mission into goals specific to the team.* Successful teams need a compelling purpose and must know that members sink or swim together. They must operationalize their goals into measurable tasks. Through this process members become committed to the team and gain ownership of its goals. Team members need to believe the team has urgent and worthwhile purposes. The more urgent and meaningful the rationale, the more likely it is that the team will live up to its performance potential.

2. *Have frequent and regular meetings that provide opportunities for team members to interact face-to-face and promote each other's success.* Team members must spend a lot of time together, scheduled and unscheduled, especially in the beginning. Creative insights as well as personal bonding require impromptu and casual interactions just as much as analyzing spreadsheets and interviewing customers. Katzenbach and Smith (1993) found that successful teams all gave themselves the time to learn to be a team. This time need not always be spent together physically; electronic, fax, and phone time can also count as time spent together.

3. *Pay particular attention to first meetings.* Initial impressions always mean a great deal (Katzenbach & Smith, 1993). When the team first gathers, members monitor the signals given by teammates to confirm, suspend, or dispel assumptions and concerns. They pay particular attention to those in authority, such as the team leader and any executives who set up, oversee, or otherwise influence the team. What such leaders do is more important than what they say. If the senior executive leaves the team kickoff to take a phone call ten minutes after the session has begun, and never returns, the members get the message.

4. *Establish clear rules of conduct.* All effective teams develop rules of conduct at the outset to help them achieve their purpose and performance goals (Katzenbach & Smith, 1993). The most critical initial rules pertain to (a) attendance (no interruptions to take phone calls), (b) discussion (no sacred cows), (c) confidentiality (the only things

to leave this room are what we agree on), (d) analytic approach (facts are friendly), (e) end-product orientation (everyone gets assignments and does them), (f) constructive confrontation (no finger pointing), and (g) contributions (everyone does real work).

5. *Ensure accountability by directly measuring the progress of the team in achieving its goals and plot it on a quality chart.* There has to be a way of measuring both team performance and the contributions of each member. The team must be accountable for achieving its goals. Each member must be accountable for contributing his or her share of the work.

6. *Show progress.* Establish a few challenging tasks the team can complete early on. Measuring results and establishing early successes help a team to congeal.

7. *Expose the team to new facts and information that help them redefine and enrich its understanding of its mission, purpose, and goals.* Teams err when they assume that all the information needed was present at the beginning of their work or exists in the collective experience and knowledge of their members.

8. *Provide training to enhance both taskwork and teamwork skills.* As the team progresses in achieving its goals, new skills will become relevant. Members need to sharpen their existing skills and gain new ones in order to keep the team progressing toward its goals.

9. *Have frequent team celebrations and seek opportunities to recognize members' contributions to team success.* Celebrations and honest, positive feedback are powerful tools in helping to shape new behaviors critical to team performance. There are many ways to recognize and reward team performance beyond direct compensation. Ulti-

mately, the satisfaction shared by a team in its own performance becomes the most cherished reward.

10. *Ensure frequent team-processing sessions.* The team needs to examine how effectively it is working and discuss ways to improve its effectiveness regularly.

Teams need to be formed, maintained, and nurtured in ways that build team commitment and increase team and individual accountability.

Building Team Commitment

Groups that become real teams are relentlessly focused on performance results. It is from the focus on performance that member commitment is built, and common commitment is the essence of a team. With it, members become a powerful unit of collective performance; without it, they perform as individuals. Ensuring that members jointly commit themselves to achieve the team's goals follows a multistep process (Katzenbach & Smith, 1993). *First, top management gives the team an initial task, problem, or assignment.* This provides the basic direction to the team's efforts. *Second, the team reframes the assignment into a mutual purpose that all members can commit themselves to.* The common purpose often relates to being on the cutting edge, being first, or revolutionizing the product or service produced by the team. The team shapes its purpose by putting its own "spin" on the demands, opportunities, timing, and approach specified by top management. *Third, the mutual goals are operationalized into a series of distinctive, unique, and specific performance goals that are measurable,* such as increasing sales by 50%. The overall goals and subgoals have to highlight the joint efforts required by team members, that is, the positive interdependence among group members (see Chapters 3 and 4). Team members become confused, pull apart, and revert to mediocre performance when (a) the team fails to establish specific performance goals or (b) the team's activities do not relate directly to the team's overall goals. Compelling mutual goals become a powerful engine of performance.

Teams develop direction, momentum, and commitment through this three-step process of working to shape meaningful purposes and goals from the general mission assigned. The combination of purpose and specific goals is essential to team performance. Each depends on the other to remain relevant and vital. Clear performance goals help a team keep track of progress and hold itself accountable; the broader and nobler aspirations in a team's purpose supply both meaning and emotional energy. The best teams invest a tremendous amount of time and effort exploring, shaping, and agreeing on a purpose that belongs to them both collectively and individually (Katzenbach & Smith, 1993). This purposing activity continues throughout the life of the team. Failed teams rarely develop clear, cooperative goals that give them a common purpose.

Transforming broad directives into specific and measurable performance goals provides a firm foundation for teams. Specific team performance goals should do the following (Katzenbach & Smith, 1993; Chapter 4 of this book):

1. *Help to define work products that are different both from the organization-wide mission and individual job objectives.* What results is a collective effort of team members to make something specific happen. Simply gathering from time to time to make decisions, by contrast, will not sustain team performance.

2. *Facilitate clear communication and constructive conflict among team members.* The clarity of the goal allows teams to resolve conflicts among members on the basis of what will facilitate the achievement of the team's goals. When goals are ambiguous or nonexistent, communication tends to break down and conflicts tend to be resolved in destructive ways.

3. *Allow teams to measure their progress and focus on getting results.*

4. *Have a leveling effect on power and status.* When a small group of people participating in Outward Bound, for example, challenge themselves to get over a wall, their respective titles fade into the background. The teams that succeed evaluate what and how each individual can best contribute to the team's goal. Teams that fail assign responsibilities on the basis of a person's status or personality.

5. *Allow a team to achieve small wins while pursuing broader purposes.* Small wins build commitment and give members the tenacity to overcome the inevitable obstacles to productive work.

6. *Be compelling symbols of accomplishment that motivate and energize.* They challenge team members to commit themselves to make a difference. Drama, urgency, and a healthy fear of failure combine to drive teams who have their collective eye on an attainable, but challenging, goal. It is the team's challenge—nobody but the team can make it happen.

Individual and Team Accountability

There are two levels of accountability that must be structured into teams. The team must be accountable for achieving its goals. Each member must be accountable for contributing his or her share of the work. The team must succeed and all team members must contribute in concrete ways to the team's success and do equivalent amounts of real work.

Mutual accountability cannot be coerced any more than people can be made to trust one another. The procedure for ensuring that team members hold each other accountable for doing their fair share of the work is as follows. *First, the team has to be clear about its purpose and goals and be able to measure its progress in achieving them.* In order for the team and each member to be accountable, it has to be clear what they are accountable for. *Second, positive interdependence is structured among group members.* Accountability begins with team members believing that they sink or swim together (positive goal interdependence) and ends with team members believing that they must hold each other accountable for doing their best to help the team achieve its goals (Katzenbach & Smith, 1993). The stronger the positive interdependence, the greater the mutual accountability among members. When a team shares a common purpose, mutual accountability grows as a natural counterpart.

Third, team members discuss how the purpose of the team may be translated into specific and measurable goals and how the goals may be accomplished. Accountability arises from the time, energy, and action invested in team discussions aimed at figuring out what the team is trying to accomplish and how best to get it done. Team members candidly explore who is best suited to each task as well as how individual roles will be integrated. Accountability is not about threats or fear of what will happen to members if they do not do their work. At its core, accountability is about the sincere promises members make to themselves and teammates. Accountability is experienced as a sense of personal responsibility to do one's best to help the team succeed.

While a team needs to know how well it is doing and what the contributions of each member are, team accountability may be more important than individual accountability. When Bell of Canada, for example, began monitoring the speed of its operators as a group rather than individually, not only did productivity stay up but the operators themselves also claimed both that their services improved and that they liked their job more (Bernstein, 1991).

When people work together towards a common objective, trust and commitment follow. Consequently, teams enjoying a strong common purpose and approach inevitably hold themselves responsible, both as individuals and as a team, for the team's performance. This sense of mutual accountability produces the rich rewards of mutual achievement in which all members share.

USE OF TEAMS IN TRAINING PROGRAMS

Teams are the heart of effective training programs (Johnson & Johnson, 1992b). Members of organizations have to be trained and continuously retrained throughout their career. The ultimate aim of training is procedural learning; that is, for trainees to be competent in performing a job such as operating and maintaining machines and equipment, conducting an interview, using a computer, piloting aircraft, or being an air-traffic controller. What is learned in a training program has to be transferred to the actual job situation and then maintained for years.

There are a number of reasons why teams are useful in training programs. *First*, in order to be proficient at a job, individuals must understand conceptually what they are supposed to do. When team members explain to each other what they are learning, the material is learned better, retained longer, and transferred to actual job situations more frequently. In addition, team members develop shared mental models of how they are supposed to perform their jobs. *Second*, team members can provide each other with appropriate feedback that individuals learning alone cannot receive. *Third*, team members can encourage and motivate each other to try hard to learn. *Fourth*, doing a job well requires that trainees develop a number of relevant attitudes and values as well as learn how to do the job. Personal commitment to do the job well, liking for the job, wanting to increase one's skills continuously are all attitudes that affect job performance. Such attitudes are better learned in groups than individually. *Finally*, learning how to do a job well affects one's view of oneself. A professional identity is adopted along with the job. This new identity is shared with other team members and with future colleagues, who make up a community of practice. Such socialization is facilitated when teammates are enthusiastically adopting the new identity.

In order to maximize the performance of teams, individuals need to be trained to do their jobs and to function effectively as part of a team. This training can take place prior to their membership in the team or concurrently while they work as part of the team. In addition, a team as a whole can receive training through team-building procedures. The result of carefully structuring teams, training team members, and building team effectiveness is high-quality products and services delivered to customers.

TEAM BUILDING

The Minnesota Timberwolves faced their first year as an NBA professional team with an emphasis on playing as a team. A game such as basketball requires elaborate teamwork if played with any degree of expertise. Each play must be practiced again and again until the athletes function as a single unit, and desire for personal success must be transformed into a desire for group success. Practices are designed to foster team spirit, formulate group goals, identify weaknesses in team play, build a desire for group success, and strive for better and better cooperation and integration. What is apparent on a basketball team is that the productivity of teams is not a simple function of team members' technical competencies and task abilities. Team goals must be set, work patterns structured and practiced, a desire for team success must be built, and a sense of team identity developed. Although technical superstars are a great asset, unless all members pursue team success over their own personal stardom, the team suffers. *There is no place for "lone rangers" on a team.* Individual members must learn how to coordinate their actions, identify any strains and stresses in working together, and continuously improve the integration of their efforts.

In order to improve the effectiveness of ongoing work teams, they may be given team-building experiences. Team building takes place at the job site. **Team building** emphasizes the analysis of work procedures and activities of ongoing work teams to improve team productivity, the quality of the relationships among members, the level of members' social skills, and the ability of the team to adapt to changing conditions and demands. The intent of the interventions is to increase long-term team effectiveness by improving the process of members working together. That is, team building focuses more on improving teamwork than on improving taskwork.

Most team-building interventions are typically based on an **action research** model of data collection, feedback, and action planning (Beckhard, 1969; Beer, 1976). Team procedures and activities are analyzed, changes are planned to improve productivity and effectiveness, the changes are implemented, and their success is assessed to see if further changes are needed. Team members are typically involved in diagnosing and planning change. The assumption is that involving team members is more likely to result in favorable consequences than imposing change. This action research model of intervening is commonly focused on (a) goal setting that clarifies the team's goals and the positive goal interdependence among members, (b) improving the interpersonal competence of members, (c) redefining and negotiating the role responsibilities of each member, and (d) identifying problems interfering with effective teamwork and taskwork (Argyris, 1964; Beer, 1980; Buller & Bell, 1986; Dyer, 1987).

In summary, teams are critical to high-quality work. Teams must be carefully formed, structured, and nurtured so that members are committed to achieving the team's goals and the team is accountable for succeeding. Team training is used to ensure team members have the taskwork and teamwork competencies they need to achieve their goals. In order to improve long-term team effectiveness, team-building activities may be periodically engaged in. If teams are able to assess their performance, the stage is set for the use of total quality management and continuous improvement of team performance.

ASSESSING QUALITY OF WORK

To improve quality, the process by which the work is completed is carefully examined so that errors can be eliminated (error-proofing the process), the process can be streamlined to make it simpler (reducing complexity), and the sources of variation can be reduced or eliminated. The stage is then set for continuously improving the process by which the team does its work. Continuous improvement is based on gathering data and displaying it so that informed decisions can be made. To assess the quality of work, two major questions have to be answered:

1. *What should we measure?* The customer is the only one who can define what quality means for a given product or service.
2. *How can we measure it?* Measurement methods should be simple, realistic, and easy for everyone involved to use and understand.

Data-based decision making demands a systematic approach supported by practical tools. Seven of the most widely used tools are (Figure 13.2):

1. Flowchart
2. Cause-and-effect diagram
3. Check sheet
4. Pareto chart
5. Run chart
6. Scatter diagram
7. Histogram

Flowcharts, cause-and-effect diagrams, check sheets, and Pareto charts are most useful when the team is trying to learn about the process and narrow the focus of the improvement process. Later, tools like run charts, scatter diagrams, and histograms can help provide a clearer picture of how the process is operating over time.

Flowchart

In order to understand how the team actually does its work, the team needs to draw a picture of the work process. The **flowchart** is a simple yet powerful visual tool to display all the steps in a process (see Figure 13.3). Flowcharts are used when teams need to identify deviations between the actual and the ideal path for a given process. The flowchart is often the first tool used to begin a process improvement project. Flowcharts are excellent tools for helping teams see the actual flow of steps in a process or procedure. They can also be used to describe the flow of people, material, and information within a designated work space. The level of detail will vary based on the needs of the team. Even without significant detail, flowcharts can help identify gaps, duplication, and other potential problems. A flowchart is created by (a) clearly defining the boundaries of the process (exactly where the process starts and stops, what the inputs and outputs are, who the customers are), (b) identifying all the steps the process actually follows (what the key steps are, who is involved, who does what, when), (c) drawing the steps in sequence, (d) drawing a second flowchart that identifies all the steps the process should follow if everything worked right, and (e) comparing the two charts.

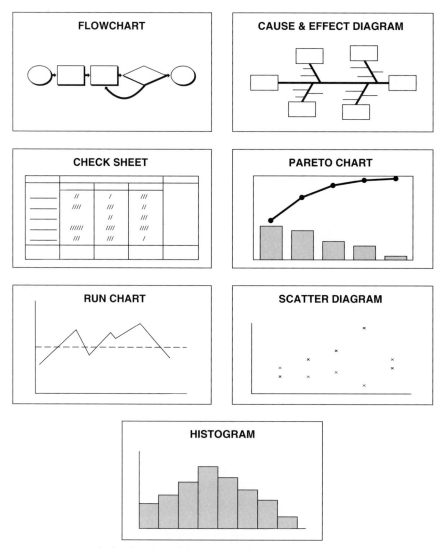

Figure 13.2   Tools for data-based decision making.

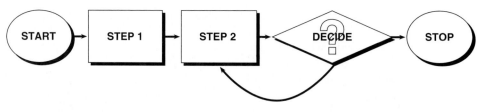

Figure 13.3   Flowchart.

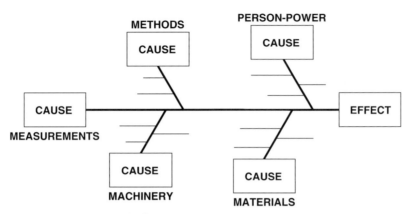

Figure 13.4 Cause-and-effect diagram.

Cause-and-Effect Diagram

A **cause-and-effect diagram** represents the relationship between some effect (the problem being studied) and its possible causes (see Figure 13.4). It is used to explore systematically cause-and-effect relationships so that the most likely causes of a problem or effect can be identified. Developed by Kauru Ishikawa, this charting technique is also referred to as a *fishbone diagram* due to its appearance when completed. A cause-and-effect diagram is usually drawn with the effect or problem on the right side of the diagram. The major causes or influences are drawn to the left of the effect. For every effect there are likely to be several major categories of causes. Any category that helps team members think creatively can be used. Examples of common categories include person-power, machinery, methods, materials, measurements. A cause-and-effect diagram is created by (a) defining the problem or effect clearly, (b) drawing a horizontal line or arrow pointing to the effect (on the right), (c) determining the major categories of possible causes (use generic terms), (d) for each major category, drawing a single line that branches off from the horizontal line, (e) thinking of possible causes in each category, (f) adding each cause as a branch of the appropriate category (ask questions like "Why?" or "Why does this happen?"), (g) identifying and circling the most basic (root) causes (start by looking for causes that appear repeatedly), and (h) using a check sheet to gather data to verify the most likely root cause(s). Use a Pareto chart to display the data collected.

Check Sheet

A **check sheet** is an easy-to-understand form used to answer the question "How often are certain events happening?" (See Figure 13.5.) Check sheets help a team tally and count the number of times an event is observed in a specified time period or amount of product. Check sheets start the process of translating opinions into facts. They are simple to construct and interpret. They help identify patterns in the data (such as the number of errors made per day). In constructing a check sheet, make sure all columns are clearly labeled and that there is enough space to enter data. A check sheet is created by (a) defining exactly what event is being observed (everyone has to be looking for the

EVENT	TIME PERIOD (days, weeks, months)			TOTAL
	1	2	3	
ERROR A	//	/	///	6
ERROR B	////	///	//	9
ERROR C		//	///	5
ERROR D	//////	////	/////	14
ERROR E	///	///	/	7
TOTAL	15	13	13	41

Figure 13.5   Check sheet.

same thing), (b) determining the time period during which the data will be collected (hours to weeks), (c) designing the form and making sure all team members can use it, (d) collecting data consistently and honestly (ensure sufficient time is made available to gather the data), (e) looking for patterns both during and after the data-gathering effort.

Pareto Chart

The **Pareto chart** is a form of vertical bar chart that helps teams separate the vital few problems and causes from the trivial many. It takes its name from the Italian economist Vilfredo Frederico Damaso Pareto (1848–1923). While studying the unequal distribution of income, Pareto found that 80% of the wealth was controlled by only 20% of the population. His findings have been generalized into the *Pareto principle (80/20 rule)*, which states that 80% of the trouble comes from 20% of the problems. The Pareto chart is used to display the frequency and relative importance of problems, causes, or conditions in order to choose the starting point for process improvement, to monitor progress, or to identify root causes of a problem. Pareto analysis allows the team to take data from basic tools (like check sheets and interviews) and present it in a simple bar-graph format. The steps in developing a Pareto chart are as follows:

1. List the condition(s) or cause(s) you wish to monitor. Absenteeism is the condition used in our example.
2. Collect the raw data on the number of times the condition occurred within a predetermined period of time. In our example, the data is the number of days absent during a thirty-day period and the names of the employees.
3. Rank the various conditions or causes from highest to lowest (most absent to least absent—see Table 13.2).
4. Under the horizontal axis, write the causes in descending order (the most important cause to the left and the least important to the right). In our example, we find David on the left with ten absences and Frank on the right with only one absence (see Figure 13.6).

Table 13.2 **Days Absent During June**

Name	Days Absent	Percent of Total Days Absent
David	10	40
Keith	8	32
Helen	4	16
Edythe	2	8
Frank	1	4
Total	25	100

5. On the left-hand vertical axis, list the measurement scale (total number of days absent).
6. On the right-hand vertical axis, note the percentage scale (the total number of absences must equal 100%).
7. Plot the data in a vertical bar graph and then draw a line for the cumulative frequencies. An example deals with the number of times each member of a team of workers was absent during the month of June (see Table 13.2). From Figure 13.6 it may be seen that David, Keith, and Helen make up 88% of the absences among them. An intervention may be planned for David and Keith and perhaps for Helen also.

A Pareto diagram is an extension of the cause-and-effect diagram in that the causes are not only identified but also listed in order of their occurrence. The advantages of the Pareto diagram are that it can be used to analyze almost anything, it is easy to do, and easy to understand. The disadvantage is that only quantifiable data can be used in constructing it.

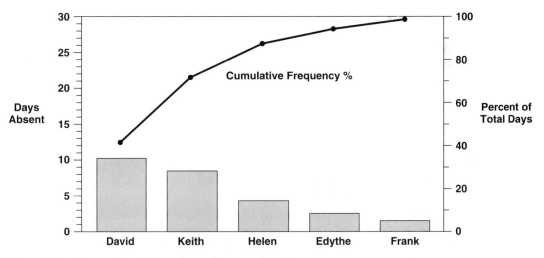

Figure 13.6 Pareto chart: Days absent from work in June per person.

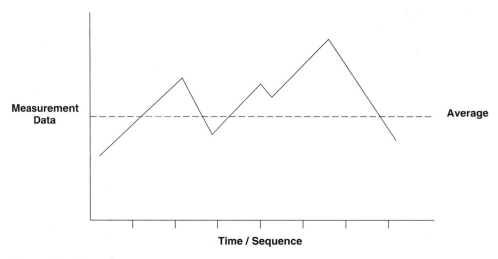

Figure 13.7 Run chart.

Run Chart

A **run chart** is a line graph used to monitor the behavior of a selected characteristic over time (see Figure 13.7). A chart provides teams an opportunity to identify changes in the average performance of a characteristic. Run charts are used to examine data for trends or patterns that occur over time. By displaying the behavior of a specific characteristic over time, the run chart shows meaningful shifts in the average. A run chart is constructed by plotting data points on an *x–y* axis in chronological order. Measurement data are represented on the vertical *(y)* axis, and time or sequence is represented on the horizontal *(x)* axis. A marked point indicates the measurement taken at one point in time. A run chart is created by (a) marking off the time period to be used along the horizontal axis (i.e., hours, days, weeks), (b) entering the unit of measurement along the left vertical axis, (c) entering the historical data as it becomes available (continue to update the chart and the average), and (d) looking for unusual patterns in the position of the data points relative to the average.

Scatter Diagram

A **scatter diagram** displays the cause-and-effect relationship between two process variables or characteristics (see Figure 13.8; Table 13.3). It is used to display what happens to one variable when another variable changes. Whereas a run chart lets you track one characteristic over time, the scatter diagram lets you observe the relationship between the two. A scatter diagram can indicate only the existence of a possible relationship (and its strength); it cannot prove it. Its main use is to test a hypothesis

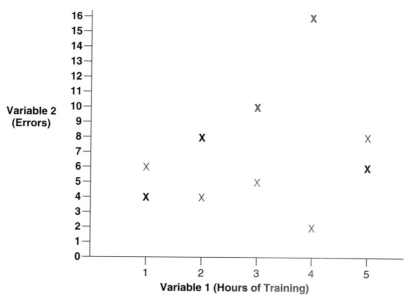

Figure 13.8   Scatter diagram.

that two variables are related (such as the amount of training received and error rates). A scatter diagram is usually constructed with the horizontal axis representing the measurement values for the possible-cause variable and the vertical axis representing the measurement values for the possible-effect variable. A scatter diagram is created by (a) collecting paired samples that may be related (the more data points the better), (b) constructing a data sheet, (c) plotting the data on the chart by placing an x on the chart at each point the paired data intersect (circle repeated data points). The ways the points are scattered about the chart will tell you if the two variables are related. A randomly scattered pattern suggests they are unrelated. If the pattern moves from bottom left to top right, a positive correlation most likely exists. If the pattern moves from top left to bottom right, a negative correlation most likely exists. The more the cluster of data points resembles a straight line, the stronger the relationship.

Table 13.3   Relationship Between Amount of Training and Error Rate

Sample	Variable 1 (Hours of Training)	Variable 2 (Errors)
1	4	6
2	8	4
3	10	5
4	16	2
5	6	8

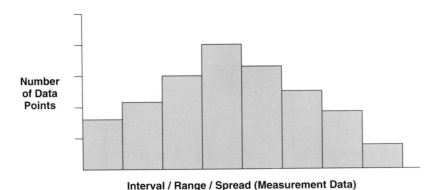

Figure 13.9   Histogram.

Histogram

A **histogram** (history diagram) shows how continuous measurement data are clustered and dispersed (see Figure 13.9). It is used when the distribution and spread of data need to be displayed. Histograms show the frequency of an occurrence and the dispersion between the highest and lowest values. By displaying measurement data across a range of values (spread), the team can learn about the process's ability to meet specifications, whether the distribution is centered in the right place, and whether the data points are evenly balanced or skewed. When large quantities of data are collected and simple tabulation does not provide easy analysis, histograms are useful. A histogram consists of a series of equal-width columns of varying height. The horizontal axis represents the range of data and the vertical axis represents the number of data points in each interval. Each column represents an interval within the range of data. Because interval size is constant, so are the column widths. Because column height represents the number of data points that occur within a given interval, column heights will vary accordingly. The number of intervals (columns) determines how much of a pattern will be visible. A histogram is created by:

1. Collecting the data to be analyzed.
2. Counting the number of data points to determine the size of the data set *(n)*.
3. Determining the range *(R)* by subtracting the smallest values from the largest.
4. Determining the number of classes *(K)* to use (such as under 50 data points = 5–7 classes, 50–100 data points = 6–10 classes, 100–250 data points = 7–12 classes, and over 250 data points = 10–20 classes).
5. Determining class width or interval size *(H)* by dividing the range *(R)* by the number of classes *(K)* *(H = R/K)*.
6. Determining class boundaries for each interval by (a) finding the lowest value data point (this is the start point for the first class boundary) and (b) finding the second class boundary by adding the class width *(H)* to the previous boundary's start point.

7. Making sure each data point can fit in one and only one class (the endpoint of each interval must always be slightly less than the start point of the next class).
8. Counting and recording the number of data points that fall within each class or interval.
9. Drawing a column above each class (horizontal axis) reflecting the appropriate frequency of occurrences.
10. Analyzing the distribution and its implications.

TOTAL QUALITY MANAGEMENT

We don't seek to be one thousand percent better at any one thing.
We seek to be one percent better at one thousand things.

　　　　Jan Carlzon, President, Scandinavian Air Systems

In a mass-production organizational structure, quality is determined by inspecting the final product to see if it is adequate or needs improvement. In a team-based, high-performance organizational structure, quality is determined by examining the process by which the product is created to determine if the process can be improved. A **process** is made up of all the tasks, organized in a sequence, that contribute to the accomplishment of one particular outcome, such as producing a product or filling an order. Flow-charts are used to display all the steps in a process. Perhaps the most profound change in improving quality is the focus on processes rather than on products. **Total quality management** refers to the use of teams to continuously improve the processes by which the product or service is produced. It requires the formation, training, and development of effective teams, a way to identify processes and measure their effectiveness, the creation of a desire to continuously improve the processes, and a focus on the customer. In other words, *where before companies sold a product, now they concentrate on being better at their processes than any other company in the world.*

　　The name most closely associated with Total Quality Management (TQM) is W. Edwards Deming. Deming was born in Sioux City, Iowa. A statistician by profession, he formed many of his theories during World War II when he taught industries how to use statistical methods to improve the quality of military production. Deming taught the Japanese his theories of quality control and continuous improvement following World War II, and he is now widely credited (along with J. Juran and others) with laying the groundwork for Japan's economic boom. Deming's great insight was that management tends to look on what goes wrong (in an organization) as the fault of individual people, not the system. Deming (along with Juran) believes in the *85/15 rule,* which states that 85% of the problems can be corrected only by changing systems (structures, practices, rules, expectations, and traditions that are largely determined by management) and less than 15% of the problems can be solved by individual workers. When problems arise, therefore, management should look for causes in the system and work to remove them before casting blame on workers.

To give some guidance to managers on how to eliminate systemic causes of problems, Deming formulated fourteen principles. Managers were to (a) create constancy of purpose for the improvement of products and services; (b) adopt the new philosophy of total quality and continuous improvement; (c) cease dependence on mass inspection; (d) end the practice of awarding business on price tag alone; (e) improve constantly and forever the system of production and service; (f) institute training on the job; (g) institute leadership; (h) drive out fear; (i) break down barriers between staff areas; (j) eliminate slogans, exhortations, and targets for the workforce; (k) eliminate numerical quotas; (l) remove barriers to pride of workmanship; (m) institute a vigorous program of education and self-improvement; and (n) take action to accomplish the transformation.

Total quality management is also based on a focus on the customer and the continuous improvement of organizational and team processes. Staying close to the customer to satisfy the customer's needs and anticipate the customer's wants is a fundamental aspect of TQM. L. L. Bean is famous for the statement "A customer is the most important person ever in this office, either in person, by mail, or over the phone. A customer is not dependent on us; we are dependent on him. A customer is not an interruption of our work; he is the purpose of it. We are not doing a favor by serving him; he is doing us a favor by giving us the chance to do so. Nobody ever won an argument with a customer." J. Juran stated that all products, goods, and services should be judged on the basis of their fitness for use by the customer. The customer thus is not the point of sale, the customer is part of the design and production process. In the 1970s and 1980s, for example, American industry lost the battle for the hearts and pocketbooks of many consumers because non-American competitors were producing products that met or exceeded consumers' expectations for quality, whereas many American companies were producing standardized goods of mediocre quality in large batches at low cost. Most companies that changed realized that quality begins and ends with the customer.

A focus on quality begins with absolute commitment to meeting the needs of the customer by listening to customers and designing products and services that meet or exceed their expectations. Achieving quality products, however, is not enough to stay competitive in today's world economy. Quality includes continuously improving all the organization processes that lead to customer satisfaction. Continuous improvement demands that how the work gets done is examined, not simply the end result. Continuous improvement leads to quality that is taken for granted. The major premise of continuous improvement is that everything an organization does can be improved by:

1. Involving everyone, from the boardroom to the mailroom, in a daily search for *incremental* improvements.
2. Providing everyone with the training, techniques, and authority they need to identify and fix problems.
3. Setting high-performance targets and measuring results.
4. Focusing the company's strategic vision on the needs of its customers.

Despite the early involvement of Americans such as Deming and Juran in the quality revolution, virtually all of the most important innovations in continuous improvement were made in Japan. Kaoru Ishikawa placed the focus on the customer and the responsibility for continuous improvement on every member of the organization. At Toshiba, for example, workers average around forty suggestions per year, and over 95% of the suggested improvements find their way into a product or service. Taiichi Ohno originated the manufacturing concept of *Just in Time,* where materials and components arrive at a factory or workstation at precisely the moment they are needed for use (no sooner and no later).

Ohno was also fanatically committed to the total elimination of waste. He believed that all waste contributes to higher costs and lower quality. To avoid wasting people, he grouped workers in teams and gave the teams the responsibility to determine how best to accomplish their missions. Of special importance for team members are (a) systematically tracing errors back to their root causes and fixing the problems upstream at their source and (b) developing personal networks throughout the organization so that team members are able to work with everyone else and understand their jobs in an organizational context. Ohno's goals included motivating workers to work smarter, to be more productive, and to do the right things right.

The work of people like Deming, Juran, Ishikawa, Ohno, and many others has resulted in a set of procedures for using total quality management.

TQM Procedure

How does TQM work? There are six steps. *The first step in making TQM work is to form a team. Nothing can get done in TQM without a team.* Teams have to be formed, trained, and developed as the first step of total quality management. Kinlaw (1991), for example, concluded that (a) team development must precede all other kinds of improvement initiatives and (b) teams, more than executive leadership, cultural change, TQM training, or any other strategy, account for most major improvements in organizations. Team development must be strategically placed at the very center of TQM and must form the hub around which other elements (customer satisfaction, supplier performance, measurement and assessment) revolve. Teams are the primary units of performance in organizations. They are the most direct sources of continuous improvement.

The second step is to select a process (subsystem) for improvement. The team needs a specific, definable process to work on. There are four questions the team asks about the process selected: (1) How significant is the process (guard against investing more time and energy in a particular subsystem than makes sense)? (2) What is the potential payoff for working on it? (3) Is it a minor modification of the status quo or a meaningful change? and (4) Is it of realistic size (can the team actually study and improve the process)?

The third step is to define the system clearly, using tools such as flowcharts and cause-and-effect diagrams. The team cannot improve a process until the process has been defined. The best way to define the process is to draw a picture of it.

The fourth step is to develop a design for gathering information about the process to analyze its effectiveness. There are three parts to this step. First, quantifiable factors (such as time) have to be identified. If it cannot be counted, it cannot be improved (conversely, to be able to improve it, you must be able to count it). Second, a design for gathering the relevant data has to be developed. This includes specifying what data will be collected, who will collect it, when will it be collected, and how will it be collected. Finally, the data have to be analyzed and portrayed in a way that team members (and other organizational members) can easily understand.

The fifth step is to generate an improvement theory or plan based on the analysis of the data collected. The theory or plan specifies how the process has to be modified or replaced in order to improve the quality of the team's work. The plan is then implemented in a few settings. The implementation is carefully evaluated (more data are gathered). If the modified process works, it is fully adopted. If it does not work, it is redesigned and tried out again on a small basis.

The sixth step is to institutionalize the changes that work and the continuous improvement process. Ensure that there is no backsliding (reverting to the old practices) by taking new data samples forever, analyzing them, revising the theory or plan, revising the process, and so forth.

DEALING WITH PROBLEM BEHAVIORS IN TEAMS

A General Electric Company (GE) plant in Salisbury, North Carolina, typically changes product models a dozen times a day by using a team system to produce lighting panel boards. This plant has increased productivity by a remarkable 250% compared with GE plants that produced the same products in 1985. The success of GE and other companies in using teams, however, does not mean that teams are problem free. Sooner or later, all teams have to deal with one or more members whose actions are causing the team problems. Problem behaviors may result from obstacles to effective team functioning. *The first obstacle is lack of team maturity.* Groups ordinarily require some time to develop and stabilize their patterns of working. *The second obstacle is the team's history.* Norms rooted in past practice can sometimes adversely influence team members' current behavior. *The third obstacle is the mixed motives of team members.* Individuals' motives are almost never purely cooperative. In varying degrees, members may desire team success, but at the same time each member may also desire to have his or her own interests satisfied. Each person may wish to be a star in order to secure individual rewards as well as contribute to the team's success. *Finally, obstructive individual behaviors may interfere with team effectiveness.* Despite good intentions, some people talk too much, argue too often, intimidate others, wander from the topic, become unnecessarily obsessed over detail, acquiesce too soon, stubbornly resist, and generally behave in a very human fashion, complete with neurotic and nonneurotic foibles that obstruct group functioning.

When individuals first start working in teams, they sometimes engage in unhelpful behaviors. Whenever inappropriate member behavior occurs, the team leader's first move should be towards strengthening the perceived interdependence within the work situation. Four of the most common behavioral problems are passive uninvolvement, active uninvolvement, independence, and taking charge.

Passive Uninvolvement

When members are turning away from the team, not participating, not paying attention to the team's work, saying little or nothing, showing no enthusiasm, or not bringing their work or materials, other members may wish to:

1. Jigsaw materials so that each team member has information the others need. If the passive and uninvolved member does not voluntarily contribute his or her information, the other team members will actively involve the member.
2. Divide up roles and assign to the passive, uninvolved member a role that is essential to the team's success.
3. Reward the team on the basis of its average performance, which will encourage other team members to derive strategies for increasing the problem member's involvement.

Active Uninvolvement

When a member is talking about everything but work, leaving the team, attempting to sabotage the team's work by giving wrong answers or destroying the team's product, refusing to do work, or refusing to work with another team member, team leaders may wish to give a reward that this member or team finds especially attractive and structure the task so that all members must work steadily and contribute in order for the team to succeed and attain the reward. Assigning the member a specific role to fulfill, making the member a team observer with high accountability to collect data about team functioning, and sitting in on the team-processing session and confronting the member are other possibilities.

Independence

When you see a team member working alone and ignoring the team discussion, you may wish to:

1. Limit the resources in the team. If there is only one set of materials or piece of equipment in the team, the member will be unable to work independently.
2. Jigsaw materials so that the member cannot do the work without the other members' information. To complete the task the independent member must interact and collaborate.

Taking Charge

When one team member is doing all the work, refusing to let other members participate, ordering other members around, bullying other members, or making decisions for the team without checking to see if the other members agree, team leaders may wish to:

1. Jigsaw resources so that the task cannot be completed without the staff member encouraging others to participate and the staff member listening carefully to the other members' contributions.
2. Assign roles so that other team members have the most powerful and dominant roles.

3. Reward the team on the basis of the lowest two performances by team members. This will place pressure on the person taking charge to encourage and help other members learn the material and complete the task.

Teams Are Not Everything

Given all the research, teams will become the primary unit of performance in high-performance organizations. But that does not mean that teams will crowd out individual opportunity and formal hierarchy and process. Rather, teams will enhance existing structures without replacing them. An opportunity to use teams exists anywhere in an organization. Every organization, furthermore, faces specific performance challenges for which teams are the most practical and powerful vehicle at management's disposal.

SUMMARY

A *team* is a set of interpersonal interactions structured to achieve established goals. Teams may be differentiated from small groups and from working groups. A team's performance includes team work products that require the joint efforts of two or more members as well as individual work products. Teams may be classified in a number of ways, such as by the setting in which they are used (work, sports, learning), their use in an organization (problem solving, special purpose, self-managing), or what they do (recommend, make or do something, run things). Through the use of modern electronics (such as e-mail, bulletin boards, and computer conferences), teams can consist of individuals who are widely separated geographically. Teams exist within organizational contexts that greatly influence their effectiveness by presenting opportunities and constraints. A general estimate is that over 85% of the behavior of members of an organization is directly attributable to the organization's structure, not the nature of the individuals involved. There are basically two organizational contexts—a mass-production organizational structure or a team-based, high-performance organizational structure. The team-based organizational structure is considered to be the wave of the future because of the relationship between teams and productivity. A number of recent meta-analyses have all found that under a wide range of conditions teams are more effective than having individuals work by themselves. The productivity of teams is not a simple function of team members' technical competencies and task abilities. To be productive, teams (like all groups) must ensure that members perceive strong positive interdependence, interact in ways that promote each other's success and well-being, be individually accountable, employ their small team skills, and process how effectively the team has been working.

If high-quality products and services are to be created, organizations are well advised to use teams. Teams are the basic unit of performance for most organizations. Teams need to be formed, carefully structured to be effective, and nurtured. Nurturing teams includes training and retraining members on both taskwork and teamwork skills as well as engaging in team-building procedures to ensure that their effectiveness keeps improving. The point of carefully structuring teams, training team members, and building team effectiveness is to deliver high-quality products and services to customers. Implementing total quality management procedures involves focusing on the process by which work gets done rather than on inspecting the finished product or service. Teams have to be able to draw flowcharts of the way they work and measure their productiveness. Finally, no matter how carefully teams are formed and developed, there are problem behaviors that must be dealt with. Through progressively refining procedures and continuously improving members' teamwork skills and the team's procedures, the problems can be solved.

Epilogue

I am cast upon a horrible, desolate island; void of all hope of recovery.
I am singled out and separated, as it were, from all the world, to be
miserable. I am divided from mankind, a solitary; one banished from
human society. I have no soul to speak to or to relieve me.

Daniel Defoe (1908, p. 51)

When Robinson Crusoe was cast up on the shore of a tropical island, the lone survivor of a shipwreck, he had everything he needed for a comfortable life. He had more than adequate food, the climate was ideal, and the setting was beautiful. Although he was thankful for being alive, he cursed his solitary life. He was emotionally miserable because he was no longer a member of any human group.

Humans are small group beings. We always have been and we always will be. The ubiquitousness of groups and the inevitability of being in them make groups one of the most important factors in our lives. As the effectiveness of our groups go, so goes the quality of our lives. Quite often groups are not very effective. To create an effective group, you need to follow a set of guidelines.

GUIDELINES FOR CREATING EFFECTIVE GROUPS

Guideline 1

The first guideline is to establish clear, operational, relevant group goals that create positive interdependence and evoke a high level of commitment from every member. Groups exist for a reason. People join groups to achieve goals they are unable to achieve by themselves. To be effective, goals must be clear so that all members understand the nature of the goals, the goals must be operational so that members understand how to achieve the goals, the goals must be relevant to members' needs so that they commit themselves to achieve the goals, and the goals must create positive interdependence among members. There are hundreds of studies indicating that group effectiveness, group cohesion, and the well-being of members depends on members believing that they "sink or swim together." If clear and operational positive goal interdependence is not established in a group, then all the following guidelines become meaningless.

Guideline 2

Once positive goal interdependence has been established, group members must communicate with each other to coordinate their efforts. The second guideline, therefore, is to establish an effective, two-way communication within which members communicate their ideas and feelings accurately and clearly. Communication is the basis for human interaction and group functioning. Members must send and receive messages effectively in order to exchange information and transmit meaning. Barriers to open and accurate communication, such as competition among members, must be minimized. Two-way communication is required for effective group work.

Guideline 3

The third guideline is to ensure that leadership and participation are distributed among all group members. All members are responsible for providing leadership. The equalization of participation and leadership makes certain that all members are involved in the group's work, committed to implementing the group's decisions, and satisfied with their membership. It also (a) assures that the resources of every member are fully utilized and (b) increases the cohesiveness of the group. Leadership is discussed in Chapter 5.

Guideline 4

The fourth guideline for creating an effective group is to ensure that the use of power is distributed among group members and patterns of influence vary according to the needs of the group as members strive to achieve their mutual goals. Members' power is based on expertise, ability, and access to information, not on authority or personality characteristics. In order to implement this guideline, there are two important principles: (a) Power exists in relationships, not individuals; and (b) for power to be constructive, the context in which it is used has to be cooperative. This dynamic-interdependent view of power assumes that (a) power inevitably exists in all relationships, (b) the use of power is essential to all aspects of group functioning, (c) the use of power is dynamic in that who is influencing whom to what degree changes constantly as the group proceeds in working to achieve its goal, and (d) power is distributed among all group members. Power is discussed in Chapter 6.

Guideline 5

The fifth guideline is to match flexibly decision-making procedures with the needs of the situation. There are many different ways groups can make decisions. There must be a balance between the availability of time and resources (such as members' skills) and the method of decision making used. Another balance must be struck among the size and seriousness of the decision, the commitment needed to put it into practice, and the method used for making the decision. The most effective way of making a decision is usually by consensus (unanimous agreement). Consensus promotes distributed participation, the equalization of power, productive controversy, cohesion, involvement, and commitment. Decision making is discussed in Chapter 7.

Guideline 6

The sixth guideline is for group members to engage in controversy by disagreeing with and challenging each other's conclusions and reasoning, thus promoting creative decision making and problem solving. In order to make effective decisions, members must present the best case possible for each major alternative course of action and subject all other alternatives to critical analysis. Controversies (conflicts among opposing ideas and conclusions) promote involvement in the group's work, quality and creativity in decision making, and commitment to implementing the group's decisions. The controversy procedure ensures that minority opinions are accepted and used. Such intellectual conflict results in more creative, effective decisions. Controversy and creativity are discussed in Chapter 8.

Guideline 7

The seventh guideline is for group members to face their conflicts of interests (conflicts promoted by incompatible needs or goals, scarce resources, and by competitiveness) and engage in problem-solving (integrative) negotiations to resolve them. There are five basic strategies to manage conflicts of interests: withdrawal, forcing (distributive, win-lose negotiations), smoothing, compromise, and problem solving (integrative negotiations). The more effective the group, the more frequently conflicts of interests will be valued for their potential constructive outcomes and resolved through problem-solving negotiations. Where problem-solving negotiations fail, another group member needs to mediate. Even in intergroup and cross-ethnic conflicts, problem-solving negotiations need to be used. When they are resolved constructively, conflicts are an important and indispensable aspect of increasing group effectiveness. Conflicts of interest are discussed in Chapter 9.

LEARNING GROUP SKILLS

To ensure that groups are effective, members must be highly skilled in small group skills. Humans are not born with these skills; they must be developed. You have completed a variety of experiences aimed at increasing your group knowledge and skills. It is hoped that you are now a more effective group member. It is hoped that you are able to apply your increased skills and knowledge in a variety of groups and under a variety of conditions. You may wish to repeat many of the exercises in this book to reinforce your knowledge and to reread much of the material to gain a more complete understanding of how to utilize group skills. There are, however, two concluding exercises that may be helpful in applying the material covered in this book to the memberships you hold in groups.

Exercise 14.1: **Terminating a Group**

The goals of this exercise are to (a) complete any unfinished business in a group, (b) relive and remember the positive group experiences the group has had, (c) synthesize what group members have received from being part of the group, and (d) describe and express constructively group members' feelings about the termination of the group. The theme of the exercise is that although every group ends, the things you as a member have given and received, the ways in which you have grown, and the skills you have learned all continue with you. Terminating relationships may be sad, but the ways in which you have grown within your relationships with other group members can be applied to group situations in the future. Here is the procedure for the group to follow in the exercise:

1. Discuss the topic, "Is there anything that needs to be resolved, discussed, dealt with, or expressed before the group ends?"
2. Discuss these questions: "What have been the most significant experiences of the group? What have I gotten out of being a member of the group? How has being a part of this group facilitated my growth as a person? What skills have I learned from being in this group?" As alternatives to a discussion, group members might make a painting, a collage, or a poem describing their experiences.
3. Discuss how you feel about the group winding up its activities and what feelings you want to express about the termination. Personal styles of handling the dissolution of a group may be discussed. If you cannot discuss this issue, the following alternatives may generate a productive discussion:
   a. Each of you in turn says goodbye to the group and leaves. Each of you then spends five minutes thinking about your feelings and returns to express anything you wanted to but did not express before.
   b. Each of you nonverbally shows how you felt when you first joined the group and then shows nonverbally how you feel now.
4. As a closing exercise, stand up in a close circle. You are all to imagine that you have the magical power to give anything you wish to another group member. You are then to give the person on your right a parting gift, each taking your turn so that everyone in the group can hear what the gifts are. Examples of what individuals might give are moonbeams, a flower, a better self-concept, an ability to commit oneself to a relationship, comfort with conflict, more empathy with others, the perfect love affair, and so on. When giving the gift, extend your hands as if actually passing something to the other person.
5. Have a group hug.

Exercise 14.2: **Self-Contract**

Write a description of yourself as a group member. Mention all the strengths and skills you can think of, and mention the areas in which you need to increase your skills. Then make a contract with yourself to make some changes in your life; the contract can involve starting something new, stopping something old, or changing some present aspect of your life. It should involve applying your group skills to the actual group situations you are now facing, or working to develop certain skills further. It may involve joining new groups and terminating old group memberships. In making the contract, pick several group memberships you now have and set a series of goals concerning how you will behave to increase your effectiveness and satisfaction as a group member. Write the contract down, place it in an envelope, address the envelope to yourself, and open it three months later.

Appendix: Answers

3.6: Broken Squares Exercise: *Directions for Making a Set of Squares*

For each five-member group you will need a set of five envelopes containing pieces of cardboard that have been cut in different patterns and that, when properly arranged with pieces from some of the other four envelopes, will form five squares of equal size. To prepare a set, cut out five cardboard squares of equal size, approximately 6 × 6 inches. Place the squares in a row and make them as below, penciling the letters "a," "b," "c," and so on lightly so that they can later be erased.

The lines should be so drawn that when the pieces are cut out, all pieces marked "a" will be ex-

actly the same size, the pieces marked "c" will be the same size, and the pieces marked "f" will be the same size. By using multiples of 3 inches, several combinations will be possible that will enable participants to form one or two squares, but one combination is possible that will form five squares 6 × 6 inches.

After drawing the lines of the 6- × 6-inch squares and labeling them with the lowercase letters, cut each square as marked into smaller pieces to make the parts of the puzzle.

Mark the five envelopes "A," "B," "C," "D," and "E," and distribute the cardboard pieces among them as follows:

Envelope A has pieces i, h, e.
Envelope B has pieces a, a, a, c.
Envelope C has pieces a, j.
Envelope D has pieces d, f.
Envelope E has pieces g, b, f, c.

Erase the penciled letter from each piece and write on it instead its appropriate envelope letter. This relabeling will make it easy, when a group has completed the task, to return the pieces to the proper envelope for later use.

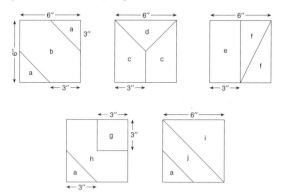

3.7: Goal Structures Exercise: *Answers*

Squares: 40
Biangles: 11
Triangles: 18

4.2: Bewise College Problem: Solution

Name	Background	Education Degree	Teaching Experience	Public Relations Experience	Administrative Experience
David Wolcott	African American	Master's	13 years	None	8 years
Roger Thornton	Upper-class family	B.A., master's	7 years	9 years; politician	16 years
Edythe Holubec	Community center director	None	8 years	2 years	7 years
Frank Pierce	Neighborhood center worker; community relations	Master's	None	14 years	14 years
Helen Johnson	Childhood in slums	B.A., master's	4 years	5 years	15 years
Keith Clement	Volunteer work: author of a book	B.A.	5 years	13 years	None

Andrews College is the smallest college in the state, and therefore it had a completely black American student body in 1952.

As is evident from the table, all candidates but Helen Johnson are disqualified because they lack one of the qualifications outlined in the data sheets.

4.3: Solstice-Shenanigans Mystery: Solution

The Solstice-Shenanigans Mystery Exercise appears on page 154. The painting by Artisimisso was stolen by Mr. Handsome, who took it with him when he left the party at 9:50. He took the painting because he was a kleptomaniac.

4.4: Liepz and Bounz Exercise: Solution

The Liepz and Bounz Exercise is on page 156. David jogged from Farmland to Muncie in one (5/5) jumpz.

4.6: Square Arrangement I: One-Way Communication

Instructions: Study the arrangement. With your back to the group members, instruct them on how to draw the squares. Begin with the top square and describe each in succession, taking particular note of the placement of each in relation to the preceding one. No questions allowed.

4.6: Square Arrangement II: Two-Way Communication

Instructions: Study the arrangement shown. Facing the group, instruct the members on how to draw the squares. Begin with the top square and describe each in succession, taking particular note of the placement of each in relation to the preceding one. Answer all questions from participants and repeat your description if necessary.

5.7: *Furniture Factory Exercise: Solution*

The more directly Mr. Day involves the workers in the change, the more likely they are to support the change.

a. 5
b. 1
c. 3
d. 4
e. 2

5.11: *Hollow Square Exercise*

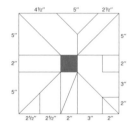

7.3: *Winter Survival Exercise*

BACKGROUND INFORMATION FOR COORDINATOR

None of the information here should be given to participants until after they have completed the decision-making parts of the exercise. Mid-January is the coldest time of the year in Minnesota and Manitoba. The first problem the survivors face, therefore, is to preserve their body heat and protect themselves against its loss. This problem can be met by building a fire, minimizing movement and exertion, using as much insulation as possible, and constructing a shelter.

The participants have just crash-landed. Many individuals tend to overlook the enormous shock reaction this has upon the human body, and the death of the pilot and copilot increases the shock. Decision making under such conditions is extremely difficult. Such a situation requires a strong emphasis upon the use of reasoning, not only for making decisions, but also for reducing the fear and panic every survivor would naturally feel. Shock is manifested in feelings of helplessness, loneliness, and hopelessness as well as in fear. These feelings have brought about more fatalities than perhaps any other cause in survival situations. Through the use of reasoning, hope for survival and the will to live can be generated. Certainly the state of shock means that the movement of the survivors should be at a minimum and that an attempt to calm them should be made.

Before taking off, a pilot always has to file a flight plan. The flight plan contains the vital information regarding the flight, such as the course, speed, estimated time of arrival, type of aircraft, and number of persons on board. Search-and-rescue operations would begin shortly after the failure of the plane to appear at its destination at its estimated time of arrival.

The twenty miles to the nearest known town is a long walk even under ideal conditions, particularly if one is not used to walking such distances. Under the circumstances of being in shock, being dressed in city clothes, and having deep snow in the woods and a variety of water barriers to cross, to attempt to walk out would mean almost certain death from freezing and exhaustion. At temperatures of minus 25 to minus 40 degrees Fahrenheit the loss of body heat through exertion is a very serious matter.

Once the survivors have found ways in which to keep warm, their immediate problem is to attract the attention of search planes and search parties. Thus, all the items the group has salvaged must be assessed for their value in signaling the group's whereabouts.

Winter Survival Exercise: Answer Key

Item	Experts' Ranking	Your Ranking	Difference Score
Ball of steel wool	2		
Newspapers (one per person)	8		
Compass	12		
Hand ax	6		
Cigarette lighter (without fluid)	1		
Loaded .45-caliber pistol	9		
Sectional air map made of plastic	11		
20 × 20-ft piece of heavy-duty canvas	5		
Extra shirt and pants for each survivor	3		
Can of shortening	4		
Quart of 100-proof whiskey	10		
Family-size chocolate bar (one per person)	7		
Total			_____

EXPLANATION OF ANSWER KEY

The following ranking of the survivors' items was made on the basis of information provided by Mark Wanvig and Roger Johnson and supplemented by Rutstrum (1973). Wanvig was an instructor in survival training for three years in the reconnaissance school in the 101st Division of the U.S. Army and later an instructor in wilderness survival for four years at the Twin City Institute for Talented Youth. He is now conducting wilderness-survival programs for Minneapolis teachers. Johnson is a national expert on environmental education.

1. *Cigarette lighter (without fluid).* The gravest danger facing the group is exposure to the cold. The greatest need is for a source of warmth and the second greatest need is for signaling devices. This makes building a fire the first order of business. Without matches something is needed to produce sparks to start a fire. Even without fluid the cigarette lighter can be used to produce sparks. The fire will provide not only warmth but also smoke for daytime signaling and firelight for nighttime signaling.
2. *Ball of steel wool.* To make a fire, the survivors need a means of catching the sparks made by the cigarette lighter. Steel wool is the best substance with which to catch a spark and support a flame, even if it is a little wet.

3. *Extra shirt and pants for each survivor.* Clothes are probably the most versatile items one can have in a situation like this. Besides adding warmth to the body they can be used for shelter, signaling, bedding, bandages, string when unraveled, and tinder to make fires. Even maps can be drawn on them. The versatility of clothes and the need for fires, signaling devices, and warmth make these items third in importance.
4. *Can of shortening.* This item has many uses—the most important being that a mirrorlike signaling device can be made from the lid. After shining the lid with the steel wool, the survivors can use it to produce an effective reflector of sunlight. A mirror is the most powerful tool they have for communicating their presence. In sunlight, a simple mirror can generate five to seven million candlepower. The reflected sunbeam can be seen beyond the horizon. Its effectiveness is somewhat limited by the trees, but one member of the group could climb a tree and use the mirror to signal search planes. If the survivors had no other means of signaling than this, they would still have a better than 80% chance of being rescued within the first twenty-four hours.

    Other uses for this item are as follows: The shortening can be rubbed on exposed areas of the body, such as the face, lips, and hands, for protection from the cold. In desperation it could be eaten in small amounts. When melted into an oil the shortening is helpful in starting fires. When soaked into a piece of cloth, melted shortening will produce an effective candlewick. The can is useful in melting snow to produce drinking water. Even in winter water is important, as the body loses water in many ways, such as through perspiration, respiration, and shock. This water must be replenished, because dehydration affects one's ability to make clear decisions. The can is also useful as a cup.

5. *Twenty by twenty-foot piece of heavy-duty canvas.* The cold makes some form of shelter necessary. The canvas can be part of a shelter, protecting the survivors from the wind and possible snow. Spread on a frame and secured, it could make a good tent as well as a ground cover. Rigged as a wind screen, it could hold heat. Its squareness, contrasting with the surrounding terrain, might also be spotted in an air search, and this makes it an important signaling device.

6. *Hand ax.* The survivors need a continuous supply of wood in order to maintain the fire. The ax is useful in obtaining wood, and also for clearing a sheltered campsite, cutting boughs for ground insulation, and constructing a frame for the shelter.

7. *Family-size chocolate bars (one per person).* To gather wood for the fire and to set up signals, the survivors need energy. The chocolate will supply the energy to sustain them for some time. Because it contains mostly carbohydrates, it supplies energy without making digestive demands upon the body.

8. *Newspapers (one per person).* The newspaper can be used for starting a fire. It will also serve as an insulator: When rolled up and placed under the clothes around a person's legs and arms, it provides dead-air space for extra protection from the cold. The survivors can use the paper for recreation by reading it, memorizing it, folding it, or tearing it. They can roll it into a cone and yell through it as a signal device. They can also spread it around an area to help signal a rescue party.

9. *Loaded .45-caliber pistol.* The pistol provides a sound-signaling device. (The international distress signal is three shots fired in rapid succession.) There have been numerous cases of survivors going undetected because they were too weak to make a loud enough noise to attract attention. The butt of the pistol can be used as a hammer. The powder from the shells will assist in fire building. By placing a small bit of cloth in a cartridge emptied of its bullet, one can start a fire by firing the gun at dry wood on the ground. At night the muzzle blast of the gun is visible, and this provides another means of signaling.

The pistol's advantages are counterbalanced by its dangerous disadvantages. Anger, frustration, impatience, irritability, and lapses of rationality may increase as the group waits to be rescued. The availability of a lethal weapon is a substantial danger to the group under these conditions. Although the pistol could be used for hunting, it would take a highly skilled marksman to kill an animal with it. Even then the animal would have to be transported through the snow to the crash area, which would probably consume more energy than would be advisable.

10. *Quart of 100-proof whiskey.* The only uses of the whiskey are as an aid in fire building and as a fuel. A torch could be made from a piece of clothing soaked in the whiskey and attached to an upright pole. The danger of whiskey is that someone might try to drink it when it is cold. Alcohol takes on the temperature it is exposed to, and a drink of it at minus 30 degrees Fahrenheit would freeze a person's esophagus and stomach and do considerable damage to the mouth. Drinking it warm would cause dehydration. Alcohol, furthermore, mixes badly with cold because it dilates the blood vessels in the skin. This results in chilled blood being carried back to the heart, which in turn chills the heart and contributes to a rapid loss of body heat. An intoxicated person is much more likely to get hypothermia than a nonintoxicated person. The bottle may be used to store heated water.

11. *Compass.* Because the compass may also encourage some survivors to try to walk to the nearest town, it too is a dangerous item. The only redeeming feature of the compass is the possible use of its glass top as a reflector of sunlight to signal search planes, but

this would be the least effective of the potential signaling devices available. That it might tempt survivors to walk away from the crash site makes it the least desirable of the twelve items.

12. *Sectional air map made of plastic.* This item is dangerous because it will encourage individuals to attempt to walk to the nearest town—thereby condemning them to almost certain death.

7.4: They'll Never Take Us Alive Exercise: Answer Key

Item	Experts' Ranking	Your Ranking	Difference Score
Swimming	5		
Railroads	7		
Police work	11		
Home appliances	9		
Alcohol	2		
Nuclear power	12		
Smoking	1		
Motor vehicles	3		
Pesticides	15		
Handguns	4		
Bicycles	8		
Firefighting	10		
Mountain climbing	13		
Vaccinations	14		
Surgery	6		
Total			_____

8.3: Stranded in the Desert Exercise: Scoring, Key

Item	Experts' Ranking	Your Ranking	Difference Score
Magnetic compass	12		
20-ft by 20-ft piece of heavy-duty canvas	7		
Book, *Plants of the Desert*	10		
Rear-view mirror	1		
Large knife	5		
Flashlight (four-battery size)	8		
One jacket per person	2		
One transparent plastic ground cloth (6 × 4 feet) per person	4		
Loaded .38-caliber pistol	9		
One 2-quart plastic canteen full of water per person	3		
Accurate map of the area	11		
Large box of kitchen matches	6		
Total			_____

Score your group's ranking by finding the absolute difference between your ranking and the experts' ranking. An absolute difference is found by recording the difference between the two rankings while ignoring all plus or minus signs. After finding all the absolute differences, sum them. The lower your total score, the more accurate your ranking.

STRANDED IN THE DESERT: RATIONALE FOR EXPERTS' RANKING

The group has just been through a traumatic situation that has had a shocking impact on all members. The fact that your advisor and the driver were killed would increase the shock reaction. Most, if not all, members of your group need to receive treatment for shock. Five of the more important problems for your group are as follows (Nesbitt, Pond, & Allen, 1959). One vital problem for the group members is dehydration from exposure to the sun, from bodily activity (causing perspiration and respiration), and from the hot dry air circulating next to the skin. To prevent dehydration the group members should (a) remain calm to reduce loss of moisture through respiration, (b) wear as many clothes as you can to reduce the loss of moisture through perspiration and having the dry desert air circulate next to your skin (by wearing sufficient clothes to keep the desert air away from your skin you can lengthen your survival time by at least a day), (c) stay in the shade, (d) minimize movement, especially during the day, and (e) drink as much water as you can. Any activity that increases heartbeat, respiration, and perspiration will speed up dehydration. Taking care to remain calm and in the shade, the group could probably survive three days without water. The need for clothes makes the jackets important. The need for shade makes the canvas important. To survive you must keep your body properly hydrated either with adequate water or by keeping body-heat production down and keeping desert heat (from sun, air, and ground reflection) out. Once the jackets are on and the sunshade is up, everyone should be as calm and inactive as possible.

Another vital problem is signaling search parties of your whereabouts so that you may be rescued. The items that may be used to signal your presence are the mirror, the canvas, the flashlight, the revolver, and a fire (matches). The mirror is the most important signaling device the group has. As Nesbitt, Pond, and Allen (1959) state, "A signal mirror is the best, the simplest, the most important piece of survival equipment ever invented for the desert." In sunlight the mirror can generate five to seven million candlepower of light, which may be seen beyond the horizon. It pays to flash the mirror at the horizon even when no plane is in view; search planes have turned toward a mirror flash even when the survivors have neither seen nor heard them. The canvas, when spread out to make a shelter, not only can reduce the temperature underneath it by as much as 20 degrees Fahrenheit, but can also be easily spotted from the air because it contrasts with the terrain. The flashlight provides a reliable and quick night signaling device. The pistol is an important sound signaling device, because speech becomes seriously impaired due to dehydration. In the desert setting there have been numerous occurrences of searchers not detecting the people they were looking for because the survivors could not make loud enough noises to attract the searchers' attention. There are important disadvantages to having the revolver in the hands of a group member who may become hysterical due to the trauma of the situation or delusional due to dehydration. Finally, building a fire at night and using smoke columns during the day will help attract the attention of searchers. "A column of smoke by day, a pillar of fire by night" is a biblical quotation worth remembering for desert signaling.

The third major problem is obtaining as much drinkable water as possible. The water you have in your canteens is enough to keep you rational for a while, but not enough to extend your survival time. That is, the water in the canteens is enough to hold off the effects of dehydration for a while; without water, within twenty-four hours you can expect to have impatience, nausea, and sleepiness interfere with rational decision making. The only way in which you may obtain purified water to drink from the shallow hole nearby is to build a solar still. The still is built by stretching the ground cloths a few inches above the waterhole and tilting them so that they drain into the canteens. The knife is helpful in cutting the stakes necessary to arrange the ground cloths. When the sun shines through the plastic onto the water, condensation forms on the underside of the plastic. The moisture is distilled and purified water.

The fourth problem is protecting yourself from the cold at night. Although the desert is hot during the day, it still gets cold at night. The jackets become important to protect the group members from the cold, as do the matches (to build a fire), and the canvas (to provide a shelter).

The fifth problem is gathering food if the group is not rescued in the first few days. It is important not to eat protein, as it takes considerable water to digest protein and flush out the waste products. The book on plants will be helpful in obtaining food. Hunting for animals, furthermore, would cause dehydration and would do far more harm than good.

If the group decides to walk out, traveling at night, all members will probably be dead by the second day. They will have walked less than thirty-three miles during the two nights. If group members decide to walk during the day, they will probably be dead by the next morning, after walking less than twelve miles. For the group to walk out, having just gone through a traumatic experience that has had a considerable impact on the body, having few if any members who have walked forty-five miles before, and having to carry the canvas and wear the jackets to prevent dehydration, would be disastrous. One further fact of great importance: Once the members start walking, they will be much harder to spot by search parties. The compass and the map, therefore, are not helpful to the group's survival.

8.5: Fallout Shelter Exercise*: Answers

_1 Containers of water. (The average person would need at least 1 quart of liquid per day. Each person should be allowed to drink according to need because studies have shown that nothing is gained by limiting the liquids below the amount demanded by the body. Two weeks is probably the maximum time needed to stay in the shelter. After that, other sources of water could be found.)

_2 Canned and dried foods. (Enough food should be on hand to feed everyone for two weeks, if possible. However, most people can get along on about half as much food as usual and can survive for several days without any. Therefore, this is not as important as the water.)

_3 1 large and 1 small garbage can with lids. (Next to water and food, the next most important concern is sanitation. Poor sanitation will attract diseases and vermin. The small garbage can can be used as a toilet and the large garbage can can be used to store garbage and human wastes until they can be taken outside and buried. Burial of the garbage is important to prevent spread of disease by rats or insects.)

_4 First-aid kit and iodine and medicines. (Useful if anyone gets hurt or falls ill; should include medicine for anyone with chronic illness. The iodine can be used to sterilize water.)

_5 Battery-powered radio. (Useful for obtaining information about what is happening outside the shelter and for information on when it is safe to come out. Useful for contact with outside world.)

_6 Soap and towels. (Useful and important for sanitation.)

_7 Liquid chlorine bleach. (Useful for sprinkling in the toilet to keep down odors and germs; it could also be used to sterilize any water that has become cloudy and thereby might contain bacteria.)

_8 Matches and candles. (They would help illuminate the shelter and thus make it more comfortable, particularly because there is not likely to be any natural source of light or electricity available.)

_9 Blankets. (They would be used for heat and comfort; they would be of important but moderate use.)

10 Flashlight and batteries. (Useful for illumination.)

11 Cooking and eating utensils. (Useful in preparing and serving foods, but not essential.)

12 Broom. (Useful for brushing radioactive fallout off anyone who had to leave the shelter for emergency reasons before he or she reentered.)

13 Canned heat stove. (Useful if a heat supply is needed. However, it can be used only if there is adequate ventilation for the fumes; it could be dangerous.)

14 Geiger counter. (Unnecessary. It could be used to check level of radiation outside the shelter to determine when it is safe to emerge, but the same information and more can be obtained from the radio. Also, fallout particles are visible and the radiation from them is given off quickly, so danger from radiation could be reduced by waiting twenty-four to forty-eight hours after the large particles have stopped falling.)

15 Foam fire extinguisher. (Useful for fighting fires outside the shelter but could not be used within the shelter because of danger from the fumes.)

*This exercise is based on information in *Protection in the Nuclear Age* (Washington, D.C.: Department of Defense, Civil Defense Preparedness Agency, February 1977).

8.6: *The Johnson School Exercise: Solution*

The following Johnsons coached the sports in the order listed.

1. Frank coached golf, basketball, wrestling, and track.
2. Roger coached basketball, golf, track, and wrestling.
3. David coached wrestling, track, basketball, and golf.
4. Helen coached track, wrestling, golf, and basketball.

8.9: *Creativity Problem: Solution*

The solution of this problem is based upon the creative insight of going outside the obvious boundaries of the dots.

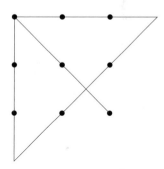

8.10: *Joe Doodlebug Exercise: Hints*

1. Joe does not always have to face the food in order to eat it.
2. Joe can jump sideways and backward, as well as forward.
3. Read the problem again: Joe was moving east when the food was presented.

Joe Doodlebug Exercise: Solution

At the moment Joe's master set down the food, Joe had already jumped once to the east. He therefore has to jump sideways three times more to the east, and once sideways back to the west, landing on top of the food. He can now eat.

9.2: Making a Profit Exercise: Buyer Profit Sheet

Oil			Gas			Coal	
Price	*Profit*		*Price*	*Profit*		*Price*	*Profit*
A	$4,000		A	$2,000		A	$1,000
B	3,500		B	1,750		B	875
C	3,000		C	1,500		C	750
D	2,500		D	1,250		D	625
E	2,000		E	1,000		E	500
F	1,500		F	750		F	375
G	1,000		G	500		G	250
H	500		H	250		H	125
I	0		I	0		I	0

The nine prices for each commodity are represented by the letters A to I. Next to each price is the profit you would make for each commodity if you sold it at that price.

You can say anything you wish during negotiations, but you may *not* show this profit sheet to the buyer you are negotiating with.

Making a Profit Exercise: Seller Profit Sheet

Oil			Gas			Coal	
Price	*Profit*		*Price*	*Profit*		*Price*	*Profit*
A	$ 0		A	$ 0		A	$ 0
B	125		B	250		B	500
C	250		C	500		C	1,000
D	375		D	750		D	1,500
E	500		E	1,000		E	2,000
F	625		F	1,250		F	2,500
G	750		G	1,500		G	3,000
H	875		H	1,750		H	3,500
I	1,000		I	2,000		I	4,000

Glossary

Acceptance: The communication of high regard towards others and their contributions to the group's work.

Action research: The use of the scientific method in solving research questions that have significant social value.

Action theory: Theory as to what actions are needed to achieve a desired consequence in a given situation.

Additive tasks: Tasks for which group productivity represents the sum of individual member efforts.

Ageism: Prejudice against the elderly.

Aggregate: Collections of individuals who do not interact with one another.

Arbitration: A form of third-party intervention in negotiations in which recommendations of the person intervening are binding on the parties involved.

Assimilation: Changing a message to fit into your own cognitive frameworks and perspective.

Attribution theory: A social-psychological explanation of how individuals make inferences about the causes of behaviors and events.

Authority: Legitimate power vested in a particular position to ensure that individuals in subordinate positions meet the requirements of their organizational role.

Autocratic leader: A leader who dictates orders and determines all policy without involving group members in decision making.

Bargaining: See **Negotiation.**

Blaming the victim: Attribution of the cause of discrimination or misfortune to the personal characteristics and actions of the victim.

Brainstorming: A procedure in which group members are asked to produce as many, and as uninhibited, ideas as they possibly can and to withhold criticism in order to optimize creativity.

Cathexis: The investment of psychological energy in objects and events outside of oneself.

Cause-and-effect diagram: Visual representation of the relationship between some effect (the problem being studied) and its possible causes.

Channel: The means of sending a message to another person, such as sound and sight.

Charisma: An extraordinary power, as of working miracles.

Charismatic leader: A person who has (1) an extraordinary power or vision and is able to communicate it to others or (2) unusual powers of practical leadership that will enable her to achieve the goals that will alleviate followers' distress.

Check sheet: Form to record the frequency with which certain events are happening.

Coercive power: When the group leader has control over positive and negative consequences for other group members.

Cognitive dissonance: When a person possesses two cognitions that contradict each other. The theory developed by Leon Festinger predicts that dissonance is uncomfortable and a person will seek to reduce it.

Cognitive structure: A set of principles and processes that organizes cognitive experience.

Cohesiveness: All the forces (both positive and negative) that cause individuals to maintain their membership in specific groups. These include attraction to other group members and a close match between individuals' needs and the goals and activities of the group. The attractiveness that a group has for its members and that the members have for one another.

Communication: A message sent by a person to a receiver (or receivers) with the conscious intent of affecting the receiver's behavior.

Communication networks: Representations of the acceptable paths of communication between persons in a group or organization.

Competitive goal structure: A negative correlation among group members' goal attainments; when group members perceive that they can obtain their goals if and only if the other members with whom they are competitively linked fail to obtain their goal.

Compliance: Behavior in accordance with a direct request. Behavioral change without internal acceptance.

Concurrence-seeking: Situation where members of a decision-making group inhibit discussion to avoid any disagreement or arguments and emphasize agreement; there is a suppression of different conclusions, an emphasis on quick compromise, and a lack of disagreement within a decision-making group.

Conflict: A conflict exists when incompatible activities occur.

Conflict of interests: When the actions of one person attempting to maximize his or her needs and benefits prevent, block, interfere with, injure, or in some way make less effective the actions of another person attempting to maximize his or her needs and benefits.

Conformity: Changes in behavior that result from group influences. Yielding to group pressures when no direct request to comply is made.

Confrontation: The direct expression of one's view of the conflict and one's feelings about it and at the same time an invitation to the opposition to do the same.

Conjunctive tasks: Tasks for which group productivity is determined by the effort or ability of the weakest member.

Consensus: A collective opinion arrived at by a group of individuals working together under conditions that permit communications to be sufficiently open and the group climate to be sufficiently supportive for everyone in the group to feel that he or she has had a fair chance to influence the decision.

Construct: A concept, defined in terms of observable events, used by a theory to account for regularities or relationships in data.

Contingency theory of leadership: A theory suggesting that leader effectiveness is determined both by characteristics of leaders and by several situational factors.

Contractual norms: Statements that spell out the rules to be observed and the penalties for violating them.

Control: When the person being influenced behaves as the one who influences intends.

Controversy: The situation that exists when one group member's ideas, information, conclusions, theories, and opinions are incompatible with those of another, and the two seek to reach an agreement.

Cooperative goal structure: A positive correlation among group members' goal attainments; when group members perceive that they can achieve their goal if and only if the other members with whom they are cooperatively linked obtain their goal.

Cooperative intentions: The expectations that you and other group members are going to behave cooperatively to achieve the group's goals.

Critical path method: Identifying the final goal and working backward to detail what must happen (tasks and subgoals) before it is achieved, what resources must be allocated, what the timetable for accomplishing each subgoal should be, and who should have what responsibilities.

Culture clash: Conflict over basic values among individuals from different cultures.

Debate: Situation where group members present the best case for positions that are incompatible with one another and a winner is declared on the basis of who presented the best position.

Decision making: Obtaining some agreement among group members as to which of several courses of action is most desirable for achieving the group's goals. The process through which groups identify problems in achieving the group's goals and attain solutions to them.

Decision-making tasks: Tasks that require consensus about the best solution to a problem when the correct answer is not known.

Deindividuation: A psychological state characterized by reduced self-awareness and major shifts in perception. It is encouraged by certain external conditions (e.g., anonymity) and enhances the performance of wild, impulsive forms of behavior.

Deliberate discourse: When the advantages and disadvantages of proposed actions are discussed in order to resolve controversy.

Delusion of individualism: When individuals believe that (1) they are separate and apart from all other individuals and, therefore, (2) others' frustration, unhappiness, hunger, despair, and misery have no significant bearing on their own well-being.

Democratic leader: A leader who sets policies through group discussion and decision, encouraging and helping group members to interact, requesting the cooperation of others, and being considerate of members' feelings and needs.

Deutsch, Morton: Social psychologist who theorized about cooperative, competitive, and individualistic goal structures.

Dilemma of honesty and openness: The risk of either being exploited for disclosing too much too quickly or seriously damaging the negotiating relationship by refusing to disclose information and thereby seeming to be deceitful or distrusting.

Dilemma of trust: Choice between believing the other negotiator and risking potential exploitation or disbelieving the other negotiator and risking no agreement.

Discretionary tasks: Tasks for which the group score is any combination of individual efforts the group wants to put together.

Discrimination: Action taken to harm a group or any of its members.

Disjunctive tasks: Tasks for which group performance is determined by the most competent or skilled member.

Disputants: The participants in the conflict who seek mediation.

Distributed-actions theory of leadership: The performance of acts that help the group to complete its task and to maintain effective working relationships among its members.

Distributive (win–lose) negotiations: In this type of negotiation the goal is to maximize your outcomes while minimizing the other person's outcomes.

Dualistic thinking: A type of thinking based on the premise that there is only one right and wrong and authority should not be questioned.

Effective communication: When the receiver interprets the sender's message in the same way the sender intended it.

Effective group: A group whose members commit themselves to the common purpose of maximizing their own and each other's success.

Egocentrism: Embeddedness in one's own viewpoint to the extent that one is unaware of other points of view and of the limitations of one's perspectives.

Equality system of distributive justice: All rewards are distributed equally among group members.

Equity or merit view of distributing rewards: A basic rule of distributive justice and equity theory: In a just distribution, rewards will be distributed among individuals in proportion to their contributions. In other words, those members who contribute the most to the group's success should receive the greatest benefits.

Ethnocentrism: Tendency to regard one's own ethnic group, nation, religion, culture, or gender as better or more correct than others.

Evaluation apprehension: Concern over being evaluated by others. Such concern may increase arousal and may play an important role in social facilitation.

Experiential learning: Generating an action theory from your own experiences and then continually modifying it to improve your effectiveness.

Expert power: When group members believe the leader has a special knowledge or skill and is trustworthy.

Expertise: A person's proficiency, adroitness, competence, and skill.

False consensus bias: A belief (often false) that most other people think and feel very much as we do, such as sharing our stereotypes (e.g., believing that poor people are lazy).

Feedback: Information that allows individuals to compare their actual performance with standards of performance.

Field experiment: A study conducted in a natural setting in which the investigator deliberately produces variations in the natural situation in order to examine their effects on group behavior.

FIRO (fundamental interpersonal relations orientation): A theory of interpersonal behavior based on three interpersonal needs: inclusion, control, and affection.

Flowchart: Visual tool to display all steps in a process.

Force field analysis: Portraying the problem as a balance between forces working in opposite directions—some helping the movement towards the desired state of affairs and others restraining such movement. The balance that results between the helping and restraining forces is the actual state of affairs—a **quasistationary equilibrium** that can be altered through changes in the forces.

Frustration-aggression process: Frustration due to the inability to achieve one's goals produces a readiness to respond in an aggressive manner that may boil over into hostility and violence if situational cues that serve as releasers are present.

Fundamental attribution error: The attribution of the causes of others' behaviors to personal (disposition) factors and the causes of one's own behavior to situational (environmental) factors. In explaining the causes of the others' behavior, the attributor overestimates the causal importance of personality, beliefs, attitudes, and values and underestimates the causal importance of situational pressures. The opposite is done in explaining the causes of one's own behavior.

Gatekeeper: Person who translates and interprets messages, information, and new developments to groupmates. Also called *opinion leader.*

Goal: A desired place towards which people are working; a state of affairs that people value.

Goal structure: The type of social interdependence specified among individuals as they strive to achieve their goals.

Great person theory of leadership: A theory suggesting that all great leaders share key traits that equip them for positions of power and authority.

Group: Two or more individuals in face-to-face interaction, each aware of his or her membership in the group, each aware of the others who belong to the group, and each aware of positive interdependence as they strive to achieve mutual goals.

Group cohesion: The mutual attraction among group members and the resulting desire to remain in the group.

Group dynamics: The area of social science that focuses on advancing knowledge about the nature of group life. The scientific study of behavior in groups to advance our knowledge about the nature of groups, group development, and the interrelations between groups and individuals, other groups, and larger entities.

Group effectiveness: Success by the group in (1) achieving its goals, (2) maintaining good working relationships among members, and (3) developing and adapting to changing conditions to improve its ability to achieve (1) and (2).

Group efficacy: The expectation of successfully obtaining valued outcomes through the joint efforts of the group members.

Group goal: A future state of affairs desired by enough members of a group to motivate the group to work towards its achievement.

Group influence: The impact of groups on their members.

Group polarization: The tendency of group members to shift towards more extreme positions than those held initially, as a function of group discussion.

Group processing: Reflecting on a group session to (1) describe what member actions were helpful and unhelpful and (2) make decisions about what actions to continue or change.

Group structure: A stable pattern of interaction among group members created by a role structure and group norms.

Groupthink: The tendency of members of highly cohesive groups led by dynamic leaders to adhere to shared views so strongly that they totally ignore external information inconsistent with these views. A mode of thinking in which group members' strivings for unanimity override their motivation to appraise alternative courses of action realistically. A strong concurrence-seeking tendency that interferes with effective group decision making.

Hawthorne effect: A change in behavior that occurs when individuals know they are being observed by researchers.

Hero–traitor dynamic: The negotiator who wins is seen as a hero, and the one who loses is perceived to be a traitor.

Hidden agendas: Personal goals that are unknown to all the other group members and are at cross-purposes with the dominant group goals.

High-performance group: A group that meets all effective group criteria and outperforms all reasonable expectations, given its membership. Most groups are unable to achieve this level of development.

Histogram: Visual representation of frequency of how continuous measurement data are clustered and dispersed across a range of values.

Illusionary correlation: Association perceived between two unrelated factors, such as being poor and being lazy, usually leading to stereotypes.

Independent variable: The variable manipulated by the researcher in an experiment; the causal factor in a cause and effect relationship.

Individual accountability: Assessing the quality and quantity of each member's contributions and giving the results to all group members.

Individualistic decision making: When isolated individuals independently decide on a course of action without any interaction or consultation with each other.

Individualistic goal structure: No correlation among group members' goal attainments; when group members perceive that obtaining their goal is unrelated to the goal achievement of other members.

Individuation: Maintaining a sense of unique individual identity.

Inducibility: Openness to influence.

Influence: Using power to change another person in a desired direction.

Influence leader: A person who exerts more influence on other group members than they exert on him.

Information dependence: Dependence on others for information about their preferences, needs, and expectations so that an agreement can be reached.

Information gatekeepers: The people who receive messages from superiors and outside sources or who read, listen, and reflect upon written reports and verbal messages to a greater extent than other group members.

Informational power: When the group leader has informational resources that are useful in accomplishing the goal and are unavailable anywhere else.

Integration: Combining several positions into one new, creative position.

Integrative negotiation: A type of negotiation where the goal is to maximize joint benefits.

Intellective tasks: Problem-solving tasks with correct answers.

Interest: Need, goal, benefit, profit, advantage, concern, right, or claim.

Interpersonal communication: A message sent by a person to a receiver with the conscious intent of affecting the receiver's behavior.

Laissez-faire leader: A leader who does not participate in a group's decision making at all.

Leader: An individual in a group who exerts the greatest influence on other members.

Leadership: The process through which leaders exert their influence on other group members.

Legitimate power: When group members believe the leader should have influence over them because of special role responsibilities (such as police officer) or position in the group (such as employer).

Level of aspiration (LOA): The compromise between ideal goals and more realistic expectations. A concept developed primarily by Kurt Lewin to explain how people set and revise goals for themselves and their groups. Generally, individuals enter situations with an ideal outcome in mind but revise their goals upward after success and downward after failure.

Leveling: Making a message shorter, more concise, and more easily grasped and told. The reciprocal of sharpening.

Lewin, Kurt: Father of group dynamics; social psychologist who originated field theory, experimental group dynamics, and applied group dynamics.

Machiavellian leadership: Leadership based on the beliefs that (1) people are basically weak, fallible, and gullible, and not particularly trustworthy; (2) others are impersonal objects; and (3) one should manipulate others whenever it is necessary in order to achieve one's ends.

Means interdependence: The second major category of interdependence. The ways in which mutual group goals and rewards are to be accomplished (includes resource, role, and task interdependence).

Mediation: A form of third-party intervention in negotiations in which a neutral person recommends a nonbinding agreement.

Mediator: A neutral person who helps two or more people resolve their conflict by assisting them with problem-solving negotiations to reach an agreement that both parties believe is fair, just, and workable.

Message: Any verbal or nonverbal symbol that one person transmits to another; the subject matter being referred to in a symbolic way (all words are symbols).

Modern racism: A more subtle form of prejudice in which people appear on the surface not to harbor prejudice, but who do in fact hold racist attitudes.

Need: A necessity for survival.

Need distribution of rewards: A situation in which the group members who are most in need of the rewards receive a disproportionate amount of them. A rule suggesting that individuals receive a share of available rewards reflecting their current needs.

Negative monitoring: Monitoring unpleasant, unrewarding, frustrating, destructive, counterproductive behaviors.

Negotiation: A process by which persons who want to come to an agreement try to work out a settlement by exchanging proposals and counterproposals.

Noise: Any element that interferes with the communication process.

Nonoperational goals: Goals that are abstract in that the specific steps required to accomplish them are indiscernible; often used to describe broad, long-range goals.

Norm of equity: Norm specifying that the benefits received or the costs assessed by the negotiators should be equal.

Norm of reciprocity: Norm that a negotiator should return the same benefit or harm given him or her by the other negotiator; "an eye for an eye and a kiss for a kiss" is an example of a norm of reciprocity.

Norms: The rules or expectations that specify appropriate behavior in the group; the standards by which group members regulate their actions.

Observational research: The systematic description and recording of events that occur in groups by observers.

Openness: The sharing of information, ideas, thoughts, feelings, and reactions to the issue the group is pursuing.

Operational goals: Goals for which specific steps to achievement are clear and identifiable.

Opinion leader: See **Gatekeeper.**

Organization effectiveness: The extent to which the organization achieves its goals with the use of minimal resources.

Organizational development: The use of diagnosis and intervention procedures to promote effective interpersonal, group, and intergroup behavior within the organization.

Outcome dependence: Dependence on others to agree to one's proposals in negotiations. Because all parties must commit themselves to an agreement, each is dependent upon the others for the outcome.

Outcome interdependence: When the goals and rewards directing individuals' actions are positively correlated; that is, if one person accomplishes his or her goal or receives a reward, all others with whom the person is cooperatively linked also achieve their goals or receive a reward.

Package deal: Several issues being negotiated are all included as part of the agreement.

Paraphrasing: Restating in your own words what the person says, feels, and means.

Pareto chart: Form of vertical bar chart that is used to display the frequency and relative importance of problems, causes, or conditions in order to choose the starting point for process improvement.

Participant-observer: A person who is skilled enough to both participate in group work and observe group process at the same time; analysis of the group process and functioning by a participating member of the group.

Participation interdependence: The understanding that it takes two to negotiate—whether it is two group members, two organizations, or two nations.

Performance tasks: Tasks that can be completed only through the proficient use of perceptual and motor skills.

Personal space: The distance that people like to keep between themselves and others.

Perspective-taking: Ability to understand how a situation appears to another person and how that person is reacting cognitively and emotionally to the situation.

Persuasive argument: An attempt to point out the validity of your position and the incorrectness of the other's opinion.

Positive goal interdependence: When members perceive that they can achieve their goals if, and only if, all other members of their group also attain their goals.

Positive interdependence: The perception that one is linked with others in such a way that success is impossible without them (and vice versa) and that group effort must be coordinated in order to complete a task.

Power: The ability to influence and control others while resisting their influence and control. Control of valuable resources. The capacity to affect rewards, costs, and goal accomplishment.

Preemptive action: A type of conflict resolution designed to resolve the conflict without the other person's consent (such as taking up residence on a disputed piece of land).

Prejudice: An unjustified negative attitude towards a person based solely on that individual's membership in a group other than one's own.

Primary groups: Small groups characterized by face-to-face interaction, interdependency, and strong group identification, such as families and very close friends.

Prisoner's Dilemma Game: Non–zero sum game used by Deutsch and others to investigate trust and conflict.

Probabilistic thinking: A type of thinking based on the premise that knowledge is available only in degrees of certainty.

Problem: A discrepancy or difference between an actual state of affairs and a desired state of affairs.

Procedural learning: Learning conceptually what the skill is, when it should be used, how to engage in the skill, practicing the skill while eliminating errors, until an automated level of mastery is attained.

Process: An identifiable sequence of events taking place over time.

Process consultation: An organizational-development procedure of analyzing group functioning by an observing expert.

Process goals: The sequence of events instrumental in achieving outcome goals.

Process loss: Losses in members' performance due to their participation in the group.

Promise: The statement that if you do as I want, I will engage in an act that will benefit you. A negotiator stating that if the other performs a desired act the negotiator will make sure the other receives benefits.

Promotive interaction: When individuals encourage and facilitate each other's efforts to complete tasks and achieve in order to reach the group's goals.

Pseudogroup: A group whose members have been assigned to work together but who have no interest in doing so.

Psychodynamic fallacy: Seeing the motivation for the other's behavior in terms of personality factors rather than the dynamics of intergroup conflict.

Psychological health: The ability to develop, maintain, and appropriately modify interdependent relationships with others to succeed in achieving goals.

Racism: Prejudice directed at people because of their ethnic membership.

Reactance: People's need to reestablish their freedom whenever it is threatened.

Receiver: The person at whom the message is aimed.

Recurring-phase theories: These theories specify the issues that dominate group interaction and that occur over and over again.

Reference group: A group people identify with, compare their attitudes to, and use as a means to evaluate those attitudes.

Referent power: Power based on the group members' identification with, attraction to, or respect for the powerholder.

Relativistic thinking: A type of thinking based on the premise that authorities are sometimes right and sometimes wrong but that right and wrong depend on your perspective.

Resource attractor: An attribute (such as ability or training) that tends to attract other resources because it gives the possessor an advantage in a competition for these other resources.

Reward power: Power based on the powerholder's control over the positive and negative reinforcements desired by other group members.

Risky shift: The tendency for individuals to recommend riskier courses of action following group discussion than they would recommend prior to such interaction. The tendency for groups to make riskier decisions than individuals.

Role: A set of expectations defining appropriate behaviors associated with a position within a group. The part played by a member of a group. Rules or understandings about the tasks persons occupying certain positions within a group are expected to perform.

Role conflict: When the demands of one role are incompatible with the demands of another.

Run chart: Line graph used to monitor the behavior of a selected characteristic over time.

Scapegoat: A guiltless but defenseless group that is attacked to provide an outlet for pent-up anger and frustration caused by another group.

Scatter diagram: Displays the cause-and-effect relationship between two process variables or characteristics.

Self-efficacy: The expectation of successfully obtaining valued outcomes through personal effort; expectation that if one exerts sufficient effort, one will be successful.

Self-fulfilling prophecy: A set of actions that provokes the other into engaging in behavior that confirms one's original assumptions. An example is assuming that the other is belligerent and then proceeding to engage in hostile behavior, thereby provoking the other into belligerent actions, which confirms the original assumption.

Self-regulation: The ability to act in socially approved ways in the absence of external monitors.

Sender: The communicator.

Sender credibility: The attitude the receiver has towards the perceived trustworthiness of the sender's statement.

Sequential-stage theories: These theories specify the typical order of the phase of group development.

Sexism: Prejudice directed at a person because of his or her gender.

Sharing: The offering of your materials and resources to others in order to help them move the group towards goal accomplishment.

Sharpening: Selective perceiving and remembering of a few high points of a message while most of the rest is forgotten. The reciprocal of leveling.

Situational approach to leadership: The view that those members of a group most likely to become leaders are those who can best help it to reach its major goals.

Small group: Two or more individuals in face-to-face interaction, each aware of positive interdependence as they strive to achieve mutual goals, each aware of his or her group membership, and each aware of the others who belong to the group.

Social dependence: The outcome of one person is affected by the actions of a second person, but not vice versa.

Social determinism: The view that historic events are determined by social forces, social movements, and changing social values; see **Zeitgeist.**

Social exchange: A form of social interaction in which participants exchange something of value. What they exchange can range from specific goods or services to information, love, and approval.

Social facilitation: The enhancement of well-learned responses in the presence of others. Effects on performance resulting from the presence of others.

Social independence: When individuals' outcomes are unaffected by each other's actions.

Social interaction: Patterns of mutual influence linking two or more persons.

Social interdependence: When individuals share common goals and the individual's outcomes are affected by the actions of the others.

Social loafing: A reduction of individual effort when working with others on an additive group task.

Social sensitivity: The ability to perceive and respond to the needs, emotions, and preferences of others.

Social skills: The interpersonal and small group skills needed to interact effectively with other people.

Social-skills training: A structured intervention designed to help participants improve their interpersonal skills. It is generally conducted in group settings.

Socioemotional activity: Behavior that focuses on interpersonal relations in the group.

Sociometry: A measurement procedure developed by Moreno that is used to summarize graphically and mathematically patterns of interpersonal attraction in groups.

Status: The degree to which an individual's contribution is crucial to the success and prestige of the group, how much power that individual has, and the extent to which the person embodies some idealized or admired characteristic.

Stereotype: Set of cognitive generalizations that summarize, organize, and guide the processing of information about members of a particular group.

Substitutability: Part of Deutsch's theory of interdependence. When the actions of one person replace the actions of another.

Superordinate goals: Goals that cannot be easily ignored by members of two antagonistic groups, but whose attainment is beyond the resources and efforts of either group alone; the two groups, therefore, must join in a cooperative effort in order to attain the goals.

Superordinate identity: Group identity that transcends the personal, gender, ethnic, and religious identities of group members.

Support: The communication to others that you recognize their strengths and believe in their capability to manage productively the situation they are in.

Survey-feedback method: An organizational development procedure that focuses on describing the current state of the organization through surveys or interviews and then sharing this descriptive information through feedback.

Synthesizing: Integrating a number of different positions containing diverse information and conclusions into a new, single, inclusive position that all group members can agree on and commit themselves to.

Team: A set of interpersonal relationships structured to achieve established goals.

Team building: The analysis of work procedures and activities to improve productivity, relationships among members, the social competence of members, and the ability of the team to adapt to changing conditions and demands.

Technological gatekeepers: The people who read more of the theory and research literature in their field and consult more with outside sources than other group members.

Theory: A set of interrelated hypotheses or propositions concerning a phenomenon or set of phenomena.

Threat: The statement that unless you do as I want you to, I will engage in an act that will harm you. One individual informing another that negative actions will follow if the recipient of the threat does (or does not) behave in some manner. A negotiator stating that unless the other agrees to the proposed settlement, the negotiator will make sure the other is harmed.

Tie-in: In negotiations, an issue considered extraneous by the other person is introduced and you offer to accept a certain settlement provided this extraneous issue will also be settled to your satisfaction.

Total quality management: Use of teams to continuously improve the processes by which the product or service is produced.

Traditional work group: A group whose members agree to work together, but see little benefit from doing so.

Transactional approach to leadership: An approach suggesting that leadership involves a complex social relationship between leaders and followers in which each exerts influence on the other.

Triggering event: An event (such as two group members being in competition, or the expression of criticism on a sensitive point) that triggers the occurrence of a conflict.

Trust: Perception that a choice can lead to gains or losses, that whether you will gain or lose depends on the behavior of the other person, that the loss will be greater than the gain, and that the person will likely behave so that you will gain rather than lose.

Trusting behavior: Openness and sharing.

Trustworthy behavior: Expressing acceptance, support, and cooperative intentions.

Unalterable position: A refusal to alter your position, thus giving the other negotiator the final opportunity to avoid a no-agreement ending—for example, plugging your ears until the other negotiator says yes.

Unitary task: Cannot be divided into subtasks. One person has to complete the entire task.

Victim derogation: The tendency for persons who take unfair advantage of others to view negatively the victims of their exploitation, believing that the victims somehow *deserve* such treatment.

Vision: An ideal and unique image of the future used to clarify the missions and goals of the group.

Want: A desire for something.

Win–lose dynamic: Seeing every action of the other as a move to dominate.

Zeitgeist: Spirit or temper of the times.

References

Abelson, R., Dasgupta, N., Park, J., & Banaji, M. (1998). Perceptions of the collective other. *Personality and Social Psychology Review, 2*(4), 243–250.

Achenback, T., & Edelbrock, C. (1981). Behavioral problems and competencies reported by parents of normal and disturbed children aged four through sixteen. *Monographs of the Society for Research in Child Development, 46*(1, Serial No. 188).

Agnew, C., Van Lange, P., Rusbult, C., & Langston, C. (1998). Cognitive interdependence: Commitment and the mental representation of close relationship. *Journal of Personality and Social Psychology, 74,* 939–954.

Aldag, R., & Fuller, S. (1993). Beyond fiasco: A reappraisal of the groupthink phenomenon and a new model of group decision processes. *Psychological Bulletin, 113,* 533–552.

Allen, V. (1965). Situational factors in conformity. In L. Berkowitz (Ed.), *Advances in experimental social psychology* (Vol. 2, pp. 133–175). New York: Academic Press.

Allport, F. (1924). *Social psychology.* Boston: Houghton Mifflin.

Allport, G. (1954). *The nature of prejudice.* Cambridge, MA: Addison-Wesley.

Allport, G., & Kramer, B. (1946). Some roots of prejudice. *Journal of Psychology, 22,* 9–39.

Allport, G., & Postman, L. (1945). The basic psychology of rumor. *Transactions of the New York Academic Sciences, 8,* Series II, 61–81.

Ames, G., & Murray, F. (1982). When two wrongs make a right: Promoting cognitive change by social conflict. *Developmental Psychology, 18,* 894–897.

Amir, Y. (1969). Contact hypothesis in ethnic relations. *Psychological Bulletin, 71,* 319–352.

Amir, Y. (1976). The role of intergroup contact in change in prejudice and ethnic relations. In P. Katz (Ed.), *Towards the elimination of racism* (pp. 245–308). New York: Pergamon.

Archer-Kath, J., Johnson, D. W., & Johnson, R. (1994). Individual versus group feedback in cooperative groups. *Journal of Social Psychology, 134*(5), 681–694.

Argyris, C. (1964). *Integrating the individual and the organization.* New York: John Wiley.

Aristotle (384-322 B.C./1991). *The art of rhetoric* (H. C. Lawson-Tancred, Trans.). New York: Penguin Books.

Aronson, E. (1972). *The social animal.* San Francisco: W. H. Freeman.

Aronson, E., Blaney, N., Stephan, C., Sikes, J., & Snapp, M. (1978). *The jigsaw classroom.* Beverly Hills, CA: Sage.

Arriaga, X., & Rusbult, C. (1998). Standing in my partner's shoes: Partner perspective taking and reactions to accommodative dilemmas. *Personality and Social Psychology Bulletin, 24*(9), 927–948.

Asch, S. (1951). Effects of group pressure upon the modification and distortion of judgments. In H. Guetzkow (Ed.), *Groups, leadership, and men* (pp. 177–190). Pittsburgh: Carnegie Press.

Asch, S. (1952). *Social psychology.* New York: Prentice Hall.

Asch, S. (1956). Studies of independence and conformity: A minority of one against a unanimous majority. *Psychological Monographs, 70,* 416.

Ashmore, R., & Del Boca, F. (1979). Sex stereotypes and implicit personality theory: Toward a cognitive-social psychological conceptualization. *Sex Roles, 5,* 219–248.

Axelrod, R. (1984). *The evolution of cooperation.* New York: Basic Books.

Babchuk, N., & Good, W. (1951). Work incentives in a self-determined group. *American Journal of Sociology, 16,* 679–687.

Bahn, C. (1964). *The interaction of creativity and social facilitation in creative problem solving.* (Doctoral Dissertation, Columbia University). Dissertation Abstracts International. (University Microfilms No. 65–7499). V24, 57.

Baldwin, T., & Ford, J. (1988). Transfer of training: A review and directions for future research. *Personality Psychology, 41,* 63–105.

Bales, R. (1950). *Interaction process analysis.* Reading, MA: Addison-Wesley.

Bales, R. (1952). Some uniformities of behavior in small social systems. In G. Swanson, T. Newcomb, and E. Hartley (Eds.), *Readings in social psychology.* New York: Holt.

Bales, R. (1953). The equilibrium problem in small groups. In T. Parsons, R. Bales, & E. Shils (Eds.), *Working papers in the theory of action* (pp. 111–162). Glencoe, IL: Free Press.

Bales, R. (1955). How people interact in conferences. *Scientific American, 192,* 31–35.

Bales, R. (1965). The equilibrium problem in small groups. In A. Hare, E. Borgatta, & R. Bales (Eds.), *Small groups: Studies in social interaction* (pp. 444–476). New York: Alfred A. Knopf.

Bales, R., & Slater, P. (1955). Role differentiation in small decision-making groups. In T. Parsons & R. Bales (Eds.), *The family, socialization, and interaction process* (pp. 159–306). Glencoe, IL: Free Press.

Bales, R., & Strodtbeck, F. (1951). Phases in group problem solving. *Journal of Abnormal and Social Psychology, 46,* 485–495.

Banas, P. (1988). Employee involvement: A sustained labor/management initiative at the Ford Motor Company. In J. Campbell & R. Campbell (Eds.), *Productivity in organizations: New perspectives from industrial and organizational psychology* (pp. 388–416). San Francisco: Jossey-Bass.

Bantel, K., & Jackson, S. (1989). Top management and innovations in banking: Does the composition of the top team make a difference? *Strategic Management Journal, 10,* 107–124.

Barnlund, D. (1959). A comparative study of individual, majority and group judgment. *Journal of Abnormal and Social Psychology, 58,* 55–60.

Baron, R. (1986). Distraction-conflict theory: Progress and problems. In L. Berkowitz (Ed.), *Advances in experimental social psychology* (Vol. 19, pp. 1–40). New York: Academic Press.

Baron, R., Baron, P., & Miller, N. (1973). The relation between distraction and persuasion. *Psychological Bulletin, 80,* 310–323.

Baron, R., Kerr, N., & Miller, N. (1992). *Group process, group decision, group action.* Pacific Grove, CA: Brooks/Cole.

Baron, R., Moore, D., & Sanders, G. (1978). Distraction as a source of drive in social facilitation research. *Journal of Personality and Social Psychology, 36,* 816–824.

Baron, R., Roper, G., & Baron, P. (1974). Group discussion and the stingy shift. *Journal of Personality and Social Psychology, 30,* 538–545.

Bartlett, F. (1932). *Remembering.* Cambridge: Cambridge University Press.

Bass, B. (1960). *Leadership, psychology, and organizational behavior.* New York: Harper & Row.

Batson, C., Early, S., & Salvarani, G. (1997). Perspective taking: Imagining how another feels versus imagining how you would feel. *Personality and Social Psychology Bulletin, 23*(7), 751–758.

Baumeister, R., Smart, L., & Boden, J. (1996). Relation of threatened egotism to violence and aggression: The dark side of high self-esteem. *Psychological Review, 103,* 5–33.

Bavelas, A. (1942). Morale and training of leaders. In G. Watson (Ed.), *Civilian morale* (pp. 143–165). Boston: Houghton Mifflin.

Bavelas, A. (1948). A mathematical model for group structures. *Applied Anthropology, 7,* 16–30.

Bavelas, A., Hostorf, A., Gross, A., & Kite, W. (1965). Experiments on the alteration of group structure. *Journal of Experimental Social Psychology, 1,* 55–70.

Beckhard, R. (1969). *Organizational development.* Reading, MA: Addison-Wesley.

Beer, M. (1976). The technology of organization development. In M. Dunnette (Ed.), *Handbook of industrial and organizational psychology* (pp. 937–994). Chicago: Rand McNally.

Beer, M. (1980). *Organization change and development: A systems view.* Glenview, IL: Scott, Foresman.

Bekhterev, W., & DeLange, M. (1924). Die ergebnisse des experiments auf dem gebiet der kollektiven reflexologie. *Zeitschrift fur Angewandte Psychologie, 24,* 305–344.

Bem, D. (1972). Self-perception theory. In L. Berkowitz (Ed.), *Advances in experimental social psychology* (Vol. 6, pp. 2–62). New York: Academic Press.

Ben-Yoav, O., & Pruitt, D. (1984a). Resistance to yielding and the expectation of cooperative future interaction in negotiation. *Journal of Experimental Social Psychology, 20,* 323–353.

Ben-Yoav, O., & Pruitt, D. (1984b). Accountability to constituents: A two-edged sword. *Organizational Behavior and Human Performance, 34,* 282–295.

Bennett, E. (1955). Discussion, decision, commitment and consensus in "group decision." *Human Relations, 8,* 251.

Berger, J., Rosenholtz, S., & Zelditch, M. (1980). Status organizing processes. *Annual Review of Sociology, 6,* 479–508.

Berkowitz, L. (1978). Whatever happened to the frustration-aggression hypothesis? *American Behavioral Scientist, 32,* 691–708.

Berlyne, D. (1965). Curiosity and education. In J. Krumboltz (Ed.), *Learning and the educational process* (pp. 67–89). Chicago: Rand McNally.

Bernstein, A. (1991, April). Quality is becoming job one in the office, too. *Business Week,* pp. 52–56.

Berscheid, E., & Walster, E. (1969). *Interpersonal attraction.* Reading, MA: Addison-Wesley.

Berscheid, E., & Walster, E. (1974). Physical attractiveness. In L. Berkowitz (Ed.), *Advances in experimental social psychology* (Vol. 7, pp. 158–215). New York: Academic Press.

Bettencourt, B., Charlton, K., & Kernahan, C. (in press). Numerical representation of groups in cooperative settings: Social orientation effects on ingroup bias. *Journal of Experimental Social Psychology.*

Bettencourt, B., & Dorr, N. (1998). Cooperative interaction and intergroup bias: Effects of numerical representation and cross-cut role assignment. *Personality and Social Psychology Bulletin, 24* (12), 1276–1293.

Bickman, L. (1974). The social power of a uniform. *Journal of Applied Social Psychology, 4,* 47–61.

Bierman, R. (1969). Dimensions for interpersonal facilitation in psychotherapy in child development. *Psychological Bulletin, 72,* 338–352.

Bion, W. (1961). *Experiences in groups.* New York: Basic Books.

Bird, C. (1940). *Social psychology.* New York: Appleton-Century-Crofts.

Blake, R., & Mouton, J. (1962). The intergroup dynamics of win–lose conflict and problem-solving collaboration in union–management relations. In M. Sherif (Ed.), *Intergroup relations and leadership,* (Vol. 5, pp. 94–140). New York: John Wiley.

Blake, R., & Mouton, J. (1964). *The managerial grid.* Houston, TX: Gulf.

Blake, R., & Mouton, J. (1983). Lateral conflict. In D. Tjosvold & D. W. Johnson (Eds.), *Productive conflict management: Perspectives for organizations.* Edina, MN: Interaction Book Company.

Blanchard, F., Lilly, T., & Vaughn, L. (1991). Reducing the expression of racial prejudice. *Psychological Science, 2,* 101–105.

Blanchard, F., Weigal, R., & Cook, S. (1975). The effect of relative competence of group members upon interpersonal attraction in cooperating interracial groups. *Journal of Personality and Social Psychology, 32,* 519–530.

Blau, P. (1954). Co-operation and competition in a bureaucracy. *American Journal of Sociology, 59,* 530–535.

Bolen, L., & Torrance, E. (1976, April). *An experimental study of the influence of locus of control, dyadic interaction, and sex on creative thinking.* Paper presented at the Annual Meeting of the American Educational Research Association, San Francisco.

Bond, C. (1982). Social facilitation: A self-presentational view. *Journal of Personality and Social Psychology, 42,* 1042–1050.

Bond, C., & Titus, L. (1983). Social facilitation: A meta-analysis of 241 studies. *Psychological Bulletin, 94,* 265–292.

Bonner, H. (1959). *Group dynamics: Principles and applications.* New York: Ronald Press.

Boster, F., & Hale, J. (1989). Responsive scale ambiguity as a moderator of the choice shift. *Communication Research, 16*(4), 532–551.

Bray, R., Kerr, N., & Atkin, S. (1978). Group size, problem difficulty, and group performance on unitary disjunctive tasks. *Journal of Personality and Social Psychology, 36,* 1224–1240.

Brehm, J. (1966). *A theory of psychological reactance.* New York: Academic Press.

Brehm, J. (1976). Responses to loss of freedom: A theory of psychological reactance. In J. Thibaut, J. Spence, & R. Carson (Eds.), *Contemporary topics in social psychology.* Morristown, NJ: General Learning Press.

Brehm, J., & Sensenig, J. (1966). Social influence as a function of attempted and implied usurpation of choice. *Journal of Personality and Social Psychology, 4,* 703–707.

Brehm, S., & Brehm, J. (1981). *Psychological reactance: A theory of freedom and control.* New York: Academic Press.

Brett, J., & Rognes, J. (1986). Intergroup relations in organizations. In P. Goodman (Ed.), *Designing effective work groups* (pp. 202–236). San Francisco: Jossey-Bass.

Brewer, M. (1988). A dual process model of impression formation. In T. Srull & R. Wyer, Jr. (Eds.), *Advances in social cognition* (Vol. 1, pp. 1–36). Hillsdale, NJ: Erlbaum.

Brewer, M., Ho, H., Lee, J., & Miller, N. (1987). Social identity and social distance among Hong Kong schoolchildren. *Personality and Social Psychology Bulletin, 13,* 156–165.

Brewer, M., Manzi, K., & Shaw, J. (1993). Ingroup identification as a function of depersonalization, distinctiveness, and status. *Psychological Science, 4,* 88–92.

Brewer, M., & Miller N. (1984). Beyond the contact hypothesis: Theoretical perspectives on desegregation. In N. Miller & M. Brewer (Eds.), *Groups in contact: The psychology of desegregation* (pp. 281–302). Orlando, FL: Academic Press.

Brickner, M. (1987). *Locked into performance: Goal setting as a moderator of the social loafing effect.* Paper presented at the annual meeting of the Midwestern Psychological Association, Chicago.

Brickner, M., Harkins, S., & Ostrom, T. (1986). Effects of personal involvement: Thought-provoking implications for social loafing. *Journal of Personality and Social Psychology, 51,* 763–769.

Bronowski, J. (1973). *The ascent of man.* Boston: Little Brown.

Brophy, J. (1945). The luxury of anti-Negro prejudice. *Public Opinion Quarterly, 9,* 456–466.

Brown, B. (1968). The effects of the need to maintain face on interpersonal bargaining. *Journal of Experimental Social Psychology, 4,* 107–122.

Brown, C., Dovidio, J., & Ellyson, S. (1990). Reducing sex differences in visual displays of dominance: Knowledge is power. *Personality and Social Psychology Bulletin, 16,* 358–368.

Brown, R. (1984). The role of similarity in intergroup relations. In H. Tajfel (Ed.), *The social dimension* (Vol. 2, pp. 603–623). Cambridge, England: Cambridge University Press.

Bruner, J., & Minturn, A. (1955). Perceptual identification and perceptual organization. *Journal of Genetic Psychology, 53,* 21–28.

Buller, P., & Bell, C. (1986). Effects of team building and goal setting on productivity: A field experiment. *Academy of Management Journal, 29,* 305–328.

Burke, P. (1972). Leadership role differentiation. In C. McClintock (Ed.), *Experimental social psychology* (pp. 514–546). New York: Holt, Rinehart & Winston.

Burke, P. (1974). Participation and leadership in small groups. *American Sociological Review, 39,* 832–842.

Burke, R. (1969, July). Methods of resolving interpersonal conflict. *Personnel Administration,* pp. 48–55.

Burke, R. (1970). Methods of resolving superior-subordinate conflict: The constructive use of subordinate differences and disagreements. *Organizational Behavior and Human Performance, 5,* 393–411.

Burnstein, E., & Vinokur, A. (1977). Persuasive argumentation and social comparison as determinants of attitude polarization. *Journal of Experimental Social Psychology, 13,* 315–332.

Bushman, B. (1984). Perceived symbols of authority and their influence on compliance. *Journal of Applied Social Psychology, 14,* 501–508.

Byrne, D. (1969). Attitudes and attraction. In L. Berkowitz (Ed.), *Advances in experimental social psychology* (Vol. 4, pp. 36–90). New York: Academic Press.

Byrne, D. (1971). *The attraction paradigm.* New York: Academic Press.

Cantrell, V., & Prinz, R. (1985). Multiple perspectives of rejected, neglected, and accepted children: Relation between sociometric status and behavioral characteristics. *Journal of Consulting and Clinical Psychology, 53,* 884–889.

Carnevale, P., & Keenan, P. (1990). *Frame and motive in integrative bargaining: The likelihood and the quality of agreement.* Paper presented at the Third Annual Meeting of the International Association for Conflict Management, Vancouver, British Columbia.

Carnevale, P., & Pegnetter, R. (1985). The selection of mediation tactics in public sector disputes: A contingency analysis. *Journal of Social Issues, 41*(2), 65–81.

Cartwright, D. (1959). A field theoretical conception of power. In D. Cartwright (Ed.), *Studies in social power.* Ann Arbor: University of Michigan Press.

Cartwright, D., & Zander, A. (Eds.). (1968). *Group dynamics: Research and theory* (3rd ed.). New York: Harper & Row.

Caspi, A. (1984). Contact hypothesis and inter-age attitudes: A field study of cross-age contact. *Social Psychology Quarterly, 47,* 74–80.

Cattell, R. (1951). New concepts for measuring leadership, in terms of group syntality. *Human Relations, 4,* 161–184.

Chertkoff, J., & Esser, J. (1976). A review of experiments in explicit bargaining. *Journal of Experimental Social Psychology, 12,* 464–487.

Chesler, M., & Franklin, J. (1968, August). *Interracial and intergenerational conflict in secondary schools.* Paper presented at the Annual Meeting of the American Sociological Association, Boston.

Christie, R., & Geis, F. (1970). *Studies in Machiavellianism.* New York: Academic Press.

Clark, K. (1953). Desegregation: An appraisal of the evidence. *Journal of Social Issues, 9*(4), 2–8.

Clement, D., & Schiereck, J. (1973). Sex composition and group performance in a visual signal detection task. *Memory and Cognition, 1,* 251–255.

Cohen, E. (1984). Talking and working together: Status, interaction and learning. In P. Peterson, L. Wilkinson, & M. Hallinan (Eds.), *The social context of instruction: Group organization and group processes* (pp. 171–187). New York: Academic Press.

Coie, J., & Kupersmidt, J. (1983). A behavioral analysis of emerging social status in boys' groups. *Child Development, 54,* 1400–1416.

Cook, S. (1957). Desegregation: A psychological analysis. *American Psychologist, 12,* 1–13.

Cook, S. (1969). Motives in a conceptual analysis of attitude-related behavior. In W. Arnold & D. Levine (Eds.), *Nebraska symposium on motivation.* Lincoln: University of Nebraska Press.

Cook, S. (1978). Interpersonal and attitudinal outcomes in cooperating interracial groups. *Journal of Research in Developmental Education, 12,* 87–113.

Cosier, R. (1981). Dialectical inquiry in strategic planning: A case of premature acceptance? *Academy of Management Review, 6,* 643–648.

Cosier, R., & Ruble, T. (1981). Research on conflict handling behavior: An experimental approach. *Academy of Management Journal, 24,* 816–831.

Cottrell, N. (1972). Social facilitation. In C. McClintock (Ed.), *Experimental social psychology* (pp. 185–236). New York: Holt.

Cottrell, N., Wack, D., Sekerak, G., & Rittle, R. (1968). Social facilitation of dominant responses by the presence of an audience and the mere presence of others. *Journal of Personality and Social Psychology, 9,* 245–250.

Cox, C. (1926). *The early mental traits of three hundred geniuses.* Stanford, CA: Stanford University Press.

Crocker, J., & Luhranen, R. (1990). Collection self-esteem and ingroup bias. *Journal of Personality and Social Psychology, 58,* 60–67.

Croizet, J. & Claire, T. (1998). Extending the concept of stereotype threat to social class: The intellectual underperformance of students from low socioeconomic backgrounds. *Personality and Social Psychology Bulletin, 24* (6), 588–594.

Dahl, R. (1957). The concept of power. *Behavioral Science, 2,* 201–218.

Dalkey, N. (1969). An experimental study of group opinion: The Delphi Method. *Futures, 1*(3), 408–426.

Dalkey, N. (1975). Toward a theory of group estimation. In H. Linstone & M. Turoff (Eds.), *The Delphi method: Techniques and applications* (pp. 236–257). Reading, MA: Addison-Wesley.

Dance, F. (1970). The "concept" of communication. *Journal of Communication, 20,* 201–210.

Darley, J., & Latane, B. (1968). Bystander intervention in emergencies: Diffusion of responsibility. *Journal of Personality and Social Psychology, 8,* 377–383.

David, G., & Houtman, S. (1968). *Thinking creatively: A guide to training imagination.* Madison: Wisconsin Research and Development Center for Cognitive Learning.

Davis, J. (1969). *Group performance.* Reading, MA: Addison-Wesley.

DeCecco, J., & Richards, A. (1974). *Growing pains: Uses of school conflict.* New York: Aberdeen Press.

Delbecq, A., Van de Ven, A., & Gustafson, D. (1975). *Group techniques for program planning.* Glenview, IL: Scott, Foresman.

Deschamps, J. (1977). Effect of crossing category membership on quantitative judgment. *European Journal of Social Psychology, 22,* 189–195.

Deschamps, J., & Doise, W. (1978). Crossed category memberships in intergroup relations. In H. Tajfel (Ed.), *Differentiation between social groups: Studies in the social psychology of intergroup relations* (pp. 141–158). New York: Academic Press.

Desforges, D., Lord, C., Ramsey S., Mason, J., Van Leeuwen, M., West, S., & Lepper, M. (1991). Effects of structured cooperative contact on changing negative attitudes toward stigmatized social groups. *Journal of Personality and Social Psychology, 60,* 531–544.

Deutsch, M. (1949a). A theory of cooperation and competition. *Human Relations, 2,* 129–152.

Deutsch, M. (1949b). An experimental study of the effects of cooperation and competition upon group process. *Human Relations, 2,* 199–231.

Deutsch, M. (1958). Trust and suspicion. *Journal of Conflict Resolution, 2,* 265–279.

Deutsch, M. (1960). The effects of motivational orientation upon trust and suspicion. *Human Relations, 13,* 123–139.

Deutsch, M. (1962). Cooperation and trust: Some theoretical notes. In M. R. Jones (Ed.), *Nebraska symposium on motivation* (pp. 275–320). Lincoln: University of Nebraska Press.

Deutsch, M. (1969). Conflicts: Productive and destructive. *Journal of Social Issues, 25,* 7–43.

Deutsch, M. (1973). *The resolution of conflict.* New Haven, CT: Yale University Press.

Deutsch, M. (1975). Equity, equality, and need: What determines which value will be used as the basis of distributive justice? *Journal of Social Issues, 31,* 137–149.

Deutsch, M. (1979). Education and distributive justice: Some reflections on grading systems. *American Psychologist, 34,* 391–401.

Deutsch, M. (1985). *Distributive justice: A social psychological perspective.* New Haven, CT: Yale University Press.

Deutsch, M., Canavan, D., & Rubin, J. (1971). The effects of size of conflict and sex of experimenter upon interpersonal bargaining. *Journal of Experimental Social Psychology, 7,* 258–267.

Deutsch, M., & Collins, M. (1951). *Interracial housing: A psychological evaluation of a social experiment.* Minneapolis: University of Minnesota Press.

Deutsch, M., & Krauss, R. (1960). The effect of threat upon interpersonal bargaining. *Journal of Abnormal and Social Psychology, 61,* 181–189.

Deutsch, M., & Krauss, R. (1962). Studies of interpersonal bargaining. *Journal of Conflict Resolutions, 6,* 52–76.

Deutsch, M., & Lewicki, R. (1970). "Locking in" effects during a game of chicken. *Journal of Conflict Resolution, 14,* 367–378.

Devine, P., Monteith, M., Zuwerink, J., & Elliot, A. (1991). Prejudice with and without compunction. *Journal of Personality and Social Psychology, 60,* 817–830.

DeVries, D., & Edwards, K. (1973). Learning games and student teams: Their effects on classroom process. *American Educational Research Journal, 10,* 307–318.

DeVries, D., & Edwards, K. (1974). Student teams and learning games: Their effects on cross-race and cross-sex interaction. *Journal of Educational Psychology, 66,* 741–749.

Diehl, M., & Stroebe, W. (1987). Productivity loss in brainstorming groups: Toward solution of a riddle. *Journal of Personality and Social Psychology, 53,* 497–509.

Dodge, K. (1983). Behavioral antecedents of peer social status. *Child Development, 54,* 1386–1389.

Dodge, K., Coie, J., & Bakke, N. (1982). Behavior patterns of socially rejected and neglected preadolescents: The roles of social approach and aggression. *Journal of Abnormal Child Psychology, 10,* 389–409.

Dovidio, J., & Gaertner, S. (1991). Changes in the expression and assessment of racial prejudice. In H. Knopke, R. Norrell, & R. Rogers (Eds.), *Opening doors: Perspectives on race relations in contemporary America* (pp. 119–148). Tuscaloosa: University of Alabama Press.

Driskell, J., Hogan, R., & Salas, E. (1987). Personality and group performance. In C. Hendrick (Ed.), *Group processes and intergroup relations* (pp. 91–112). Newbury Park, CA: Sage.

Drucker, P. (1974). Multinationals and developing countries: Myths and realities. *Foreign Affairs, 53,* 121–134.

Dunnette, M., Campbell, J., & Jaastad, K. (1963). The effect of group participation on brainstorming effectiveness of two industrial samples. *Journal of Applied Psychology, 47,* 30–37.

Dunning, D., & Ross, L. (1988). Overconfidence in individual and group prediction: Is the collective any wiser? Unpublished manuscript, Cornell University.

Duval, S., & Wicklund, R. (1972). *A theory of objective self-awareness.* New York: Academic Press.

Dyer, W. (1987). *Team building: Issues and alternatives.* Reading, MA: Addison-Wesley.

Ehrlich, H., & Lee, D. (1969). Dogmatism, learning, and resistance to change: A review and a new paradigm. *Psychological Bulletin, 71*(4), 249–260.

Emerson, R. (1954). Deviation and rejection: An experimental replication. *American Sociological Review, 19,* 688–693.

Epstein, S., & Taylor, S. (1967). Instigation to aggression as a function of degree of defeat and perceived aggressive intent of the opponent. *Journal of Personality, 35,* 265–289.

Espenshade, T., & Calhoun, C. (1993). An analysis of public opinion toward undocumented immigration. *Population Research and Policy Review, 12,* 189–224.

Falbe, C., & Yukl, G. (1992). Consequences for managers of using single influence tactics and combination of tactics. *Academy of Management Journal, 35,* 638–652.

Falk, D., & Johnson, D. W. (1977). The effects of perspective-taking and egocentrism on problem solving in heterogeneous and homogeneous groups. *Journal of Social Psychology, 102,* 63–72.

Fay, B. (1929). *Benjamin Franklin: The apostle of modern times.* Boston: Little, Brown.

Fenelon, J., & Megaree, E. (1971). Influence of race on the manifestation of leadership. *Journal of Applied Psychology, 55,* 353–358.

Festinger, L. (1950). Informal social communication. *Psychological Review, 57,* 271–292.

Festinger, L. (1954). A theory of social comparison processes. *Human Relations, 7,* 117–140.

Festinger, L. (1957). *A theory of cognitive dissonance.* Evanston, IL: Row, Peterson.

Festinger, L., Pepitone, A., & Newcomb, T. (1952). Some consequences of deindividuation in a group. *Journal of Abnormal and Social Psychology, 47,* 382–389.

Festinger, L., Schachter, S., & Back, K. (1950). *Social pressures in informal groups: A study of human factors in housing.* New York: Harper Collins.

Fiedler, F. (1967). *A theory of leadership effectiveness.* New York: McGraw-Hill.

Fiedler, F. (1978). Recent developments in research on the contingency model. In L. Berkowitz (Ed.), *Group processes.* New York: Academic Press.

Fiedler, R., Meuwese, W., & Conk, S. (1961). An exploratory study of group creativity in laboratory tasks. *Acta Psychologie,* pp. 100–119.

Filley, A. (1975). *Interpersonal conflict resolution.* Glenview, IL: Scott Foresman.

Filley, A., House, R., & Kerr, S. (1976). *Managerial process and organizational behavior.* Glenview, IL: Scott Foresman.

Fine, G. (1979). The Pinkston settlement: An historical and social psychological investigation of the contact hypothesis. *Phylon, 40,* 229–242.

Fisher, R., & Ury, W. (1981). *Getting to yes: Negotiating agreement without giving in.* Boston: Houghton Mifflin.

Fiske, S. (1993). Controlling other people: The impact of power on stereotyping. *American Psychologist, 48,* 621–628.

Fiske, S., & Morling, B. (1996). Stereotyping as a function of personal control motives and capacity constraints: The odd couple of power and anxiety. In R. Sorrentino and E. Higgins (Vol. Eds.), *Handbook of motivation and cognition: Vol. 3. The interpersonal context* (pp. 322–346). New York: Guilford.

Fiske, S., & Neuberg, S. (1990). A continuum of impression formation, from category-based to individuating processes: Influences of information and motivation on attention and interpretation. In M. Zanna (Ed.), *Advances in experimental social psychology* (Vol. 23, pp. 1–74). New York: Academic Press.

Flowers, M. (1977). A laboratory test of some implications of Janis' groupthink hypothesis. *Journal of Personality and Social Psychology, 35,* 888–896.

Foley, J., & MacMillan, F. (1943). Mediated generalization and the interpretation of verbal behavior: V. Free association as related to differences in professional training. *Journal of Experimental Psychology, 33,* 299–310.

Follet, M. (1940). Constructive conflict. In H. Metcalf & L. Urwick (Eds.), *Dynamic administration: The collected papers of Mary Parker Follet* (pp. 30–49). New York: Harper.

Fox, D. (1985). Psychology, ideology, utopia, and the commons. *American Psychologist, 40,* 48–58.

Frank, M. (1984). *A comparison between an individual and group goal structure contingency that differed in the behavioral contingency and performance-outcome components.* Unpublished doctoral thesis, University of Minnesota, Minneapolis, MN.

Frankfort, H., Frankfort, H., Wilson, J., & Jacobson, T. (1949). *Before philosophy.* Baltimore, MD: Penguin.

Fraser, C. (1971). Group risk-taking and group polarization. *European Journal of Social Psychology, 1,* 493–510.

French, J. (1941). The disruption and cohesion of groups. *Journal of Abnormal Social Psychology, 36,* 361–377.

French, J., & Coch, L. (1948). Overcoming resistance to change. *Human Relations, 1,* 512–532.

French, J., & Raven, B. (1959). The basis of social power. In D. Cartwright (Ed.), *Studies in social power* (pp. 150–167). Ann Arbor: University of Michigan Press.

Freud, S. (1922). *Group psychology and the analysis of the ego.* London, Vienna: The International Psychoanalytical Press.

Frick, F. (1973). *Study of peer training with the Lincoln Training System* (AFATC Report KE 73–116). Harrison, MS: Keesler Air Force Base.

Gabbert, B., Johnson, D., & Johnson, R. (1986). Cooperative learning, group-to-individual transfer, process gain, and the acquisition of cognitive reasoning strategies. *Journal of Psychology, 120,* 265–278.

Gabrenya, W. K., Wang, Y., & Latanne, B. (1983). Social loafing in cross-cultural perspective: Chinese on Taiwan. *Journal of Cross Cultural Psychology, 14* (3), 368–384.

Gaertner, S., & Dovidio, J. (1986). The aversive form of racism. In J. Dovidio & S. Gaertner (Eds.), *Prejudice, discrimination, and racism* (pp. 61–89). New York: Academic Press.

Gaertner, S., Dovidio, J., Anastasio, P., Bachman, B., & Rust, M. (1993). The common ingroup identity model: Recategorization and the reduction of intergroup bias. In W. Stroebe & M. Hewstone (Eds.), *European review of social psychology* (Vol. 4, pp. 1–26). Chichester, England: Wiley.

Gardin, J., Kaplan, K., Firestone, I., & Cowan, G. (1973). Proxemic effects on cooperation, attitude, and approach-avoidance in a prisoner's dilemma game. *Journal of Personality and Social Psychology, 27,* 13–18.

Geen, R. (1976). Test anxiety, observation, and range of cue utilization. *British Journal of Social and Clinical Psychology, 15,* 253–259.

Geen, R. (1980). The effects of being observed on performance. In P. Paulus (Ed.), *Psychology of group influence* (pp. 61–97). Hillsdale, NJ: Erlbaum.

Georgesen, J., & Harris, M. (1998). Why's my boss always holding me down? A meta-analysis of power effects on performance evaluations. *Personality and Social Psychology Review, 2*(3), 184–195.

Gerard, H., & Hoyt, M. (1974). Distinctiveness of social categorization and attitude toward ingroup members. *Journal of Personality and Social Psychology, 27,* 836–842.

Gerard, H., Wilhelmy, R., & Conolley, E. (1968). Conformity and group size. *Journal of Personality and Social Psychology, 8*(1), 79–82.

Ghiselli, E., & Lodahl, T. (1958). Patterns of managerial traits and group effectiveness. *Journal of Abnormal and Social Psychology, 57,* 61–66.

Gibb, J. (1951). The effects of group size and of threat upon certainty in a problem-solving siutation. *American Psychologist, 6,* 324.

Gibb, J. (1961). Defensive communication. *Journal of Communication, 11,* 141–148.

Giffin, K. (1967). The contribution of studies of source credibility to a theory of interpersonal trust in the communication process. *Psychological Bulletin, 68,* 104–121.

Gilbert, D., & Malone, P. (1995). The correspondence bias. *Psychological Bulletin, 117,* 21–38.

Gilbert, D., McNulty, S., Giuliano, T., & Benson, J. (1992). Blurry words and fuzzy deeds: The attribution of obscure behavior. *Journal of Personality and Social Psychology, 62,* 18–25.

Gilbert, P. (1992). *Depression: The evolution of powerlessness.* New York: Guilford.

Glass, D., & Singer, J. (1973). Experimental studies of uncontrollable and unpredictable noise. *Representative Research in Social Psychology, 4*(1), 165–183.

Glass, G. (1977). Integrating findings: The meta-analysis of research. In L. Schulman (Ed.), *Review of research in education* (Vol. 5, pp. 351–379). Itasca, IL: Peacock.

Glasser, W. (1984). *Control theory.* New York: Harper & Row.

Glidewell, J. (1953). *Group emotionality and productivity.* Unpublished doctoral dissertation, University of Chicago.

Goldman, M., Dietz, D., & McGlynn, A. (1968). Comparison of individual and group performance related to heterogeneous-wrong responses, size, and patterns of interaction. *Psychological Reports, 23*(2), 459–465.

Gordon, K. (1924). Group judgments in the field of lifted weights. *Journal of Experimental Psychology, 7,* 398–400.

Gordon, W. (1961). *Synectics.* New York: Harper & Row.

Gottman, J. (1993). The roles of conflict engagement, escalation, and avoidance in marital interaction: A longitudinal view of five types and couples. *Journal of Consulting and Clinical Psychology, 61*(1), 6–15.

Gottschalk, L. (1966). Psychoanalytic notes on T-groups at the Human Relations Laboratory, Bethel, Maine. *Comprehensive Psychiatry, 7*(6), 472–487.

Graham, S. (1991). A review of attribution theory in achievement contexts. *Educational Psychology Review, 3,* 5–39.

Gray, J., & Thompson, A. (1953). The ethnic prejudices of white and Negro college students. *Journal of Abnormal and Social Psychology, 48,* 311–313.

Green, D. (1977). The immediate processing of sentences. *Quarterly Journal of Experimental Psychology, 29,* 135–146.

Gundlach, R. (1950). The effect of on-the-job experience with Negroes upon social attitudes of white workers in union shops. *American Psychologist, 5,* 300.

Hackman, J., & Morris, C. (1975). Group tasks, group interaction process and group performance effectiveness: A review and proposed integration. In L. Berkowitz (Ed.), *Advances in Experimental Social Psychology* (Vol. 8, pp. 47–99). New York: Academic Press.

Hackman, J., & Oldham, G. (1980). *Work redesign.* Reading, MA: Addison-Wesley.

Hackman, J., & Walton, R. (1986). Leading groups in organizations. In P. Goodman (Ed.), *Designing effective work groups* (pp. 72–119). San Francisco: Jossey-Bass.

Hall, J., & Veccia, E. (1990). More "touching" observations: New insights on men, women, and interpersonal touch. *Journal of Personality and Social Psychology, 59,* 1155–1162.

Hall, J., & Williams, M. (1966). A comparison of decision making performance in established and ad hoc groups. *Journal of Personality and Social Psychology, 3,* 214–222.

Halle, L. J. (1967, June). Overestimating the power of power. *The New Republic,* pp. 15–17.

Hamilton, D. (1979). A cognitive-attributional analysis of stereotyping. In L. Berkowitz (Ed.), *Advances in experimental social psychology* (Vol. 12, pp. 53–84). New York: Academic Press.

Hamilton, D., & Sherman, J. (1994). Stereotypes. In R. Wyer, Jr., & T. Srull (Eds.), *Handbook of social cognition* (2nd ed., Vol. 2, pp. 1–68). Hillsdale, NJ: Erlbaum.

Harding, J., & Hogerge, R. (1952). Attitudes of white department store employees toward Negro co-workers. *Journal of Social Issues, 8,* 18–28.

Hare, A. (1976). *Handbook of small group research* (2nd ed.). New York: Free Press.

Harlan, H. (1942). Some factors affecting attitude toward Jews. *American Sociological Review, 7,* 816–827.

Harkins, S. (1987). Social loafing and social facilitation. *Journal of Experimental Social Psychology, 23,* 1–18.

Harkins, S., & Jackson, J. (1985). The role of evaluation in eliminating social loafing. *Personality and Social Psychology Bulletin, 11,* 457–465.

Harkins, S., & Petty, R. (1982). The effects of task difficulty and task uniqueness on social loafing. *Journal of Personality and Social Psychology, 43,* 1214–1229.

Harkins, S., & Szymanski, K. (1987). Social loafing and self-evaluation with an objective standard. *Journal of Experimental Social Psychology, 24,* 354–365.

Harkins, S., & Szymanski, K. (1989). Social loafing and group evaluation. *Journal of Personality and Social Psychology, 56,* 934–941.

Harris, M., & Schaubroeck, J. (1988). A meta-analysis of self-supervisor, self-peer, and peer-supervisor ratings. *Personnel Psychology, 41,* 43–62.

Haunschild, P., Moreland, R., & Murrell, A. (1994). Sources of resistance to mergers between groups. *Journal of Applied Social Psychology, 24,* 1150–1178.

Haythorn, W. (1968). The composition of groups: A review of the literature. *Acta Psychologica, 28,* 97–128.

Heider, F. (1958). *The psychology of interpersonal relations.* New York: John Wiley.

Herek, G., & Capitanio, J. (1996). "Some of my best friends": Intergroup contact, concealable stigma, and heterosexuals' attitudes toward gay men and lesbians. *Personality and Social Psychology Bulletin, 22,* 412–424.

Herek, G., Janis, I., & Huth, P. (1987). Decision-making during international crises: Is quality of process related to outcome? *Journal of Conflict Resolution, 31,* 203–226.

Hersey, P., & Blanchard, K. (1977). *Management of organizational behavior: Utilizing human resources* (3rd ed.). Englewood Cliffs, NJ: Prentice Hall.

Hewstone, M., & Brown, R. (Eds.). (1986). *Contact and conflict in intergroup relations.* Oxford, England, Basil Blackwell.

Hill, G. (1982). Group versus individual performance: Are $n + 1$ heads better than one? *Psychological Bulletin, 91,* 517–539.

Hill, W., & Gruner, L. (1973). A study of development in open and closed groups. *Small Group Behavior, 4,* 355–381.

Hinkin, R., & Schriesheim, C. (1989). Development and application of new scales to measure the French and Raven (1959) bases of social power. *Journal of Applied Psychology, 74,* 561–567.

Hoffman, L. (1959). Group problem solving. In L. Berkowitz (Ed.), *Advances in experimental social psychology* (Vol. 2, pp. 99–132). San Diego, CA: Academic Press.

Hoffman, L. (1961). Conditions for creative problem solving. *Journal of Psychology, 52,* 429–444.

Hoffman, L. (1979). Applying experimental research on group problem solving to organizations. *Journal of Applied Behavioral Science, 15,* 375–391.

Hoffman, L., Harburg, E., & Maier, N. (1962a). Differences and disagreement as factors in creative problem solving. *Journal of Abnormal and Social Psychology, 64,* 206–214.

Hoffman, L., Harburg, E., & Maier, N. (1962b). Quality and acceptance of problem solutions by members of homogeneous and heterogeneous groups. *Journal of Abnormal and Social Psychology, 64,* 206–214.

Hoffman, L., & Maier, N. (1961). Quality and acceptance of problem solutions by members of homogeneous and heterogeneous. *Journal of Abnormal and Social Psychology, 62*(2), 401–407.

Hollander, E., & Willis, R. (1967). Some current issues in the psychology of conformity and nonconformity. *Psychological Bulletin, 68,* 62–76.

Homans, G. (1950). *The human group.* New York: Harcourt, Brace.

Homans, G. (1961). *Social behavior: Its elementary forms.* New York: Harcourt, Brace & World.

Hong, O., & Harrod, W. (1988). The role of reasons in the in-group bias phenomenon. *European Journal of Social Psychology, 18,* 537–545.

Hook, S. (1955). *The hero in history.* Boston: Beacon Press.

Hopper, R. (1950). The revolutionary process. *Social Forces, 28,* 270–279.

Horai, J. (1977). Attributional conflict. *Journal of Social Issues, 33*(1), 88–100.

Horowitz, E. (1936). The development of attitude toward the Negro. *Archives of Psychology,* (Whole No. 194).

Horwitz, M. (1954). The recall of interrupted group tasks: An experimental study of individual motivation in relation to group goals. *Human Relations, 7,* 3–38.

Hovland, C., Janis, I., & Kelley, H. (1953). *Communication and persuasion.* New Haven, CT: Yale University Press.

Hovland, C., Lumsdaine, A., & Sheffield, F. (1949). *Experiment on mass communication.* Princeton, NJ: Princeton University Press.

Hovland, C., & Weiss, W. (1952). The influence of source credibility on communication effectiveness. *Public Opinion Quarterly, 15,* 635–650.

Howells, L., & Becker, S. (1962). Seating arrangement and leadership emergence. *Journal of Personality and Social Psychology, 64,* 148–150.

Hunt, P., & Hillery, J. (1973). Social facilitation in a coaction setting: An examination of the effects over learning trials. *Journal of Experimental Social Psychology, 9,* 563–571.

Hwong, N., Caswell, A., Johnson, D. W., & Johnson, R. (1993). Effects of cooperative and individualistic learning on prospective elementary teachers' music achievement and attitudes. *Journal of Social Psychology, 133,* 53–64.

Illing, H. (1957). C. Jung on the present trends in group psychotherapy. *Human Relations, 10,* 77–84.

Indik, B. (1965). Organization size and member participation: Some empirical tests of alternative explanations. *Human Relations, 18*(4), 339–350.

Ingham, A., Levinger, G., Graves, J., & Peckham, V. (1974). The Ringelmann effect: Studies of group size and group performance. *Journal of Experimental Social Psychology, 10,* 371–384.

Irish, D. (1952). Reactions of Caucasian residents to Japanese-American neighbors. *Journal of Social Issues, 8,* 10–17.

Isenberg, D. (1986). Group polarization: A critical review and meta-analysis. *Journal of Personality and Social Psychology, 50,* 1141–1151.

Islam, M., & Hewstone, M. (1993). Intergroup attributions and affective consequences in majority and minority groups. *Journal of Personality and Social Psychology, 64,* 936–950.

Iverson, M., & Schwab, H. (1967). Ethnocentric dogmatism and binocular fusion of sexually and racially discrepant stimuli. *Journal of Personality and Social Psychology, 7,* 73–81.

Jackman, M., & Crane, M. (1986). "Some of my best friends are black. . . ." Interracial friendship and whites' racial attitudes. *Public Opinion Quarterly, 50,* 459–486.

Jackson, S. (1992). Team composition in organizational settings: Issues in managing an increasingly diverse work force. In S. Worchel, W. Wood, & J. Simpson (Eds.), *Group process and productivity* (pp. 138–173). Newbury Park, CA: Sage.

Jackson, S., Brett, J., Sessa, V., Cooper, D., Julin, J., & Peyronnin, K. (1991). Some differences make a difference: Interpersonal dissimilarity and group heterogeneity as correlates of recruitment, promotion, and turnover. *Journal of Applied Psychology, 76,* 675–689.

Jacobson, N., & Margolin, G. (1979). *Marital therapy: Strategies based on social learning and behavior exchange principles.* New York: Brunner/Mazel.

Jahoda, M., & West, P. (1951). Race relations in public housing. *Journal of Social Issues, 7,* 132–139.

James, N., & Johnson, D. W. (1983). The relationship between attitudes toward social interdependence and psychological health within three criminal populations. *Journal of Social Psychology, 121,* 131–143.

James, S., & Johnson, D. W. (1988). Social interdependence, psychological adjustment, orientation toward negative life stress, and quality of second marriage. *Journal of Social Psychology, 128*(3), 287–304.

Janis, I. (1972). *Victims of groupthink.* Boston: Houghton Mifflin.

Janis, I. (1982). *Groupthink* (revised and enlarged edition of *Victims of groupthink*). Boston: Houghton Mifflin.

Janis, I., & Mann, L. (1977). *Decision making.* New York: Free Press.

Janz, T., & Tjosvold, D. (1985). Costing effective vs. ineffective work relationships: A method and first look. *Canadian Journal of Administrative Sciences, 2,* 51–53.

Johnson, D., & Rusbult, C. (1989). Resisting temptation: Devaluation of alternative partners as a means of maintaining commitment in close relationships. *Journal of Personality and Social Psychology, 57,* 967–980.

Johnson, D. W. (1970). *The social psychology of education.* New York: Holt, Rinehart & Winston.

Johnson, D. W. (1971). Role reversal: A summary and review of the research. *International Journal of Group Tensions, 1,* 318–334.

Johnson, D. W. (1973). *Contemporary social psychology.* Philadelphia: Lippincott.

Johnson, D. W. (1974). Communication and the inducement of cooperative behavior in conflicts. *Speech Monographs, 41,* 64–78.

Johnson, D. W. (1977). Distribution and exchange of information in problem solving dyads. *Communication Research, 4,* 283–298.

Johnson, D. W. (1978). *Human relations and your career* (1st ed.). Englewood Cliffs, NJ: Prentice Hall.

Johnson, D. W. (1979). *Educational psychology.* Englewood Cliffs, NJ: Prentice Hall.

Johnson, D. W. (1980a). Group processes: Influences on student-student interaction on school outcomes. In J. McMillan (Ed.), *Social psychology of school learning* (pp. 123–168). New York: Academic Press.

Johnson, D. W. (1980b). Attitude modification methods. In F. Kanfer and A. Goldstein (Eds.), *Helping people change* (pp. 51–88). New York: Pergamon Press.

Johnson, D. W. (2000). *Reaching out: Interpersonal effectiveness and self-actualization* (6th ed.). Boston: Allyn & Bacon.

Johnson, D. W., & Allen, S. (1972). Deviation from organizational norms concerning the relations between status and power. *Sociological Quarterly, 13,* 174–182.

Johnson, D. W., Johnson, F., & Johnson, R. (1976). Promoting constructive conflict in the classroom. *Notre Dame Journal of Education, 7,* 163–168.

Johnson, D. W., & Johnson, R. (1974). Instructional goal structure: Cooperative, competitive, or individualistic. *Review of Educational Research, 44,* 213–240.

Johnson, D. W., & Johnson, R. (1979). Conflict in the classroom: Controversy and learning. *Review of Educational Research, 49,* 51–70.

Johnson, D. W., & Johnson, R. (1981). Effects of cooperative and individualistic learning experiences on interethnic interaction. *Journal of Educational Psychology, 73,* 454–459.

Johnson, D. W., & Johnson, R. (1983). The socialization and achievement crisis: Are cooperative learning experiences the solution? In L. Bickman (Ed.), *Applied social psychology annual 4* (pp. 119–164). Beverly Hills, CA: Sage.

Johnson, D. W., & Johnson, R. (1987). *Creative conflict.* Edina, MN: Interaction Book Company.

Johnson, D. W., & Johnson, R. (1989). *Cooperation and competition: Theory and research.* Edina, MN: Interaction Book Company.

Johnson, D. W., & Johnson, R. (1992a). *Positive interdependence: The heart of cooperative learning.* Edina, MN: Interaction Book Company.

Johnson, D. W., & Johnson, R. (1992b). *Positive interdependence: The heart of cooperative learning* (Video). Edina, MN: Interaction Book Company.

Johnson, D. W., & Johnson, R. (1994). *Leading the cooperative school* (2nd ed.). Edina, MN: Interaction Book Company.

Johnson, D. W., & Johnson, R. (1995a). *Teaching students to be peacemakers* (3rd ed.). Edina, MN: Interaction Book Company.

Johnson, D. W., & Johnson, R. (1995b). *My mediation notebook* (3rd ed.). Edina, MN: Interaction Book Company.

Johnson, D. W., & Johnson, R. (1995c). *Creative controversy: Intellectual challenge in the classroom* (3rd ed.). Edina, MN: Interaction Book Company.

Johnson, D. W., & Johnson, R. (1996). *Meaningful and manageable assessment through cooperative learning.* Edina, MN: Interaction Book Company.

Johnson, D. W., & Johnson, R. (1997). *Learning to lead teams: Developing leadership skills.* Edina, MN: Interaction Book Company.

Johnson, D. W., & Johnson, R. (1999a). *Learning together and alone: Cooperative, competitive, and individualistic learning* (5th ed.). Boston: Allyn & Bacon.

Johnson, D. W., & Johnson, R. (1999b). *Human relations: Valuing diversity.* Edina, MN: Interaction Book Company.

Johnson, D. W., & Johnson, R. (1999c). *Learning together and alone: Cooperation and competition, and individualization* (6th ed.). Boston: Allyn & Bacon.

Johnson, D. W., Johnson, R., Buckman, L., & Richards, P. (1986). The effect of prolonged implementation of cooperative learning on social support within the classroom. *Journal of Psychology, 119,* 405–411.

Johnson, D. W., Johnson, R., & Holubec, E. (1994). *Nuts and bolts of cooperative learning.* Edina, MN: Interaction Book Company.

Johnson, D. W., Johnson, R., & Holubec, E. (1998a). *Cooperation in the classroom* (7th ed.). Edina, MN: Interaction Book Company.

Johnson, D. W., Johnson, R., & Holubec, E. (1998b). *Advanced cooperative learning* (5th ed.). Edina, MN: Interaction Book Company.

Johnson, D. W., Johnson, R., & Krotee, M. (1986). The relation between social interdependence and psychological health on the 1980 U.S. Olympic ice hockey team. *Journal of Psychology, 120* (3), 279–291.

Johnson, D. W., Johnson, R., & Maruyama, G. (1983). Interdependence and interpersonal attraction among heterogeneous and homogeneous individuals: A theoretical formulation and a meta-analysis of the research. *Review of Educational Research, 53,* 5–54.

Johnson, D. W., Johnson, R., Ortiz, A., & Stanne, M. (1991). Impact of positive goal and resource interdependence on achievement, interaction, and attitudes. *Journal of General Psychology, 118*(4), 341–347.

Johnson, D. W., Johnson, R., Stanne, M., & Garibaldi, A. (1990). Impact of group processing on achievement in cooperative groups. *Journal of Social Psychology, 130,* 507–516.

Johnson, D. W., Kavanagh, J., & Lubin, B. (1973). Tests, t-groups, and tension. *Comparative Group Studies, 4,* 81–88.

Johnson, D. W., & Matross, R. (1977). The interpersonal influence of the psychotherapist. In A. Gurman & A. Razin (Eds.), *Effective psychotherapy: A handbook of research* (pp. 395–432). Elmsford, NY: Pergamon Press.

Johnson, D. W., McCarty, K., & Allen, T. (1976). Congruent and contradictory verbal and nonverbal communications of cooperativeness and competitiveness in negotiations. *Communication Research, 3,* 275–292.

Johnson, D. W., & Noonan, P. (1972). Effects of acceptance and reciprocation of self-disclosures on the development of trust. *Journal of Counseling Psychology, 19,* 411–416.

Johnson, D. W., & Norem-Hebeisen, A. (1977). Attitudes toward interdependence among persons and psychological health. *Psychological Reports, 40,* 843–850.

Johnson, D. W., Skon, L., & Johnson, R. (1980). The effects of cooperative, competitive and individualistic goal structures on student achievement on different types of tasks. *American Educational Research Journal, 17,* 83–93.

Johnson, R., Johnson, D. W., Scott, L., & Ramolae, B. (1985). Effects of single-sex and mixed-sex cooperative interaction on science achievement and attitudes and cross-handicap and cross-sex relationship. *Journal of Research in Science Teaching, 22,* 207–220.

Jones, E., & Gerard, H. (1967). *Foundations of social psychology.* New York: John Wiley.

Jones, E., & Nesbett, R. (1972). The actor and the observer: Divergent perceptions of the causes of behavior. In E. Jones et al., (Eds.), *Attribution: Perceiving the causes of behavior* (pp. 79–94). Hillsdale, NJ: Erlbaum.

Jones, M. (1974). Regressing group on individual effectiveness. *Organizational Behavior and Human Performance, 11,* 426–451.

Kaplan, M., & Miller, C. (1987). Group decision making and normative versus information influence: Effects of type of issue and assigned decision rule. *Journal of Personality and Social Psychology, 53,* 306–313.

Katz, D., & Braly, K. (1933). Racial stereotypes of 100 college students. *Journal of Abnormal and Social Psychology, 28,* 280–290.

Katz, I., & Hass, R. (1988). Racial ambivalence and American value conflict: Correlational and priming studies of dual cognitive structures. *Journal of Personality and Social Psychology, 55,* 893–905.

Katz, I., Wachenhut, J., & Hass, R. (1986). Racial ambivalence, value duality, and behavior. In J. Dovidio & S. Gaertner (Eds.), *Prejudice, discrimination, and racism* (pp. 35–60). New York: Academic Press.

Katzenbach, J., & Smith, D. (1993). *The wisdom of teams.* Cambridge, MA: Harvard Business School Press.

Kelley, H. (1979). *Personal relationships.* Hillsdale, NJ: Erlbaum.

Kelley, H., & Stahelski, A. (1970). Social interaction basis of cooperators' and competitors' beliefs about others. *Journal of Personality and Social Psychology, 16,* 66–91.

Kelley, H., & Thibaut, J. (1978). *Interpersonal relations: A theory of interdependence.* New York: John Wiley.

Kerr, N. (1983). The dispensability of member effort and group motivation losses: Free-rider effects. *Journal of Personality and Social Psychology, 44,* 78–94.

Kerr, N. (1989). Illusions of efficacy: The effects of group size on perceived efficacy in social dilemmas. *Journal of Experimental Social Psychology, 35,* 287–313.

Kerr, N., Atkin, R., Stasser, G., Meek, D., Holt, R., & Davis, J. (1976). Guilt beyond a reasonable doubt: Effects of concept definition and assigned decision rule on the judgments of mock jurors. *Journal of Personality and Social Psychology, 34,* 282–294.

Kerr, N., & Bruun, S. (1981). Ringelmann revisited: Alternative explanations for the social loafing effect. *Personality and Social Psychology Bulletin, 7,* 224–231.

Kerr, N., & Bruun, S. (1983). The dispensability of member effort and group motivation losses: Freerider effects. *Journal of Personality and Social Psychology, 44,* 78–94.

Kerr, N., Davis, J., Meek, D., & Rissman, A. (1975). Group position as a function of member attitudes: Choice shift effects from the perspective of social decision scheme theory. *Journal of Personality and Social Psychology, 31,* 574–593.

Key, V. (1949). *Southern politics in state and nation.* New York: Alfred A. Knopf.

Kiesler, S., Siegel, J., & McGuire, T. (1984, October). Social psychological aspects of computer-mediated communication. *American Psychologist, 39*(10), 1123–1134.

Kim, S., Smith, R., & Brigham, N. (1998). Effects of power imbalance and the presence of third parties on reactions to harm: Upward and downward revenge. *Personality and Social Psychology Bulletin, 24*(4), 353–361.

Kipnis, D. (1972). Does power corrupt? *Journal of Personality and Social Psychology, 24,* 33–41.

Kipnis, D. (1987). Psychology and behavioral technology. *American Psychologist, 42,* 30–36.

Kipnis, D., Castell, J., Gergen, M., & Mauch, D. (1976). Metamorphic effects of power. *Journal of Applied Psychology, 61,* 127–135.

Kipnis, D., Schmidt, S., Prince K., & Stitt, C. (1981). Why do I like thee: Is it your performance or my orders? *Journal of Applied Psychology, 66,* 324–328.

Kolb, D. (1985). To be a mediator: Expressive tactics in mediation. *Journal of Social Issues, 41*(2), 11–26.

Kostick, M. (1957). An experiment in group decision. *Journal of Teacher Education, 8,* 67–72.

Kouzes, J., & Posner, B. (1987). *The leadership challenge.* San Francisco: Jossey-Bass.

Kramer, G. (1951). *Residential contact as a determinant of attitudes toward Negroes.* Unpublished doctoral dissertation, Harvard University.

Kramer, R. (1996). Divergent realities and convergent disappointments in the hierarchic relation: Trust and the intuitive auditor at work. In R. Kramer & T. Tyler (Eds.), *Trust in organizations: Frontiers of theory and research* (pp. 216–245). Thousand Oaks, CA: Sage.

Kramer, R., & Brewer, M. (1986). Social group identity and the emergence of cooperation in resource conservation dilemmas. In H. Wilke, D. Messick, & C. Rutte (Eds.), *Experimental social dilemmas* (pp. 205–234). Frankfurt am Main: Verlag Peter Lang.

Kressel, K., & Pruitt, D. (1985). Themes in the mediation of social conflict. *Journal of Social Issues, 41*(2), 179–198.

Labarre, W. (1972). *The ghost dance.* New York: Delta.

Lakin, M. (1972). *Interpersonal encounter: Theory and practice in sensitivity training.* New York: McGraw-Hill.

Lamm, H., & Trommsdorff, G. (1973). Group versus individual performance on tasks requiring ideational proficiency (Brainstorming): A review. *European Journal of Social Psychology, 3,* 361–388.

Langer, E., Blank, A., & Chanowitz, B. (1978). The mindlessness of ostensibly thoughtful action: The role of "placebic" information in interpersonal interaction. *Journal of Personality and Social Psychology, 36,* 635–642.

Langer, E., & Rodin, J. (1976). The effects of choice and enhanced personal responsibility for the aged: A field experiment in an institutional setting. *Journal of Personality and Social Psychology, 34*(2), 191–198.

Latane, B., & Nida, S. (1981). Ten years of research on group size and helping. *Psychological Bulletin, 89,* 308–324.

Latane, B., Williams, K., & Harkins, S. (1979). Many hands make light the work: The causes and consequences of social loafing. *Journal of Personality and Social Psychology, 37,* 822–832.

Latham, G., & Baldes, J. (1975). The "practical significance" of Locke's theory of goal setting. *Journal of Applied Psychology, 60,* 122–124.

Laughlin, P. (1980). Social combination processes of cooperative problem-solving groups on verbal intellective tasks. In M. Fishbein (Ed.), *Progress in social psychology* (Vol. 1, pp. 127–155). Hillsdale, NJ: Erlbaum.

Laughlin, P., & Adamopoulos, J. (1980). Social combination processes and individual learning for six-person cooperative groups on an intellective task. *Journal of Personality and Social Psychology, 38,* 941–947.

Laughlin, P., & Bitz, D. (1975). Individual versus dyadic performance on a disjunctive task as a function of initial ability level. *Journal of Personality and Social Psychology, 31,* 487–496.

Laughlin, P., & Early, P. (1982). Social combination models, persuasive arguments theory, social comparison theory and choice shift. *Journal of Personality and Social Psychology, 42,* 273–280.

Lawrence, P., & Lorsch, J. (1967). *Organization and environment: Managing differentiation and integration.* Cambridge: Harvard University, Division of Research, Graduate School of Business Administration.

Leana, C. (1985). A partial test of Janis' groupthink model: Effects of group cohesiveness and leader behavior on defective decision making. *Journal of Management, 11,* 5–17.

Leavitt, H. (1951). Some effects of certain communication patterns on group performance. *Journal of Abnormal and Social Psychology, 46,* 38–50.

Levine, J., & Butler, J. (1952). Lecture vs. group decision in changing behavior. *Journal of Applied Psychology, 36,* 29–33.

Levine, R., Chein, I., & Murphy, G. (1942). The relation of the intensity of a need to the amount of perceptual distortion: A preliminary report. *Journal of Psychology, 13,* 283–293.

Levinger, G. (1980). Toward the analysis of close relationships. *Journal of Experimental Social Psychology, 16,* 510–544.

Lew, M., Mesch, D., Johnson, D. W., & Johnson, R. (1986a). Postive interdependence, academic and collaborative-skills group contingencies and isolated students. *American Educational Research Journal, 23,* 476–488.

Lew, M., Mesch, D., Johnson, D. W., & Johnson, R. (1986b). Components of cooperative learning: Effects of collaborative skills and academic group contingencies on achievement and mainstreaming. *Contemporary Educational Psychology, 11,* 229–239.

Lewin, K. (1943). Forces behind food habits and methods of change. *Bulletin of the National Research Council, 108,* 35–65.

Lewin, K. (1944). Dynamics of group action. *Educational Leadership, 1,* 195–200.

Lewin, K. (1948). *Resolving social conflicts.* New York: Harper.

Lewin, K. (1951). *Field theory in social science.* New York: Harper.

Lewin, K., Dembo, T., Festinger, L., & Sears, P. (1944). Level of aspiration. In J. Hunt (Ed.), *Personality and the behavior disorders* (pp. 333–378). New York: Ronald Press.

Lewin, K., Lippitt, R., & White, R. (1939). Patterns of aggressive behavior in experimentally created "social climates." *Journal of Social Psychology, 10,* 271–299.

Lewis, H. (1944). An experimental study of the role of the ego in work. I. The role of the ego in cooperative work. *Journal of Experimental Psychology, 34,* 113–126.

Lewis, H., & Franklin, M. (1944). An experimental study of the role of the ego in work. II. The significance of task-orientation in work. *Journal of Experimental Psychology, 34,* 195–215.

Lewis, S., & Pruitt, D. (1971). Organization, aspiration level, and communication freedom in integrative bargaining. *Proceedings of the 79th Annual Convention of the American Psychological Association, 6,* 221–222.

Lieberman, M., Lakin, M., & Whitaker, D. (1968). The group as a unique context for therapy. *Psychotherapy: Theory, Research and Practice, 5*(1), 29–36.

Lieberman, M., Yalom, I., & Miles, M. (1973). *Encounter groups: First facts.* New York: Basic Books.

Lieberman, M., Yalom, I., & Miles, M. (1980). Group methods. In F. Kanfer & A. Goldstein (Eds.), *Helping people change* (pp. 433–485). New York: Pergamon Press.

Likert, R. (1961). *New patterns of management.* New York: McGraw-Hill.

Lindskold, S., & Arnoff, J. (1980). Conciliatory strategies and relative power. *Journal of Experimental Social Psychology, 16,* 187–198.

Linville, P., Fisher, G., & Salovey, P. (1989). Perceived distribution of the characteristics of in-group and out-group members: Empirical evidence and a computer simulation. *Journal of Personality and Social Psychology, 57,* 165–188.

Lippmann, W. (1922). *Public opinion.* New York: Harcourt, Brace, Jovanovich.

Lissner, K. (1933). The resolution of needs by substitutive acts: Studies of action and affect psychology, edited by K. Lewin. *Psychologische Fortung, 18,* 27–87.

Longley, D., & Pruitt, D. (1980). Groupthink: A critique of Janis's theory. In L. Wheeler (Ed.), *Review of personality and social psychology* (Vol. 1). Beverly Hills, CA: Sage.

Lord, C., Ross, L., & Lepper, M. (1979). Biased assimilation and attitude polarization: The effects of prior theories on subsequently considered evidence. *Journal of Personality and Social Psychology, 37*(11), 2098–2109.

Lorge, I., Fox, D., Davitz, J., & Brenner, M. (1958). A survey of studies contrasting the quality of group performance and individual performance, 1920–1957. *Psychological Bulletin, 55,* 337–372.

Luce, R. & Raiffa, H. (1957). *Games and decisions.* New York: John Wiley.

Luchins, A. (1942). Mechanization in problem solving: The effect of Einstellung. *Psychological Monographs, 54* (Whole No. 248).

MacKenzie, B. (1948). The importance of contact in determining attitudes toward Negroes. *Journal of Abnormal and Social Psychology, 43,* 417–441.

Magnuson, E. (1986, March 10). A serious deficiency: The Rogers Commission faults NASA's flawed decision-making process. *Time,* pp. 40–42.

Mahler, W. (1933). Substitution acts of a different degree of reality. Students of action and affect psychology, edited by K. Lewin. *Psychologishe Fortschung, 18,* 27–89.

Maier, N. (1970). *Problem solving and creativity in individuals and group.* Belmont, CA: Brooks/Cole.

Maier, N., & Hoffman, L. (1964). Financial incentives and group decision in motivating change. *Journal of Social Psychology, 64,* 369–378.

Maier, N., & Solem, A. (1952). The contribution of a discussion leader to the quality of group thinking: The effective use of minority opinions. *Human Relations, 5,* 277–288.

Maier, N., & Thurber, J. (1969). Innovative problem-solving by outsiders: A study of individuals and groups. *Personal Psychology, 22*(3), 237–249.

Major, B., Schmidlin, A., & Williams, L. (1990). Gender patterns in social touch: The impact of setting and age. *Journal of Personality and Social Psychology, 58,* 634–643.

Mann, L., & Janis, I. (1983). Decisional conflict in organizations. In D. Tjosvold & D. Johnson (Eds.), *Productive conflict management* (pp. 16–45). New York: Irvington.

Mann, R. (1959). A review of the relationship between personality and performance in small groups. *Psychological Bulletin, 56,* 241–270.

Mannheimer, D., & Williams, R. (1949). A note on Negro troops in combat. In S. Stouffer, E. Suchman, L. DeVinney, S. Star, & R. Williams (Eds.), *The American Soldier,* Vol. 1. Princeton, N.J.: Princeton University Press.

Marcus-Newhall, A., Miller, N., Holtz, R., & Brewer, M. (1993). Cross-cutting category membership with role assignment: A means of reducing inter-group bias. *British Journal of Social Psychology, 32*, 124–146.

Markman, H. (1981). Prediction of marital distress: A 5-year follow-up. *Journal of Consulting and Clinical Psychology, 49*, 760–762.

Markus, H. (1978). The effect of mere presence on social facilitation: An unobtrusive test. *Journal of Experimental Social Psychology, 14*, 389–397.

Marrow, A. (1957). *Making management human.* New York: McGraw-Hill.

Maslow, A. (1954). *Motivation and personality.* New York: Harper & Row.

Maslow, A. (1962). *Toward a psychology of being.* Princeton, NJ: Van Nostrand.

Matsui, N., Kakuyama, T., & Onglateo, M. (1987). Effects of goals and feedback on performance in groups. *Journal of Applied Psychology, 72*(3), 416–425.

McCain, B., O'Reilly, C., & Pfeffer, J. (1983). The effects of departmental demography on turnover. *Academy of Management Journal, 26*, 626–641.

McCauley, C. (1989). The nature of social influence in groupthink: Compliance and internalization. *Journal of Personality and Social Psychology, 57*, 250–260.

McClelland, D., & Atkinson, J. (1948). The projective expression of needs: I. The effect of different intensities of the hunger drive on perception. *Journal of Psychology, 25*, 205–222.

McConahay, J. (1986). Modern racism, ambivalence, and the modern racism scale. In J. Dovidio & S. Gaertner (Eds.), *Prejudice, discrimination, and racism* (pp. 91–125). New York: Academic Press.

McDavid, J., & Harari, H. (1968). *Social psychology: Individuals, groups, societies.* New York: Harper & Row.

McGrath, J. (1984). *Groups: Interaction and performance.* Englewood Cliffs, NJ: Prentice Hall.

McGregor, D. (1967). *The human side of enterprise.* New York: McGraw-Hill.

McGuire, T., Kiesler, S., & Siegel, J. (1987). Group and computer-mediated discussion effects in risk decision making. *Journal of Personality and Social Psychology, 52*, 917–930.

McGuire, W. (1964). Inducing resistance to persuasion. In L. Berkowitz (Ed.), *Advances in experimental social psychology* (Vol. 1, pp. 192–232). New York: Academic Press.

McGuire, W. (1969). The nature of attitudes and attitude change. In B. Lindsey and E. Aronson (Eds.), *Handbook of social psychology* (Vol. 3, pp. 136–314). Reading, MA: Addison-Wesley.

McGuire, W., McGuire, C., Child, P., & Fujioka, P. (1978). Salience of ethnicity in the spontaneous self-concept as a function of one's ethnic distinctiveness in the social environment. *Journal of Personality and Social Psychology, 36*, 511–520.

McGuire, W., McGuire, C., & Winton, W. (1979). Effects of household sex composition on the salience of one's gender in the spontaneous self-concept. *Journal of Experimental Social Psychology, 15*, 77–90.

Medin, D. (1988). Social categorization: Structures, processes, and purposes. In R. Wyer, Jr. & T. Srull (Eds.), *Handbook of social cognition,* (2nd ed.) (Vol. 2, pp. 1–68). Hillsdale, NJ: Erlbaum.

Meer, B., & Freedman, E. (1966). The impact of Negro neighbors on White house owners. *Social Forces, 45*, 11–19.

Mehrabian, A. (1971). *Silent messages.* Belmont, CA: Wadsworth.

Mesch, D., Johnson, D. W., & Johnson, R. (1988). Impact of positive interdependence and academic group contingencies on achievement. *Journal of Social Psychology, 128*, 345–352.

Mesch, D., Lew, M., Johnson, D. W., & Johnson, R. (1986). Isolated teenagers, cooperative learning and the training of social skills. *Journal of Psychology, 120*, 323–334.

Messe, L., Kerr, N., & Sattler, D. (1992). "But some animals are more equal than others": The supervisor as a privileged status in group contexts. In S. Worchel, W. Wood, & J. Simpson (Eds.), *Group process and productivity* (pp. 203–223). Newburn Park, CA: Sage.

Messe, L., Stollak, G., Larson, R., & Michaels, G. (1979). Interpersonal consequences of person perception in two social contexts. *Journal of Personality and Social Psychology, 37*, 369–379.

Messick, D., & Brewer, M. (1983). Solving social dilemmas: A review. In L. Wheeler & P. Shaver (Eds.), *Review of personality and social psychology* (Vol. 4, pp. 11–44). Newbury Park, CA: Sage.

Miller, N., Brewer, M., & Edwards, K. (1985). Cooperative interaction in desegregated settings: A laboratory analogue. *Journal of Social Issues, 41*(3), 63–79.

Miller, N., & Davidson-Podgorny, G. (1987). Theoretical models of intergroup relations and the use of cooperative teams as an intervention for desegregated settings. In C. Hendrick (Ed.), *Annual review of personality and social psychology: Group processes and intergroup relations* (Vol. 9, pp. 23–39). Newbury Park, CA: Sage.

Mills, T. (1967). *The sociology of small groups.* Englewood Cliffs, NJ: Prentice Hall.

Minard, R. (1952). Race relationships in the Pocahontas coal field. *Journal of Social Issues, 8*, 29–44.

Mitchell, T., & Silver, W. (1990). Individual and group goals when workers are interdependent:

Effects on task strategies and performance. *Journal of Applied Psychology, 75*(2), 185–193.

Moede, W. (1920). *Experimentelle massenpsychologie.* Leipzig: S. Hirzel.

Moede, W. (1927). Die richtlinien der leistungs-psycholgie. *Industrielle Psychotechnik, 4,* 193–207.

Monteith, M. (1996a). Affective reactions to prejudice-related discrepant responses: The impact of standard salience. *Personality and Social Psychology Bulletin, 22,* 48–59.

Monteith, M. (1996b). Contemporary forms of prejudice-related conflict: In search of a nutshell. *Personality and Social Psychology Bulletin, 22,* 416–473.

Monteith, M., Devine, P., & Zuwerink, J. (1993). Self-directed versus other-directed affect as a consequence of prejudice-related discrepancies. *Journal of Personality and Social Psychology, 64,* 198–210.

Monteith, M., & Walters, G. (1998). Egalitarianism, moral obligation, and prejudice-related personal standards. *Personality and Social Psychology Bulletin, 24*(2), 186–199.

Moreland, R., & Levine, J. (1982). Socialization in small groups: Temporal changes in individual-group relations. In L. Berkowitz (Ed.), *Advances in experimental social psychology* (Vol. 15, pp. 137–192). New York: Academic Press.

Morgan, B., Coates, G., & Rebbin, T. (1970). *The effects of Phlebotomus fever on sustained performance and muscular output* (Tech. Rep. No. ITR-70-14). Louisville, KY: University of Louisville, Performance Research Laboratory.

Moscovici, S. (1985a). Innovation and minority influence. In S. Moscovici, G. Mugny, & E. Van Avermaet (Eds.), *Perspectives on minority influence* (pp. 9–51). Cambridge: Cambridge University Press.

Moscovici, S. (1985b). Social influence and conformity. In G. Lindzey & E. Aronson, (Eds.), *The handbook of social psychology* (3rd ed.) (Vol. 2, pp. 347–412). New York: Random House.

Mullen, B., Brown, R., & Smith, C. (1992). Ingroup bias as a function of salience, relevance, and status: An integration. *European Journal of Social Psychology, 22,* 103–122.

Mullen, B., & Cooper, C. (1994). The relation between group cohesiveness and performance: An integration. *Psychological Bulletin, 115*(2), 210–227.

Mullen, B., Johnson, C., & Salas, E. (1991). Productivity loss in brainstorming groups: A meta-analytic integration. *Basic and Applied Social Psychology, 12,* 3–25.

Murnighan, J., & Pillutla, M. (1995). Fairness versus self-interest: Asymmetric moral imperatives in ultimatum bargaining. In R. Kramer & D. Messick (Eds.), *Negotiation as a social process* (pp. 240–267). Thousand Oaks, CA: Sage.

Myers, D. (1978). The polarizing effects of social comparison. *Journal of Experimental Social Psychology, 14,* 554–563.

Myers, D. (1982). Polarizing effects of social interaction. In H. Brandstatter, J. Davis, & G. Stocker-Kreichgauer (Eds.), *Group decision making.* New York: Academic Press.

Myers, D., & Bishop, G. (1970). Discussion effects on racial attitudes. *Science, 169,* 778–789.

Myers, D., & Lamm, H. (1976). The group polarization phenomenon. *Psychological Bulletin, 83,* 602–627.

Myrdal, G. (1944). *An American dilemma: The Negro problem and modern democracy.* New York: Harper.

Nadler, D., Hackman, J., & Lawler, E. (1979). *Managing organizational behavior.* Boston: Little, Brown.

Neisser, U. (1954). On experimental distinction between perceptual process and verbal response. *Journal of Experimental Psychology, 47,* 399–402.

Nemeth, C. (1977). Interaction between jurors as a function of majority vs. unanimity decision rules. *Journal of Applied Social Psychology, 7,* 38–56.

Newcomb, T. (1943). *Personality and social change.* New York: Dryden.

Newcomb, T. (1956). The prediction of interpersonal attraction. *American Psychologist, 11,* 575–586.

Nijhof, W., & Kommers, P. (1982, July). *Analysis of cooperation in relation to cognitive controversy.* Paper presented at International Conference on Cooperation in Education, Provo, UT.

Oakes, P. (1987). The salience of social categories. In J. Turner, M. Hogg, P. Oakes, S. Reicher, & M. Wetherell (Eds.), *Rediscovering the social group: A self-categorization theory* (pp. 117–141). Oxford, UK: Basil Blackwell.

Oakes, P., & Turner, J. (1986). Distinctiveness and the salience of social category memberships: Is there an automatic perceptual bias toward novelty? *European Journal of Social Psychology, 16,* 325–344.

Oakes, P., Turner, J., & Haslam, S. (1991). Perceiving people as group members: The role of fit in the salience of social categorizations. *British Journal of Social Psychology, 30,* 125–144.

Ohbuchi, K., & Saito, M. (1986). Power imbalance, its legitimacy, and aggression. *Aggressive Behavior, 12,* 33–40.

Olson, M. (1965). *The logic of collective action: Public goods and the theory of groups.* Cambridge, MA: Harvard University Press.

O'Reilly, C., Caldwell, D., & Barnett, W. (1989). Work group demography, social integration, and turnover. *Administrative Science Quarterly, 34,* 21–37.

Ortiz, A., Johnson, D. W., & Johnson, R. (1996). Effects of positive goal and resource interdependence on individual performance. *Journal of Social Psychology, 136*(2), 243–249.

Orvis, B., Kelley, H., & Butler, D. (1976). Attributional conflict in young couples. In J. Harvey, W. Ickles, & R. Kidd (Eds.), *New directions in attribution research* (Vol. 1). Hillsdale, NJ: Erlbaum.

Palmer, P. (1991). The courage to teach. *National Teaching and Learning Forum, 1*(2), 1–3.

Palmer, P. (1992, March–April). Divided no more. *Change,* pp. 11–17.

Pelz, D. (1956). Some social factors related to performance in a research organization. *Administrative Science Quarterly, 1,* 310–325.

Pelz, E. (1958). Some factors in "group decision." In E. Maccoby, T. Newcomb, & E. Hartley (Eds.), *Readings in social psychology.* New York: Holt.

Pelz, E., & Andrews, F. (1966). *Scientists in organizations.* New York: John Wiley.

Pennebaker, J. W. (1982). Social and perceptual factors affecting symptom reporting and mass psychogenic illness. In M. J. Colligan, J. W. Pennebaker, & L. R. Murphy (Eds.), *Mass psychogenic illness: A social psychological analysis.* Hillsdale, NJ: Erlbaum.

Pennington, D., Haravey, F., & Bass, B. (1958). Some effects of decision and discussion on coalescence, change, and effectiveness. *Journal of Applied Psychology, 42,* 404–408.

Pepinsky, P., Hemphill, J., & Shevitz, R. (1958). Attempts to lead, group productivity, and morale under conditions of acceptance and rejection. *Journal of Abnormal and Social Psychology, 57,* 47–54.

Pepitone, A. (1952). *Responsibility to the group and its effects on the performance of members.* Unpublished doctoral dissertation, University of Michigan, Ann Arbor.

Pepitone, E. (Ed.). (1980). *Children in cooperation and competition.* Lexington, MA: Lexington Books.

Perdue, C., Dovidio, J., Gutman, M., & Tyler, R. (1990). Us and them: Social categorization and the process of intergroup bias. *Journal of Personality and Social Psychology, 59,* 475–486.

Peters, D. (1966). *Identification and personal change in laboratory training.* Unpublished doctoral dissertation, Massachusetts Institute of Technology, Boston.

Peterson, R., Johnson, D. W., & Johnson, R. (1991). Effects of cooperative learning on perceived status of male and female pupils. *Journal of Social Psychology, 13,* 717–735.

Pettigrew, T. (1997). Generalized intergroup contact effects on prejudice. *Personality and Social Psychology Bulletin, 23*(2), 173–185.

Petty, M., Harkins, S., Williams, K., & Latane, B. (1977). Effects of group size on cognitive effort and evaluation. *Journal of Personality and Social Psychology, 3*(4), 579–582.

Petty, R., Cacioppo, J., & Krasmer, J. (1985). *Individual differences in social loafing on cognitive tasks.* Paper presented at the annual meeting of the Midwestern Psychological Association, Chicago.

Phoon, W. H. (1982) Outbreaks of mass hysteria at workplaces in Singapore: Some patterns and modes of presentation. In M. J. Colligan, J. W. Pennebaker, & L. R. Murphy (Eds.), *Mass psychogenic illness: A social psychological analysis* (pp. 21–31). Hillsdale, NJ: Erlbaum.

Preston, M., & Heintz, R. (1949). Effects of participatory vs. supervisory leadership on group judgment. *Journal of Abnormal and Social Psychology, 44,* 345–355.

Pruitt, D., & Johnson, D. (1970). Mediation as an aid to face saving in negotiation. *Journal of Personality and Social Psychology, 14,* 239–246.

Pruitt, D., & Rubin, J. (1986). *Social conflict.* New York: Random House.

Pruitt, D., & Syna, H. (1983). Successful problem solving. In D. Tjosvold & D. W. Johnson (Eds.), *Conflict in organizations* (pp. 62–81). New York: Irvington.

Putallaz, M. (1983). Predicting children's sociometric status from their behavior. *Child Development, 54,* 1417–1426.

Putnam, J., Rynders, J., Johnson, D. W., & Johnson, R. (1989). Collaborative skills instruction for promoting positive interactions between mentally handicapped and nonhandicapped children. *Exceptional Children, 55,* 550–557.

Qin, A., Johnson, D. W., & Johnson, R. (1995). Cooperative versus competitive efforts and problem solving. *Review of Educational Research, 65*(2), 129–143.

Radke, M., & Klisurich, D. (1947). Experiments in changing food habits. *Journal of the American Dietetics Association, 23,* 403–409.

Rahim, M. (1983). A measure of styles of handling interpersonal conflict. *Academy of Management Journal, 26,* 368–376.

Rahim, M. (1989). Relationships of leader power to compliance and satisfaction with supervision: Evidence from a national sample of managers. *Journal of Management, 15,* 545–556.

Raven, B. (1993). The origins of power: Origins and recent developments. *Journal of Social Issues, 49,* 227–251.

Raven, B., & Kruglanksi, A. (1970). Conflict and power. In P. Swingle (Ed.), *The structure of conflict* (pp. 69–110). New York: Academic Press.

Raven, B., & Rietsema, J. (1957). The effects of varied clarity of group goal and group path upon the individual and his relation to his group. *Human Relations, 10,* 29–44.

Raven, B., & Rubin, J. (1976). *Social psychology: People in groups.* New York: Wiley.

Rawls, J. (1971). *A theory of justice.* Cambridge: Harvard University Press.

Reed, B. (1947). Accommodation between Negro and white employees in a west coast aircraft industry, 1942–1944. *Social Forces, 26,* 76–84.

Reeder, G. (1993). Trait-behavior relations and dispositional inference. *Personality and Social Psychology Bulletin, 19,* 586–593.

Regan, D., & Totten, J. (1975). Empathy and attribution: Turning observers into actors. *Journal of Personality and Social Psychology, 32,* 850–856.

Ringelmann, M. (1913). Research on animate sources of power: The work of man. *Annales de L'Instite National Agronomique, 2e, serietome* XII, 1–40.

Robins, J., et al. (1984). Lifetime prevalence of specific psychiatric disorders in three sites. *Archives of General Psychiatry, 41,* 949–958.

Rodin, J., & Langer, E. (1977). Long-term effects of a control-relevant intervention with the institutionalized aged. *Journal of Personality and Social Psychology, 35,* 897–902.

Rodin, J., Solomon, J., & Metcalf, J. (1978). Role of control in mediating perceptions of density. *Journal of Personality and Social Psychology, 36(9),* 988–999.

Roethlisberger, F., & Dickson, W. (1939). *Management and the worker.* Cambridge, MA: Harvard University Press.

Roff, J., & Wirt, R. (1984). Childhood aggression and social adjustment antecedents of delinquency. *Journal of Abnormal Child Psychology, 12(1),* 111–126.

Rogers, C. (1970). Towards a theory of creativity. In P. Vernon (Ed.), *Creativity: selected readings* (pp. 137–151). London: Penguin.

Rogers, M., Hennigan, K., Bosman, C., & Miller, N. (1984). Intergroup acceptance in classroom and playground settings. In N. Miller & M. Brewer (Eds.), *Groups in contact: The psychology of desegregation* (pp. 187–212). Orlando, FL: Academic Press.

Rokeach, M. (1960). *The open and closed mind.* New York: Basic Books.

Rokeach, M. (1968). *Beliefs, attitudes, and values.* San Francisco: Jossey-Bass.

Rose, A. (1948). Race relations in a Chicago industry. In M. Rose (Ed.), *Studies in the reduction of prejudice.* Chicago: American Council on Race Relations.

Rosenberg, L. (1961). Group size, prior experience, and conformity. *Journal of Abnormal and Social Psychology, 63(2),* 436–447.

Rosenblith, J. (1949). A replication of "some roots of prejudice." *Journal of Abnormal and Social Psychology, 44,* 470–489.

Roskow-Ewoldsen, D., & Fazio, R. (1992). The accessibility of source likeability as a determinant of persuasion. *Personality and Social Psychology Bulletin, 18,* 19–25.

Ross, L. (1977). The intuitive psychologist and his shortcomings: Distortions in the attributional process. In L. Berkowitz (Ed.), *Advances in experimental social psychology* (Vol. 10, pp. 174–220). New York: Academic Press.

Ross, L., & Nisbett, R. (1991). *The person and the situation.* New York: McGraw-Hill.

Rothbart, M., Evans, M., & Fulero, S. (1979). Recall for confirming events: Memory processes and the maintenance of social stereotypes. *Journal of Experimental Social Psychology, 15,* 343–355.

Rothgerber, H., & Worchel, S. (1997). The view from below: Intergroup relations from the perspective of the disadvantaged group. *Journal of Personality and Social Psychology, 73,* 1191–1205.

Rotter, J. (1971). Generalized expectancies for interpersonal trust. *American Psychologist, 26,* 443–452.

Rubin, J., Pruitt, D., & Kim, S. (1994). *Social conflict.* New York: McGraw-Hill.

Rusbult, C., & Van Lange, P. (1996). Interdependent processes. In E. Higgins & A. Kruglanski (Eds.), *Social psychology: Handbook of basic principles* (pp. 564–596). New York: Guilford.

Rusbult, C., Yovetich, N., & Verette, J. (1996). An interdependence analysis of accommodation processes. In G. Fletcher & J. Fitness (Eds.), *Knowledge structures in close relationships: A social psychological approach* (pp. 63–90). Mahwah, NJ: Lawrence Erlbaum.

Sachdev, I., & Bourhis, R. (1984). Minimal majorities and minorities. *European Journal of Social Psychology, 14,* 35–52.

Sachdev, I., & Bourhis, R. (1991). Power and status differentials in minority and majority group relations. *European Journal of Social Psychology, 21,* 1–24.

Sanders, G. (1981). Driven by distraction: An integrative review of social facilitation theory and research. *Journal of Experimental Social Psychology, 17,* 227–251.

Sanders, G., & Baron, R. (1975). The motivating effects of distraction on task performance. *Journal of Personality and Social Psychology, 32,* 956–963.

Schachter, S. (1951). Deviation, rejection, and communication. *Journal of Abnormal and Social Psychology, 46,* 190–207.

Schachter, S., Ellertson, N., McBride, D., & Gregory, D. (1951). An experimental study of cohesiveness and productivity. *Human Relations, 4,* 229–238.

Schachter, S., Nuttin, J., Demonchaux, C., Maucorps, P., et al. (1954). Cross-cultural experiments on threat and rejection. *Human Relations, 7,* 403–439.

Schein E. (1969). *Process consultation.* Reading, MA: Addison-Wesley.

Schmidt, W. (1974). Conflict: A powerful process for (good and bad) change. *Management Review, 63,* 4–10.

Schultz, W. (1958). *FIRO: A three dimensional theory of interpersonal behavior.* New York: Rinehart.

Schultz, W. (1966). *The interpersonal underworld.* Palo Alto: Science and Behavior Books.

Schweiger, D., Sandberg, W., & Rechner, P. (1989). Experiential effects of dialectical inquiry, devil's advocacy, and consensus approaches to strategic decision making. *Academy of Management Journal, 32,* 722–745.

Schwenk, C. (1983). Laboratory research on ill-structured decision aids: The case of dialectical inquiry. *Decision Sciences, 14,* 140–144.

Seashore, S. (1954). *Group cohesiveness in the industrial work group.* Ann Arbor, MI: Institute for Social Research.

Seligman, M. (1975). *On depression, development, and death.* San Francisco: Freeman.

Seligman, M. (1988). Boomer blues. *Psychology Today, 22,* 50–55.

Selman, R. (1981). The development of interpersonal competence: The role of understanding in conduct. *Departmental Review, 1,* 401–422.

Seta, J., Paulus, P., & Schkade, J. (1976). Effects of group size and proximity under cooperative and competitive conditions. *Journal of Personality and Social Psychology, 34,* 47–53.

Shambaugh, P. (1978). The development of the small group. *Human Relations, 31,* 283–295.

Shaw, M. (1932). A comparison of individuals and small groups in the rational solution of complex problems. *American Journal of Psychology, 44,* 491–504.

Shaw, M. (1964). Communication networks. In L. Berkowitz (Ed.), *Advances in experimental social psychology* (Vol. 1, pp. 111–147). New York: Academic Press.

Shaw, M. (1976, 1981). *Group dynamics: The psychology of small group behavior.* New York: McGraw-Hill.

Shepperd, J. (1993). Productivity loss in performance groups: A motivation analysis. *Psychological Bulletin, 113*(1), 67–81.

Sherif, M. (1936). *The psychology of group norms.* New York: Harper.

Sherif, M. (1966). *In common predicament.* Boston: Houghton Mifflin.

Sherif, M., & Sherif, C. (1956). *An outline of social psychology.* New York: Harper & Row.

Sherif, M., & Sherif, C. (1969). *Social psychology.* New York: Harper & Row.

Sherman, J. (1996). Development and mental representation of stereotypes. *Journal of Personality and Social Psychology, 70,* 1126–1141.

Sherman, J., Lee, A., Bessenoff, G., & Frost, L. (1998). Stereotype efficiency reconsidered: Encoding flexibility under cognitive load. *Journal of Personality and Social Psychology, 75*(3), 589–606.

Shinagawa, L. (1997). *Atlas of American diversity.* Thousand Oaks, CA: Sage.

Short, J., Williams, E., & Christie, B. (1976). *The social psychology of telecommunications.* London: John Wiley.

Siegel, J., Dubrovsky, V., Kiesler, S., & McGuire, T. (1986). Group processes in computer-mediated communication. *Organizational Behavior and Human Decision Processes, 37,* 157–187.

Sigelman, L., & Welch, S. (1993). The contact hypothesis revisited: Black–white interaction and positive racial attitudes. *Social Forces, 71,* 781–795.

Simon, H. (1976). *Administrative behavior: A study of decision-making processes in administrative organization* (3rd ed.). New York: Free Press.

Simon, H. (1979). *The science of the artificial* (2nd ed.). Cambridge, MA: Massachusetts Institute of Technology Press.

Simonton, D. (1979). Multiple discovery and invention: *Zeitgeist,* genius or chance? *Journal of Personality and Social Psychology, 37,* 1603–1616.

Singh, R., Choo, W., & Poh, L. (1998). In-group bias and fair-mindedness as strategies of self-presentation in intergroup perception. *Personality and Social Psychology Bulletin, 24*(2), 147–162.

Skon, L., Johnson, D. W., & Johnson, R. (1981). Cooperative peer interaction versus individual competition and individualistic efforts: Effects of the acquisiton of cognitive reasoning strategies. *Journal of Educational Psychology, 73,* 83–92.

Slavin, R. (1986). *Using student team learning.* Baltimore, MD: Center for Research on Elementary & Middle Schools, Johns Hopkins University.

Smith, F. (1943). *An experiment in modifying attitudes toward the Negro* (Teachers College Contributions to Education, 887). New York: Columbia University.

Smith, M. (1945). Social situation, social behavior, and social group. *Psychological Review, 52,* 224–229.

Spencer, S., Fein, S., Wolfe, C., Fong, C., & Dunn, M. (1998). Automatic activation of stereotypes: The role of self-image threat. *Personality and Social Psychology Bulletin, 24*(11), 1139–1152.

Stanne, M., Johnson, D. W., & Johnson, R. (1999). Does competition enhance or inhibit motor performance: A meta-analysis. *Psychological Bulletin, 125*(1), 1–22.

Star, S., Williams, R., & Stouffer, S. (1965). Negro infantry platoons in white companies. In H. Proshansky & B. Seidenberg (Eds.), *Basic studies in social psychology.* New York: Holt, Rinehart & Winston.

Stasser, G., & Titus, W. (1987). Effects of information load and percentage shared information on the dissemination of unshared information during discussion. *Journal of Personality and Social Psychology, 53,* 81–93.

Stein, M. (1968). *The creative individual.* New York: Harper & Row.

Stein, R., & Heller, T. (1979). An empirical analysis of the correlations between leadership status and participation rates reported in the literature. *Journal of Personality and Social Psychology, 37,* 1993–2002.

Steiner, I. (1959). Human interaction and interpersonal perception. *Sociometry, 22,* 230–235.

Steiner, I. (1966). Models for inferring relationships between group size and potential group productivity. *Behavioral Science, 11,* 273–283.

Steiner, I. (1972). *Group process and productivity.* New York: Academic Press.

Steinzor, B. (1950). The spatial factor in face-to-face discussion groups. *Journal of Abnormal and Social Psychology, 45,* 552–555.

Stephan, F., & Mishler, E. (1952). The distribution of participation in small groups: An exponential approximation. *American Sociological Review, 17,* 598–608.

Stephan, W. (1978). School desegregation: An evaluation of predictions made in *Brown vs. Board of Education. Psychological Bulletin, 85,* 217–238.

Stogdill, R. (1959). *Individual behavior and group achievement.* New York: Oxford University Press.

Stogdill, R. (1974). *Handbook of leadership.* New York: Free Press.

Stoner, J. (1961). *A comparison of individual and group decisions involving risk.* Unpublished master's thesis, Massachusetts Institute of Technology, Boston.

Storm, H. (1972). *Steven arrows.* New York: Ballantine Books.

Storms, M. (1973). Videotape and the attribution process: Reversing actors' and observers' points of view. *Journal of Personality and Social Psychology, 27,* 165–175.

Stotle, J. (1978). Power structure and personal competence. *Journal of Social Psychology, 38,* 72–83.

Strodtbeck, F., & Hook, L. (1961). The social dimensions of a twelve man jury table. *Sociometry, 24,* 397–415.

Stroebe, W., Diehl, M., & Abukoumkin, G. (1992). The illusion of group effectivity. *Personality and Social Psychology Bulletin, 18,* 643–650.

Sundstrom, E., Perkins, M., George, J., Futrell, D., & Hoffman, D. (1990, April). *Work-team context, development, and effectiveness in a manufacturing organization.* Paper presented at the Fifth Annual Conference of the Society for Industrial and Organizational Psychology, Miami.

Swann, W. (1984). Quest for accuracy in person perception: A matter of pragmatics. *Psychological Review, 91,* 457–477.

Sweeney, J. (1973). An experimental investigation of the free-rider problem. *Social Science Research, 2,* 277–292.

Swim, K., Aikin, K., Hall, W., & Hunter, B. (1995). Sexism and racism: Old fashioned and modern prejudices. *Journal of Personality and Social Psychology, 68,* 199–214.

Szymanski, K., & Harkins, S. (1987). Social loafing and self-evaluation with a social standard. *Journal of Personality and Social Psychology, 53,* 891–897.

Tajfel, H. (1969). Cognitive aspects of prejudice. *Journal of Social Issues, 25,* 79–87.

Tajfel, H. (1974). Social identity and intergroup behavior. *Social Science Information, 13,* 65–93.

Tajfel, H. (1978). Social categorization, social identity, and social comparison. In H. Tajfel (Ed.), *Differentiation between social groups* (pp. 61–76). London: Academic Press.

Tajfel, H. (1981). *Human groups and social categories.* Cambridge, UK: Cambridge University Press.

Tajfel, H. (1982). Social psychology of intergroup relations. *Annual Review of Psychology, 33,* 1–39.

Tajfel, H., & Turner, J. (1979). An integrative theory of intergroup conflict. In W. Austin & S. Worchel (Eds.), *Psychology of intergroup relations* (pp. 33–47). Monterey, CA: Brooks/Cole.

Tajfel, H., & Turner, J. (1986). The social identity theory of intergroup relation. In S. Worchel & W.

Austin (Eds.), *Psychology of intergroup relations* (pp. 7–24). Chicago: Nelson-Hall.

Taylor, D., & Faust, W. (1952). Twenty questions: Efficiency in problem solving as a function of size of group. *Journal of Experimental Psychology, 44,* 360–368.

Taylor, S. (1980). The interface of cognitive and social psychology. In J. H. Harvey (Ed.), *Cognition, social behavior, and the environment* (pp. 189–211). Hillsdale, NJ: Erlbaum.

Teger, A. (1980). *Too much invested to quit.* New York: Pergamon.

Terborg, J., Castore, C., & DeNinno, J. (1976). A longitudinal field investigation of the impact of group composition on group performance and cohesion. *Journal of Personality and Social Psychology, 34,* 782–790.

Terman, L., & Odor, M. (1947). *The gifted child grows up.* Stanford, CA: Stanford University Press.

Tetlock P. (1979). Identifying victims of groupthink from public statements of decision makers. *Journal of Personality and Social Psychology, 37,* 1314–1324.

Thibaut, J., & Kelly, H. (1959). *The social psychology of groups.* New York: John Wiley.

Thomas, E., & Fink, C. (1961). Models of group problem solving. *Journal of Abnormal and Social Psychology, 63,* 53–63.

Thomas, K. (1976). Conflict and conflict management. In M. Dunnette (Ed.), *Handbook of industrial and organizational psychology,* (pp. 889–935). Chicago: Rand McNally.

Thomas, K., & Schmidt, W. (1976). A survey of managerial interests with respect to conflict. *Academy of Management Journal, 19,* 315–318.

Thorndike, R. (1938). On what type of task will a group do well? *Journal of Abnormal Social Psychology, 30,* 409–413.

Tjosvold, D. (1974). Threat as a low-power person's strategy in bargaining: Social face and tangible outcomes. *International Journal of Group Tensions, 4,* 494–510.

Tjosvold, D. (1977). Low-power person's strategies in bargaining: Negotiability of demand, maintaining face, and race. *International Journal of Group Tensions, 7,* 29–42.

Tjosvold, D. (1978). Alternative organizations for schools and classrooms. In D. Bar-Tal & L. Saxe (Eds.), *Social psychology of education: Theory & research* (pp. 275–298). Washington, DC: Hemisphere.

Tjosvold, D. (1981). Unequal power relationships within a cooperative or competitive context. *Journal of Applied Social Psychology, 11,* 137–150.

Tjosvold, D. (1986). *Working together to get things done.* Lexington, MA: Lexington.

Tjosvold, D. (1989). Interdependence and power between managers and employees: A study of the leader relationship. *Journal of Management, 15,* 49–62.

Tjosvold, D. (1990a). Power in cooperative and competitive organizational contexts. *Journal of Social Psychology, 130,* 249–258.

Tjosvold, D. (1990b). *The team organization: Applying group research to the workplace.* New York: John Wiley.

Tjosvold, D. (1991a). *Team organization.* New York: John Wiley.

Tjosvold, D. (1991b). *The conflict-positive organization.* Reading, MA: Addison-Wesley.

Tjosvold, D. (1993). Experiencing a given base of power as a reward or punishment. *Psychological Reports, 73,* 178.

Tjosvold, D. (1995a). Cooperation theory, constructive controversy, and effectiveness: Learning from crisis. In R. Guzzo & E. Salas (Eds.), *Team effectiveness and decision making in organizations* (pp. 79–112). San Francisco: Jossey-Bass.

Tjosvold, D. (1995b). Effects of power to reward and punish in cooperative and competitive contexts. *Journal of Social Psychology, 135*(6), 723–736.

Tjosvold, D., & Johnson, D. W. (1982). *Productive conflict.* New York: Irvin.

Tjosvold, D., Johnson, D. W., & Johnson, R. (1981). Effect of partner's effort and ability on liking for partner after failure on a cooperative task. *Journal of Psychology, 109,* 147–152.

Tjosvold, D., & Sagaria, D. (1978). Effects of relative power of cognitive perspective-taking. *Personality and Social Psychology Bulletin, 4,* 256–259.

Torrance, E. (1954). Some consequences of power differences in decision making in permanent and temporary three-man groups. *Research Studies, State College of Washington, 22,* 130–140.

Torrance, E. (1957). Group decision-making and disagreement. *Social Forces, 35,* 314–318.

Torrance, E. (1961). Can grouping control social stress in creative activity? *Elementary School Journal, 62,* 391–394.

Treffinger, D., Speedie, S., & Brunner, W. (1974). Improving children's creative problem solving ability: The Purdue creativity project. *The Journal of Creative Behavior, 8,* 20–29.

Trevino, L., Lengel, R., & Draft, R. (1987). Media symbolism, media richness, and media choice in organizations: A symbolic interactionist perspective. *Communication Research, 14,* 553–574.

Triandis, H., Bass, A., Ewen, R., & Mieksele, E. (1963). Teaching creativity as a function of the members. *Journal of Applied Psychology, 47*, 104–110.

Triandis, H., Hall, D. & Ewen, R. (1965). Member heterogeneity and dyadic creativity. *Human Relations, 18*, 33–55.

Triplett, N. (1898). The dynamogenic factors in pacemaking and competition. *American Journal of Psychology, 9*, 507–533.

Tuckman, B. (1965). Developmental sequence in small groups. *Psychological Bulletin, 63*, 384–399.

Tuckman, B., & Jensen, M. (1977). Stages of small group development revisited. *Group and Organizational Studies, 2*, 419–427.

Turner, J. (1978). Social comparison, similarity and ingroup favoritism. In H. Tajfel (Ed.), *Differentiation between social groups* (pp. 235–250). London: Academic Press.

Turner, J. (1987). *Rediscovering the social group: A self-categorization theory.* New York: Basil Blackwell.

Turner, J., & Oakes, P. (1989). Self-categorization theory and social influence. In P. Paulus (Ed.), *Psychology of group influence* (2nd ed., pp. 233–275). Hillsdale, NJ: Erlbaum.

Turner, M., Pratkanis, A., Probasco, P., & Leve, C. (1992). Threat, cohesion, and group effectiveness: Testing a social identity maintenance perspective on groupthink. *Journal of Personality and Social Psychology, 63*, 781–796.

Turner, R., & Killian, L. (1972/1987). *Collective behavior* (3rd ed.). Englewood Cliffs, NJ: Prentice Hall.

Tversky, A., & Kahneman, D. (1981). The framing of decisions and the psychology of choice. *Science, 211*, 453–458.

Tyler, T., Lind, E., Ohbuchi, K., Sugawara, I., & Huo, Y. (1998). Conflict with outsiders: Disputing within and across cultural boundaries. *Personality and Social Psychology Bulletin, 24*(2), 137–146.

Urban, L., & Miller, N. (in press). A theoretical analysis of crossed categorization effects: A meta-analysis. Manuscript submitted for publication.

Vacchiano, R. B., Strauss, P. S., & Hochman, L. (1968). The open and closed mind: A review of dogmatism. *Psychological Bulletin, 71*(4), 261–273.

Vanbeselaere, N. (1987). The effects of dichotomous and crossed social categorizations upon intergroup discrimination. *European Journal of Social Psychology, 17*, 143–156.

Vanbeselaere, N. (1991). The different effects of simple and crossed categorization: A result of the category differentiation process or of differential category salience? In W. Stroebe & M. Hewstone (Eds.), *European review of social psychology* (Vol. 2, pp. 143–156). Chichester, UK: John Wiley.

Villasenor, V. (1977). *Jury: The people vs. Juan Corona.* New York: Bantam.

Voiers, W. (1956). *Bombing accuracy as a function of the group-school proficiency structure of the B-29 bomb team.* (Research Report AFDTRC-TN-56-4.) Lackland Air Force Base, TX: Air Force Personnel and Training Research Center.

Von Mises, L. (1949). *Human action: A treatise on economics.* New Haven, CT: Yale University Press.

Wagner, U., Hewstone, M., & Machleit, U. (1989). Contact and prejudice between Germans and Turks. *Human Relations, 42*, 561–574.

Walton, R. (1987). *Managing conflict.* Reading, MA: Addison-Wesley.

Walton, R., & McKersie, R. (1965). *A behavioral theory of labor negotiations.* New York: McGraw-Hill.

Watson, G. (1928). Do groups think more effectively than individuals? *Journal of Abnormal and Social Psychology, 23*, 328–336.

Watson, G. (1931). Do groups think more effectively than individuals? In G. Murphy & L. Murphy (Eds.), *Experimental social psychology.* New York: Harper.

Watson, G. (1947). *Action for unity.* New York: Harper.

Watson, G., & Johnson, D. W. (1972). *Social psychology: Issues and insights* (2nd ed.). Philadelphia: Lippincott.

Webb, N. (1977). *Learning in individual and small group setting* (Tech. Report No. 7). Stanford, CA: Stanford University, School of Education, Aptitude Research Project.

Weick, K. (1990). The vulnerable system: An analysis of the Tenerife air disaster. *Journal of Management, 16*, 571–593.

Weigel, R., & Howes, P. (1985). Conceptions of racial prejudice. *Journal of Social Issues, 41*(3), 117–138.

Weiner, N., Pandy, J., & Latane, B. (1981). *Individual and group productivity in the United States and India.* Paper presented at the American Psychological Association, Los Angeles.

West, C., & Zimmerman, D. (1983). Small insults: A study of interruptions in cross-sex conversations between unacquainted persons. In B. Thorne, C. Dramarge, & N. Henley (Eds.), *Language, gender, and society* (pp. 102–117). Rowley, MA: Newbury House.

Wheeler, R., & Ryan, F. (1973). Effects of cooperative and competitive classroom environments on the attitudes and achievement of elementary school students engaged in social studies inquiry activities. *Journal of Educational Psychology, 65*, 402–407.

Whyte, W. F. (1943). *Street corner society.* Chicago: University of Chigaco Press.

Wiggam, A. (1931). The biology of leadership. In H. Metcalf (Ed.), *Business leadership.* New York: Pitman.

Wilder, D. (1977). Perception of group, size of opposition, and social influence. *Journal of Experimental Social Psychology, 13*, 253–268.

Wilder, D. (1978a). Perceiving persons as a group: Effects on attributions of causality and beliefs. *Social Psychology, 41*, 13–33.

Wilder, D. (1978b). Reduction of intergroup discrimination through individuation of the out-group. *Journal of Personality and Social Psychology, 36*, 1361–1374.

Wilder, D. (1986). Social categorization: Implications for creation and reduction of intergroup bias. *Advances in Experimental Social Psychology, 19*, 291–355.

Wilder, D. (1990). Some determinants of the persuasive power of in-groups and the out-groups: Organization of information and attribution of independence. *Journal of Personality and Social Psychology, 59*, 1202–1213.

Wilder, D., & Shapiro, P. (1989a). Effects of anxiety on impression formation in a group context: An anxiety-assimilation hypothesis. *Journal of Experimental Social Psychology, 25*, 481–499.

Wilder, D., & Shapiro, P. (1989b). Role of competition-induced anxiety in limiting the beneficial impact of positive behavior by an out-group member. *Journal of Personality and Social Psychology, 56*, 60–69.

Wilder, D., & Shapiro, P. (1991). Facilitation of out-group stereotypes by enhanced ingroup identity. *Journal of Experimental Social Psychology, 27*, 431–452.

Wilkinson, I., & Kipnis, D. (1978). Interfirm use of power. *Journal of Applied Psychology, 63*, 315–320.

Willems, E., & Clark, R. (1971). Shift toward risk and heterogeneity of groups. *Journal of Experimental and Social Psychology, 7*, 304–312.

Williams, D. (1948). The effect of an interracial project upon the attitudes of Negro and white girls within the YWCA. In A. Rose (Ed.), *Studies in the reduction of prejudice.* Chicago: American Council of Race Relations.

Williams, K. (1981). Developmental characteristics of a forward roll. *Research Quarterly for Exercise and Sport, 51*(4), 703–713.

Williams, K., Harkins, S., & Latane, B. (1981). Identifiability as a deterrent to social loafing: Two cheer-

ing experiments. *Journal of Personality and Social Psychology, 40*, 303–311.

Williams, K., & Williams, K. (1984). *Social loafing in Japan: A cross-cultural development study.* Paper presented at the Midwestern Psychological Association, Chicago.

Williams, R. (1947). *Reduction of intergroup tension: A survey of research on problems of ethnic, racial, and religious group relations,* Bulletin 57. New York: Social Science Research Council.

Williams, R., & Ryan, M. (Eds.). (1954). *Schools of transition: Community experiences in desegregation.* Chapel Hill: University of North Carolina Press.

Wilner, D., Walkley, R., & Cook, S. (1952). Residential proximity and intergroup relations in public housing projects. *Journal of Social Issues, 8*, 45–69.

Winder, A. (1952). White attitudes toward Negro–white interaction in an area of changing racial composition. *American Psychologist, 7*, 330–331.

Wolfe, J., & Box, T. (1988). Team cohesion effects on business game performance. *Simulation and Games, 19*(1), 82–98.

Wolman, B., & Stricker, G. (Eds.). (1983). *Handbook of family and marital therapy.* New York: Plenum.

Wood, W. (1987). Meta-analytic review of sex differences in group performance. *Psychological Bulletin, 102*, 53–71.

Wood, W., Lundgren, S., Quelletter, J., Busceme, S., & Blackstone, T. (1994). Minority influence: A meta-analytic review of social influence processes. *Psychological Bulletin, 115*(3), 323–345.

Woods, F. (1913). *The influence of monarchs.* New York: Macmillan.

Worchel, S., & Brehm, J. (1971). Direct and implied social restoration of freedom. *Journal of Personality and Social Psychology, 18*, 294–304.

Worchel, S., Coutant-Sassic, D., & Grossman, M. (1992). A developmental approach to group dynamics: A model and illustrative research. In S. Worchel, W. Wood, & J. Simpson (Eds.), *Group process and productivity.* Newbury Park, CA: Sage.

Worchel, S., Andreoli, V., & Folger, R. (1977). Intergroup cooperation and intergroup attraction: The effect of previous interaction and outcome on combined effort. *Journal of Experimental Social Psychology, 13*, 131–140.

Wright, J. (1979). *On a clear day you can see General Motors.* New York: Avon.

Wright, S., Aron, A., McLaughlin-Volpe, T., & Ropp, S. (1997). The extended contact effect: Knowledge of cross-group friendships and prejudice. *Journal of Personality and Social Psychology, 73*(1), 73–90.

Yager, S., Johnson, D. W., & Johnson, R. (1985). Oral discussion, group-to-individual transfer, and achievement in cooperative learning groups. *Journal of Educational Psychology, 77,* 60–66.

Yarrow, M., Campbell, J., & Yarrow, L. (1958). Interpersonal dynamics in racial integration. In E. Maccoby, T. Newcomb, & E. Hartley (Eds.), *Readings in social psychology.* New York: Holt, Rinehart, & Winston.

Young, D. (1932). *American minority people: A study in racial and cultural conflicts in the United States.* New York: Harper.

Yukl, G., & Falbe, C. (1991). Importance of different power sources in downward and lateral relations. *Journal of Applied Psychology, 76,* 416–423.

Yukl, G., & Tracey, J. (1992). Consequences of influence attempts used with subordinates, peers, and the boss. *Journal of Applied Psychology, 77,* 525–535.

Zaccaro, S. (1984). Social loafing: The role of task attractiveness. *Personality and Social Psychology Bulletin, 10,* 99–106.

Zajonc, R. (1965). Social facilitation. *Science, 149,* 269–272.

Zander, A. (1971). *Motives and goals in groups.* New York: Academic Press.

Zander, A. (1979). The psychology of group process. In A. Inkeles, J. Coleman, & R. Turner (Eds.), *Annual review of sociology* (Vol. 5). Palo Atlo, CA: Annual Review Inc.

Zander, A., & Armstrong, W. (1972). Working for group pride in a slipper factory. *Journal of Applied Social Psychology, 2,* 293–307.

Zander, A., & Medow, H. (1963). Individual and group levels of aspiration. *Human Relations, 16,* 89–105.

Zdep, S., & Oakes, W. (1967). Reinforcement of leadership behavior in group discussion. *Journal of Experimental Social Psychology, 3,* 310–320.

Ziller, R. (1957). Group size: A determinant of the quality and stability of group decision. *Sociometry, 20,* 165–173.

Ziller, R., Behringer, R., & Goodchilds, J. (1962). Group creativity under conditions of success or failure and variations in group stability. *Journal of Applied Psychology, 46,* 43–49.

Zimbardo, P. (1970). The human choice: Individuation, reason, and order versus deindividuation, impulse, and chaos. In W. Arnold & D. Levine (Eds.), *Nebraska symposium on motivation* (pp. 237–307). Lincoln: University of Nebraska Press.

Zimbardo, P. (1972). Pathology of imprisonment. *Transactional/Society, 4,* 8a.

Zimbardo, P. (1973, April 8). The mind is a formidable jailer: A Pirandellian prison. *New York Times,* p. 38.

Zimbardo, P. (1975). Transforming experimental research into advocacy for social change. In M. Deutsch & H. Hornstein (Eds.), *Applying social psychology* (pp. 33–66). Hillsdale, NJ: Erlbaum.

Zuwerink, J., Monteith, M., Devine, P., & Cook, D. (1996). Prejudice towards Blacks: With and without compunction? *Basic and Applied Social Psychology, 18,* 131–150.

Index

Note: Page numbers followed by a *t* or *f* indicate tables or figures, respectively.

Photo Credits:

Will Faller: *Chapter 14*; Robert Harbison: *Chapters 1, 3, 6, 7, 9, 12*; Will Hart: *Chapters 2, 4, 8, 10, 11*; MaryEllen Lepionka: *Chapter 13*; Library of Congress: *Chapter 5.*